Bartholomew's

Touring Atlas
and Gazetteer
of the
British Isles

by

John Bartholomew f.r.g.s.

John Bartholomew & Son, Ltd
The Geographical Institute, Park Road, Edinburgh.

PUBLISHER'S NOTE

This Bartholomew Touring Atlas and Gazetteer of the British Isles has been recreated from the Practical Motorist's Touring Maps and Gazetteer published by John Bartholomew and Sons Ltd. Edinburgh.

These maps were produced between 1897-1903 from reduced Ordnance Surveys at a scale of 4 miles to 1 inch. The original map series was hand-drawn, hand-lettered and printed from copper-engraved plates at the Bartholomew premises in Park Road, Edinburgh.

Subsequent additions and corrections to the maps were made directly onto the copper plates, consequently some of the pages may carry later additions to the original cartography. The atlas does however, accurately, represent the first ever Bartholomew Motorist's Atlas and shows in detail the roads, railways, canals and settlements as they existed at that time.

The Gazetteer, originally compiled in 1900, lists many of the important settlements and physical features shown on the map pages. This Gazetteer may also contain some later corrections.

In order to make the original documents easier to interpret this edition has been published at a slightly enlarged scale.

The Atlas and Gazetteer is introduced by text extracted from The Highways and Byways of England by T. W. Wilkinson and published by Iliff and Sons Ltd. London and Coventry in 1900. This introduction charts the history and development of our road system and predicts, with uncanny accuracy, the future of both road and rail transport within Britain.

Mike Cottingham.

Published by Collins
An Imprint of HarperCollins*Publishers*
77-85 Fulham Palace Road, Hammersmith, London W6 8JB

Copyright © HarperCollins*Publishers* Ltd 1998
Mapping © Bartholomew Ltd

First published 1897-1903

Printed in China

ISBN 978 0 00 793487 4

This special edition for Sandpiper Books / Postscript published 2013   LC9949

INTRODUCTION

Within living memory the King's highway has undergone changes to which it is difficult to find a parallel. First it was thronged with traffic, then deserted, and now it is thronged with traffic again. This expansion and growth, its decline, and its revivification with the advent of cycling, and still more of motoring, have all taken place in a span of about seventy years.

As a result of the return of traffic to the old roads, the faults of these roads are no longer, as they were during the great development of railways in the Victorian era, matters of merely academic or antiquarian interest; they are matters of practical importance, and, as such, are steadily forcing themselves upon public notice. The condition of our roads is already a serious impediment to cheap, rapid, and safe communication. Upon whether they can be remedied, and our roads thereby made suitable for modern methods of transport, may depend the solution to many great problems that confront the nation.

One of those problems may be the retention of our place in the domain of trade. Nearly a century before the opening of railways, when our roads were the principal channels of communication, much of our prosperity and commercial eminence was attributed to the circumstances that our highways, bad though they were judged by the engineering standard, were superior to those of other countries. Adam Smith's contention, that the increasing wealth of England was mainly due to improvements in her roads, was endorsed by other political economists; and about 1840 the French Minister of Commerce eulogised our highways, declaring that it was principally owing to them that England had an advantage over France in the markets of the world. But while we neglected our roads, allowing the existing system to fall into decay and making very few additions to it, both France and Germany displayed great activity in highway construction, and are today intersected by routes which are to our own what the Holyhead Road (in many respects the best of our trunk lines) is to a meandering byway. As long as railways were the controlling agencies in our internal transport this circumstance was practically negligible; but now that motor traffic is rapidly increasing in England and on the Continent it is of great importance, and may have to be taken seriously into account in connection with our competition with our countries.

The history of our highways not only shows how the faults which handicap us originated and have come down to us, but also indicates how the needed improvements may be effected. It tells us that our roads, with their erratic lines and severe gradients, their narrowness and sinuosity, their breakneck hills and dangerous corners, were made so nearly as often from choice as from necessity and that opportunities for improving them were not always taken.

Though our highway system is made up of bits of all the ages, it still curiously reflects, as a whole, the physical state of England in the earliest days of our history. About one-third of the country was then covered with dense wood, thicket, or scrub, and over much of the rest stretched dismal swamps. In general, therefore, animals and carriers travelled over the high lands, and thus, in a large measure, our roads acquired their principal characteristic.

Centuries later, when regular communication had been established between different parts of the country, the same conditions were still factors in road-making. Clearings and drainage had greatly extended the open areas; but numerous forests remained, and there were many tracts of clay impassable for half the year, as well as series of bogs as perilous to travellers as those of Dartmoor are to the incautious tourist of our own times.

Owing to the danger of becoming engulfed in clay or of sinking into a bog, carriers, like the early road-makers, kept to the high lands. Their packhorse trains wore tracks over the hill ranges, and these became recognised trade routes, and were ultimately, in many cases, turned into roads. The conversion began towards the end of the seventeenth century, when carts and wagons had come into general use. As ways suitable for wheeled traffic were then called for, and as the contemporary road-makers could not throw such ways over soft ground, or, at all events, could not make a hard way except on a naturally good and stable foundation, such as rock or stone, the packhorse lines were followed in all their climbing and twisting and abrupt turnings.

Instances of this are many. The Wells-Shepton Mallet road, the Whitby-Ruswarp road, and scores of the emphatic highways linking Lancashire and Yorkshire are unquestionably on packhorse routes, running as they do over steep hills instead of through valleys along the line of least resistance. But it is enough to note that the unscientific race of road-makers never crossed low-lying ground if they could possibly avoid it, and that in consequence they intensified the circuitous and hilly nature of our highways in general.

The turnpike system, introduced as a solution of the 'road problem' as it existed in Stuart times, and peculiar to this country, no other having ever adopted it, was the next factor in moulding our roads, to which it gave many of the bad qualities they now possess. To it we owe many of the extremely erratic lines that vex the engineer and cause so vast a waste of energy. These were brought about in many ways. A prolific cause of the resultant expense and loss of time to generations of travellers was squabbling between two highway authorities. One opposed a turnpike Bill promoted by the other, and in consequence a scheme was held up for years or abandoned altogether. The effect can be seen to this day even in connection with so important a highway as the Great North Road, the remarkable line of which is, in some parts of its course, due to fights over obtaining power to turnpike.

Besides hampering communication in this manner, the trusts added largely to the number of hilly roads. As one of the necessary results of making a highway was a material increase in the value of the adjoining lands, the line was frequently taken precisely where it would best suit the pockets of the promoters, sometimes over hills that might easily have been avoided. It is for this reason that certain of the roads extending from Manchester into Cheshire, Derbyshire, and Staffordshire across the summits of hills. A number of similar highways, in the construction of which public requirements were subordinated to private interests, have now practically disappeared; for so little did they return in tolls that they brought nothing but sorrow to their bondholders, and, being neglected in consequence, are represented at the present time by a few parallel ruts. The construction of some of such roads, however, was beneficial to the districts through which they pass, because otherwise those districts would have lacked roads practicable for wheeled vehicles, and of great service, therefore, to agriculturists, till many years later.

In numerous cases, again, turnpike trusts made their roads so narrow that on them two coaches could not run abreast. They considered that it was enough to provide semi-circular refuges, into which a coach could draw and wait while another, travelling in the opposite direction, passed it. Some of these makeshifts are still in existence, and curiously exemplify the haphazard and un-systematic manner in which our highway system was formed.

There was, in truth, insufficient Parliamentary supervision over turnpike trusts, which, bound and restricted though they were in many particulars, were allowed far too much liberty in the making of roads. Had they been placed under the control of a central authority, investors would have been spared some bitter pangs, and our highway system would have been extended with more regard to national requirements and less to purely local needs.

Public attention was first sharply focused on the many faults and shortcomings in the products of the early road-makers and of the turnpike trusts by the Rebellion of 1745. General Wade's failure to relieve Carlisle owing to the vileness of the highway between that city and his headquarters at Newcastle, and the ease with which the Highlanders, unencumbered by baggage or wagon, outstripped the royal army, and left the cavalry and artillery far in the rear, compelled Parliament to direct its attention to the highways in the northern part of the kingdom, with the result that it passed an Act for the formation of a road for wheeled traffic between Newcastle and Carlisle, which were then connected by nothing but a bridle-way. This was carried into effect in 1756, General Wade employing his army on the undertaking. The line of the Roman Wall was followed for thirty miles, and a long stretch of that structure was pulled down to furnish materials for the work, which has ever since been known as the 'Military Road'. Subsequently other highways were made for military and civil purposes, and the impulse thus given to the construction of roads resulted in a vast improvement in communication, particularly in Cumberland.

A new era then dawned, an era of road-making and mending. Side by side with the construction of new highways was carried on the improvement of the principal old roads, all of which were modernised to a greater or lesser degree. Every trunk road in the kingdom was added to in some parts and taken from in others, straightened out, and generally made less trying to horse and man alike. Long hollows were filled up by embankments; hills were cut through, crossed at a lower level, or altogether removed; widenings were effected to facilitate the flow of traffic; and loops and dangerous corners were cut off.

While, however, our highway system was revolutionised by the numerous works carried out in this coaching age, it could not be freed from all of its old faults. Ineffaceable were the marks of the packhorse and of the early road-maker. The accumulated defects of centuries could not be remedied without a combined effort and an outlay impossible to the trusts, which, besides being heavily in debt, were neither responsible for nor specially interested in roads other than those under their own management. Nothing short of State action would have sufficed to accomplish so stupendous a task.

The principal faults of our highways are, therefore, relics of far-off days, and they have patently descended to us, through many generations, mainly because of insufficient public care for internal communication. For this neglect the blame must be laid at the door of the State, which, since the departure of the Romans, has not taken upon itself the provision of roads for general use. Parliament has probably devoted more care and time to the subject of highways than to any other. It has debated every phase of it at great length, called in to its aid eminent engineers and other experts, held costly inquiries, and by legislative enactments dealt with the most minute details respecting traffic, down to the shape of the heads of nails for affixing the tyres to wheels and the precise form of axles to be used in given circumstances. But the making of roads it has nearly always left to philanthropic effort and municipal and private enterprise; and, as a natural corollary, system and co-ordination have been conspicuously lacking, and no large, well-conceived scheme of road construction has ever been carried out.

It is probable that, had not traffic temporarily left the roads, England would have followed the example of France, which solved her 'road problem' by constituting a Minister of Roads and Bridges, in whose hands was placed the supervision of her highway system. Under his directions the roads were divided into several classes, the most important of which are *Routes Nationales* (constructed and maintained by the various departments at the expense of the Government). By this means the whole of the French highway system was re-made and brought up to its present high standard. The scheme, on its inauguration, attracted much notice in this country, and many times it was proposed that we should adopt it or a modification of it. Weary of the turnpike system, which had always been costly and irksome, and was then plainly moribund, as well as disgusted with the chicanery and negligence in connection with parochial highways, reformers saw in the bold measures taken in France a means of disposing once for all of controversies and nuisances which had lasted for centuries. But railways were monopolising the attention of the public at large, and partly for this reason, and partly because the general opinion was that there would be little further use for roads, the Legislature continued on its old course.

By 1840 the traffic which had ebbed and flowed for centuries ceased, apparently for ever, on some main roads, and soon afterwards there were many miles of highway deserted save for idle toll-collectors, whose time was profitlessly spent in mourning the life which had surged past them and in cursing the railways. The Brighton Road did not retain its old-time glories much later than September, 1840, when the railway was opened. In 1846 coaches stopped running on the Norwich Road, the last mail through Bury St. Edmunds covering the familiar ground on January 6th of that year. Four months later ended the Southampton and Oxford service. In the same year, too, railways extended along the whole course of the Great North Road. With the opening of the Edinburgh and Berwick Railway the last stretch of the ancient way to the north was superseded, and coaches disappeared from every part of it. Before 1845, in fact, coaching was patently moribund all over the country, though it survived here and there for years afterwards, nowhere, perhaps, more strangely than at Manchester, the last four-horse coach out of that city, the "Derby Dilly," not finishing its course before October, 1858.

One of the earliest results of the growth of the railways was the abandonment of any highway improvements. A few years before railways were initiated there had been contemplated some road works which, had they been completed, would have been the most important carried out in this country since the Roman era, including as they did nothing less than a road to replace, or, at least, supplement, the ancient way to Scotland. The course of this undertaking, of which Telford was appointed engineer, was to be as straight as possible. About 1824 the section from Edinburgh to Morpeth was actually completed, and some years later the other and larger portion was begun; but the coming of the railways stopped further work for many years to come. All that was finished of the proposed new Great North Road was the highway from Morpeth to Wooler, Coldstream, and Edinburgh. This road, though hilly, is much shorter and better than that by the coast, and indicates that the planned road has been a great improvement.

Other schemes of a similar nature were also abandoned. Relics of one of these ill-starred enterprises remain for years at Ferrybridge, near Doncaster. When the coaching age was rapidly nearing its end, some speculators proposed to cut off a part of the Great North Road, and substitute for it a straight and level road across the valley. The work was started, and pushed forward rapidly, the promoters calculating on a satisfactory return from the tolls for which Parliamentary powers had been obtained. When, however, the enterprise was nearing completion, traffic deserted the North Road for the railway, and consequently it was left unfinished. For years a lofty embankment was the most prominent feature of the derelict work, in connection with which a large sum was lost.

On wayside inns also the diversion of traffic was disastrous, practically all their trade going away at once. Even large houses gladly welcomed customers whom they had aforetime openly despised. These were foot travellers, the scorned of all the coaching inns in pre-railway days.

Little imagination is needed to visualise the King's highway itself undergoing, in these circumstances, rapid decay and becoming again cut up into longitudinal strips by infantile ruts; but the actual degeneration was far greater than the conditions warrant us in picturing. As early as 1846, the year when the Norfolk Railway was opened, roads in that county were stated to be "half-a-yard deep in mud" and almost impassable. "Heavy goods in large quantities," it is said, were "sent from Norwich to London and from thence to Ipswich by rail, 196 miles, instead of [by] the direct route of 40 miles by road, the rail conveyance being cheaper and quicker." If the deterioration was not so rapid in other parts of the country, it was, at all events, marked and continuous. In many places the old coaching highways became like sheep tracks; and before 1870 parts of even the Great North Road were covered with grass. The public apathy was such, too, that once more greedy landowners were allowed to practise that filching which Harrison had denounced in the reign of Elizabeth, and to add to their estates by annexing the grassy strips which the trusts had used as summer roads, and which they had had to purchase from those same landowners at grossly extortionate rates. There was, moreover, a recrudescence of road diverting, the effect of which was to make our highway system still more tortuous.

A great change for the worse, in fact, took place in the condition of the King's highway. As turnpike trusts expired the roads again became wholly under the jurisdiction of parishes, which had always been responsible for them, and also partly liable, except for a short period, for their maintenance. "The obligation to maintain all public roads, with the exception of those which are to be repaired *ratione tenurÉ* or *clausurÉ*, is," a royal commission reported in 1840, "a public obligation and in the nature of a public tax." It then proceeded to point out that "when a highway has been converted into a turnpike road and placed under the management of trustees, with power to collect tolls to be applied to the repairs, if the way be out of repair, the parish (or township, as the case may be) are the only parties who are liable to be indicted, and must seek their remedies against the trustees, which they have, after conviction, by motion for relief against the trustees under the Turnpike Act 3 George IV., c. 126, sec. 10." During most of the time that the turnpike system was in operation, moreover, trustees were empowered to, and frequently did, call upon parishes to assist in the maintenance of their roads either by statute labour or by a payment in lieu. The only alteration brought about by the abolition of the turnpike system, therefore, was that parishes had to repair all their roads without any help from tolls. For this reason the position of those bodies after the discontinuance of trusts was not very different from what it had been before. Since, however, parishes had for so many years been relieved of part, at least, of the cost of their highways, they sustained by the abolition of turnpikes a shock which paralysed them, and, there being nobody sufficiently interested in road communication to galvanise them into activity the old lines of traffic suffered greatly.

While roads in rural districts were rapidly deteriorating, those in towns and their environs steadily improved. A reform which gave rise to much bitterness was the sweeping away of obstructions. London rid itself of many relics, including Temple Bar, for centuries its western gate. Pulled down in 1879, the fabric lay dismembered for some time, and then the stones were given to Sir H.B. Meux, who re-erected them at the principal entrance to Theobald's Park, near Cheshunt, Herts. The removal of so famous a landmark had some influence in sealing the fate of impediments to traffic in other parts of the country, though it was not a precedent recognised when the Bar, at Southampton, was threatened with demolition or when iconoclasts wished to remove Hotspur's Gate, Alnwick. In some towns, most of them in manufacturing districts where the growth of industries and the consequent increase of traffic had brought on numbers of old structures the scorn of the utilitarian, a middle course was taken, and relics which obstructed the way were transplanted on fresh sites belonging to the public. A sweeping removal of this kind took place at Bingley, in the West Riding, where a market, a cross, and a set of stocks were transferred to the public park, and the main street, which had been nearly blocked, was cleared from side to side. This kind of improvement, however, was not confined to the industrial parts of England, several villages clearing the way in the comparatively simple method adopted by Nether Stowey, near Bridgwater.

Here a clock tower and a lock-up which stood in the middle of the road were moved to the side, and are now as much out of the way as is the local gazebo, a summerhouse from which many a party witnessed the passing of the Minehead coach.

About 1870 the King's highway reached its low-water mark. For twenty years scarcely a new road had then been made except in urban districts, and the repairs to the old highways, even those which formed arteries of communication, had been of the most contemptible character. Roads in general were in consequence in a worse condition than they had been for a generation. In summer multitudinous weeds luxuriated in their depths, and in winter they bore a thick coat of rutty mud, through which the pedestrian struggled with difficulty and the horseman at no little risk. Our whole highway system, outside of towns, was well-nigh derelict, and a traveller might have journeyed over it for many leagues without encountering any traffic other than local.

Then begun that remarkable revival which still continues and gathers force yearly. It was with the advent of the cycle that the renaissance set in. The "ordinary" had a vogue, and before its novelty had time to pall the tricycle was introduced and taken up with enthusiasm by the middle-aged. Next came the "safety," with the aid of which the open road may be said to have been "discovered" by the present generation. Just as cycling began to wane the automobile was brought forward, or, rather, brought forward again, and, though for a time its progress was checked by reactionary legislation similar to that which had killed self-propelled traffic in the early part of the century, its course was ultimately cleared by the "Emancipation" Act of 1896, which relieved the driver of such a vehicle from the necessity of being proceeded by a man bearing a red flag, such as it had been obligatory to carry in front of a traction engine.

Finally, from the automobile for personal conveyance sprang motor vans for the delivery of goods, merchandise, etc.

As a result of this unparalleled series of improvements in transport, there has been a remarkable drift back to the open road. If the adventurous youths who bestrode the high wheel did not make much impression on the countryside, the tricyclists, and still more the riders of the "safety," roused the King's highway from its somnolence and brought a measure of prosperity to wayside inns. Greater far are the results which the automobile has since achieved; for it has not only resuscitated the whole of our highway system, but strangled the railway monopoly, which can never again dominate the country as it did less than twenty years ago.

In the service of the Royal Mail alone the automobile is now doing work of great interest and value. The Post Office, with which the history of road communication is very closely connected, never wholly deserted the King's highway, but clung to it, and retained much of the nomenclature of stage-coach days. When the parcels post was introduced, and the railway companies claimed about one-half of the postage paid on the parcels, it strengthened its old ties by introducing a service of road vans, which are now being displaced by big and fast motor vans, with "guards," as of old, only the present race carry a truncheon and whistle, instead of loaded firearms. The Post Office, by thus acting in accordance with its traditions, has materially helped in the return to the road.

It cannot be said that the improvements in highways have kept pace with those in transport; but our roads are certainly better now than they ever were. Twenty years' steady effort has not been wasted; it has borne some fruit, though not so much as was expected. The general improvement was started by cyclists, who, while everywhere preventing the King's highway from deteriorating further, actually stimulated some local authorities to bring their share of it into passable condition. Besides taking individual action to this end, they moved through their organisation, the Cyclists' Touring Club, which was formed in 1878, when touring awheel became popular. The club became known to the general public by the danger-boards which it placed on hills. It had been preceded in this useful work by the Bicycle Union (now the National Cyclists' Union), which set up a number of similar warnings, the first on the top of Muswell Hill, in the north of London. The "C.T.C." boards, indeed, probably attracted attention more by their number than by their novelty, though they were the first seen in many parts of the country. However this may be, the club missed no opportunity of stirring up highway authorities, and doubtless paved the way for many reforms. It was most successful in its efforts after the establishment of county councils. Before those bodies were formed the number of highway authorities was so great, and the views they took of their responsibilities were so divergent, that it was impossible to rouse them to effective action. When, however, main roads came under the control of county councils, some of the absurdities of highway administration were abolished, and real progress was made. That progress, thanks to the persistent agitation carried on by automobilists, has continued, and the institution of the Road Board marks an important stage in it. Already the dreams of old cyclists have thereby been realised, and that still greater improvements will be carried out in the near future, some of them of incalculable value to the country, cannot for a moment be doubted.

A pleasing vista thus opens out - a vista of a transformed countryside, of the decline of railways, of their relegation to very fast and very heavy traffic, of the road as the dominating feature in internal communication and as the greatest factor in the affairs of the nation.

It has been said that the coming question is, "first, roads; second, roads; and third and last, roads"; and it cannot be doubted that time will speedily justify the proposition.

T.W. WILKINSON. 1899

MAP 1

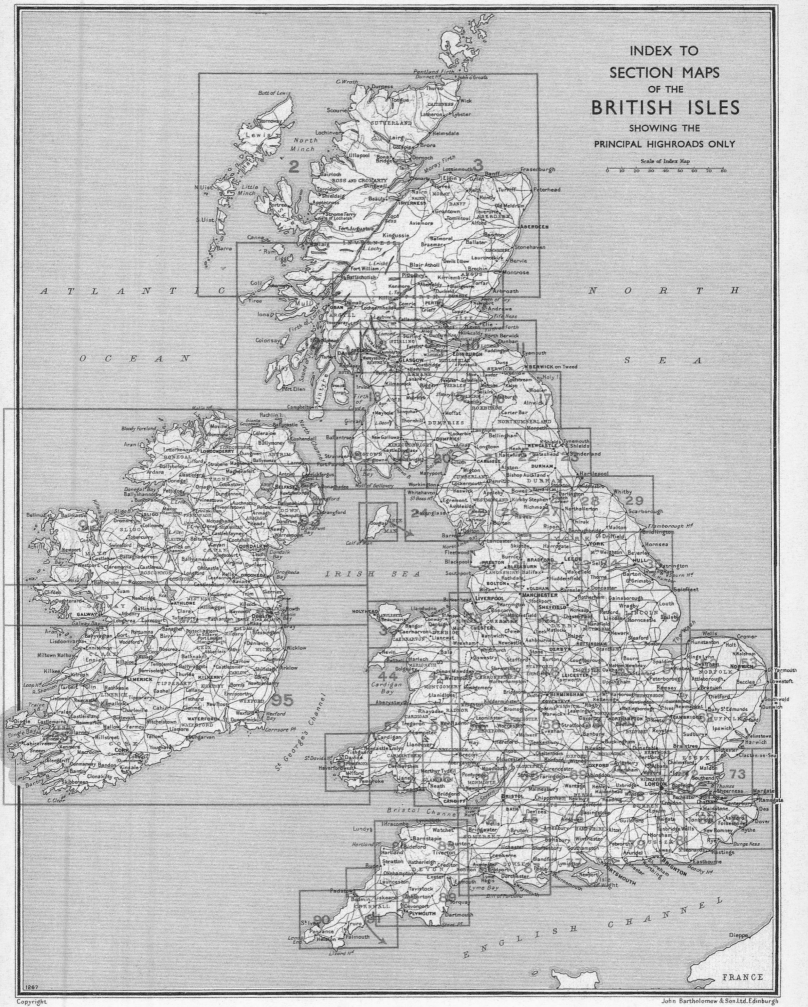

INDEX TO
SECTION MAPS
OF THE
BRITISH ISLES
SHOWING THE
PRINCIPAL HIGHROADS ONLY

John Bartholomew & Son.Ltd.Edinburgh

MAP 2

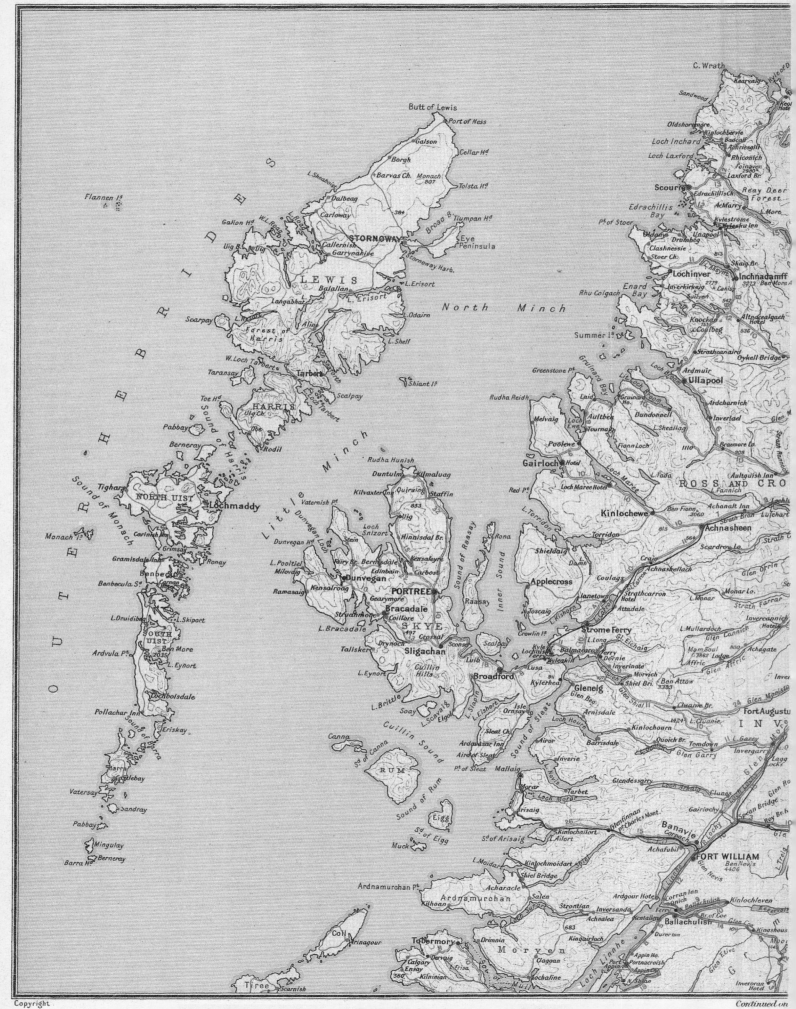

Copyright

Main Roads _____ 20 _____   **Other Roads** _____   **Railways** _____

Red Figures indicate distances between places with **Black Dots**

MAP 3

MAP 4
Continued on

MAMORE FOREST

BLACKWATER RESERVOIR

Glen Gour · Glen Tarbert · Glen Duror

BALLACHULISH · North Ballachulish · Ballachulish Pier · Loch Leven · Loch Leven Hotel

Bridge of Coe · Pap of Glencoe · Glen Coe · Kingshouse Hotel

Royal Forest · Buachaille Etive Mòr 3345 · Buachaille Etive Beag 3120

Bidean nam Bian 3766 · Aonach Eagach 3118 · Devil's Staircase

Black Mount · Moor of Rannoch · Loch Bà · Stob Ghabhar 3565 · Clashgour

Ben Starav 3541 · Glas Bheinn Mhòr 3258 · Glen Etive · Glen Kinglass

PORT APPIN · Portnacroish · LOCH LINNHE · LYNN OF LORNE

LOCH CRERAN · BENDERLOCH · Barcaldine · Ledaig · Beregonium

Dunstaffnage Cas. · Connel Ferry Sta. · TAYNUILT · Ben Cruachan 3689

Pass of Brander · Loch Awe · LORN

OBAN · Dunollie Cas. · Loch Nell · Kilbride

Bridge of Orchy · Beinn Dòrain 3523 · GLEN ORCHY · Glen Lochy

DALMALLY · Ben Lui 3708 · Ben Oss · Beinn a' Chleibh 3008

Loch Awe · Ardanaiseig · Kilchrenan · Portsonachan

LOCH AWE · Loch Avich · Loch Scammadale

A R G Y L L

Inveraray · INVERARAY · LOCH FYNE · Glen Shira · Glen Fyne

Ben Vorlich 3092 · Ben Vane 3004 · Ben Ime 3318 · The Cobbler 2891

ARROCHAR · LOCH LONG · Rest & be Thankful · Glen Croe

Glen Kinglas · Cairndow · Ardkinglas

Continued on Map 12

Scale of Miles
0 1 2 3 4 5 6 7 8 9 10

Continued on

PERTH

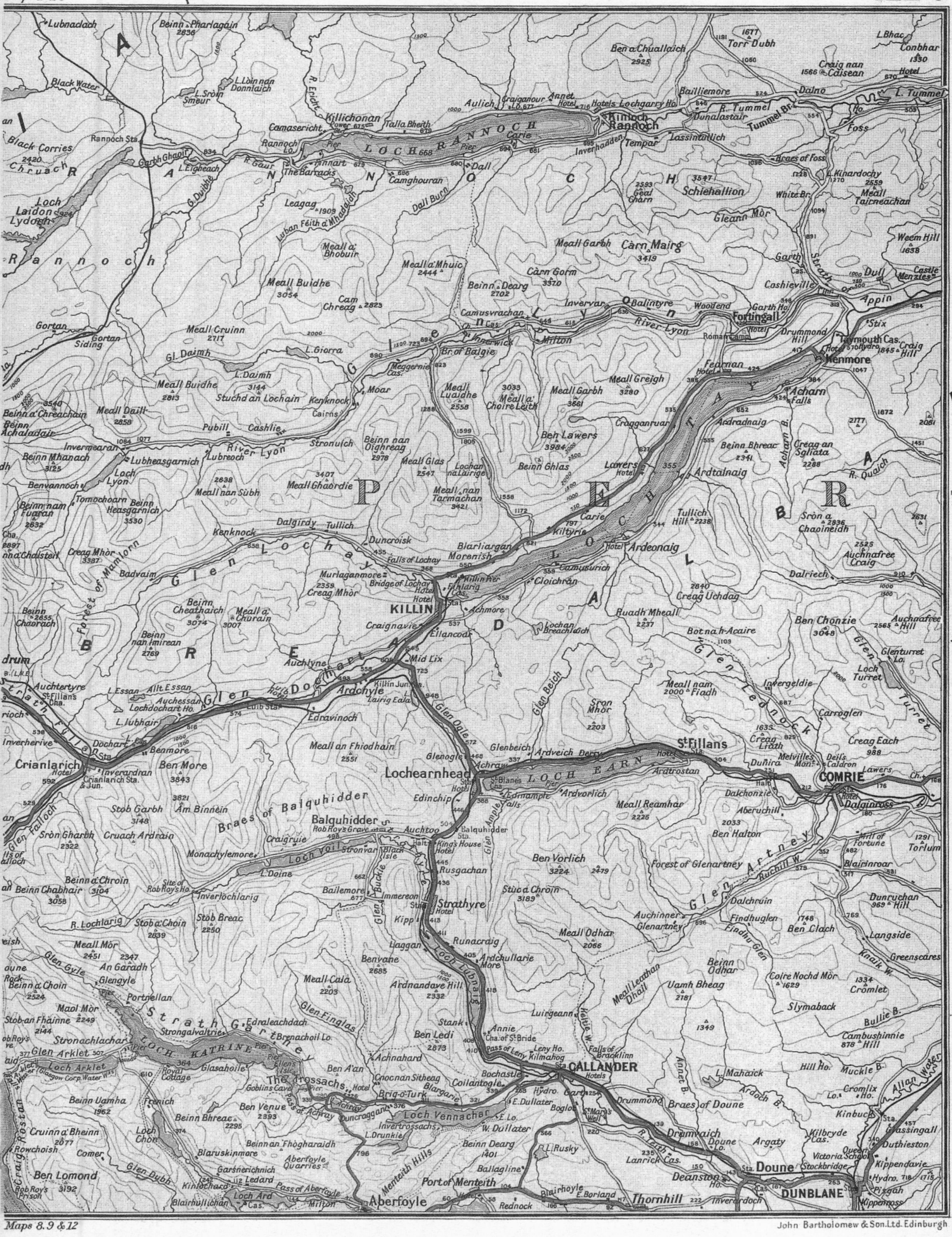

Continued on Map 6

Main Roads ══════ Other Roads ══════ Railways ──────

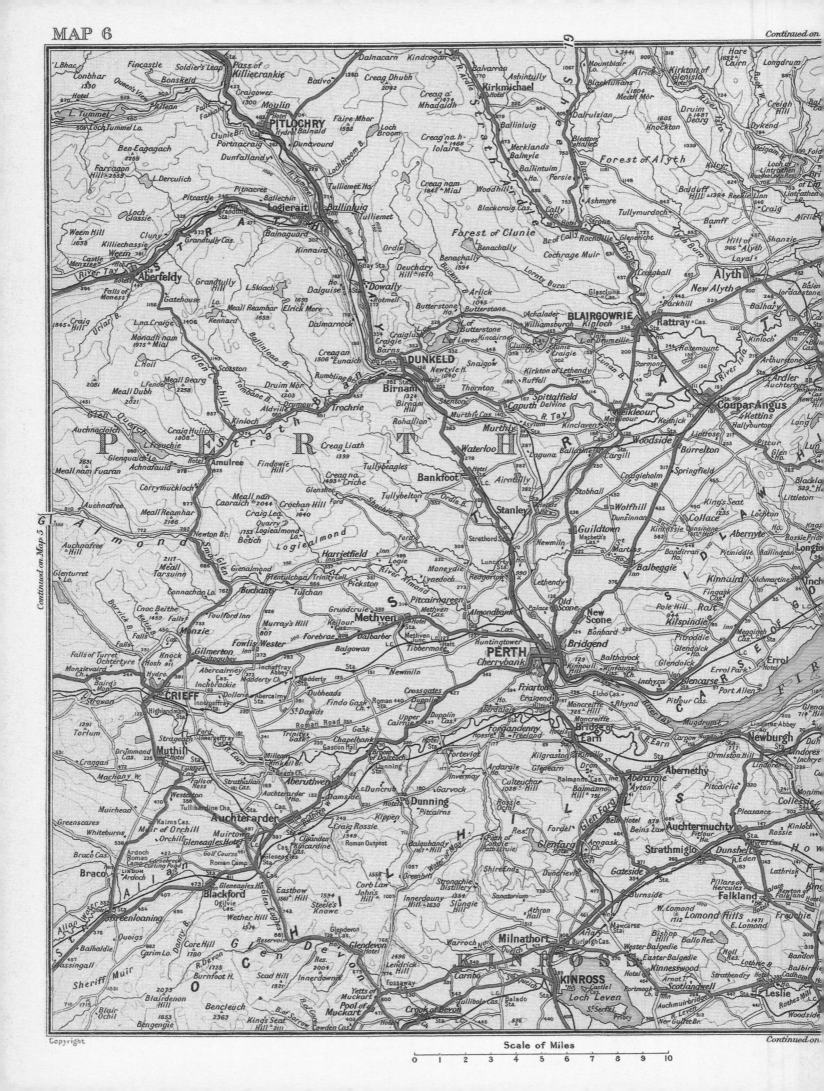

MAP 7

John Bartholomew & Son.Ltd.Edinburgh

Main Roads —————— Other Roads —————— Railways ——————

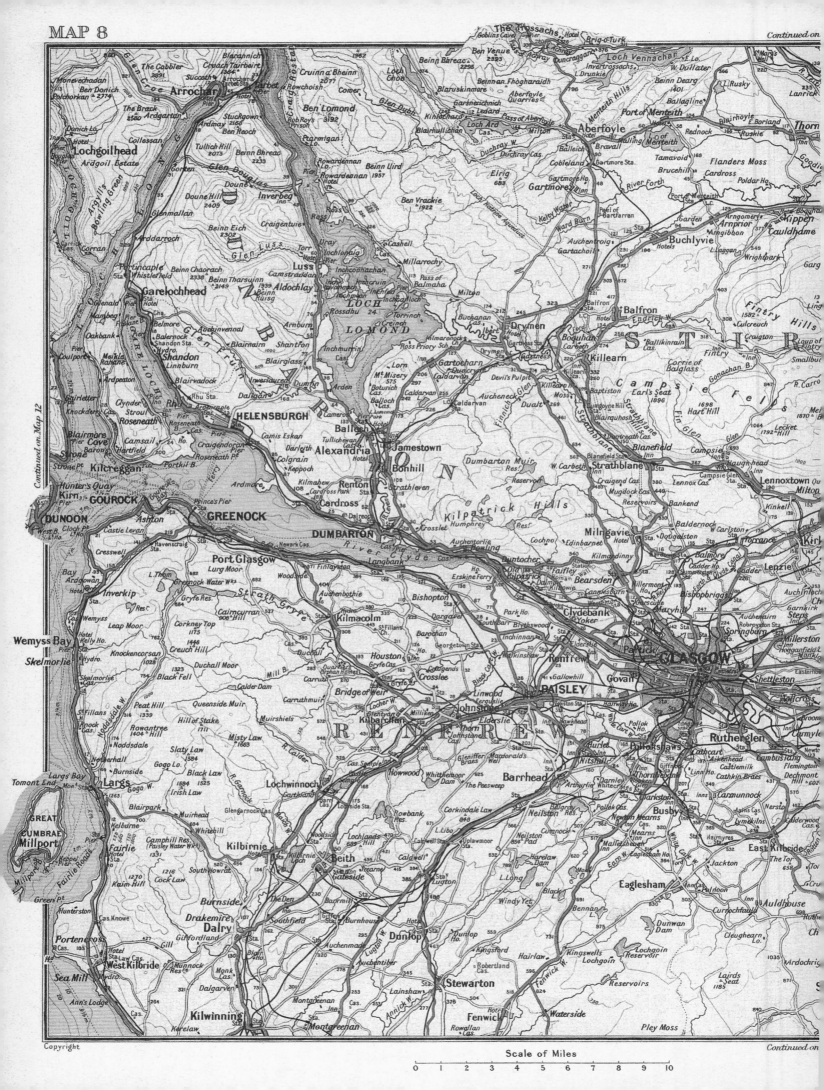

MAP 8

Continued on

Continued on Map 12

The Trossachs
Goblins Cave
Brig-o-Turk
Ben Venue 2393
L. of Achray
Duncraggan
Loch Vennachar
Invertrossachs
W. Dullater
L. Drunkie
Beinn Dearg 1401
Ballagline
L. Rusky
Lanrick
Thor

The Cobbler 2891
Cruach Tairbeirt
Blaranich
Beinn an Fhògharaidh 796
Menteith Hills
Port of Menteith
Blairhoyle
E. Borland
Ruskie
Goodie

Ben Donich 2774
Arrochar
Tarbet
Cruinn a' Bheinn 2077
Comer
Glen Dubh
Aberfoyle Quarries
Aberfoyle
L. of Menteith

The Brack 2580
Ardgartan
Ardmay 2168
Ben Reoch
Ben Lomond 3192
Rob Roy's Prison
Kinlochard
Ledard
Pass of Aberfoyle
Milton
Rednock
168

Lochgoilhead
Ardgoil Estate
Ptarmigan L
Rowardennan Lo.
Beinn Uird
Elrig 683
Gartmore Ho.
Brucehill
Cardross
Flanders Moss
Poldar Ho.

Doune Hill 2409
Inverbeg
Rowardennan Hotel 1957
River Forth
Port o Menteith

Glenmallan
Beinn Bhreac 2233
Ben Vrackie 1922
Gartmore Inn
Arngomery
Arnprior
Kippen
Cauldhame

Arddarroch
Beinn Eich 2302
Loch Lomond
Cashell
Millarrochy
Buchanan Cas.
Garden
Buchlyvie
Wrightpark
Garg

Portincaple
Whistlefield
Beinn Chaorach 2338
Beinn Tharsuinn 2149
Aldochlay
Inchlonaig
Inchfad
Pass of Balmaha
Milton
Balfron Sta.
Balfron 1582
Fintry Hills

Garelochhead
Beinn Ruisg 1939
Luss
Camstradden
Inchmoan
Inchcailloch
Drymen
Culreuch

Glenald
Belmore
Shandon Sta.
Arnburn
Rossdhu 24
Torrinch
Creinch
Inchmurrin
Drymen Sta.
Boguhan Carbeth
Killearn
Corrie of Balglass
Loup of Fintry

Shandon
Linnburn
Blairnairn
Shanton
Lorn
Mt. Misery 575
Boturich Cas.
Caldarvan
Gartocharn
Gartness
Baptiston
Lungoyne Hill
Earl's Seat 1896
Hart Hill 1698

Blairvadock
Rhu Sta.
Ardencaple
Inverlauren
Dunfin
Arden
Ballagan Cas.
Caldarvan
Auchineck Glen
Dualt
Strathblane
Blanefield
Campsie

Helensburgh
Camis Eskan
Cameron
Balloch
Pier Park
Jamestown
Dumbarton Muir Res.
W. Carbeth
Strathblane
Campsie Glen

Craigendoran
Colgrain
Keppoch
Bonhill
Strathleven
Kilmahew
Renton
Cardross
Milngavie
Lennoxtown
Milton

Gourock
Greenock
Dumbarton
River Clyde
Bowling
Old Kilpatrick
Dalmuir
Bearsden
Clydebank
Yoker
Partick
GLASGOW
Shettleston

Dunoon
Port Glasgow
Langbank
Erskine Ferry
Inchinnan
Renfrew
Govan
Rutherglen

Wemyss Bay
Skelmorlie
Inverkip
Kilmacolm
Bishopton
Houston
Bridge of Weir
Johnstone
PAISLEY
Linwood
Pollokshaws
Cathcart
Busby

Largs
Lochwinnoch
Kilbarchan
Elderslie
Barrhead
Neilston
Newton Mearns
East Kilbride

Great Cumbrae
Millport
Kilbirnie
Beith
Caldwell
Uplawmoor
Eaglesham

West Kilbride
Dalry
Dunlop
Stewarton
Fenwick
Auldhouse

Kilwinning

Continued on

Scale of Miles

0 1 2 3 4 5 6 7 8 9 10

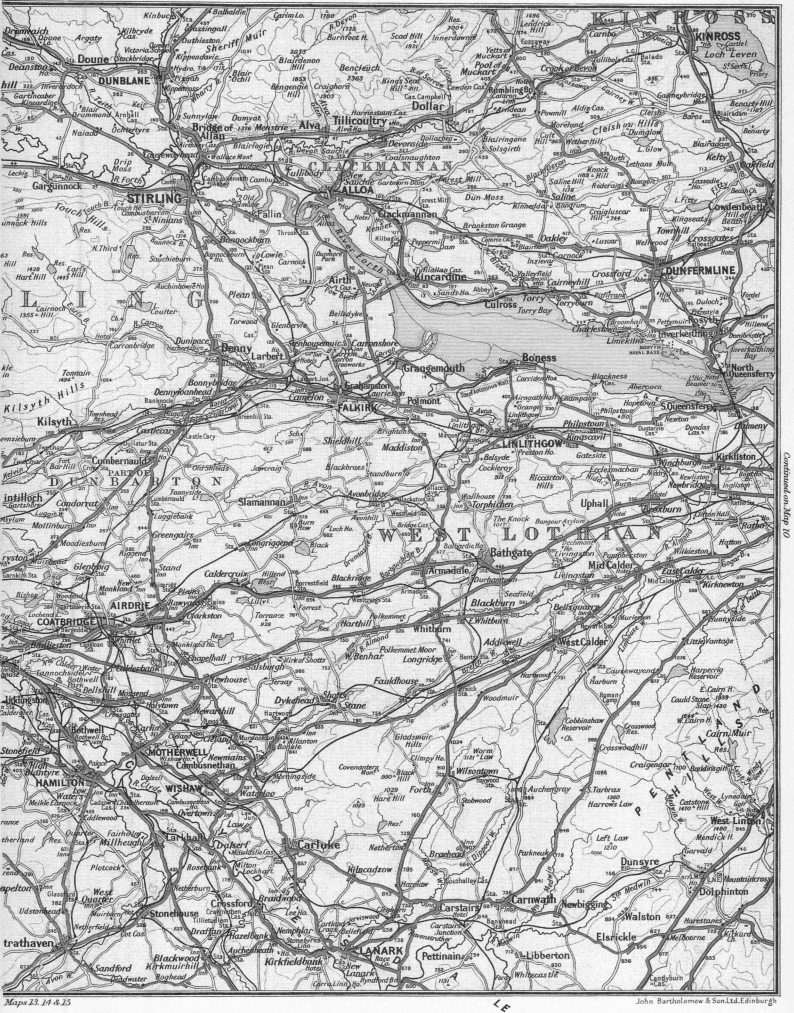

Continued on Map 10

Main Roads ━━━━━   Other Roads ═════   Railways ━━━━━

MAP 10

Continued on Maps 6 & 7

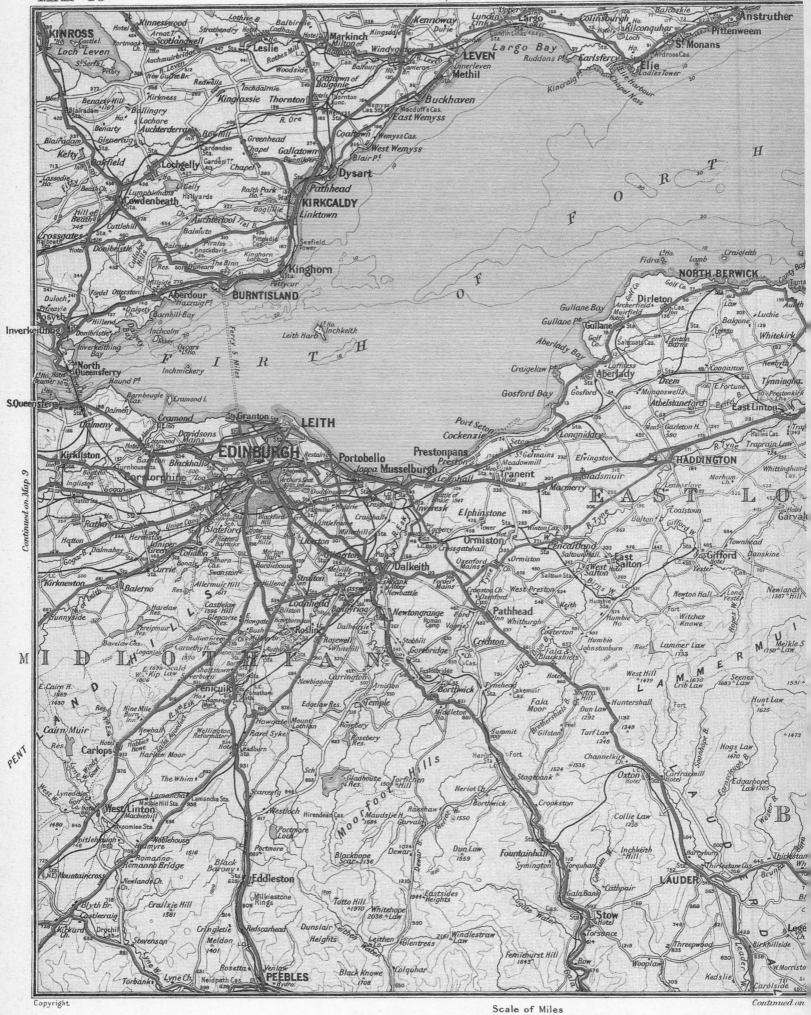

MAP 11

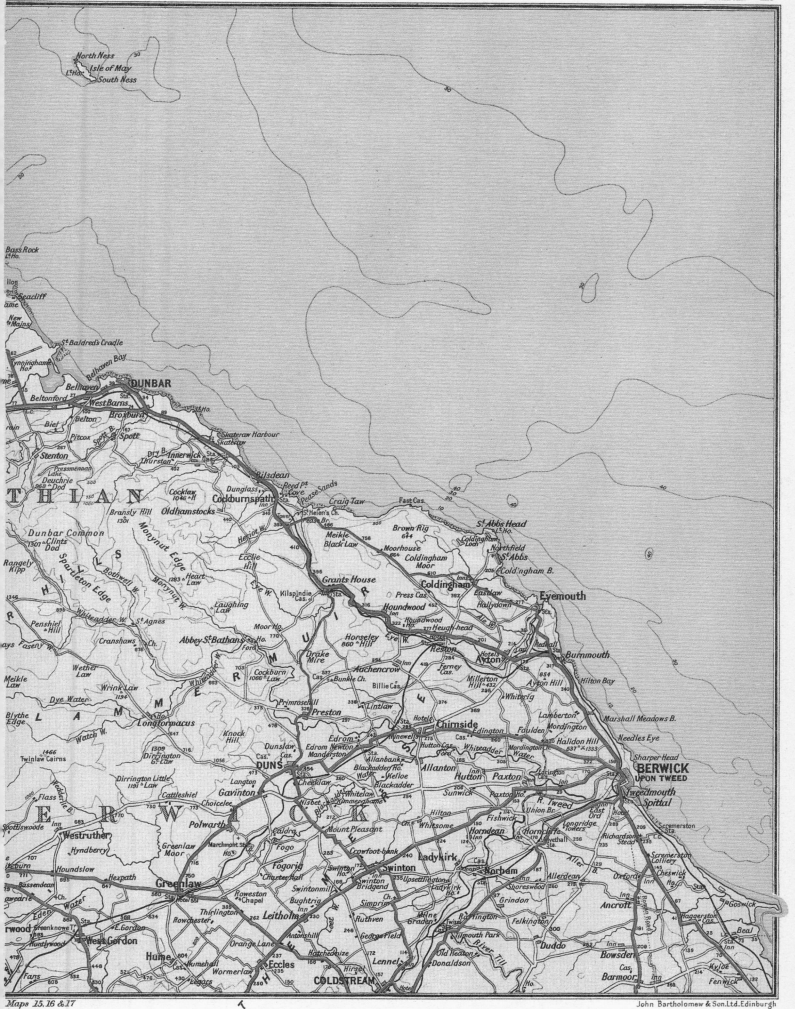

North Ness
Isle of May
Lᵗʰ Hoˢ
South Ness

Bass Rock
Lᵗ Ho.

Ilon
Seacliff
ame
New Mains

Sᵗ Baldred's Cradle
ynninghame
Hoˢ
Belhaven Bay

Belhaven
Beltonford
West Barns
DUNBAR
Sta.
Lᵗ Ho.
Biel
Broxburn
Belton
Pitcox
Spott
Spot B.
Stenton
Dry B.
Innerwick
Sta.
Thurston
Pressmennan
Lake
Deuchrie
Dod
Bilsdean
Dunglass
Reed Pᵗ
Cove
Pease Sands
Cocklaw
1046 H.
Cockburnspath
Inn
Craig Taw
Fast Casᵗ.
Bransly Hill
1301
Oldhamstocks
Heriot W.
Sᵗ Helen's Ch.
Br.
Brown Rig
644
Sᵗ Abbs Head
Lᵗ Ho.

THIAN

Dunbar Common
1307
Clints
Dod
Meikle
Black Law
758
Moorhouse
664
Coldingham
Moor
Coldingham
Loch
Northfield
Sᵗ Abbs
Coldʼngham B.

Rangely
Kipp
Ecclie
Hill
Grants House
Sta.
Press Casᵗ.
Enslaw
Eyemouth

Penshiel
Hill
Whiteadder W.
Sᵗ Agnes
Laughing
Law
Houndwood
Inn
Houndwood
Heugh-head
Hallydown

RRHILL
Fasenʸ W.
Cranshaws
Ch.
Moor Hoˢ
Abbey Sᵗ Bathans
ford
Horseley
Hill
860
Eye W.
Reston
Sta.
Ayton
Burnmouth

Wether
Law
Wrink Law
1194
Drake
Mire
Auchencrow
Inn
Ferney
Casᵗ.
Millerton
Hill
432
Ayton Hill
340
Hilton Bay

Meikle
Law
Dye Water
Cockburn
Law
1066
Bunkle Ch.
Billie Casᵗ.
Whiterig

Blythe
Edge
LAMMER
Watch W.
Primrosehill
Preston
Linzlaw
Whitelaw
Lamberton
Mordington
Marshall Meadows B.

Longformacus
Knock
Hill
Dunslaw
Edrom
Edrom Newton
Manderston
Ninewells
Chirnside
Edington
Faulden
Halidon Hill
537
1333
Needles Eye

Twinlaw Cairns
1466
Dirrington
Gᵗ Law
1309
Allanbank
Hoˢ
Hutton Cot
ford
Whiteadder
Water
Mordington Ch.
Sharper Head

Dirrington Little
1191 Law
Langton
Duns
Sta.
Cheeklaw
Kelloe
Allanton
Hutton
Paxton
Edrington
BERWICK
UPON TWEED

Cattleshiel
Gavinton
Choicelee
Nisbet
Blackadder
Kimmerghame
Sunwick
Paxton Hoˢ
Tweedmouth
Spittal

ERW
Inn
Polwarth
Caldra
Fogo
Mount Pleasant
Hilton
Whitsome
Fishwick
R. Tweed
Union Br.
East
Ord
Longridge
Towers
Richardson's
Stead

Spottiswoode
Inn
Westruther
Greenlaw
Moor
Marchmont
Sta.
Crowfoot-bank
Horndean
Horncliffe
Allerdean
Scremerston
Colliery

Hyndberry
Fogoris
Charterhall
Swinton
Ladykirk
Norham
Inn
Ancroft
Cheswick

Houndslow
Hexpath
Greenlaw
Sta.
Roweston
Chapel
Bughtrig
Swinton
Bridgend
Upsettlington
Ladykirk
Casᵗ.
Shoreswood
Oxford
Inn

Bassendean
Thirlington
Fogorig
Simprim
Grindon
Felkington

Eden
Water
E. Gordon
Rowchester
Leitholm
Ruthven
Georgefield
Nine
Graden
Barrington
Duddo
Bowsden
Beal

wood
greenknowe Tᵗ
West Gordon
Orange Lane
Antonshill
Hatchednize
Lennel
Old Heaton
Donaldson
Tilmouth Park
River Till
Barmoor
Cas.

Huntlywood
Hume
Humehall
Wormerlaw
Eccles
Hirsel
COLDSTREAM
Hotel
Fenwick

Fans
Legars
Coldingham
Goswick
Haggerston
Cas.

John Bartholomew & Son.Ltd.Edinburgh

Main Roads ══════ Other Roads ══════ Railways ───────

MAP 12

Continued on Maps 2 & 3

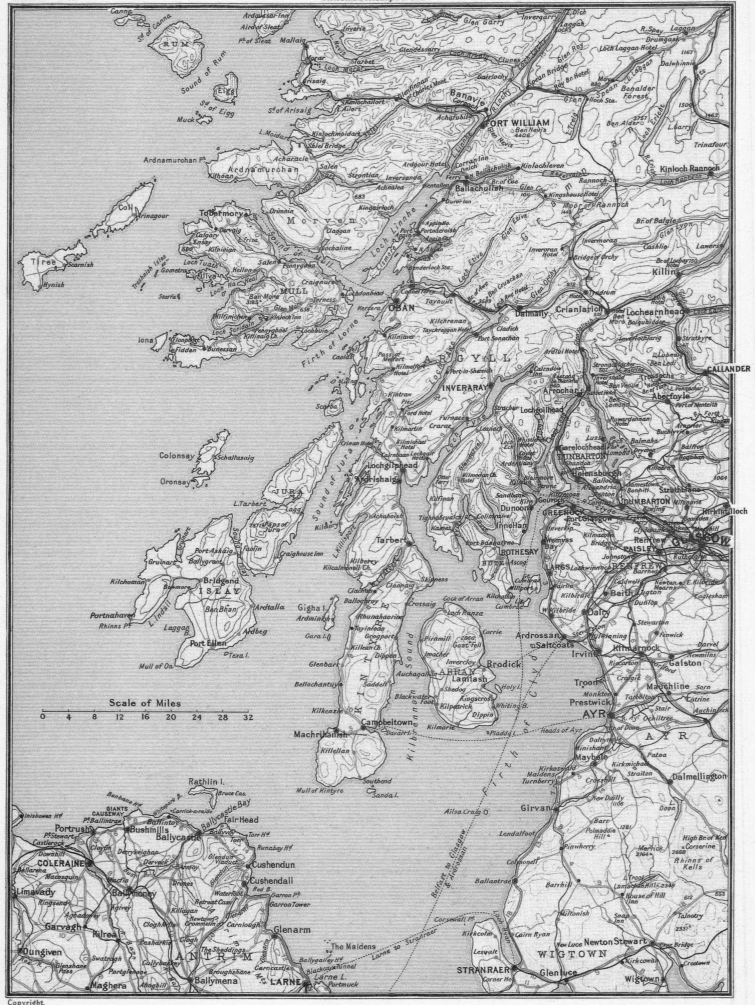

Scale of Miles

0   4   8   12   16   20   24   28   32

Main Roads ——20——   Other Roads ———————   Railways ———————
Red Figures indicate distances between places with Black Dots

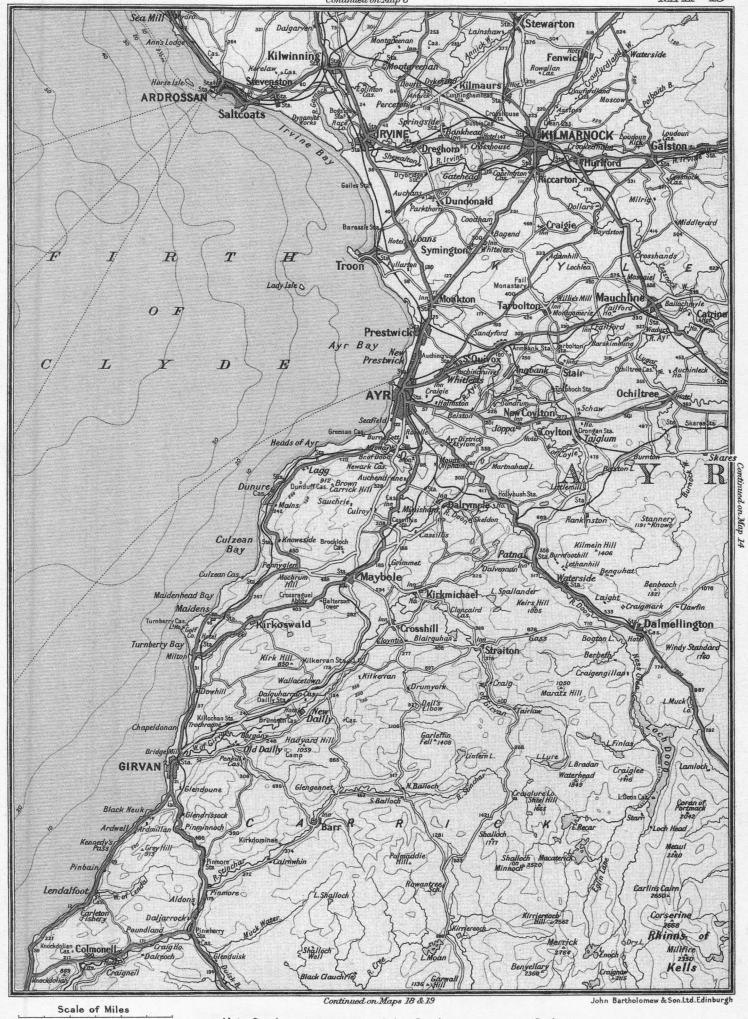

Scale of Miles

0 1 2 3 4 5 6

Main Roads ━━━━━   Other Roads ━━━━━   Railways ━━━━━

MAP 14

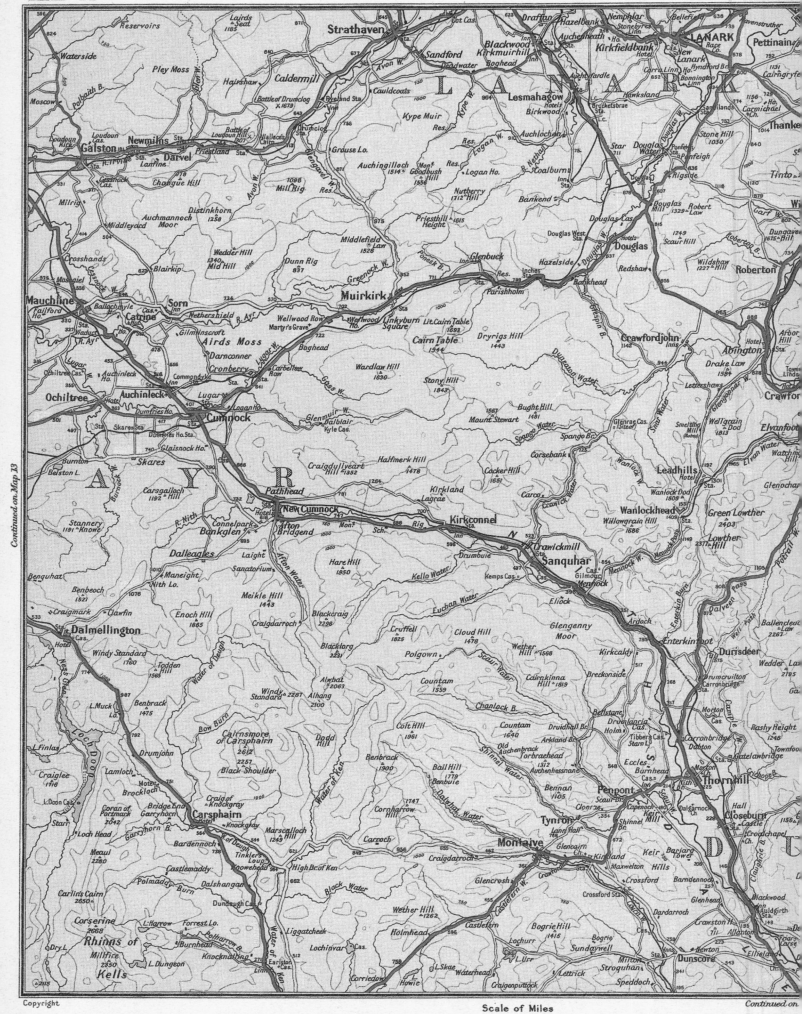

Continued on Map 13

Continued on

Scale of Miles

0 1 2 3 4 5 6 7 8 9 10

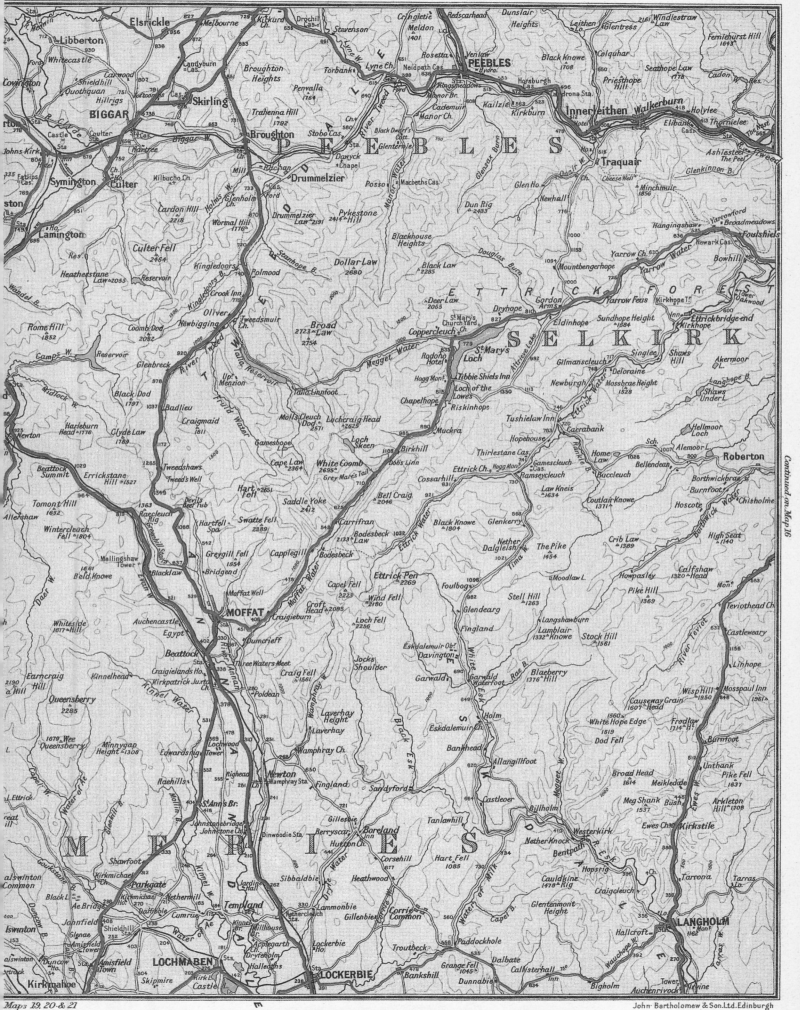

Continued on Map 16

Main Roads ——————   Other Roads ——————   Railways ——————

MAP 16

Continued on
Continued on Map 15
Continued on

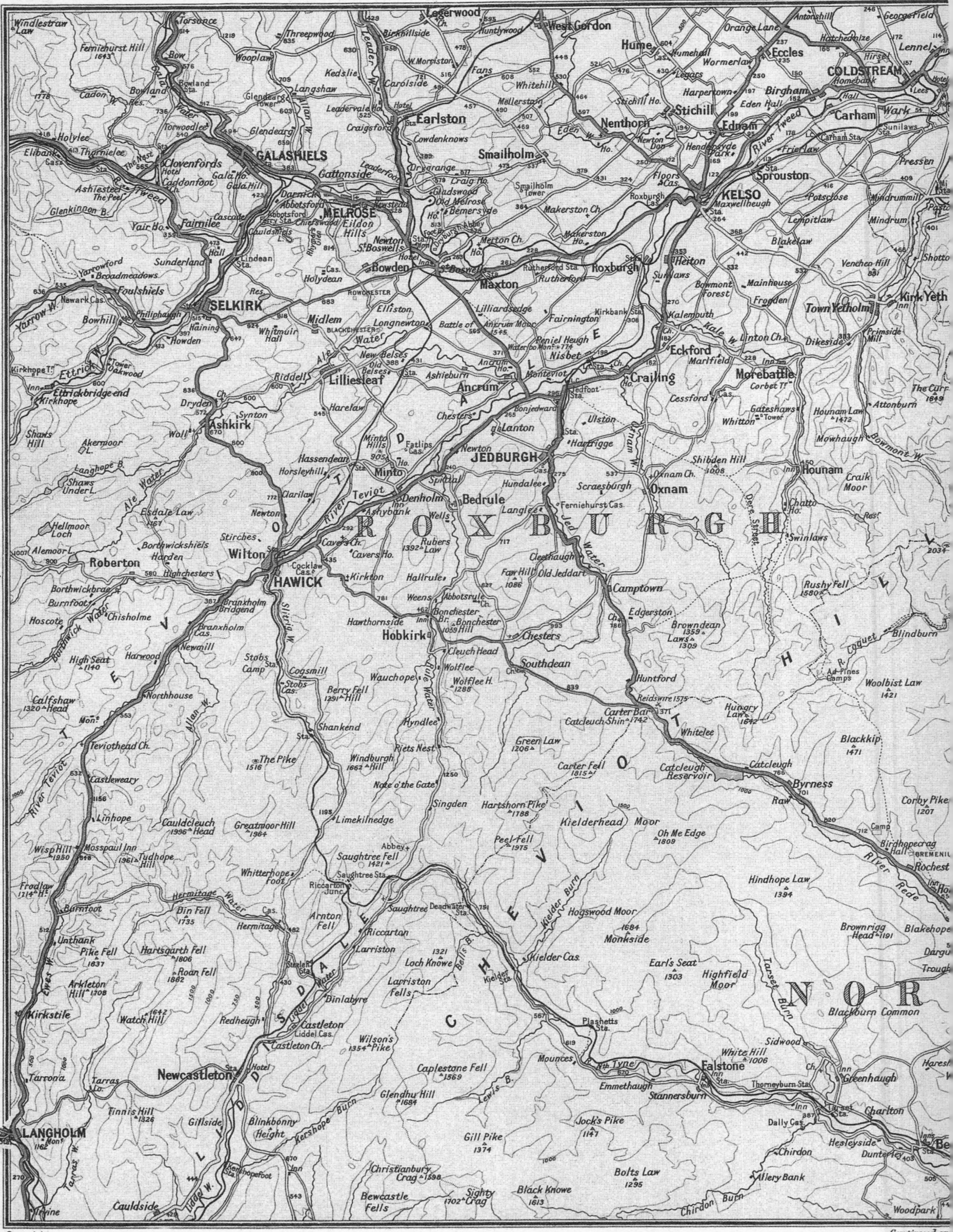

ROXBURGH

CHEVIOT HILLS

NOR

GALASHIELS · MELROSE · SELKIRK · EARLSTON · Smailholm · HUME · West Gordon · Eccles · COLDSTREAM · Lennel · CARHAM · Wark · Stichill · Ednam · KELSO · Sprouston · Birgham · Nenthorn

HAWICK · Wilton · Roberton · JEDBURGH · Bedrule · Denholm · Ancrum · Nisbet · Crailing · Eckford · Morebattle · Town Yetholm · Kirk Yetholm · Oxnam · Camptown

Lilliesleaf · Ashkirk · Ettrickbridge end · Kirkhope · Minto · Hassendean · Hobkirk · Bonchester · Chesters · Southdean · Carter Bar · Byrness · Catcleugh Reservoir

Newcastleton · Castleton · Kielder Cas. · Falstone · Stannersburn

LANGHOLM · Kirkstile · Tarras · Hermitage · Riccarton · Larriston · Saughtree · Deadwater · Plashetts

Scale of Miles
0 1 2 3 4 5 6 7 8 9 10

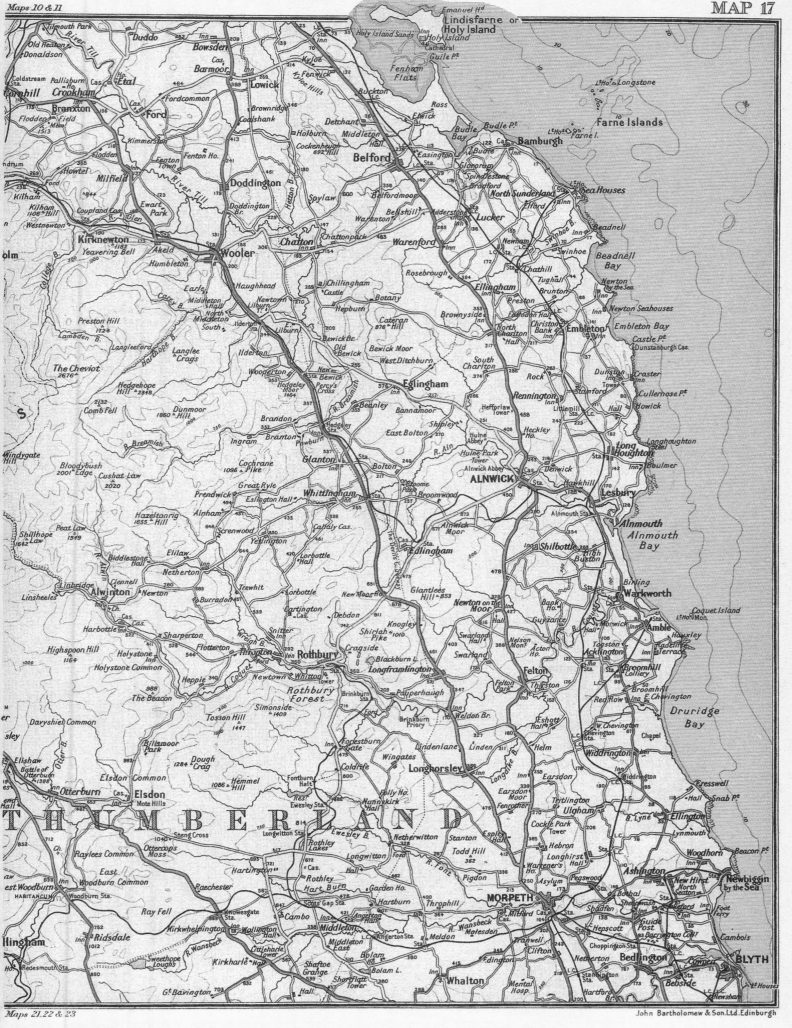

MAP 17

Lindisfarne or
Holy Island

Farne Islands

T H U M B E R L A N D

Main Roads ═══ Other Roads ═══ Railways ═══

MAP 18

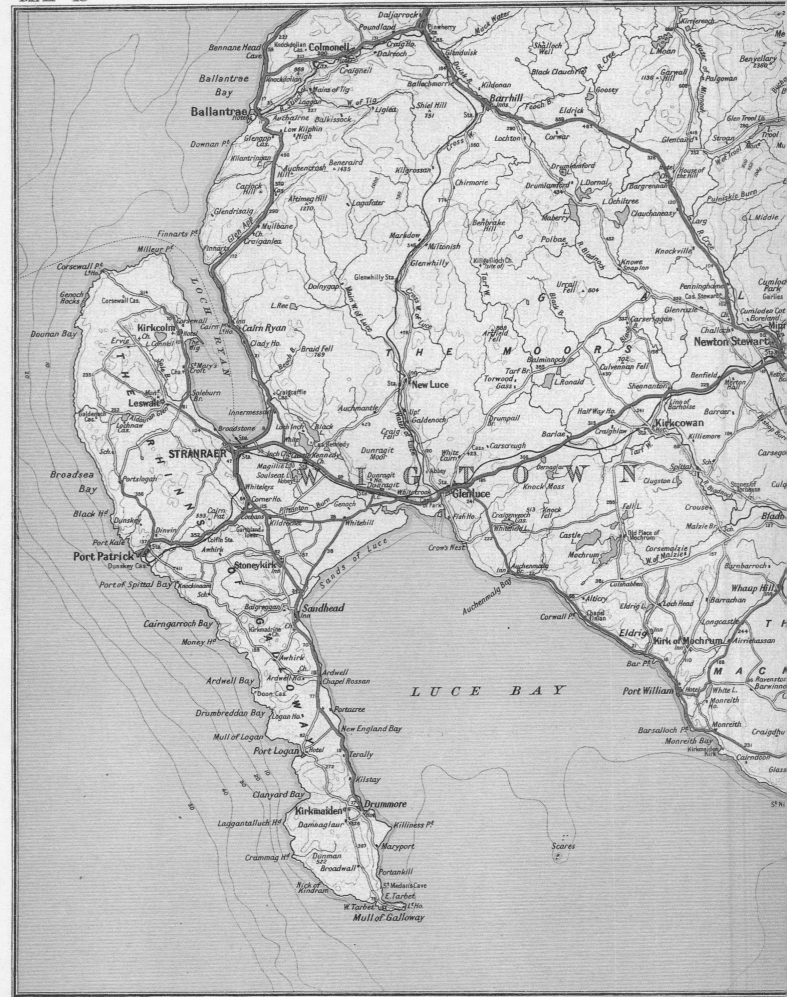

Daljarrock
Poundland
Pinwherry Sta.
Muck Water
Kirriereoch
Bennane Head Cave
Knockdolian Cas.
Colmonell
Craig Ho.
Dalreoch
Glenduisk
Shalloch Well
L. Moan
Water of Minnoch
Benyellary 2360
Me
Ballantrae Bay
Knockdolian
Craigneil
Mains of Tig
Ballochmorrie
Black Clauchrie
Kildonan
L. Goosey
Garwall Hill
Glen Trool Mt
608
Stron
1136
969
Craigs
Barrhill
Sta.
Eldrick
Glencaird
Trool
L. Troo
Ballantrae
Hotel
R. Stinchar
Laggan
W. of Tig
Liglea
Shiel Hill 751
Feoch B.
Corwar
559
487
Hotel Ch.
House of the Hill
W. of Trool
Auchairne
Balkissock
Cross
Lochton
290
Downan Pt
Glenapp Cas.
Low Kilphin High
560
526
755
Kilantringan Hill
498
Auchencrosh
Beneraird 1435
Kilgrossan
Chirmorie
Drumlamford
L. Dornal
434
Bargrennan
418
Corlock Hill
510
Altimeg Hill 1270
Lagafater
Drumlamford
Penninghame
Cumloden Park Garlies
L. Middie
Glendrisaig
290
Benbrake Hill
L. Ochiltree
Clauchaneasy
120
L. Middie
Finnarts Pt
Markdow
Miltonish
Maberry
R. Bladnoch
Knockville
R. Cree
Milleur Pt
Glen App
Ch.
549
Killigallioch Ch. (site of)
Polbae
Knowe Snap Inn
Penninghame
Corsewall Pt
Lt. Ho.
Finnarts
Craiganlea
Glenwhilly
432
Urrall Fell 604
104
Cumloden Ch.
112
Dolnygap
Glenwhilly Sta.
Tarf W.
Boreland
Genoch Rocks
Corsewall Cas.
L. Ree
Cross W. of Luce
888 Artfield Fell
Glenrazie
Challoch
Mull
Dounan Bay
20
Cairn Pt
Inn
Cairn Ryan
Braid Fell 769
T H E   M O O R S
Black B.
Carseriggan
332
Newton Stewart
Kirkcolm
Corsewall Ch.
70
Hotel The Tig
Clady Ho.
Beoch B.
Balminnoch
Culvennan Fell 430
Benfield
Merton Hall
Nethe Bo
Ervie
L. Connell
St. Mary's Croft
21
Tarf Br. 385
L. Ronald
Shennanton
229
Barraer
235
Mont
Cha.
Soleburn Br.
Craigcaffie Cas.
Auchmantle
Torwood Gass
Drumpail Br.
Half Way Ho.
Linn of Barhoise
Barraer
252
Leswalt
Aldouran Glen
81
Broadstone
Loch Inch
White
Black
Cas. Kennedy
Up Galdenoch
Waters of Luce
Carscreugh
Barlae
315
Kirkcowan
Hotel
Killiemore
104
Galdenoch Cas.
Lochnaw Cas.
Sta.
Inch Ch.
Castle Kennedy
Dunragit Moor
White Cairn
Cass
Craighlaw
Sta.
Spittal
Sch.
STRANRAER
47
Sta.
Magillie
Ch. Sta.
Dunragit Ho.
Abbey
120
423
Dernaglar L.
Carsego
Broadsea Bay
Portslogan
356
Soulseat Abbey
Whiteleys
Corner Ho.
W I G T O W N
59
Sta.
Dunragit
Abbey Sta.
165
Knock Moss
Clugston L.
Crouse
R. Bladnoch
Bladn
137
Black Hd
Dunskey
593
Cairn Pat
115
Pilanton Burn
Genoch
Whitecrook
Glenluce
Fish Ho.
Craigenveoch Cas.
513
Knock Fell
255
Fell L.
Malzie Br.
Sch.
Dinvin
352
Lochans
Kildrochet
28
Whitehill
241
Whitefield L.
222
Castle
Old Place of Mochrum
Corsemalzie W. of Malzie
157
Port Kale
Sta.
Colfin Sta.
Garthland Tower
Crow's Nest
Mochrum L.
Burnbarroch
Port Patrick
Dunskey Cas.
Awhirk
38
Auchenmalg Br.
Alticry
Culshabben
361
Whaup Hill Inn
Port of Spittal Bay
Knockinaam Sch.
Stoneykirk Inn
Sands of Luce
Auchenmalg Bay
Eldrig L.
Loch Head
Barrachan
Cairngarroch Bay
Balgreggan
35
Corwall Pt
Chapel Finian
Eldrig Inn
Longcastle
Kirkmadrine Ch.
Money Hd
Awhirk Ch.
21
Kirk of Mochrum Inn
Airriehassan
244
Ardwell Bay
Ardwell Ho.
18
Ardwell Chapel Rossan
Bar Pt
16
110
188
M A C
Ardwell
Doon Cas.
77
L U C E   B A Y
Port William
Hotel
White L.
Drumbreddan Bay
Logan Ho.
Portacree
Monreith Ho.
Ravenstor
Barwinno
Mull of Logan
New England Bay
Barsalloch Pt
Monreith
Craigdhu
Port Logan
Hotel
19
Terally
Monreith Bay
231
10
272
Kilstay
Kirkmaiden Kirk
Cairndoon
St. Ni
Clanyard Bay
Drummore
Glass
20
30
Hotel
Kirkmaiden
77
40
Damnaglaur
526
Killiness Pt
Scares
Laggantalluch Hd
367
Maryport
Crammag Hd 522
Dunman
Broadwall
Portankill
Nick of Kindram
St. Medan's Cave
E. Tarbet
W. Tarbet
Lt. Ho.
Mull of Galloway

Scale of Miles

0 1 2 3 4 5 6 7 8 9 10

MAP 19

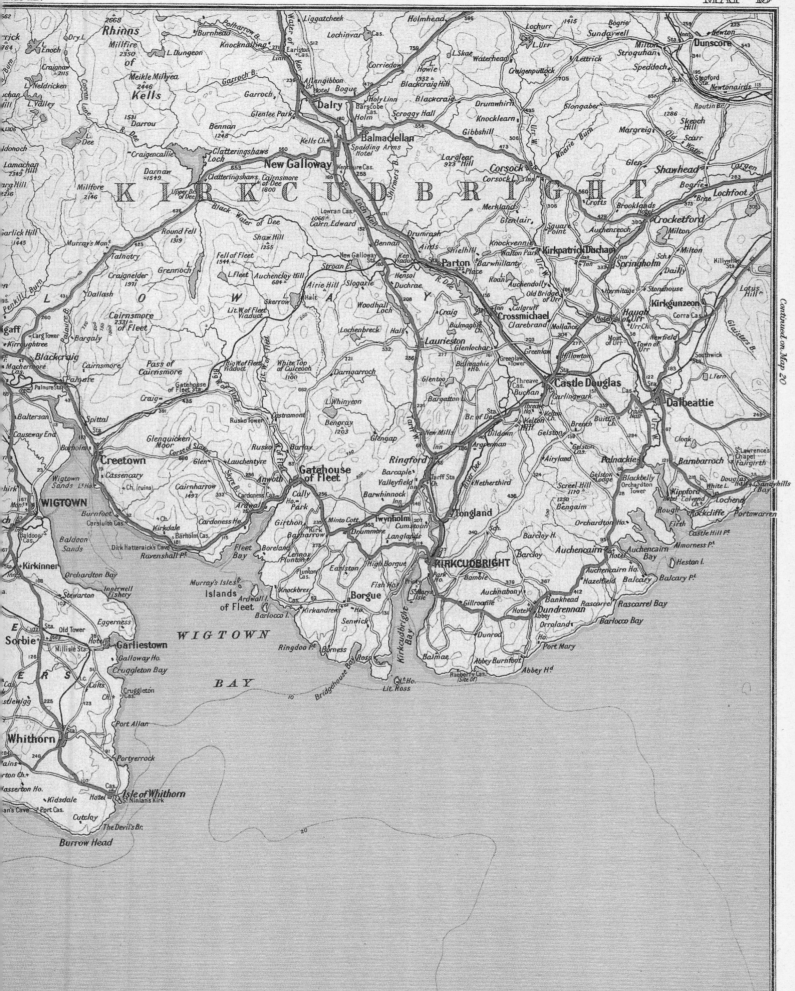

Continued on Map 20

Main Roads —————— Other Roads —————— Railways ——————

MAP 20

Continued o

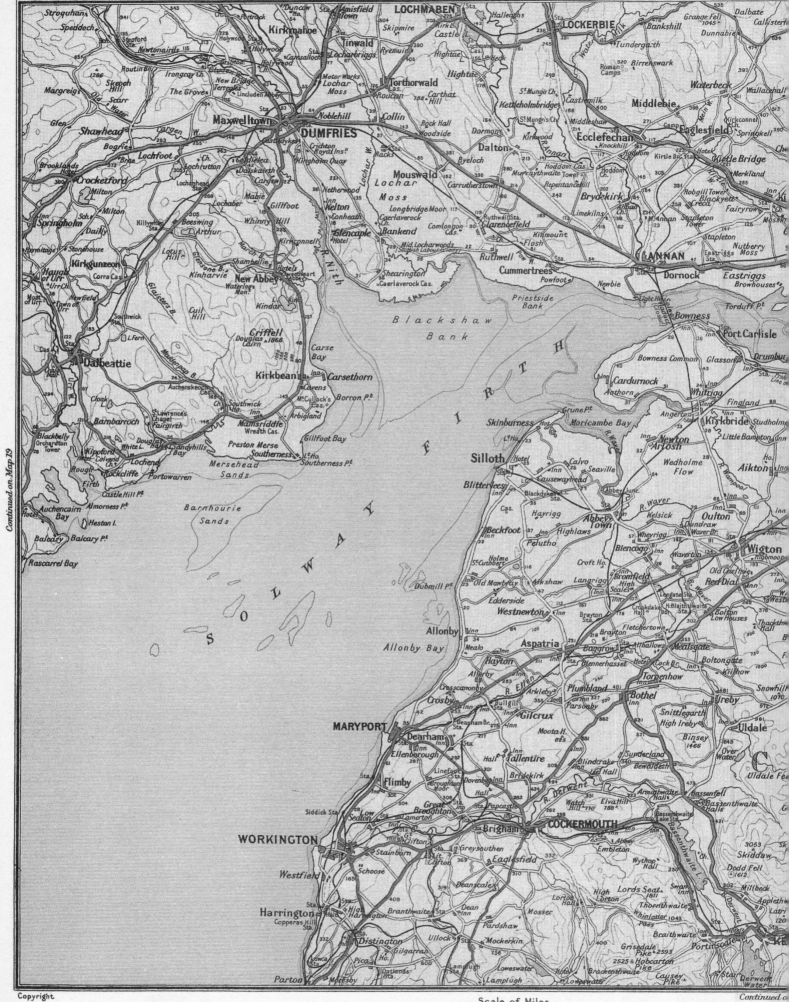

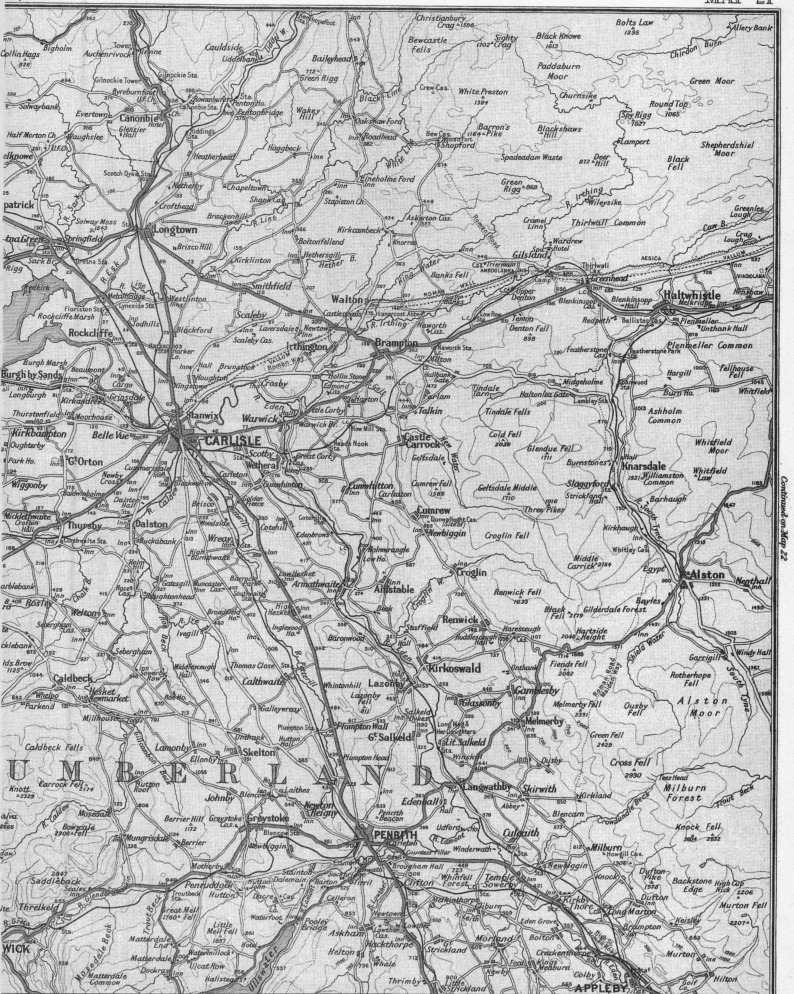

Main Roads —————— Other Roads ═══════ Railways ——————

MAP 22

Continued on Maps 16 & 17

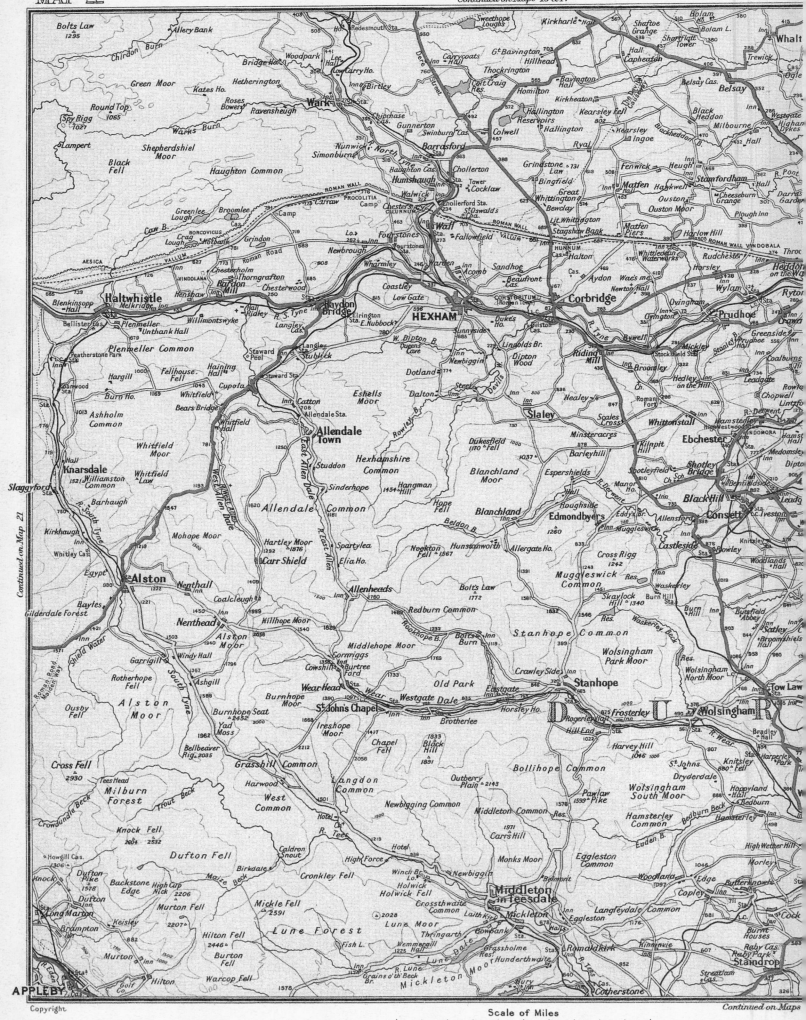

Continued on Map 21

Scale of Miles

0 1 2 3 4 5 6 7 8 9 10

Copyright

Continued on Maps

MAP 23

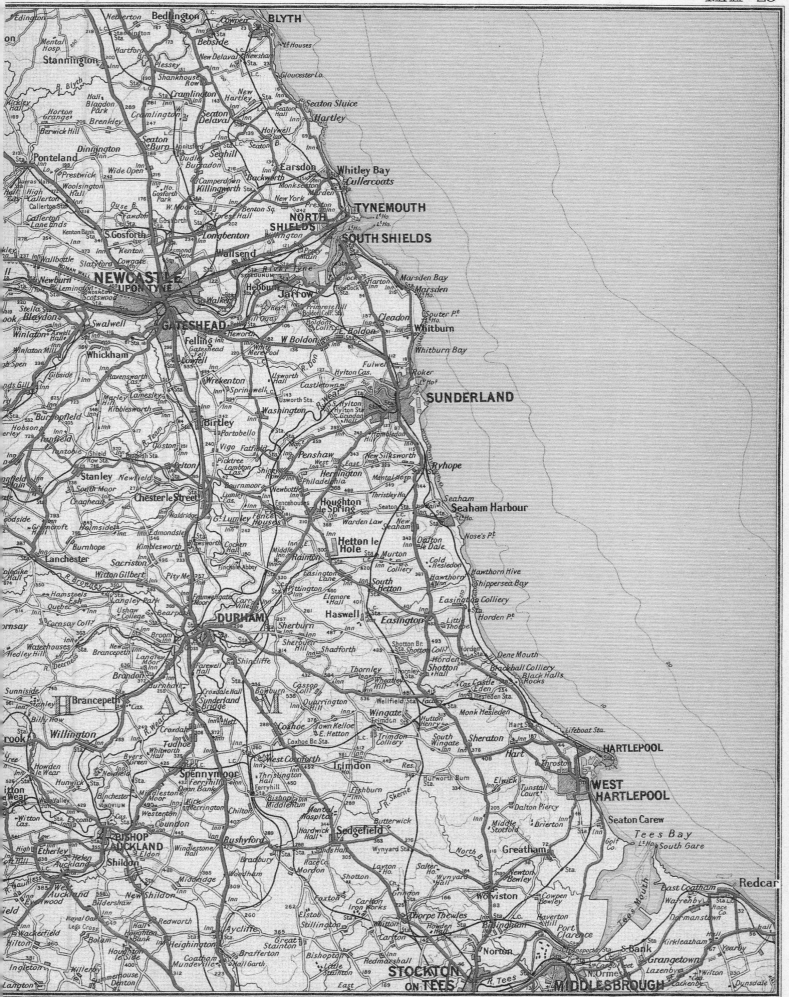

John Bartholomew & Son.Ltd.Edinburgh

Main Roads ——————— Other Roads ——————— Railways ————

MAP 24

Continued on

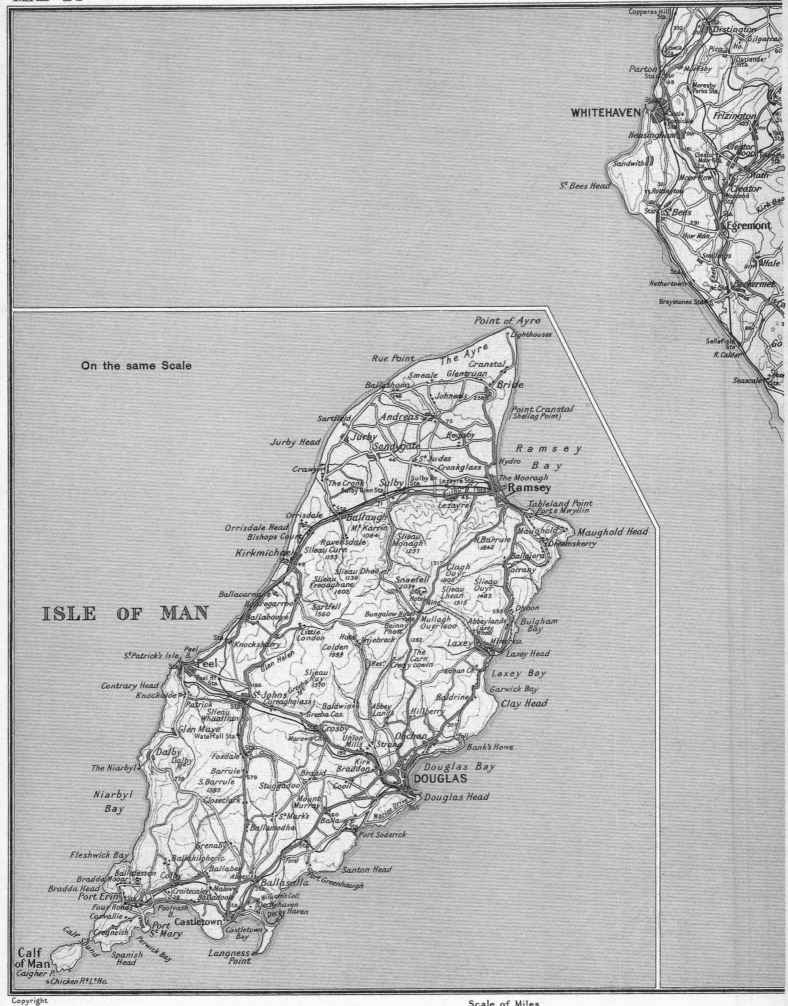

On the same Scale

ISLE OF MAN

WHITEHAVEN

Point of Ayre
Lighthouses

The Ayre
Rue Point
Cranstal
Smeale Glentruan
Ballaghona Bride
Johneis
Point Cranstal
(Shellag Point)
Sartfield Andreas
Jurby Head 75
Jurby Regaby Ramsey
Sandygate Bay
Crawyn St. Judes Cronkglass Hydro
The Cronk Sulby The Mooragh
Sulby Sta. Sulby Br. Lezayre Sta. Ramsey
Orrisdale Sulby Glen Sta. Sulby R. Sta.
Sta. Lezayre
Orrisdale Head Ballaugh Tableland Point
Bishops Court Mt. Karrin Port e Mwyllin
Ravensdale 1084 Slieau
Kirkmichael Slieau Curn Monagh N.Barrule Maughold
1153 1257 1842 Dreemskerry
Slieau Dhoo 1317 Balljora
Ballacarnane 1139 Snaefell Clagh Torrany
Barregarroo Slieau 2034 Ouyr Slieau
Ballabooye Freoaghane Sta. 1808 Ouyr
1602 Sartfell Hotel Slieau 1483
Sartfell 1560 Bungalow Hotel Lhean Dhoon
Beinny 1515 595
Knocksharry Little Phott Mullagh Abbeylands Bulgham
London Colden Injebreck Ouyr 1600 Laxey Bay
St. Patrick's Isle Hotel 1599 1282 Wheel
Peel B. Res. The Laxey Minorca
Peel Glen Helen Carn Laxey Head
Peel Rd. Slieau Cregy cowin Eonan Ch.
Contrary Head Sta. Ruy Laxey Bay
Knockaloe 186 1570 Garwick Bay
St. Johns Greeba Baldwin Baldrine Clay Head
Patrick Curraghglass Mt. Abbey
Slieau Greeba Cas. Lands Hillberry
Whaalllan Bank's Howe
Glen Maye Crosby Onchan
Waterfall Sta. Marown Ch. Union Strang Toll
Dalby Mills 357
Dalby Foxdale 192 Kirk Douglas Bay
Mt. Braddon DOUGLAS
The Niarbyl 739 Barrule Braaid Douglas Head
679 Cooil
Niarbyl S. Barrule Stuggadoo Mount Marine Drive Toll
Bay 1585 Murray Ballavere
Closeclark St. Mark's Port Soderick
Ballamodha
Grenaby Santon Head
Fleshwick Bay Ballakilpheric ford Port Greenhaugh
Bradda Mooar Colby Ballabeg
Bradda Head Balladesson Abbey
Port Erin Croitecaley Malew Williams Coll.
Four Roads Poolvash Balladoole Derbyhaven
Corvallie Sta. Derby Haven
Calf Port Cregneish Castletown
of Man St. Mary Castletown
Caigher P. Spanish Bay
Chicken Rk. L. Ho. Perwick Bay Head Langness
Calf Sound Point

Copyright.

Scale of Miles
0 1 2 3 4 5 6 7 8 9 10

MAP 25

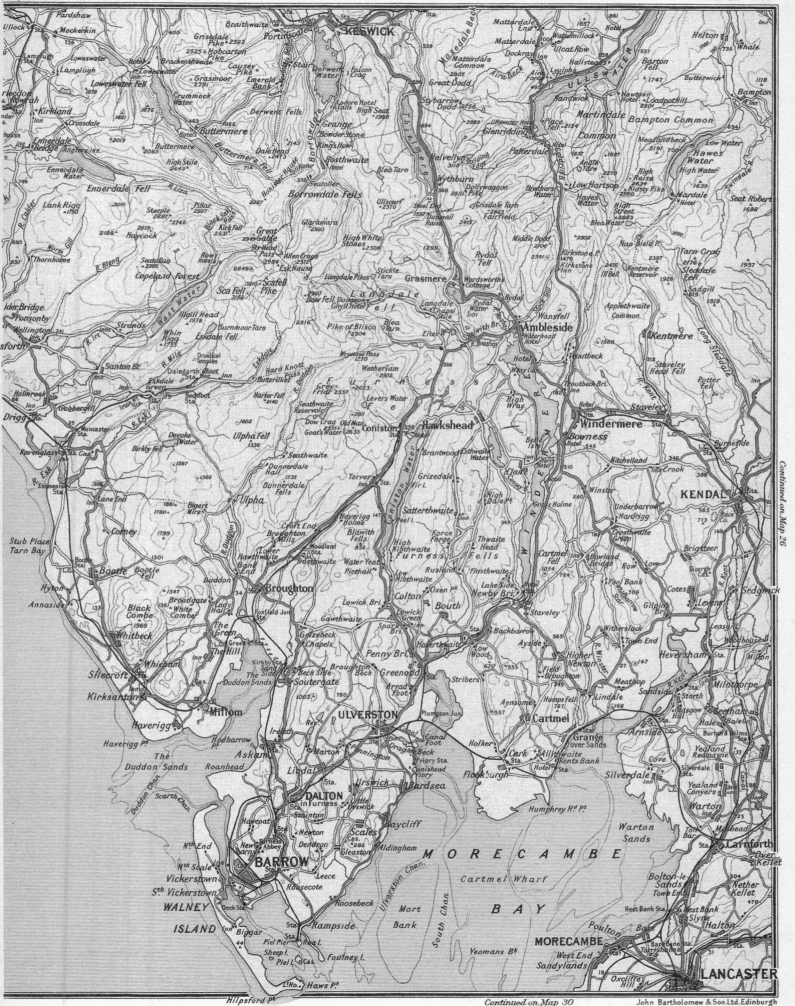

Continued on Map 26

Continued on Map 30

John Bartholomew & Son. Ltd. Edinburgh

Main Roads ———— Other Roads ———— Railways ————

MAP 26

Continued on Maps

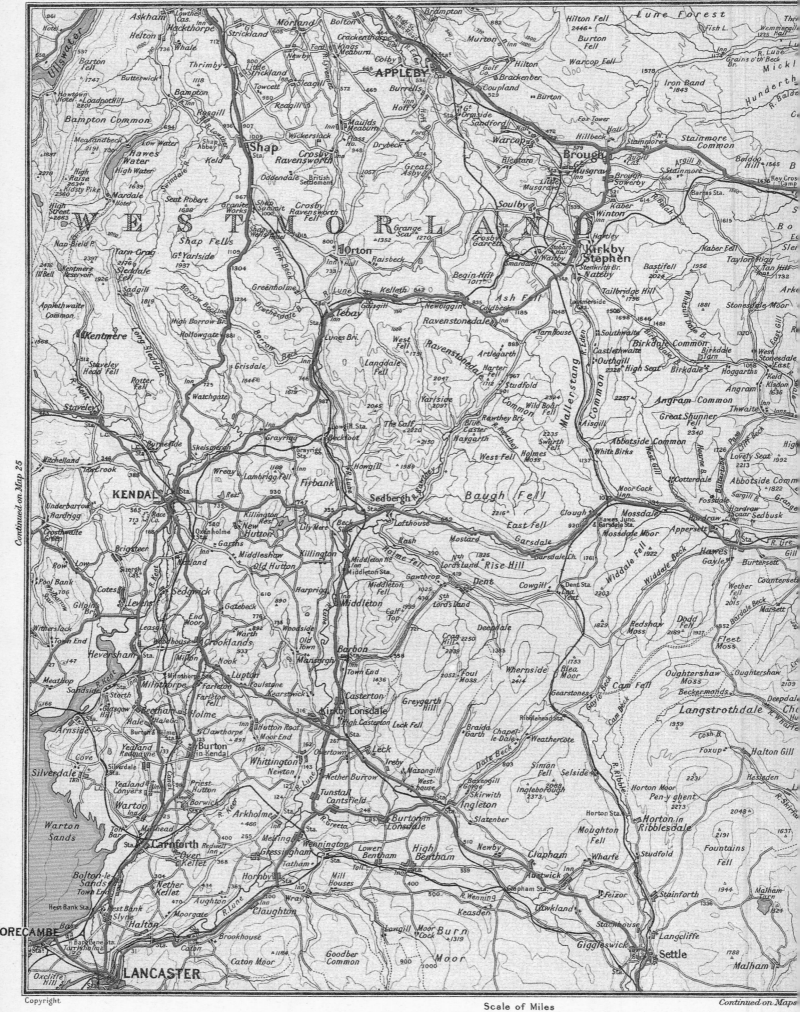

Continued on Map 25

Continued on Maps

Scale of Miles

0 1 2 3 4 5 6 7 8 9 10

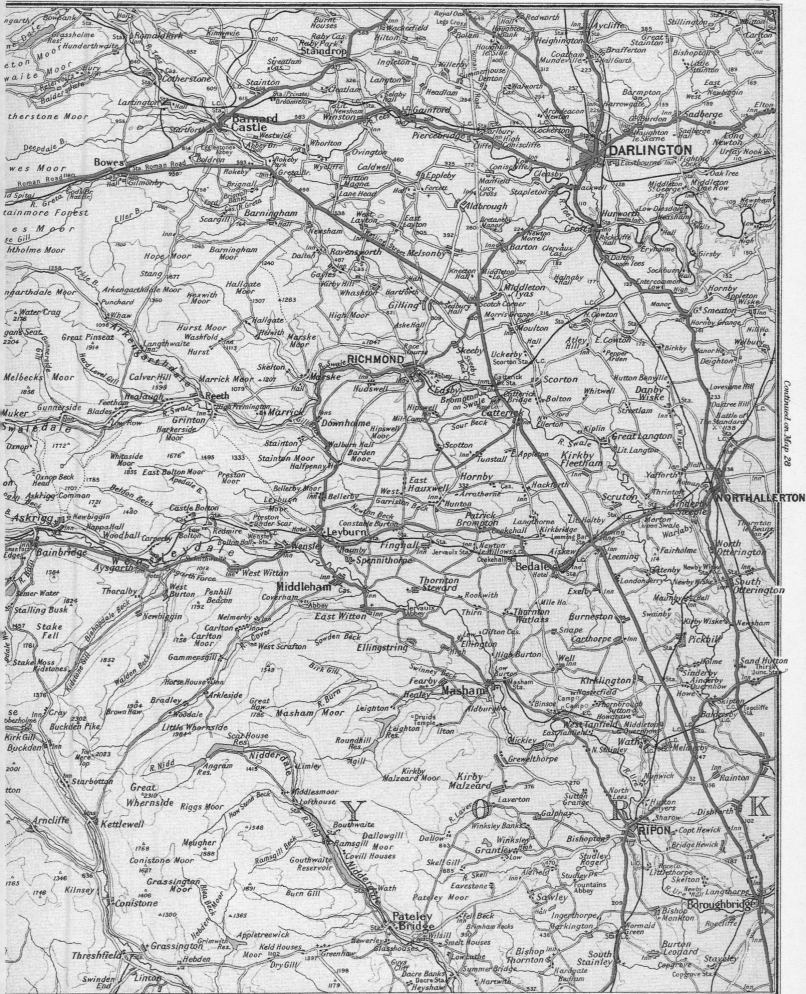

Main Roads ━━━━━ Other Roads ═══════ Railways ────────

John Bartholomew & Son Ltd. Edinburgh

Continued on Map 28

MAP 28

Continued on Map 23

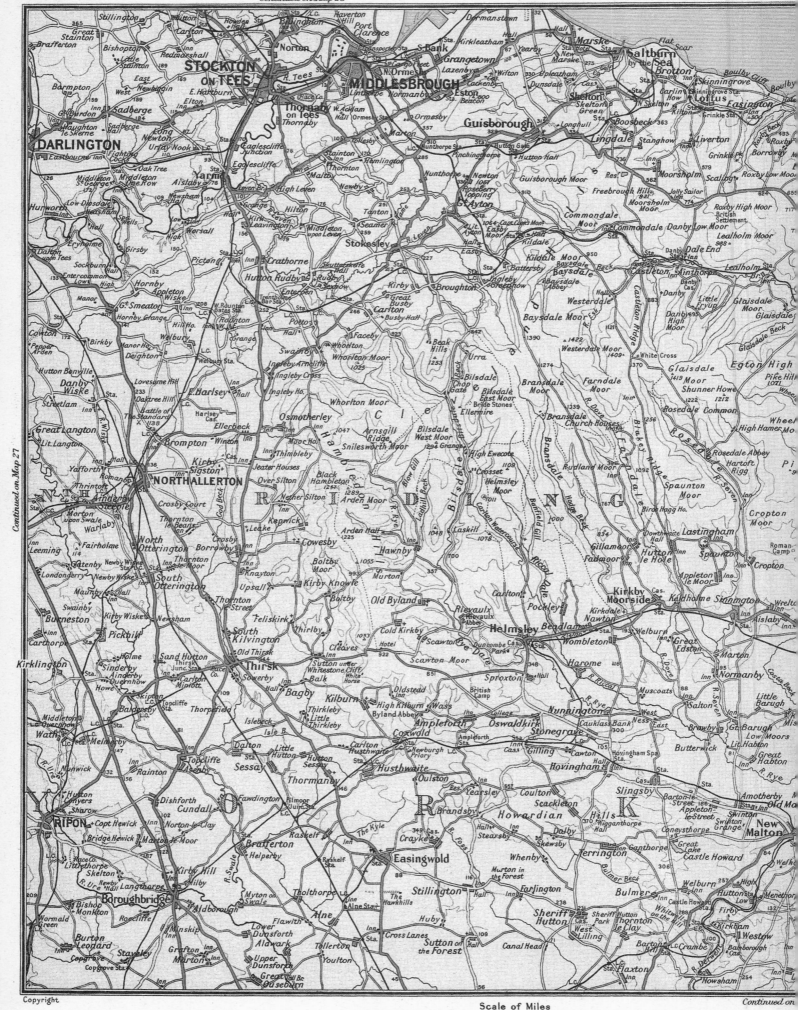

Continued on Map 27

Scale of Miles

0 1 2 3 4 5 6 7 8 9 10

Continued on

MAP 29

Staithes
Dalehouse
Port Mulgrave
Hinderwell
Runswick B.
Runswick Sta.
Inn
Kettle Ness
Kettleness
grave
Mickleby
Goldsborough
Sta.
Lythe
Sandsend Ness
erby
W. Barnby
Mulgrave
Sandsend
Les.
Upgang
Lt. Ho.
Ugthorpe
Dunsley
West Cliff Sta.
Abbey
Baltwick B.
Newholm
WHITBY
718
Swarthoe Cross
235
Hall
Egton
682
Ruswarp
Low Moor
R. Esk
Aislaby
Stainsacre
Priory
Sneaton
Low
Sta.
Egton
Egton Br.
Sleights
Inn
High Hawsker
Roman Camp
Grosmont
Little Beck
562
Fylingdales
Sleights Moor
Fylingthorpe
Inn
Hotel
Robin Hood's Bay
930
700
Falling
Low Moor
Beck Hole
Sta.
613
Goathland
Foss
Hotel
558
Flask Inn
Ravenscar
Gill
Goathland Moor
700
Golf Co.
Ravenscar Sta.
dale
825
564
959
Fylingdales Moor
Staintondale
Sta.
Lockton High
661
Falcon Inn
Hayburn Wyke
Moor
Allerston High
Hotel
ering Moor
701
Saltergate
Moor
Wykeham
Cloughton
Inn
Newlands
Manley Cross
920
High Moor
Hackness Moor
Inn
Cloughton
Stape
Black Beck
R. Derwent
Sta.
Lockton Low
743
Jerry
801
Noddle
Burniston
Levisham
Moor
Broxa
Inn
Newton
Lockton
Allerston Low
Langdale
Silpho
Inn
Dalby Beck
Moor
End
Suffield
Scalby
amp
808
Hall
Hackness
Sta.
Haugh Rigg
783
Trout Dale
Newby
Blansby
449
Wykeham
North
Toll
iddleton
Park
Moor
670
Bay
Cas. Hotel
12 Cas.
Dalby Warren
Falsgrave
Ho.
294
Forge Valley
SCARBOROUGH
Pickering
Sawdon
Irton
South
Ellerburn
Inn
W. Ayton
Moor
Bay
Wilton
Hutton
E. Ayton
Race Co.
Inn
Allerston
Bushel
300
Golf Co.
Thornton Dale
Ebberston
Ruston
Wykeham
Irton
162
Osgodby
Cayton Bay
62
L.C.
Inn
Brompton
Seamer
Sta.
Inn
Ebberston Sta.
L.C.
Snainton
Sawdon Sta.
Cayton
Letterston
Wilton Carr
L.C.
L.C.
Gristhorpe
Filey Brigg
Abbey
R. Derwent
The Cars
Hertford R.
Sta.
Marishes Road
Yedingham
Willerby
Flixton
Folkton
Muston
Filey
erton
70
Sta.
Inn
Staxton
Lang Camp
Sta. L.C.
Marishes
L.C.
Weaverthorpe
Golf Co.
441
Golf
Inn
Hesterton Sta.
Sta.
Ganton
Intrenchment
Co.
Filey
L.C.
160
Sherburn
Hall
Bay
Rillington
Knapton
E. Heslerton
572
Hunmanby
Scampston
165
Inn
Fordon
Sta.
Rillington
W. Heslerton
Sherburn Wold
Reighton
Speeton
Sta.
510
409
L.C.
Wintringham
Inn
Wold
273
Buckton
Thorpe
Newton
Newton
382
Bempton
Bassett
367
251
North Burton or
310
Hotel
Scagglethorpe
Place Newton
Foxholes
Burton Fleming
Inn
Norton
186
Grindale
L.C.
68
Weaverthorpe
Butterwick
143
238
Hotel
Settrington
Inn
Thwing
285
Flamborough
654
Octon
Ho.
Lt. Ho.
angton Wold
East Lutton
Helperthorpe
537
Flamborough Hd.
50
Sta.
442
Ancient
100
Sewerby
Race
306
Village
Co.
West Lutton
Swaythorpe
Rudston
Boynton
210
369
281
The Gypsey Race
Bridlington
Langton
North Grimston
Inn
Langtoft
Kirby Grindalythe
200
Bridlington Quay
561
400
300
Bessingby
Duggleby
579
Carnaby
Birdsall
Cowlam
BRIDLINGTON
Kennythorpe
Wharram-le-Street
Haisthorpe
Sledmere
Cottam
400
West End
Carnaby Moor
Burythorpe
688
Ho.
356
Kilham
Thornholme
Aldro
Wharram
477
300
Burton
78
L.C. Sta.
ening
Percy
Agnes
55
Towthorpe
Carnaby Moor
26
Burdale
345
97 Hill
Sta.
BAY

John Bartholomew & Son. Ltd. Edinburgh

Main Roads ———   Other Roads ———   Railways ———

MAP 30
Continued on Maps

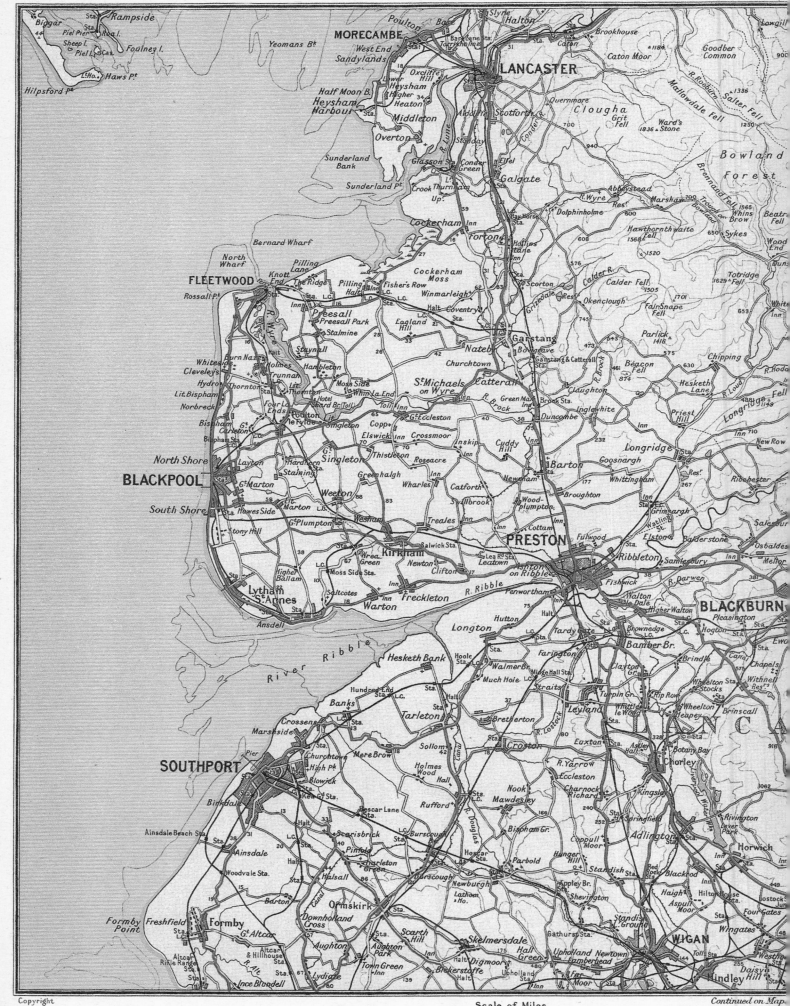

Continued on Map

Scale of Miles

0 1 2 3 4 5 6 7 8 9 10

MAP 31

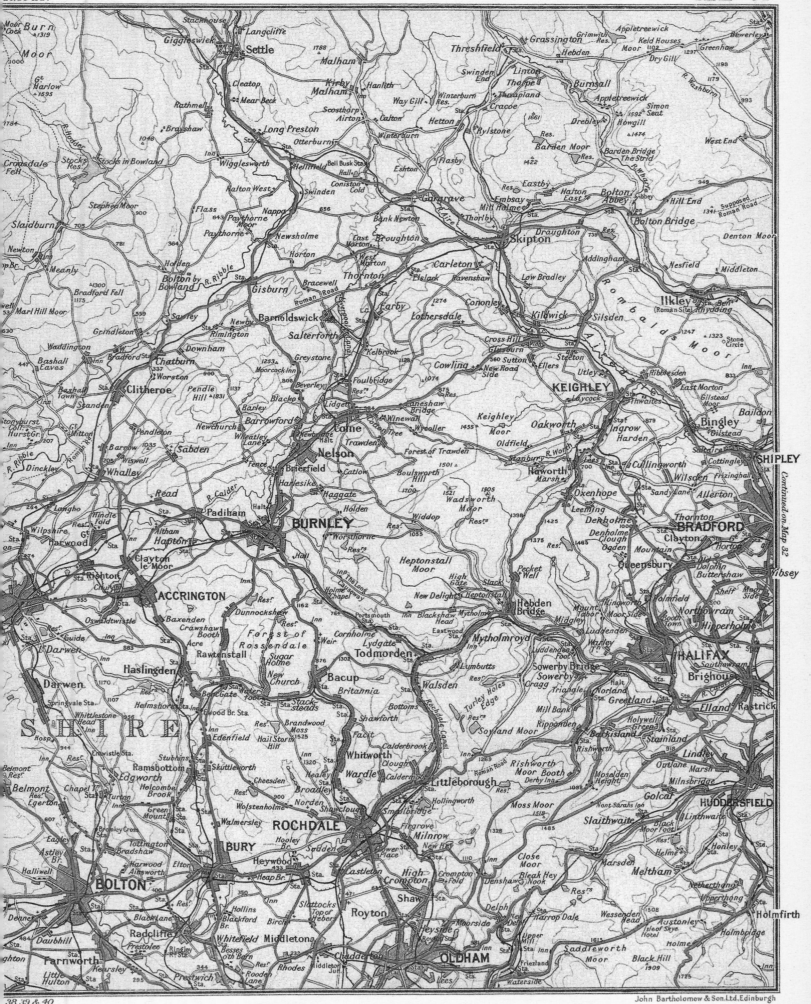

Continued on Map 32

John Bartholomew & Son.Ltd.Edinburgh

Main Roads ━━━━━ Other Roads ━━━━━ Railways ━━━━━

MAP 32

Continued on

Continued on Map 31

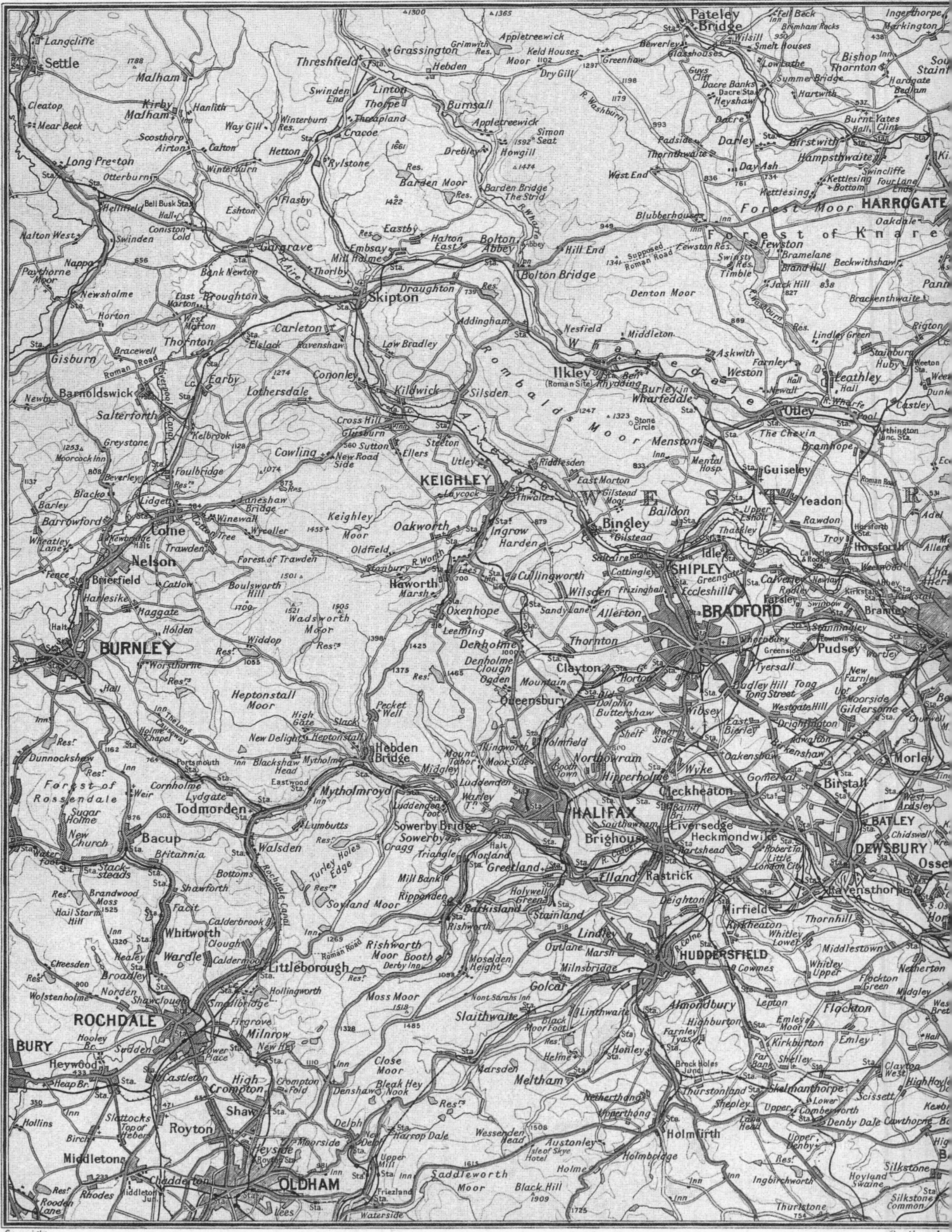

Settle
Langcliffe
Cleatop
Mear Beck
Long Preston
Otterburn
Malham
Kirby Malham
Hanlith
Scosthorp
Airton
Calton
Winterburn
Way Gill
Hetton
Cracoe
Threshfield
Linton
Thorpe
Theapland
Burnsall
Swinden End
Rylstone
Grassington
Hebden
Appletreewick
Keld Houses
Dry Gill
Grimwith Res.
Greenhow
Pateley Bridge
Bewerley
Glasshouses
Wilsill
Brimham Rocks
Ingerthorpe
Markington
Smelt Houses
Low Lathe
Summer Bridge
Bishop Thornton
Hargate
Bedlam
Dacre Banks
Heyshaw
Dacre
Darley
Birstwith
Hampsthwaite
Burnt Yates
Clint
Helifield
Bell Busk Sta
Coniston Cold
Gargrave
Eshton
Flasby
Thorlby
Embsay
Mill Holme
Halton East
Bolton Abbey
Hill End
Bolton Bridge
Blubberhouses
Fewston
Swinsty Res.
Timble
Bramelane
Brand Hill
Beckwithshaw
HARROGATE
Forest of Knare
Forest Moor
Oakdale
Skipton
Draughton
Addingham
Nesfield
Middleton
Denton Moor
Ilkley
(Roman Site)
Ben Rhydding
Burley in Wharfedale
Askwith
Weston
Farnley
Leathley
Otley
The Chevin
Bramhope
Guiseley
Rombalds Moor
Stone Circle
Menston
Mental Hosp.
Yeadon
Rawdon
Horsforth
Carleton
Elslack
Ravenshaw
Low Bradley
Kildwick
Silsden
Cross Hill
Glusburn
Sutton
New Road Side
Ellers
Steeton
Utley
Riddlesden
East Morton
Gilstead Moor
Bingley
Gilstead
Baildon
Shipley
Idle
Eccleshill
BRADFORD
Pudsey
Thornton
Earby
Lothersdale
Kelbrook
Cowling
Stanbury
Keighley Moor
Oakworth
Oldfield
KEIGHLEY
Laycock
Thwaites
Ingrow
Harden
Cullingworth
Wilsden
Sandy Lane
Allerton
Barnoldswick
Salterforth
Gisburn
Newsholme
Horton
Foulridge
Blacko
Lidget
Laneshaw Bridge
Winewall
Wycoller
Colne
Trawden
Forest of Trawden
Haworth Marsh
Lees
Oxenhope
Leeming
Denholme
Denholme Clough
Ogden
Clayton
Queensbury
Mountain
Horton
Nelson
Brierfield
Harlesike
Haggate
Holden
Catlow
Boulsworth Hill
Wadsworth Moor
Widdop
BURNLEY
Worsthorne
Heptonstall Moor
High Gate
Slack
Pecket Well
New Delights
Heptonstall
Hebden Bridge
Midgley
Luddenden
Warley
Mytholm
Blackshaw Head
Eastwood
Mytholmroyd
Luddenden Foot
Sowerby Bridge
Sowerby
Cragg
Triangle
Wainstalls
Mount Tabor
Moor Side
Illingworth
Holmfield
Northowram
Booth Town
Shelf
Moor Side
Hipperholme
Wyke
Cleckheaton
Liversedge
Heckmondwike
HALIFAX
Southowram
Brighouse
Elland
Rastrick
Greetland
Norland
Ripponden
Backisland
Stainland
Rishworth
Mill Bank
Soyland Moor
Lindley
Outlane
Marsh
Milnsbridge
HUDDERSFIELD
Deighton
Mirfield
Kirkheaton
Whitley Lower
Middlestown
Golcar
Slaithwaite
Linthwaite
Almondbury
Highburton
Farnley Tyas
Lepton
Flockton
Emley
Kirkburton
Shelley
Todmorden
Bacup
Britannia
Walsden
Cornholme
Lydgate
Stacksteads
Shawforth
Facit
Calderbrook
Littleborough
Whitworth
Wardle
Healey
Broadley
Shawclough
Smallbridge
ROCHDALE
Milnrow
Newhey
Moss Moor
Rishworth Moor
Mosalden Height
Marsden
Black Moor Foot
Helme
Meltham
Honley
Brockholes
Holmfirth
Holmbridge
Thurstonland
Shepley
Denby Dale
Scissett
Clayton West
Forest of Rossendale
Sugar Home
New Church
Waterfoot
Brandwood Moss
Hail Storm Hill
Cheesden
Wolstenholme
Norden
Hooley Br.
BURY
Heywood
Heap Br.
Hollins
Slattocks
Top of Hebers
Royton
Middleton
Rhodes
Rooden Lane
Castleton
High Crompton
Crompton Fold
Shaw
Denshaw
Delph
Moorside
Upper Mill
Friezland
Heyside
OLDHAM
Lees
Waterside
Saddleworth Moor
Harrop Dale
Wessenden Head
Isle of Skye Hotel
Austonley
Black Hill
Upperthong
Netherthong
Upper Denby
Hoyland Swaine
Ingbirchworth
Thurlstone
Silkstone Common

Scale of Miles
0 1 2 3 4 5 6 7 8 9 10

Continued on

MAP 33

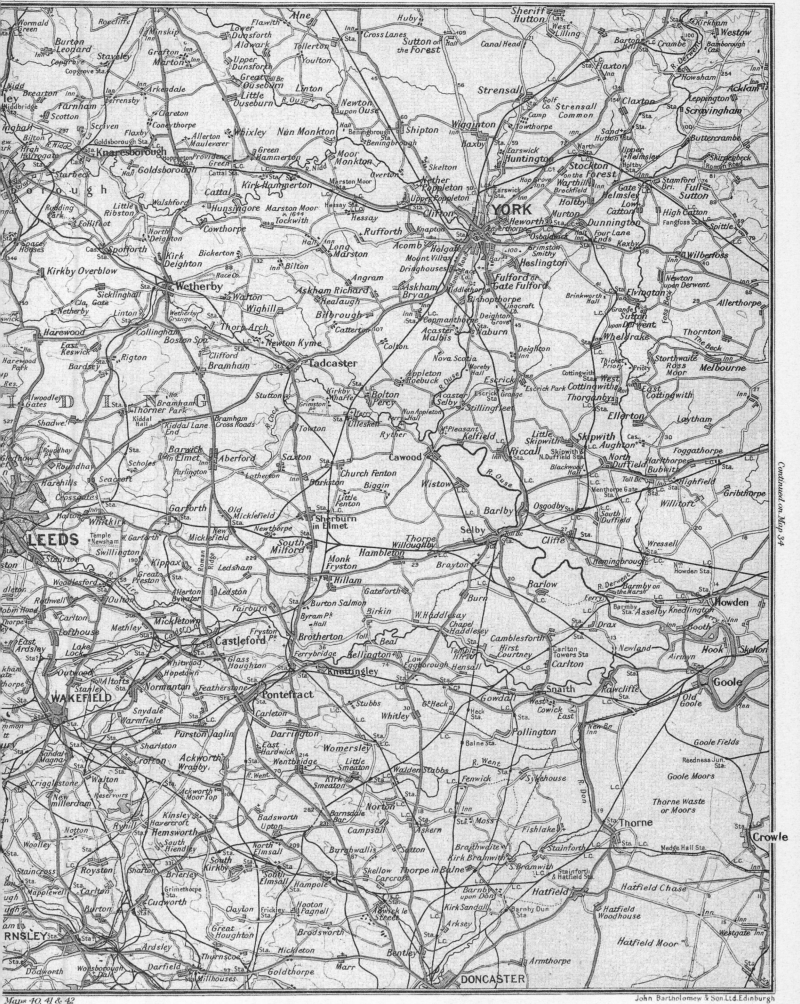

John Bartholomew & Son.Ltd.Edinburgh.

Main Roads ━━━━━━   Other Roads ━━━━━━   Railways ━━━━━━

MAP 34
Continued on

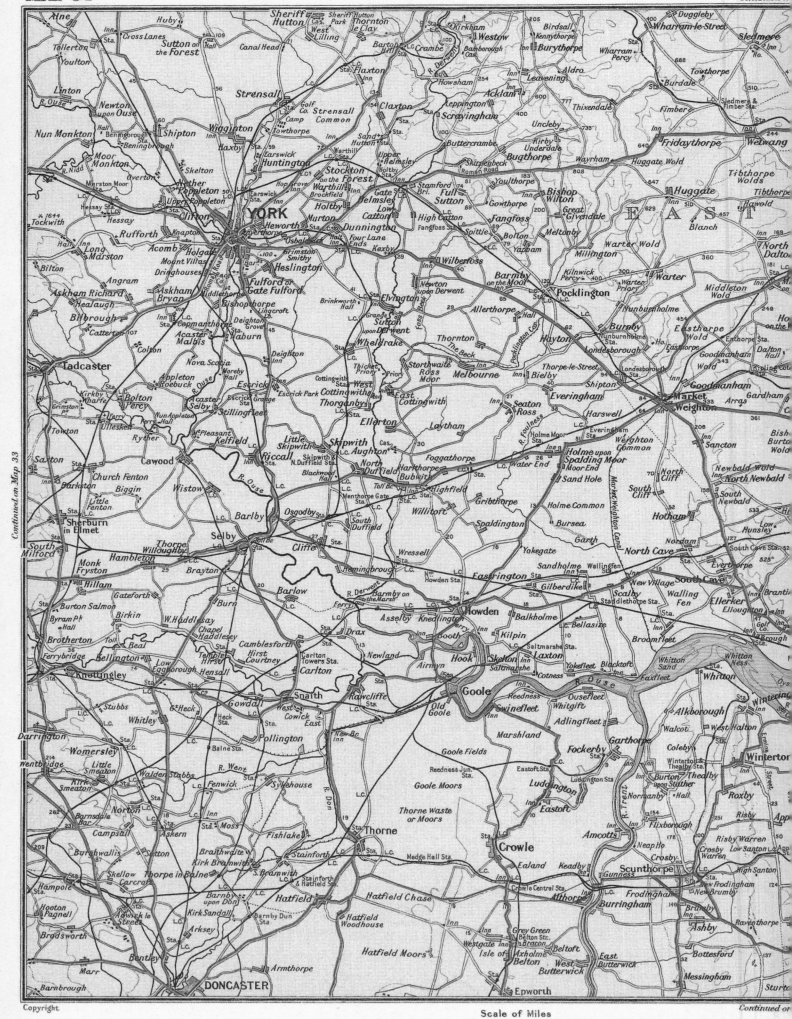

Scale of Miles

0 1 2 3 4 5 6 7 8 9 10

Continued on

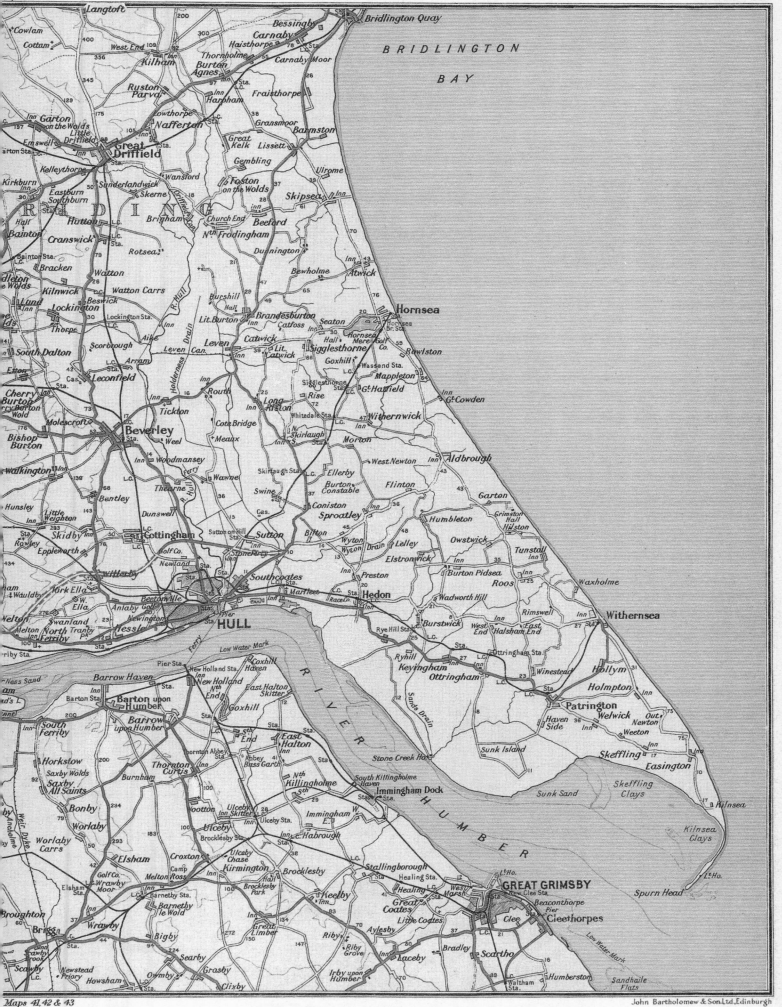

Main Roads   Other Roads   Railways

MAP 36

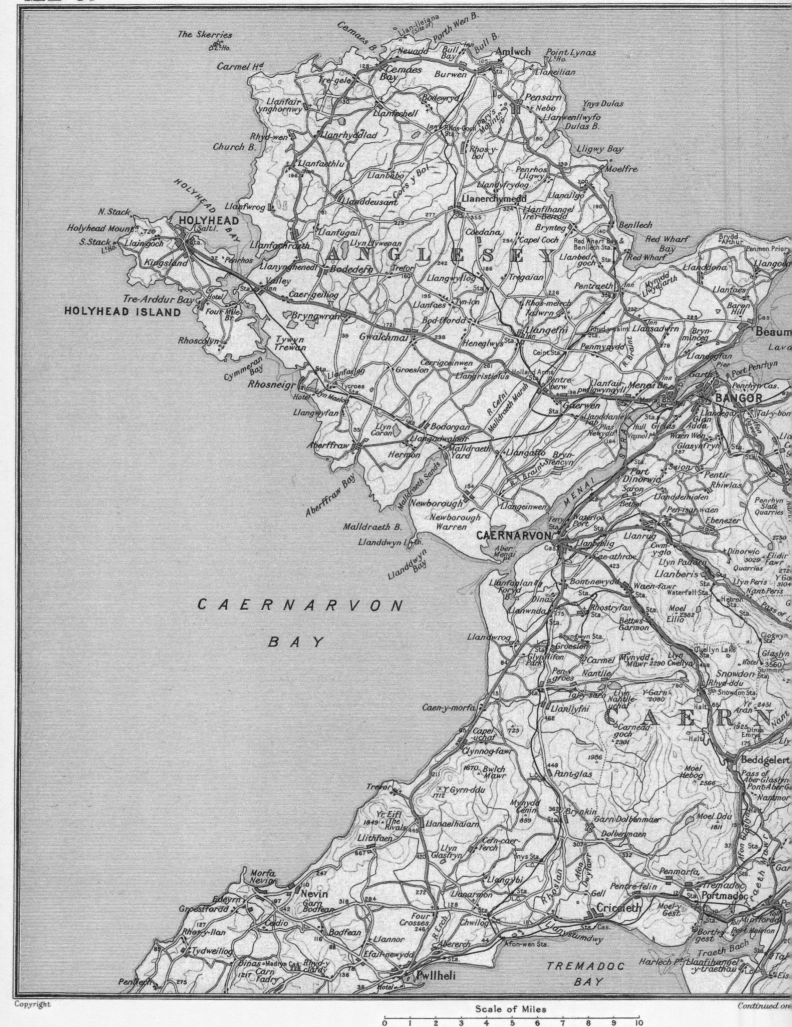

The Skerries
L¹.Ho.
Cemaes B.
Carmel Hᵈ
Llan-lleiana (Site of)
Porth Wen B.
Neuadd
Inn
Bull B.
Bull
Bay
Amlwch
Point Lynas
L¹.Ho.
Tre-gele
Cemaes
Bay
Burwen
105
Sta.
Llaneilian
Llanfair
ynghornwy
Llanfechell
Bodewryd
Pensarn
Nebo
Llanwenllwyfo
Ynys Dulas
Rhyd-wen
Church B.
Rhos-goch
Inn
Parys
Mountain
Dulas B.
Llanrhyddlad
Rhos-y-
bol
180
Lligwy Bay
Llanfaethlu
196
Cors y Bol
Llanbabo
Penrhos
Lligwy
Moelfre
HOLYHEAD
Llandyfrydog
39
N. Stack
Holyhead Mount
720
HOLYHEAD (Salt.)
Llanddeusant
Sta.
277
Llanerchymedd
355
Llanallgo
190
Llanfihangel
Tre'r-Beirdd
S. Stack
L¹.Ho.
Llaingoch
Kingsland
32
Penrhos
Llanfugail
229
324
Coedana
Brynteg
140
Benllech
Valley
Sta.
242
294
Capel Coch
Red Wharf Bay &
Benllech Sta.
Red Wharf
Brydd
Arthur
Tre-Arddur Bay
Hotel
Four Mile
Bᵉ
Caer-geiliog
Bodedern
Llangwyllog
186
Llanbedr
goch
Sta.
Red Wharf
Penmon Priory
HOLYHEAD ISLAND
Rhoscolyn
Bryngwran
195
Llanfaes
Tyn-lon
Rhos-meirch
Talwrn
226
Pentraeth
Inn
Mynydd
Llwydiarth
252
Llanddona
Llanfaes
Llangoed
Tywyn
Trewan
ANGLESEY
Gwalchmai
172
Bod-ffordd
Llangefni
Rhyd-y-saint
Llansadwrn
Baron
Hill
Beaum
Cymmeran Bay
Sta.
238
Heneglwys
Ceint Sta.
Penmynydd
278
Bryn-
minceg
Lava
Rhosneigr
Cerrigceinwen
261
Holland Arms
Inn
Pentre-
berw
Llanddyfnan
Llanddaniel
Fab Plas
Newydd
Llangefni
Hotel
Groeslon
Llangristiolus
198
Llanfair
P.G.
Pwllgwyngyll
Menai Bᵉ
Llandegfan
Garth
Port Penrhyn
Llenfaelog
Tycroes
Sta.
R. Cefni
Malldraeth Marsh
Sta.
Gaerwen
Pier
Penrhyn Cas.
BANGOR
Llangwyfan
35
Llyn Maelog
Llyn
Coron
Bodorgan
Sta.
Caein Sta.
164
Menai Br.
Hull Gias.
Llandegai
Glan
Adda
Tal-y-bon
Aberffraw
Hermon
Llangadwaladr
Malldraeth
Yard
Llangaffo
Bryn-
Siencyn
R. Brain
Vaynol Pk.
Waen Wen
Seion
Glasynfryn
287
Aberffraw Bay
134
R. Braint
Port
Dinorwic
Pentir
Rhiwlas
Malldraeth Sands
Newborough
Llangeinwen
Saron
Bethel
Llanddeiniolen
Perfsarwaen
Ebenezer
Penrhyn
Slate
Quarries
Malldraeth B.
Newborough
Warren
CAERNARVON
MENAI
Fern
Sta.
Waterloo
Port
Cwm-
y-glo
2730
Llanddwyn I. ch.
Aber
Menai
Bᵉ
Llanbeblig
Cas.
Llanrug
Cae-athron
423
Llyn Padarn
Dinorwic
Quarries
Elidir
Fawr
3104
Llanddwyn Bay
Llanfaglan
Foryd
B.
Dinas
Sta.
Waen-fawr
Llanberis
Sta.
Llyn Peris
Nant Peris
Y Garn
3104
Pass of
Llanwnda
175
Rhostryfan
Bettws
Garmon
Moel
Eilio
2382
Waterfall Sta.
Hebron Sta.
Llandwrog
Sta.
Bryngwyn Sta.
Groeslon
Carmel
Mynydd
Mawr 2290
Llyn
Cwellyn
Quellyn Lake
Hotel
Glaslyn
3560
Clogwyn
Sta.
C A E R N A R V O N
Glyn
Llifon
Park
Pen-
groes
Nantlle
Rhyd-ddu
Llyn
Nantlle
uchaf
Y-Garn
2080
Snowdon
780
Snowdon Sta.
Snowdon Sta.
Halt
Yr
Aran
2451
B A Y
Caen-y-morfa
84
Tal-y-sarn
Llanllyfni
162
C A E R N
Carnedd
goch
2301
Dinas
Emrys
175
Capel-uchaf
65
725
1986
Beddgelert
Clynnog-fawr
1670
Bwlch
Mawr
Pant-glas
449
Moel
Hebog
2566
Pass of
Aber Glaslyn
Pont Aber G
Nanmor
Trevor
211
Y Gyrn-ddu
1712
Mynydd
Cennin
359
Brynkir
Sta.
Garn Dolbenmaen
Moel Ddu
1811
Yr Eifl
(The Rivals)
1849
Sta.
445
Llanaelhaiarn
Llithfaen
667
Cefn-caer-
ferch
420
Dolbenmaen
501
Penmarfa
37
Morfa
Nevin
247
116
Llyn Glasfryn
Inys Sta.
332
Pentre-felin
Tremadoc
Sta.
Portmadoc
Edeyrn
97
Nevin
Garn
Bodfean
318
284
Llangybi
L.C.
Llanarmon
128
Gell
Criccieth
Moel-y-
Gest
Groesffordd
Cadio
142
Four
Crosses
246
R. Erch
Chwilog
Llanystumdwy
Cas.
Afon
Dwyfawr
Borthy
gest
Port Meirion
Rhos-y-llan
127
Bodfean
116
Llannor
68
Efail-newydd
Abererch
44
Afon-wen Sta.
Harlech Pt.
Llanfihangel
y-traethau
Traeth Bach
Tydweiliog
89
Dinas
Madryn Cas.
Rhyd-y-
clafdy
125
136
38
Hotel
Pwllheli
TREMADOC
BAY
Penllech
275
Carn
Fadryn
1217

Scale of Miles
0 1 2 3 4 5 6 7 8 9 10

Continued on

MAP 37

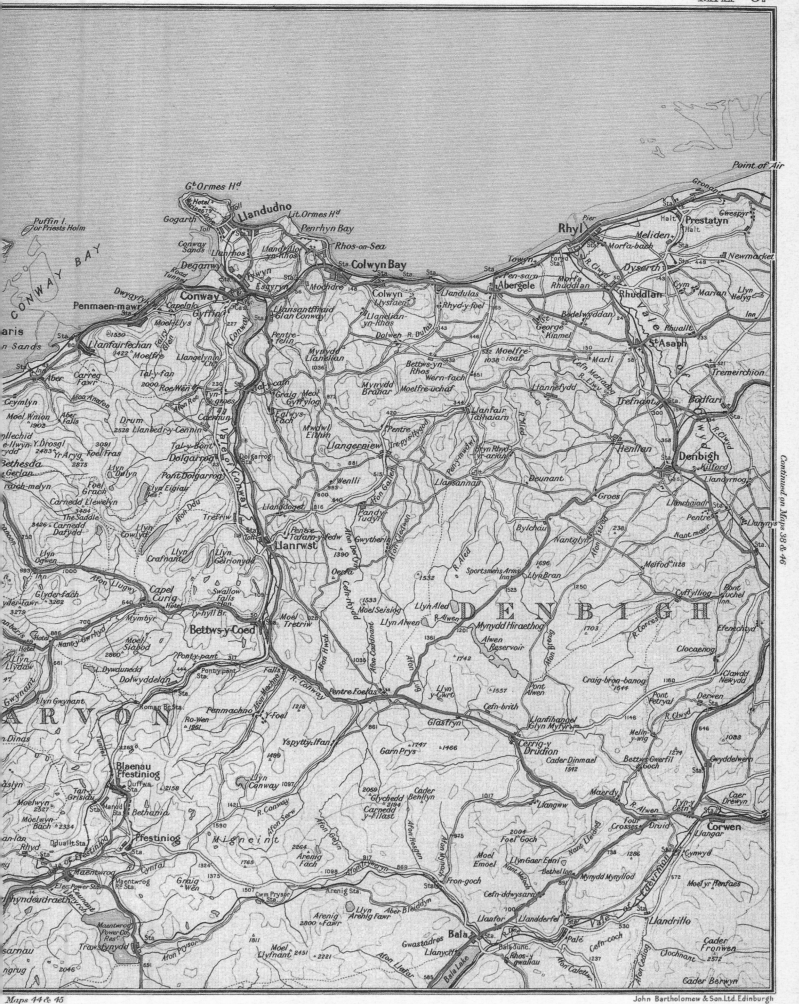

Continued on Maps 38 & 46

Point of Air

Puffin I.
or Priests Holm

CONWAY BAY

G.^t Ormes H^d

Gogarth

Conway Sands

Llandudno

Lit.Ormes H^d

Penrhyn Bay

Rhos-on-Sea

Colwyn Bay

Deganwy

Llanrhos

Llandrillo yn-Rhos

Conway

Penmaen-mawr

Capelulo

Deganwy

Esgyryn

Mochdre

Colwyn

Llysfaen

Llandulas

Rhyd-y-foel

Abergele

Morfa Rhuddlan

Rhyl

Pier

Towyn

Ten-sarn

Bodelwyddan

Rhuddlan

Meliden

Prestatyn

Gwespyr

Morfa-bach

Newmarket

Dyserth

R. Clwyd

Cefn

Marian

Llyn Helyg

Inn

Rhuallt

St^t George

Kinmel

Llandulas

Moelfre isaf

St Asaph

Cefn Meriadog

Tremeirchion

Bodfari

Trefnant

Llannefydd

Llanfair Talhaiarn

R. Aled

R. Elwy

Henllan

Denbigh

Kilford

Llandyrnog

Llanrhaiadr

Pentre

Llanynys

Llansantffraid Glan Conway

Llanelian-yn-Rhos

Dolwen

R. Dulas

Bettws-yn Rhos

Wern-fach

Moelfre-uchaf

Pentre-felin

Mynydd L.lanelian

Graig Meol Gyffylog

Eglwys-fach

Mynydd Brafar

Mwdwl Eithin

Llangerniew

Tre-pys-tygiad

Penymynydd

Blyn Rhyd yr arian

Deunant

Groes

Llanfairfechan

Moelfre

Llangelynin Ch^l

Tal-y-fan

Roe Wen

Aber

Carreg Fawr

Moel Llys

Gyffin

Llansantffraid Glan Conway

Wenlli

Pandy Tudyr

Llansannan

Bylchau

Nantglyn

Meifod

Cyffylliog

Pont uchel Inn

Y Drosgl

Moel Fras

Drum

Llanbedr-y-Cennin

Dolgarrog

Pont Dolgarrog

Trefriw

Llandoget

Pense Tafarn-y-fedw

Gwytherin

Afon Cledwen

Oerfa

Cefn-rhyd

Moel Seisiog

Llyn Aled

R. Alwen

Mynydd Hiraethog

Sportsmens Arms Inn

Llyn Bran

Craig-bron-banog

Clocaenog

Clawdd Newydd

Carnedd Llewelyn

The Saddle

Carnedd Dafydd

Llyn Eigiau Res.

Llyn Cowlyd

Llanrwst

Llyn Crafnant

Llyn Geirionydd

Capel Curig

Swallow Falls

Moel Tretriw

Afon Hwch

Afon Gadnant

Alwen Reservoir

Pont Alwen

Derwen Sta.

Glyder-fach

Glyder-fawr

Mymbyr

Bettws-y-Coed

Pont-y-pant

Falls

R. Conway

Pentre Foelas

Cefn-brith

Llanfihangel Glyn Myfyr

Melin-y-wig

Gwyddelwern

Llanberis

Hotel

Nant y Gwryd

Moel Siabod

Ponty-pant Sta.

Roman Bridge

Dolwyddelan

Penmachno

Afon Machno

Y-Foel

Ro-Wen

Yspytty-Ifan

Garn Prys

Glasfryn

Cerrig-y-Drudion

Cader Dinmael

Bettws Gwerfil Goch

Maerdy

R. Clwyd

Llyn Gwynant

Llyn Llydaw

Y-Foel

Blaenau Ffestiniog

Tan-y-Grisiau

Duffws Sta.

Bethania

Ffestiniog

Migneint

Llyn Conway

R. Conway

Cader Benllyn

Llangwm

Foel Goch

Moel Emoel

Llyn Gaer Edni

Bethel Inn

Mynydd Mynyllod

Caer Drewyn

Corwen

Llangar

Cynwyd

Moelwyn

Moelwyn-Bach

Maentwrog

Elec. Power Sta.

Afon Serw

Arenig Fach

Glychedd

Carnedd y-Fllast

Afon Gelyn

Moel Llyfnant

Arenig Fawr

Afon Tryweryn

Afon Hesgyn

Fron-goch

Cefn-ddwysarn

Llanuwchllyn

Llandderfel

Pale

Cefn-coch

Druid

Tyn-y Cefn

Moel yr Henfaes

Llandrillo

Traws-fynydd

Maentwrog Power Res.

Cwm Prysor Sta.

Arenig Sta.

Afon Prysor

Moel Llyfnant

Llyn Arenig Fawr

Aber Bleiddyn

Bala

Bala Junc.

Rhos-y gwaliau

Afon Lliafar

Gwastadros

Llanycil

Bala Lake

R. Dee

Afon Ceidiog

Cader Fronwen

Cader Berwyn

CARNARVON

DENBIGH

Maps 44 & 45

John Bartholomew & Son.Ltd.Edinburgh

Main Roads ———— Other Roads ———— Railways ————

MAP 38

Continued on

Continued on Maps 37

Scale of Miles

0 1 2 3 4 5 6 7 8 9 10

Continued on

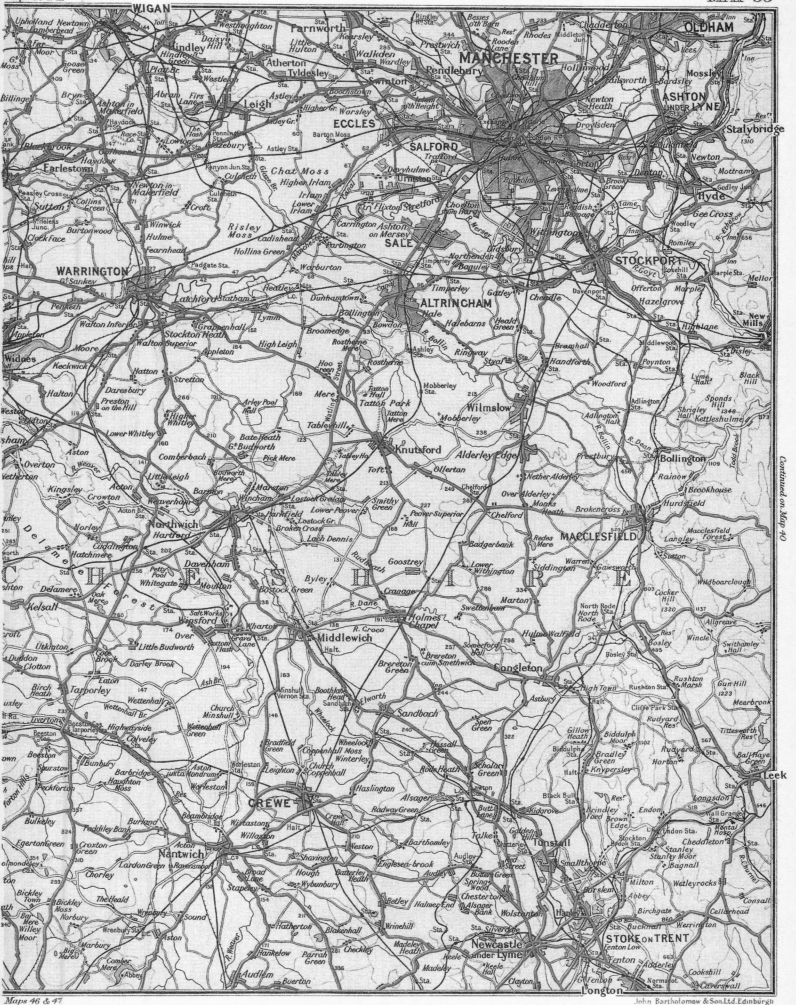

Main Roads ━━━━━━   Other Roads ═════   Railways ━━━━━━

MAP 40

Continued on

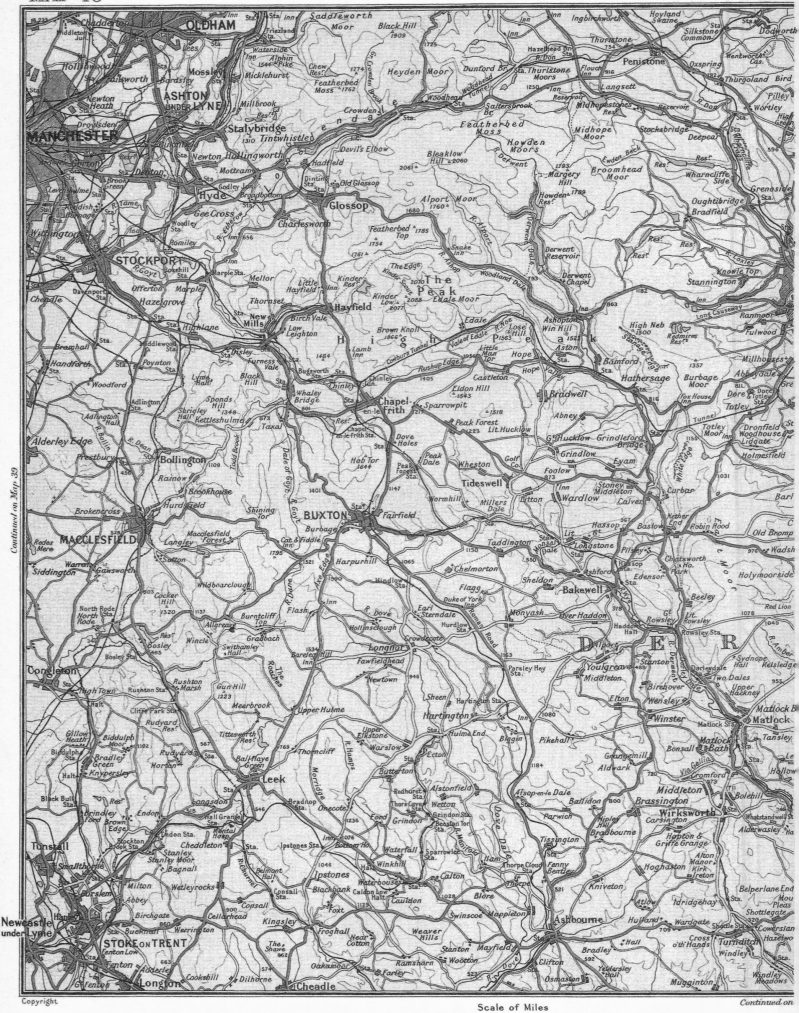

Continued on Map 39

Continued on

Scale of Miles

0 1 2 3 4 5 6 7 8 9 10

Continued on Map 42

Maps 48 & 49

Worsbrough Dale · Darfield · Thurnscoe · Goldthorpe · Marr · Armthorpe · Epworth

Lovecliffe · Wombwell · Millhouses · Barnbrough · High Melton · Sprotbrough · DONCASTER · Race Co. · Cantley Common · Wroot · Low Burnham

Hoyland Nether · Jump · West Melton · Bolton-upon-Dearne · Adwick · Cadeby · Balby · Cantley · Branton · Auckley · Blaxton · Westwoodside · Owston Ferry

Elsecar · Wath upon Dearne · Mexborough · New Edlington · Loversall · Finningley Sta. · Finningley · Park Drain · Haxey · E. Lound

Wentworth · Swinton · Denaby Main · Conisbrough · Kilnhurst · Rossington · Rossington Hall · Finningley Hall · Craiselound · Haxey Jun. Sta. · Gunthorpe

Chapeltown · Thorpe Hesley · Rawmarsh · Park Gate · Hooton Roberts · Edlington · Wadworth · Hesley Hall · Austerfield · Mission · Misterton · West Stockwith

Ecclesfield · Greasbrough · Thrybergh · Ravenfield · Braithwell · Tickhill & Wadworth Sta. · Bawtry · Misterton Carr · Walkeringham

Bickley Carr · Wadsley Br. · Eastwood · ROTHERHAM · Bramley · Maltby · Tickhill · Harworth · Scaftworth · Everton · Chesterfield Canal · Gringley on the Hill · Morton · Gainsborough

SHEFFIELD · Tinsley · Brinsworth · Whiston · Wickersley · Sandbeck Hall · Styrrup · Scrooby · Mattersey · Clayworth · Saundby · Bole

Handsworth · Catcliffe · Treeton · Ulley · Laughton en le Morthen · Firbeck · Oldcoats · Ranskill · Lound · Wheatley · Sturton le Steeple

Heeley · Intake · Brampton-en-le-Morthen · Letwell · N. Carlton · Torworth · Sutton · Hayton · Clarborough · Littleborough

Norton Woodseats · Woodhouse · Swallow Nest · Aston · Dinnington · Gildingwells · Carlton in Lindrick · S. Carlton · Barnby Moor · N. Leverton with Habblesthorpe

Highlane Ridgeway · Beighton · Wales · North Anston · Woodsetts · Winthorpe · Welham · S. Leverton · Cottam

Coal Aston · Ford · Mosbrough · Halfway · Nether Moor · South Anston · Gateford · Scofton · Ranby · Retford Sta. · East Retford · Ordsall · Grove · Treswell

Dronfield · Eckington · Harthill · Killamarsh · Thorpe Salvin · Shireoaks · Worksop Sta. · Checker House · Eaton · Nether Headon · Headon · Stokeham · Rampton

Unstone · Spinkhill · Barlborough · Whitwell · WORKSOP · Manton · Gamston · Elksley · Upton · Askham · East Drayton · Laneham · Dunham

New Whittington · Barrowhill · Clowne · Manor · The Dukeries · Clumber Park · West Drayton · Markham Moor · East Markham · Ragnall · Darlton

Whittington · Newbold Moor · Staveley · Elmton · Creswell · Welbeck Abbey · Normanton Inn · Bothamsall · Milton · Clinton · Tuxford · Fledborough Sta.

CHESTERFIELD · Brimington · Bolsover · Whaley · Holbeck · Welbeck Park Great Lake · Carburton · Haughton · Perlethorpe · Markham Clinton · Walesby · High Marnham

New Brampton · Calow · Long Duckmanton · Nether Langwith · Cuckney · Norton · Lake · Thoresby Park · Kirton · Egmanton · Normanton upon Trent

Walton · Hasland · Cock Alley · Sutton Scarsdale · Upper Longwith · Shirebrook Nth. Sta. · Cuckney Hill · Budby · Welbeck Colly Village · Boughton · Boughton Sta. · Weston · Sutton upon Trent · Crow Park Sta.

Wingerworth · Grassmoor · Heath · Palterton · Scarcliffe · Shirebrook · Church Warsop · Ollerton · Moorhouse · Ossington

Nether Moor · New Tupton · Heath Sta. · Williamthorpe · Glapwell · Stony Houghton · Market Warsop · Edwinstowe · Wellow · Ompton · Kneesall · Norwell Woodhouse

Alton · North Wingfield · Rowthorpe · New Houghton · Sookholme · R. Maun · Clipstone Park · Rufford Abbey · Eakring · The Beck · Norwell · Carlton on Trent

Ashover · Clay Cross · Hardstoft · Hardwick Hall · Pleasley · Clipstone Village · Rufford Park · Maplebeck · Caunton · Cromwell

Fallgate · Danesmoor · Pilsley · Teversall · Lane End · Mansfield Woodhouse · Clipstone Forest · Bilsthorpe · Bathley · North Muskham · Holme

Brackenfield · Higham · Stretton · Tibshelf · Doehill Sta. · Stantonhill · Sutton in Ashfield · Ratcher Hill · Rufford Forest · Winkburn · South Muskham

Wessington · Shirland · Newton · Blackwell · MANSFIELD · Skegby · Robin Down's Hill · Rainworth · Kirklington · Hockerton · Kelham

South Wingfield · Stonebroom · Morton · Shirland · South Normanton · Huthwaite · Sutton Jun. · Rainworth Water · Red Br. · Farnsfield · Normanton · Upton

Crich Carr · Fourlane Ends · Kirkby in Ashfield · East Kirkby · Fishpool · Blidworth · Edingley · Halam · Averham

Wessington · Riddings · Pinxton · Pinxton Green · New Annesley · Newstead Abbey · Blidworth Bottoms · Westhorpe · Southwell · Rolleston · Newark

Ambergate Jun. · Fritchley · Swanwick · Somercotes · Selston · Annesley Woodhouse · Newstead · Sherwood · Hallolughton · Fiskerton Sta. · Fiskerton · Ferndon

Heage · Butterley · Somercotes · Annesley · Annesley Park · Papplewick · Linby · Oxton · Morton · Bleasby · East Stoke

Belper · Greenhillock · Codnor · New Brinsley · Bagthorpe · Friezeland · Beauvale Priory · Bestwood · Calverton · Thurgarton · Epperstone · Hoveringham · Elston

White Moor · Cross Hill · Loscoe · Langley Mill · Eastwood · Watnall Chaworth · Moor Green · Butlers Hill · Redhill · Bestwood Lo. · Highbury Vale · Arnold · Woodborough · Lowdham · Gonalston · Syerston

Holbrook · Kilburn · Denby · Heanor · Langley · Smalley · Hucknall Torkard · Bestwood · Sherwood Sta. · Lambley · Burton Joyce · East Bridgford · Screveton · Flintham

Horsley Woodhouse · Marlpool · Kimberley · Awsworth · Bulwell · Nuthall · Marshall Hill · Gunthorpe · Caythorpe · Shelton · Staunton

Horsley · Coxbench · Mapperley · Cotmanhay · Coddnay

MAP 42

Continued on

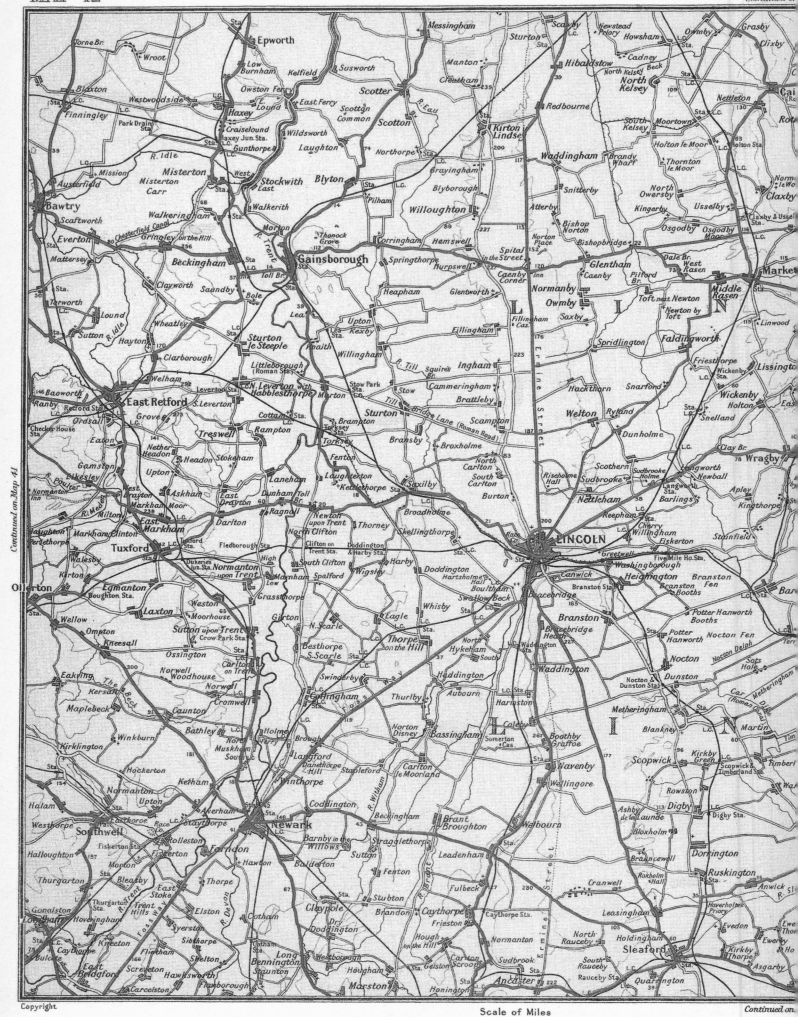

Continued on Map 41

Continued on

Scale of Miles

0 1 2 3 4 5 6 7 8 9 10

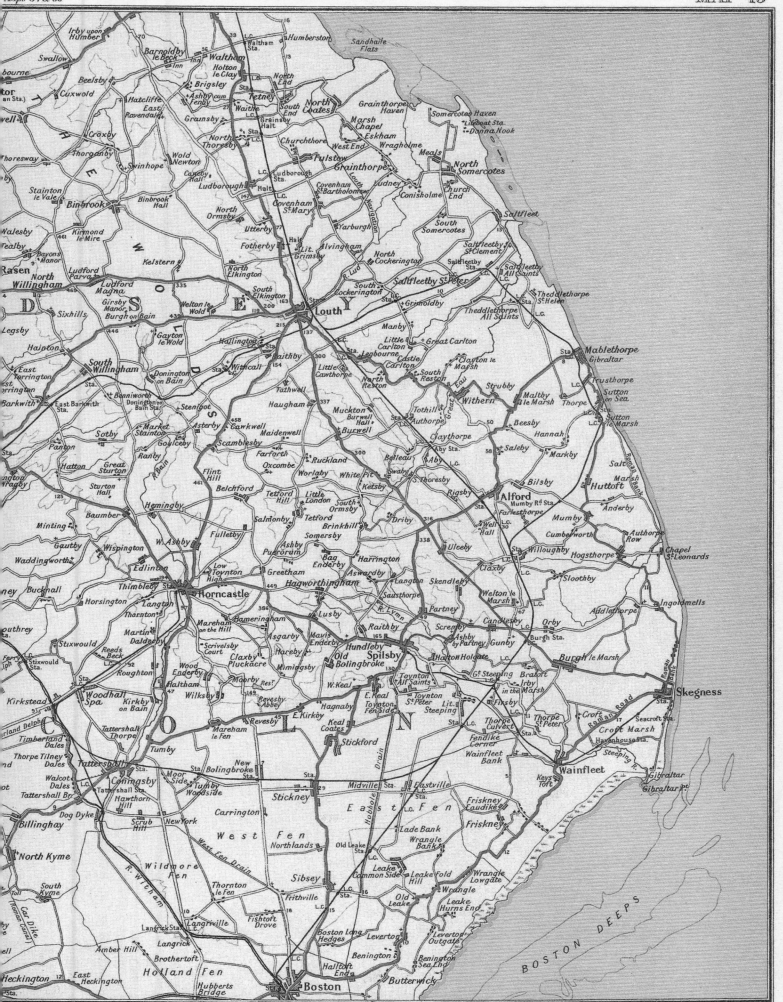

Main Roads ════════ Other Roads ════════ Railways ────────

MAP 44

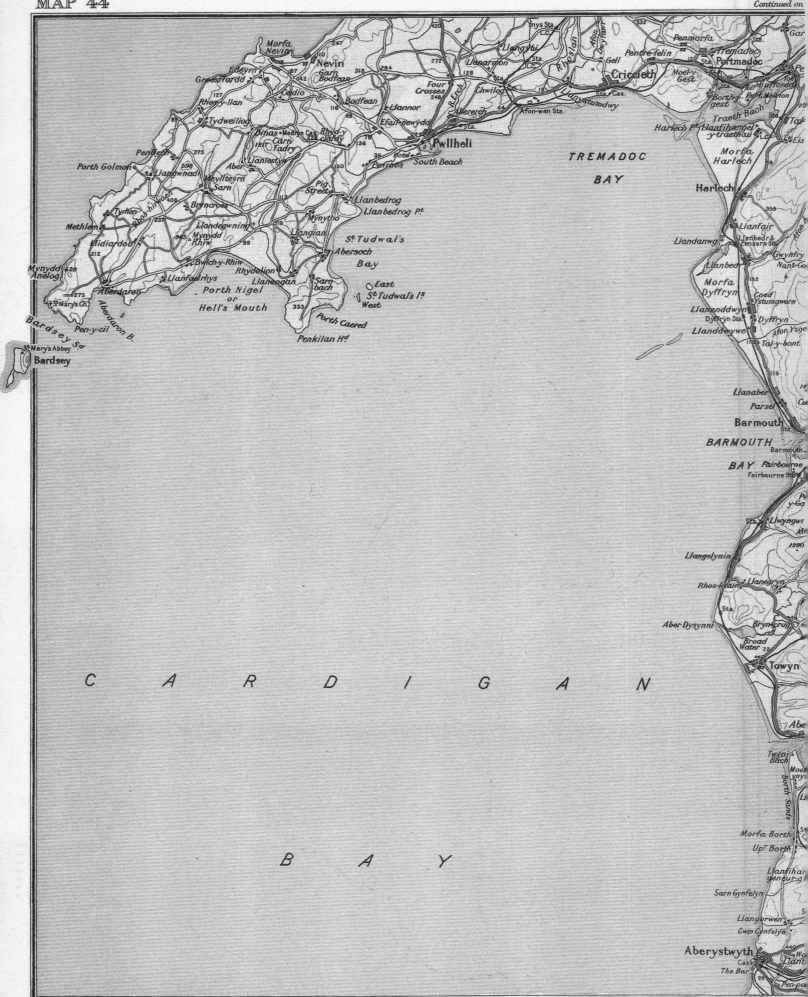

Penmarfa
Tremadoc
Portmadoc

Llangybi Sta.
Llanarmon Sta.
Penthe-felin
Gell
Criccieth
Moel-y Gest
Borth y-gest
Traeth Bach

Morfa Nevin
Nevin
Garn Bodfean
Four Crosses
Chwilog
Llanystumdwy
Afon-wen Sta.
Harlech Pt
Llanfihangel-y-traethau

Edeyrn
Greesffordd
Ceidio
Bodfean
Llannor
Aberarch
Sta.
Morfa Harlech

Rhos-y-llan
Efail-newydd
Tydweiliog
Rhyd-y clafdy
Pwllheli
Harlech

Binas
Madryn Cas.
Carn Fadry
Penrhos
South Beach
Llanfair
Llanbedr & Pensarn Sta.

Penllech
Aber
Llaniestyn
Llandanwg
Gwynfryn
Nant-coll

Porth Golmon
Llangwnad
Meyllteyrn
Sarn
Pig Street
Llanbed
Morfa Dyffryn

Tynllan
Rhoshirwaen
Bryncroes
Llanbedrog
Llanbedrog Pt
Llanddwye
Dyffryn Sta.
Dyffryn

Methlem
Llandegwning
Mynytho
Mynydd Rhiw
Llangian
St Tudwal's
Abersoch Bay
Llanddwywe
Tal-y-bont

Midiardou
Bulch-y-Rhiw
Rhydolion
Llanfaelrhys
Llanengan
Sarn bach
East St Tudwal's Is West

Mynydd Anelog
Aberdaron
Porth Nigel or Hell's Mouth
Llanaber
Parsel

St Mary's Ch.
Aberdaron B.
Porth Caered
Penkilan Hd.
Barmouth

Bardsey Sd.
Pen-y-cil
BARMOUTH BAY
Fairbourne

St Mary's Abbey
Bardsey
Fairbourne Sta

Pen-y-Ga
Llwyngwr

TREMADOC BAY

Llangelynin

Rhos-y-gun
Llanegryn

Aber Dysynni
Bryncrug
Broad Water

Towyn

C A R D I G A N

Twyni Bach
Moel-y-nys

B A Y

Morfa Borth
Upr Borth

Llanfihangel-geneur-g

Sarn Gynfelyn

Llangorwen
Cwm Cynfelyn

Aberystwyth
The Bar

Continued on

Scale of Miles
0 1 2 3 4 5 6 7 8 9 10

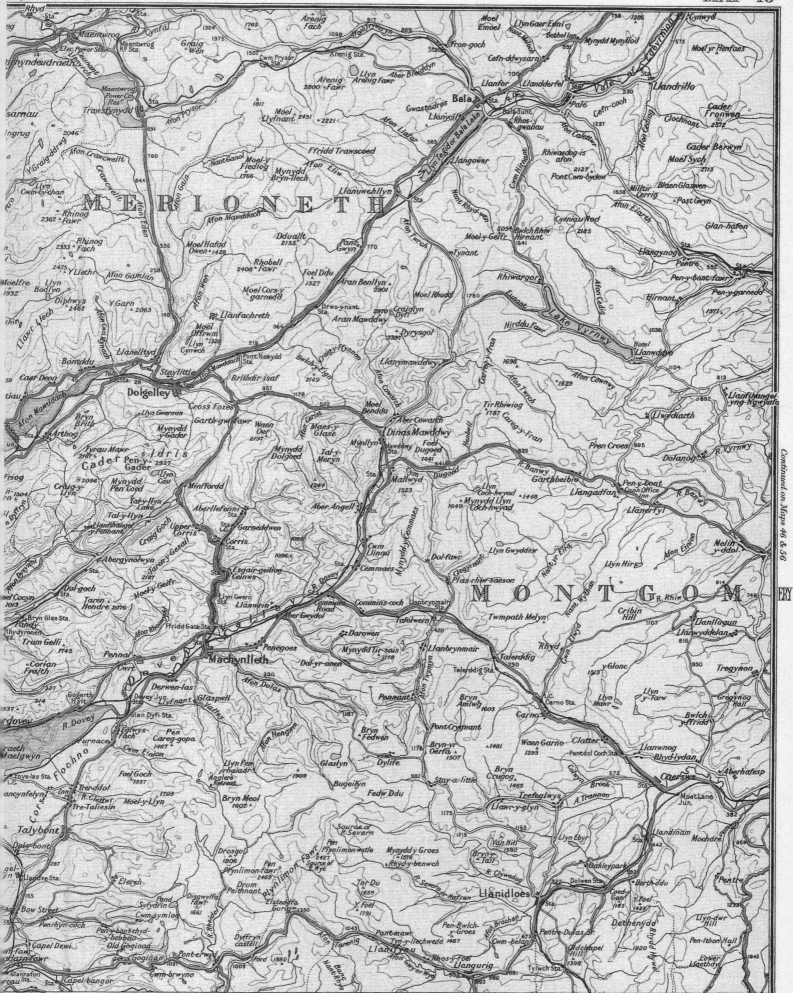

MAP 45

John Bartholomew & Son.Ltd.,Edinburgh

Main Roads ══════ Other Roads ════════ Railways ════════

MAP 46
Continued on

PART OF FLINT

MONTGOMERY

SHRO...

Corwen
Llangollen
Rhosllanerchrugog
Johnstown
Bangor
Threapwood
Cuddington Heath
Oldcastle Heath
Worthenbury
Wych B.
Higher Wych
Gwyddelwern
Bryn-Eghwys
Gernant
Stryt-issa
Gyfellia
Eyton
Tallarn Green
Llantysilio Mountain
Moel Morfydd 1804
Moel-y-Gamelin 1897
Valle Crucis Abbey
Pen-y-cae
Ruabon
Wynnstay
Overton
Penley
Eglwys Cross
Whit...
Druid
Llangar
Cynwyd
Carrog
Glyn Dyfrdwy
Derwen
Castell Dinas Bran
Trevor
Acrefair
Cefn-mawr
R. Dee
Overton on Dee Sta.
Lightwood Green
Hanmer
Arowry
Higher Wych
Moel Ferna 2071
Moel yr Henfaes
N. Foel 1713
Llansantffraid Glyn-Ceiriog
Fron Cysyllte
Pentre Halt
Sedylt Bank
Street Dinas
Shell Brook
Park Lane
Gredington
Bettisfield Pk.
Fenns Moss
Llandrillo
Pen-plaenau 1773
Nant Rhyd Wilym 1845
Pandy
Halt Dol-y-wern
Weston Rhyn
Chirk Cas.
Chirk
Ifton Heath
Gledrid
S. Martins
Dudleston Heath
Higher Grange
Welshampton
Oteley
Welsh Mere
Bettisfield
Whixa...
Poolbank
Northwood
Eastaston
Cader Fronwen 2572
Clochnant
Nant-cwm-llauenog
Tregeiriog
R. Ceiriog
Peny-y-gwely
Selattyn
Gobowen
Brogyntyn
Whittington
Perthy
Tetchill
Lee
White Mere
Crose Mere
Lyneal
Colemere
English Frankton
Wem
Cader Berwyn
Moel Sych 2713
Blaen Glaswen
Post Gwyn
Llanarmon Dyffryn Ceiriog
Garnedwen 1628
Cefn hir Fynydd
Rhyd-y-croesau
Res.
OSWESTRY
Shropshire Union Canal
Mile End
Halston Hall
Hordley
Cockshutt
Loppington
Noneley
Filley
Glan-hafon 1753
Gyrn Moelfre
Llyn Moelfre
Llansilin
Croesau-bach
R. Morda
Morda
Ball
Queens Head
Maesbury Marsh
W. Felton
The Cross
Rednal
Grimpo
Eardiston
Weirbrook
R. Perry
Stanwardine in the Wood
Burlton
Sleap Br.
Llanrhaiadr yn-Mochnant
Pentre
Pen-y-bont-fawr
Llanrhaiadr Sta.
Trefonen
Treflach Wood
Porth-y-waen
Llanymynech
Knockin
Ruyton of the Eleven Towns
Weston Lullingfields
Myddle
Alderton
Myddlewood
Hirnant
Pen-y-garnedd
Pedair Ffordd Halt
Llangedwyn
Pany-bont
Llynclys
Pant
Blodwell Jun. Sta.
Morton
Woolston
Wykey
Stanwardine in the Fields
Baschurch
Prescott
Milford
Walford
Oldwood
Merrington
Bomere Heath
Lit. Ness
Nesscliff
Gt. Ness
Grafton
Leaton
Harmer...
Bwlch-y-ddar
Llansantffraid yn Mechain
Llanfechain
Llanfyllin
Godor
Llandysilio
Crosslanes
Four Crosses
Edgerley
Pentre
Wilcott
Kinnerley
Dovaston
Kinnerley Junc. Sta.
Kinton
Maesbrook Green
Nessel & Pentre Sta.
Alderton
Fitz
Albrig...
Bryngwyn Sta.
Bwlch-y-Cibau
R. Vyrnwy
Llandrinio
Melverley Green
Melverley
Crew Green
Shrawardine
Montford
Bicton
Leaton C.
Battlefield
Ha...
Plas-nant y-Meichiaid
Llanfihangel-yng-Ngwynfa
Allt-y-main 1168
Sarnau
Arddleen
Criggion
Breidden Hill 1202
Cefn-y-Castell
Ford & Crossgates
Rowton Cas.
Montford
Montford Bri.
Shelton
Berwick Ho.
Frankwell
Sh...
Llwydiarth
Geuffordd
Middletown
Moel-y-Golfa
Wollaston
Ivyend
Cardeston
Cruckton
Bicton Heath
Belle Vu...
Meadle Brace
Dolanog
R. Vyrnwy
Meifod
Brolearth Hill 760
Groes-lwyd
Pont Robert
Guilsfield
Poolquay
Trewern
Westbury Sta.
Cardeston
Shoot Hill
Cruckmeole
Cruckton Sta.
Edgebold Sta.
Rea Br.
R. Banwy
Maes-mawr
Inn
Buttington
Frochas
Westbury
Yockleton
Stoney Stretton
Edge
Gt. Hanwood
Hookagate
Redhill
Annscroft
Bayston...
Bomere Pool
Heniarth Sta.
Cyfronydd Sta.
Welshpool
Leighton Br.
Long Mountain
L. Wallop
Westley
Asterley
Plealey
Exfordsgreen
Longden
Condover Sta.
Melin y-ddol
Castle Caereinion
Halt
Golfa Sta.
Leighton Pk.
Leighton
Rowley
Minsterley
Pontesford
Longden
Stapleton
Ryton
Dorrington
Actor...
Afon Einion
Llanfair Caereinion
Fron
Kingswood
Marton
Brockton
Worthen
Hope
Habberley
Wrentnall
Church Pulverbatch
Cothercott
Longn...
Llanllugan
Manafon
Slingwern Hill 816
Berriew
Forden
Rorrington
Perkinsbatch
Pennerley
Snailbeach
Picklescott
Woolstaston
Matling Street
Tregynon
Brooks
Garthmyl
Camlad
Shiregrove Br.
Chirbury
Middleton
Shelve
Shelve
Priestweston
Corndon Hill 1684
The Bog
Rhadley Hill
Linley Hill
Ratlinghope
Leebotwood
Gregynog Hall
Bettws Cedewain
Fron
Montgomery Sta.
Montgomery
All Stretton
Caer Caredoc
Bwlch y-ffridd
Llandyssil
Brompton Hall
Church Stoke
Hyssington
Norbury
R.E. Onney
Wentnor
Church Stretton
Hope Bowdler Hill
Longvil...
Rhyd-lydan
Aberhafesp
Cefn-y Coed 1158
Pentreheyling
Sned
More
Lydham
Asterton
Little Stretton
Hope Bowdler
Rushbu...
Caersws
Moat Lane Jun.
Newtown
Hodley
Sarn
R. Mule
Camlad
Lydhamheath Sta.
Myndtown
Marshbrook Sta.
Harton Rd. Sta.
Acton Scott
Ticklerton
Mochdre
Dolfor 1022
Cefn-gwyn
Mainstone
Bishops Castle
Colebatch
Lydbury North
Plowden Sta.
Eaton
Horderley
Wistanstow
Corfton Hall
Corft...
Llandinam
Pentre
Kerry Hill
Anchor
Clun Forest
Offa's Dyke
Cefn Einion
Bryn
Lower Down
Walcot
Stratfordbridge Junc.
Lydbury...
Totterton Hall
Plowder Hall
Up. Affcot
Alcaston
Milford Lo...
The Long Mynd
Hop Dale

Copyright.
Continued on Maps 37 & 45
Continued on

MAP 47

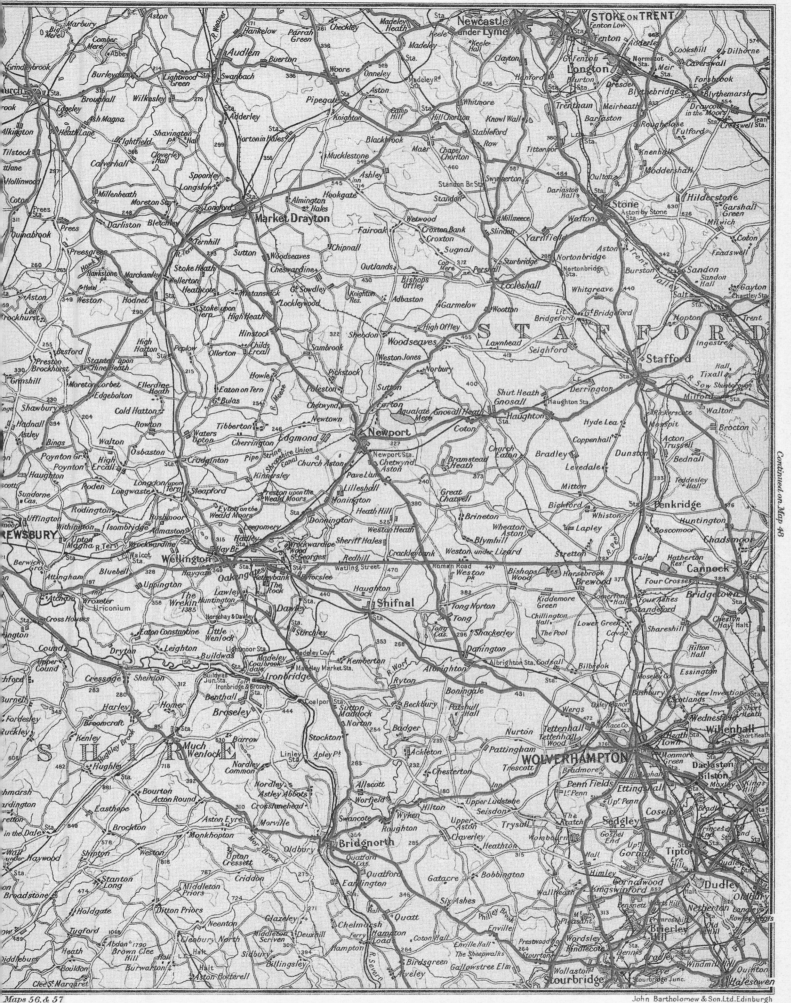

Continued on Map 48

John Bartholomew & Son Ltd. Edinburgh

Main Roads ━━━━━   Other Roads ━━━━━   Railways ━━━━━

MAP 48

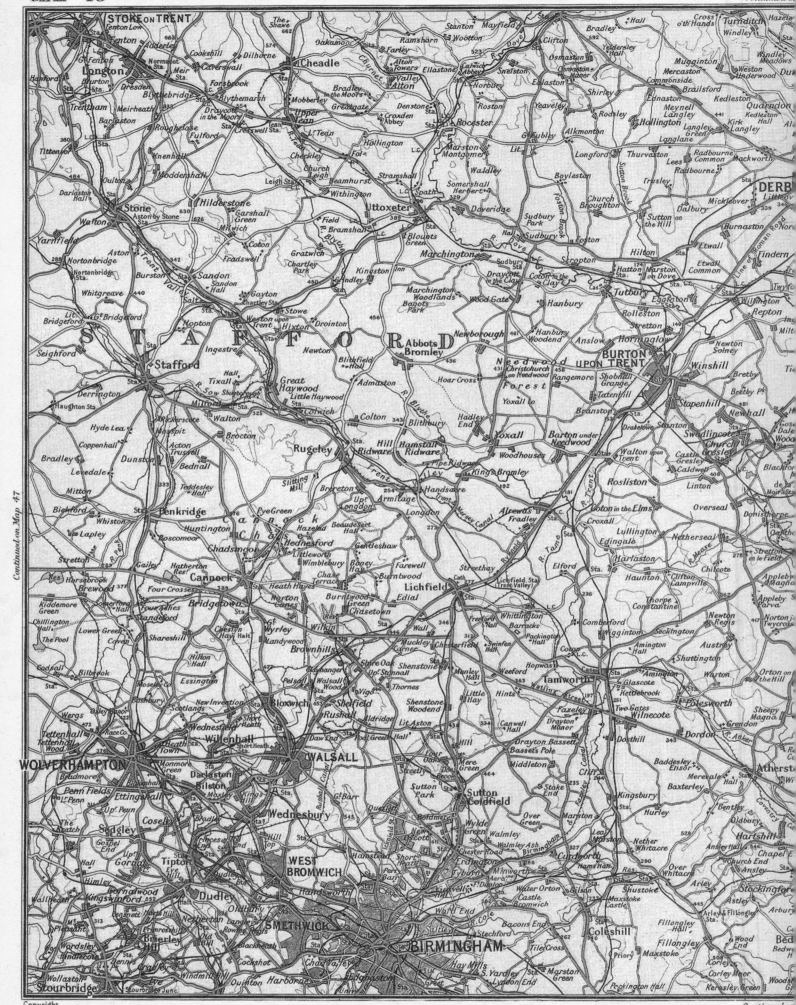

Continued o.

Continued on Map 47

Continued o

Scale of Miles

0 1 2 3 4 5 6 7 8 9 10

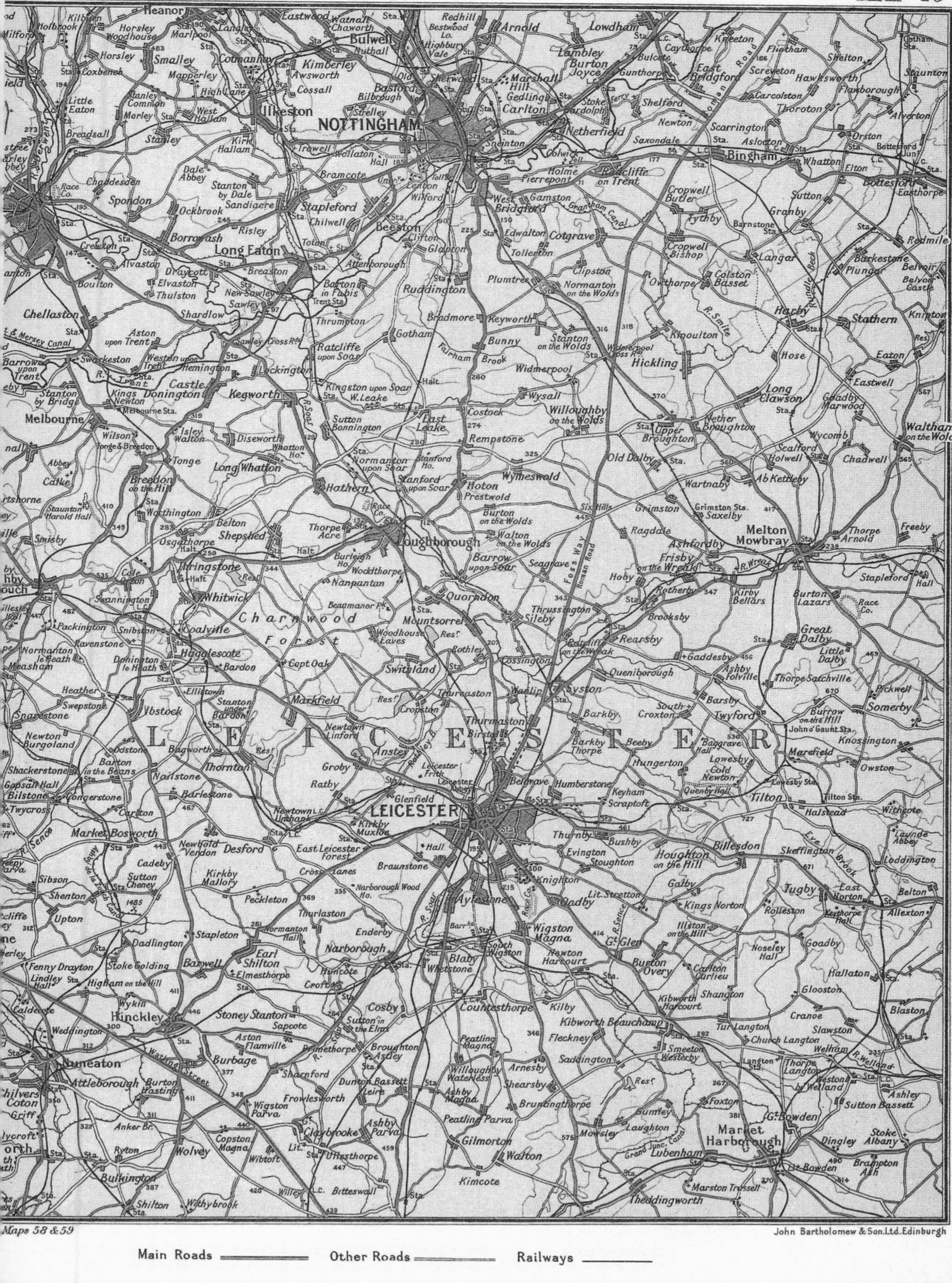

NOTTINGHAM

LEICESTER

Charnwood Forest

Continued on Map 50

Main Roads ——— Other Roads ——— Railways ———

MAP 50
Continued

KESTEVEN

RUTLAND

SOKE OF PETERBOROUGH

Sleaford · Ancaster · Grantham · Bourne · Stamford · Melton Mowbray · Oakham · Uppingham · Market Harborough · Bingham · Oundle · Rockingham · Corby · King's Cliffe

East Bridgford · Flintham · Shelton · Long Bennington · Westborough · Hougham · Marston · Carlton Scroop · Sudbrook · South Rauceby · Rauceby Sta. · Kirkby Thorpe · Asgarby

Screveton · Hawksworth · Staunton · Foston · Honington · Wilsford · Kelby · Swarby · Burton Pedwardine

Scarrington Sta. · Aslocton · Orston · Normanton · Allington · Syston Hall · Belton Ho. · Londonthorpe · Welby · Aisby · Osbournby · Spanby · Swaton

Bingham · Whatton · Elton · Gt. Gonerby · Manthorpe · Culverthorpe · Oasby · Dembleby · Scott Willoughby · Scredington · Horbling

Cropwell Butler · Sutton · Granby · Sedgebrook · Barrowby · Grantham · Braceby · Haceby · Newton · Threekingham · Billingborough

Tythby · Barnstone Sta. · Bottesford · Muston · Nottington & Grantham Canal · Ropsley · Sapperton · Folkingham · Birthorpe · Pointon

Cropwell Bishop · Langar · Redmile · Belvoir · Woolsthorpe · Harlaxton · Old Somerby · Humby · Boothby Pagnell · Pickworth · Dowsby · Keisby

Owthorpe · Colston Basset · Barkestone · Plungar · Belvoir Castle · Harston · Denton · Little Ponton · Lenton · Ingoldsby · Aslackby · Rippingale · Dunsby

Kinoulton · Hose · Stathern · Knipton · Stroxton · Great Ponton · Bitchfield · Laughton · Hawthorpe · Dunsby Fen

Hickling · Long Clawson · Eastwell · Croxton Kerrial · Wyville · Stoke Rochford Hall · South Stoke · Bassingthorpe · Irnham · Bulby · Kirkby Underwood

Nether Broughton · Goadby Marwood · Croxton Abbey · Saltby · Skillington · Crabtree Ho · Easton Hall · Burton Coggles · Hall · Corby · Elsthorpe · Morton · Morton Fen

Upper Broughton · Waltham on the Wolds · Stonesby · Sproxton · Woolsthorpe · Colsterworth · Swayfield · Grimsthorpe · Castle · Cowthorpe · Edenham · Bourne North Fen Twenty

Sealford Holwell · Chadwell · Stainby · North Witham · Counthorpe · Grimsthorpe Park · Scottlethorpe · Creeton · Dyke

Wartnaby · Ab Kettleby · Coston · Buckminster · Sewstern · Gunby · South Witham · Bourne · Eastgate

Grimston Sta. · Saxelby · Melton Mowbray · Thorpe Arnold · Freeby · Garthorpe · Saxby · Castle Bytham · Little Bytham · Manthorpe · Thurlby

Ashfordby · Frisby · Stapleford Hall · Edmondthorpe & Wymondham Sta. · Thistleton · Clipsham · Holywell Hall · Careby · Witham on the Hill · Northorpe · Baston Common

Rotherby · Kirby Bellars · Burton Lazars · Whissendine Sta. · Market Overton · Stretton · Pickworth · Carlby · Wilsthorpe · Baston

Great Dalby · Little Dalby · Whissendine · Teigh · Barrow · Ashwell · Greetham · Essendine · Bracebrough · Greatford · Langtoft

Gaddesby · Ashby Folville · Thorpe Satchville · Pickwell · Somerby · Cold Overton · Langham · Cottesmore · Exton Park · Losecoat Field Site of Battle · Ryhall · Barholm · Market Deeping

Barsby · Twyford · Burrow on the Hill · John O'Gaunt Sta. · Knossington · Barleythorpe · Burley · Whitwell · Tickencote · Lit. Casterton · Belmesthorpe · Casewick Hall · West Deeping · Deeping Gate

Baggrave · Lowesby · Cold Newton · Quenby Hall · Marefield · Owston · Braunston · Oakham · Catmose · Fox Br. · Empingham · Great Casterton · Ufington · Tallington · Maxey

Tilton · Halstead · Witcote · Brooke · Manton · Normanton Park · Stamford · Tinwell · Burghley Ho. · Burton · Etton

Billesdon · Skeffington · Loddington · Ridlington · Preston · Wing · Pilton · Ketton · Easton on the Hill · Collyweston Br. · Pilsgate · Barnack · Ufford Sta. · Helpston

Tugby · East Norton · Belton · Ayston · Wardley · Allexton · Glaston · Morcott · Lyndon · N. Luffenham · S. Luffenham · Colly Weston · Wittering · Southorpe · Marholm

Kings Norton · Rolleston · Keythorpe Hall · Uppingham · Bisbrooke · Barrowden · Duddington · Collyweston Cross Roads · Thornhaugh · Upton · PETERBOROUGH

Illston on the Hill · Goadby · Hoseley Hall · Stockerston · Stoke Dry · Seaton · Liddington · Harringworth · Laxton Hall · Fineshade Abbey · King's Cliffe · Wansford · Wansford Rd. Sta. · Milton Hall · Ailsworth

Carlton Curlieu · Hallaton · Horninghold · Thorpe by Water · Laxton · Park · Blatherwycke · Apethorpe · Nassington · Sutton · Castor · Water Newton · Orton Roman Camp

Shangton · Glooston · Blaston · Nevill Holt · Caldecott · Gretton · Bulwick · Deene · Woodnewton · Fotheringhay · Kates Cabin · Chesterton · Alwalton

Tur Langton · Church Langton · Slawston · Gt. Easton · Medbourne Drayton · Bringhurst · Rockingham Sta. · Deene Pk. · Deenethorpe · Southwick · Glapthorn · Cotterstock · Tansor · Warmington · Morborne

Foxton · Gt. Bowden · Welham · Thorpe Langton · Weston by Welland · Ashley · Middleton · Cottingham · Rockingham · Weldon · Corby · Biggin Hall · Oundle · Haddon · Elton

Market Harborough · Lubenham · Dingley · Stoke Albany · Wilbarston · E. Carlton · Corby · Up. Benefield · Oundle Sta. · Ashton · Polebrook · Folksworth

Lit. Bowden · Marston Trussell · Brampton Ash · Sutton Bassett · Weldon & Corby Sta. · Benefield · Stanion · Stoke Doyle · Armston · Barnwell · Lutton · Denton

East Farndon · Gt. Oxendon · Desborough · Pipewell · Gt. Oakley · Lit. Oakley · Brigstock · Barnwell St. Andrew · Barnwell All Saints · Hemington · Luddington · Glatton

Glendon & Rushton Sta. · Geddington · R. Ise · Lilford Hall · Newberry Hall

R. Trent · R. Smite · R. Devon · R. Eye · R. Wreak · R. Gwash · R. Chater · R. Welland · R. Nene · R. Glen · Ermine Street · Roman Road · Car Dike (Roman Canal) · Rockingham Forest · Willow Brook

Continued on Map 49
Continued

Scale of Miles
0 1 2 3 4 5 6 7 8 9 10

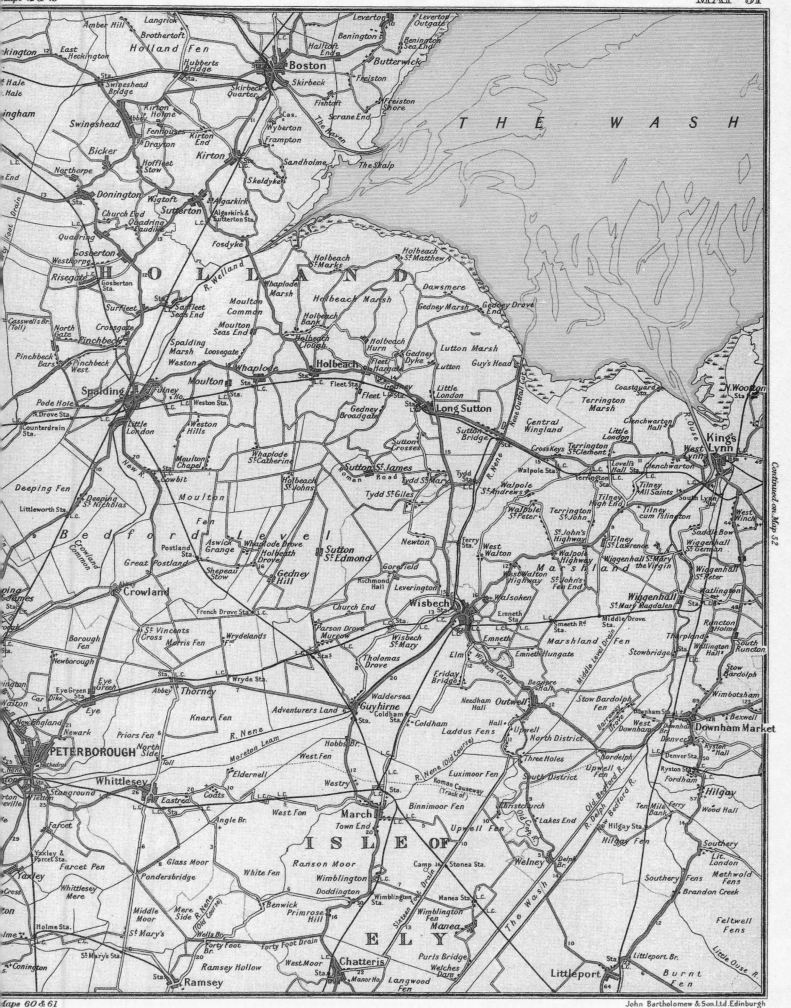

THE WASH

HOLLAND

Boston

Holland Fen

Amber Hill
Langrick
Brothertoft
East Heckington
Hubberts Bridge
Swineshead Bridge
Swineshead
Kirton Holme
Fenhouses
Drayton
Bicker
Northorpe
Hoffleet Stow
Kirton End
Kirton
Donington
Wigtoft
Church End
Quadring Eaudike
Quadring
Sutterton
Algarkirk
Algarkirk & Sutterton Sta.
Fosdyke
Gosberton
Westhorpe
Risegate
Gosberton Sta.
Surfleet
Crossgate
North Gate
Pinchbeck
Pinchbeck Bars
Pinchbeck West
Spalding
Pode Hole
Little London
Weston Sta.
Weston Hills
Deeping Fen
Deeping St. Nicholas
Littleworth Sta.
Bedford Level
Crowland Common
Great Postland
Postland Sta.
Crowland
Borough Fen
Newborough
Eye Green
Car Dike
Abbey
Thorney
New England
Newark
Priors Fen
Peterborough
Whittlesey
Stanground
Fletton
Farcet
Yaxley & Farcet Sta.
Yaxley
Farcet Pen
Whittlesey Mere
Holme Sta.
Middle Moor
St. Mary's
Ramsey Hollow
Ramsey

Leverton
Benington
Halton End
Butterwick
Leverton Outgate
Benington Sea End
Skirbeck Quarter
Skirbeck
Fishtoft
Freiston
Freiston Shore
Wyberton
Frampton
Scrane End
The Haven
Sandholme
The Skalp
Skeldyke

Saffleet Seas End
Moulton Common
Moulton Seas End
Spalding Marsh
Loosegate
Weston
Whaplode
Moulton
Moulton Chapel
Cowbit
Moulton Fen
Whaplode St. Catherine
Aswick Grange
Whaplode Drove
Shepeau Stow
Holbeach Drove
Gedney Hill
Sutton St. Edmond
Gorefield
Newton
Richmond Hall
Leverington
Church End
Parson Drove
Murrow
Wisbech St. Mary
Tholomas Drove
Waldersea
Coldham
Guyhirne
Coldham
Hobbs Br.
West Fen
Moreton Leam
West Fen
March
Town End
Eldernell
Westry
Angle Br.
Coats
Eastrea
Glass Moor
White Fen
Ranson Moor
Wimblington
Doddington
Benwick
Primrose Hill
Mere Side
Wells Br.
Forty Foot Br.
Forty Foot Drain
West Moor
Chatteris
Manor Ho.
Langwood Fen
Purls Bridge
Welches Dam

Holbeach St. Marks
Holbeach Marsh
Holbeach Bank
Holbeach Clough
Holbeach Hurn
Holbeach
Fleet Hargate
Fleet Sta.
Fleet
Gedney
Holbeach St. Johns
Whaplode Marsh
Moulton Common
Holbeach St. Matthew
Dawsmere
Gedney Marsh
Gedney Drove End
Lutton Marsh
Gedney Dyke
Lutton
Guy's Head
Gedney Broadgate
Little London
Long Sutton
Sutton Crosses
Sutton St. James
St. James Road
Tydd St. Mary
Tydd St. Giles
Sutton Bridge
Central Wingland
Cross Keys
Walpole Sta.
Walpole St. Andrews
Walpole St. Peter
Ferry Sta.
West Walton
Walsoken
Wisbech
Emneth
Emneth Sta.
Elm
Friday Bridge
Begdale Hall
Needham Hall
Outwell
Upwell
Laddus Fens
North District
Three Holes
South District
Euximoor Fen
Roman Causeway (Track of)
R. Nene (Old Course)
Binnimoor Fen
Upwell Fen
Stonea Sta.
Camp
Manea Sta.
Manea
Wimblington Fen
Sixteen Foot Drain
Delph Br.
Welney
Isle of Ely

R. Welland
R. Nene

Terrington Marsh
Coastguard Sta.
Clenchwarton
N. Wootton
King's Lynn
West Lynn
Terrington St. Clement
Terrington St. John
Lovell's Hall
Clenchwarton
Tilney All Saints
South Lynn
Tilney High End
St. John's Highway
Tilney cum Islington
Tilney St. Lawrence
West Winch
Saddle Bow
Wiggenhall St. German
Wiggenhall St. Mary the Virgin
Wiggenhall St. Peter
Wiggenhall St. Mary Magdalen
Watlington
Runcton Holme
Tharpland
Wellington Hall
South Runcton
Stow Bardolph
Stowbridge
Wimbotsham
Downham Market
Stow Bardolph Fen
Barroway Drove
West Downham
Nordelph
Upwell Fen
Denver
Ryston Hall
Ryston Sta.
Denver Sta.
Fordham
Hilgay
Wood Hall
Ten Mile Bank
R. Delph
New Bedford R.
Old Bedford R.
Hilgay Fen
New Hilgay Sta.
Lakes End
Christchurch
Southery
Southery Fens
Lit. London
Methwold Fens
Brandon Creek
Feltwell Fens
The Wash
Littleport
Littleport Br.
Burnt Fen
Little Ouse R.

Continued on Map 52

Main Roads ——— Other Roads ——— Railways ———

MAP 52

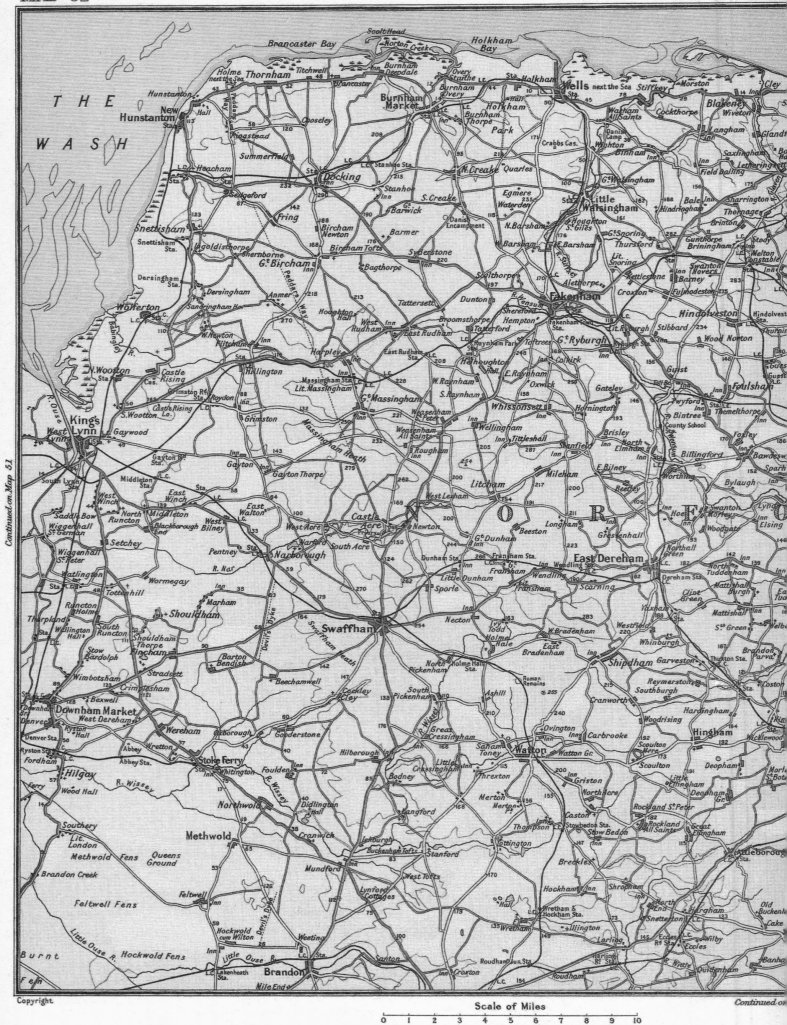

THE
WASH

Continued on Map 51

Scale of Miles

0 1 2 3 4 5 6 7 8 9 10

Copyright

Continued on

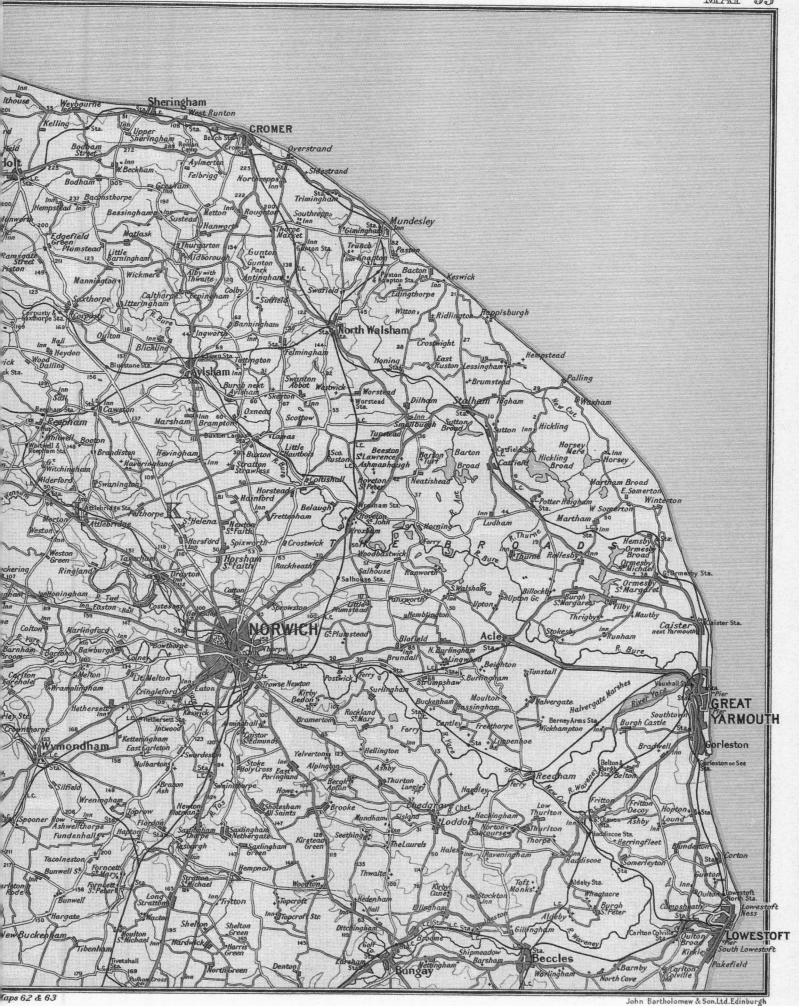

MAP 53

Main Roads ━━━━━━ Other Roads ══════ Railways ━━━━━━

John Bartholomew & Son.Ltd.Edinburgh

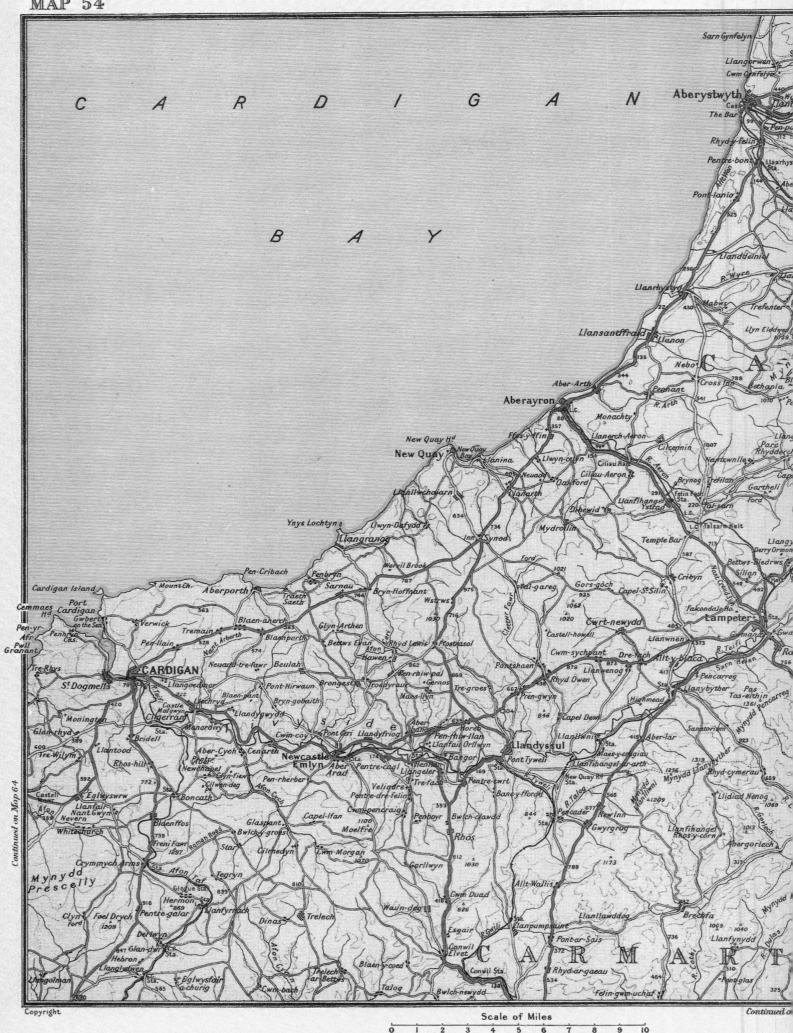

MAP 55

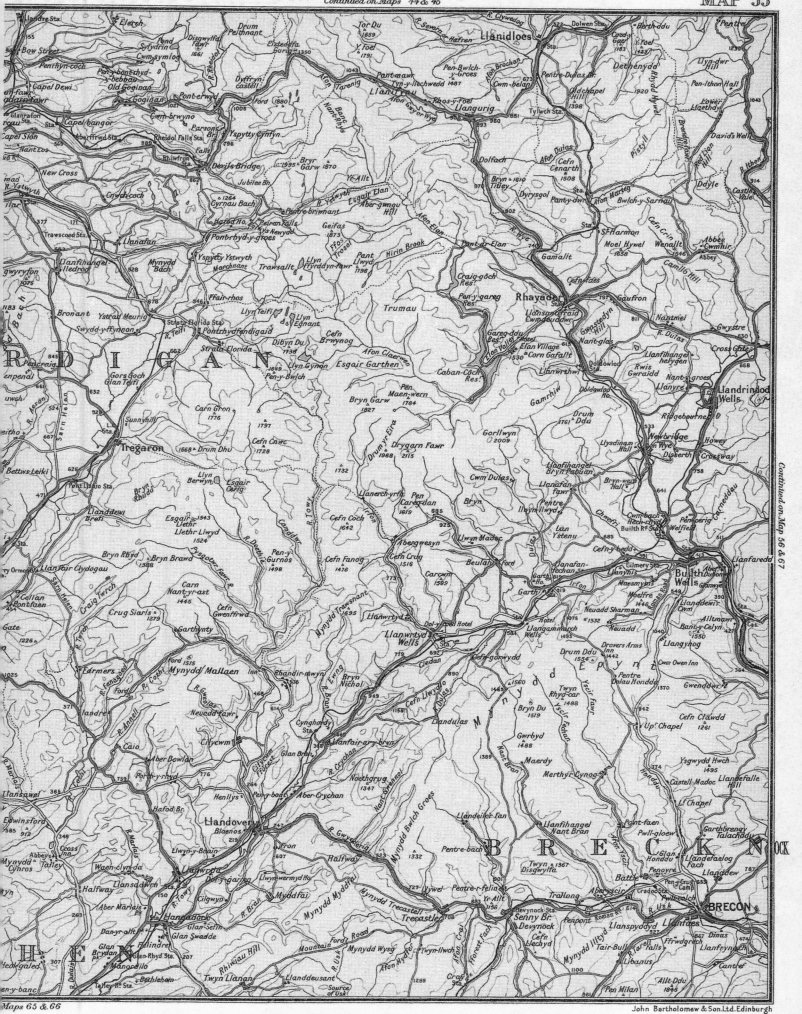

Continued on Map 56 & 57

John Bartholomew & Son. Ltd. Edinburgh

Main Roads ————— Other Roads ========= Railways —————

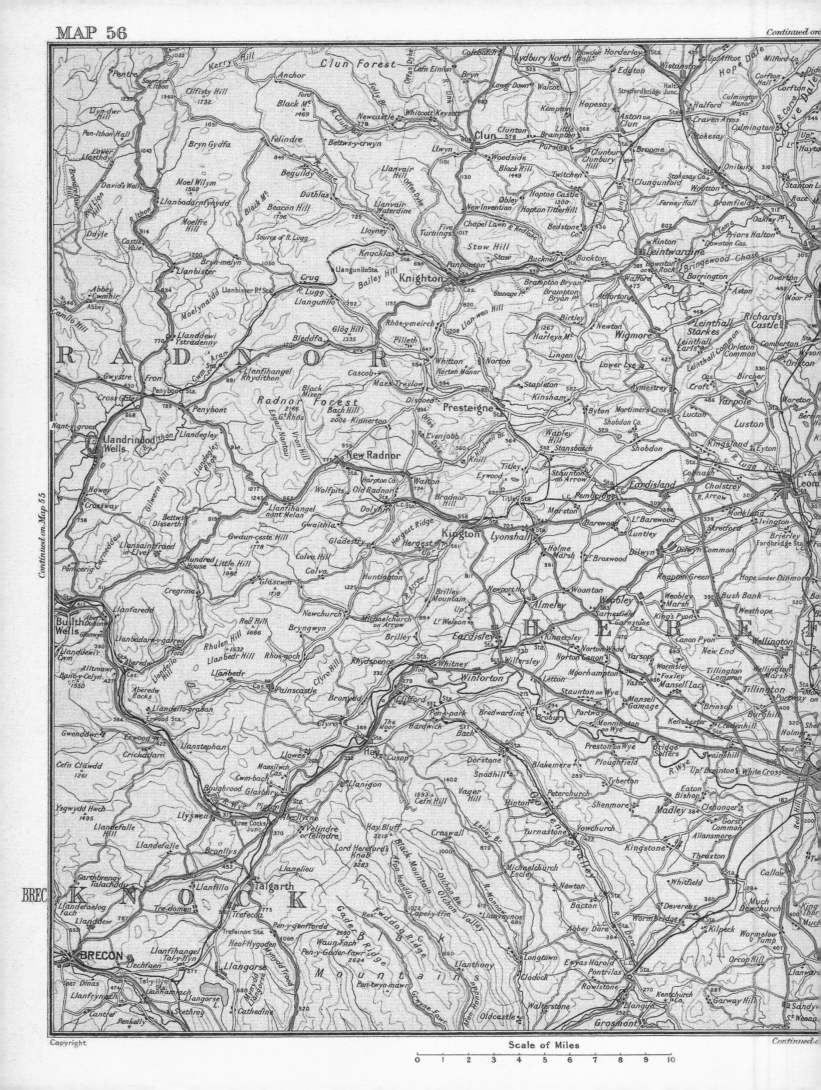

MAP 56

Scale of Miles

0 1 2 3 4 5 6 7 8 9 10

Continued on Map 55

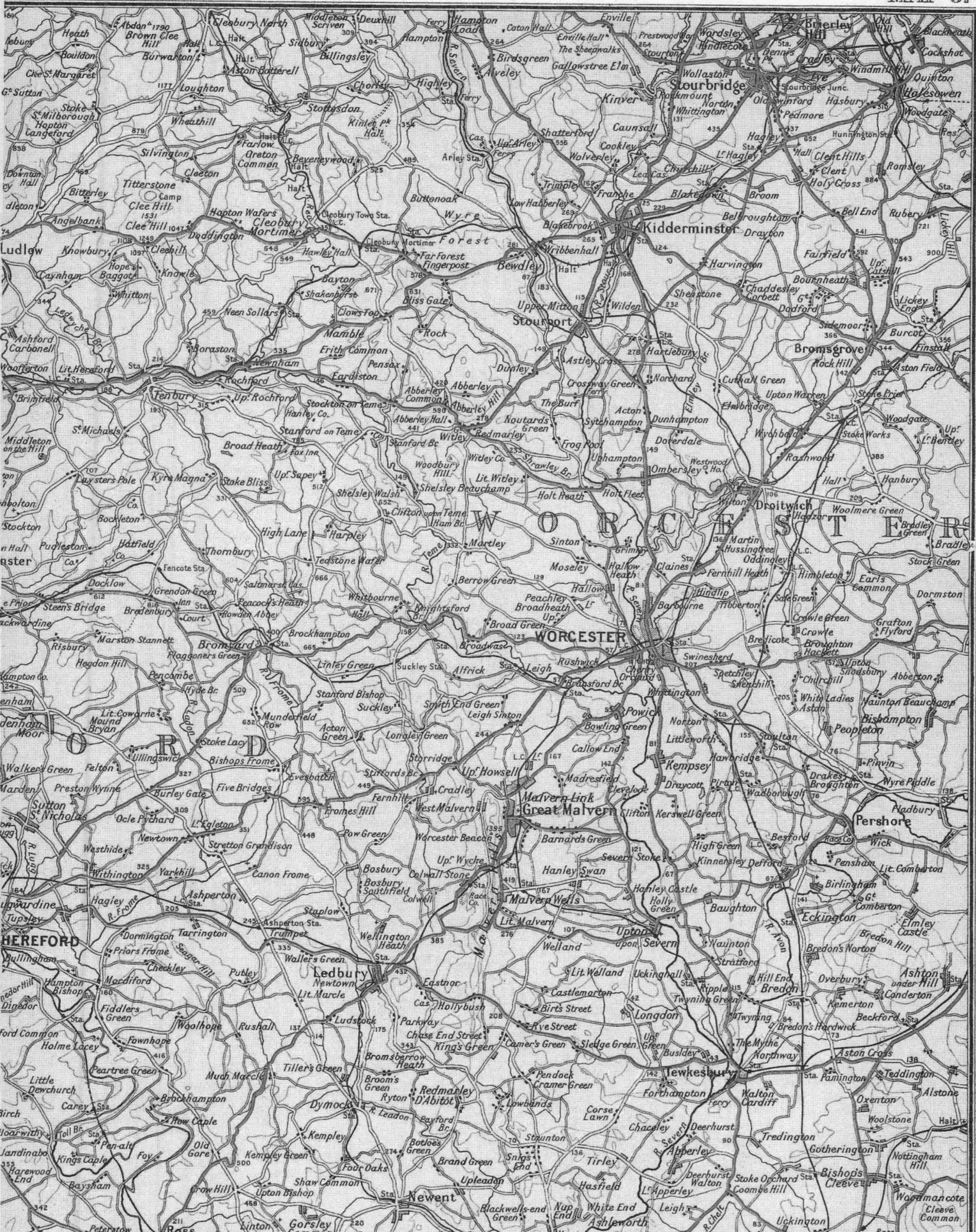

Abdon 1790
Brown Clee Hill
Cleobury North
Middleton Scriven
Deuxhill
Hampton Load
Coton Hall
Enville
Prestwood
Wordsley
Brierley Hill
Old Hill
Blackheath
Cockshot

Heath
Bouldon
Burwarton
Halt
Sidbury
Hampton
R. Severn
Birdsgreen
Enville Hall
The Sheepwalks
Stourton
Wollaston
Pedmore
Stourbridge
Hasbury
Windmill Hill
Quinton

Clee St. Margaret
Gt. Sutton
Loughton
Billingsley
Highley
Ferry
Aveley
Gallowstree Elm
Kinver
Stourbridge Junc.
Old Swinford
Halesowen
Woodgate

Stoke St. Milborough
Wheathill
Stottesdon
Chorley
Kinlet
Shatterford
Caunsall
Cookley
Whittington
North
Hagley
Clent Hills

Silvington
Oreton Common
Cleeton
Bevereywood
Kinlet Pk. Hall
Arley Sta.
Up. Arley
Wolverley
Trimpley
Franche
Churchill
Broom
Bell End
Rubery

Titterstone Clee Hill
Camp
Cleobury Mortimer
Wyre
Blakebrook
Kidderminster
Harvington
Fairfield
Up. Catshill
Bournheath

Clee Hill
Deddington
Hopton Wafers
Cleobury Town Sta.
Forest
Wribbenhall
Bewdley
Shenstone
Chaddesley Corbett
Dodford
Sidemoor
Burcot
Finstall

Ludlow
Knowbury
Cleehill
Hawley Hall
Far Forest Fingerpost
Upper Mitton
Wilden
Bromsgrove
Rock Hill
Aston Fields

Ashford Carbonel
Woofferton
Bayton
Shakenhurst
Bliss Gate
Clows Top
Rock
Stourport
Astley Cross
Hartlebury
Crossway Green
Norchard
Cutnall Green
Upton Warren
Stoke Prior

Tenbury
Newnham
Frith Common
Pensax
Mamble
Dunley
Hartlebury
Acton
Sytchampton
Dunhampton
Wychbold
Stoke Works

St. Michaels
Rochford
Stockton on Teme
Eardiston
Abberley Common
Abberley
Noutards Green
Frog Pool
Ombersley
Rashwood
Hanbury

Lysters Pole
Kyre Magna
Stoke Bliss
Up. Sapey
Stanford on Teme
Witley Co.
Redmarley
Ushampton
Doverdale
Hanbury

Bockleton
Hatfield
Thornbury
Tedstone Wafer
Shelsley Walsh
Shelsley Beauchamp
Woodbury Hill
Lit. Witley
Holt Heath
Holt Fleet
Droitwich
Woolmere Green
Bradley Green

WORCESTER

High Lane
Harpley
Clifton upon Teme
Martley
Sinton
Hallow Heath
Claines
Fernhill Heath
Himbleton
Earls Common
Dormston

Fencote Sta.
Saltmarsh Las.
Berrow Green
Moseley
Grimley
Barbourne
Hindlip
Tibberton
Sale Green
Crowle Green
Grafton Flyford

Docklow
Grendon Green
Peacock's Heath
Rowden Abbey
Whitbourne
Knightsford
Broadheath Up.
Broad Green
Hindlip
Crowle
Broughton Hackett

Risbury
Hegdon Hill
Bredenbury
Court
Hall
Broadwas
WORCESTER
Rushwick
Bredicote
Upton Snodsbury
Abberton

Bromyard
Flaggoners Green
Brockhampton
Linley Green
Suckley Sta.
Alfrick
Leigh
Bransford Br.
Whittington
Spetchley
Shenhill
Churchill

Marston Stannett
Pencombe
Hyde Br.
Stanford Bishop
Suckley
Smith End Green
Leigh Sinton
Broadford Br.
Norton
White Ladies Aston
Naunton Beauchamp
Peopleton

Hampton Co.
Lit. Cowarne
Mound Bryan
Munderfield Row
Acton Green
Longley Green
Powick
Bowling Green
Littleworth
Stoulton
Bishampton

Stoke Lacy
Ullingswick
Bishops Frome
Evesbatch
Storridge
Up. Howsell
Callow End
Kempsey
Hawbridge
Drakes Broughton
Pinvin
Wyre Piddle

Felton
Preston Wynne
Burley Gate
Five Bridges
Stifford's Br.
Cradley
West Malvern
Madresfield
Clevelode
Draycott
Pirton
Wadborough
Pershore

Sutton St. Nicholas
Marden
Ocle Pychard
Lr. Egleton
Fromes Hill
Fernhill
Malvern Link
Great Malvern
Clifton
Kerswell Green
Besford
Wick
Pensham

Withington
Yarkhill
Stretton Grandison
Pow Green
Worcester Beacon
Barnards Green
Severn Stoke
High Green
Kinnersley
Defford
Lit. Comberton

Ugwardine
Tupsley
HEREFORD
Hagley
Ashperton
Canon Frome
Bosbury
Colwall Stone
Hanley Swan
Hanley Castle
Holly Green
Baughton
Eckington
Elmley Castle

Dormington
Priors Frame
Checkley
Putley
Staplow
Ashperton Sta.
Trumpet
Bosbury Southfield
Colwall
Malvern Wells
Upton upon Severn
Wainton
Stratford
Bredon Hill
Conderton

Mordiford
Fiddlers Green
Tarrington
Wallers Green
Wellington Heath
Lit. Malvern
Welland
Lit. Welland
Uckinghall
Ripple
Hill End
Bredon
Overbury
Ashton under Hill

Holme Lacey
Fownhope
Ledbury
Newtown
Lit. Marcle
Eastnor
Castlemorton
Hollybush
Birts Street
Longdon
Twyning Green
Kemerton
Beckford

Peartree Green
Much Marcle
Ludstock
Parkway
Chase End Street
King's Green
Rye Street
Camer's Green
Sledge Green
Twyning
Bredon's Hardwick
Aston Cross
Teddington

Brockhampton
Tillers Green
Bromsberrow Heath
Broom's Green
Ryton
Redmarley D'Abitot
Lowbands
Corse Lawn
Forthampton
The Mythe
Northway
Tewkesbury
Pamington
Alstone

Carey
Dymock
R. Leadon
Payford Br.
Botloe's Green
Staunton
Chaceley
Apperley
Deerhurst
Tredington
Gotherington
Nottingham Hill

Kings Caple
Foy
Old Gore
Kempley
Kempley Green
Brand Green
Tirley
Hasfield
Lt. Apperley
Stoke Orchard
Coombe Hill
Bishops Cleeve
Woodmancote

Ross
Bromsash
Linton
Gorsley Common
Four Oaks
Upleadon
Newent
Kent's Green
Blackwells-end Green
White End
Ashleworth
Hartpury
Withy Br.
Swindon
Uckington
Cleeve Common

Main Roads ═══════ Other Roads ═══════ Railways ═══════

MAP 58

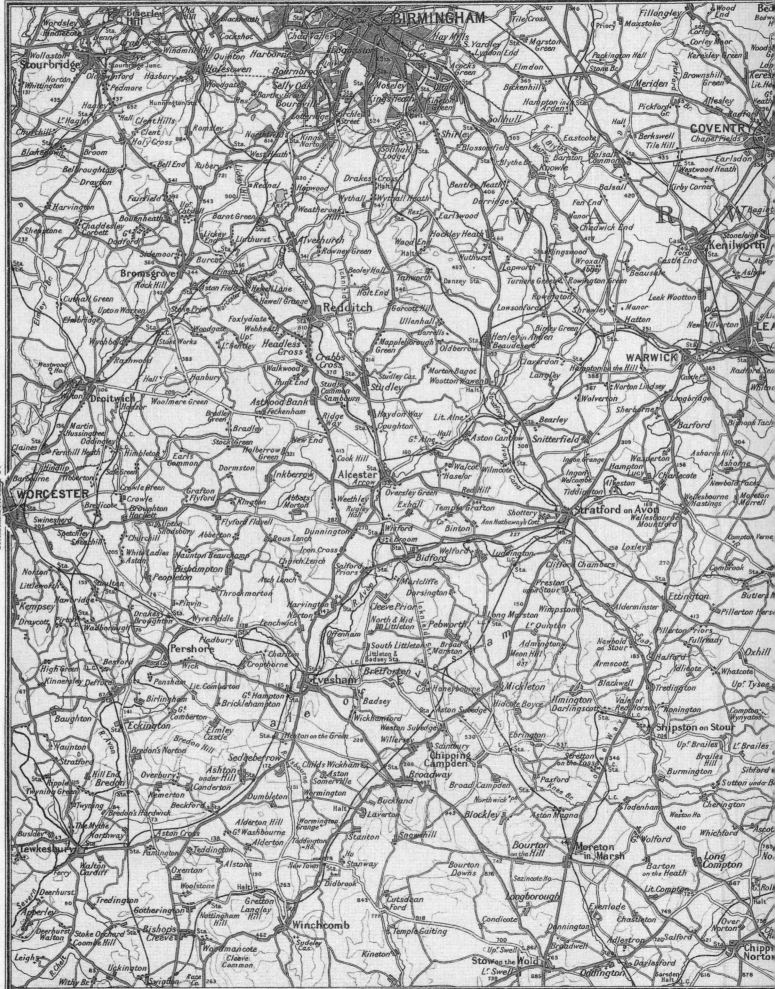

Scale of Miles

0 1 2 3 4 5 6 7 8 9 10

Continued on Map 57

Continued o

MAP 59

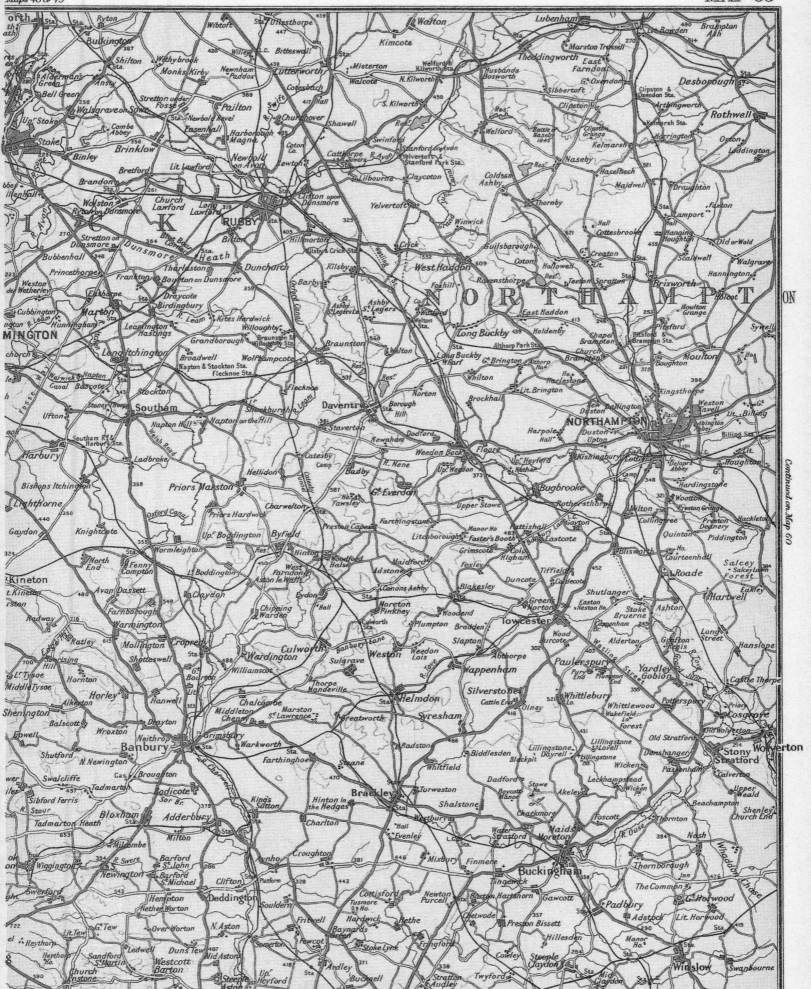

John Bartholomew & Son Ltd. Edinburgh

Main Roads ——— Other Roads ═══ Railways ━━━

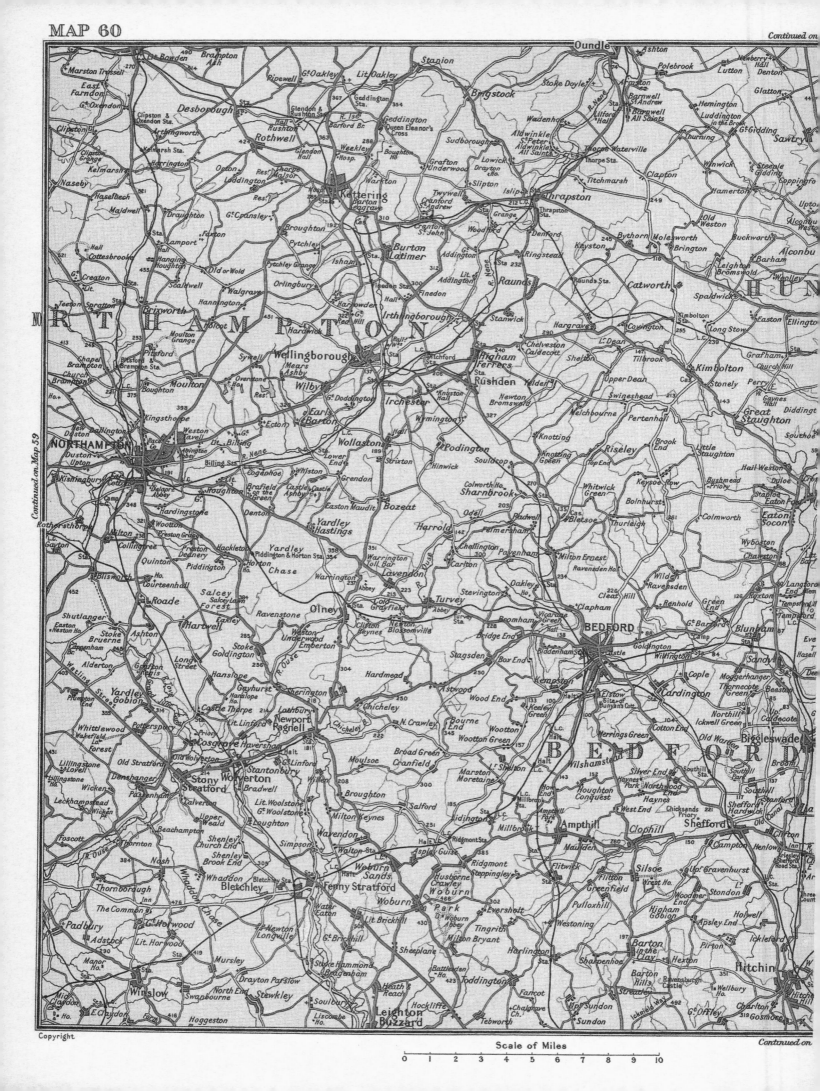

MAP 60

Scale of Miles

0 1 2 3 4 5 6 7 8 9 10

MAP 61

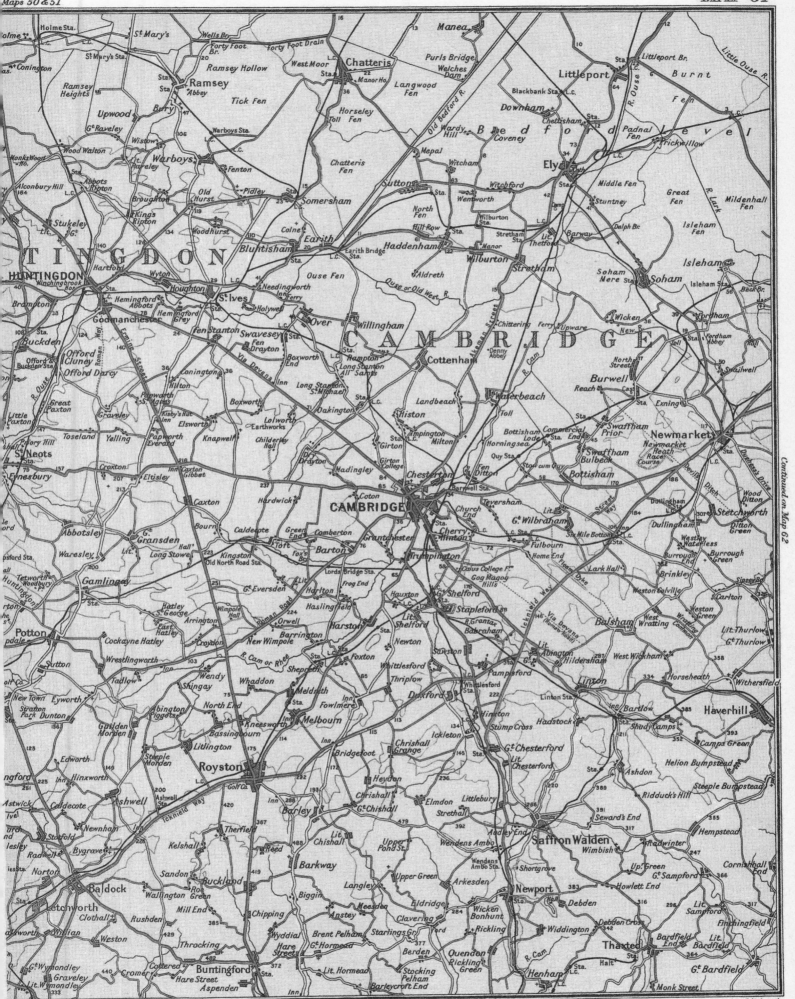

John Bartholomew & Son.Ltd Edinburgh

Main Roads ━━━━━ Other Roads ═══════ Railways ━━━━━━

MAP 62

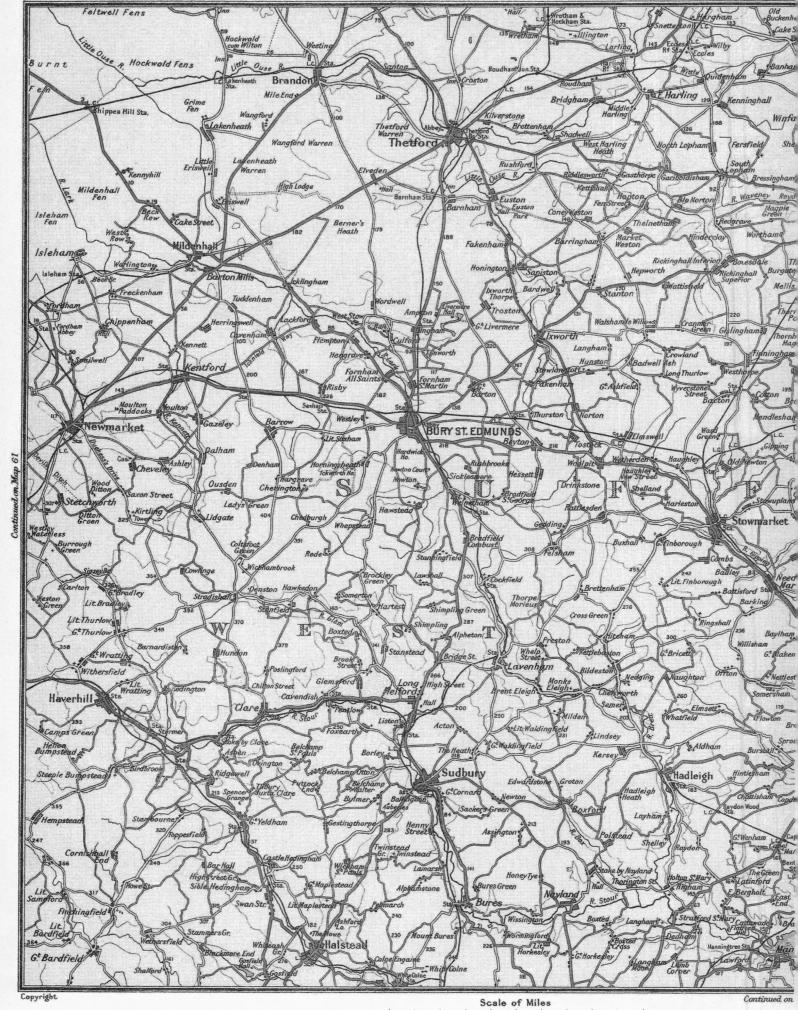

Continued on Map 61

Scale of Miles

0 1 2 3 4 5 6 7 8 9 10

MAP 63

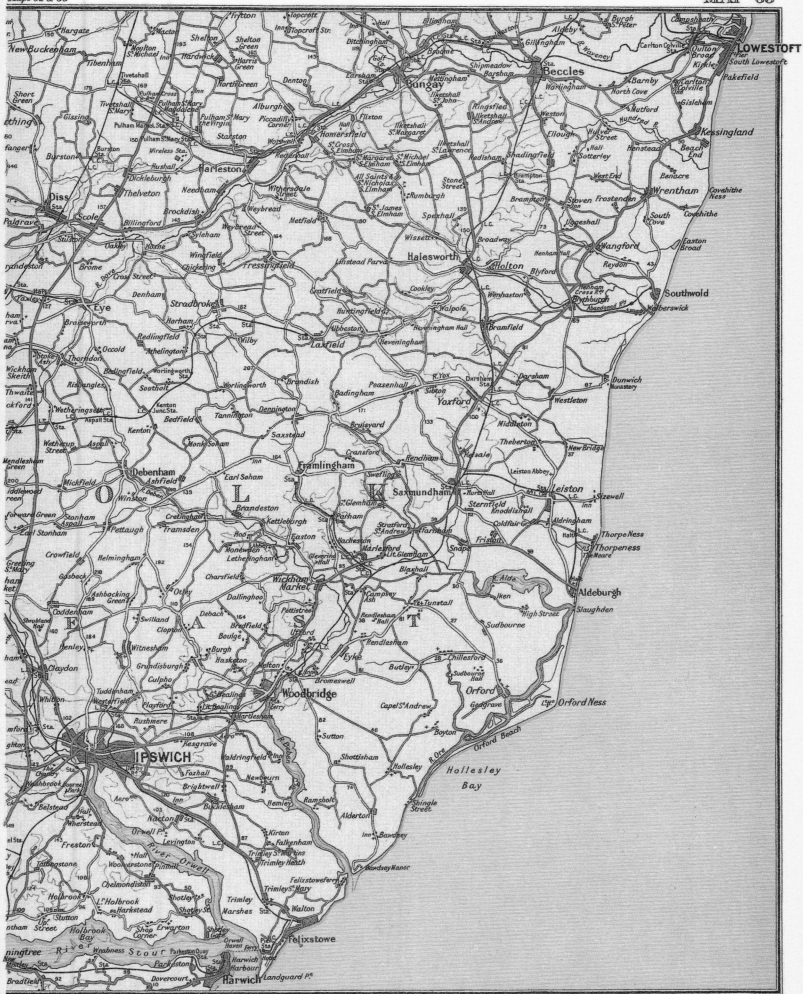

John Bartholomew & Son.Ltd.,Edinburgh

Main Roads ——————   Other Roads ——————   Railways ——————

MAP 64

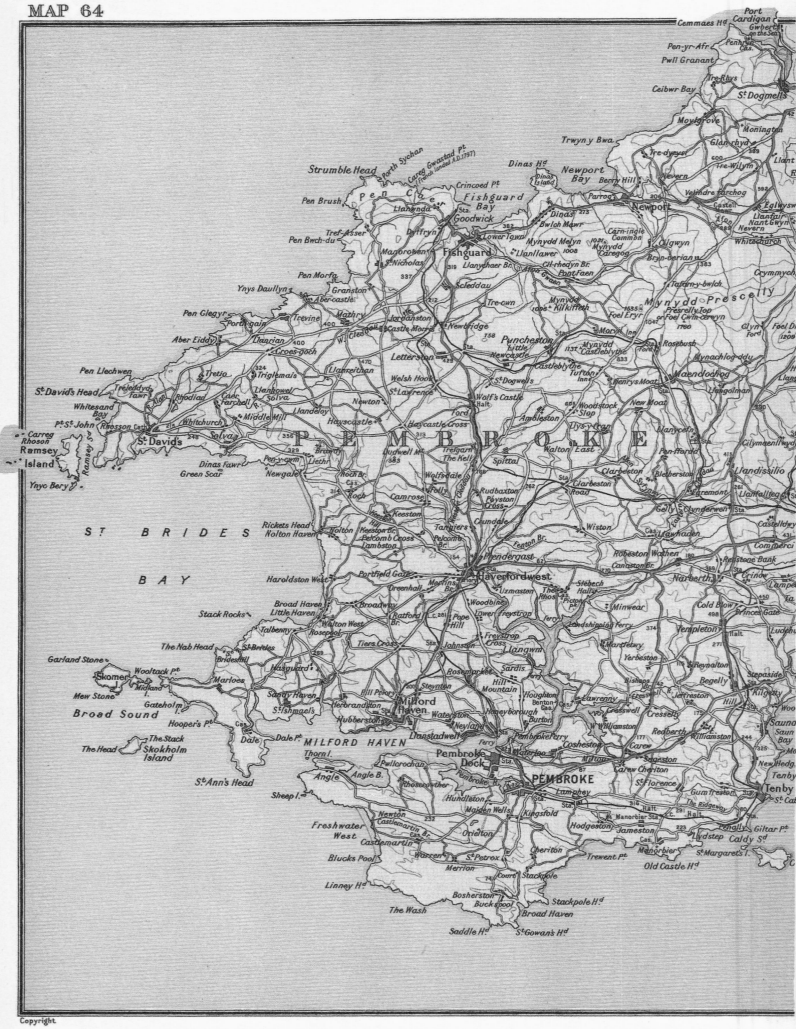

Main Roads ⎯⎯⎯⎯⎯   Other Roads ⎯⎯⎯⎯⎯   Railways ⎯⎯⎯⎯⎯

MAP 65

CARMARTHEN

CARMARTHEN

BAY

Scale of Miles

0 1 2 3 4 5 6 7 8 9 10

John Bartholomew & Son.Ltd.,Edinburgh

MAP 66

Scale of Miles

0 1 2 3 4 5 6 7 8 9 10

Continued on Map 68

Main Roads ━━━━━━ Other Roads ═════ Railways ┅┅┅┅┅

MAP 68

Continued on

CHELTENHAM

Newent

Ross

MONMOUTH

GLOUCESTER

Forest of Dean

Cinderford

Coleford

Chepstow

Lydney

Stroud

Painswick

Tetbury

Malmesbury

Dursley

Wotton under Edge

Nailsworth

Minchinhampton

Chipping Sodbury

Thornbury

Wickwar

Marshfield

CHIPPENHAM

BRISTOL

Keynsham

BATH

Melksham

Corsham

Continued on Map 67

Copyright

Continued on

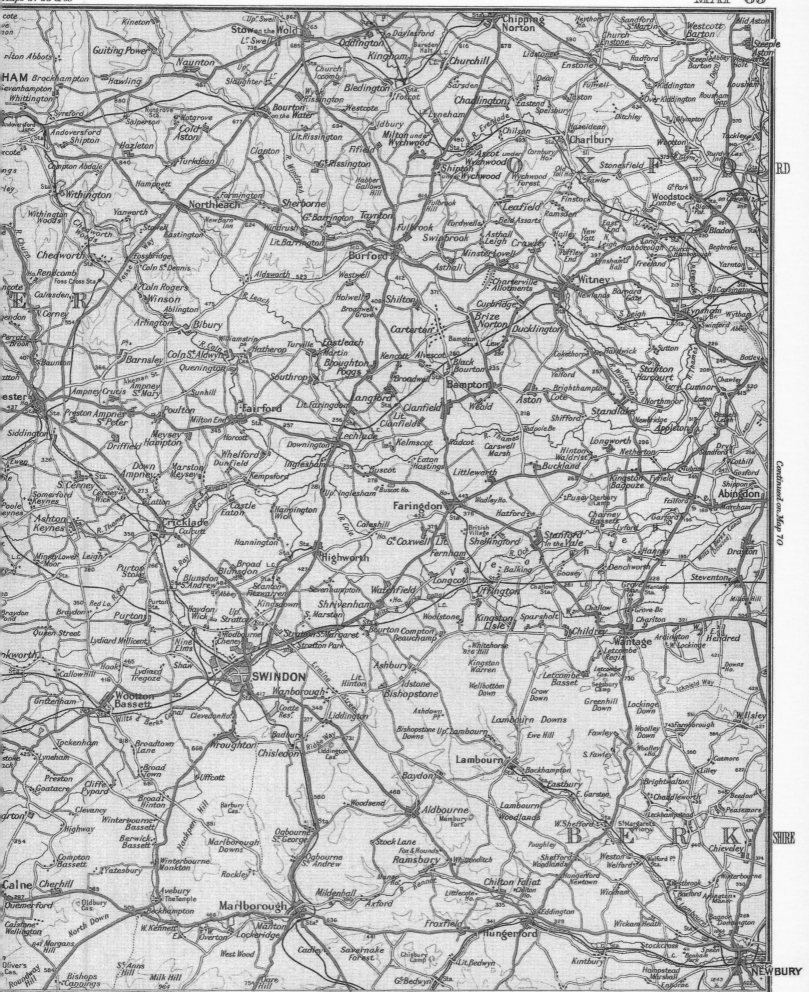

Main Roads ━━━━━   Other Roads ━━━━━   Railways ━━━━━

MAP 70

Continued

OXF ... WOODSTOCK ... OXFORD ... BUCKINGH... ... Bicester ... Winslow ... Linslade

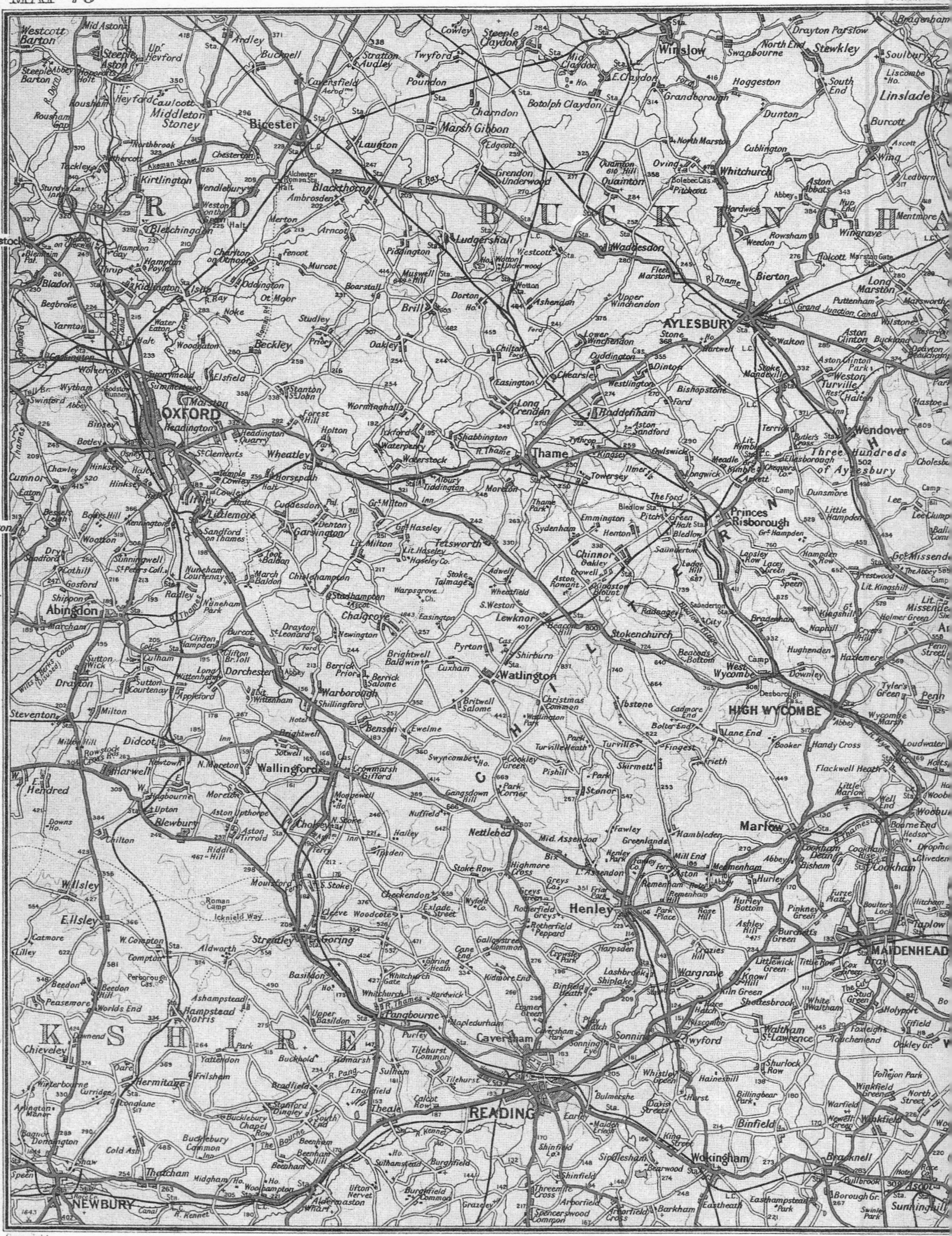

AYLESBURY

Thame ... Wendover ... Princes Risborough

HIGH WYCOMBE ... Marlow ... MAIDENHEAD

Abingdon ... Wallingford ... Watlington ... Henley

BER KSHIRE

Didcot ... Goring ... Pangbourne ... Caversham ... Twyford

READING ... Wokingham ... Bracknell

NEWBURY

Continued on Map 69

Scale of Miles

0 1 2 3 4 5 6 7 8 9 10

Copyright.

MAP 71

Maps 59, 60 & 61

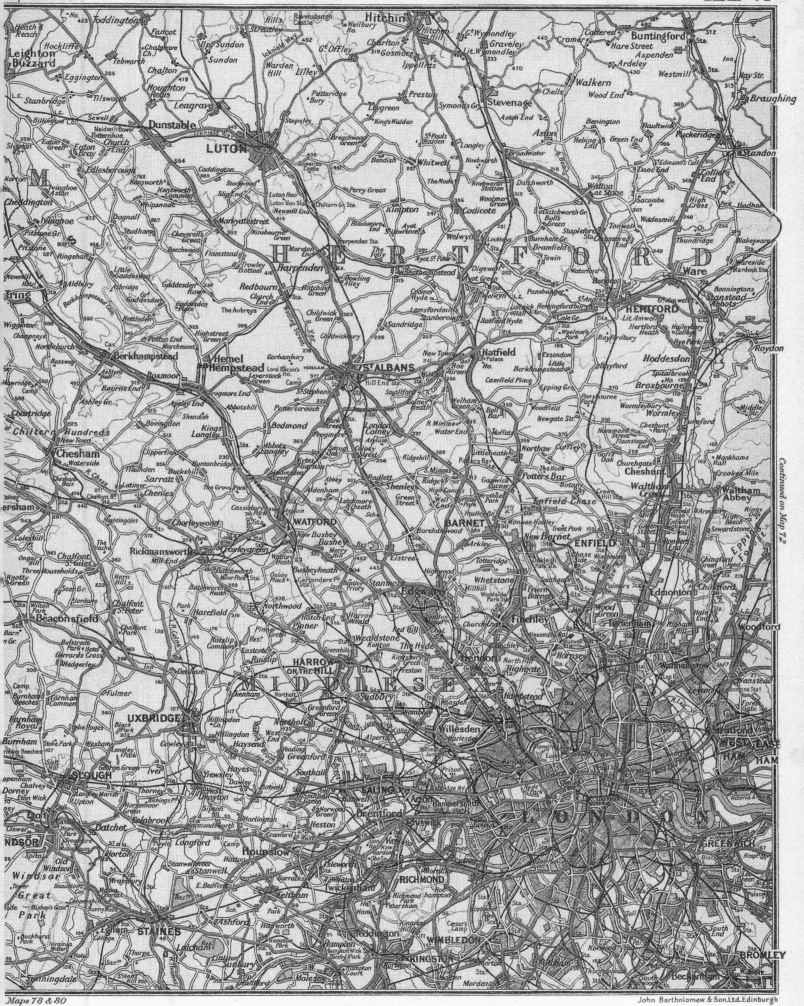

Continued on Map 72

John Bartholomew & Son, Ltd., Edinburgh.

Main Roads —————— Other Roads —————— Railways ——————

MAP 72

Continued on

Continued on Map 71

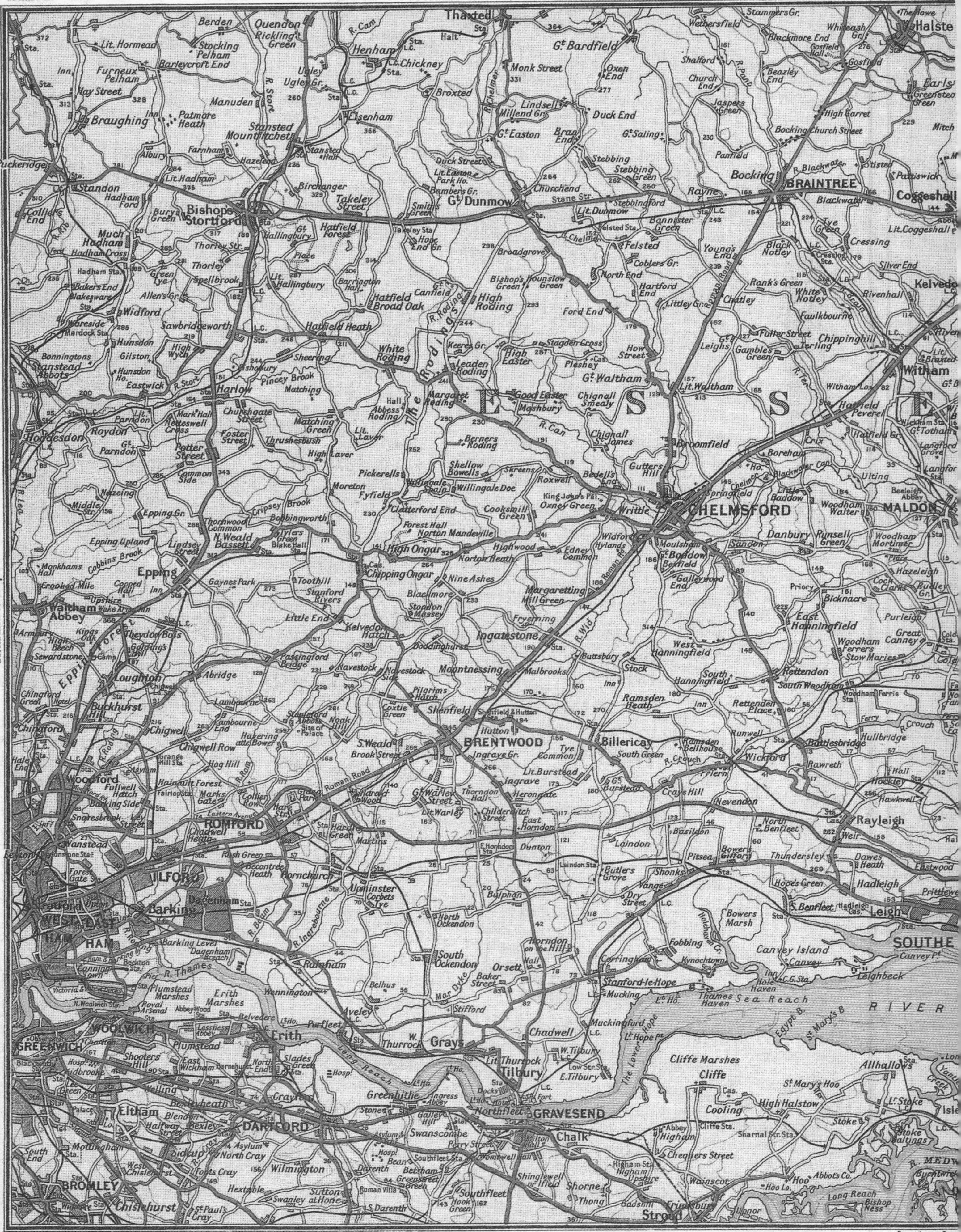

Thaxted · Halste · Wethersfield · Stammers Gr. · The Howe · Whiteash Gr. · Gosfield

Braughing · Furneux Pelham · Stocking Pelham · Berden · Quendon · Rickling Green · Henham · Gt. Bardfield · Shalford · Blackmore End · Gosfield Hall

Puckeridge · Lit. Hormead · Hay Street · Manuden · Ugley · Broxted · Monk Street · Oxen End · Duck End · Beazley End · High Garret

Standon · Hadham Ford · Bishops Stortford · Birchanger · Takeley Street · Gt. Dunmow · Lindsell · Duck End · Bocking · BRAINTREE · Coggeshall

Much Hadham · Thorley · Hatfield Forest · Broadgrove · Felsted · Young's End · White Notley · Kelvedon · Rivenhall

Widford · Sawbridgeworth · Hatfield Broad Oak · High Roding · Hounslow Green · North End · Hartford End · Faulkbourne · Witham

Ware · Hunsdon · Gilston · Sheering · White Roding · Leaden Roding · High Easter · Gt. Waltham · Lit. Waltham · Hatfield Peverel · Gt. Totham

Hoddesdon · Roydon · Harlow · Matching · Margaret Roding · Good Easter · Mashbury · Broomfield · Boreham · Ulting · Langford

Nazeing · Epping Gr. · Cripsey Brook · Moreton · Fyfield · Willingale · Roxwell · Writtle · CHELMSFORD · Woodham Walter · MALDON

Epping · N. Weald Bassett · High Ongar · Chipping Ongar · Norton Heath · Highwood · Gt. Baddow · Danbury · Runsell Green · Woodham Mortimer

Waltham Abbey · Loughton · Abridge · Stanford Rivers · Blackmore · Stondon Massey · Margaretting · Ingatestone · Stock · East Hanningfield · Great Canney

Buckhurst Hill · Chigwell · Lambourne · Passingford Bridge · Navestock · Mountnessing · West Hanningfield · South Hanningfield · Rettendon · Stow Maries

Woodford · Chigwell Row · Pilgrims Hatch · Shenfield · Hutton · Billericay · Ramsden Heath · Runwell · Wickford · Battlesbridge · Hullbridge

Wanstead · Romford · S. Weald · BRENTWOOD · Ingrave · Gt. Warley · Herongate · Gt. Burstead · Crays Hill · Nevendon · Rayleigh · Hawkwell

ILFORD · Hornchurch · Upminster · Childerditch · East Horndon · Laindon · Basildon · North Benfleet · Weir · Hockley

Barking · Dagenham · North Ockendon · Bulphan · Dunton · Pitsea · Bowers Gifford · Thundersley · Hadleigh · Leigh · SOUTHE

WEST HAM · EAST HAM · Rainham · South Ockendon · Orsett · Stanford-le-Hope · Corringham · Fobbing · Canvey Island · Canvey Pt.

Woolwich · GREENWICH · Erith · Purfleet · Aveley · Mucking · Thames Haven · Sea Reach · RIVER

Plumstead · Welling · Crayford · W. Thurrock · Grays · Chadwell · Muckingford · Cliffe Marshes · Allhallows

Eltham · Bexley · DARTFORD · Greenhithe · Northfleet · GRAVESEND · Chalk · Cooling · High Halstow · St. Mary's Hoo

BROMLEY · Chislehurst · Swanley · Sutton at Hone · Southfleet · Swanscombe · Cliffe · Cliffe Sta. · Strod · R. MEDW

ESSEX

Scale of Miles
0 1 2 3 4 5 6 7 8 9 10

Continued on

Main Roads ——— Other Roads ——— Railways ———

MAP 74

Continued on

Senghenydd
Llanbradach
M. Machen
Machen Upper
Sirhowy
Risca
Bettws
Caerleon
Malpas
Christchurch
Penhow
S.t Bride's Netherwent
Crick
Aust
Ingst
Ol
Aber
Bedwas
Pont y Mister
Rhiw derin
Rogerstone
Maindee
NEWPORT
Llangstone
Lianmartin
Llanvihangel near Roggiett
Caldicot
Portskewett
Northwick
Worthy
Redwick
Pilning
Easter
Compto
Caerphilly
Rudry
Ruperra Cas
Pentre-peoth
Bassaleg
Lis Werry
Bishton
Milton
Roggiett
Severn Tunnel Junc.
Severn Tunnel
Cha
Upr. Boat
Machen
Tredegar Ho.
Broadstreet Common
Magor
Undy
Caldicot Level
Cross Hands
Nant-garw
Thornhill
Cefn Mably
Michaelston Fedwy
Whitson Common
Redwick
Severn Beach Sta.
Glany Llan
Castleton
Nash
Goldcliff

Continued on Map 67

Taffs well
Ton-gwynlais
Lisvane
Begen
Marshfield
St Bride's Wentlloog
Redwick

Radyr
Llanishen
Llandaff North
Whitchurch
Llandeyrn
Blacktown
S.t Mellons
Peterstone Wentlloog
Battery Pt
West Hill
Sheepway
Portishead
Le Portbury
Easton in Gordano
Abbots Leigh
Clifton
Henbury
Avonmouth
Westbury on Trym

St fagans
Llandaff
Ely
Canton
Grangetown
Roath
CARDIFF
Dock
Weston in Gordano
Walton in Gordano
Halt
Clapton in Gordano
Cadbury Camp
Wraxall
L. Fairland
BRISTOL

Leckwith
Llandough juxta Cardiff
Dock
Clevedon
West End
Nailsea
East End
Farleigh
Flax Bourton
Burrow Gurney
Long Ashton

Wenvoe
Dinas Powis
Cogan
Penarth
Kingston St. Lawrence
R. Kenn
Kenn
Chelvey
Blackwell
Dundry
Dundry Hill

Wenvoe Cas
Cadoxton
L. Penarth
Halt
Lavernock
Lavernock Pt
Broadstone Sta.
Kingston Seymour
North End
Claverham
Yatton
Cleeve
Downside
Felton
Winford

Barry
Sully
Sully I.
Sand Bay
Wick St. Lawrence
Kewstoke
Bourton
R. Yeo
Congresbury
Redhill
Butcombe
Chew

Barry Island
Flat Holme
Worle
Milton
Puxton Sta.
Wrington
Ridgehill
Butcombe
Nemptnett Thrubwell
Bish Sutton

Steep Holme
Weston super Mare
Weston Bay
Locking
East Rolstone
Churchill
Langford
Burrington
Blagdon
Richford
Yeo Res.
Ubley
Harpt

BRIDGWATER BAY
Uphill
Hutton
Banwell
Sandford
Rowberrow
Shipham
Sidcot
Charterhouse
Compton Martin
E. Harptree

Brean
Bleadon Hill
Bleadon
Christon
Shiplate
Woodborough
Winscombe
Cross
Mendip
Cheddar Cliffs
Castle of Comfort Inn
Miner's Arms Inn

R. Axe
Loxton
L. Weare
Axbridge
Caverns
Cheddar
Nyland Hill
Draycott
Priddy
Hunters Lodge Inn

Lympsham
Rooks Bridge
Tarnock
Weare
Clewer
Cocklake
Rodney Stoke
Westbury

Berrow
Brent Knoll
East Brent
Badgworth Stone
Allerton Chapel
West Stoughton
Blackford
Wedmore
Lodgehill Sta.
Wookey Hole
Easton

R. Parrett
Burnham
Stert I.
Highbridge
Mark Causeway
Mark
Theale
R. Axe
Wookey
Henton
Wells
Dulcote

Huntspill
Bason Bridge
Cote
Tadham Moor
Panborough
Westhay Moor
Yarley
Coxley

Stolford
Knighton
Stockland Bristol
Stert
Huntspill Level
Catcott Burtle
Westhay
L. Godney
Polsham
Queens Sedge Moor

Kilve
Kilton
Burton
Fairfield Ho.
Shurton
Otterhampton
Pawlett
Edington Junc.
Meare
Shapwick
L. Godney
N. H.

East Quantoxhead
Putsham
Stogursey
Combwich
Coultings
Rodway
Down End
Puriton
Woolavington
Shapwick
Cossington
Edington
Glastonbury
Isle of Avalon
Glastonbury Tor

West Quantoxhead
Holford
Stringston
Dodington
Fiddington
Nether Stowey
Brymore Ho.
Cannington
Dunball
Knowle Hall
Chilton
Catcott
Athcott Sta.
Abbey
W. Pennar

Bicknoller
Over Stowey
Chilton Trinity
Bawdrip
Stawell
Chedzoy
Polden
Hills
Ashcott
Street
Walton
Edgarley
E.

Stogumber
Crowcombe
Quantock Lo.
Spaxton
Fourforks
Enmore
Wembdon
BRIDGWATER
Battle of Sedgemoor 1685
Weston Zoyland
Moorlinch
Greinton
Ashcott
Overleigh
Baltonsborough
Ham

Quantock Hills
SOMERSET
Durleigh
Sutton Mallet
King's Sedge Moor
Nythe
Compton
Dundon
Butleigh
Barton St David

Willett
Lydeard St. Lawrence
West Bagborough
Merridge
Halswell Ho.
Goathurst
Woolmersdon
N. Petherton
Huntworth
Middlezoy
Greylake
Henley
Henley Corner
Littleton
Copley Wood
Kempton

Tolland
Pitsford Hill
Combe Florey
Cothelstone
Toulton
Thurloxton
North Newton
Northmoor Green or Moorland
Burrow Bridge
Pathe
High Ham
Aller
Bramwell
Pitney
Charlton Mackrell
Somerton

Ash Priors
Bishop's Lydeard
Kingston
Adsborough
Lyng
Isle of Athelney
Stathe
Othery
Low
Kingweston

Continued on Map 85

RIVER SEVERN

Scale of Miles
0 1 2 3 4 5 6 7 8 9 10

Continued on

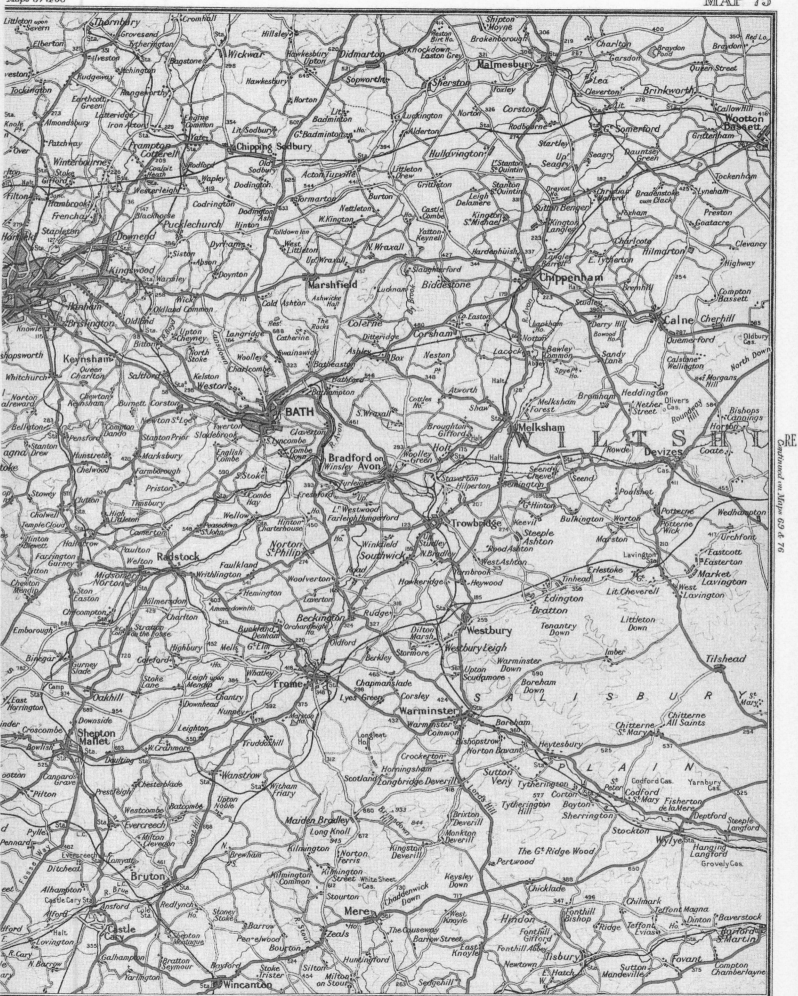

Main Roads ——— Other Roads ═══ Railways ———

MAP 76

Continued on

Continued on Maps 68 & 69

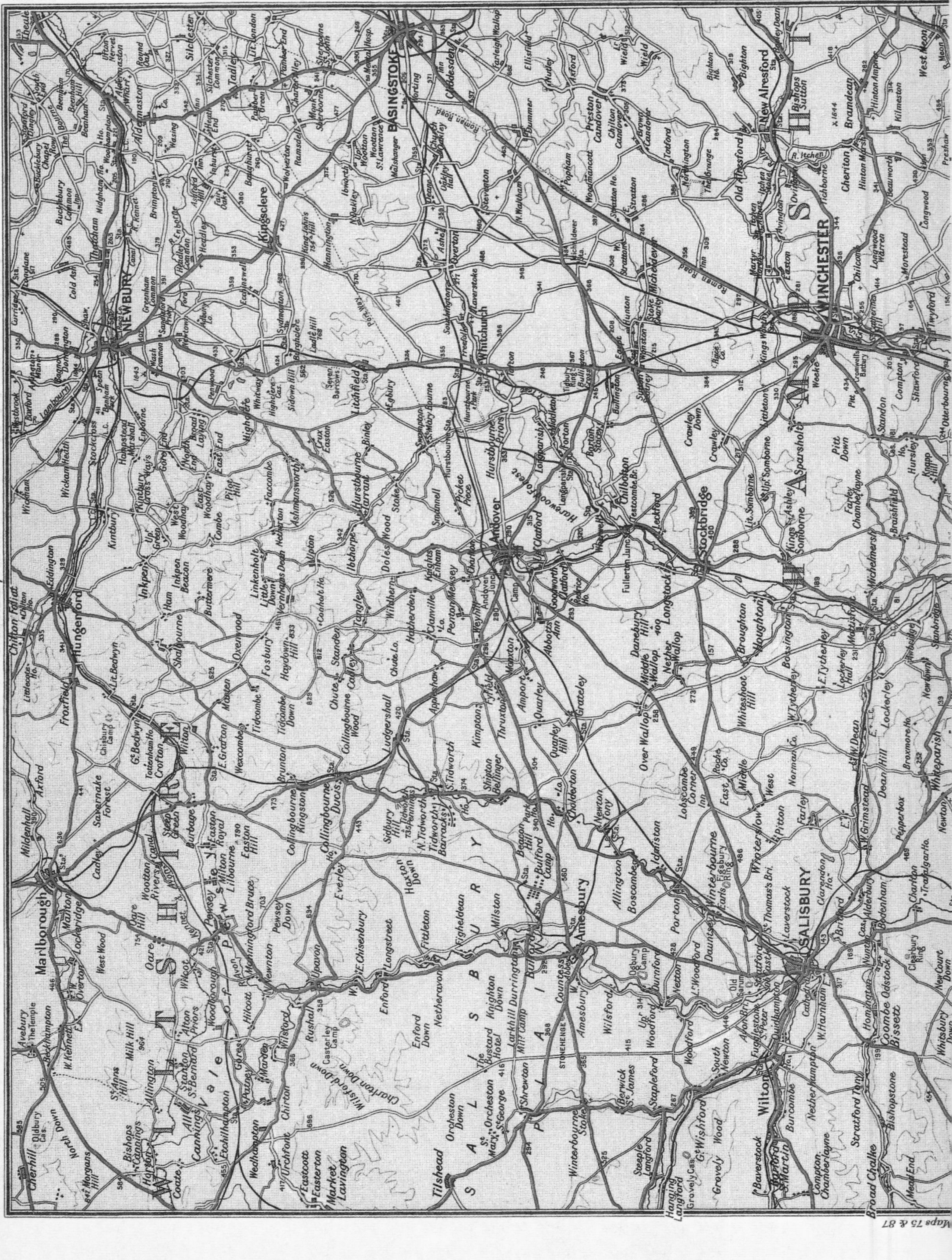

BASINGSTOKE

NEWBURY

WINCHESTER

New Alresford

Bishops Sutton

Cheriton

Kingsclere

Whitchurch

Litchfield

Andover

Stockbridge

Hungerford

Marlborough

Pewsey

Ludgershall

Amesbury

SALISBURY

Wilton

STONEHENGE

Tilshead

Market Lavington

HANTS.

WILTS.

BERKS.

SALISBURY PLAIN

Vale of Pewsey

Maps 75 & 87

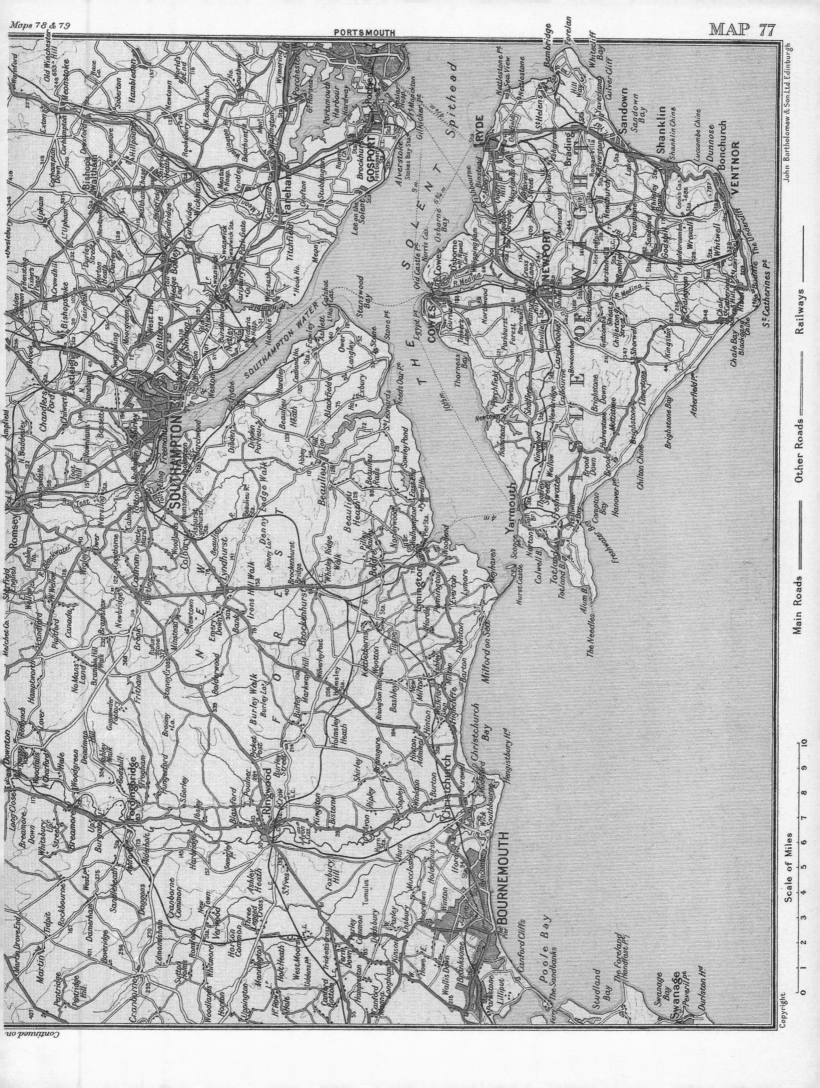

MAP 77

GOSPORT

Fareham

SOUTHAMPTON WATER

SOUTHAMPTON

Romsey

N E W

F O R E S T

Lyndhurst

BOURNEMOUTH

Poole Bay

Ringwood

Christchurch

Yarmouth

COWES

Newport

RYDE

Spithead

Sandown

Shanklin

Ventnor

Bonchurch

ISLE OF WIGHT

THE SOLENT

St Catherines Pt

Swanage

Swanage Bay

John Bartholomew & Son Ltd Edinburgh

Scale of Miles

0 1 2 3 4 5 6 7 8 9 10

Main Roads ═══ Other Roads ═══ Railways ═══

MAP 78

Continued on

Continued on Maps 70 & 71

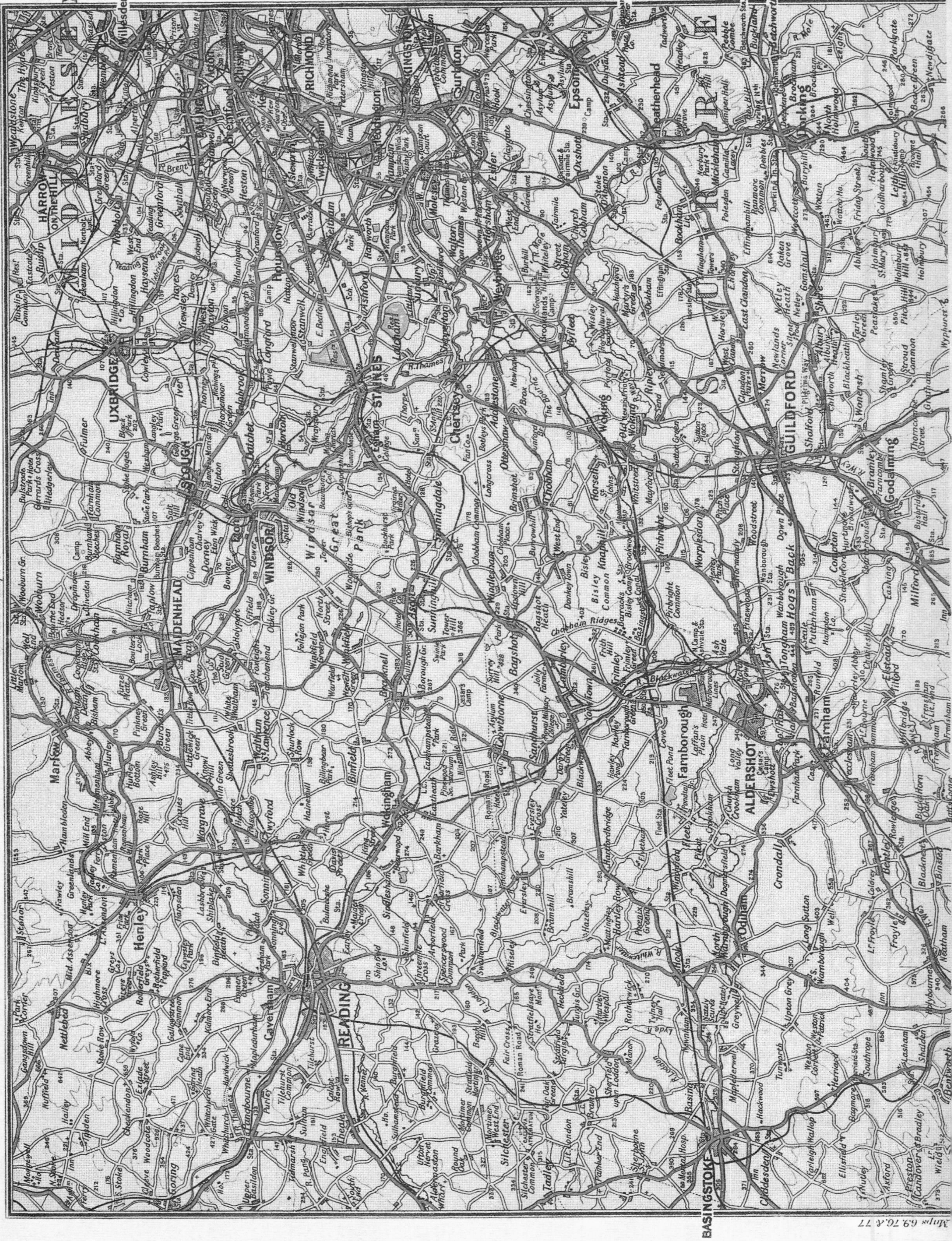

MIDDLESEX

SURREY

Major towns and places shown on the map:

HARROW ON THE HILL · RICHMOND · UXBRIDGE · SLOUGH · MAIDENHEAD · WINDSOR · STAINES · CHERTSEY · WEYBRIDGE · EPSOM · LEATHERHEAD · GUILDFORD · GODALMING · WOKING · FARNBOROUGH · ALDERSHOT · FARNHAM · READING · HENLEY · MARLOW

Great Park · R. Thames · Sunningdale · Bagshot Heath · Chobham Ridges · Camberley · Blackwater · Crondall

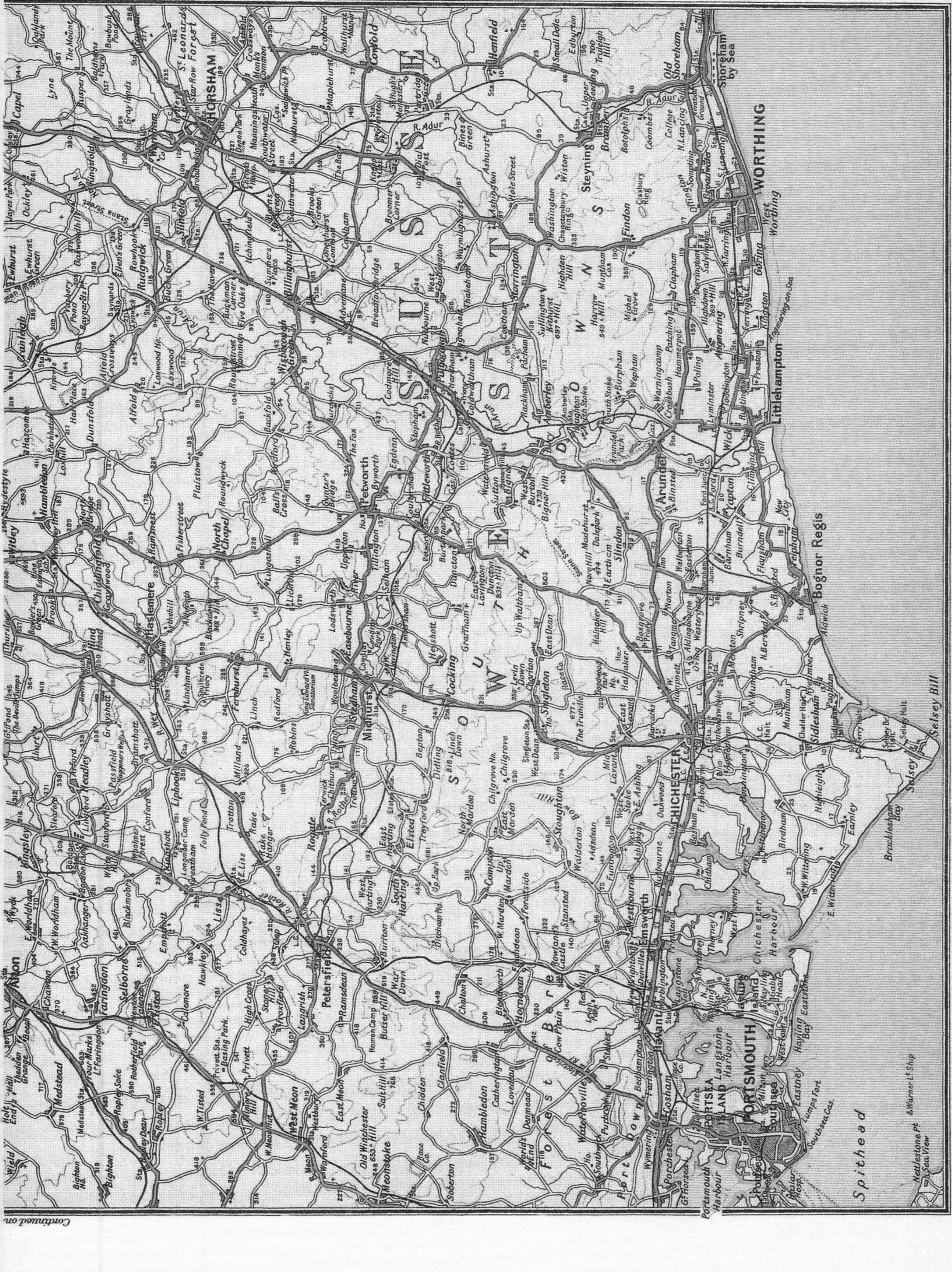

SUSSEX

WEST

S U S S E X

HORSHAM

WORTHING

WEST WORTHING

Shoreham by Sea

Old Shoreham

Steyning

Littlehampton

Bognor Regis

Arundel

CHICHESTER

Midhurst

Haslemere

Petersfield

PORTSMOUTH

Southsea

Emsworth

Havant

Hayling Island

Selsey Bill

Selsey

Bracklesham Bay

Chichester Harbour

Langstone Harbour

Spithead

Forest of Bere

Hindhead

Alton

Capel

R. Adur

R. Arun

R. Rother

Scale of Miles

0 1 2 3 4 5 6 7 8 9 10

Main Roads   Other Roads   Railways

John Bartholomew & Son,Ltd.Edinburgh

Copyright.

Continued on

MAP 80

Continued on

Continued on Maps 70 71 & 72

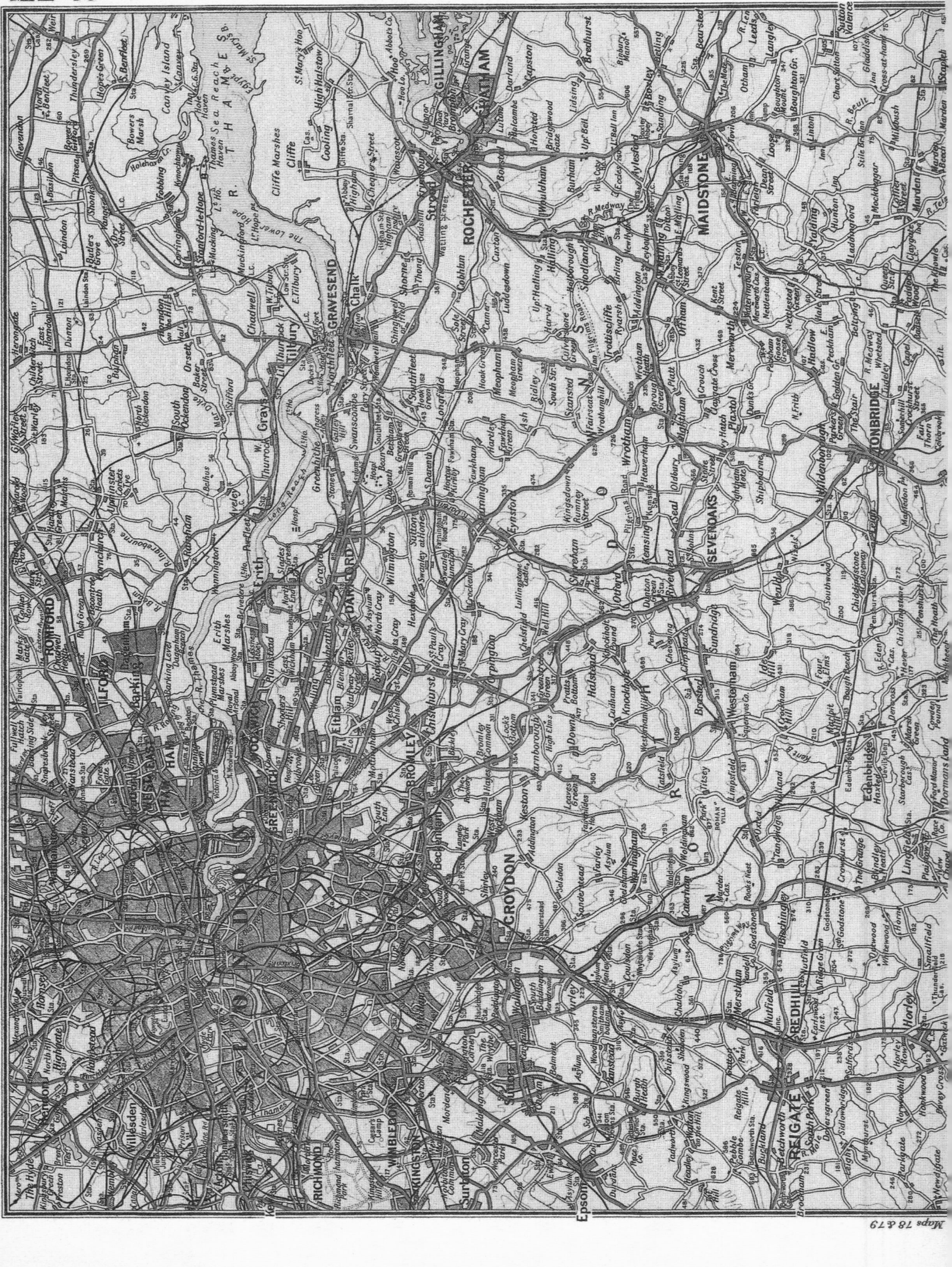

GILLINGHAM

CHATHAM

ROCHESTER

Strood

MAIDSTONE

GRAVESEND

TILBURY

DARTFORD

ERITH

TONBRIDGE

SEVENOAKS

ROMFORD

ILFORD

Barking

BROMLEY

CROYDON

EDENBRIDGE

WIMBLEDON

KINGSTON

RICHMOND

EPSOM

REDHILL

REIGATE

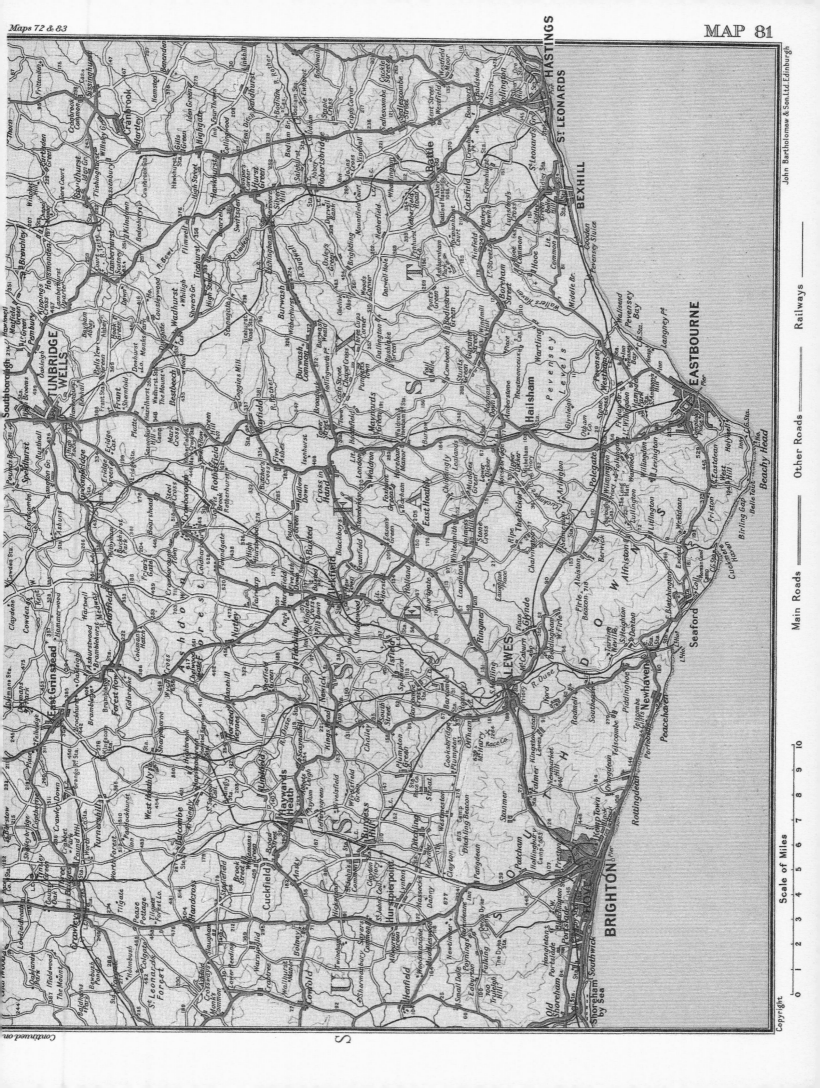

MAP 82

Continued on

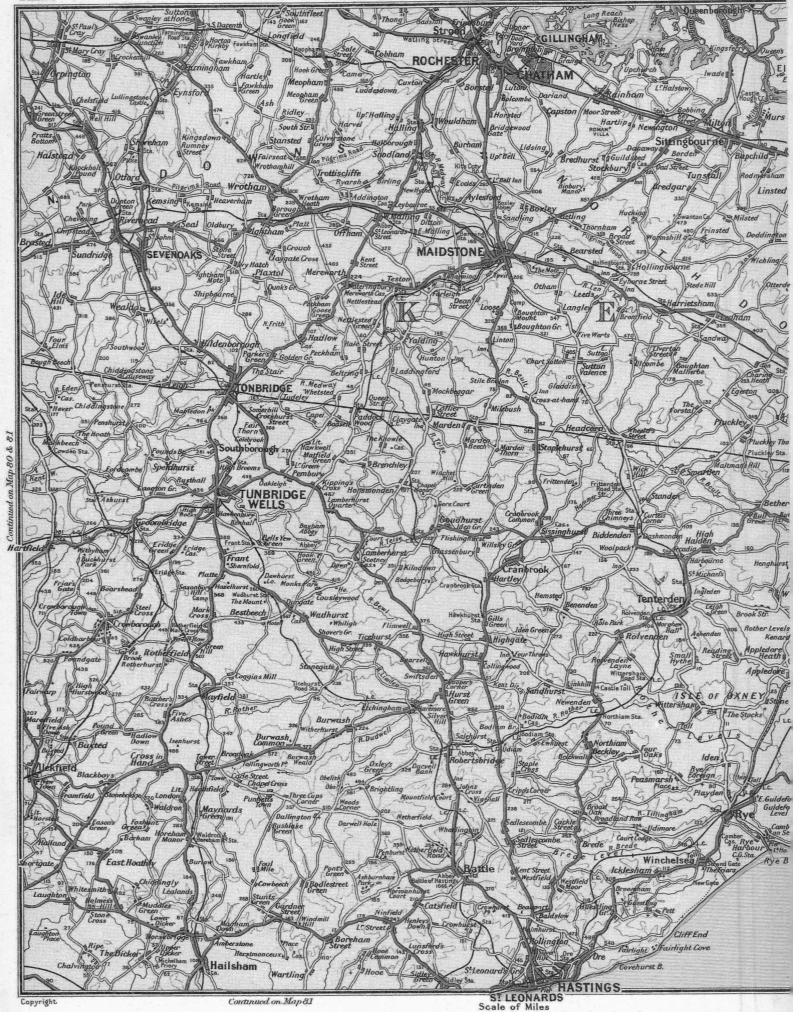

Scale of Miles

0 1 2 3 4 5 6 7 8 9 10

MAP 83

Main Roads ━━━━━   Other Roads ═════   Railways ━━━━━

MAP 84

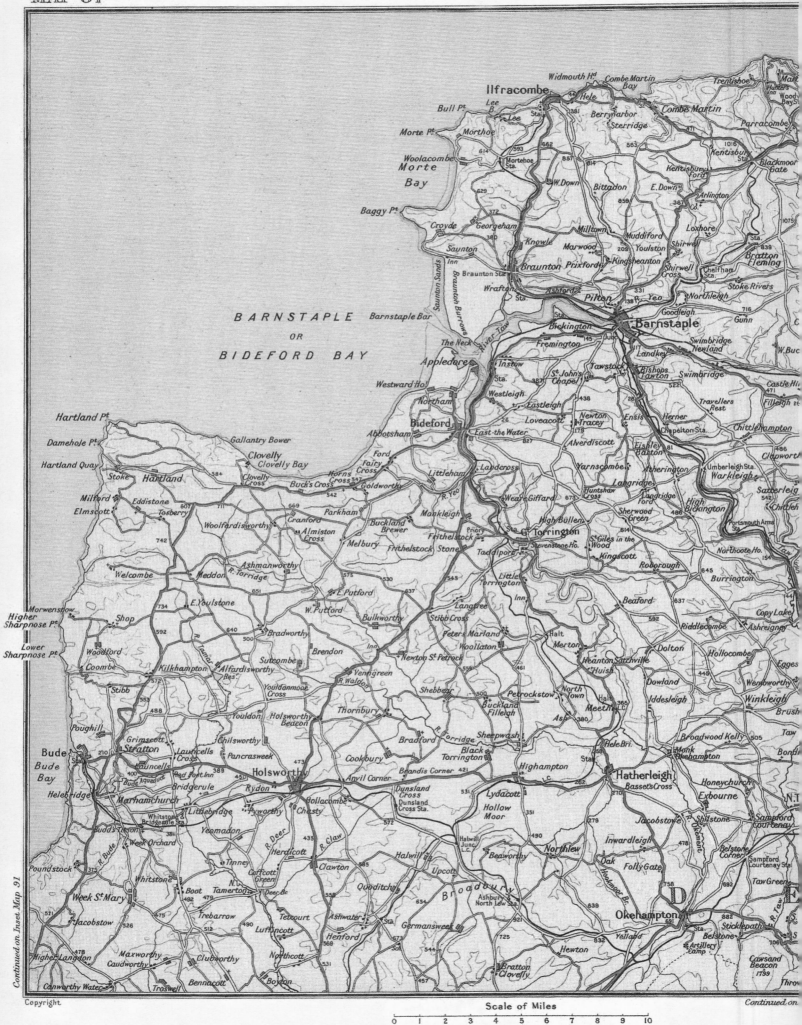

BARNSTAPLE

OR

BIDEFORD BAY

Ilfracombe

Barnstaple

Bideford

Bude

Holsworthy

Okehampton

Continued on Inset Map 91

Scale of Miles

0 1 2 3 4 5 6 7 8 9 10

Continued on

MAP 85

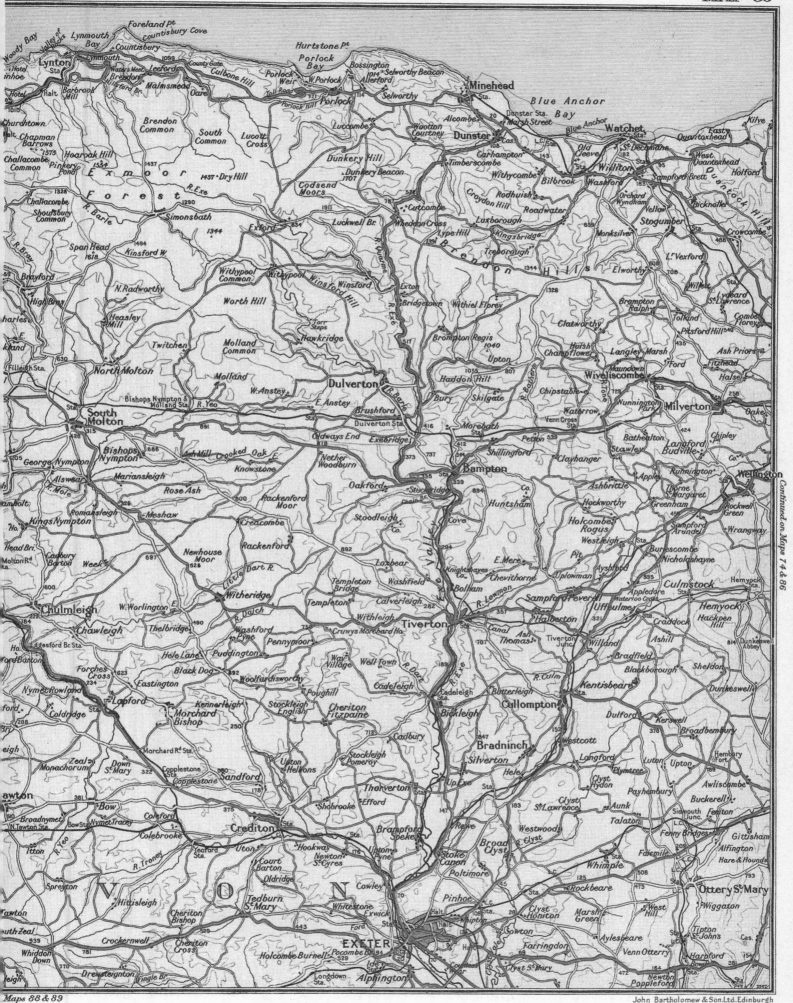

Continued on Maps 74 & 86

John Bartholomew & Son.Ltd.Edinburgh

Main Roads ———— Other Roads ═══════ Railways ─────

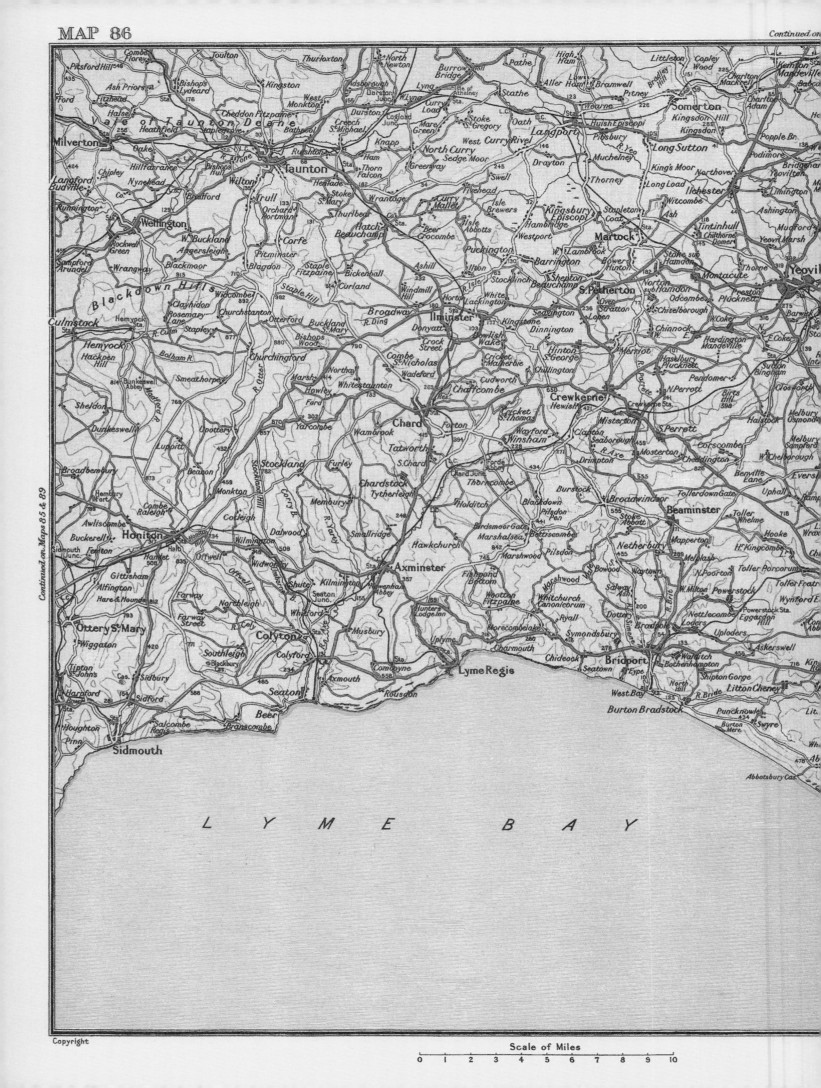

MAP 86

L Y M E   B A Y

Scale of Miles

0 1 2 3 4 5 6 7 8 9 10

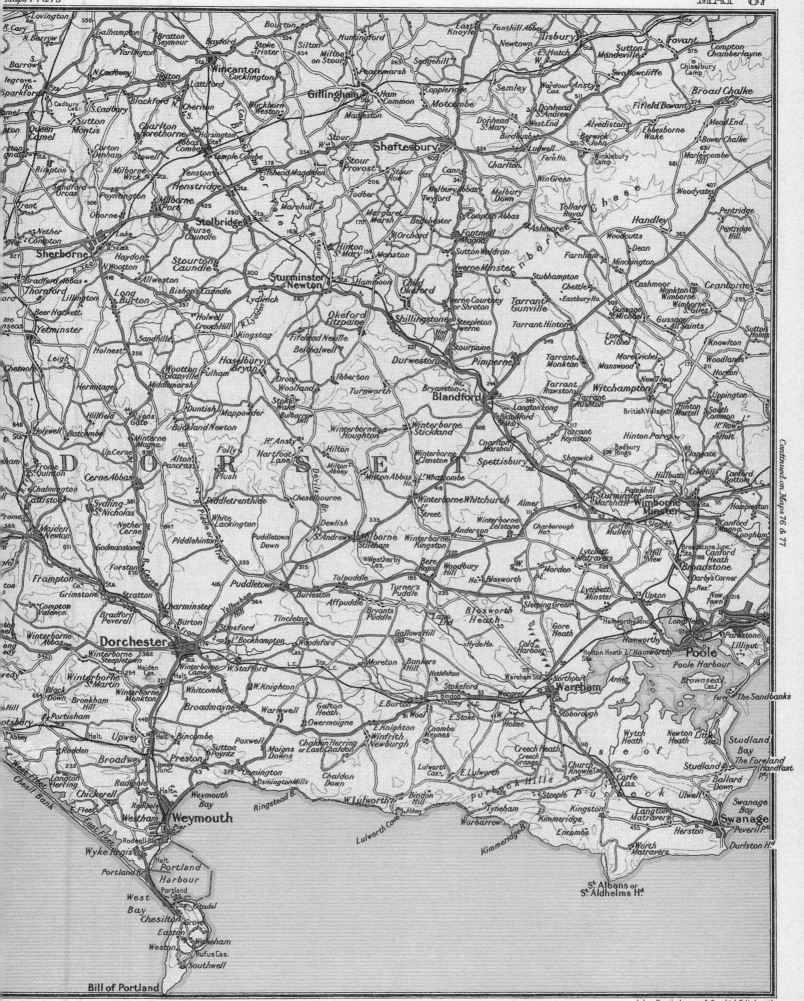

John Bartholomew & Son.Ltd.Edinburgh

Main Roads ━━━━━━ Other Roads ━━━━━━ Railways ━━━━━━

MAP 88

Continued on

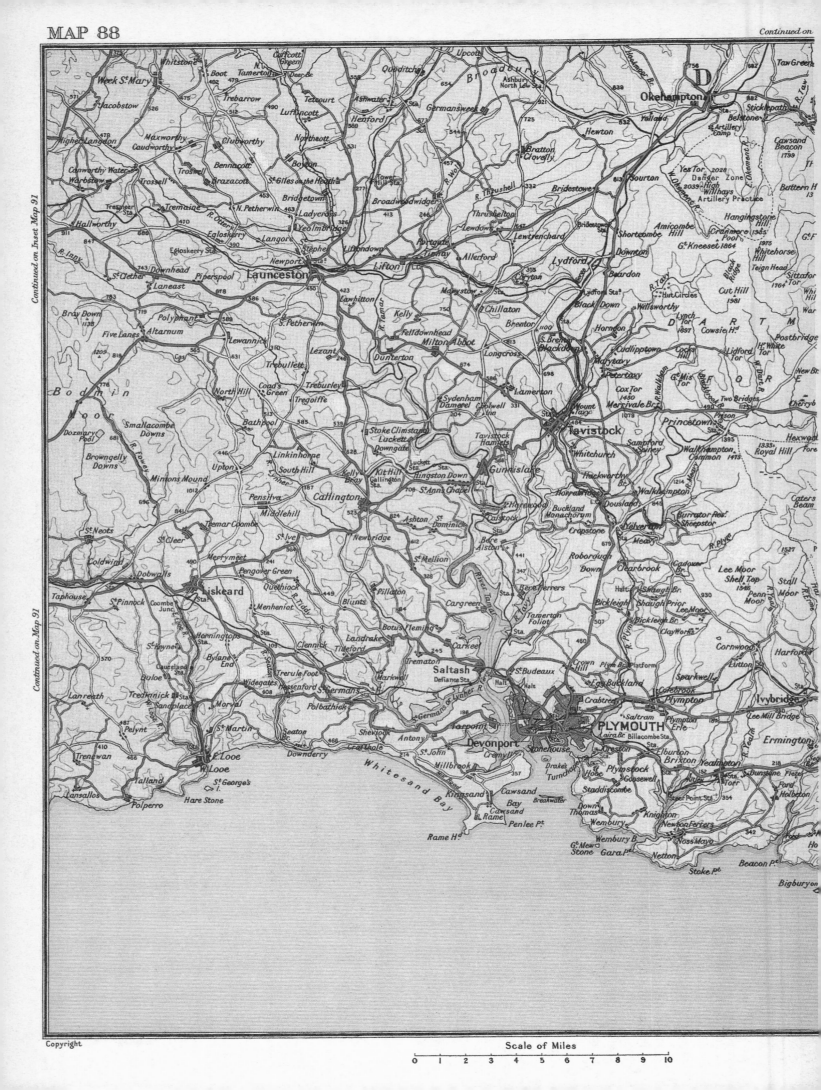

Continued on Inset Map 91

Continued on Map 91

Scale of Miles

0 1 2 3 4 5 6 7 8 9 10

MAP 89

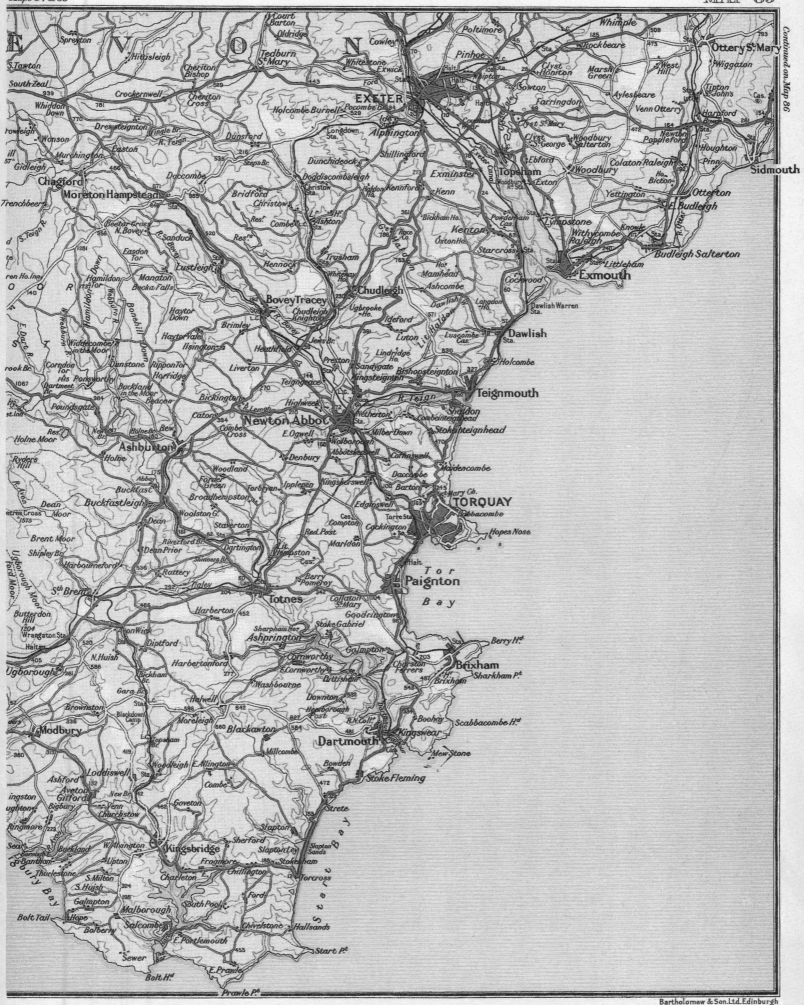

Bartholomew & Son. Ltd. Edinburgh

Main Roads ━━━━━━ Other Roads ━━━━━━ Railways ━━━━━━

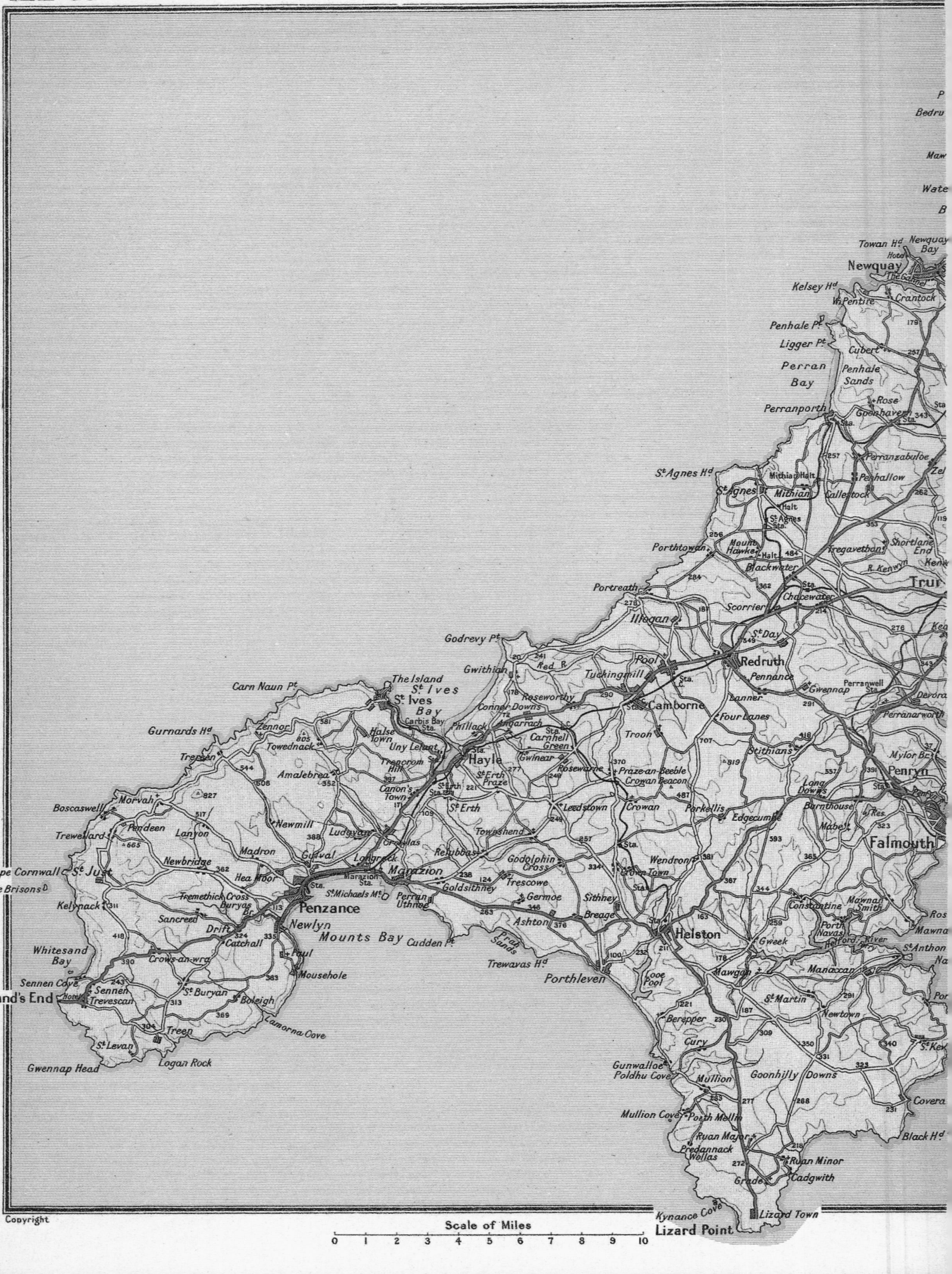

MAP 90

Bedru

Maw

Wate

B

Towan Hd — Newquay Bay

Newquay — Hotel — The

Kelsey Hd

Pentire — Crantock

Penhale Pt

Ligger Pt — Cubert — 179

Perran Bay — Penhale Sands — 251

Perranporth — Rose — Goonhavern — 343

Sta.

St Agnes Hd — Mithian Halt — 257 — Perranzabuloe — Zel

St Agnes — Penhallow — 262

Mithian — 553 — Callestock — 119

St Agnes Sta.

256 — Mount Hawke — Halt — 484 — Tregavethan — Shortlane End — Kenw

Porthtowan — Blackwater — Sta.

Portreath — 284 — 362 — Chacewater — Trur

278 — Illogan — 181 — Scorrier — 214 — 276

Pool — St Day — 549 — Kea

Godrevy Pt — 20 — 241 — Redruth — 543

Gwithian — Red R. — Pennance — Perranwell — Devora

The Island — Carn Naun Pt — Roseworthy — 290 — Tuckingmill — Sta. — Gwennap — Sta.

St Ives — St Ives Bay — Conner Downs — 72 — Camborne — Banner — 291 — Perranarworth

Carbis Bay Sta. — Phillack — Angarrack — Four Lanes

Gurnards Hd — Zennor — 581 — Halse Town — Carnhell — Trooh — 707 — Stithians — 418 — Mylor Br.

Trenon — 805 — Towednack — 391 — Green — 819 — Penry

Amalebrea — 552 — Trencrom Hill — Hayle — Gwinear — Rosewarne — 370 — Praze-an-Beeble — 557 — 391 — Penry

544 — 508 — Uny Lelant — 277 — Crowan Beacon — Long Downs

827 — Canon's — St Erth Sta. — St Erth Praze — 487 — Porkellis — Burnthouse — Res. — 323

Boscaswell — Morvah — 517 — Town — 221 — Leedstown — Crowan — Edgcumbe — Mabe — Falmouth

Trewellard — Pendeen — Newmill — Lanyon — Ludgvan — 105 — St Erth — 249 — 593 — 365

665 — Madron — 388 — 257 — Sta. — Townshend — Wendron — 381 — Constantine — Mawnan Smith

Cape Cornwall — St Just — Newbridge — 362 — Guval — Longreck — Relubbas — Godolphin — 334 — Chy — 367 — 163 — 259 — Port Navas — Ros

The Brisons — Hea Moor — Marazion — 238 — Cross — 344 — Helford River — Mawna

Kelynack — 311 — Tremethick Cross — Buryas — Marazion Sta. — Goldsithney — Trescowe — Sta. — St Anthon — Na

Sancreed — Drift — Br. — 113 — St Michaels Mt — Perran Uthnoe — 124 — Germoe — 346 — Mawgan — Gweek — Manaxxan — Por

418 — Catchall — 324 — 335 — Penzance — 263 — Ashton — 376 — Sithney — Breage — Sta. 4 — Helston — St Key

Whitesand Bay — Crows-an-wra — Newlyn — Mounts Bay — Cudden Pt — Prah Sands — 100 — 232 — 211 — 176 — Gunwalloe — Covera

243 — 390 — Paul — Trewavas Hd — Looe Pool — Mawgan — 231

Sennen Cove — Sennen — 383 — Mousehole — Porthleven — 221 — Berepper — 230 — St Martin — 291

Land's End — Hotel — Trevescan — St Buryan — Boleigh — Camorna Cove — 187 — Cury — Newtown — 350 — 340

304 — Treen — 313 — 369 — Gunwalloe — Poldhu Cove — Mullion — Goonhilly Downs — 268 — 323

St Levan — Logan Rock — 277

Gwennap Head — Mullion Cove — Porth Mellin — Black Hd

Ruan Major — 218

Predannack Wollas — 272 — Ruan Minor — Cadgwith

Grade — Kynance Cove — Lizard Town

Lizard Point

Scale of Miles

0 1 2 3 4 5 6 7 8 9 10

MAP 91

Continued on Inset & Map 88

Continued on Map 88

CORNWALL

Bodmin

Wadebridge
Egloshayle

Liskeard

St Columb
Major

St Austell

Lostwithiel

St Blazey

Fowey

Mevagissey
Bay

Mevagissey

Veryan
Bay

Falmouth
Bay

Boscastle

Tintagel H?

Tintagel

Camelford

Davidstow
Moor

Lower
Moor

Brown Willy

Bodmin
Moor

Port Isaac
Bay

Port Isaac

Padstow

Trevose
Head

Wadebridge
Egloshayle

John Bartholomew & Son Ltd. Edinburgh

Main Roads ——————— Other Roads ═══════ Railways ———————

MAP 92

Tory I. Sheep Haven Doagh
Horn H^d Rosapenna
Inishbofin Dunfanaghy
Bloody Foreland
Gola I. Bedlam Creeslough
Derrybeg Altan
Gweedore Kilmacrenan
Aran I. Burtonport Crolly Veagh Gartan
L. Anure Glend^d Breenagh Letterken
Dungloe
Crohy H^d Doochary
DONEGAL
Gweebarra B. Fintown
Portnoo Maas Commeen Cloghan
Narin 800
Rosbeg Glenties Ballybofey
Loughros More B. Bluestacks Barnesmore
Glencolumbkille Croaghe Gap
Malin More Meenaneary Mount
Rathlin O'Birne I. Carrick Charles
St. League Killybegs Inver DONEGAL
Carrigan H^d Dunkineely Laghy
St. Johns P^t Ballintra

Donegal Bay R. Erne BALLYSHANNON
Bundoran Belleek
Inishmurray Mullaghmore L. Melvin Garrison
Cliffony Kinlough Bundrowse
Grange Truskmore Rossinver
St. Johns Point Carney Manor Macnean Up.
Drumcliff Hamilton Belco
Sligo B. Glencar LEITRIM
SLIGO Dromahair
Easky Strandhill Gill Killargue Swan
Dromore Ballysadare Ballintogher Drumkeeran
Knocklong Colloney Ballygawley Coola Glengavlen
Ox Coolaney Tobercurry Lecarrow Carrow
Mountains Curryontary Drumfin Riverstown Geevagh
Bunnyconnellan SLIGO L. Allen
Ardnaree Gleneask Cloonacool Ballyfarnan St. Amerin
BALLINA Mullany's Cross Ballymote Keadeu Drumshanbo
Crossmolina Aclare Bunnanaddan Corrigeehros L. Key Leitrim
Foxford Curry Gorteen Ballinafad Garvagh
Callow Charlestown Mullaghroe Boyle Cootehall
Cuilin Ardcarn CARRICK ON SHAN
Swineford Bellavary Ballyglass Frenchpark Drumsna
Kilkelly Carracastle Ballaghaderreen Rathlien Jamestown
Boholo Hill Str. Elphin
CASTLEBAR Manulla Kilkelly Bellanagare Shankill Drumod
Balla Kiltamagh Carrowbelly Loughglinn ROSCOMMON
Knock Castlerea Strokestown
Ballycarra Ballyhaunis Tulsk (Scramoge)
WESTPORT Ballyglass Castleplunket
Kiltamagh Ballinlough Ballymoe Killashee
Claremorris Cloonfad Four Mile Ho. Ballyclare Lanesborough
Hollymount Ballinmore Oran ROSCOMMON Carrowroe
Dunmore Milltown Glennamaddy Athleague L. Ree
Ballinrobe Neale Foxhall Clonbern Ballygar Tang
Kilmaine Shrule Clonbern Athleague Knockcroghery
TUAM Mount Bellew Lecarron
Headford Liss Moylough Ballyforan Bellaua ATHLONE
Half Way Ho. Horseleap Glentane Cornafulla
Oughterard Audgoggen Manivea Ahascragh Ballinasloe
Lightgeorge Kilconnell BALLINASLOE Aughrim
Claregalway New Inn Clonmacnoise
ATHENRY Shannonbridge
GALWAY Oranmore Kiltormer Clonfert Laurencetown
Barna Clarinbridge Craughwell
Spiddle Inveran Dunbulcaun B. Kilcolgan Kilreekill Cloch
North Sound Galway Bay LOUGHREA

Termoncarragh Benwee H^d Stags of Broadhaven
Erris H^d Broad Haven Portacloy Ballinapark Downpatrick H^d B.
Belmullet Belderg Maumakeogh Rathlackan Lacken B. Lenadoon P^t
Barnatra Benmore Glenamoy Br. Ballycastle Killala Bay
Binghamstown Carrowmore Palmerstown
Bunnahowen Killala
Inishkea Is. Bangor Bellacorick Br. Inishcrone
Termon Geedalia Crossmolina
Achill H^d Ballycroy Slieve Car Nephin Conn
Saddle H^d Doogort Nephin Beg Boghadoon Pontoon
Keel Achill Cushcamcarragh Beltra
Dooagh L. Feeagh Beltra Ross West
Dooega Mallaranny Newport
Camport Newport B.
Achillbeg I. Derrycoosh
Clare I. Clew Bay Westport B.
Inishturk Louisburgh Croagh Patrick The Triangle Listarney
Caher I. Cregganbaun Carrowkennedy
Cross Lough Guilmore Partry
Inishbofin Killary Loe Nuiltea Doo Lough
Inishshark Cashleen Mamturk Toormakeady Trean Lough Mask
High I. Tully Cross Leenaun Glendane Clonbur Cornamona
Omey I. Letterfrack Mamturk Mts Maam Cong Cross
Mannin B. Moyard Twelve Pins Griggins Glaggan Lough Corrib
Clifden Ballinaboy Maam Cross Ross Abbey
Ballyconneely Recess Farravaun
Slyne H^d Toombeola Cashel Goirtmore Screeb
Roundstone Glinsk Knockferry
Croaghnakeel Moyrus Carna Kinvarra Moycullen
Mweenish I. Kilkieran Costelloe
Gorumna I. Cashla
Golam H^d

Copyright.

Continued on

Main Roads ——20—— Other Roads ———— Railways ————
Red Figures indicate distances between places with Black Dots

MAP 93

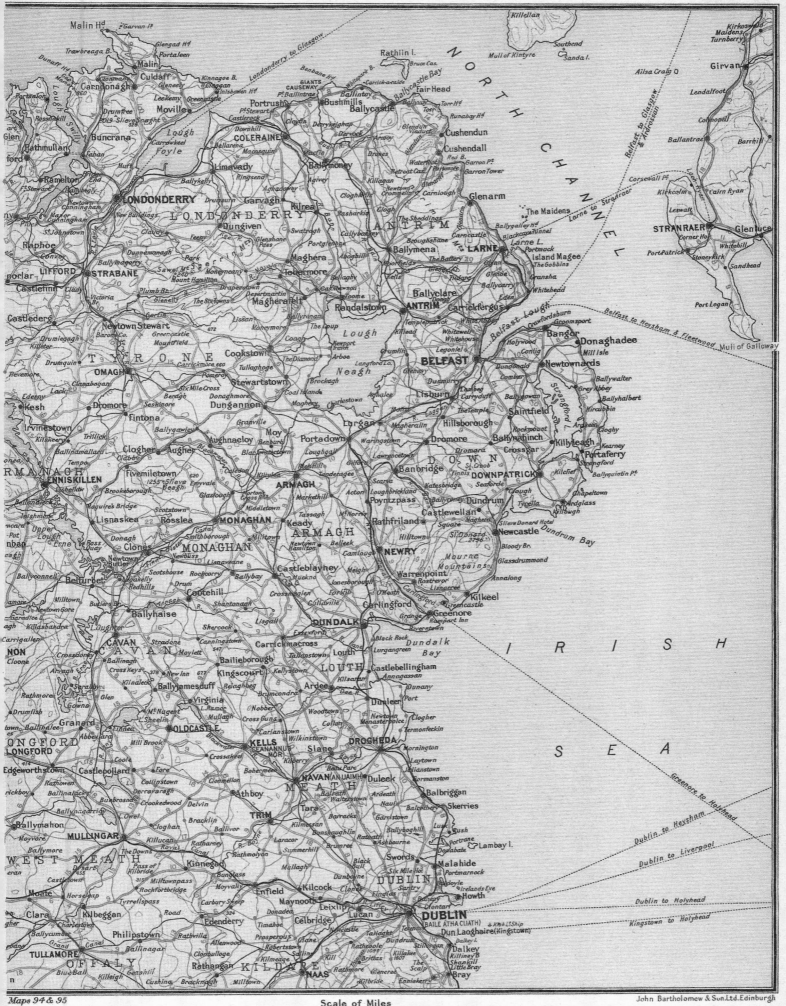

Scale of Miles

0 4 8 12 16 20 24 28 32 36 40

John Bartholomew & Son.Ltd.Edinburgh

MAP 94

Continued on

Main Roads _____ 20 _____   Other Roads _____   Railways _____
Red Figures indicate distances between places with Black Dots

MAP 95

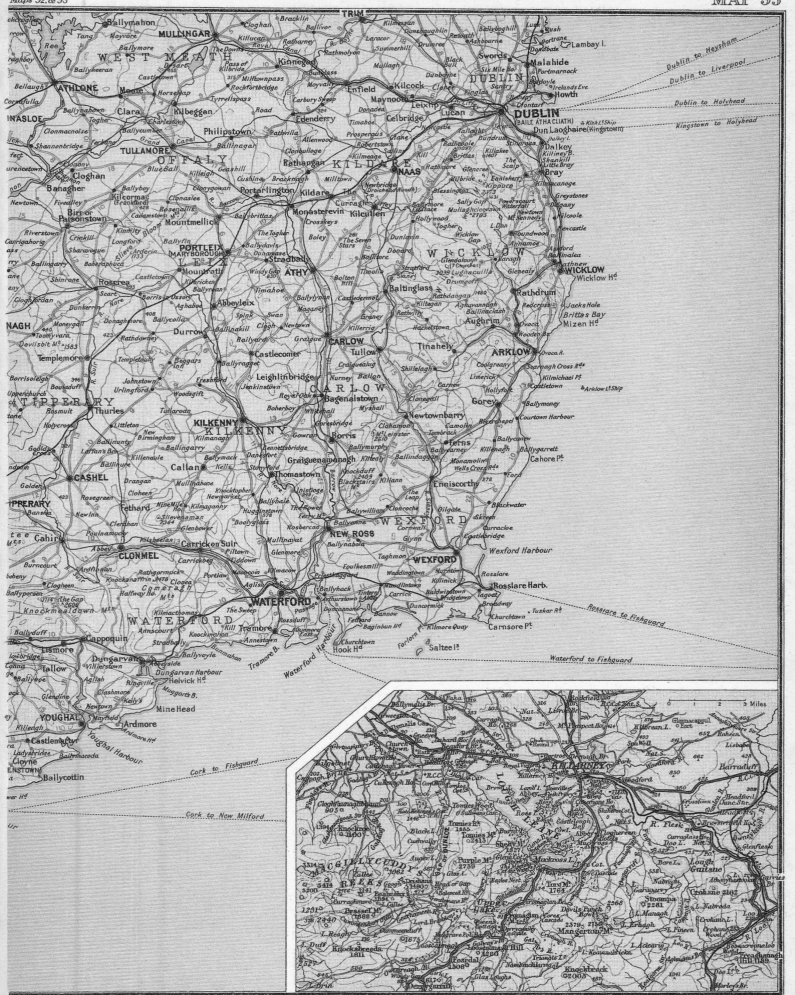

Scale of Miles

0 4 8 12 16 20 24 28 32 36 40

John Bartholomew & Son Ltd. Edinburgh

MAP 96

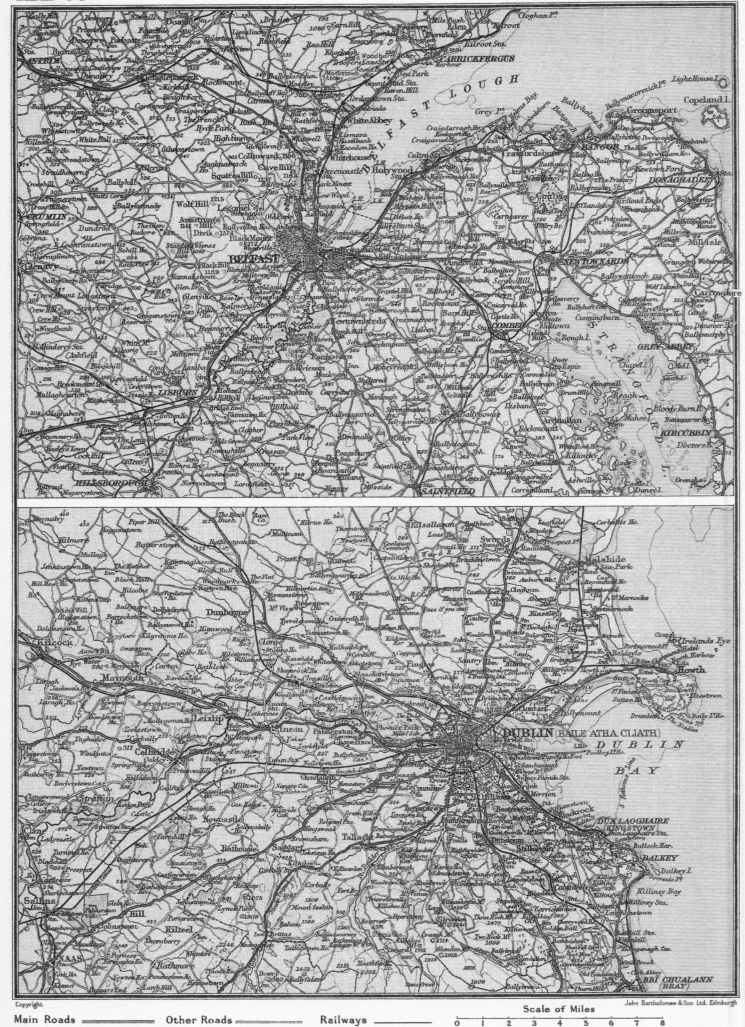

John Bartholomew & Son Ltd. Edinburgh

Scale of Miles

Main Roads Other Roads Railways

0 1 2 3 4 5 6 7 8

GAZETTEER INDEX TO PLACES

Abbreviations.—Alt., altitude; bor., borough; bur., burgh (in Scotland); civ., civil; co., county; dist., district; E.R., East Riding; eccl., ecclesiastical; ft., feet; ham., hamlet; isl., island; m., mile or miles; met., metropolitan; mun., municipal; N.R., North Riding; par., parish; pop., population; *q.s., quoad sacra* (in Scotland); r., river; ry. sta., railway station; spt., seaport; tn., town urb., urban; vil., village; W.R., West Riding.

ABBERLEY, par., Worcestershire, 4 m. S.W. of Stourport; pop. 467. Map 57.
Abbeycwmhir, par. and vil., Radnorshire, 6 m. N.E. of Rhayadir; pop. 336. Map 56.
Abbey Town, vil., N.W. Cumberland, 4½ m. E.S.E. of Silloth. Map 20.
Abbots Bromley, par. and town, Staffordshire, 4½ m. N.E. of Rugeley; pop. 1516. Map 48.
Abbotsley, par. and vil., Huntingdonshire, 3½ m. S.E. of St Neots; pop. 321. Map 61.
Aberaman, vil. and ry. sta., Glamorganshire, 2 m. S.E. of Aberdare. Map. 66.
Aberavon, Glamorganshire, now in Port Talbot. Map 66.
Aberayron, urb. dist. and seaport, Cardiganshire, 15 m. S.W. of Aberystwyth; pop. 1155. Map 54.
Abercarn, urb. dist. and par., Monmouthshire, 10½ m. N.W. of Newport; pop. 20,554. Map 67.
Aberdare, par. and urb. dist., Glamorganshire, 4 m. S.W. of Merthyr Tydfil; pop. 48,751. Map 66.
Aberdaron, par. and vil., Carnarvonshire, 14 m. S.W. of Pwllheli; pop. 1075. Map 44.
Aberdeen, parl. and mun. bur. and co. town of Aberdeenshire, 130½ m. N.E. of Edinr.; pop. 167,259. Map 3.
Aberdour, coast par. and vil., Fifeshire, 3 m. W. of Burnt-island; pop. 3063. Map 10.
Aberdovey, seaport, Merionethshire, in urb. dist. and 3½ m. S. of Towyn. Map 44.
Aberdulais, vil. and ry. sta., Glamorganshire, 1¾ m. N.E. of Neath. Map 66.
Aberfeldy, police burgh, Perthshire, 32½ m. N.W. of Perth; pop. 1505. Map 6.
Aberffraw, par. and seaport vil., S. Anglesey, 12 m. S.E. of Holyhead; pop. 861. Map 36.
Aberffrwd, ry. sta., Cardiganshire, 7 m. S.E. of Aberystwyth. Map 55.
Aberford, par. and vil., W.R. Yorkshire, 5 m. S.W. of Tadcaster; pop. 570. Map 33.
Aberfoyle, par. and vil., Perthshire, 6 m. N.W. of Buchlyvie; pop. 1169. Map 8.
Abergavenny, mun. bor. and par., Monmouthshire, 20 m. N. of Newport; pop. 8608. Map 67.
Abergele, coast par. and market town, Denbighshire, 4½ m. W. of Rhyl; pop. 2651. Map 37.
Aber Glaslyn, mt. pass on boundary between Carnarvon and Merioneth., 1 m. S. of Beddgelert. Map 36.
Abergwili, par. and vil., in co. and 1½ m. N.E. of Carmarthen; pop. 1393. Map. 65.
Aberlady, par. and vil., E. Lothian, 16½ m. E. of Edinburgh; pop. 1100. Map 10.
Abernethy, par. and police bur., Perthshire, 8½ m. S.E. of Perth; pop. 595. Map 6.
Aberporth, coast par. and vil., in co. and 6½ m. N.E. of Cardigan; pop. 371. Map 54.
Aber-Sychan, urb. dist. and par., Monmouthshire, 2¼ m. N.N.W. of Pontypool; pop. 25,627. Map 67.
Abertillery, urb. dist. and par., Monmouthshire, 15 m. N.W. of Newport; pop. 31,799. Map 67.
Aberystwyth, mun. bor. and seaport, in co. and 38½ m. N.E. of Cardigan; pop. 9474. Map 54.
Abingdon, mun. bor. and par., Berkshire, 6 m. S. of Oxford; pop. 7240. Map 70.
Abington, vil. and ry. sta., Lanarkshire, 15½ m. S.W. of Carstairs Junction. Map 14.
Aboyne, vil. and ry. sta., Aberdeenshire, 10½ m. E. of Ballater; pop. 890. Map 3.
Abram, urb. dist., Lancashire, 2 m. S.E. of Wigan; pop. 6660. Map 39.
Accrington, par. and mun. bor., market tn. and par., E. Lancs, 20 m. N. of Manchester; pop. 42,973. Map 31.
Achnasheen, ry. sta., Ross and Cromarty, 28 m. W. of Dingwall. Map 2.
Ackworth, par. and seat, W.R. Yorkshire, 3 m. S. of Pontefract; pop. 4831. Map 33.
Acle, par. and vil., Norfolk, 8 m. W.N.W. of Great Yarmouth; pop. 1042. Map 53.
Acton, mun. bor., Middlesex, 4½ m. W. of Paddington; pop. 70,523. Map 71.
Acton Turville, par. and vil., S.E. Gloucestershire, 9½ m. S.W. of Tetbury; pop. 269. Map 68.
Adderbury, vil. and ry. sta., Oxon, 5¼ m. S. of Banbury. Map 59.
Adderley, par. and ry. sta., Salop, 4 m. N. of Market Drayton; pop. 283. Map 47.
Addiewell, par. and vil., Midlothian, 1½ m. S.W. of West Calder; pop. 2146. Map 9.
Addlestone, eccl. par. and vil., N.W. Surrey, 1½ m. S.E. of Chertsey; pop. 7818. Map 78.
Adlington, urb. dist. and par., N. Lancashire, 3½ m. S.E. of Chorley; pop. 4179. Map 30.
Adwick-le-Street, urb. dist. and par., W.R. Yorkshire, 4 m. N.W. of Doncaster; pop. 20,257. Map 33.
Adwick-upon-Dearne, par., W.R. Yorkshire, 6½ m. N.E. of Rotherham; pop. 751. Map 41.
Aikton, par. and vil., Cumberland, 4 m. N.E. of Wigton; pop. 641. Map 20.
Ainderby Steeple, par., Yorkshire, 3 m. S.W. of Northallerton; pop. 241. Map 27.
Ainstable, par. and vil., E. Cumberland, 11 m. N.E. of Penrith; pop. 363. Map 21.
Aintree, par. and vil., S.W. Lancs, 4¾ m. N.E. of L'pool; well-known racecourse here; pop. 7372. Map 38.
Airdrie, mun. bur., par., and market town, Lanarkshire, 11 m. E. of Glasgow; pop. 25,954. Map 9.
Airth, par. and vil., in co. and 8¼ m. S.E. of Stirling; pop. 1777. Map 9.
Albrighton, par. and vil., Salop, 5 m. S.E. of Shifnal; pop. 1028. Map 47.
Albury, par. and vil., W. Surrey, 4 m. S.E. of Guildford; pop. 1172. Map 78.
Alcester, par. and market town, in co. and 15 m. S.W. of Warwick; pop. 2259. Map 58.
Alconbury, par. and vil., in co. and 4 m. N.W. of Huntingdon; pop. 523. Map 61.

Aldbourne, par. and vil., N. Wiltshire, 6 m. N.E. of Marlborough; pop. 980. Map 69.

Aldbrough, par. and vil., E.R. Yorkshire, $11\frac{1}{2}$ m. N.E. of Hull, coastguard sta.; pop. 743. Map 35.

Aldeburgh, mun. bor. and seaport, E. Suffolk, 6 m. S.E. of Saxmundham; pop. 2480. Map 63.

Aldermaston, par. and vil., S. Berkshire, 9 m. S.W. of Reading; pop. 533. Map 78.

Aldershot, mun. bor., N. Hants, 3 m. N.E. of Farnham; pop. 34,281. Map 78.

Aldringham, par. and vil., E. Suffolk, 3 m. N. of Aldeburgh; pop. 901. Map 63.

Alexandria, *q.s.* par. and town, Dumbartonshire, $3\frac{1}{2}$ m. N. of Dumbarton; pop. 10,359. Map 8.

Alford, urb. dist. and par., Lindsey, Lincolnshire, $23\frac{1}{4}$ m. N.E. of Boston; pop. 2227. Map 43.

Alford, par. and vil., in co. and $29\frac{1}{2}$ m. N.W. of Aberdeen; pop. 994. Map 3.

Alfreton, urb. dist., Derbyshire, 14 m. N.N.E. of Derby; pop. 21,232. Map 41.

Alfriston, par. and vil., E. Sussex, $3\frac{1}{2}$ m. N.E. of Seaford; pop. 667. Map 81.

Allendale, par. and vil., Northumberland, $13\frac{1}{2}$ m. S.W. of Hexham; pop. 3012. Map 22.

Allerton, eccl. par. and vil., W.R. Yorkshire, $3\frac{1}{2}$ m. N.W. of Bradford; pop. 4016. Map 32.

Allhallows, par. and vil., Kent, 8 m. N.E. of Rochester; pop. 314. Map 72.

Alloa, par. and police bur., Clackmannanshire, $6\frac{1}{2}$ m. E. of Stirling; pop. 13,322. Map 9.

Allonby, par. and seaport, Cumberland, 5 m. N.E. of Maryport; pop. 660. Map 20.

Almond, Glen, or **Sma' Glen,** Perthshire, 6 m. N. of Crieff. Map 6.

Alness, par. and vil., Ross and Cromarty, $9\frac{3}{4}$ m. N.E. of Dingwall; pop. 917. Map 3.

Alnmouth, par. and seaport, Northumberland, 4 m. S.E. of Alnwick; pop. 933. Map 17.

Alnwick, urb. dist. and par., Northumb., $37\frac{3}{4}$ m. N.W. of Newcastle-on-Tyne by rail; pop. 6882. Map 17.

Alpheton, par. and vil., W. Suffolk, 6 m. N. of Sudbury; pop. 213. Map 62.

Alphington, par. and vil., Devonshire, 2 m. S. of Exeter; pop. 1053. Map 89.

Alresford, New, par., Hants, $6\frac{1}{2}$ m. N.E. of Winchester; pop. 1709. Map 76.

Alresford, Old, par., Hants, 1 m. N. of New Alresford; pop. 499. Map 76.

Alsop-en-le-Dale, vil., N. Derbyshire, 6 m. N. of Ashbourne; pop. 652. Map 40.

Alston, par. and market town, E. Cumberland, 13 m. S. of Haltwhistle; pop. 3344. Map 22.

Altcar Rifle Range Station, S.W. Lancashire, $9\frac{1}{2}$ m. N.W. of Liverpool. Map 38.

Altguish Inn, Ross and Cromarty, $13\frac{1}{2}$ m. W.N.W. of Dingall. Map 2.

Althorpe, par. and vil., Lindsey, Lincolnshire, $4\frac{1}{2}$ m. S.E. of Crowle; pop. 689. Map 34.

Alton, market town and par., N. Hants, $8\frac{3}{4}$ m. S.W. of Farnham; pop. 6172. Map 79.

Altrincham, urb. dist. and par., Cheshire, 8 m. S.W. of Manchester; pop. 21,356. Map 39.

Alva, par. and police bur., Clackmannanshire, 8 m. N.E. of Stirling; pop. 3820. Map 9.

Alyth, par. and town, Perthshire, $4\frac{1}{2}$ m. E.N.E. of Blairgowrie; pop. 1662. Map 6.

Amberley, par. and vil., W. Sussex, 4 m. N. of Arundel; pop. 489. Map 79.

Amble, urb. dist. and par., Northumberland, 7 m. S.E. of Alnwick; pop. 4208. Map 17.

Ambleside, urb. dist. and par., Westmorland, 12 m. N.W. of Kendal; pop. 2343. Map 25.

Amersham, market town and par., Buckinghamshire, 15 m. S.E. of Aylesbury; pop. 4221. Map 70.

Amesbury, town and par., S. Wiltshire, $7\frac{1}{2}$ m. N. of Salisbury; pop. 1530. Map 76.

Amlwch, par., urb. dist., and seaport, N. Anglesey, 24 m. N.W. of Bangor; pop. 2561. Map 36.

Ammanford, urb. dist. and par., Carmarthenshire, 7 m. S. of Llandilo; pop. 7160. Map 66.

Ampleforth, par. and vil., N.R. Yorkshire, 4 m. S.W. of Helmsley; pop. 877. Map 28.

Ampthill, urb. dist. and par., in co. and 7 m. S. of Bedford; pop. 2167. Map 60.

Amulree, *q.s.* par. and vil., Perthshire, 11 m. N.N.E. of Crieff; pop. 292. Map 6.

Ancaster, par. and vil., Kesteven, Lincolnshire, 6 m. W. of Sleaford; pop. 566. Map 50.

Ancrum, par. and vil., N. Roxburghshire, $3\frac{1}{2}$ m. N.W. of Jedburgh; pop. 912. Map 16.

Andover, mun. bor., Hants, on r. Anton, $17\frac{1}{4}$ m. N.E. of Salisbury; pop. 9692. Map 76.

Annan, royal bur. and seaport, in co. and $15\frac{1}{2}$ m. S.E. of Dumfries; pop. 3959. Map 20.

Annfield Plain, urb. dist., Durham, 4 m. E. of Consett; pop. 15,922. Map 23.

Anstruther, seaport and market town, Fifeshire, $18\frac{3}{4}$ m. E. of Thornton Junction; pop. 1673. Map 7.

Antrim, par. and market town, co. Antrim, $27\frac{3}{4}$ m. N.W. of Belfast; pop. 4160. Map 93.

Appleby, mun. bor., par. and co. town of Westmorland, 14 m. S.W. of Penrith; pop. 1618. Map 26.

Applecross, par. and ham., Ross and Cromarty, 11 m. N.W. of Lochcarron; pop. 1119. Map 2.

Appledore, eccl. par. and seaport vil., N. Devon, 3 m. N. of Bideford; pop. 2706. Map 84.

Arbirlot, coast par. and vil., Angus, $2\frac{1}{2}$ m. W. of Arbroath; pop. 789. Map 7.

Arbroath, mun. bur. and seaport, Angus, 17 m. N.E. of Dundee; pop. 17,637. Map 7.

Ardee, par. and town, co. Louth, 14 m. N.W. of Drogheda; pop. of town, 1730. Map 93.

Ardlui, vil. with ry. sta. at N. end of Loch Lomond, Dumbartonshire. Map 12.

Ardmore, par. and vil., Waterford, $5\frac{1}{2}$ m. E. of Youghal; pop. 2197. Map 95.

Ardnadam, vil., Argyllshire, on Holy Loch, 2 m. N. of Dunoon. Map 12.

Ardnamurchan, par., W. Argyllshire, with lighthouse on **Ardnamurchan Point**; pop. 1369. Map 2.

Ardrishaig, par. and seaport, Argyllshire, 2 m. S. of Lochgilphead; pop. 1244. Map 12.

Ardrossan, par., police bur. and seaport, Ayrshire, 6 m. N.W. of Irvine; pop. 6888. Map 12.

Arklet, Loch, Stirlingshire, $\frac{3}{4}$ m. S.W. of Loch Katrine, depth 67 feet. Map 5.

Arklow, par., market town and seaport, co. Wicklow, 49 m. S.E. of Dublin; pop. 4526. Map 95.

Armadale, par. and town, W. Lothian, $2\frac{1}{2}$ m. W. by S. of Bathgate; pop. (town) 4854. Map 9.

Armagh, parl. bur. and co. town of Armagh, $35\frac{3}{4}$ m. S.W. of Belfast; pop. 7356. Map 93.

Arncliffe, par. and vil., W.R. Yorkshire, 9 m. N.E. of Settle; pop. 101. Map 27.

Arnold, urb. dist., Nottinghamshire, 3 m. N.E. of Nottingham; pop. 14,470. Map 49.

Arran, Isle of, in Firth of Clyde, forms part of Buteshire; pop. 8294. Map 12.

Arrochar, vil. and pier, Dumbartonshire, at head of Loch Long, $17\frac{1}{4}$ m. N. of Helensburgh. Map 12.

Artney, Glen, traversed by the Ruchill Water, Perthshire, 8 m. S.W. of Comrie. Map 5.

Arundel, mun. bor. and par., W. Sussex, 10 m. E. of Chichester; pop. 2489. Map 79.

Ascot, vil., S.E. Berks., $6\frac{3}{4}$ m. S.W. of Windsor. Map 78.

Ash, par. and vil., W. Surrey, 2 m. E. of Aldershot; pop. 5479. Map 78.

Ashbourne, urb. dist. and par., in co. and 13 m. N.W. of Derby; pop. 4507. Map 40.

Ashburton, urb. dist. and par., Devon, $9\frac{1}{2}$ m. N. of Totnes; pop. 2505. Map 89.

Ashby-de-la-Zouch, urb. dist. and par., in co. and $21\frac{1}{4}$ m. N.W. of Leicester; pop. 5093. Map 49.

Ashford, par. and vil., Middlesex, 2 m. E. of Staines; pop. 7673. Map 71.

Ashford, urb. dist. and par., Kent, 14 m. S.W. of Canterbury; pop. 15,239. Map 83.

Ashington, urb. dist. and par., Northumberland, 4 m. E.N.E. of Morpeth; pop. 29,418. Map 17.

Ashperton, par. and vil., Herefordshire, 5 m. N.W. of Ledbury; pop. 352. Map 57.

Ashprington, par. and vil., Devon, $2\frac{3}{4}$ m. S.E. of Totnes; pop. 387. Map 89.

Ashridge, Bonar Law Unionist College, Herts, 3 m. N. of Berkhamsted. Map 71.

Ashtead, par. and vil., mid Surrey, 2 m. S.W. of Epsom; pop. 3226. Map 78.

Ashton-in-Makerfield, par. and urb. dist., S.W. Lancs., 7 m. N.W. of Warrington; pop. 20,541. Map 39.

Ashton-under-Lyne, par., parl. and mun. bor., Lancashire, 6 m. E. of Manchester; pop. 51,573. Map 39.

Ashton-upon-Ribble, eccl. dist., N. Lancashire, 2 m. W. of Preston; pop. 8042. Map 30.

Ashwell, par. and vil., Hertfordshire, $4\frac{1}{2}$ m. N.E. of Baldock; pop. 1163. Map 61.

Askam, vil. with ry. sta., Lancashire, 6 m. N.N.E. of Barrow-in-Furness. Map 25.

Askeaton, par. and town, in co. and $16\frac{1}{4}$ m. W.S.W. of Limerick; pop. 594. Map 94.

Askrigg, par. and vil., N.R. Yorkshire, 12 m. W. of Leyburn; pop. 481. Map 27.

Aspatria, urb. dist., Cumberland, $7\frac{1}{2}$ m. N.E. of Maryport; pop. 3239. Map 20.

Aston Cantlow, par. and vil., Warwickshire, $5\frac{1}{2}$ m. N.W. of Stratford-on-Avon; pop. 878. Map 58.

Aston-on-Clun, vil., Salop, 3 m. W.S.W. of Craven Arms. Map 56.

Athenry, market town, in co. and 12 m. E. of Galway; pop. 791. Map 94.

Atherstone, market town and par., Warwickshire, 8 m. S.E. of Tamworth; pop. 5957. Map 48.

Atherton, urb. dist., town and par., S.W. Lancashire, 11 m. N.W. of Manchester; pop. 19,985. Map 39.

Athleague, par. and vil., cos. Galway and Roscommon, 6 m. S.W. of Roscommon; pop. 155. Map 92.

Athlone, urb. dist., cos. Roscommon and Westmeath, $48\frac{1}{2}$ m. E. of Galway; pop. 7546. Map 95.

Athy, urb. dist., co. Kildare, $44\frac{3}{4}$ m. S.W. of Dublin; pop. 3549. Map 95.

Attleborough, eccl. dist. and vil., Warwickshire, 1 m. S.S.E. of Nuneaton; pop. 4782. Map 49.

Attleborough, par. and market town, Norfolk, 16 m. S.W. of Norwich; pop. 2453. Map 52.

Attlebridge, par. and ry. sta., Norfolk, 8 m. N.W. of Norwich; pop. 88. Map 53.

Auchterarder, par. and market town, S.E. Perthshire, 14 m. S.W. of Perth; pop. 2254. Map 6.

Auchterderran, par. and vil., Fifeshire, 5 m. N.W. of Kirkcaldy; pop. 19,088. Map 10.

Auchtermuchty, par., bur. and market town, N.W. Fifeshire, $4\frac{1}{2}$ m. W. of Ladybank Jct.; pop. 1253. Map. 6.

Auchtertool, par. and vil., Fifeshire, 4 m. W. of Kirkcaldy; pop. 257. Map 10.

Audlem, par. and town, Cheshire, $5\frac{1}{2}$ m. S. of Nantwich; pop. 1394. Map 39.

Audley, urb. dist., Staffordshire, $4\frac{1}{2}$ m. N.W. of Newcastle-under-Lyme; pop. 13,619. Map 39.

Aughrim, vil. and ry. sta., co. Wicklow, 8 m. S.S.W. of Rathdrum; pop. 291. Map 95.

Aveley, par. and vil., S. Essex, 7 m. S.E. of Romford; pop. 1567. Map 80.

Avening, par. and vil., Gloucestershire, 5 m. S.E. of Stroud; pop. 828. Map 68.

Aviemore, vil. and ry. sta., Inverness-shire, $12\frac{1}{2}$ m. S.W. of Grantown. Map 3.

Avonmouth, eccl. par. and seaport, Gloucestershire, $6\frac{1}{4}$ m. N.W. of Bristol; pop. 2949. Map 67.

Awe, Loch, N. Argyllshire, extends 24 m. N.N.E. to the base of Ben Cruachan. Map 12.

Axbridge, par. and small town, N.W. Somerset, $9\frac{1}{2}$ m. N.W. of Wells; pop. 919. Map 74.

Axminster, urb. dist. and par., Devonshire, 27 m. N.E. of Exeter; pop. 2327. Map 86.

Axmouth, par. and fishing vil., Devonshire, 6 m. S.W. of Axminster; pop. 594. Map 86.

Aycliffe, par. and vil., S. co. Durham, $5\frac{1}{2}$ m. N. of Darlington; pop. 820. Map 27.

Aylesbury, mun. bor. and par., in co. and 17 m. S.E. of Buckingham; pop. 13,382. Map 70.

Aylesford, par. and vil., Kent, $3\frac{1}{2}$ m. N.W. of Maidstone; pop. 3113. Map 82.

Aylsham, par. and market town, Norfolk, 12 m. N. of Norwich; pop. 2466. Map 53.

Ayr, seaport, parl. and mun. bur., and co. town of Ayrshire, $41\frac{1}{2}$ m. S.W. of Glasgow; pop. 36,784. Map 12.

Ayton, par. and vil., Berwickshire, $7\frac{1}{4}$ m. N.W. of Berwick-on-Tweed; pop. 1521. Map 11.

Ayton, Great, and Little, 2 pars., N.R. Yorkshire, 3 m. N.E. of Stokesley, pop. 2708 and 144. Map 28.

BACTON, coast par. and vil., Norfolk, $4\frac{1}{2}$ m. N.E. of N. Walsham; pop. 585. Map 53.

Bacup, mun. bor., par. and market town, Lancashire, $21\frac{3}{4}$ m. N. of Manchester; pop. 20,606. Map 31.

Bagenalstown, market town, in co. and 10 m. S. of Carlow; pop. 1825. Map 95.

Bagshot, eccl. par. and town, W. Surrey, 3 m. S. of Ascot; pop. 2198. Map 78.

Baildon, urb. dist., Yorkshire, $1\frac{1}{2}$ m. N.E. of Shipley; pop. 7794. Map 32.

Bainbridge, par., N.R. Yorkshire, $1\frac{1}{2}$ m. S.W. of Askrigg; pop. 632. Map 27.

Bakewell, urb. dist., par. and market town, in co. and 25 m. N.W. of Derby; pop. 3012. Map 40.

Bala, urb. dist. and par., Merionethshire, $10\frac{3}{4}$ m. S.W. of Corwen; pop. 1395. Map 45.

Bala Lake, Merionethshire, 4 m. long by $\frac{1}{2}$ m. broad. Map 45.

Balbriggan, seaport town, in co. and $21\frac{3}{4}$ m. N.N.E. of Dublin; pop. 2278. Map 93.

Baldock, urb. dist. and par., Hertfordshire, $4\frac{3}{4}$ m. N.E. of Hitchin; pop. 3171. Map 61.

Balerno, vil., Midlothian, $7\frac{1}{2}$ m. S.W. of Edinburgh pop. 651. Map 10.

Balfron, par. and vil., W. Stirlingshire, 3 m. N.E. of Killearn; vil. pop. 873. Map 8.

Ballachulish, vil., Argyllshire, on Loch Leven, $16\frac{1}{2}$ m. S. of Fort William; pop. 714. Map 12.

Ballaghaderreen, town, Roscommon, $12\frac{1}{4}$ m. N.W. of Castlerea; pop. 1317. Map 92.

Ballantree, coast vil., Ayrshire, 13 m. S.W. of Girvan. Map 18.

Ballater, police bur., in co. and $43\frac{1}{4}$ m. S.W. of Aberdeen; pop. 1198. Map 3.

Ballaugh, par. and vil., Isle of Man, 7 m. W. of Ramsey; pop. 648. Map 24.

Ballina, urb. dist. and seaport, co. Mayo, $7\frac{3}{4}$ m. S. of Killala; pop. 4872. Map 92.

Ballinasloe, urb. dist., co. Roscommon, 12 m. S.W. of Athlone; pop. 5243. Map 92.

Ballinluig, village and ry. junct., Perthshire, 8 m. N.W. of Dunkeld. Map 6.

Ballinrobe, market town and par., co. Mayo, $12\frac{1}{2}$ m. S.W. of Claremorris; pop. 1585. Map 92.

Balloch, vil., Dumbartonshire, at foot of Loch Lomond, $19\frac{1}{2}$ m. N.W. of Glasgow. Map 12.

Ballybofey, vil. and ry. sta., in E. of co. Donegal. Map 92.

Ballycastle, vil., co. Mayo, 18 m. N.W. of Ballina. Map 92.

Ballycastle, seaport and market town, co. Antrim, $16\frac{1}{2}$ m. N. of Ballymoney; pop. 1435 Map 93.

Ballyclare, market town, W. Antrim, $12\frac{1}{2}$ m. N.E. of Belfast; pop. 3369. Map 95.

Ballycottin, vil., co. Cork, 11½ m. S.E. of Midleton; pop. 431. Map 95.

Ballyhaise, vil., in co. and 4½ m. N.E. of Cavan; pop. 92. Map 93.

Ballylongford, vil., co. Kerry, 8 m. N. of Listowel; pop. 484. Map 94.

Ballymahon, market town, in co. and 13½ m. S. of Longford; pop. 661. Map 93.

Ballymena, urb. dist. and market town, in co. and 11½ m. N. of Antrim; pop. 11,381. Map 93.

Ballymoney, urb. dist. and market town, co. Antrim, 20 m. N.W. of Ballymena; pop. 3100. Map 93.

Ballynahinch, market town, co. Down, 21½ m. S. of Belfast; pop. 1667. Map 93.

Ballyshannon, seaport town, in co. and 14 m. S.W. of Donegal; pop. 2112. Map 92.

Ballyvaughan, fishing vil., co. Clare, 10 m. N.E. of Lisdoonvarna; pop. 116. Map 94.

Balmerino, par. and vil., Fifeshire, 3½ m. W. of Wormit; pop. 699. Map 7.

Balmoral, royal residence, on r. Dee, in co. and 52½ m. W. of Aberdeen. Map 3.

Balquhidder, par. and vil., Perthshire, 3 m. S.W. of Lochearnhead; pop. 875. Map 12.

Baltinglass, market town, co. Wicklow, 10½ m. N. of Tullow; pop. 860. Map 95.

Bamber Bridge, vil., N.E. Lancashire, 3 m. S.E. of Preston; pop. 3018. Map 30.

Bamburgh, coast par., Northumberland, 5 m. E. of Belford; pop. 734. Map 17.

Bampton, par. and vil., N.W. Westmorland, 3 m. N.W. of Shap; pop. 424. Map 26.

Bampton, urb. dist. and par., Devonshire, 7 m. N.W. of Tiverton; pop. 1392. Map 85.

Bampton, market town and par., Oxon, 5 m. S.W. of Witney; pop. 1104. Map 69.

Banagher, market town, Offaly co., 8 m. N.W. of Birr; pop. 891. Map 95.

Banavie, vil., Inverness-shire, 2½ m. N.N.E. of Fort William. Map 2.

Banbridge, urb. dist., co. Down, 24½ m. S.W. of Belfast; pop. 5101. Map 93.

Banbury, mun. bor. and par., in co. and 22 m. N. of Oxford; pop. 13,953. Map 59.

Banchory, police bur., Kincardineshire, 16¾ m. S.W. of Aberdeen; pop. 1690. Map 3.

Bandon, market town on r. Bandon, in co. and 20 m. S.W. of Cork; pop. 2816. Map 94.

Banff, mun. bur., par. and cap. of Banffshire, 64½ m. N.W. of Aberdeen; pop. 3489. Map 3.

Bangor, par., bor. and city, Carnarvonshire, nr. Menai Strait, 59¾ m. W. of Chester; pop. 10,959. Map 36.

Bangor, par., urb. dist. and seaport, co. Down, 12 m. N.E. of Belfast; pop. 11,515. Map 93.

Bankfoot, vil., S.E. Perthshire, 4 m. N.W. of Strathord; pop. 713. Map 6.

Bannockburn, par. and town, in co. and 2½ m. S.E. of Stirling; town pop. 4223. Map 9.

Banstead, par. and vil., mid Surrey, 3 m. E. of Epsom; pop. 7337. Map 80.

Bantry, seaport town, co. Cork, 17¾ m. N.W. of Skibbereen; pop. 2681. Map 94.

Banwell, par. and vil., N.W. Somersetshire, 3½ m. N.W. of Axbridge; pop. 1416. Map 74.

Bapchild, par. and vil., Kent, 1½ m. E.S.E. of Sittingbourne; pop. 486. Map 82.

Bardsey, isl. in Cardigan Bay, S.W. Carnarvonshire; pop. 58. Map 44.

Bardwell, par. and vil., Suffolk, 8 m. N.E. of Bury St. Edmunds; pop. 653. Map 62.

Bargoed, ward of Gelligaer urb. dist., Glamorganshire, 18½ m. N. of Cardiff. Map 67.

Barham, par. and ham., Kent, 6 m. S.E. of Canterbury; pop. 905. Map 83.

Barking, mun. bor., S.W. Essex, 7½ m. E. of London; pop. 51,277. Map 80.

Barkisland, urb. dist. and par., W.R. Yorkshire, 5 m. S.W. of Halifax; pop. 1552. Map 31.

Barkway, par. and vil., Hertfordshire, 4½ m. S.E. of Royston; pop. 568. Map 61.

Barlby, par. and vil., E.R. Yorkshire, 1¾ m. N.E. of Selby; pop. 2593. Map 33.

Barmouth, urb. dist., par. and seaport, Merionethshire, 9¼ m. W.S.W. of Dolgelley; pop. 2491. Map 44.

Barnack, par. and vil., Soke of Peterborough, Northants, 3½ m. S.E. of Stamford; pop. 548. Map 50.

Barnard Castle, urb. dist. and par., S.W. Durham, 15½ m. W. of Darlington; pop. 3883. Map 27.

Barnes, urb. dist., Surrey, 7 m. S.W. of Waterloo Sta., London; pop. 42,439. Map 71.

Barnet, urb. dist. and market town, Hertfordshire, 11½ m. N. of London; pop. 14,721. Map 71.

Barnham, par. and ry. sta., W. Suffolk, 2½ m. S. of Thetford; pop. 384. Map 62.

Barnoldswick, urb. dist., W.R. Yorkshire, 9½ m. S.W. of Skipton; pop. 11,915. Map 31.

Barnsley, parl. and co. bor. and market town, W.R. Yorks, 16 m. N. of Sheffield; pop. 71,522. Map 32.

Barnstaple, mun. bor. and seaport town, N. Devon, 39¼ m. N.W. of Exeter; pop. 14,693. Map 84.

Barnwood, par. and vil., in co. and 2 m. E. of Gloucester; pop. 1333. Map 68.

Barrasford, vil., Northumberland, 8½ m. N.W. of Hexham. Map 22.

Barrhead, police bur., Renfrewshire, 7½ m. S.W. of Glasgow; pop. 12,308. Map 8.

Barrington, par. and vil., Somersetshire, 3 m. N.E. of Ilminster; pop. 358. Map 86.

Barrowby, par. and vil., Kesteven, Lincolnshire, 2 m. W. of Grantham; pop. 812. Map 50.

Barrowford, urb. dist., N.E. Lancashire, 2 m. W. of Colne; pop. 5299. Map 31.

Barrow-in-Furness, parl. and co. bor. and seaport, Lancs, 50 m. N.W. of Liverpool; pop. 66,366. Map 25.

Barry, coast par., vil. and military camp, Angus, 9½ m. N.E. of Dundee; pop. 6133. Map 7.

Barry, urb. dist., Glamorganshire, 7 m. S.W. of Cardiff; pop. 38,916. Map 67.

Barton-in-the-Clay, par. and vil., Bedfordshire, 6 m. N. of Luton; pop. 783. Map 60.

Barton Mills, par. and vil., W. Suffolk, 1 m. S.E. of Mildenhall; pop. 464. Map 62.

Barton-upon-Humber, par., urb. dist. and market town, N. Lincs, 6 m. S.W. of Hull; pop. 6330. Map 35.

Baschurch, par. and vil., Salop, 7½ m. N.W. of Shrewsbury; pop. 1435. Map 46.

Basingstoke, mun. bor., N. Hants, 48 m. S.W. of London; pop. 13,862. Map 78.

Baslow-with-Bubnell, Derbyshire, 3 m. N.E. of Bakewell; pop. 854. Map 40.

Bassenthwaite, par., lake and sta., Cumberland, 7½ m. N.W. of Keswick; pop. 437. Map 20.

Bassett, vil., Hampshire, 2 m. N. of Southampton. Map 77.

Bath, city, co. and parl. bor., N.E. Somersetshire, 11¾ m. S.E. of Bristol; pop. 68,801. Map 75.

Bathgate, par. and market town, W. Lothian, 18½ m. W.S.W. of Edinburgh; pop. 10,097. Map 9.

Batley, mun. bor. and par., W.R. Yorkshire, 8 m. S.W. of Leeds; pop. 34,573. Map 32.

Battle, urb. dist. and par., E. Sussex, 6¾ m. N.W. of Hastings; pop. 3490. Map 82.

Battlesbridge, vil., S.E. Essex, 9¾ m. S.W. of Maldon. Map 72.

Bawtry, par. and market town, W.R. Yorkshire, 9 m. S.E. of Doncaster; pop. 1219. Map 41.

Beachy Head, prom. on S. Coast of Sussex, 3 m. N.W. of Eastbourne; alt. 530 ft. Map 81.

Beaconsfield, urb. dist. and par., Buckinghamshire, 5½ m. S. of Amersham; pop. 4843. Map 71.

Beaminster, market town and par., Dorsetshire, 6 m. N. of Bridport; pop. 1651. Map 86.

Bearsden, town, S.E. Dumbartonshire, 5 m. N.W. of Glasgow; pop. 3362. Map 8.

Beattock, vil. and ry. sta., Dumfriesshire, 2 m. S.W. of Moffat. Map 15.

Beaulieu, par. and vil., Hants, 6 m. N.E. of Lymington; pop. 1011. Map 77.

Beauly, town and ry. sta., in co. and 10 m. W. of Inverness; pop. 805. Map 3.

Beaumaris, mun. bor., par. and seaport, Anglesey, 7 m. N.E. of Bangor; pop. 1708. Map 36.

Bebington and Bromborough, urb. dist., Cheshire, 5 m. S.E. of Birkenhead; pop. 26,742. Map 38.

Bebside, colliery vil., Northumberland, 1 m. S.E. of Bedlington. Map 17.

Beccles, mun. bor. and par., E. Suffolk, 8½ m. W. of Lowestoft; pop. 6544. Map 63.

Beckenham, urb. dist., N.W. Kent, 2 m. W. of Bromley; pop. 43,834. Map 80.

Beckfoot, vil., Cumberland, 3½ m. S. of Silloth. Map 20.

Beckington, par. and vil., E. Somersetshire, 3 m. N.E. of Frome; pop. 727. Map 75.

Bedale, par. and market town, N.R. Yorkshire, 7½ m. S.W. of Northallerton; pop. 1064. Map 27.

Beddgelert, par. and vil., in co. and 12½ m. S.E. of Carnarvon; pop. 1055. Map 36.

Beddington and Wallington, urb. dist., Surrey, 1½ m. W. of Croydon; pop. 26,249. Map 80.

Bedford, mun. bor. and co. town of Bedfordshire, 49¾ m. N.W. of London; pop. 40,573. Map 60.

Bedlington, par. co-extensive with **Bedlingtonshire** urb. dist., Northumberland, 5 m. S.E. of Morpeth; pop. 27,315. Map 17.

Bedrule, par. and ham., Roxburghshire, 4 m. S.W. of Jedburgh; pop. 180. Map 16.

Bedwas and Machen, urb. dist., Monmouthshire, 9 m. W. of Newport; pop. 9190. Map 67.

Bedwellty, urb. dist., Monmouthshire, 3½ m. S. of Tredegar; pop. 30,069. Map 67.

Bedworth, par. and town, Warwickshire, 3½ m. S. of Nuneaton; pop. 12,058. Map 49.

Beer, coast par. and vil., Devonshire, 5½ m. S.W. of Axminster; pop. 1257. Map 86.

Beeston, urb. dist. and par., in co. and 3¼ m. S.W. of Nottingham; pop. 16,016. Map 49.

Beith, par. and market town, Ayrshire, 18½ m. S.W. of Glasgow; town pop. 4098. Map 8.

Belfast, parl. and co. bor. on **B. Lough**, cos. Antrim and Down, 113 m. N. of Dublin; pop. 414,844. Map 93.

Belford, par. and market town, Northumberland, 15¼ m. S.E. of Berwick; pop. 663. Map 17.

Belleek, par. and vil., co. Fermanagh, 22 m. N.W. of Enniskillen; pop. 1276. Map 92.

Bellingham, par. and vi., Northumberland, 17 m. N.W. of Hexham; pop. 1392. Map 16.

Belmullet, fishing vil., N.W. co. Mayo, 38¾ m. W.N.W. of Ballina; pop. 681. Map 92.

Belper, urb. dist., par. and market town in co. and 7¾ m. N. of Derby; pop. 13,023. Map 41.

Belton, par. and vil., Lincolnshire, in Isle of Axholme, 1½ m. N.E. of Epworth; pop. 1528. Map 42.

Bembridge, par. and vil., S. Hants, 2½ m. N.E. of Brading, Isle of Wight; pop. 1973. Map 77.

Bempton, coast par. and vil., E.R. Yorkshire, 3½ m. N. of Bridlington; pop. 300. Map 29.

Benfieldside, urb. dist., Durham, 13 m. S.W. of Gateshead; pop. 9193. Map 22.

Benfleet, urb. dist., Essex, 3 m. S.W. of Rayleigh; pop. 12,091. Map 72.

Benfleet, South, coast par., S. Essex, 6 m. W. of Southend; pop. 1918. Map 72.

Bennington, Long, par. and vil., Kesteven, Lincolnshire, 8 m. N.W. of Grantham; pop. 756. Map 50.

Bentley, Gt., par. and vil., N.E. Essex, 8 m. S.E. of Colchester; pop. 1093. Map 73.

Bentley with Arksey, urb. dist., W.R. Yorkshire, 2 m. N. of Doncaster; pop. 16,458. Map 41.

Bentworth, par. and vil., N.E. Hants, 3½ m. N.W. of Alton; pop. 522. Map 78.

Berkeley, town in co. and 15 m. S.W. of Gloucester. Map 68.

Berkhamsted, urb. dist., W. Herts, 10 m. N.W. of Watford; pop. 8053. Map 71.

Berriew, par. and vil., in E. of co. and 3½ m. N.W. of Montgomery; pop. 1479. Map 46.

Bervie, par., parl. and royal bur., mkt. tn., Kincardineshire, 13 m. N.E. of Montrose; pop. 2153. Map 3.

Berwick-upon-Tweed, co. of a town, mun. bor., par. and seaport town, Northumberland, 57½ m. E.S.E. of Edinburgh; pop. 12,299. Map 11.

Bessingby, par., vil. and seat, E.R. Yorkshire, 1½ m. S.W. of Bridlington; pop. 429. Map 29.

Betchworth, par. and vil., mid Surrey, 2¾ m. W.S.W. of Reigate; pop. 1908. Map 80.

Bethersden, par. and vil., S. Kent, 5 m. S.W. of Ashford; pop. 922. Map 82.

Bethesda, urb. dist. and par., Carnarvonshire, 5 m. S.E. of Bangor; pop. 4476. Map 37.

Bettws Garmon, par. and ham., in N.W. of co. and 5 m. S.E. of Carnarvon; pop. 340. Map 36.

Bettwys-y-Coed, urb. dist. and par., E. Carnarvonshire, 4 m. S. of Llanrwst; pop. 912. Map 37.

Beverley, mun. bor. and market town, E.R. Yorkshire, 8¼ m. N.N.W. of Hull; pop. 14,011. Map 35.

Bewdley, mun. bor., Worcestershire, 3 m. W.S.W. of Kidderminster; pop. 2868. Map 57.

Bexhill, mun. bor. and coast par., E. Sussex, 5 m. S.W. of Hastings; pop. 21,229. Map 81.

Bexley, urb. dist., Kent, 4½ m. W. of Dartford; pop. 32,940. Map 80.

Bexleyheath, eccl. par. and vil., N.W. Kent, 3 m. W.N.W. of Dartford; pop. 11,140. Map 80.

Bicester, urb. dist., seat and market town, in N.E. of co. and 12 m. N.E. of Oxford; pop. 3109. Map 70.

Bickleigh, par. and seat, E. Devon, on r. Exe, 10 m. N. of Exeter; pop. 191. Map 85.

Biddenham, par. and vil., in co. and 2 m. W. of Bedford; pop. 460. Map 60.

Biddestone, par. and vil., N. Wiltshire, 4 m. W. of Chippenham; pop. 418. Map 68.

Biddulph, urb. dist., Staffordshire, 4 m. S.E. of Congleton; pop. 8346. Map 39.

Bideford, mun. bor. and seaport, N. Devon, 8¾ m. S.W. of Barnstaple; pop. 8782. Map 84.

Biggar, par. and town, Lanarkshire, 13½ m. S.E. of Lanark; pop. 1323. Map 15.

Biggleswade, urb. dist. and par., in co. and 9 m. E.S.E. of Bedford; pop. 5844. Map 60.

Billericay, eccl. par. and market town, S. Essex, 5¼ m. E. of Brentwood; pop. 1500. Map 72.

Billesdon, par. and vil., in S. of co. and 8½ m. S.E. of Leicester; pop. 514. Map 49.

Billinge and Winstanley, urb. dist., Lancashire, 4½ m. S.W. of Wigan; pop. 5111. Map 39.

Billingham, urb. dist., Durham, 2½ m. N.E. of Stockton-on-Tees; pop. 17,972. Map 23.

Billinghay, par. and vil., S. Lincolnshire, 8 m. N.E. of Sleaford; pop. 1226. Map 43.

Billingshurst, par. and vil., W. Sussex, 6 m. S.W. of Horsham; pop. 1873. Map 79.

Bilston, urb. dist., par. and market town, S. Staffs, 2½ m. S.E. of Wolverhampton; pop. 31,248. Map 47.

Bingham, par. and market town, in co. and 8½ m. E. of Nottingham; pop. 1576. Map 49.

Bingley, urb. dist., par. and mkt. town, W.R. Yorkshire, 5½ m. N.W. of Bradford; pop. 20,553. Map 32.

Birchington, coast par. and vil., N.E. Kent, 3½ m. W.S.W. of Margate; pop. 3503. Map 83.

Birkenhead, co. and parl. bor., seaport town and par., Cheshire, on left bank of Mersey, opp. Liverpool, 13 m. N.N.W. of Chester; pop. 147,946. Map 38.

Birkenshaw, urb. dist., W.R. Yorkshire, $3\frac{1}{2}$ m. S.E. of Bradford; pop. 2816. Map 32.

Birmingham, city, parl., mun. and co. bor., Warwicksh., 113 m. N.W. of London; pop. 1,002,413. Map 48.

Birnam, vil., E. Perths., $\frac{3}{4}$ m. S.E. of Dunkeld; pop. 711. Map 6.

Birr, or **Parsonstown,** par., market town and urb. dist., $11\frac{3}{4}$ m. N. of Roscrea; pop. 5405. Map 95.

Birstall, urb. dist. and par. town, W.R. Yorkshire, 2 m. N.W. of Batley; pop. 7205. Map 32.

Birtley, par., vil. and seat, Durham, $5\frac{1}{2}$ m. S.E. of Gateshead; pop. 11,279. Map 23.

Bishop Auckland, urb. dist., par. and mkt. tn., S. Durham, 11 m. S.W. of Durham; pop. 12,269. Map 23.

Bishopbriggs, now a district in Glasgow, $3\frac{1}{2}$ m. N.E. of Queen Street ry. sta. Map 8.

Bishop's Castle, mun. bor., Salop, 18 m. S.W. of Shrewsbury; pop. 1352. Map 46.

Bishop's Cleave, par. and vil., N. Gloucestershire, 3 m. N. of Cheltenham; pop. 615. Map 57.

Bishop's Frome, par., Herefordshire, 4 m. S. of Bromyard; pop. 696. Map 57.

Bishop's Nympton, par. and vil., N. Devon, $4\frac{1}{2}$ m. S.E. of South Molton; pop. 843. Map 85.

Bishop's Stortford, urb. dist., par. and mkt. tn., in E. of co. and 14 m. N E. of Hertford; pop. 9509. Map 72.

Bishops-Tawton, par. and vil., N. Devon, 2 m. S.E. of Barnstaple; pop. 779. Map 84.

Bishopsteignton, par. and vil., E. Devon, 2 m. W. of Teignmouth; pop. 1066. Map 89.

Bishopstone, par. and vil., N. Wiltshire, on verge of co., 6 m. E. of Swindon; pop. 427. Map 69.

Bishop's Waltham, par. and mkt. town, S.E. Hampshire, $9\frac{1}{2}$ m. S.E. of Winchester; pop. 2597. Map 77.

Bishopthorpe, par., W.R. Yorkshire, on r. Ouse, $2\frac{1}{2}$ m. S. of York; contains **B. Palace**; pop. 486. Map 33.

Bishopton, vil., N. Renfrewshire, $5\frac{3}{4}$ m. N.W. of Paisley; pop. 739. Map 8.

Bitterne, par. and seat, S. Hampshire, in co. bor. of Southampton; pop. 3882. Map 77.

Blackawton, par. and vil., S. Devon, 4 m. W. of Dartmouth; pop. 943. Map 89.

Black Borong, hotel, in co. and $4\frac{1}{2}$ m. N. of Peebles. Map 10.

Blackburn, parl., co. bor. and par., mid Lancashire, 11 m. E. of Preston; pop. 122,695. Map 30.

Blackford, par. and vil., S. Perthshire, 10 m. N.E. of Dunblane; pop. 1593. Map 6.

Black Hill, eccl. dist. and vil., N.W. Durham, between Consett and Shotley Bridge; pop. 5342. Map 22.

Blackpool, parl. and co. bor., par., seaport and lifeboat sta., N. Lancashire, $16\frac{1}{2}$ m. N.W. of Preston; pop. 101,543. Map 30.

Blackrod, urb. dist., Lancashire, 5 m. S.E. of Chorley; pop. 3599. Map 30.

Blackwater, vil., N.E. Hants, $3\frac{1}{2}$ m. N.W. of Farnborough. Map 78.

Blackwood, vil., W. Monmouthshire, $7\frac{1}{2}$ m. W.N.W. of Pontypool. Map 67.

Blackwood, vil. and ry. sta., Lanarkshire, 2 m. S. of Stonehouse. Map 14.

Blaenau Ffestiniog, vil., N.W. Merionethshire, $2\frac{1}{2}$ m. N. of Ffestiniog Duffws. Map 37.

Blaen-Avon, urb. dist. and par., N.W. Monmouthshire, $5\frac{1}{2}$ m. N.W. of Pontypool; pop. 11,075. Map 67l

Blaengarw, mining vil., S. Glamorganshire, $9\frac{1}{2}$ m. N. of Bridgend. Map 66.

Blaengwynfi, vil., N. Glamorganshire, 10 m. N.E. of Port Talbot. Map 66.

Blagdon, par. and vil., N. Somersetshire, 11 m. S.W. of Bristol; pop. 958. Map 74.

Blair-Atholl, par. and vil., N. Perthshire, $35\frac{1}{4}$ m. N.W. of Perth; pop. 1824. Map 3.

Blairgowrie and Rattray, burgh, E. Perthshire, $4\frac{3}{4}$ m. N.W. of Coupar-Angus; pop. 4676. Map 6.

Blakeney, eccl. dist. and vil., W. Gloucestershire, $3\frac{1}{2}$ m. S.W. of Newnham; pop. 849. Map 68.

Blakeney, par. and vil., Norfolk, $5\frac{1}{2}$ m. N.W. of Holt; pop. 662. Map 52.

Blanchland, eccl. dist. and vil., Northumberland, 9 m. S.E. of Hexham; pop. 222. Map 22.

Blandford, par., mun. bor. and market town, E. Dorset, 16 m. N.E. of Dorchester; pop. 3371. Map 87.

Blanefield, vil., S.W. Stirlingshire, $16\frac{3}{4}$ m. N.W. of Glasgow. Map 8.

Blantyre, town, Lanarkshire, $3\frac{1}{2}$ m. W. by N. of Hamilton. Map 9.

Blaydon, urb. dist., Durham, $4\frac{1}{2}$ m. W. of Newcastle; pop. 32,259. Map 23.

Blean, par., E. Kent, 2 m. N.W. of Canterbury; pop. 601. Map 83.

Bleasby, par. and vil., in co. and 11 m. N.E. of Nottingham; pop. 288. Map 41.

Bletchingdon, par. and seat, Oxfordshire, 7 m. N. of Oxford; pop. 492. Map 70.

Bletchingley, par. and vil., Surrey, 3 m. E. of Redhill; pop. 2190. Map 80.

Bletchley, ham., N. Shropshire, $3\frac{1}{2}$ m. W. of Market Drayton. Map 47.

Bletchley, urb. dist., Buckinghamshire, $45\frac{3}{4}$ m. N.W. of London; pop. 6169. Map 60.

Bloxham, par. and vil., Oxon, $3\frac{1}{2}$ m. S.W. of Banbury; pop. 1384. Map 59.

Bloxwich, eccl. dist. and vil., Staffordshire, $2\frac{3}{4}$ m. N.N.W. of Walsall; pop. 8662. Map 48.

Blundell Sands, eccl. dist., Lancashire, $6\frac{1}{4}$ m. N.W. of Liverpool; pop. 3991. Map 38.

Blunham, par. and vil., in co. and 6 m. E. of Bedford; pop. 603. Map 60.

Blunsdon Broad, eccl. dist. and vil., N. Wiltshire, 4 m. N. of Swindon; pop. 750. Map 69.

Bluntisham cum Earith, par. and vil., Huntingdonshire, $3\frac{3}{4}$ m. N.E. of St Ives; pop. 1006. Map 61.

Blyth, mun. bor., seaport and par., Northumberland, 9 m. S.E. of Morpeth; pop. 31,808. Map 17.

Blyth, par. and vil., N. Notts, 7 m. N.E. of Worksop; pop. 600. **B. Hall,** seat of Lord Barnby. Map 41.

Blyth, river, S. Northumberland, flows 20 miles to North Sea at Blyth. Map 23.

Blythburgh, par. and vil., E. Suffolk, $3\frac{1}{2}$ m. W.S.W. of Southwold; pop. 673. Map 63.

Blythebridge, ham. and ry. sta., Staffordshire, $5\frac{1}{2}$ m. S.E. of Stoke-on-Trent. Map 47.

Boat of Garten, vil., Inverness-shire, 5 m. N.E. of Aviemore; pop. 322. Map 3.

Bodenham, par. and vil., Herefordshire, $5\frac{1}{2}$ m. S.E. of Leominster; pop. 685. Map 56.

Bodmin, mun. bor. and par., Cornwall, 29 m. N.W. of Plymouth; pop. 5526. Map 91.

Bodorgan, seat and ry. sta., S.W. Anglesey, 12 m. S.E. of Holyhead. Map 36.

Bognor Regis, urb. dist., par. and watering place, S.W. Sussex, $6\frac{3}{4}$ m. S.E. of Chichester; pop. 13,510. Map 79.

Boldon, E. and **W.,** par., N. Durham, $3\frac{1}{2}$ m. N.W. of Sunderland; pop. 4179. Map 23.

Boldre, par., S.W. Hampshire, $2\frac{1}{2}$ m. N. of Lymington; pop. 2395. Map 77.

Bollington, urb. dist. and par., Cheshire, $2\frac{1}{2}$ m. N.E. of Macclesfield; pop. 5027. Map 39.

Bolsover, urb. dist. and par., E. Derbyshire, $5\frac{3}{4}$ m. E. of Chesterfield; pop. 11,811. Map 41.

Bolton, par., co. and parl. bor., and mfr. town, S. Lancs, $10\frac{1}{2}$ m. N.W. of Manchester; pop. 177,253. Map 31.

Bolton Abbey, par., W.R. Yorkshire, 5½ m. N.W. of Ilkley ; pop. 186. Map 31.

Bolton-by-Bowland, par., W.R. Yorkshire, 6 m. N.E. of Clitheroe ; pop. 633. Map 31.

Bolton-le-Sands, par. and vil., N.W. Lancashire, 4¾ m. N. of Lancaster ; pop. 994. Map 25.

Bolton-upon-Dearne, urb. dist. and par., W.R. York., 7 m. N. of Rotherham ; pop. 14,242. Map 41.

Bonar Bridge, vil., S.E. Sutherlandshire, 13½ m. N.W. of Tain ; pop. 331. Map 3.

Bonawe, vil. and seat, N. Argyllshire, on r. Awe, 13½ m. E.N.E. of Oban. Map 12.

Boncath, vil. and ry. sta., Pembrokeshire, 4½ m. N.N.E. of Crymmych Arms. Map 65.

Bonchurch, par. and vil., in S.E. of Isle of Wight, Hampshire, 1 m. E. of Ventnor ; pop. 501. Map 77.

Bo'ness, par. and seaport, W. Lothian, 24 m. W.N.W. of Edinburgh ; pop. 10,095. Map 9.

Bonhill, par. and town, Dumbartonshire, adjacent to Alexandria ; pop. 16,622. Map 8.

Bonnybridge, par. and town, Stirlingshire, 4 m. W. of Falkirk ; pop. 5969. Map 9.

Bonnyrigg and Lasswade, town, Midlothian, 9½ m. S.E. of Edinburgh ; pop. 4483. Map 10.

Bonsall, urb. dist., Derbyshire, 2 m. S.W. of Matlock ; pop. 1173. Map 40.

Boosbeck, eccl. dist. and vil., N.R. Yorkshire, 3 m. E.N.E. of Guisborough ; pop. 5866. Map 28.

Boothby Pagnell, par. and vil., Kesteven, Lincolnshire, 5 m. S.E. of Grantham ; pop. 136. Map 50.

Bootle, parl. and co. bor. adjg. Liverpool, S.W. Lancs, on r. Mersey ; pop. 76,799. Map 38.

Bootle, coast par. and vil., Cumberland, 4½ m. S. of Ravenglass ; pop. 806. Map 25.

Boroughbridge, par. and market town, W.R. Yorks, 11 m. N.E. of Harrogate ; pop. 807. Map 28.

Borris, vil. and seat, in co. and 18 m. S. of Carlow ; pop. 469. Map 95.

Borrowdale, romantic valley, W. Cumberland. Map 25.

Boscastle, vil. and coastguard sta., N. Cornwall, 5 m. N. of Camelford. Map 91.

Boston, mun. bor. and seaport, Holland, Lincolnshire, 30 m. S.E. of Lincoln ; pop. 16,597. Map 51.

Bothwell, par. and town, Lanarkshire, 8 m. S.E. of Glasgow ; pop. 3511. Map 9.

Botley, par. and vil., S. Hampshire, 3¾ m. S.W. of Bishop's Waltham ; pop. 1166. Map 77.

Bottesford, par. and vil., Leicestershire, 7 m. N.W. of Grantham ; pop. 1204. Map 50.

Bottisham, par. and vil., in co. and 6 m. E.N.E. of Cambridge ; pop. 624. Map 61.

Boughrood, par., Radnor, 11 m. S.E. of Builth ; pop. 215. Map 56.

Boulmer, fishing vil., Northumberland, 5 m. E. of Alnwick. Map 17.

Bourne, urb. dist., Kesteven, Lincolnshire, 9¼ m. W. of Spalding ; pop. 4889. Map 50.

Bournemouth, parl. and co. bor., par. and watering place, S.W. Hants, 3½ m. S.W. of Christchurch ; pop. 116,780. Map 77.

Bournville, vil., Worcestershire, 4½ m. S.W. of Birmingham. Map 58.

Bourton-on-the-Hill, par. and vil., Gloucestershire, 4½ m. N.W. of Stow-on-the-Wold ; pop. 363. Map 58.

Bourton-on-the-Water, par. and vil., E. Gloucestershire, 17¾ m. E. of Cheltenham ; pop. 1073. Map 69.

Bovey Tracey, par. and vil., S.E. Devon, 6¼ m. S.E. of Moreton Hampstead ; pop. 2788. Map 89.

Bow, par. and vil., N. Devon, 16 m. W.N.W. of Exeter ; pop. 616. Map 85.

Bowden, par. and vil., Roxburghshire, 1 m. W. of St Boswells ; pop. 638. Map 16.

Bowdon, urb. dist., Cheshire, 9 m. S. of Manchester ; pop. 3285. Map 30.

Bowes, par. and vil., N.R. Yorkshire, 4 m. S.W. of Barnard Castle ; pop. 655. Map 27.

Bowness, par., E. Cumberland, on Solway Firth, 2½ m. S. of Annan (Scotland) ; pop. 1107. Map 20.

Bowness, par., Westmorland, on E. side of Lake Windermere ; pop. 3860. Map 25.

Boxford, par. and vil., W. Suffolk, 6 m. E.S.E. of Sudbury ; pop. 479. Map 62.

Boyle, par. and market town, N. co. Roscommon, on r. Boyle, 28 m. S.E. of Sligo ; pop. 5654. Map 92.

Bozeat, par. and vil., Northamptonshire, 6 m. S. of Wellingborough ; pop. 1145. Map 60.

Bracadale, par., and sea loch, Skye, Inverness-shire, 10 m. S.W. of Portree ; pop. (incl. Soay isl.) 740. Map 2.

Brackley, mun. bor., par. and mkt. tn., S. Northants, 7 m. W.N.W. of Buckingham ; pop. 2181. Map 59.

Bracknell, eccl. par. and vil., S.E. Berkshire, 4½ m. E. of Wokingham ; pop. 2696. Map 78.

Braco, vil., S. Perthshire, 7½ m. S. of Crieff. Map 6.

Bradford, parl. and co. bor. and par., W.R. Yorkshire, 9 m. W. of Leeds ; pop. 298,041. Map 32.

Bradford-on-Avon, urb. dist. and market town, W. Wiltshire, 9 m. S.E. of Bath : pop. 4735. Map 75.

Brading, par. and town, Isle of Wight, Hants, 4 m. S. of Ryde ; pop. 1696. Map 77.

Bradninch, par. and town, E. Devon, 8¼ m. N.E. of Exeter ; pop. 1486. Map 85.

Bradpole, par. and vil., S.W. Dorsetshire, 1 m. N.E. of Bridport ; pop. 581. Map 86.

Bradwell, par., N. Derbyshire, 2 m. S.E. of Castleton ; stalactite cavern here ; pop. 1325. Map 40.

Braemar, vil., Crathie and Braemar par., Aberdeensh., 16½ m. W. of Ballater ; pop. 1029. Map 3.

Braintree, urb. dist., par. and market town, N.E. Essex, 45 m. N.E. of London ; pop. 8912. Map 72.

Bramber, par. and vil., N. Sussex, 4 m. N.W. of New Shoreham ; pop. 255. Map 79.

Bramfield, par., E. Suffolk, 2½ m. S. of Halesworth ; pop. 530. Map 63.

Bramham, vil., W.R. Yorkshire, 3½ m. W. of Tadcaster ; pop. 984. Map 33.

Bramley, par., S.W. Surrey, 5 m. S.S.E. of Guildford ; pop. 2006. Map 78.

Brampton, ham., N Westmorland, 2 m. N. of Appleby. Map 22.

Brampton, par. and market town, N.E. Cumberland, 9 m. N.E. of Carlisle ; pop. 2590. Map 21.

Brampton and Walton, urb. dist., Derbyshire, 3 m. S.W. of Chesterfield ; pop. 2323. Map 41.

Brampton Bryan, par. and vil., Herefordshire, 5½ m. E. of Knighton ; pop. 280. Map 56.

Brancaster, par. and fishing vil., Norfolk, 8½ m. W. of Wells ; pop. 974. Map 52.

Brancepeth, par. and vil., mid Durham, 4¼ m. S.W. of Durham ; pop. 355. Map 19.

Brandesburton, par. and vil., E.R. Yorkshire, 8 m. N.E. of Beverley ; pop. 577. Map 35.

Brandon, par. and market town, W. Suffolk, 6 m. N.W. of Thetford ; pop. 2462. Map 62.

Brandon and Byshottles, urb. dist., Durham, 3 m. S.W. of Durham ; pop. 17,099. Map 23.

Branksome, urb. dist. and par., S.E. Dorsetshire, now in bor. of Poole ; pop. 7202. Map 87.

Bran, Strath, valley of r. Bran and vil., Little Dunkele, par. Perthshire. Map 6.

Brant Broughton, par. and vil., Lincolnshire, 7 m. S.E. of Newark ; pop. 515. Map 42.

Branxton, par. and vil., Northumberland, 2 m. S.E. of Coldstream ; pop. 184. Map 17.

Brassington, par. and vil., N. Derbyshire, 3 m. W. of Wirksworth ; pop. 602. Map 40.

Brasted, par. and vil., W. Kent, 1½ m. N.E. of Westerham ; pop. 1327. Map 80.

Bratton Fleming, par. and vil., N. Devon, 7 m. N.E. of Barnstaple; pop. 486. Map 84.

Braughing, par. and vil., E. Hertfordshire, 3½ m. S.S.E. of Buntingford; pop. 928. Map 71.

Braunston, par. and vil., Rutland, 2½ m. S.W. of Oakham; pop. 294. Map 50.

Braunton, par. and vil., N.W. Devon, 5¾ m. N.W. of Barnstaple; pop. 2644. Map 84.

Brawnhills, urb. dist., Staffordshire, 6 m. W. of Lichfield; pop. 18,248. Map 48.

Bray (Bri Chualann), urb. dist., cos. Wicklow and Dublin, 12¼ m. S.E. of Dublin; pop. 7691. Map 95.

Bray, par. and vil., E. Berkshire, 1½ m. S.E. of Maidenhead; pop. 3803. Map 78.

Brechin, par., parl., royal and mun. bur., Angus, 9½ m. W. of Montrose; pop. 6838. Map 3.

Brecon, mun. bor. and co. town of Brecknockshire, 40 m. N.E. of Swansea; pop. 5334. Map 55.

Bredbury and Romiley, urb. dist., Cheshire, 2 m. N.E. of Stockport; pop. 10,878. Map 39.

Bredwardine, par. and vil., Herefordshire, 6½ m. E.N.E. of Hay; pop. 244. Map 56.

Breedon-on-the-Hill, par., N.W. Leicestershire, 5 m. N.E. of Ashby-de-la-Zouch; pop. 730. Map 49.

Brentford and Chiswick, urb. dist. and market town, W. Middlesex, 10½ m. W. of London; pop. 62,617. Map 71.

Brentwood, urb. dist., par. and market town, S. Essex, 11 m. S.W. of Chelmsford; pop. 7209. Map 72.

Brewood, par. and town, Staffordshire, 7 m. N.N.W. of Wolverhampton; pop. 2578. Map 47.

Bridgend, urb. dist. and market town, Glamorganshire, 20 m. W. of Cardiff; pop. 10,033. Map 66.

Bridgend, Islay, Argyllshire. Map 12.

Bridge of Allan, *q.s.* par. and town, in co. and 2½ m. N.W. of Stirling; pop. 2897. Map 9.

Bridge of Earn, vil., S.E. Perthshire, on r. Earn, 4½ m. S.E. of Perth. Map 6.

Bridge of Weir, *q.s.* par. and town, Renfrewshire, 6 m. W.N.W. of Paisley; town pop. 2487. Map 8.

Bridgham, par. and vil., Norfolk, 6 m. N.E. of Thetford; pop. 235. Map 62.

Bridgnorth, mun. bor., Salop, 14¼ m. W.S.W. of Wolverhampton; pop. 5151. Map 47.

Bridgwater, mun. bor. and seaport, W. Somersetshire, 33¼ m. S.W. of Bristol; pop. 17,139. Map 74.

Bridlington, mun. bor. and par., E.R. Yorkshire, 31 m. N.N.E. of Hull; pop. 19,704. Map 29.

Bridlington Quay, port of Bridlington; favourite seacoast resort. Map 29.

Bridport, seaport town, mun. bor. and par., S.W. Dorsetshire, 15½ m. W. of Dorchester; pop. 5917. Map 86.

Brierfield, urb. dist. and par., N.E. Lancashire, 2¼ m. N.E. of Burnley; pop. 7696. Map 31.

Brierley Hill, urb. dist. and par., Staffordshire, 2½ m. N.E. of Stourbridge; pop. 14,344. Map 47.

Brigg, urb. dist. and par., Lindsey, Lincs, 10 m. S. of Barton upon Humber; pop. 4019. Map 35.

Brigham, par. and vil., Cumberland, 2½ m. W. of Cockermouth; pop. 772. Map 20.

Brighouse, mun. bor. and par., W.R. Yorkshire, 5¼ m. N. of Huddersfield; pop. 19,756. Map 32.

Brightlingsea, urb. dist., par. and seaport, N.E. Essex, 8 m. S.E. of Colchester; pop. 4145. Map 73.

Brighton, parl. and co. bor., par. and watering place, Sussex, 50½ m. S. of London; pop. 147,427. Map 81.

Brill, par., vil. and seat, W. Buckinghamshire, 6 m. N.W. of Thame; pop. 1019. Map 70.

Brinklow, par. and vil., Warwickshire, 5½ m. N.W. of Rugby; pop. 681. Map 59.

Brinkworth, par. and ham., N. Wiltshire, 4 m. N.W. of Wootton Bassett; pop. 932. Map 68.

Brislington, par. and vil., N. Somersetshire, 2 m. S.E. of Bristol; pop. 3493. Map 75.

Bristol, city, co. bor. and seaport, Glos. and Somersetshires, 117½ m. W. of London; pop. 396,918. Map 74.

Briton Ferry, par., S.W. Glamorganshire, 7¼ m. E. of Swansea; pop. 9165. Map 66.

Brixham, urb. dist., par. and seaport town, S.E. Devon, 6 m. S. of Torquay; pop. 8147. Map 89.

Brixworth, par. and vil., in co. and 7½ m. N. of Northampton; pop. 1184. Map 59.

Brize Norton, par. and vil., S.W. Oxon, 4¼ m. S.W. of Witney; pop. 492. Map 69.

Broad Chalk, par. and vil., S. Wiltshire, 5 m. S.W. of Wilton; pop. 661. Map 75.

Broad Clyst, par. and vil., E. Devon, 5¼ m. N.E. Exeter; pop. 1859. Map 85.

Broadford, fishing vil., Isle of Skye, 8¼ m. W. of Kyle of Lochalsh; pop. 151. Map 2.

Broadmayne, par., S. Dorsetshire, 4½ m. S.E. of Dorchester; pop. 343. Map 87.

Broadstairs and St Peter's, urb. dist. and par., E. Kent, 2 m. N.E. of Ramsgate; pop. 12,748. Map 83.

Broadstone, eccl. dist. and vil., S.E. Dorsetshire, 3½ m. N.N.W. of Poole; pop. 1537. Map 87.

Broadway, par. and vil., S.E. Worcestershire, 5 m. S.E. of Evesham; pop. 1860. Map 58.

Broadway, par. and vil., S. Somersetshire, 2 m. W. of Ilminster; pop. 307. Map 86.

Broadwinsor, par. and vil., W. Dorsetshire, 3 m. N.W of Beaminster; pop. 901. Map 86.

Brockenhurst, par. and vil., S.W. Hampshire, 5 m. N. of Lymington; pop. 2159. Map 77.

Brodick, par., vil., pier and bay, Arran I., Buteshire, 4 m. N.W. of Lamlash; pop. 1760. Map 12.

Bromborough, port and urb. dist., N.W. Cheshire, 5 m. S.E. of Birkenhead; pop. 2557. Map 38.

Bromfield, par. and vil., Salop, 2½ m. N.W. of Ludlow; pop. 545. Map 56.

Bromley, mun. bor., N.W. Kent, 5½ m. N.E. of Croydon; pop. 45,348. Map 80.

Brompton, par. and seat, N.R. Yorkshire, 7 m. S.W. of Scarborough; pop. 598. Map 29.

Brompton, par., N.R. Yorkshire, 3 m. N. of Northallerton; pop. 1452. Map 28.

Brompton-on-Swale, par. and vil., N.R. Yorkshire, 3½ m. E. of Richmond; pop. 362. Map 27.

Bromsgrove, urb. dist. and par., in co. and 12 m. N.E. of Worcester; pop. 9520. Map 58.

Bromsgrove, North, urb. dist., Worcestershire, 7 m. N.E. of Droitwich; pop. 10,982. Map 57.

Bromyard, urb. dist., Herefordshire, 10½ m. E.S.E. of Leominster; pop. 1571. Map 57.

Brora, vil. and loch, Sutherlandshire, 6½ m. N.E. of Golspie; pop. 744; loch 66 ft. deep. Map 3.

Broseley, par. in mun. bor. of Wenlock, S.E. Shropshire, 13½ m. S.E. of Shrewsbury; pop. 3037. Map 47.

Brotton, par., N.R. Yorkshire, 2 m. S.E. of Saltburn; pop. 4428. Map 28.

Brough, par. and market town, E. Westmorland, 5 m. N. of Kirkby Stephen; pop. 620. Map 26.

Broughton, vil., in co. and 11 m. S.W. of Peebles; alt. 636 ft. Map 15.

Broughton, urb. dist., par. and vil., Lincolnshire, 3 m. N.W. of Brigg; pop. 1744. Map 35.

Broughton, par. and vil., N.R. Yorkshire, 2 m. S.E. of Stokesley; pop. 659. Map 28.

Broughton, par., N.E. Lancashire, 7 m. N.E. of Ulverston; pop. 210. Map 25.

Broughty Ferry, *q.s.* par. and dist. in E. of Dundee; pop. 5278. Map 7.

Brownhills, urb. dist., Staffordshire, 6 m. W. of Lichfield; pop. 18,368. Map 48.

Broxbourne, par. and vil., in co. and 5 m. S.E. of Hertford; pop. 790. Map 71.

Broxburn, *q.s.* par. and mining town, W. Lothian, 10½ m. W. of Edinburgh; pop. 7578. Map 9.

Bruisyard, par. and vil., E. Suffolk, 4 m. N.W. of Saxmundham; pop. 212. Map 63.

Bruton, par. and market town, S.E. Somersetshire, 10½ m. S.W. of Frome; pop. 1724. Map 75.
Brydekirk, *q.s.* par. and vil., Dumfriesshire, 3 m. N. of Annan; pop. 701. Map 20.
Brynamman, vil., S.E. Carmarthenshire, 5¾ m. E.N.E. of Ammanford. Map 66.
Bryn-Mawr, urb. dist. and par., S.E. Brecon, 8 m. W.N.W. of Abergavenny; pop. 7247. Map 67.
Buchanty, vil., mid Perthshire, on r. Almond, 10 m. N.E. of Crieff. Map 6.
Buchlyvie, vil. and par., N.W. Stirlingshire, 4½ m. N.N.E. of Balfron; pop. 409. Map 8.
Buckfastleigh, urb. dist., Devonshire, 3¾ m. N.W. of Totnes; pop. 2406. Map 89.
Buckhaven, parl. and police bur., Fifeshire, 1¼ m. S.W. of Methil; pop. 17,643. Map 10.
Buckhurst Hill, urb. dist. and par., S.W. Essex, 10¾ m. N.E. of London; pop. 5486. Map 72.
Buckie, *q.s.* par. and fishing town, Banffshire, 13¾ m. N. of Keith; pop. 8688. Map 3.
Buckingham, mun. bor. and par., Bucks, on r. Ouse, 17 m. N.W. of Aylesbury; pop. 3082. Map 59.
Buckland, vil. and paper mill, E. Kent, 1½ m. N.W. of Dover; pop. 10,087. Map 83.
Buckland, par., N.E. Hertfordshire, 3 m. N. of Buntingford; pop. 237. Map 61.
Bucklesham, par. and vil., E. Suffolk, 5 m. S.E. of Ipswich; pop. 272. Map 63.
Buckley, urb. dist. and ry. sta., Flintshire, 2 m. E. of Mold; pop. 6900. Map 38.
Bucknell, par. and vil., Salop, 5½ m. S.E. of Clun; pop. 419. Map 56.
Bude, ward of Stratton and Bude urb. dist., Cornwall, 10½ m. W.N.W. of Holsworthy; pop. 2069. Map 84.
Budleigh, E., par. and vil., E. Devon, 5 m. S.W. of Sidmouth; pop. 756. Map 89.
Budleigh Salterton, urb. dist., par. and watering pl., Devon, 4½ m. E. of Exmouth; pop. 3162. Map. 89.
Bugbrooke, par. and vil., in co. and 5½ m. S.W. of Northampton; pop. 734. Map 59.
Buglawton, urb. dist., Cheshire, 1 m. N.E. of Congleton; pop. 1651. Map 39.
Bugsworth, Derbyshire. *See* Buxworth.
Builth Road, ry. sta., Radnorshire, 2 m. W.N.W. of Builth Wells. Map 55.
Builth Wells, urb. dist., Brecknock, 16 m. N. of Brecon; pop. 1663. Map 55.
Bulford, par. and vil., Wiltshire, 2 m. N.E. of Amesbury; pop. 3797. Map 76.
Bulkington, urb. dist. and par., Warwickshire, 3½ m. S.S.E. of Nuneaton; pop. 2749. Map 49.
Buncrana, market town, co. Donegal, 12 m. N.W. of Londonderry; pop. 1848. Map 93.
Bungay, urb. dist. and par., E. Suffolk, 6 m. W. of Beccles; pop. 3098. Map 63.
Buntingford, town on r. Rib, Hertfordshire, 7 m. S. of Royston. Map 61.
Bures, par. and vil., N.E. Essex, 6 m. S.E. of Sudbury; pop. 423. Map 62.
Burford, par. and town, in co. and 18½ m. W.N.W. of Oxford; pop. 987. Map 69.
Burgess Hill, urb. dist., E. Sussex, 9 m. N. of Brighton; pop. 5975. Map 81.
Burgh-by-Sands, par. and vil., N.W. Cumberland, 5 m. N.W. of Carlisle; pop. 754. Map 21.
Burghead, spt., Morayshire, 10¾ m. N.W. of Elgin; pop. 1255. Map 3.
Burgh-next-Aylsham, par. and ham., Norfolk, 2 m. S.E. of Aylsham; pop. 212. Map 53.
Burley-in-Wharfedale, urb. dist., W.R. Yorkshire, 3¼ m. E.S.E. of Ilkley; pop. 3960. Map 32.
Burnham, par. and vil., Bucks., 2½ m. N.E. of Maidenhead; pop. 4113. Contains **B. Beeches**. Map 71.
Burnham, urb. dist. and coast par., W. Somersetshire, 7½ m. N. of Bridgwater; pop. 5120. Map 74.
Burnham Market, vil., Norfolk, 6 m. W. of Wells. Map 52.
Burnham-on-Crouch, urb. dist. and seaport, E. Essex, 9 m. S.E. of Maldon; pop. 3395. Map 73.
Burnley, parl. and co. bor. and par., N.E. Lancashire, 23 m. E. of Preston; pop. 98,259. Map 31.
Burntisland, par., parl., royal and mun. bur., spt., Fife, 5 m. by ferry N. of Edinburgh; pop. 5389. Map 10.
Burringham, par. and vil., Lincolnshire, on r. Trent, 4½ m. S.E. of Crowle; pop. 706. Map 34.
Burry Port, urb. dist., par. and seaport, Carmarthenshire, 4 m. W. of Llanelly; pop. 5752. Map 65.
Burslem, par., Staffordshire, in Stoke-on-Trent co. bor.; pop. 41,566. Map 39.
Burstwick, par. and vil., E.R. Yorkshire, 7½ m. S.E. of Hull; pop. 586. Map 35.
Burton Agnes, par. and vil., E.R. Yorkshire, 5½ m. S.W. of Bridlington; pop. 342. Map 35.
Burton Bradstock, par., S.W. Dorsetshire, 4 m. S.E. of Bridport; pop. 624. Map 86.
Burton Coggles, par. and vil., Kesteven, Lincolnshire, 7½ m. S.S.E. of Grantham; pop. 192. Map 50.
Burton Constable, seat, E.R. Yorkshire, 7 m. N.E. of Hull. Map 35.
Burton-in-Kendal, par. and town, Westmorland, 10½ m. S. of Kendal; pop. 460. Map 26.
Burton-in-Lonsdale, par., W.R. Yorkshire, 12 m. N.W. of Settle; pop. 565. Map 26.
Burton Joyce, par. and vil., in co. and 5 m. N.E. of Nottingham; pop. 1010. Map 49.
Burton Latimer, par. and vil., Northamptonshire, 3 m. S.E. of Kettering; pop. 3586. Map 60.
Burton Pidsea, par. and vil., E.R. Yorkshire, 7½ m. N.W. of Patrington; pop. 313. Map 35.
Burton-upon-Trent, co. bor. and par., Staffordshire, 11 m. S.W. of Derby; pop. 49,485. Map 48.
Burwash, par., vil. and seat, E. Sussex, 8 m. N.W. of Battle; pop. 1942. Map 82.
Burwell, par. and vil., in co. and 10 m. N.E. of Cambridge; pop. 2108. Map 61.
Bury, parl. and co. bor. and par., S.E. Lancashire, 5½ m. E. of Bolton; pop. 56,186. Map 31.
Bury St Edmunds, mun. bor. and par., W. Suffolk, 27 m. N.W. of Ipswich; pop. 16,708. Map 62.
Busby, vil., Lanarkshire, 7½ m. S. of Glasgow; pop. 538. Map 8.
Bushey, urb. dist. and par., S.W. Hertfordshire, 16 m. N.W. of London; pop. 11,243. Map 71.
Busheyheath, eccl. dist., Bushey par., Hertfordshire; pop. 2251. Map 71.
Bushmills, market town, co. Antrim, 8 m. N.E. of Coleraine; pop. 970. Map 93.
Buttermere, par., vil. and lake, W. Cumberland, 9½ m. S.W. of Keswick; pop. 130. Map 25.
Buttertubs, pass, N.W. Yorkshire, 5½ m. long, between Hawes and Muker. Map 26.
Butterwick, coast par., Holland, Lincolnshire, 4 m. E. of Boston; pop. 498. Map 51.
Buttington, dist., Montgomeryshire, 2¾ m. N.E. of Welshpool. Map 46.
Buxton, mun. bor. and watering place, Derbyshire, 36 m. N.W. of Derby; pop. 15,353. Map 40.
Buxworth, ham., N.W. Derbyshire, 3 m. W.N.W. of Chapel-en-le-Frith. Map 40.
Bwlch-y-Sarnau, hamlet, Radnorshire, 6½ m. N.E. of Rhayader. Map 55.
Byfleet, par. and vil., N.W. Surrey, 2¼ m. S.S.W. of Weybridge; pop. 4173. Map 78.
Bynea, vil. and ry. sta., Carmarthenshire, 2¾ m. E.S.E. of Llanelly. Map 65.
Byrness, eccl. dist. and ham., N. Northumberland, 9 m. N.W. of Otterburn; pop. 140. Map 16.
Bytham, Little, par. and vil., Kesteven, Lincolnshire, 7 m. N. of Stamford; pop. 390. Map 50.
CADER IRIS, mountain ridge in S.W. of Merionethshire. Map 45.
Cadnam, ham., Hampshire, 4 m. N. of Lyndhurst. Map 77.

Caergwrie, ham., Flintshire, on R. Alyn, 5¼ m. N.W. of Wrexham. Map 38.

Caerlaverock, par. and ruined castle, in co. and 7½ m. S.E. of Dumfries; pop. 799. Map 20.

Caerleon, urb. dist. and par., Monmouthshire, 2½ m. N.E. of Newport; pop. 2326. Map 67.

Caerphilly, urb. dist., Glamorganshire, 7 m. N. of Cardiff; pop. 35,760. Map 74.

Caersws, ham. and ry. sta., Montgomeryshire, 5¾ m. N.W. of Newton. Map 46.

Cahir, market town and par., in co. and 13¼ m. S.E. of Tipperary; pop. of town 1707. Map 95.

Cahirciveen, market town, co. Kerry, 3½ m. N.E. of Valencia; pop. 1773. Map 94.

Cairnwell, pass, Perthshire and Aberdeenshire, 10 m. S. of Braemar. Map 3.

Caister-on-Sea, coast par. and vil., Norfolk, 3 m. S. of Yarmouth; pop. 2346. Map 53.

Caistor, par. and town, Lindsey, Lincolnshire, 8 m. S.E. of Brigg; pop. 1571. Map 42.

Caldbeck, par. and vil., Cumberland, 6½ m. S.E. of Wigton; pop. 775. Map 21.

Caldecott, par., Rutland, 4 m. S. of Uppingham; pop. 264. Map 50.

Caldercruix, *q.s.* par. and vil., Lanarkshire, 4½ m. N.E. of Airdrie; pop. 2370. Map 9.

Caldicot, par. and vil., Monmouthshire, 5 m. S.W. of Chepstow; pop. 1770. Map 67.

Caldy and St Margaret, 2 isls. off S.E. coast of Pembrokeshire, 2½ m. S. of Tenby. Map 64.

Callan, market town and par. in co. and 13 m. S.W. of Kilkenny; pop. 1510. Map 95.

Callander, police bur., Perthshire, 16 m. N.W. of Stirling; pop. of town, 1572. Map 5.

Callington, urb. dist. and par., Cornwall, 9½ m. S. of Launceston; pop. 1801. Map 88.

Cally, Bridge of, Perthsh., 4½ m. N.W. of Blairgowrie. Map 6.

Calne, mun. bor., N. Wiltshire, 5½ m. S.E. of Chippenham; pop. 3463. Map 75.

Calverley, urb. dist. and par., W.R. Yorkshire, 5¾ m. W.N.W. of Leeds; pop. 3655. Map 32.

Calverton, par. and vil., in co. and 6½ m. N.E. of Nottingham; pop. 1040. Map 49.

Camberley, place, W. Surrey, 2½ m. S.W. of Bagshot. Here is a Military Staff College. Map 78.

Cambois, colliery vil., Northumberland, 2½ m. N.W. of Blyth. Map 17.

Camborne, urb. dist. and par., Cornwall, 12½ m. S.W. of Truro, pop. 14,157. Map 90.

Cambridge, parl. and mun. bor., and co. town of Cambs., 57 m. N. of London by rail; pop. 66,803. Map 61.

Cambuslang, town, Lanarkshire, 5 m. S.E. of Glasgow. Map 9.

Cambusnethan, par. and vil., Lanarkshire, 1½ m. N.E. of Wishaw; pop. 36,737. Map 9.

Camelford, market town, Cornwall, 17½ m. W. of Launceston. Map 91.

Camelon, *q.s.* par., forming part of Falkirk, Stirlingshire; pop. 8137. Map 9.

Campbeltown, mun. bur. and spt., Kintyre, Argyllshire, 83 m. S.W. of Glasgow by sea; pop. 6309. Map 12.

Campsie, par., Stirlingshire, containing Lennoxtown; pop. 5335. Map 8.

Cannington, par. and vil., W. Somersetshire, 3½ m. N.W. of Bridgwater; pop. 871. Map 74.

Cannock, urb. dist. and par., Staffordshire, 8 m. N.N.W. of Walsall; pop. 34,588. Map 48.

Canonbie, par. and vil., S.E. Dumfriesshire, 6 m. S.E. of Langholm; pop. 1756. Map 21.

Canterbury, city, co. bor. and par., Kent, 16 m. N.W. of Dover; pop. 24,450. Map 83.

Canvey Island, urb. dist., Essex, 4½ m. S.W. of Rayleigh; pop. 3530. Map 72.

Capel, par. and vil., S. Surrey, 5½ m. S. of Dorking; pop. 1459. Map 78.

Capel Bangor, vil. and sta., Cardiganshire, 4½ m. E.S.E. of Aberystwyth. Map 55.

Capel Curig, par. and ham., E. Carnarvonshire, 6 m. W. of Bettws-y-Coed; pop. 359. Map 37.

Cappamore, vil., in co. and 12 m. S.E. of Limerick; pop. 531. Map 94.

Cappoquin, town, co. Waterford, 10½ m. W.N.W. of Dungarvan; pop. 1069. Map 95.

Caputh, par. and vil., Perthshire, 1½ m. N.W. of Murthly sta.; pop. 1046. Map 6.

Cardiff, co. bor., co. town and seaport, Glamorganshire, 38 m. W. of Bristol; pop. 223,648. Map 67.

Cardigan, mun. bor. and co. town of Cardiganshire, 42 m. N.W. of Carmarthen by rail; pop. 3309. Map 54.

Cardington, par. and vil., in co. and 2 m. S.E. of Bedford; pop. 377. Map 60.

Cardross, coast par. and vil., in co. and 3¾ m. W.N.W. of Dumbarton; pop. 1662. Map 8.

Carew, par. and ham., in co. and 4½ m. E.N.E. of Pembroke; pop. 756. Map 64.

Carham, par. and vil., Northumberland, near boundary with Scotland; pop. 841. Map 16.

Carisbrooke, par., vil. and castle, Isle of Wight, 1 m. S.W. of Newport; pop. 4767. Map 77.

Carlisle, city, bor. and co. town of Cumberland, 60 m. W. of Newcastle; pop. 57,107. Map 21.

Carlops, vil., Peeblesshire, on N. Esk, 15 m. S.W. of Edinburgh. Map 10.

Carlow, urb. dist. and par., co. Carlow, 56 m. S.W. of Dublin; pop. 7175. Map 95.

Carlton, urb. dist. and par., in co. and 3½ m. N.E. of Nottingham; pop. 22,336. Map 49.

Carluke, town and par., Lanarkshire, 5½ m. N.W. of Lanark; town pop. 5436. Map 9.

Carmarthen, par. and mun. bor., Carmarthenshire, 27¾ m. N.W. of Swansea by rail; pop. 10,310. Map 65.

Carnaby, par. and ham., E.R. Yorkshire, 2¼ m. S.W. of Bridlington; pop. 194. Map 29.

Carnarvon, co. town of Carnarvonshire, parl. and mun. bor., 8½ m. S.W. of Bangor; pop. 8469. Map 36.

Carndonagh, vil. and ry. sta., co. Donegal, 18 m. N.E. of Buncrana; pop. 668. Map 93.

Carnforth, urb. dist. and par., N. Lancashire, 6½ m. N.N.E. of Lancaster; pop. 3193. Map 26.

Carnoustie, coast town, Angus, 10½ m. N.E. of Dundee; pop. 4806. Map 7.

Carnwath, par. and vil., Lanarkshire, 26 m. S.W. of Edinburgh; vil. pop. 964. Map 9.

Carrbridge, vil. and ry. sta., in co. and 28 m. S.E. of Inverness. Map 3.

Carrickfergus, seaport and urb. dist., co. Antrim, 9½ m. N. of Belfast; pop. 8669. Map 93.

Carrickmacross, urb. dist. and par., co. Monaghan, 14 m. W. of Dundalk; pop. 2000. Map 93.

Carrick-on-Shannon, market town, co. Leitrim, 37 m. S.E. of Sligo; pop. 1013. Map 92.

Carrick-on-Suir, urb. dist., co. Tipperary, 13¾ m. E. of Clonmel; pop. 4675. Map 95.

Carr Shield, vil., Northumberland, 7 m. S.W. of Allendale. Map 22.

Carshalton, urb. dist., Surrey, 1½ m. E. of Sutton; pop. 28,769. Map 80.

Carstairs, par. and vil., Lanarkshire, 27½ m. S.W. of Edinburgh; vil. pop. 492. Map 9.

Carter Bar, road summit, Cheviot Hills, between Roxburgh and Northumberland; alt. 1371 ft. Map 16.

Cartmel, market town, N. Lancashire, 6 m. E. of Ulverston; pop. 313. Map 25.

Cashel, city and urb. dist., co. Tipperary, 8 m. N. of Cahir; pop. 2945. Map 95.

Castle Acre, par. and vil., Norfolk, 4 m. N. of Swaffham; pop. 955. Map 52.

Castle Bar, urb. dist. and cap. of co. Mayo, 11 m. N.E. of Westport; pop. 4256. Map 92.

Castleblayney, urb. dist., co. Monaghan, 18 m. N.W. of Dundalk; pop. 1553. Map 93.

Castle Carrock, par. and vil., N.E. Cumberland, 4 m. S. of Brampton; pop. 346. Map 21.

Castle Cary, par. and market town, Somersetshire, 12 m. N.E. of Yeovil; pop. 1646. Map 75.

Castlecomer, market town and par., in co. and 11¼ m. N.N.E. of Kilkenny; pop. of town 872. Map 95.

Castlederg, vil. and ry. sta., co. Tyrone, 10 m. S.W. of Strabane; pop. 835. Map 93.

Castle Donington, par. and town, Leicestershire, 11 m. S.W. of Nottingham; pop. 2736. Map 49.

Castle Douglas, police bur., Kirkcudbrightshire, 10½ m. S.W. of Dumfries; pop. 3008. Map 19.

Castleford, urb. dist. and par., W.R. Yorkshire, 10 m. S.E. of Leeds; pop. 21,781. Map 33.

Castle Hedingham, par. and vil., Essex, 5 m. N. of Halstead; pop. 961. Map 62.

Castleisland, par. and town, co. Kerry, 11½ m. S.E. of Tralee; pop. 1333. Map 94.

Castlemartyr, vil., co. Cork, 1¼ m. S. of Mogeely ry. sta.; pop. 274. Map 95.

Castlemorris, vil., Pembrokeshire, 5 m. S.S.W. of Fishguard. Map 64.

Castlerea, market town, in co. and 16½ m. N.W. of Roscommon; pop. 1224. Map 92.

Castle Rising, par. and vil., Norfolk, 4 m. N.E. of King's Lynn; pop. 236. Map 52.

Castleton, par. and vil., Derbyshire, 10 m. N.E. of Buxton; pop. 646. Map 40.

Castleton, par. and vil., S. Roxburghshire, 21½ m. S. of Hawick; pop. 1853. Map 16.

Castleton, vil. and ry. sta., N.R. Yorkshire, 6½ m. S.E. of Guisborough. Map 28.

Castletown, seaport town and coastguard station, Isle of Man, 10 m. S.W. of Douglas; pop. 1898. Map 24.

Castlewellan, market town, co. Down, 4 m. N.W. of Newcastle; pop. 819. Map 93.

Castor, par. and vil., Soke of Peterborough, Northants, 4 m. W. of Peterborough; pop. 576. Map 50.

Catcleugh, ham. and reservoir, N. Northumberland, on r. Rede, 12 m. N.W. of Otterburn. Map 16.

Caterham and Warlingham, urb. dist., E. Surrey, 7 m. S. of Croydon; pop. 19,503. Map 80.

Catterall, par. and vil., N. Lancashire, 2 m. S.E. of Garstang; pop. 330. Map 30.

Catterick, par. and vil., N.R. Yorkshire, 4½ m. S.E. of Richmond; pop. 564. Map 27.

Cattistock, par. and vil., Dorsetshire, 4½ m. W.S.W. of Cerne Abbas; pop. 434. Map 87.

Catwick, par. and vil., E.R. Yorkshire, 5½ m. W.S.W. of Hornsea; pop. 213. Map 35.

Catworth, par. and vil., Huntingdonshire, 4 m. N. of Kimbolton; pop. 384. Map 60.

Cavan, urb. dist. and co. town of Cavan, 79¾ m. S.W. of Belfast; pop. 2961. Map 93.

Caversham, eccl. par. in N. of co. bor. of Reading, Berkshire; pop. 10,432. Map 78.

Cawood, par. and vil., W.R. Yorkshire, 5¼ m. N.W. of Selby; pop. 983. Map 34.

Cawston, par. and vil., Norfolk, 4 m. S.W. of Aylsham; pop. 970. Map 53.

Caxton, par. and vil., in co. and 9 m. W. of Cambridge; pop. 398. Map 61.

Caythorpe, par. and vil., Kesteven, Lincolnshire, 8½ m. N.N.E. of Grantham; pop. 764. Map 50.

Cefn-Coed-y-Cymmer, vil. and ry. sta., Brecon, 2½ m. N.W. of Merthyr-Tydfil. Map 66.

Celbridge, vil., co. Kildare, 10¼ m. W. of Dublin. Map 93.

Cellardyke, fishing vil. and q.s. par., Fifeshire, adjoining Anstruther; pop. 1472. Map 7.

Ceres, par. and vil., Fifeshire, 2½ m. S.E. of Cupar; pop. 1445. Map 7.

Cerne Abbas, market town and par., Dorsetshire, 7 m. N. of Dorchester; pop. 511. Map 87.

Cerney, South, par. and vil., Gloucestershire, 4 m. S.E. of Cirencester; pop. 873. Map 69.

Cerrig-y-Druidion, par. and vil., in co. and 13 m. S.W. of Denbigh; pop. 1072. Map 37.

Chadderton, urb. dist., Lancashire, 1 m. W. of Oldham; pop. 27,455. Map 31.

Chadlington, par. and vil., Oxon, 3½ m. S. of Chipping Norton; pop. 496. Map 69.

Chaffcombe, par. and vil., Somersetshire, 3 m. S. of Ilminster; pop. 230. Map 86.

Chagford, market town and par., Devonshire, 3 m. N.W. of Moreton Hampstead; pop. 1715. Map 89.

Chalfont St Giles, par. and vil., Buckinghamshire, 3 m. S.E. of Amersham; pop. 2074. Map 71.

Chalford, par. and vil., Gloucestershire, 3½ m. S.E. of Stroud; pop. 2985. Map 68.

Chalgrove, par. and vil., Oxon, 5 m. S.W. of Tetsworth; pop. 359. Map 70.

Chalk, par. and vil., N. Kent, on r. Thames, 1½ m. S.E. of Gravesend; pop. 517. Map 80.

Chandler's Ford, par. and vil., Hants, 5 m. E. of Romsey; pop. 1831. Map 77.

Chapel-en-le-Frith, market town and par., Derbyshire, 5¼ m. N. of Buxton; pop. 5283. Map 40.

Chard, mun. bor. and par., Somersetshire, 12 m. S.E. of Taunton; pop. 4053. Map 86.

Chardstock, par. and vil., Devonshire, 4 m. N. of Axminster; pop. 916. Map 86.

Charing, town and par., mid Kent, 5½ m. N.W. of Ashford; pop. 1207. Map 83.

Charlbury, market town and par., in co. and 13¼ m. N.W. of Oxford; pop. 1231. Map 69.

Charlestown, seaport vil., Fifeshire, 3½ m. S.W. of Dunfermline. Map 9.

Charlestown, seaport, Cornwall, 2 m. S.E. of St Austell; pop. of eccl. dist. 2973. Map 91.

Charlestown of Aberlour, town, Banffshire, 2¼ m. S.W. of Craigellachie; pop. 1175. Map 3.

Charlesworth, par. and vil., N. Derbyshire, 2 m. W.S.W. of Glossop; pop. 1772. Map 40.

Charleville, market town, in co. and 33 m. N. of Cork; pop. 1684. Map 94.

Charlton Kings, urb. dist., Gloucestershire, sub. of Cheltenham; pop. 4764. Map 68.

Charminster, par. and vil., Dorsetshire, 2 m. N.W. of Dorchester; pop. 1762. Map 87.

Charmouth, par. and watering place, Dorsetshire, 6 m. S.E. of Axminster; pop. 668. Map 86.

Chatburn, par., Lancashire, 2 m. N.E. of Clitheroe; pop. 1168. Maps 26 and 31.

Chatham, mun. bor. and seaport town, N. Kent, 7¾ m. N. of Maidstone; pop. 42,996. Map 80.

Chat Moss, peat bog, Lancashire, 7 m. W. of Manchester; area 12 sq. m., 30 ft. deep in places. Map 39.

Chatsworth, par., N. Derbyshire, on r. Derwent, 2½ m. N.E. of Bakewell; pop. 50. Map 40.

Chatteris, urb. dist. and par., Isle of Ely, Cambs, 8 m. S. of March; pop. 5153. Map 51.

Chatton, par. and vil., Northumberland, 3 m. E. of Wooler; pop. 891. Map 17.

Cheadle and Gatley, urb. dist., Cheshire, 2½ m. S.W. of Stockport; pop. 18,469. Map 39.

Cheddar, par. and vil., N. Somersetshire, 1¾ m. S.E. of Axbridge; pop. 2007. Map 74.

Chedworth, par. and vil., Gloucestershire, 6¾ m. N.E. of Cirencester; pop. 671. Map 69.

Chelmondiston, par. and vil., E. Suffolk, 5 m. S.S.E. of Ipswich; pop. 801. Map 63.

Chelmsford, mun. bor. and co. town of Essex, 29¾ m. N.E. of London by rail; pop. 26,537. Map 72.

Cheltenham, parl. and mun. bor., Gloucestershire, 7 m. N.E. of Gloucester; pop. mun. bor. 49,385. Map 68.

Chepstow, urb. dist. on r. Wye, in co. and 14¾ m. S. of Monmouth; pop. 4303. Map 67.

Cheriton, coast par. and urb. dist., Kent, 2 m. W.N.W. of Folkestone; pop. 8089. Map 83.
Cherry Burton, par. and vil., E.R. Yorkshire, 3½ m. N.W. of Beverley; pop. 378. Map 35.
Cherry Hinton, par., in co. and 2½ m. S.E. of Cambridge; pop. 1164. Map 61.
Chertsey, market town and par., N. Surrey, on r. Thames, 9½ m. W.S.W. of Kingston; pop. 17,130. Map 78.
Chesham, urb. dist. and par., Buckinghamshire, 5 m. S.W. of Berkhampstead; pop. 8809. Map 71.
Cheshunt, urb. dist. and par., Hertfordshire, 16¼ m. N. of London; pop. 14,651. Map 71.
Chesilton, vil., on W. side of Portland Isle, Dorsetshire. Map 87.
Chester, co. bor., city and co. in itself and par., 16 m. S. of Liverpool; pop. 41,438. Map 38.
Chesterfield, mun. bor. and par., Derbyshire, 12¼ m. S. of Sheffield; pop. 64,146. Map 41.
Chesterford, Great and **Little,** 2 pars., Essex, 4 m. N.W. of Saffron Walden; pop. 766 and 176. Map 61.
Chester-le-Street, urb. dist. and par., in co. and 5½ m. N. of Durham; pop. 16,639. Map 23.
Chesterton, par. and ward of Wolstanton United, Staffordshire; pop. 7439. Map 39.
Cheveley, par. and vil., Cambridgeshire, 3 m. S.E. of Newmarket; pop. 599. Map 61.
Chevington, East, par. and vil., Northumberland, 3½ m. S. of Amble; pop. 3671. Map 17.
Chevington, West, par. and vil., Northumberland, 7½ m. N.N.E. of Morpeth; pop. 359. Map 17.
Cheviot Hills, mtn. range, extending about 35 m. along border of England and Scotland. Map 16.
Chew Magna, par. and vil., E. Somersetshire, 7 m. S. of Bristol; pop. 1594. Map 74.
Chew Stoke, par. and vil., N. Somerset, 8 m. S. of Bristol; pop. 622. Map 74.
Chichester, city and mun. bor., W. Sussex, 28 m. W. of Brighton; pop. 13,911. Map 79.
Chickerell, par. and vil., Dorsetshire, 3 m. N.W. of Weymouth; pop. 1016. Map 87.
Chiddingfold, par. and vil., S.W. Surrey, 4¼ m. N.E. of Haslemere; pop. 2156. Map 79.
Chigwell, par. and vil., W. Essex, 13½ m. N.E. of London; pop. 2943. Map 72.
Childrey, par. and vil., Berkshire, 2½ m. W. of Wantage; pop. 476. Map 69.
Childwall, par., S.W. Lancashire, in S.E. of co. bor. of Liverpool; pop. 1970. Contains **C. Hall.** Map 38.
Chillingham, par., vil. and seat (**C. Castle**), Northumberland, 4½ m. S.E. of Wooler; pop. 95. Map 17.
Chilton Foliat, par. and vil., E. Wiltshire, 2 m. N.W. of Hungerford; pop. 336. Map 69.
Chingford, mun. bor. and par., W. Essex, 12¼ m. N.E. of London; pop. 22,051. Map 71.
Chinnor, par. and vil., Oxon, 5 m. S.E. of Thame; pop. 973. Map 70.
Chippenham, par. and vil., Cambridgeshire, 4½ m. N.E. of Newmarket; pop. 481. Map 62.
Chippenham, mun. bor., N.W. Wiltshire, 13 m. N.E. of Bath; pop. 8493. Map 68.
Chipping Campden, par. and market town, Gloucestershire; 9½ m. S.E. of Evesham; pop. 1627. Map 58.
Chipping Norton, mun. bor. and par., Oxon, 13 m. S.W. of Banbury; pop. 3489. Map 58.
Chipping Ongar, par. and vil., Essex, 23½ m. N.E. of London; pop. 1142. Map 72.
Chipping Sodbury, par. and market town, Gloucestershire, 11 m. N.E. of Bristol; pop. 952. Map 68.
Chirk, par. and vil., Denbighshire, 9 m. S. of Wrexham; pop. 2576. Map 46.
Chirnside, par. and vil., Berwickshire, 4¾ m. N.E. of Duns; pop. 1402. Map 11.
Chisledon, par. and vil., Wiltshire, 3 m. S.E. of Swindon; pop. 1688. Map 69.
Chislehurst, urb. dist., N.W. Kent, 11¼ m. S.E. of London; pop. 9876. Map 80.
Chiswick. *See* Brentford and Chiswick.
Chobham, par. and vil., W. Surrey, 3 m. N.W. of Woking ry. sta.; pop. 4085. Map 78.
Chorley, mun. bor., market town and par., N. Lancashire, 9 m. S.E. of Preston; pop. 30,795. Map 30.
Chorleywood, urb. dist., Herts, 2 m. N.W. of Rickmansworth; pop. 3296. Map 71.
Christchurch, mun. bor., seaport and par., Hants, 25½ m. S.W. of Southampton by rail; pop. 9183. Map 77.
Chryston, *q.s.* par., Cadder par., Lanarkshire, 7 m. N.E. of Glasgow; pop. 6837. Map 8.
Chudleigh, market town and par., Devonshire, 14¾ m. S.W. of Exeter by rail; pop. 1869. Map 89.
Chulmleigh, market town and par., Devonshire, 8 m. S. of S. Molton; pop. 1143. Map 85.
Church, urb. dist., Lancs, 1 m. W. of Accrington; pop. 6185. Map 31.
Churchingford, vil. in Somersetshire, 7½ m. S. of Taunton. Map 86.
Church Lawford, par. and vil., Warwickshire, 3½ m. W.N.W. of Rugby; pop. 271. Map 59.
Church Stretton, urb. dist., Salop, 12¾ m. S.S.W. of Shrewsbury; pop. 1705. Map 46.
Cilfynydd, vil. and ry. sta., Glamorganshire, 2¼ m. N. of Pontypridd. Map 67.
Cilgerran, par. and vil., Pembrokeshire, 3 m. S.S.E. of Cardigan; pop. 904. Map 54.
Cinderford, vil. and ry. sta., Gloucestershire, 3 m. N.W. of Newnham. Map 68.
Cirencester, urb. dist. and par., Gloucestershire, 20¾ m. S.E. of Cheltenham by rail; pop. 7200. Map 68.
Clackmannan, par. and co. town of Clackmannanshire, 2 m. S.E. of Alloa; pop. 2373. Map 9.
Clacton-on-Sea, urb. dist. and par., Essex, 19 m. S.E. of Colchester; pop. 15,851. Map 73.
Clapham, vil., W.R. Yorkshire, 4 m. S.E. of Ingleton; pop. 642. Map 26.
Clare, par. and market town, W. Suffolk, 7 m. W.N.W. of Sudbury; pop. 1340. Map 62.
Clare, town and ry. sta. (**C. Castle**), mid co. Clare, 2 m. S.E. of Ennis; pop. 538. Map 94.
Clavering, par., Essex., 6½ m. S.W. of Saffron Walden; pop. 799. Map 61.
Claybrook, vil., Leicestershire, 3½ m. N.W. of Lutterworth. Map 49.
Clay Cross, urb. dist., Derbyshire, 4½ m. S. of Chesterfield; pop. 8493. Map 41.
Claydon, par. and vil., E. Suffolk, 5 m. N.W. of Ipswich; pop. 613. Map 63.
Claypole, par. and vil., Kesteven, Lincolnshire, 4 m. S.E. of Newark; pop. 547. Map 42.
Clayton, urb. dist and par., Yorkshire 3½ m. S.W. of Bradford; pop. 5043. Map 31.
Clayton-le-Moor, urb. dist. and par., N.E. Lancashire, 5½ m. N.E. of Blackburn; pop. 7910. Map 31.
Clayton, West, urb. dist., W.R. Yorkshire, 12 m. S.E. of Huddersfield; pop. 1846. Map 32.
Cleator, par. and urb. dist. (**C. Moor**), Cumberland, 4¼ m. S.E. of Whitehaven; pop. 6582. Map 24.
Cleckheaton, W.R. Yorkshire, 5½ m. S.E. of Bradford, now part of Spenborough. Map 32.
Cleethorpes, urb. dist. and par., ry. terminus, N. Lincs, 2¼ m. S.E. of Gt. Grimsby; pop. 28,624. Map 43.
Cleobury Mortimer, market town, Salop, 7 m. N.E. of Tenbury; pop. 1487. Map 57.
Clevedon, seaside town and par., N.W. Somersetshire, 15¼ m. W.S.W. of Bristol; pop. 7033. Map 74.
Cliddesden, par. and vil., N. Hants, 3 m. S. of Basingstoke; pop. 316. Map 78.
Clifden, seaport and market town, in co. and 49 m. N.W. of Galway; pop. 809. Map 92.
Cliffe, par. and vil., N. Kent, 5½ m. E.N.E. of Gravesend; pop. 2581. Map 72.
Clifford, par. and vil., Herefordshire, 2¼ m. N.E. of Hay; pop. 729. Map 56.

Clifton, par. and vil., N. Lancashire, 3 m. S.E. of Kirkham; pop. 460. Map 30.

Clifton, par. and vil., Westmorland, 2½ m. S.E. of Penrith; pop. 397. Map 21.

Clifton, watering place, forming W. suburb of Bristol. Map 68.

Clifton, par., N.R. Yorkshire, 1 m. N. of York city; pop. 808. Map 33.

Clitheroe, mun. bor. and market town, N.E. Lancashire, 10½ m. N.E. of Blackburn; pop. 12,008. Map 31.

Cloghan, vil. and ry. sta., Offaly co., 5 m. N.E. of Banagher; pop. 256. Map 95.

Clogheen, market town, Tipperary, 8 m. S. of Cahir ry. sta.; pop. 734. Map 95.

Clonakilty, urb. dist. and seaport, co. Cork, 13 m. S.W. of Bandon; pop. 2771. Map 94.

Clones, urb. dist. and market town, co. Monaghan, 39½ m. N.W. of Dundalk; pop. 2358. Map 93.

Clonmel, mun. bor., cos. Tipperary and Waterford, 28 m. N.W. of Waterford; pop. 8989. Map 95.

Clophill, par. and vil., Bedfordshire, 3½ m. E. of Ampthill; pop. 909. Map 60.

Clovelly, coast par. and vil., Devonshire, 11 m. S.W. of Bideford; pop. 634. Map 84.

Clovenfords, ham., N.E. Selkirkshire, 3½ m. W. of Galashiels. Map 16.

Clun, market town and par., Salop, 5½ m. N.N.E. of Knighton; pop. 1774. Map 56.

Clydach-on-Tawe, vil. and ry. sta., Glamorganshire, 5 m. N. of Swansea. Map 66.

Clydebank, police bur., Dumbartonshire, 6¼ m. N.W. of Glasgow; pop. 46,963. Map 8.

Clynderwen, vil. and ry. sta., Pembroke and Carmarthen, 6½ m. E. of Clarbeston Road sta. Map 64.

Coalville, urb. dist. and par., Leicestershire, 5 m. S.E. of Ashby-de-la-Zouch; pop. 21,886. Map 49.

Coatbridge, mun. bur., Lanarkshire, 8¾ m. E. of Glasgow; pop. 43,056. Map 9.

Cobh (Queenstown), seaport town, in co. and 13 m. S.E. of Cork; pop. 7070. Map 94.

Cobham, or **Church Cobham**, par. and vil., Surrey, 6½ m. W. of Epsom; pop. 5103. Map 78.

Cockburnspath, par. and vil., Berwickshire, 7½ m. S.E. of Dunbar; pop. 941. Map 11.

Cockenzie and Port Seton, seaport, E. Lothian, 9¾ m. E. of Edinburgh; pop. 2526. Map 10.

Cockerham, par. and vil., N. Lancashire, 6 m. S. of Lancaster; pop. 569. Map 30.

Cockermouth, urb. dist. and par., Cumberland, 32 m. S.W. of Carlisle; pop. 4789. Map 20.

Cockfield, par. and vil., Durham, 7 m. N.E. of Barnard Castle; pop. 2693. Map 22.

Cockfield, par., W. Suffolk, 7 m. S.E. of Bury St Edmunds; pop. 816. Map 62.

Cocking, par. and vil., W. Sussex, 2½ m. S. of Midhurst; pop. 427. Map 79.

Coddenham, par. and vil., E. Suffolk, 3 m. E. of Needham Market; pop. 671. Map 63.

Coggeshall, town, Essex, 6 m. E. of Braintree; pop. of par. (**Great C.**) 2300. Map 72.

Colbury, par. and vil., Hants, 3 m. N.E. of Lyndhurst; pop. 1066. Map 77.

Colby, vil., Isle of Man, 3 m. N.W. of Castletown. Map 24.

Colchester, mun. bor. and river-port, Essex, 22 m. N.E. of Chelmsford; pop. 48,607. Map 73.

Coldingham, par. and vil., Berwickshire, 3 m. N.W. of Eyemouth; pop. 2830. Map 11.

Coldstream, police bur. and par., Berwickshire, 13½ m. S.W. of Berwick-on-Tweed; pop. 1233. Map 16.

Coleford, urb. dist. and par., Gloucestershire, 4½ m. E.S.E. of Monmouth; pop. 2777. Map 68.

Coleraine, seaport, urb. dist. and par., in co. and 33½ m. N.E. of Londonderry; pop. 7785. Map 93.

Colerne, par. and vil., N. Wiltshire, 8 m. W.S.W. of Chippenham; pop. 912. Map 75.

Coleshill, market town and par., Warwickshire, 8½ m. E.N.E. of Birmingham; pop. 3177. Map 48.

Colinsburgh, vil., Fifeshire, 2 m. N.W. of Kilconquhar sta.; pop. 304. Map 7.

Colinton, eccl. par., in S.W. of city of Edinburgh; pop. 4778. Map 10.

Coll Island, par., Argyllshire, 9½ m. W.S.W. of Ardnamurchan Point; pop. 383. Map 2.

Collace, par. and vil., in co. and 8 m. N.E. of Perth; pop. 349. Map 6.

Collessie, par. and vil., Fifeshire, 2½ m. N.W. of Ladybank Junction; pop. 2014. Map 6.

Collingbourne Ducis, par. and vil., Wiltshire, 2½ m. N.W. of Ludgershall; pop. 366. Map 76.

Collingbourne Kingston, par. and vil., Wiltshire, 3½ m. N.W. of Ludgershall; pop. 669. Map 76.

Collingham, vil., Nottinghamshire, 5½ m. N.E. of Newark. Map 42.

Collooney, vil., in co. and 6½ m. S. of Sligo; pop. 330. Map 92.

Colne, mun. bor., market town and par., N.E. Lancashire, 5¼ m. N.E. of Burnley; pop. 23,790. Map 31.

Coln St Aldwyn, par. and vil., Gloucestershire, 6½ m. S.E. of Northleach; pop. 325. Map 69.

Colsterworth, par. and vil., Kesteven, Lincolnshire, 7½ m. S. of Grantham; pop. 764. Map 50.

Coltishall, par. and vil., Norfolk, 8 m. N.E. of Norwich; pop. 955. Map 53.

Colwyn Bay, watering place with ry. sta., Denbighshire, 6 m. W. of Abergele; pop. 20,885. Map 37.

Colyton, market town and par., Devonshire, 2¾ m. N. of Seaton; pop. 1886. Map 86.

Combe Martin, coast par. and vil., N. Devonshire, 5 m. E. of Ilfracombe; pop. 2004. Map 84.

Combe St Nicholas, par. and vil., Somersetshire, 2 m. N.W. of Chard; pop. 929. Map 86.

Commercial, ham., Pembrokeshire, 3 m. N.E. of Narberth. Map 64.

Compstall, urb. dist., Cheshire, 5 m. E. of Stockport; pop. 865. Map 40.

Compton, par. and vil., W. Sussex, 6 m. S.E. of Petersfield; pop. 249. Map 79.

Comrie, par. and town, Perthshire, 6¾ m. W. of Crieff; pop. 2208. Map 5.

Congleton, mun. bor., mkt. town and par., E. Cheshire, 8½ m. S.S.W. of Macclesfield; pop. 12,885. Map 39.

Congresbury, par. and vil., N.W. Somersetshire, on r. Yeo, 11½ m. S.W. of Bristol; pop. 1258. Map 74.

Coningsby, par. and vil., Lindsey, Lincolnshire, 7 m. S.S.W. of Horncastle; pop. 1031. Map 43.

Conisborough, urb. dist., W.R. Yorkshire, 5 m. S.W. of Doncaster; pop. 18,179. Map 41.

Coniston, par., vil. and lake, Lancashire, 6 m. N.W. of Ambleside; pop. 1098. Map 25.

Connah's Quay, par. and urb. dist. on Dee estuary, in co. and 3½ m. S.E. of Flint; pop. 5982. Map 38.

Connel Ferry, vil. and ry. sta., Argyllshire, 6 m. N.E. of Oban; pop. 458. Map 12.

Consett, urb. dist. and par., Durham, 12 m. S.W. of Newcastle; pop. 12,251. Map 22.

Conway, market town and spt., Carnarvonshire, 3½ m. S. of Llandudno; pop. 8769. Map 37.

Conwil Elvet, par. and vil., in co. and 5¼ m. N.N.W. of Carmarthen; pop. 1225. Map 65.

Cookham, par. and vil., Berkshire, 3 m. N. of Maidenhead; pop. 5848. Map 70.

Coombe Bissett, par., S. Wiltshire, 3 m. S.W. of Salisbury; pop. 248. Map 76.

Cootehill, urb. dist., co. Cavan, 33½ m. N.W. of Dundalk; pop. 1534. Map 93.

Corbridge, par. and town, Northumberland, 3½ m. E. of Hexham; pop. 2415. Map 22.

Corby, par. and vil., Kesteven, Lincolnshire, 8 m. S.E. of Grantham; pop. 664. Map 50.

Corby, par. and vil., Northants, 7½ m. N. of Kettering. Map 50.
Corfe, par. and vil., Somersetshire, 3½ m. S. of Taunton; pop. 230. Map 86.
Corfe Castle, par. and town, Isle of Purbeck, Dorsetshire, 6 m. S.E. of Wareham; pop. 1402. Map 87.
Cork, seaport, mun. bor. and co. town of Cork, 166½ m. S.W. of Dublin by rail; pop. 78,468. Map 94.
Cornhill, par. and vil., Northumberland, adjoining Coldstream. Map 17.
Cornworthy, par. and vil., Devonshire, 4 m. S.E. of Totnes; pop. 355. Map 89.
Corpusty, par. and vil., Norfolk, 5 m. N.W. of Aylsham; pop. 424. Map 53.
Corsham, market town and par., N. Wiltshire, 4¼ m. S.W. of Chippenham; pop. 3940. Map 68.
Corwen, market town and par., Merionethshire, 11 m. N.E. of Bala; pop. 2690. Map 37.
Coseley, urb. dist., Staffordshire, 2¾ m. S.E. of Wolverhampton; pop. 25,137. Map 47.
Cosgrove, par. and vil., Northamptonshire, 1½ m. N. of Stony Stratford; pop. 584. Map 60.
Cosheston, par. and vil., in co. and 2 m. N.E. of Pembroke; pop. 508. Map 64.
Cotherstone, par. and ham., N.R. Yorkshire, 3½ m. N.W. of Barnard Castle; pop. 701. Map 27.
Cotmanhay, eccl. dist. and ham., Derbyshire, 1½ m. N. of Ilkeston; pop. 6636. Map 49.
Cottenham, par. and vil., in co. and 6½ m. N. of Cambridge; pop. 2470. Map 61.
Cottesmore, par. and vil., Rutlandshire, 4½ m. N.E. of Oakham; pop. 363. Map 50.
Cottingham, urb. dist. and par., E.R. Yorkshire, 4 m. N.W. of Hull; pop. 6182. Map 35.
Coulsdon and Purley, urb. dist., Surrey, 5 m. S. of Croydon; pop. 37,666. Map 80.
County School, ry. sta., Norfolk, 6 m. N. of East Dereham. Map 52.
Coupar-Angus, police bur. and par., in co. and 15¾ m. N.E. of Perth; pop. 1883. Map 6.
Cove and Kilcreggan, bur. and wtg. place, Dumbartonshire, 4½ m. N.W. of Greenock; pop. 954. Map 12.
Coventry, city, parl. and co. bor., Warwickshire, 19 m. S.E. of Birmingham; pop. 167,046. Map 58.
Cowbit, par. and vil., Holland, Lincolnshire, 3½ m. S. of Spalding; pop. 528. Map 51.
Cowbridge, mun. bor., Glamorganshire, 12¼ m. W. of Cardiff; pop. 1018. Map 66.
Cowden, Great, par., E.R. Yorkshire, 4 m. S.E. of Hornsea; pop. (with **Little Cowden**) 102. Map 35.
Cowdenbeath, police bur., Fifeshire, 5¾ m. N.E. of Dunfermline; pop. 12,731. Map 10.
Cowes, urb. dist. and seaport, Isle of Wight, 4½ m. N. of Newport; pop. 10,179, **E. Cowes** 4595. Map 77.
Cowie, mining vil., 4 m. S.E. of Stirling. Map 9.
Coxwell, Great, par., Berkshire, 1½ m. S.W. of Faringdon; pop. 259. Map 69.
Coxwold, par. and vil., N.R. Yorkshire, 7½ m. S.E. of Thirsk; pop. 251. Map 28.
Craigendoran, pier, Dumbartonshire, 1 m. E. of Helensburgh. Map 8.
Crail, seaport and bur., Fifeshire, 11 m. S.E. of St Andrews; pop. 1058. Map 7.
Crailing, par. and vil., Roxburghshire, 3½ m. N.E. of Jedburgh; pop. 488. Map 16.
Cramlington, urb. dist. and par., Northumberland, 7 m. S.E. of Morpeth; pop. 8238. Map 23.
Cranborne, par. and vil., Dorsetshire, 10 m. N.E. of Wimborne Minster; pop. 657. Map 87.
Cranbrook, market town and par., Kent, 4 m. N. of Hawkhurst; pop. 3829. Map 82.
Cranford, vil. and ry. sta., Northamptonshire, 4½ m. E.S.E. of Kettering. Map 60.
Cranleigh, par. and vil., W. Surrey, 8 m. S.E. of Guildford; pop. 3746. Map 79.
Cranswick, vil., E.R. Yorkshire, 3 m. S. of Great Driffield. Map 35.
Cranwell, par., vil., Kesteven, Lincolnshire, 4 m. N.W. of Sleaford; pop. 2191. Map 42.
Craven Arms and Stokesay, ry. junct., Salop, 7 m. S. of Church Stretton. Map 56.
Crawford, par. and vil., Lanarkshire, 2¾ m. S.E. of Abington; pop. 2041. Map 14.
Crawley, par. and vil., W. Sussex, 7 m. N.E. of Horsham; pop. 453. Map 81.
Crawley, par. and vil., N. Hants, 5½ m. N.W. of Winchester; pop. 563. Map 76.
Crayford, urb. dist., Kent, 15½ m. S.E. of London; pop. 15,887. Map 80.
Creake, North, par., Norfolk, 3 m. S.E. of Burnham Market; pop. 499. Map 52.
Creake, South, par., Norfolk, 3½ m. S. of Burnham Market; pop. 658. Map 52.
Crediton, urb. dist. and par., Devonshire, 7½ m. N.W. of Exeter; pop. 3490. Map 85.
Creeslough, coast vil. and ry. sta., co. Donegal, 20 m. N.W. of Letterkenny; pop. 150. Map 92.
Creetown, seaport, Kirkcudbrightshire, 6½ m. S.E. of Newton Stewart; pop. 757. Map 19.
Cressingham, Great and **Little**, 2 pars., Norfolk, 4 m. W. of Watton; pop. 286 and 197. Map 52.
Crewe, mun. bor., Cheshire, 24½ m. N.W. of Stafford; pop. 46,061. Map 39.
Crewkerne, urb. dist. and par., Somersetshire, 8 m. S.W. of Yeovil; pop. 3509. Map 86.
Crianlarich, vil. and ry. station, Perthshire, 28¾ m. N.W. of Callander. Map 12.
Criccieth, par. and urb. dist., Carnarvonshire, 4 m. W.S.W. of Portmadoc; pop. 1449. Map 44.
Crich, par. and mining vil., N. Derbyshire, 4 m. W.S.W. of Alfreton; pop. 3056. Map 41.
Crickhowel, market town and par., Brecon, 14½ m. S.E. of Brecknock; pop. 1307. Map 67.
Cricklade, market town and par., Wiltshire, 8½ m. N.W. of Swindon; pop. 1425. Map 69.
Crieff, police bur. and par., in co. and 17¾ m. W. of Perth; pop. 5544. Map 6.
Cringleford, par. and vil., Norfolk, 3 m. S.W. of Norwich; pop. 261. Map 53.
Croesgoch, vil., Pembrokeshire, 6 m. N.E. of St Davids. Map 64.
Croft, par. and vil., N.R. Yorkshire, 3 m. S. of Darlington; pop. 509. Map 27.
Crofton, par. and seat, W.R. Yorkshire, 3¾ m. S.E. of Wakefield; pop. 2817. Map 33.
Cromarty, mun. bur., par. and seaport, Ross and Crom., 15½ m. N.E. of Inverness; pop. 837. Map 3.
Cromer, urb. dist. and watering place, Norfolk, 24 m. N. of Norwich; pop. 4177. Map 53.
Crompton, urb. dist., Lancashire, 3 m. N. of Oldham; pop. 14,750. Map 31.
Crook, urb. dist. and par., Durham, 6 m. N.W. of Bishop Auckland; pop. 11,690. Map 23.
Crookham, vil., Northumberland, 8½ m. N.W. of Wooler. Map 17.
Crooklands, ham., Westmorland, 6 m. S.E. of Kendal. Map 26.
Crook of Devon, vil., on r. Devon, in co. and 6 m. S.W. of Kinross. Map 6.
Croom, par. and town, in co. and 12½ m. S.W. of Limerick; pop. of par. 2038. Map 94.
Cropredy, par. and vil., Oxon, 3½ m. N. of Banbury; pop. 409. Map 59.
Crosby Ravensworth, par., N. Westmorland, 6 m. S.W. of Appleby; pop. 722. Map 26.
Crossford, vil., Lanarkshire, 3 m. S.W. of Carluke. Map 9.
Crossgates, mining vil., Fifeshire, 3½ m. N.E. of Dunfermline; pop. 2602. Map 10.

Cross Hands, vil., Carmarthenshire, 4½ m. W. of Ammanford. Map 65.

Cross Keys, ham. and ry. sta., Monmouthshire, 8 m. N.W. of Newport. Map 67.

Crossmolina, market town and par., co. Mayo, 7 m. W. of Ballina; pop. 4065. Map 92.

Croston, urb. dist. and par., S.W. Lancashire, 8 m. N.E. of Ormskirk; pop. 1935. Map 30.

Crowborough, par. and vil., E. Sussex, 7 m. N.E. of Uckfield; pop. 5846. Map 82.

Crowland, market town, Holland, Lincolnshire, 8 m. N.E. of Peterborough; pop. 2707. Map 51.

Crowland, vil., W. Suffolk, 5 m. E. of Ixworth. Map 62.

Crowle, urb. dist. and par., Lincolnshire, 6 m. E. of Thorne; pop. 2833. Map 33.

Crowthorne, par. and vil., Berkshire, 2½ m. S.E. of Wokingham; pop. 3980. Map 78.

Croxleygreen, eccl. par., S.W. Hertfordshire, 2 m. S.W. of Watford; pop. 2649. Map 71.

Croxton, eccl. dist. and ham., Staffordshire, 3 m. N.W. of Eccleshall; pop. 548. Map 47.

Croydon, mun. bor., N.E. Surrey, 10 m. S. of London Bridge; pop. 233,115. Map 80.

Cruden Bay, watering-place, Aberdeenshire, 8 m. S.S.W. of Peterhead. Map 3.

Crymmych Arms, vil. with ry. sta., Pembrokeshire, 11 m. S. of Cardigan. Map 65.

Cuckfield, urb. dist. and par., E. Sussex, 14 m. N. of Brighton; pop. 2114. Map 81.

Cudworth, urb. dist. and par., W.R. Yorkshire, 4¼ m. N.E. of Barnsley; pop. 9380. Map 33.

Culdaff, coast par. and vil., Donegal, 5 m. N.E. of Carndonagh; pop. 3075. Map 93.

Culgaith, par., E. Cumberland, 7 m. N.W. of Appleby; pop. 313. Map 21.

Cullen, mun. bur., par. and seaport, Banffshire, 5½ m. W.N.W. of Portsoy; pop. of bur. 1688. Map 3.

Cullercoats, eccl. dist. and ry. sta., in Tynemouth bor., Northumberland; pop. 5063. Map 23.

Culloden Moor, pl. with ry. sta., in co. and 7 m. E. of Inverness. Map 3.

Cullompton, market town and par., Devonshire, 12½ m. N.E. of Exeter; pop. 2737. Map 85.

Culmington, par. and vil., Salop, 5 m. N.N.W. of Ludlow; pop. 483. Map 56.

Culmstock, par. and vil., Devonshire, 9¾ m. N.E. of Tiverton; pop. 760. Map 85.

Culross, royal and mun. bur. and small seaport, Fifeshire, 7½ m. S.E. of Alloa; pop. 495. Map 9.

Cumbernauld, par. and vil., Dumbartonshire, 13 m. N.E. of Glasgow; pop. 5261. Map 9.

Cumbrae Islands, Buteshire, in Firth of Clyde. Map 8.

Cummertrees, par. and vil., Dumfriesshire, 3¼ m. W. of Annan; pop. 1084. Map 20.

Cumnock, par. and police bur., on r. Lugar, in co. and 16 m. E. of Ayr; pop. 3653. Map 12.

Cumwhitton, par. and vil., N.E. Cumberland, 6½ m. S.E. of Carlisle; pop. 444. Map 21.

Cupar, par., mun. bur. and co. town of Fifeshire, 44½ m. N.E. of Edinburgh by rail; pop. 4596. Map 7.

Curdworth, par. and vil., Warwickshire, 2½ m. N.N.W. of Coleshill; pop. 413. Map 48.

Cushendall, coast vil., co. Antrim, 17 m. N.E. of Ballymena; pop. 306. Map 93.

Cushendun, coast vil., co. Antrim, 4 m. N. of Cushendall. Map 93.

Cwmaman, vil. and ry. sta., Glamorganshire, 2 m. S. of Aberdare. Map 66.

Cwmamman, urb. dist., Carmarthenshire, 4 m. E.N.E. of Ammanford; pop. 5214. Map 66.

Cwmbach, vil., Glamorganshire, 2 m. E. of Aberdare. Map 66.

Cwm-bran, vil., Monmouthshire, 3½ m. S. of Pontypool. Map 67.

Cwm-felin-fach, ham., Monmouthshire, 1¼ m. W.N.W. of N ne M le Point ry. sta. Map 7.

DAGENHAM, par. and urb. dist., Essex, 3 m. E. of Barking; pop. 89,365. Map 72.

Dalbeattie, police bur., Kirkcudbrightshire, 5¼ m. E. of Castle Douglas; pop. 3011. Map 19.

Dalby, vil., Isle of Man, 4 m. S. of Peel. Map 24.

Dale End, vil., N.R. Yorkshire, 6 m. W.N.W. of Egton. Map 28.

Dalkeith, police bur. and par., Midlothian, 6½ m. S.E. of Edinburgh; pop. 7502. Map 10.

Dalkey, urb. dist. and par., in co. and 9 m. S.E. of Dublin; pop. 4135. Map 93.

Dalmally, vil. and ry. sta., Argyllshire, 24½ m. E. of Oban. Map 12.

Dalmellington, par. and vil., in co. and 15 m. S.E. of Ayr; pop. 6155. Map 12.

Dalmeny, par. and vil., West Lothian, 9½ m. N.W. of Edinburgh; pop. 4557. Map 10.

Dalry, par. and town, Ayrshire, 3½ m. N. of Kilwinning; pop. 7243. Map 12.

Dalserf, par. and vil., Lanarkshire, 7 m. S.E. of Hamilton; pop. 19,465. Map 9.

Dalston, par., N.E. Cumberland, 4½ m. S.W. of Carlisle; pop. 1746. Map 21.

Dalton, par. and vil., Dumfriesshire, 6 m. S.S.W. of Lockerbie; pop. 548. Map 20.

Dalton-in-Furness, urb. dist. and par., Lancashire, 3½ m. N.E. of Barrow-in-Furness; pop. 10,338. Map 25.

Danby Wiske, par. and vil., N.R. Yorkshire, 3½ m. N.W. of Northallerton; pop. 297. Map 28.

Darfield, urb. dist., W.R. Yorkshire, 5 m. E.S.E. of Barnsley; pop. 5268. Map 33.

Darlaston, urb. dist., Staffordshire, within Wednesbury; pop. 19,736. Map 47.

Darleydale, locality, Derbyshire, in N. Derby urb. dist. Map 40.

Darlington, parl. and co. bor., market town and par., S. Durham, 9½ m. W.S.W. of Stockton-on-Tees; pop. 72,093. Map 27.

Darliston, ham., Salop, on r. Tern, 5½ m. N.E. of Wem. Map 46.

Dartford, urb. dist. and market town, W. Kent, 6¼ m. W. of Gravesend; pop. 28,928. Map 80.

Dartmoor Forest, upland tract, Devonshire, from Brent to Okehampton. Maps 88, 89.

Dartmouth, mun. bor., par. and seaport, Devonshire, opposite Kingswear; pop. 6707. Map 89.

Darton, urb. dist., W.R. Yorkshire, 3½ m. N.W. of Barnsley; pop. 12,595. Map 32.

Darvel, town, Ayrshire, 9 m. E. of Kilmarnock; pop. 3232. Map 12.

Darwen, mun. bor., mkt. and mfg. town, par., N.E. Lancs, 4 m. S. of Blackburn; pop. 36,010. Map 31.

Darwen, Lower, eccl. dist., N.E. Lancashire, 1½ m. S. of Blackburn; pop. 1874. Map 31.

Datchet, par. and vil., S. Buckinghamshire, on r. Thames, 2 m. E. of Windsor; pop. 2406. Map 78.

Daventry, mun. bor. and par., in co. and 12 m. W.N.W. of Northampton; pop. 3608. Map 59.

Dawley, urb. dist. and par., Salop, 4 m. S.E. of Wellington; pop. 7363. Map 47.

Dawlish, urb. dist., Devonshire, 3 m. N.E. of Teignmouth; pop. 4578. Map 89.

Deal, mun. bor., par. and Cinque port, Kent, 8 m. N.E. of Dover; pop. 13,680. Map 83.

Dearham, par. and vil., Cumberland, 7½ m. N.W. of Cockermouth; pop. 2075. Map 20.

Debenham, par. and market town, E. Suffolk, 8 m. S. of Eye; pop. 1085. Map 63.

Deddington, market town and par., Oxon, 6 m. S. of Banbury; pop. 1339. Map 59.

Deeping St Nicholas, par. and vil., Holland, Lincolnshire, 4½ m. S.W. of Spalding; pop. 1540. Map 51.

Deganwy, ry. sta., Denbighshire, 1 m. N.W. of Llandudno Junction. **D. Castle** in vicinity. Map 37.

Delph, vil., W.R. Yorkshire, 6 m. N.E. of Ashton-under-Lyne. Map 31.

Denbigh, mun. bor., market town and par., Denbighshire, 29½ m. W. of Chester; pop. 7249. Map 37.

Denby and Cumberworth, urb. dist., W.R. Yorkshire, 8 m. W. of Barnsley; pop. 3396. Map 32.

Denholm, vil., Roxburghshire, 5 m. N.E. of Hawick; pop. 384. Map 16.

Denholme, urb. dist., par. and ham., W.R. Yorkshire, 6½ m. W. of Bradford; pop. 2662. Map 31.

Denny, town and par., in co. and 12 m. S. of Stirling; pop. of par. 5512. Map 9.

Dennyloanhead, vil. and ry. sta., Stirlingshire, 1¾ m. S. of Denny; pop. 3378. Map 9.

Dent, par. and vil., W.R. Yorkshire, 5 m. S.E. of Sedbergh; pop. 996. Map 26.

Denton, urb. dist. and par., Lancashire, 7 m. E.S.E. of Manchester; pop. 17,383. Map 39.

Denwick, par. and vil., Northumberland, 1½ m. N.E. of Alnwick; pop. 668. Map 17.

Derby, parl. and co. bor., cap. of Derbyshire, 42½ m. N.E. of Birmingham; pop. 142,406. Map 48.

Dereham, East, urb. dist. and par., Norfolk, 16 m. W.N.W. of Norwich; pop. 5641. Map 52.

Derwent, par., N. Derbyshire, on r. Derwent, 5 m. N.E. of Castleton; pop. 174. Map 40.

Derwent Water, lake, in basin of r. Derwent, Cumberland. Map 20.

Desborough, urb. dist. and par., Northamptonshire, 5½ m. S.E. of Market Harborough; pop. 4407. Map 60.

Devil's Bridge, ham. and ry. sta., Cardiganshire, 11¾ m. E.S.E. of Aberystwyth. Map 55.

Devil's Elbow, crook on road over the Grampians, 9½ m. S. of Braemar. Map 3.

Devizes, mun. bor., N. Wiltshire, 25½ m. N.W. of Salisbury; pop. 6058. Map 75.

Devonport, dist. in Plymouth, Devonshire. Map 88.

Dewsbury, co. and parl. bor., mkt. town and par., W.R. Yorkshire, 9¼ m. S. of Leeds; pop. 54,303. Map 32.

Dibden, par. and vil., Hants, 1 m. W.N.W. of Hythe; pop. 2144. Map 77.

Diddlebury, par., Salop, 6½ m. N. of Ludlow; pop. 727. Map 56.

Didmarton, par. and ham., Gloucestershire, 5½ m. S.W. of Tetbury; pop. 318. Map 68.

Didsbury, ward in S. Manchester. Map 39.

Digby, par. and vil., Kesteven, Lincolnshire, 6 m. N. of Sleaford; pop. 368. Map 42.

Dilton Marsh, par., S. Wiltshire, 5 m. S. of Trowbridge; pop. 1525. Map 75.

Dinas, coast par. and vil., Pembrokeshire, 3½ m. N.E. of Fishguard; pop. 691. Map 64.

Dinas, ham., in co. and 3 m. S. of Carnarvon. Map 36.

Dinas Mawddwy, market town, Merionethshire, 10 m. S.E. of Dolgelley. Map 45.

Dinas Powis, vil., Glamorganshire, 6 m. S.W. of Cardiff. Map 67.

Dingle, seaport town and par., co. Kerry, 31¼ m. S.W. of Tralee; pop. of town 1998. Map 94.

Dingwall, mun. bur., par. and cap. of Ross and Cromarty, 18½ m. N.W. of Inverness; pop. 2554. Map 3.

Dinnington, par. and vil., Northumberland, 6½ m. N.N.W. of Newcastle; pop. 1078. Map 23.

Dinorwic, vil., 1½ m. N.E. of Llanberis, co. Carnarvon; slate quarries. Map 36.

Dirleton, coast par. and vil., E. Lothian, 20¼ m. E.N.E. of Edinburgh; pop. 2623. Map 10.

Diss, urb. dist. and par., Norfolk, 20 m. S.W. of Norwich; pop. 3422. Map 63.

Distington, par. and vil., Cumberland, 3½ m. S. of Workington; pop. 2093. Map 20.

Ditchingham, par. and vil., Norfolk, 1½ m. N. of Bungay; pop. 997. Map 53.

Ditchling, par. and vil., E. Sussex, 6 m. N. of Brighton; pop. 1414. Map 81.

Ditton Priors, par. and vil., Salop, 7½ m. S.W. of Bridgnorth; pop. 650. Map 47.

Docking, par. and vil., Norfolk, 5¾ m. S.W. of Burnham Market; pop. 1127. Map 52.

Dodworth, urb. dist., W.R. Yorkshire, 2 m. S.W. of Barnsley; pop. 4248. Map 33.

Dolgarrog, par., Carnarvonshire, 7½ m. S. of Conway; pop. 364. Map 37.

Dolgelley, urb. dist. and par., Merionethshire, 9¼ m. E. of Barmouth; pop. 2261. Map 43.

Dollar, police bur. and par., Clackmannanshire, 6½ m. N.E. of Alloa; pop. 1485. Map 9.

Dolphinton, par., Lanarkshire, 11 m. N.E. of Carstairs; pop. 252. Map 9.

Dolton, par. and vil., Devonshire, 7 m. N.E. of Hatherleigh; pop. 359. Map 84.

Dolyhir, ry. sta., Radnorshire, 2½ m. S.E. of New Radnor. Map 56.

Donaghadee, seaport town and par., co. Down, 21½ m. E. of Belfast; pop. of par. 4878. Map 93.

Doncaster, mun. bor., mkt. tn. and par., W.R. Yorks, on r. Don, 32 m. S. of York; pop. 63,308. Map 41.

Donegal, spt., par. and cap. of co. Donegal, 18 m. S.W. of Stranorlar; pop. of town 1104. Map 92.

Donington, par. and vil., Kesteven, Lincolnshire, 8½ m. N.N.W. of Spalding; pop. 1604. Map 51.

Donnington, market town, Salop, 3½ m. S.W. of New port. Map 47.

Dorchester, mun. bor. and capital of Dorsetshire, 6 m. N. of Weymouth; pop. 10,030. Map 87.

Dorking, urb. dist. and par., Surrey, 5½ m. S.W. of Reigate; pop. 10,109. Map 78.

Dornoch, mun. bur., spt. and capital of Sutherlandshire, 8¾ m. N.E. of Tain; pop. 725. Map 3.

Dornock, par. and vil., Dumfriesshire, 3 m. E. of Annan; pop. 2475. Map 20.

Dorrington, par. and vil., Kesteven, Lincolnshire, 5 m. N. of Sleaford; pop. 410. Map 42.

Douglas, spt. and mkt. tn., cap. of I. of Man, 10¾ m. N.E. of Castletown; pop. 27,604. Map 24.

Doune, police bur., Perthshire, 8¾ m. N.W. of Stirling; pop. 822. Map 9.

Dove Holes, vil., N.W. Derbyshire, 3 m. N.N.W. of Buxton. Map 40.

Dover, mun. bor., par. and Cinque port, Kent, 78½ m. S.E. of London by rail; pop. 41,095. Map 83.

Dovercourt, par., Essex, in Harwich mun. bor.; pop. 7695. Map 73.

Dowally, vil., Perthshire, 4½ m. N.W. of Dunkeld. Map 6.

Dowlais, colliery and iron dist., Glamorganshire, round Merthyr-Tydfil. Map 66.

Downend, eccl. par. and vil., S.E. Gloucestershire, 4½ m. N.E. of Bristol; pop. 9448. Map 68.

Downham Market, urb. dist. and par., Norfolk, 11 m. S. of King's Lynn; pop. 2463. Map 51.

Downholland, par. and ry. sta., Lancashire, 6½ m. S.E. of Southport; pop. 618. Map 30.

Downpatrick, market town and cap. of co. Down, 27 m. S.E. of Belfast; pop. 3199. Map 93.

Downton, town and par., Wiltshire, 7 m. S.E. of Salisbury; pop. 1906. Map 77.

Drayton, par. and vil., Norfolk, 4½ m. N.W. of Norwich; pop. 557. Map 53.

Drigg, par. and ham., Cumberland, 2 m. N.W. o Ravenglass; pop. 446. Map 25.

Drighlington, urb. dist., par. and vil., W.R. York shire, 6½ m. S.E. of Bradford; pop. 4064. Map 32.

Drogheda, mun. bor. and seaport, co. Louth, 32 m. N. of Dublin; pop. 12,688. Map 93.

Droitwich, mun. bor., in co. and 6 m. N.E. of Wor cester; pop. 4553. Map 57.

Dromcolliher, par. and vil., co. Limerick, 10 m. S.E. of Newcastle; pop. 948. Map 94.

Dromore, urb. dist. and par., co. Down, 17½ m. S.W. of Belfast; pop. of town, 2364. Map 93.

Dronfield, urb. dist. and par., E. Derbyshire, 6 m. N.W. of Chesterfield; pop. 4530. Map 41.

Dronfield Woodhouse, par., E. Derbyshire, 2 m. N. of Dronfield; pop. 902. Map 41.

Droylsden, urb. dist. and par., S.E. Lancs, 4¾ m. N.E. of Manchester; pop. 13,277. Map 40.

Drymen, par. and vil., in co. and 23½ m. S.W. of Stirling; vil. pop. 279. Map 8.

Dublin (Baile Atha Cliath), city co. bor. and spt., on Dublin Bay, cap. of Ireland, 112¾ m. by rail S. of Belfast; pop., with environs, 419,176. Map 93.

Ducklington, par. and vil., Oxon, 1½ m. S. of Witney; pop. 386. Map 69.

Dudley, parl. and co. bor., Worcestershire, 8 m. N.W. of Birmingham; pop. 59,579. Map 48.

Dufftown, police bur., Banffshire, 64 m. N.W. of Aberdeen; pop. 1454. Map 3.

Dukeries Junction, sta. adjoining Tuxford, Nottinghamshire, 6½ m. S.E. of Retford. Map 41.

Dukinfield, mun. bor. and par., Cheshire, 1½ m. W.S.W. of Stalybridge; pop. 19,309. Map 40.

Duleek, par. and vil., co. Meath, 4¾ m. S.W. of Drogheda; pop. 1810. Map 93.

Dulverton, par. and market town, W. Somersetshire, 20 m. W. of Taunton; pop. 1298. Map 85.

Dumbarton, mun. bur., par. and cap. of Dumbartonshire, 15½ m. N.W. of Glasgow; pop. 21,546. Map 12.

Dumfries, bur., par. and cap. of Dumfriesshire, 33 m. N.W. of Carlisle; pop. 22,795. Map 20.

Dunbar, mun. bur., par. and seaport, E. Lothian, 29¼ m. E. of Edinburgh; pop. 3751. Map 11.

Dunblane, police bur. and par., Perthshire, 5 m. N. of Stirling; pop. 2692. Map 9.

Dunchurch, par. and vil., Warwickshire, 2 m. S.W. of Rugby; pop. 963. Map 59.

Dundalk, urb. dist., seaport, par. and cap. of co. Louth, 54 m. N. of Dublin; pop. 14,007. Map 93.

Dundee, parl. and co. bur. and city, Angus, 59½ m. N. of Edinburgh; pop. 175,583. Map 7.

Dundrum, seaport and vil., co. Down, 7 m. S.W. of Downpatrick; pop. 474. Map 93.

Dunfermline, parl. and mun. bur., Fifeshire, 16¾ m. N.W. of Edinburgh; pop. 34,954. Map 9.

Dungannon, urb. dist., co. Tyrone, 40 m. W. of Belfast; pop. 3830. Map 93.

Dungarvan, urb. dist., par. and seaport, in co. and 28½ m. S.W. of Waterford; pop. 4977. Map 95.

Dungeness, headland, S. Kent, 10½ m. E.S.E. of Rye. Map 83.

Dunipace, town and par., Stirlingshire, forms part of Denny and Dunipace. Map 9.

Dunkeld, market town, in co. and 15½ m. N.W. of Perth; pop. 529. Map 6.

Dunlop, par. and vil., Ayrshire, 7½ m. N.W. of Kilmarnock; pop. 1335. Map 8.

Dunmanway, market town, in co. and 37¾ m. S.W. of Cork; pop. 1619. Map 94.

Dunmore, market town and par., co. Galway, 8 m. N.E. of Tuam; pop. of par. 5986. Map 92.

Dunmow, Great, market town and par., Essex, 8½ m. W. of Braintree; pop. 2506. Map 72.

Dunning, par. and vil., in co. and 10 m. S.W. of Perth; pop. 1136. Map 6.

Dunoon, police bur., Argyllshire, on Firth of Clyde, 27 m. by water from Glasgow; pop. 8780. Map 12.

Duns, police bur. and par., Berwickshire, 7¼ m. N.E. of Greenlaw; pop. of bur. 1788. Map 11.

Dunshelt, vil., Fifeshire, 1 m. S.E. of Auchtermuchty. Map 6.

Dunstable, mun. bor. and par., Bedfordshire, 4¼ m. W. of Luton; pop. 8972. Map 71.

Dunstan, coast par., Northumberland, 6 m. N.E. of Alnwick; pop. 357. Map 17.

Dunstanburgh Castle, ruin, Northumberland, 7 m. N.E. of Alnwick. Map 17.

Dunster, par. and market town, W. Somersetshire, 5 m. W. of Watchet; pop. 705. Map 85.

Dunsyre, par. and vil., Lanarkshire, 8½ m. E.N.E. of Carstairs; pop. 161. Map 9.

Dunvegan, vil. and loch, N.W. Skye Isl., Inverness-shire, 22½ m. N.W. of Portree. Map 2.

Durham, city and cap. of co. Durham, 14½ m. S. of Newcastle; pop. 16,223. Map 23.

Durrow, market town, Leix co., 15 m. N.N.W. of Kilkenny; pop. 548. Map 95.

Dursley, market town and par., in co. and 15 m. S.S.W. of Gloucester; pop. 2792. Map 68.

Duxford, par. and vil., in co. and 8 m. S.S.E. of Cambridge; pop. 734. Map 61.

Dymchurch, coast par. and vil., Kent, 4 m. N.E. of New Romney; pop. 891. Map 83.

Dymock, par. and vil., Gloucestershire, 4 m. S. of Ledbury; pop. 1215. Map 57.

Dysart, seaport, Fifeshire, 2 m. N.E. of Kirkcaldy, to which it has been annexed. Map 10.

EAGLESFIELD, par. and vil., Cumberland, 2½ m. S.W. of Cockermouth; pop. 232. Map 20.

Eaglesham, par. and vil., Renfrewshire, 8½ m. S.S.W. of Glasgow; pop. 1519. Map 8.

Ealing, mun. bor., Middlesex, 5¾ m. W. of Paddington; pop. 117,688. Map 71.

Earby, urb. dist., W.R. Yorkshire, 6½ m. S.W. of Skipton; pop. 5522. Map 32.

Eardington, par. and vil., Salop, 2 m. S. of Bridgnorth; pop. 271. Map 47.

Eardisland, par. and vil., Herefordshire, 5 m. W. of Leominster; pop. 496. Map 56.

Eardisley, par. and vil., Herefordshire, 5 m. S. of Kington; pop. 702. Map 56.

Earith, vil., Huntingdonshire, 5¾ m. N.E. of St Ives. Map 61.

Earls Barton, par. and vil., in co. and 6½ m. E. of Northampton; pop. 2574. Map 60.

Earls Colne, par. and vil., Essex, 2½ m. S.E. of Halstead; pop. 1806. Map 73.

Earlston, market town and par., S.W. Berwickshire, 4½ m. N. of St Boswells; pop. 1061. Map 16.

Earn, Loch, Perthshire, 12 m. W. of Crieff, 6½ m. long by ½ m. broad. Map 5.

Earn, River, Perthshire, from Loch Earn flows 46 m. E. to Tay, 6½ m. S.E. of Perth. Map 6.

Earsdon, urb. dist. and coast par., Northumberland, 4 m. N.W. of North Shields; pop. 13,086. Map 23.

Easebourne, par. and vil., W. Sussex, 1 m. N. of Midhurst; pop. 1514. Map 79.

Easington, coast par., E.R. Yorkshire, 5 m. S.E. of Patrington; pop. 336. Map 35.

Easington, par. and vil., N.R. Yorkshire, 10½ m. N.W. of Whitby; pop. 768. Map 28.

Easingwold, town and par., N.R. Yorkshire, 13 m. N.W. of York; pop. 2045. Map 28.

East Barnet Valley, urb. dist., Hertfordshire, adjoining Barnet; pop. 18,542. Map 71.

Eastbourne, co. bor. and par., E. Sussex, 66 m. S.S.E. of London; pop. 57,435. Map 81.

East Grinstead, urb. dist. and par., E. Sussex, 14 m. N.E. of Horsham; pop. 7981. Map 81.

East Halton, par. and vil., N. Lincolnshire, 7 m. S.E. of Barton; pop. 662. Map 35.

Eastham, par. and vil., N. Cheshire, on r. Mersey, 6 m. S.E. of Birkenhead; pop. 1098. Manchester Ship Canal enters Mersey here. Map 38.

East Ham, co. bor., S.W. Essex, 6 m. E. of Fenchurch St. Sta., London; pop. 142,460. Map 71.

Eastington, par. and vil., Gloucestershire, 5 m. W. of Stroud; pop. 1182. Map 68.

East Kilbride, town and par., Lanarkshire, 12 m. S. of Glasgow; pop. 2046. Map 8.

East Leake, par. and vil., Nottinghamshire, 5 m. N.E. of Loughborough; pop. 1023. Map 49.

Eastleigh and Bishopstoke, urb. dist., Hampshire, 5½ m. N.E. of Southampton; pop. 18,333. Map 77.

East Linton, town, East Lothian, 6 m. W. of Dunbar; pop. 882. Map 10.

East Markham, par. and vil., Nottinghamshire, $1\frac{1}{2}$ m. N. of Tuxford; pop. 737. Map 41.

East Retford, mun. bor., market town and par., Notts, $18\frac{1}{2}$ m. N.W. of Newark; pop. 14,228. Map 41.

Eastrington, par. and vil., E.R. Yorkshire, 3 m. N.E. of Howden; pop. 531. Map 34.

East Wemyss, town, Fifeshire, 1 m. S.W. of Buckhaven; pop. 2805. Map 10.

Eastwood, urb. dist., in co. and 9 m. N.W. of Nottingham; pop. 5360. Map 41.

Eatington or **Ettington,** par. and vil., Warwickshire, $5\frac{1}{2}$ m. S.E. of Stratford-on-Avon; pop. 500. Map 58.

Eaton Bray, par. and vil., Bedfordshire, $3\frac{1}{2}$ m. S.W. of Dunstable; pop. 975. Map 71.

Eaton Socon, par. and vil., Bedfordshire, $1\frac{1}{2}$ m. W.S.W. of St Neots; pop. 2231. Map 60.

Ebberston, par., vil. and seat, N.R. Yorkshire, 6 m. E. of Pickering; pop. 462. Map 29.

Ebbw Vale, urb. dist. and par., Monmouthshire, 6 m. N.W. of Aberbeeg Junction; pop. 31,695. Map 67.

Ebchester, par. and vil., Durham, $12\frac{3}{4}$ m. S.W. of Newcastle; pop. 710. Map 22.

Ebenezer, vil. in co. and 6 m. S.W. of Carmarthen. Map 65.

Ecclefechan, vil. and ry. sta., Dumfriesshire, $5\frac{3}{4}$ m. S.E. of Lockerbie; pop. 680. Map 20.

Eccles, parl. and mun. bor. and par., S.E. Lancashire, 4 m. W. of Manchester; pop. 44,415. Map 39.

Eccleshall, market town and par., in co. and 7 m. N.W. of Stafford; pop. 3630. Map 47.

Eckford, par. and vil., Roxburghshire, 6 m. S. of Kelso; pop. 665. Map 16.

Eckington, par. and vil., in co. and 9 m. S.E. of Worcester; pop. 623. Map 57.

Eckington, par. and town, E. Derbyshire, 6 m. S.E. of Sheffield; pop. 12,624. Map 41.

Eddleston, par. and vil., in co. and 4 m. N. of Peebles; pop. 527. Map 10.

Edenbridge, par. and town, W. Kent, 5 m. S. of Westerham; pop. 2890. Map 80.

Edenderry, town, Offaly co., 37 m. W. of Dublin; pop. 2093. Map 93.

Edenfield, eccl. dist. and vil., S.E. Lancashire, $5\frac{1}{2}$ m. N. of Bury; pop. 3385. Map 31.

Edgbaston, parl. div. in S.W. of Birmingham; pop. 71,459. Map 58.

Edgeworthstown, town, in co. and 9 m. E.S.E. of Longford; pop. 654. Map 93.

Edgware, par. and vil., Middlesex, $11\frac{1}{4}$ m. N.W. of London; pop. 1516. Map 71.

Edgworth, par., S.E. Lancashire, 5 m. N.N.E. of Bolton; pop. 2557. Map 31.

Edinburgh, city, parl. and mun. bur. and capital of Scotland, on Firth of Forth, $392\frac{1}{4}$ m. N. of London by rail; pop. 438,998. Map 10.

Edington, par., N. Wiltshire, $3\frac{1}{2}$ m. N.E. of Westbury; pop. 748. Map 75.

Edlington, par. and ham., W.R. Yorkshire, $4\frac{1}{4}$ m. S.W. of Doncaster; pop. 5289. Map 41.

Edmondbyers, par. and vil., Durham, $5\frac{1}{2}$ m. W.S.W. of Consett; pop. 285. Map 22.

Edmonton, urb. dist. and par., Middlesex, $8\frac{3}{4}$ m. N. of London; pop. 77,652. Map 71.

Ednam, par. and vil., Roxburghshire, $2\frac{1}{2}$ m. N.E. of Kelso; pop. 413. Map 16.

Edzell, par. and vil., Angus, $6\frac{1}{2}$ m. N. of Brechin; pop. 745. Map 3.

Egham, urb. dist. and par., W. Surrey, $1\frac{1}{2}$ m. W. of Staines; pop. 15,915. Map 78.

Egremont, urb. dist., Cumberland, 5 m. S.E. of Whitehaven; pop. 6015. Map 24.

Egremont, eccl. dist., W. Cheshire, on r. Mersey, 2 m. N.W. of Birkenhead; pop. 16,727. Map 38.

Egten, par. and vil., N.R. Yorkshire, $6\frac{1}{2}$ m. S.W. of Whitby; pop. 993. Map 29.

Eigg, isl., Inverness-shire, 5 m. S.W. of Sleat Point; pop. 197. Map 2.

Elan Valley, reservoirs of Birmingham Water Supply, Rhayader, Radnorshire. Map 55.

Elgin, bur., par. and capital of co. Moray, 37 m. N.E. of Inverness; pop. 8810. Map 3.

Elie, police bur., Fifeshire, on Firth of Forth, $5\frac{1}{4}$ m. S.E. of Largo; pop. 1098. Map 7.

Elland, urb. dist., par. and town, W.R. Yorkshire, 3 m. S.E. of Halifax; pop. 10,327. Map 32.

Ellerby, par. and ham., E.R. Yorkshire, $7\frac{1}{2}$ m. N.E. of Hull; pop. 339. Map 35.

Ellerker, par. and vil., E.R. Yorkshire, 11 m. W. of Hull; pop. 299. Map 34.

Ellerton, vil., E.R. Yorkshire, 3 m. N. of Bubwith. Map 33.

Ellesmere, urb. dist. and par., Salop, 11 m. S.W. of Whitchurch; pop. 1872. Map 46.

Ellesmere Port, urb. dist. and par., W. Cheshire, 7 m. N. of Chester; pop. 18,898. Map 38.

Ellington, par. and vil., Northumberland, 6 m. N.E. of Morpeth; pop. 786. Map 17.

Ellon, police bur. and par., in co. and $19\frac{1}{2}$ m. N.E. of Aberdeen; pop. of town 1300. Map 3.

Elloughton, par. on estuary of r. Ouse, E.R. Yorkshire, 9 m. W. of Hull; pop. 1230. Map 34.

Elphin, par. and town, co. Roscommon, 9 m. S.W. of Carrick-on-Shannon; pop. of par.: 208. Map 92.

Elsham, par. and vil., N. Lincolnshire, on the Wolds, $2\frac{3}{4}$ m. N.W. of Barnetby; pop. 421. Map 35.

Elstow, par. and vil., in co. and $1\frac{1}{4}$ m. S. of Bedford; pop. 412. Map 60.

Elstree, par. and vil., S. Herefordshire, 7 m. S. of St Albans; pop. 2238. Map 71.

Elstronwick, par. and vil., E.R. Yorkshire, $3\frac{1}{2}$ m. N.E. of Hedon; pop. 101. Map 35.

Eltham, par. and town in met. bor. of Woolwich, co. of London; pop. 28,308. Map 72.

Elvanfoot, ham., Lanarkshire, 5 m. S.E. of Abington. Map 14.

Ely, city, Isle of Ely, in co. and 15 m. N.E. of Cambridge; pop. 8382. Map 61.

Embleton, par. and vil., Northumberland, $6\frac{1}{2}$ m. N.E. of Alnwick; pop. 639. Map 17.

Emley, urb. dist., W.R. Yorkshire, 7 m. S.E. of Huddersfield; pop. 1635. Map 32.

Empingham, par. and vil., Rutlandshire, 6 m. W.N.W. of Stamford; pop. 559. Map 50.

Emsworth, eccl. dist. and port, Hampshire, 2 m. S.S.E. of Havant; pop. 2459. Map 79.

Enfield, vil., co. Meath, 11 m. S.W. of Trim; pop. 182. Map 93.

Enfield, market town and par., Middlesex, $10\frac{3}{4}$ m. N. of London; pop. 67,869. Map 71.

Ennerdale Bridge, vil., Cumberland, $6\frac{1}{2}$ m. S.E. of Whitehaven. Map 25.

Ennerdale Water, lake, Cumberland, $7\frac{1}{2}$ m. S.E. of Whitehaven. Map 25.

Ennis, urb. dist., co. Clare, $24\frac{3}{4}$ m. N.W. of Limerick; pop. 5517. Map 94.

Enniscorthy, urb. dist., co. Wexford, $77\frac{1}{2}$ m. S. of Dublin; pop. 5545. Map 95.

Enniskillen, co. town of co. Fermanagh, $61\frac{3}{4}$ m. N.W. of Dundalk; pop. 4847. Map 93.

Ennistimon, town, co. Clare, 15 m. N.W. of Ennis pop. 1204. Map 94.

Enterkinfoot, hamlet, Dumfries-shire, 6 m. N.W. of Thornhill. Map 14.

Epping, market town and par., W. Essex, 17 m. N.E. of London; pop. 4956. Map 72.

Epsom, urb. dist. and market town, mid Surrey, $17\frac{1}{4}$ m. S.W. of London; pop. 27,089. Map 78.

Epworth, market town and par., N. Lincolnshire, in Isle of Axholme, $8\frac{1}{2}$ m. N.N.W. of Gainsborough; pop. 1822. Map 42.

Erdington, eccl. par. in N.E. of Birmingham; pop. 35,380. Map 48.

Ericht, River, E. Perthshire, flows 10 m. S.E. to the Isla, 2 m. N.E. of Coupar-Angus. Map 6.
Eriswell, par. and vil., W. Suffolk, 2½ m. N.E. of Mildenhall; pop. 317. Map 62.
Erith, urb. dist., N.W. Kent, 5 m. E. of Woolwich; pop. 32,780. Map 72.
Erpingham, par. and vil., Norfolk, 3 m. N. of Aylsham; pop. 357. Map 53.
Errol, par. and vil., in co. and 10½ m. E. of Perth; pop. 738. Map 6.
Escrick, par. and vil., E.R. Yorkshire, 7 m. S. of York; pop. 597. Map 34.
Esher and the Dittons, urb. dist., N. Surrey, 14½ m. S.W. of London; pop. 17,075. Map 78.
Etal, vil., Northumberland, 8 m. N.W. of Wooler. Map 17.
Eton, urb. dist. and par., S. Buckinghamshire, 21 m. W.S.W. of London; pop. 2005. Map 78.
Ettingshall, ward in Bilston urb. dist., Staffordshire. Map 47.
Euston, par. and vil., W. Suffolk, 4 m. S.E. of Thetford; pop. 248. Map 62.
Evenjobb, par. and vil., Radnorshire, 3½ m. S.W. of Presteigne; pop. 204. Map 56.
Evenlode, par. and vil., Gloucester, 3 m. N.E. of Stow-on-the-Wold. Map 58.
Evercreech, par. and vil., E. Somersetshire, 3½ m. S.E. of Shepton Mallet; pop. 1265. Map 75.
Everdon, Great, par. and vil., Northamptonshire, 4 m. S.E. of Daventry; pop. 436. Map 59.
Evesham, mun. bor., in co. and 15 m. S.E. of Worcester; pop. 8799. Map 58.
Ewell, town and par., N. Surrey, 1½ m. N.E. of Epsom; pop. 4187. Map 80.
Exbourne, par. and vil., Devonshire, 4½ m. S.E. of Hatherleigh; pop. 311. Map 84.
Exeter, bor. and co. town of Devon, 171¾ m. S.W. of London; pop. 66,039. Map 89.
Exminster, par. and vil., Devonshire, 3½ m. S.E. of Exeter; pop. 2404. Map 89.
Exmouth, urb. dist., and seaport, Devonshire, 10½ m. S.E. of Exeter; pop. 14,584. Map 89.
Eye, mun. bor. and par., E. Suffolk, 19 m. N. of Ipswich; pop. 1733. Map 63.
Eyemouth, coast town, Berwickshire, 5½ m. N.W. of Berwick-upon-Tweed; pop. 2231. Map 11.
Eynsford, par. and vil., W. Kent, 6½ m. N. of Sevenoaks; pop. 2567. Map 82.
FAILSWORTH, urb. dist., Lancashire, 3¾ m. N.E. of Manchester; pop. 15,724. Map 39.
Fairford, par. and vil., Gloucestershire, 8 m. E. of Cirencester; pop. 1347. Map 69.
Fakenham, market town and par., Norfolk, 12 m. N.W. of E. Dereham; pop. 2966. Map 52.
Fakenham Magna, par., W. Suffolk, 5½ m. S.E. of Thetford; pop. 163. Map 62.
Falkirk, mun. bur. and par., Stirlingshire, 25½ m. W.N.W. of Edinburgh; pop. 36,565. Map 9.
Falkland, bur. and par., Fifeshire, 10 m. N. of Kirkcaldy; pop. of bur. 791. Map 6.
Fallin, mining vil., in co. and 3 m. S.E. of Stirling. Map 9.
Falmouth, mun. bor., seaport and par., Cornwall, 11¾ m. S. of Truro; pop. 13,492. Map 90.
Falstone, eccl. dist. and vil., S. Northumberland, 8 m. W.N.W. of Bellingham; pop. 834. Map 16.
Fareham, urb. dist. and par., Hampshire, 11 m. S.E. of Eastleigh; pop. 11,575. Map 77.
Faringdon, par. and vil., E. Hampshire, 3 m. S. of Alton; pop. 439. Map 79.
Faringdon, Great, par., Berkshire, 5½ m. S.E. of Lechlade; pop. 2758. Map 69.
Farnborough, urb. dist. and par., N. Hampshire, 33 m. S.W. of London; pop. 16,359. Map 78.
Farnham, market town and par., W. Surrey, 3 m. S.W. of Aldershot; pop. 18,294. Map 78.
Farningham, town and par., W. Kent, 12 m. W. of Rochester; pop. 1395. Map 80.
Farnworth, urb. dist. and par., S.E. Lancashire, 3 m. S.E. of Bolton; pop. 28,711. Map 31.
Farsley, urb. dist. and par., W.R. Yorkshire, 4 m. N.E. of Bradford; pop. 6158. Map 32.
Fauldhouse, town, West Lothian, 6½ m. S.W. of West Calder; pop. 4106. Map 9.
Faversham, mun. bor. and river port, N. Kent, 9¾ m. N.W. of Canterbury; pop. 10,091. Map 83.
Featherstone, urb. dist., W.R. Yorkshire, 2½ m. S.W. of Pontefract; pop. 14,952. Map 33.
Felindre, vil., Radnorshire, 9½ m. N.W. of Knighton. Map 56.
Felixstowe, coast par. and urb. dist., E. Suffolk, 11 m. S.E. of Ipswich; pop. 12,037. Map 63.
Felling, urb. dist., Durham, 1½ m. S.E. of Gateshead pop. 27,041. Map 23.
Felsted, par. and vil., Essex, 3½ m. S.E. of Dunmow pop. 2089. Map 72.
Feltham, urb. dist., Middlesex, 15 m. W.S.W. of London; pop. 16,316. Map 78.
Felton, par. and vil., Northumberland, 8 m. S. of Alnwick; pop. 547. Map 17.
Fen Ditton, par. and vil., in co. and 2 m. N.E. of Cambridge; pop. 781. Map 61.
Fenny Compton, par. and vil., in co. and 12 m. S.E. of Warwick; pop. 443. Map 59.
Fen Stanton, par. and vil., Huntingdonshire, 2 m. S. of St Ives; pop. 798. Map 61.
Fenton, Staffordshire, now in Stoke-on-Trent. Map 40.
Fenwick, par. and vil., Ayrshire, 3½ m. N.E. of Kilmarnock; pop. 330. Map 12.
Fermoy, urb. dist., co. Cork, 16 m. E. of Mallow; pop. 4505. Map 94.
Ferndale, vil., Glamorganshire, 6 m. N.W. of Pontypridd Junction. Map 66.
Ferns, town and par., co. Wexford, 7¾ m. N. of Enniscorthy; pop. 1576. Map 95.
Ferryside, vil., in co. and 7 m. S.S.W. of Carmarthen. Map 65.
Fethard, par. and town, co. Tipperary, 8¾ m. N. of Clonmel; pop. 1599. Map 95.
Fettercairn, par. and vil., Kincardineshire, 4½ m. N.W. of Laurencekirk; pop. 1290. Map 3.
Ffestiniog, urb. dist. and par., Merionethshire, 16 m. S.W. of Llanrwst; pop. 9072. Map 37.
Fife Ness, the Eastern extremity of Fifeshire, 2 m. N.E. of Crail. Map 7.
Filey, urb. dist. and watering place, E.R. Yorkshire, 9½ m. S.E. of Scarborough; pop. 3730. Map 29.
Fillongley, par. and vil., Warwickshire, 6 m. S.W. of Nuneaton; pop. 1408. Map 48.
Finchley, urb. dist. and par., Middlesex, 7¼ m. N. of London; pop. 58,961. Map 71.
Findern, par. and vil., in co. and 5 m. S.W. of Derby; pop. 381. Map 48.
Findochty, seaport, Banffshire, 3½ m. N.E. of Buckie; pop. 1675. Map 3.
Finedon, urb. dist., Northants, 3 m. N.E. of Wellingborough; pop. 4100. Map 60.
Fintona, town, co. Tyrone, 5¼ m. S. of Omagh; pop. 1100. Map 93.
Fishguard, urb. dist., seaport and par., Pembrokeshire, 13 m. N. of Haverfordwest; pop. 2963. Map 64.
Fittleworth, par. and vil., W. Sussex, 2¼ m. S.E. of Petworth; pop. 639. Map 79.
Flamborough, par. and vil., E.R. Yorkshire, 4 m. N.E. of Bridlington; pop. 1325. Map 29.
Fleet, urb. dist. and par., Hampshire, 3½ m. W. of Farnborough; pop. 4528. Map 78.
Fleetwood, urb. dist., seaport and par., Lancashire, 20 m. N.W. of Preston; pop. 22,983. Map 30.
Fletching, par. and vil., E. Sussex, 8 m. N. of Lewes; pop. 1151. Map 81.
Flimby, coast par. and vil., Cumberland, 1¾ m. S.E. of Maryport; pop. 2498. Map 20.
Flint, mun. bor., market town and par., Flintshire, 11½ m. N.W. of Chester; pop. 7635. Map 38.

Flockton, par. and urb. dist., W.R. Yorkshire, 7 m. S.W. of Wakefield; pop. 1471. Map 32.

Floore, par. and vil., Northamptonshire, 5½ m. S.E. of Daventry; pop. 815. Map 59.

Fobbing, par. and vil., S. Essex, 2½ m. E.N.E. of Stanford-le-Hope; pop. 607. Map 72.

Fochabers, vil., Morayshire, 6¼ m. S.E. of Elgin; pop. 867. Map 3.

Folkestone, mun. bor., seaport and par., Kent, 5 m. S.W. of Dover; pop. 35,890. Map 83.

Folkton, par. and vil., E.R. Yorkshire, 5½ m. S. of Scarborough; pop. 419. Map 29.

Fontmell Magna, par. and vil., Dorsetshire, 4 m. S. of Shaftesbury; pop. 460. Map 87.

Ford, ham., Argyllshire, at head of Loch Awe, 13 m. N. of Ardrishaig. Map 12.

Ford, par. and vil., Northumberland, 6½ m. N.W. of Wooler; pop. 950. Map 17.

Ford Bridge, ry. sta., Herefordshire, 2½ m. S.E. of Leominster. Map 56.

Fordham, par. and vil., Cambridgeshire, 5 m. N. of Newmarket; pop. 1461. Map 61.

Fordingbridge, market town and par., Hants, 14½ m. S. of Salisbury; pop. 3394. Map 77.

Forest Row, par. and vil., E. Sussex, 3½ m. S.E. of E. Grinstead; pop. 3303. Map 81.

Forfar, bur. and co. town of Angus, 21½ m. N.E. of Dundee; pop. 9660. Map 7.

Forgandenny, par. and vil., Perthshire, 4 m. S.W. of Perth; pop. 678. Map 6.

Forge Valley, resort and ry. stn., N.R. Yorks., 6½ m. S.W. of Scarborough. Map 29.

Formby, urb. dist. and coast par., S.W. Lancashire, 7 m. S.W. of Southport; pop. 7957. Map 30.

Fornham, vil., W. Suffolk, 2 m. N.W. of Bury St Edmunds. Map 62.

Forres, mun. bur. and par., Morayshire, 12½ m. W. of Elgin; pop. 4169. Map 3.

Fort Augustus, vil. and monastery, at head of Loch Ness, Inverness-shire. Map 2.

Fortingall, par. and vil., Perthshire, 8 m. W.S.W. of Aberfeldy; pop. 1629. Map 5.

Fortrose, mun. bur., Ross and Cromarty, 10½ m. N.E. of Inverness; pop. 875. Map 3.

Fort William, police bur., in co. and 65½ m. S.W. of Inverness; pop. 2527. Map 12.

Foston, par. and vil., Kesteven, Lincolnshire, 5½ m. N.W. of Grantham; pop. 279. Map 50.

Foston-on-the-Wolds, par. and vil., E.R. Yorkshire, 5 m. S.E. of Driffield; pop. 211. Map 35.

Foulness, insular par. and vil., Essex, 7 m. N.E. of Shoeburyness; pop. 460. Map 73.

Foulsham, par. and vil., Norfolk, 8 m. N.E of E. Dereham; pop. 869. Map 52.

Fountainhall, ham. and ry. junct., 22½ m. S.E. of Edinburgh. Map 10.

Four Crosses, ry. sta., Montgomeryshire, 7½ m. S.W. of Oswestry. Map 46.

Fovant, par. and vil., S. Wiltshire, 6 m. S.W. of Wilton; pop. 474. Map 87.

Fowey, bor., seaport and par., Cornwall, 10 m. S.S.E. of Bodmin; pop. 2382. Map 91.

Fowlis Wester, par. and vil., Perthshire, 4½ m. N.E. of Crieff; pop. 939. Map 6.

Foyle, Lough, sea inlet between cos. Donegal and Londonderry. Map 93.

Framlingham, par. and market town, E. Suffolk, 7 m. E. of Debenham; pop. 2397. Map 63.

Frampton, Cotterell, par. and vil., Gloucestershire, 3½ m. W.S.W. of Chipping Sodbury; pop. 2122. Map 68.

Frankford, town, Offaly co., 11 m. S.W. of Tullamore; pop. 518. Map 95.

Fraserburgh, police bur., seaport and par., in co. and 47½ m. N. of Aberdeen; pop. of bur. 9720. Map 3.

Freckleton, par. and vil., N. Lancashire, 7½ m. W. of Preston; pop. 1438. Map 30.

Freiston, par. and vil., Holland, Lincolnshire, 3 m. E. of Boston; pop. 984. Map 51.

Freshwater, par. and vil., Isle of Wight, 1½ m. S.W. of Yarmouth; pop. 3439. Map 77.

Fressingfield, par. and vil., E. Suffolk, 8 m. W. of Halesworth; pop. 986. Map 63.

Freuchie, *q.s.* par. and vil., Falkland par., Fifeshire; pop. 1059. Map 6.

Friarton, isle in r. Tay, in co. and 1 m. S. of Perth. Map 6.

Friern Barnet, urb. dist., Middlesex, 1½ m. N. of Finchley; pop. 23,081. Map 71.

Frimley, par. and vil., W. Surrey, 1¾ m. S. of Camberley; pop. 16,472. Map 78.

Frinton-on-Sea, urb. dist., Essex, 1½ m. S. of Walton-on-the-Naze; pop. 2196. Map 73.

Friockheim, *q.s.* par. and vil., Angus, 6½ m. N.W. of Arbroath; pop. 701. Map 7.

Friskney, par. and vil., Lindsey, Lincolnshire, 3 m. S.W. of Wainfleet; pop. 1508. Map 43.

Friston, par. and vil., E. Suffolk, 3 m. S.E. of Saxmundham; pop. 491. Map 63.

Frizington, eccl. dist. and vil., Cumberland, 4 m. E.S.E. of Whitehaven; pop. 3656. Map 24.

Frodingham, North, par. and vil., E.R. Yorkshire, 5½ m. S.E. of Gt. Driffield; pop. 543. Map 35.

Frodsham, market town and par., Cheshire, 10 m. N.E. of Chester; pop. 3025. Map 38.

Frome, market town and par., E. Somersetshire, 24½ m. S.E. of Bristol; pop. 10,738. Map 75.

Frosterly, eccl. dist. and vil., Durham, 3 m. S.E. of Stanhope; pop. 1315. Map 22.

Froxfield, par. and vil., E. Wiltshire, 3 m. W. of Hungerford; pop. 285. Map 69.

Fulford (Gate Fulford), eastern suburb of York city. Map 33.

Fulwood, urb. dist., Lancashire, in parl. bor. of Preston; pop. 7387. Map 30.

Furnace, vil., Argyllshire, on Loch Fyne, 7 m. S.S.W. of Inverary. Map 12.

Furness Vale, vil., N.E. Cheshire, 4½ m. N.W. of Chapel-en-le-Frith. Map 40.

Fyne, Loch, sea loch, Argyllshire, 40½ m. long, and from 1 to 5 m. broad. Map 12.

GAINSBOROUGH, urb. dist. and par., Lindsey, in co. and 17¾ m. N.W. of Lincoln; pop. 18,684. Map 42.

Gairloch, par. and vil., Ross and Cromarty, 29½ m. N.W. of Achnasheen; pop. 2781. Map 2.

Galashiels, mun. bur., town and par., Selkirkshire, 33½ m. S.E. of Edinburgh; pop. 13,102. Map 16.

Galloway, Mull of, headland, Wigtown; most southerly point of Scotland. Map 18.

Galston, police bur. and par., Ayrshire, 5½ m. E.S.E. of Kilmarnock; pop. of bur. 4601. Map 14.

Galway, seaport, urb. dist. and co. town of Galway, 20 m. S. of Tuam; pop. 14,223. Map 94.

Gamblesby, par. and vil., Cumberland, 3½ m. S.E. of Kirkoswald; pop. 189. Map 21.

Gamlingay, par. and vil., in co. and 15¾ m. S.W. of Cambridge; pop. 1645. Map 61.

Ganton, par. and vil., E.R. Yorkshire, 7½ m. S.W. of Scarborough; pop. 351. Map 29.

Gareloch, right arm of Firth of Clyde, Dumbartonshire. Map 12.

Garelochhead, par. and vil., with pier, Dumbartonshire, 7½ m. N.W. of Helensburgh; pop. 1116. Map 12.

Garforth, urb. dist. and par., W.R. Yorkshire, 7 m. E. of Leeds; pop. 3774. Map 33.

Gargrave, par. and vil., W.R. Yorkshire, 4 m. N.W. of Skipton; pop. 1166. Map 31.

Gargunnock, par. and vil., in co. and 6 m. W. of Stirling; pop. 586. Map 9.

Garstang, market town and par., N.W. Lancashire, 10½ m. S. of Lancaster; pop. 837. Map 30.

Garston, par., S.W. Lancashire, on r. Mersey, 6½ m. S.E. of Liverpool; pop. 16,645. Map 38.

Garthorpe, par. and vil., Lindsey, Lincolnshire, on r. Old Don, 6½ m. N.E. of Crowle; pop. 453. Map 34.

Gartly, par., Aberdeenshire, 5 m. S. of Huntly; pop. 684. Map 3.

Gartmore, vil., Perthshire, 2 m. S. of Aberfoyle; pop. 351. Map 8.

Garton-on-the-Wolds, par. and vil., E.R. Yorkshire, 3 m. N.W. of Great Driffield; pop. 438. Map 35.

Garvagh, town, co. Londonderry, 12½ m. S. of Coleraine; pop. 494. Map 93.

Gatehouse of Fleet, police bur. and river port, in co. and 9 m. W. of Kirkcudbright; pop. 888. Map 19.

Gateshead, co. bor. and par., Durham, on Tyne, opposite Newcastle; pop. 122,379. Map 23.

Gattonside, vil., Roxburghshire, 1 m. N.W. of Melrose; pop. 272. Map 16.

Gazeley, par. and vil., Suffolk, 4½ m. E. of Newmarket; pop. 430. Map 62.

Geddington, par. and vil., Northamptonshire, 3 m. N.E. of Kettering; pop. 958. Map 60.

Gedney, par. and vil., Holland, Lincolnshire, 3¼ m. E. of Holbeach; pop. 1985. Map 51.

Gelligaer, urb. dist., Glamorganshire, 14 m. N. of Cardiff; pop. 41,042. Map 67.

Gerrard's Cross, par. and vil., Buckinghamshire, 3 m. S.E. of Beaconsfield; pop. 2208. Map 71.

Giant's Causeway, promontory of columnar basalt, on N. coast of co. Antrim. Map 93.

Gifford, vil., East Lothian, 4 m. S.S.E. of Haddington; pop. 345. Map 10.

Giggleswick, par. and vil., W.R. Yorkshire, 10 m. S.E. of Ingleton; pop. 954. Map 26.

Gilcrux, par. and vil., Cumberland, 5½ m. N.W. of Cockermouth; pop. 463. Map 20.

Gildersome, urb. dist. and par., W.R. Yorkshire, 5 m. S.W. of Leeds; pop. 3041. Map 32.

Gillingham, market town and par., N. Dorsetshire, 4 m. N.W. of Shaftesbury; pop. 3294. Map 87.

Gillingham, mun. bor., Kent, on r. Medway, 1½ m. N.E of Chatham; pop. 60,983. Map 80.

Gilmerton, vil., Perthshire, 2 m. N.E. of Crieff. Map 6.

Gilsland, eccl. dist. and vil., Northumberland, 7 m. N.E. of Brampton; pop. 781. Map 21.

Girvan, police bur., seaport and par., in co. and 21½ m. S.W. of Ayr; pop. 5292. Map 12.

Gisburn, par. and vil., W.R. Yorkshire, 7½ m. N.E. of Clitheroe; pop. 416. Map 31.

Glamis, par. and vil., Angus, 5½ m. S.W. of Forfar; pop. 1099. Map 7.

Glanton, par. and vil., Northumberland, 11½ m. W. of Alnwick; pop. 421. Map 17.

Glasbury, par. and vil., Radnorshire, 4 m. S.W. of Hay; pop. 468. Map 56.

Glasgow, co. of a city and mun. bur., on r. Clyde, Lanarkshire, 47¼ m. W. of Edinburgh; pop. 1,088,417. Map 8.

Glassonby, par. and vil., E. Cumberland, 7 m. N.E. of Penrith; pop. 147. Map 21.

Glastonbury, mun. bor. and market town, mid Somersetshire, 5 m. S.W. of Wells; pop. 4515. Map 74.

Glemsford, urb. dist., Suffolk, 2½ m. N.W. of Long Melford; pop. 1262. Map 62.

Glenarm, seaport town, co. Antrim, 11 m. N.W. of Larne; pop. 951. Map 93.

Glenboig, vil., Lanarkshire, 2½ m. N. of Coatbridge. Map 9.

Glencaple, vil., in co. and 5 m. S. of Dumfries; pop. 225. Map 20.

Glencoe, vil. and glen, Argyllshire, 2 m. E. of Ballachulish. Map 12.

Glendalough, mtn. vale, co. Wicklow, 8 m. N.W. of Rathdrum. Map 95.

Glen Devon, valley of r. Devon and par., S. Perthshire; pop 134. Map 6.

Gleneagles, Perthshire, 2 m. S.W. of Auchterarder; palatial hotel with golf courses, etc. Map 6.

Glenelg, par. and vil., Inverness-shire, 7 m. S.W. of Lochalsh; pop. 1643. Map 2.

Glenfarg, vil., in co. and 10½ m. S. of Perth; pop. 409. Map 6.

Glenfinnan, ham., Inverness-shire, at head of Loch Shiel, 17 m. W. of Fort William. Map 2.

Glengariff, vil., co. Cork, 8 m. N.W. of Bantry. Map 94.

Glenluce, vil., Wigtownshire, 8¾ m. S.E. of Stranraer; pop. 806. Map 18.

Glenridding, ham. and mt. vale, N.W. border of Westmorland. Map 25.

Glentham, par. and vil., Lindsey, Lincolnshire, 7 m. W.N.W. of Market Rasen; pop. 340. Map 42.

Glenties, vil., co. Donegal, 24½ m. W. of Stranorlar; pop. 425. Map 92.

Glossop, mun. bor., mkt. tn. and par., N. Derbyshire, 13 m. S.E. of Manchester; pop. 19,510. Map 40.

Gloucester, city, co. bor., par. and co. tn. of Gloucestershire, 37 m. N.N.E. of Bristol; pop. 52,937. Map 68.

Glusburn, par. and vil., W.R. Yorkshire, 4 m. S. of Skipton; pop. 2587. Map 31.

Glyncorwg, urb. dist., Glamorganshire, 2 m. N.E. of Cymmer; pop. 10,208. Map 66.

Glynde, par. and vil., E. Sussex, 3 m. S.E. of Lewes; pop. 274. Map 81.

Glyn Neath, vil. and ry. sta., Glamorganshire, 12 m. N.E. of Neath. Map 66.

Goathland, par. and vil., N.R. Yorkshire, 7½ m. S.W. of Whitby; pop. 712. Map 29.

Godalming, mun. bor. and market town, W. Surrey, 34½ m. S.W. of London; pop. 10,400. Map 78.

Godmanchester, mun. bor. and par., in co. and adjoining Huntingdon; pop. 1991. Map 61.

Godshill, par. and vil., Isle of Wight, 5½ m. N.W. of Ventnor; pop. 972. Map 77.

Godstone, par. and vil., E. Surrey, 4½ m. N.E. of Redhill; pop. 2943. Map 80.

Goginan, vil., Cardiganshire, 7 m. E. of Aberystwyth. Map 55.

Gogmagog Hills, in co. and 4 m. S.E. of Cambridge. Map 61.

Goil, sea loch, Argyllshire, west arm of Loch Long. Map 12.

Golborne, urb. dist., Lancashire, 5¼ m. S.E. of Wigan; pop. 7322. Map 39.

Golcar, urb. dist., par. and vil., W.R. Yorkshire, 3 m. S.W. of Huddersfield; pop. 9812. Map 32.

Golspie, coast par. and vil., Sutherlandshire, 84 m. N.E. of Inverness; pop. 890. Map 3.

Gomersal, Yorkshire, in Spenborough urb. dist. Map 32.

Goodwick, urb. dist., Pembrokeshire, 1½ m. N.W. of Fishguard; pop. 2279. Map 64.

Goodwood, seat and racecourse, W. Sussex, 3 m. N.E. of Chichester. Map 79.

Goole, urb. dist., par., mkt. tn. and r. port, W.R. Yorks, 23¾ m. S.W. of Hull; pop. 20,238. Map 34.

Gorey, market town, co. Wexford, 10½ m. S.W. of Arklow; pop. 2291. Map 95.

Goring, par. and vil., Oxon, on r. Thames, 8¾ m. N.W. of Reading; pop. 1989. Map 70.

Gorleston, par., in S. of Great Yarmouth bor., Norfolk; pop. 20,391. Map 53.

Gornal, Lower and **Upper**, 2 eccl. dists., Staffs, 4½ m. S. of Wolverhampton; pop. 7399 and 5122. Map 47.

Gornalwood, vil., Staffordshire, 1 m. N.W. of Dudley. Map 47.

Gorseinon, vil. and ry. sta., Glamorganshire, 5 m. N. of Swansea. Map 65.

Gosforth, par. and vil., Cumberland, 6¼ m. S.E. of Egremont; pop. 922. Map 25.

Gosforth, urb. dist. and par., Northumberland, 2½ m. N. of Newcastle; pop. 18,042. Map 23.
Gosport, mun. bor., seaport and par., Hants, on W. side of Portsmouth Harbour; pop. 37,928. Map 77.
Goudhurst, par. and town, Kent, 3½ m. N.W. of Cranbrook; pop. 2967. Map 82.
Gourock, police bur., Renfrewshire, 2 m. below Greenock; pop. 8844. Map 12.
Govan, par. in S.W. of Glasgow. Map 8.
Grafton Underwood, par. and vil., Northamptonshire, 4 m. N.E. of Kett ing; pop. 212. Map 60.
Graiguenamanagh, town and par., co. Kilkenny, 5 m. S. of Borris ry. sta.; pop. of town 844. Map 95.
Grainthorpe, par. and vil., Lindsey, Lincolnshire, 7 m. N.E. of Louth; pop. 659. Map 43.
Grampound, par. and vil., Cornwall, 6 m. S.W. of St Austell; pop. 419. Map 91.
Grange-over-Sands, urb. dist. and par., Lancashire, 8 m. E. of Ulverston; pop. 2648. Map 25.
Grangemouth, seaport town, pol. bur. and par., E. Stirlingshire, 3 m. N.E. of Falkirk; pop. 11,798. Map 9.
Grangetown, eccl. dist., N.R. Yorkshire, 3½ m. E. of Middlesbrough; pop. 7021. Map 28.
Grantchester, par. and vil., in co. and 2½ m. S.W. of Cambridge; pop. 489. Map 61.
Grantham, mun. bor., Kesteven, in co. and 25 m. S.S.W. of Lincoln; pop. 19,709. Map 50.
Grantown-on-Spey, police bur., Morayshire, 23½ m. S. of Forres; pop. 1577. Map 3.
Grantshouse, ham., Berwickshire, 16½ m. N.W. of Berwick-on-Tweed. Map 11.
Grappenhall, par. and vil., Cheshire, 2½ m. S.E. of Warrington; pop. 1945. Map 39.
Grasmere, urb. dist., par. and lake, Westmorland, 3½ m. N.W. of Ambleside; pop. 988. Map 25.
Gravesend, mun. bor. on S. bank of r. Thames, 24 m. E. of London; pop. 35,490. Map 72.
Grayrigg, par., Westmorland, 5 m. N.E. of Kendal; pop. 202. Map 26.
Grays Thurrock, urb. dist. and market town, S. Essex, 19½ m. S.E. of London; pop. 18,172. Map 80.
Greasbrough, urb. dist., W.R. Yorkshire, 2 m. N.W. of Rotherham; pop. 3599. Map 41.
Great Coates, par. and vil., N.E. Lincs, on r. Humber, 2½ m. W. of Gt. Grimsby; pop. 493. Map 35.
Great Crosby, coast town, S.W. Lancashire, 6½ m. N.W. of Liverpool; pop. 18,283. Map 38.
Great Dalby, par. and vil., Leicestershire, 3½ m. S.W. of Melton Mowbray; pop. 317. Map 49.
Great Driffield, urb. dist. and par., E.R. Yorkshire, 36 m. E. of York; pop. 5916. Map 35.
Great Gidding, par. and vil., in co. and 10 m. N.W. of Huntingdon; pop. 271. Map 60.
Great Grimsby, parl. and co. bor. and par., Lincolnshire, 15 m. S.E. of Hull; pop. 92,463. Map 35.
Greatham, par. and vil., Durham, 3½ m. S.W. of W. Hartlepool; pop. 1128. Map 23.
Great Haywood, eccl. dist. and vil., in co. and 5 m. E. of Stafford; pop. 618. Map 48.
Great Torrington, mun. bor., Devonshire, 6 m. E. of Bideford; pop. 2913. Map 84.
Greenford, dist., Middlesex, 7½ m. W.N.W. of Paddington; pop. 1461. Map 71.
Greenhead, eccl. dist. and vil., S. Northumberland, 3 m. N.W. of Haltwhistle; pop. 1349. Map 21.
Greenhithe, eccl. par. and vil., W. Kent, 2½ m. E.N.E. of Dartford; pop. 3361. Map 80.
Greenhow, vil., W.R. Yorks, 3½ m. S.W. of Pateley Bridge. Map 27.
Greenlcaning, vil., Perthshire, 5½ m. N.E. of Dunblane. Map 6.
Greenock, mun. bur., par. and seaport, Renfrewshire, 22½ m. N. W. of Glasgow; pop. 78,948. Map 12.
Greenore, coast town, co. Louth, on S. side of Carlingford Lough; pop. 289. Map 93.
Greenwich, met. bor., co. London, 3½ m. S.E. of London Bridge; pop. 100,879. Map 80.
Greetland, urb. dist., par. and town, W.R. Yorks, 2 m. S.W. of Halifax; pop. 4298. Map 31.
Gretna, par. and town, Dumfriesshire, 9½ m. N.W. of Carlisle; pop. 2969. Map 21.
Greystoke, par. and vil., E. Cumberland, 5 m. W. of Penrith; pop. 495. Map 21.
Greystones, coast town, co. Wicklow, 4½ m. S.E. of Bray; pop. 1592. Map 95.
Griffithstown, par. and vil., Monmouthshire, 1½ m. S. of Pontypool; pop. 4151. Map 67.
Grimsthorpe, ham. and seat, Kesteven, Lincolnshire, 3½ m. N.W. of Bourne. Map 50.
Grimston, par. and vil., Norfolk, 6½ m. N.E. of King's Lynn; pop. 1058. Map 52.
Grindon, par. and vil., N. Staffordshire, 13¾ m. E.S.E. of Leek; pop. 325. Map 40.
Grinton, par., vil. and seat, N.R. Yorkshire, 1 m. S.E. of Reeth; pop. 262. Map 27.
Grosmont, eccl. dist. and vil., N.R. Yorkshire, 5½ m. S.W. of Whitby; pop. 879. Map 29.
Grosmont, par. and vil., in co. and 10 m. N.W. of Monmouth; pop. 521. Map 67.
Grundisburgh, par. and vil., E. Suffolk, 3 m. W.N.W. of Woodbridge; pop. 762. Map 63.
Guildford, mun. bor. and co. town of Surrey, 30½ m. S.W. of London; pop. 30,753. Map 78.
Guisborough, urb. dist. and par., N.R. Yorkshire, 8 m. S. of Middlesbrough; pop. 6306. Map 28.
Guiseley, urb. dist., par. and vil., W.R. Yorkshire, 2 m. S. of Otley; pop. 5607. Map 32.
Gullane, vil., East Lothian, 4 m. S.W. of North Berwick; pop. 1354. Map 12.
Gunnislake, market vil., Cornwall, 3 m. S.W. of Tavistock. Map 88.
Gunthwaite and Ingbirchworth, urb. dist., W.R. Yorkshire, 2½ m. N. of Penistone; pop. 338. Map 40.
Guyhirn, vil. and ry. sta., Cambridgeshire, 3½ m. N.W. of March. Map 51.
Gwaun-cae-Gurwen, ham., Glamorganshire, 1½ m. S.E. of Garnant. Map 66.
Gwbert-on-the-Sea, vil., in co. and 2¾ m. N.W. of Cardigan. Map 54.
Gweedore, vil., co. Donegal, 38 m. N.W. of Letterkenny. Map 92.
Gwytherin, par. and vil., Denbighshire, 5½ m. E. of Llanrwst. Map 37.
HABROUGH, par. and vil., Lindsey, Lincolnshire, 8 m. N.W. of Grimsby; pop. 411. Map 35.
Hacheston, par. and vil., E. Suffolk, 2 m. N. of Wickham Market; pop. 390. Map 63.
Hackington, par., Kent, adjoining Canterbury; pop. 632. Map 83.
Hackthorp, vil., Westmorland, 5 m. S.E. of Penrith. Map 21.
Haddenham, par. and vil., Isle of Ely, Cambridgeshire, 5¾ m. S.W. of Ely; pop. 1655. Map 61.
Haddenham, par. and vil., Buckinghamshire, 3 m. N.E. of Thame; pop. 1403. Map 70.
Haddington, mun. bur., par. and co. town of East Lothian, 18 m. E. of Edinburgh; pop. 4405. Map 10.
Haddon, West, par. and vil., Northamptonshire, 8 m. N.E. of Daventry; pop. 706. Map 59.
Hadleigh, urb. dist. and par., W. Suffolk, 9½ m. W.S.W. of Ipswich; pop. 2952. Map 62.
Hadleigh, par. and vil., S. Essex, 2 m. N.E. of Benfleet sta.; pop. 2246. Map 72.
Hadlow, par. and vil., Kent, 4 m. N.E. of Tonbridge; pop. 2264. Map 82.
Hailsham, par. and town, Sussex, 7 m. N. of Eastbourne; pop. 4907. Map 81.
Hale, par. and vil., Cumberland, 2½ m. S.E. of Egremont; pop. 291. Map 24.
Hale, urb. dist. and par., Cheshire, 1 m. S.E. of Altrincham; pop. 10,669. Map 39.
Halesowen, urb. dist. and par., Worcestershire, 7 m. S.W. of Birmingham; pop. 31,058. Map 58.

Halesworth, urb. dist. and par., E. Suffolk, 9 m. S.W. of Beccles ; pop. 2024. Map 63.

Halifax, parl. and co. bor. and par., W.R. Yorks, 7 m. W. of Bradford ; pop. 98,122. Map 31.

Halkyn, par. and vil., in co. and 2½ m. S.W. of Flint ; pop. 1297. **H. Castle,** seat. Map 38.

Halkirk, par. and vil., Caithness-shire, 8¼ m. S.W. of Thurso ; pop. 1969. Map 3.

Halstead, urb. dist. and par., Essex, 16 m. N.W. of Colchester ; pop. 5878. Map 62.

Halstead, par. and vil., W. Kent, 4½ m. N.N.W. of Sevenoaks ; pop. 565. Map 80.

Halton, par. and vil., N. Lancashire, 2½ m. N.E. of Lancaster ; pop. 825. Map 26.

Haltwhistle, par. and market town, Northumberland, 16½ m. W. of Hexham ; pop. 4500. Map 22.

Ham, urb. dist., Surrey, 1½ m. N.N.W. of Kingston ; pop. 2206. Map 71.

Hambledon, par. and vil., Hants, 6½ m. N.E. of Fareham ; pop. 2185. Map 79.

Hambledon, par. and vil., S.W. Surrey, 3 m. S. of Godalming ; pop. 838. Map 79.

Hambleton, par. and vil., W.R. Yorkshire, 4¼ m. W. of Selby ; pop. 526. Map 33.

Hamilton, mun. bur. and par., Lanarkshire, 11½ m. S.E. of Glasgow ; bur. pop. 37,863. Map 9.

Hampstead, met. bor., co. of London ; pop. 86,153. **Hampstead Heath** is here. Map 71.

Hampstead Norris, par. and vil., Berkshire, 7½ m. N.E. of Newbury ; pop. 1321. Map 70.

Hampsthwaite, par. and vil., W.R. Yorkshire, 2 m. S.W. of Ripley ; pop. 425. Map 32.

Hampton, urb. dist. and vil., Middlesex, 3¼ m. W. of Kingston ; pop. 13,053. Map 71.

Hampton, par., Cheshire, 2 m. N.E. of Malpas ; pop. 384. Map 38.

Hampton in Arden, par. and vil., Warwickshire, 9 m. N.W. of Coventry ; pop. 1157. Map 58.

Hampton Lucy, par. and vil., Warwickshire, 4 m. N.E. of Stratford-on-Avon ; pop. 367. Map 58.

Hampton Wick, urb. dist., Middlesex, suburb of Kingston ; pop. 2957. Map 71.

Hamstall Ridware, par. and vil., Staffordshire, 4 m. E.N.E. of Rugeley ; pop. 312. Map 48.

Handforth, urb. dist., Cheshire, 5 m. S.W. of Stockport ; pop. 1031. Map 39.

Handley, par. and vil., Dorsetshire, 5 m. N.W. of Cranborne ; pop. 724. Map 87.

Handsworth, par. in N.W. of Birmingham. Map 48.

Hanley, par. and parl. div. of Stoke-on-Trent, in co. and 18¼ m. N. of Stafford ; par. pop. 67,891. Map 39.

Hanningfield, East, par. and vil., W. Essex, 5 m. S.E. of Chelmsford ; pop. 474. Map 72.

Happisburgh, coast par. and vil., Norfolk, 6 m. E. of N. Walsham ; pop. 574. Map 53.

Hapton, par. and vil., N.E. Lancashire, 3 m. N.E. of Accrington ; pop. 1950. Map 31.

Harborne, a S.W. ward of Birmingham. Map 58.

Harbury, par. and vil., Warwickshire, 5 m. S.E. of Leamington ; pop. 1192. Map 58.

Harlech, ancient coast town, Merionethshire, 11¼ m. N. of Barmouth. Map 44.

Harleston, market town, Norfolk, 6½ m. S.W. of Bungay ; pop. of par. 1789. Map 63.

Harling, East, par. and town, Norfolk, 7½ m. N.E. of Thetford ; pop. 880. Map 62.

Harlow, market town and par., Essex, 24¼ m. N.E. of London by rail ; pop. 2962. Map 72.

Harpenden, urb. dist. and par., Hertfordshire, 5 m. S.E. of Luton by rail ; pop. 8349. Map 71.

Harrietfield, vil., S.E. Perthshire, 3½ m. N.W. of Methven. Map 6.

Harrietsham, par. and vil., Kent, 7 m. S.E. of Maidstone ; pop. 722. Map 82.

Harrington, urb. dist. and par., Cumberland, 4½ m. N. of Whitehaven ; pop. 4125. Map 20.

Harris, par. and lower part of Lewis Isl., Outer Hebrides, Inverness-shire ; pop. 5276. Map 2.

Harrogate, mun. bor., par. and market town, W.R. Yorks, 18 m. N. of Leeds ; pop. 39,785. Map 32.

Harrow-on-the-Hill, urb. dist., Middlesex, 10 m. N.W. of London ; pop. 26,378. Map 71.

Hartfield, par. and vil., E. Sussex, 6¾ m. S. of East Grinstead ; pop. 1861. Map 81.

Hartington, town, N. Derbyshire, 8 m. S.W. of Bakewell ; pop. 405. Map 40.

Hartland, par. and vil., N. Devonshire, 13½ m. W. of Bideford ; pop. 1483. Map 84.

Hartlepool, mun. bor., par. and seaport, Durham, 11 m. N.E. of Stockton ; pop. 20,545. Map 23.

Hartlepool, West, co. bor. and par. within the parl. limits of Hartlepool ; pop. 68,134. Map 23.

Hartley, ward of Seaton Delaval, Northumberland, 4 m. S.E. of Blyth. Map 23.

Hartshill, par. and vil., Warwickshire, 3 m. S.S.E. of Atherstone ; pop. 2560. Map 48.

Harwich, mun. bor., seaport and par., Essex, 10 m. S.E. of Ipswich ; pop. 12,700. Map 73.

Harwood, Great, urb. dist., town and par., N.E. Lancs, 4½ m. N.E. of Blackburn ; pop. 12,787. Map 31.

Haselbury Bryan, par., Dorsetshire, 4 m. S.W. of Sturminster Newton ; pop. 484. Map 87.

Haslemere, urb. dist. and par., S.W. Surrey, 12¾ m. S.W. of Guildford ; pop. 4340. Map 79.

Haslingden, mun. bor., mkt. tn. and par., N.E. Lancs, 3½ m. S. of Accrington ; pop. 16,637. Map 31.

Hastings, co. bor., par. and Cinque port, E. Sussex, 34 m. E. of Brighton ; pop. 65,199. Map 82.

Haswell, par. and vil., Durham, 9¼ m. S.S.W. of Sunderland ; pop. 6199. Map 23.

Hatfield, market town and par., in co. and 6 m. S.W. of Hertford ; pop. 5965. Map 71.

Hatfield, par., W.R. Yorkshire, 7 m. N.E. of Doncaster ; pop. 1820. Map 33.

Hatherleigh, par. and vil., Devonshire, 10¾ m. S.S.E. of Torrington ; pop. 1206. Map 84.

Hathern, par. and ry. sta., Leicestershire, 3 m. N.W. of Loughborough ; pop. 1124. Map 49.

Hathersage, par., N. Derbyshire, on r. Derwent, 10 m. N. of Bakewell ; pop. 1694. Map 40.

Hatherton, par. and vil., Staffordshire, 3 m. S.E. of Penkridge ; pop. 532. Map 47.

Haughton, par. and vil., in co. and 4 m. S.W. of Stafford ; pop. 567. Map 47.

Havant, urb. dist. and par., Hants, 7½ m. N.E. of Portsmouth ; pop. 4264. Map 79.

Haverfordwest, mun. bor. and cap. of Pembrokeshire, 9 m. N.N.W. of Pembroke ; pop. 6113. Map 64.

Haverhill, urb. dist. and par., W. Suffolk, 12 m. S.S.E. of Newmarket ; pop. 3827. Map 61.

Haveringland, par. and vil., Norfolk, 8 m. N.W. of Norwich ; pop. 126. Map 53.

Haverrigg, vil., Cumberland, 1¼ m. S.W. of Millom. Map 25.

Hawarden, market town and par., Flintshire, 6 m. N.W. of Chester ; pop. 8016. **H. Castle** is a seat. Map 38.

Hawes, par. and market town, N.R. Yorkshire, 16 m. W. of Leyburn ; pop. 1437. Map 26.

Hawes Water, lake, Westmorland, 2¼ m. long, 694 ft. above sea level. Map 26.

Hawick, mun. bur., town and par., Roxburghshire, 53¾ m. S.E. of Edinburgh ; pop. 17,059. Map 16.

Haworth, urb. dist., par. and town, W.R. Yorkshire, 3¼ m. S.W. of Keighley ; pop. 5912. Map 32.

Hawstead, par. and vil., W. Suffolk, 3 m. S. of Bury St Edmunds ; pop. 266. Map 62.

Haxey, par. and vil., Lindsey, Lincolnshire, 7¼ m. N.W. of Gainsborough ; pop. 1944. Map 42.

Hay, urb. dist. and par., Breconshire, 7 m. N.E. of Brecon ; pop. 1509. Map 56.

Haydock, urb. dist. and par., S.W. Lancashire, 3 m. N.E. of St Helens ; pop. 10,352. Map 39.

Haydon Bridge, town and ry. sta., Northumberland, 6 m. W. of Hexham; pop. of eccl. dist. 2464. Map 22.

Hayes, par. and vil., Kent, 2 m. S. of Bromley; pop. 1010. Map 80.

Hayes and Harlington, urb. dist. and par., Middlesex, 3 m. S.E. of Uxbridge; pop. 23,646. Map 71.

Hayesend, ham., Middlesex, 2 m. S.E. of Uxbridge. Map 71.

Hayfield, par. and vil., N. Derbyshire, 9 m. S.E. of Stockport; pop. 2644. Map 40.

Hayle, urb. dist. and seaport, Cornwall, 7 m. N.E. of Penzance; pop. 915. Map 90.

Hayling Island, Hants, comprising the pars. of N. and S. Hayling, 4 m. S. of Havant; pop. 3288. Map 79.

Hayton, par. and vil., Cumberland, 3 m. S.W. of Brampton; pop. 1210. Map 21.

Hayton, vil., Cumberland, 5 m. N.E. of Maryport. Map 20.

Haywards Heath, urb. dist. and par., E. Sussex, 13 m. N. of Brighton; pop. 5382. Map 81.

Hazel Grove and Bramhall, urb. dist., Cheshire, 2½ m. S.E. of Stockport; pop. 13,300. Map 39.

Headcorn, par. and vil., Kent, 9 m. S.E. of Maidstone; pop. 1492. Map 82.

Headford, vil., co. Galway, 12 m. W. of Tuam ry. sta. Map 94.

Headley, par. and vil., E. Hants, 3 m. E. of Bordon sta.; pop. 4888. Map 79.

Heage, urb. dist. and par., Derbyshire, 2½ m. N.E. of Belper; pop. 4054. Map 41.

Heasor, urb. dist. and par., Derbyshire, 3¼ m. N.W. of Ilkeston; pop. 22,386. Map 41.

Hebburn, urb. dist. and par., Durham, 4 m. W.S.W. of South Shields; pop. 24,125. Map 23.

Hebden Bridge, urb. dist. and par., W.R. Yorkshire, 4 m. N.E. of Todmorden; pop. 6312. Map 32.

Heckington, par. and vil., Kesteven, Lincolnshire, 5 m. E.S.E. of Sleaford; pop. 1551. Map 50.

Heckmondwike, urb. dist. and par., W.R. Yorkshire, 2 m. N.W. of Dewsbury; pop. 8991. Map 32.

Heddon-on-the-Wall, par. and vil., Northumberland, 7 m. W.N.W. of Newcastle; pop. 676. Map 22.

Hednesford, eccl. dist. and ward in Cannock urb. dist., Staffordshire; pop. 11,868. Map 48.

Hedon, mun. bor. and par., E.R. Yorkshire, 5¼ m. E. of Hull; pop. 1509. Map 35.

Hele Bridge, place, Devonshire, on r. Torridge, 1½ m. N. of Hatherleigh. Map 84.

Helensburgh, police bur., Dumbartonshire, on Firth of Clyde, opposite Greenock; pop. 8893. Map 8.

Helmdon, par. and vil., Northamptonshire, 7¾ m. S.W. of Towcester; pop. 409. Map 59.

Helmsdale, seaport, Sutherlandshire, 17½ m. N.E. of Golspie; pop. 691. Map 3.

Helmsley, town and par., N.R. Yorkshire, 20 m. N. of York; pop. 1303. Map 28.

Helperthorpe, par., E.R. Yorkshire, 9 m. N.W. of Great Driffield; pop. 124. Map 29.

Helpringham, par. and vil., Kesteven, Lincolnshire, 5 m. S.E. of Sleaford; pop. 733. Map 50.

Helston, mun. bor. and par., Cornwall, 10 m. S.W. of Falmouth; pop. 2544. Map 90.

Hemel Hempstead, mun. bor. and par., Hertfordshire, 12 m. S.W. of Luton; pop. 15,122. Map 71.

Hempstead with Eccles, coast par., Norfolk, 8 m. S.E. of N. Walsham; pop. 125. Map 53.

Hemsworth, urb. dist. and par., W.R. Yorkshire, 8¼ m. S.E. of Wakefield; pop. 13,001. Map 33.

Hemyock, par. and vil., Devonshire, 7½ m. E. of Tiverton Junction; pop. 882. Map 85.

Henbury, par. and vil., S. Gloucestershire, 7¾ m. N.W. of Bristol; pop. 2260. Map 74.

Hendon, urb. dist., Middlesex, 8 m. N.W. of St Paul's, London; pop. 115,682. Map 71.

Hendy, vil., Carmarthenshire, 5¾ m. N.E. of Llanelly. Map 65.

Henfield, par. and vil., W. Sussex, 4 m. N.E. of Steyning; pop. 1948. Map 79.

Hengrave, par. and vil., W. Suffolk, 3 m. N.W. of Bury St Edmunds; pop. 186. Map 62.

Henham, par. and vil., Essex, 6 m. N.E. of Bishop's Stortford; pop. 726. Map 72.

Henley-in-Arden, eccl. par. and town, in co. and 8½ m. W. of Warwick; pop. 1192. Map 58.

Henley-on-Thames, mun. bor., S.E. Oxon, 35½ m. W. of London; pop. 6618. Map 78.

Herbrandston, par. and vil., Pembrokeshire, 2½ m. W.N.W. of Milford; pop. 267. Map 64.

Hereford, city, mun. bor. and co. town of Herefordshire, 144 m. N.W. of London; pop. 24,159. Map 57.

Herne, par. and vil., Kent, 5½ m. N.N.E. of Canterbury; pop. 1964. Map 83.

Herne Bay, urb. dist. and par., Kent, 11 m. S.W. of Margate; pop. 11,244. Map 83.

Hersham, eccl. par. and vil., N. Surrey, 2½ m. E. of Weybridge; pop. 6110. Map 78.

Hertford, mun. bor. and capital of Hertfordshire, 24½ m. N. of London; pop. 11,376. Map 71.

Hesketh Bank, ham., on coast of W. Lancashire, 9 m. N.E. of Southport. Map 30.

Hessle, urb. dist., E.R. Yorkshire, 4½ m. S.W. of Hull; pop. 6430. Map 35.

Heston and Isleworth, urb. dist., Middlesex, 1½ m. N.N.W. of Hounslow; pop. 75,446. Map 71.

Hethersett, par. and vil., Norfolk, 6¼ m. S.W. of Norwich; pop. 1119. Map 53.

Hetton-le-Hole, urb. dist. and par., Durham, 7 m. S. of Sunderland; pop. 17,672. Map 23.

Hevingham, par. and vil., Norfolk, 8½ m. N.N.W. of Norwich; pop. 698. Map 53.

Hexham, urb. dist. and par., Northumberland, 20 m. W. of Newcastle-on-Tyne; pop. 8888. Map 22.

Heybridge, par. and vil., Essex, 9 m. E. of Chelmsford; pop. 1934. Map 73.

Heysham, dist. in bor. of Morecambe, Lancaster; pop. 5027. Map 30.

Heytesbury, par. and vil., S. Wiltshire, 4 m. S.E. of Warminster; pop. 496. Map 75.

Heywood, mun. bor. and par., S.E. Lancashire, 3 m. E. of Bury; pop. 25,967. Map 31.

Higham Ferrers, mun. bor. and par., Northamptonshire, 4½ m. E. of Wellingborough; pop. 2928. Map 60.

High Bentham, par. and market town, W.R. Yorkshire, 14¾ m. N.W. of Hellifield; pop. 2463. Map 31.

High Bickington, par. and vil., Devonshire, 7½ m. E. of Torrington; pop. 56. Map 84.

Highbridge, urb. dist., N.W. Somersetshire, 6½ m. N. of Bridgwater; pop. 2584. Map 74.

Highclere, par. and vil., N. Hants, 4 m. S.W. of Newbury sta.; pop. 529. Map 76.

High Crompton, eccl. dist. and vil., S.E. Lancashire, 3 m. N. of Oldham; pop. 1873. Map 31.

Higher Newton, ham., N. Lancashire, 3 m. N.E. of Cartmel. Map 25.

Highgate, N. suburb of London, in Hornsey mun. bor., E. Middlesex. Map 71.

High Halden, par. and vil., Kent, 2½ m. N.N.E. of Tenterden; pop. 632. Map 82.

High Ongar, par. and vil., Essex, 6 m. E. of Epping; pop. 1209. Map 72.

High Roding, par., Essex, on r. Roding, 4 m. S.W. of Dunmow; pop. 351. Map 72.

Highworth, town and par., Wiltshire, 6 m. N.E. of Swindon; pop. 2072. Map 69.

Hildenborough, par. and vil., W. Kent, 2 m. N.W. of Tonbridge; pop. 1727. Map 82.

Hilderstone, par. and vil., Staffordshire, 3 m. E. of Stone; pop. 377. Map 47.

Hilgay, par. and vil., Norfolk, 3 m. S. of Downham; pop. 1491. Map 51.

Hillsborough, market town and par., co. Down, 12 m. S.S.W. of Belfast; pop. (town) 544. Map 93.
Hilmarton, par. and vil., N. Wiltshire, 3½ m. N.E. of Calne; pop. 718. Map 75.
Hinckley, urb. dist. and par., in co. and 14½ m. S.W. of Leicester; pop. 16,030. Map 49.
Hinderwell, urb. dist. and par., N.R. Yorkshire, 7½ m. N.W. of Whitby; pop. 2147. Map 29.
Hindhead, eccl. dist., Surrey, 2 m. N.W. of Haslemere; pop. 1536. Map 79.
Hindley, urb. dist. and par., Lancashire, 2½ m. S.E. of Wigan; pop. 21,629. Map 39.
Hindlow, ry. sta., N.W. Derbyshire, 3½ m. S. of Buxton. Map 40.
Hindolveston, par. and vil., Norfolk, 8 m. E. of Fakenham; pop. 571. Map 52.
Hindon, par. and vil., S. Wiltshire, 9 m. S.E. of Warminster; pop. 415. Map 75.
Hingham, par. and vil., Norfolk, 6 m. W. of Wymondham; pop. 1413. Map 52.
Hinton-on-the-Green, par., vil. and ry. stn., Worcestershire, 2½ m. S.S.W. of Evesham. Map 58.
Hinton St George, par. and vil., Somersetshire, 2 m. N.W. of Crewkerne; pop. 433. Map 86.
Hipperholme, urb. dist. and par., W.R. Yorkshire, 2 m. N.E. of Halifax; pop. 5383. Map 31.
Hirnant, par. and vil., Montgomeryshire, 6½ m. N.W. of Llanfyllin; pop. 208. Map 46.
Hirwain, vil. and ry. sta., Glamorganshire, 3½ m. N.W. of Aberdare. Map 66.
Hitchin, urb. dist. and par., in co. and 13½ m. N.W. of Hertford; pop. 14,382. Map 71.
Hoath, par. and vil., Kent, 5 m. N.E. of Canterbury; pop. 317. Map 83.
Hobkirk, par., Roxburghshire, 6 m. S.E. of Hawick; pop. 555. Map 16.
Hoddesdon, urb. dist. and par., in co. and 4 m. S.E. of Hertford; pop. 6811. Map 71.
Holbeach, urb. dist., Holland, Lincolnshire, 7½ m. E.N.E. of Spalding; pop. 6111. Map 51.
Holcombe, vil., S. Devonshire, 1½ m. S.W. of Dawlish. Map 89.
Holkham, par. and vil., Norfolk, 2¼ m. W. of Wells; pop. 426. Map 52.
Holland Arms, ry. sta., 2½ m. S.E. of Llangefni, Anglesey. Map 36.
Hollington Rural, par. and vil., E. Sussex, 2½ m. N.W. of Hastings; pop. 451. Map 82.
Hollingworth, urb. dist., Cheshire, 3½ m. S.E. of Stalybridge; pop. 2299. Map 40.
Holme, par. and vil., Westmorland, 1½ m. N. of Burton in Kendal; pop. 626. Map 26.
Holme, urb. dist., W.R. Yorkshire, 9 m. S.W. of Huddersfield; pop. 368. Map 32.
Holme Cultram, urb. dist., Cumberland pop. 4735. Map 20.
Holme Hale, par. and vil., Norfolk, 5 m. E.S.E. of Swaffham; pop. 343. Map 52.
Holme-on-the-Wolds, par. and vil., E.R. Yorkshire, 6½ m. N.W. of Beverley; pop. 136. Map 35.
Holmes Chapel, vil., mid Cheshire, 4 m. N.E. of Sandbach. Map 39.
Holme upon Spalding Moor, par. and vil., E.R. Yorks, 5½ m. S.W. of Market Weighton; pop. 1596. Map 34.
Holmfirth, urb. dist. and par., W.R. Yorkshire, 6 m. S. of Huddersfield; pop. 10,407. Map 31.
Holsworthy, urb. dist. and par., Devonshire, 15 m. W. of Hatherleigh; pop. 1403. Map 84.
Holt, market town and par., Norfolk, 10 m. W.S.W. of Cromer; pop. 2249. Map 53.
Holt, par. and vil., N. Wiltshire, 3 m. N.E. of Bradford-on-Avon; pop. 991. Map 75.
Holt, par., Denbighshire, on r. Dee, 5½ m. N.E. of Wrexham; pop. 1265. Map 38.
Holton, par. and vil., E. Suffolk, 1 m. E. of Halesworth; pop. 500. Map 63.
Holyhead, spt., urb. dist., par., coastguard and lifeboat sta., Holyhead I., Anglesey; pop. 10,707. Map 36.
Holyhead Island, on W. side of and forming part of co. of Anglesey, 8 m. long, 3½ m. wide. Map 36.
Holy Island, or **Lindisfarne,** par. off coast of N. Northumberland; pop. 586. Map 17.
Holy Loch, arm of Clyde, Dunoon and Kilmun par., Argyllshire. Map 12.
Holytown, town and *q.s.* par., Lanarkshire, 11 m. S.E. of Glasgow; town pop. 12,537. Map 9.
Holywell, urb. dist. and par., on Dee estuary, Flintshire, 4½ m. N.W. of Flint; pop. 3423. Map 38.
Honeyborough, vil., Pembrokeshire, 3 m. E. of Milford Haven. Map 64.
Honiton, mun. bor. and par., Devonshire, 16½ m. N.E. of Exeter; pop. 3008. Map 86.
Honley, urb. dist., W.R. Yorkshire, 6 m. S. of Huddersfield; pop. 4619. Map 32.
Hook, ham., Hants, 5½ m. N.E. of Basingstoke. Map 78.
Hoole, urb. dist., adjoining Chester; pop. 5889. Map 38.
Hope Bowdler, par. and vil., Salop, 2 m. S.E. of Church Stretton; pop. 121. Map 46.
Hopton, par. and vil., W. Suffolk, 8 m. E.S.E. of Thetford; pop. 420. Map 62.
Horbury, urb. dist., par. and vil., W.R. Yorkshire, 3¾ m. S.W. of Wakefield; pop. 7791. Map 32.
Horley, par. and residential vil., S. Surrey, 5 m. S.S.E. of Reigate; pop. 6100. Map 80.
Hornby, par. and vil., N. Lancashire, 8½ m. N.E. of Lancaster; pop. 421. Map 26.
Horncastle, urb. dist. and par., Lindsey, Lincolnshire, 21 m. E. of Lincoln; pop. 3496. Map 43.
Hornchurch, urb. dist., Essex, 2 m. S.E. of Romford; pop. 28,417. Map 72.
Horndon-on-the-Hill, par. and vil., S. Essex, 2 m. N.E. of Orsett; pop. 683. Map 72.
Hornsea, urb. dist. and par., E.R. Yorkshire, on N. sea, 15½ m. N.E. of Hull; pop. 4450. Map 35.
Hornsey, mun. bor., Middlesex, 4½ m. N. of King's Cross sta.; pop. 95,524. Map 71.
Horsforth, urb. dist. and par., W.R. Yorkshire, 5 m. N.W. of Leeds; pop. 11,770. Map 32.
Horsham, urb. dist. and par., W. Sussex, 26 m. N.W. of Brighton; pop. 13,579. Map 79.
Horsham St Faith with Newton St Faith, par. and vil., Norfolk, 4 m. N. of Norwich; pop. 843. Map 53.
Horton in Ribblesdale, par. and vil., W.R. Yorkshire, 6 m. N.N.W. of Settle; pop. 704. Map 26.
Horwich, urb. dist. and par., S.E. Lancashire, 18 m. N.W. of Manchester; pop. 15,680. Map 30.
Hospital, par. and vil., co. Limerick, 3 m. N. of Knocklong sta.; pop. 1235. Map 94.
Hotham, par. and vil., E.R. Yorkshire, 5 m. S.E. of Market Weighton; pop. 279. Map 34.
Hoton, par. and vil., Leicestershire, 3 m. N.E. of Loughborough; pop. 250. Map 49.
Houghton, vil., in co. and 5¾ m. N. of Pembroke. Map 64.
Houghton, par. and vil., S. Hants, 8½ m. W.N.W. of Winchester; pop. 391. Map 76.
Houghton-le-Spring, urb. dist. and par., in co. and 6½ m. N.E. of Durham; pop. 10,492. Map 23.
Hounslow, town, Heston and Isleworth pars., S.W. Middlesex, 2½ m. S.W. of Brentford. Map 71.
Houston, vil., Renfrewshire, 6 m. N.W. of Paisley. Map 8.
Hove, mun. bor. adjoining Brighton on the west, Sussex; pop. 54,994. Map 81.
Hovingham, par. and vil., N.R. Yorkshire, 8 m. W.N.W. of Malton; pop. 411. Map 28.
Howden, market town and par., E.R. Yorkshire, 21 m. W. of Hull; pop. 2052. Map 34.
Howick, coast par. and vil., Northumberland, 5 m. N.E. of Alnwick; pop. 245. Map 17.
Hoxne, par. and vil., E. Suffolk, 3½ m. N.E. of Eye; pop. 769. Map 63.

Hoylake, urb. dist. and par., Cheshire, 6 m. W. of Birkenhead. Golfing, watering place, racecourse ; pop. 16,628. Map 38.

Hoyland, Nether, urb. dist., W.R. Yorkshire, 5½ m. S.E. of Barnsley ; pop. 15,215. Map 41.

Hoyland Swaine, urb. dist., W.R. Yorkshire, 5¼ m. W.S.W. of Barnsley ; pop. 793. Map 32.

Hubberston, par. and vil., Pembrokeshire, on Milford Haven ; pop. 255. Map 64.

Hucknall Torkard, urb. dist. and par., in co. and 8 m. N.W. of Nottingham ; pop. 17,338. Map 41.

Huddersfield, parl. and co. bor. and par., W.R. Yorks, 16½ m. S.W. of Leeds ; pop. 113,467. Map 31.

Huggate, par. and vil., E.R. Yorkshire, on the Wolds, 7 m. N.E. of Pocklington ; pop. 403. Map 34.

Hull, parl. and co. bor., city, spt. and co. in itself, E.R. Yorkshire ; pop. 313,366. Map 35.

Hullavington, par. and vil., N. Wiltshire, 5 m. S.W. of Malmesbury ; pop. 478. Map 68.

Hulton, Little, urb. dist., Lancashire, 3½ m. S. of Bolton ; pop. 7878. Map 31.

Humshaugh, par. and vil., Northumberland, 5 m. N.N.W. of Hexham ; pop. 487. Map 22.

Hungerford, mkt. tn. and par., Berks., on r. Kennet, 27 m. W.S.W. of Reading ; pop. 2784. Map 76.

Hunmanby, par. and vil., E.R. Yorkshire, 12 m. S.E. of Scarborough by rail ; pop. 1501. Map 29.

Hunstanton, New, urb. dist. and par., N.W. Norfolk, on the Wash ; pop. 3131. Map 52.

Hunsworth, urb. dist., W.R. Yorkshire, 3½ m. S.E. of Bradford ; pop. 1318. Map 32.

Hunter's Quay, part of Dunoon, Argyllshire. Map 12.

Huntingdon, mun. bor. and co. town of Huntingdonshire, 59 m. N. of London ; pop. 4108. Map 61.

Huntington, par., N.R. Yorkshire, 3 m. N. of York ; pop. 2219. Map 34.

Huntly, town and par., in co. and 41 m. N.W. of Aberdeen ; pop. of bur. 3778. Map 3.

Hurstbourne Priors, par. and vil., N. Hants, 3½ m. N.E. of Andover ; pop. 394. Map 76.

Hurstbourne Tarrant, par. and vil., N. Hants, 5½ m. N. of Andover ; pop. 619. Map 76.

Hurst Green, eccl. dist. and ham., E. Sussex, 2½ m. N. of Robertsbridge ; pop. 703. Map 82.

Hurstpierpoint, par. and market town, E. Sussex, 8 m. N. of Brighton ; pop. 3099. Map 81.

Hurworth, par. and vil., S. Durham, 3 m. S. of Darlington ; pop. 1444. Map 27.

Husbands Bosworth, par. and vil., Leicestershire, 6 m. S.W. of Market Harborough ; pop. 732. Map 59.

Husthwaite, par. and vil., N.R. Yorkshire, 4 m. N. of Easingwold ; pop. 376. Map 28.

Huthwaite, urb. dist., Nottinghamshire, 3 m. S.W. of Mansfield ; pop. 5092. Map 41.

Hutton Bushel, par. and vil., N.R. Yorkshire, 5 m. S.W. of Scarborough ; pop. 313. Map 29.

Hutton-le-Hole, par. and vil., N.R. Yorkshire, 2½ m. N.N.E. of Kirkby Moorside ; pop. 242. Map 28.

Hutton Rudby, par. and vil., N.R. Yorkshire, 4 m. S.W. of Stokesley ; pop. 894. Map 28.

Huyton, urb. dist., par. and vil., S.W. Lancashire, 5½ m. E. of Liverpool ; pop. (with Roby) 5198. Map 38.

Hyde, mun. bor., mkt. tn. and par., E. Cheshire, 7½ m. E. of Manchester ; pop. 32,066. Map 39.

Hythe, parl. and mun. bor., E. Kent, 68 m. S.E. of London ; mun. bor. pop. 8397. Map 83.

Hythe, eccl. dist. and vil., S. Hants, 2½ m. S. of Southampton sta. ; pop. 1076. Map 77.

IBSLEY, par. and vil., Hampshire, 3 m. N. of Ringwood ; pop. 220. Map 77.

Ibstock, par. and vil., Leicestershire, 14 m. S.W. of Loughborough ; pop. 5211. Map 49.

Ibstone, par. and vil., Buckinghamshire, 8 m. W. of High Wycombe ; pop. 241. Map 70.

Icklesham, par. and vil., E. Sussex, 1½ m. W. of Winchelsea ; pop. 1474. Map 82.

Icklingham, par. and vil., W. Suffolk, 4 m. S.E. of Mildenhall ; pop. 285. Map 62.

Iddesleigh, par. and vil., S. Devon, 3 m. N.E. of Hatherleigh. Map 84.

Idridgehay, ham., N. Derbyshire, in par. and 3 m. S. of Wirksworth ; pop. 572. Map 40.

Iffley, par. and vil., Oxon, 1½ m. S.E. of Oxford ; pop. 405. Map 70.

Ightham, par. and vil., W. Kent, 4½ m. N.E. of Sevenoaks ; pop. 1596. Map 82.

Ilchester, par. and vil., S. Somersetshire, 5 m. N.W. of Yeovil ; pop. 449. Map 86.

Ilford, urb. dist., S. Essex, 3½ m. N.E. of Stratford ; pop. 131,046. Map 72.

Ilfracombe, urb. dist. and market town, N. Devonshire, 14 m. N.W. of Barnstaple ; pop. 9174. Map 84.

Ilkeston, mun. bor., market town and par., in co. and 8 m. N.E. of Derby ; pop. 32,809. Map 49.

Ilkley, urb. dist., par. and watering place, W.R. Yorkshire, 9 m. S.E. of Skipton ; pop. 9721. Map 32.

Ilminster, urb. dist. and par., S. Somersetshire, 5 m. N.E. of Chard ; pop. 2232. Map 86.

Ilsley, East, small town and par., Berkshire, 9 m. N. of Newbury ; pop. 429. Map 70.

Immingham Dock, par. and port, Lincolnshire, 4¼ m. N.W. of Grimsby ; pop. 2150. Map 35.

Ince Blundell, par. and seat, S.W. Lancashire, 8 m. N. of Liverpool ; pop. 440. Map 38.

Ince-in-Makerfield, urb. dist. Lancashire, sub. of Wigan ; pop. 21,763. Map 30.

Inchcolm, isl. in Firth of Forth, Fifeshire. Map 10.

Inchkeith, isl. in Firth of Forth, Fifeshire. Map 10.

Inchnadamff, ham., S.W. Sutherlandshire, at S.E. end of Loch Assynt. Map 2.

Inchture, par. and vil., Perthshire, 8 m. S.W. of Dundee ; pop. 490. Map 6.

Ingatestone, par. and vil., W. Essex, 6 m. S.W. of Chelmsford ; pop. 2012. Map 72.

Ingleby Cross, ham., N.R. Yorkshire, 7 m. N.E. of Northallerton. Map 28.

Ingleton, par. and vil., W.R. Yorkshire, 4 m. N.W. of Clapham ; pop. 2464. Map 26.

Ingoldsby, par. and vil., Kesteven, Lincolnshire, 8 m. S.E. of Grantham ; pop. 239. Map 50.

Ingrow, vil., W.R. Yorks, 1 m. S.W. of Keighley. Map 31.

Ingworth, par. and vil., Norfolk, 2 m. N. of Aylsham ; pop. 143. Map 53.

Inkberrow, par. and vil., Worcestershire, 5 m. W. of Alcester ; pop. 1360. Map 58.

Inkpen, par. and vil., S.W. Berkshire, 4 m. S.E. of Hungerford ; pop. 575. Map 76.

Innellan, q.s. par. and vil., Argyllshire, 3¾ m. S. of Dunoon ; pop. 1409. Map 12.

Innerleithen, town and par., in co. and 6¼ m. S.E. of Peebles ; bur. pop. 2359. Map 15.

Innerwick, par. and vil., East Lothian, 5 m. S.E. of Dunbar ; pop. 146. Map 11.

Insch, par. and vil., Aberdeenshire, 13½ m. S.E. of Huntly ; pop. 1377. Map 3.

Inveraray, mun. bur., par. and co. town of Argyllshire, 15 m. S.W. of Dalmally ; bur. pop. 455. Map 12.

Inverbervie, mun. bur., Kincardineshire, 13 m. N.E. of Montrose ; pop. 1032. Map 3.

Invergarry, ham., Inverness-shire, 7 m. S.W. of Fort Augustus. Map 2.

Invergordon, police bur. and tn., E. Ross and Cromarty, 13 m. N.E. of Dingwall ; pop. 1417. Map 3.

Inverkeilor, coast par. and vil., Angus, 6 m. N. of Arbroath ; pop. 1297. Map 7.

Inverkeithing, mun. bur. and par., Fifeshire, 13¼ m. N.W. of Edinburgh ; pop. 3185. Map 10.

Inverkip, par. and vil., Renfrewshire, 6 m. S.W. of Greenock ; pop. 12,901. Map 12.

Inverness, mun. bur., spt. and mkt. tn., Inverness-shire, 108 m. from Aberdeen; pop. 22,582. Map 3.
Inverurie, police bur. and par., in co. and 16½ m. N.W. of Aberdeen; pop. 4524. Map 3.
Iona, isl., off S.W. coast of Mull Isl., Argyllshire. Map 12.
Ipstones, par. and vil., Staffordshire, 4½ m. N. of Cheadle; pop. 1757. Map 40.
Ipswich, parl. and co. bor. and seaport, E. Suffolk, 68¾ m. N.E. of London; pop. 87,557. Map 63.
Irchester, par. and vil., Northamptonshire, 2 m. S.E. of Wellingborough; pop. 2304. Map 60.
Ireby, par., N. Lancashire, 3½ m. S.E. of Kirkby Lonsdale; pop. 71. Map 26.
Irlam, urb. dist., Lancashire, 8 m. S.W. of Manchester; pop. 12,898. Map 39.
Ironbridge, eccl. dist. and town, Shropshire, 13¾ m. S.E. of Shrewsbury; pop. 2371. Map 47.
Irthington, par. and vil., Cumberland, 2 m. N.W. of Brampton; pop. 671. Map 21.
Irthlingborough, urb. dist. and par., Northamptonshire, 2 m. N.W. of Higham Ferrers; pop. 4715. Map 60.
Irvine, mun. bur., market town and par., Ayrshire, 30½ m. S.W. of Glasgow; pop. of bur. 12,032. Map 12.
Isfield, par. and vil., Sussex, 3 m. S.W. of Uckfield; pop. 478. Map 81.
Islay, Isle of, in Argyllshire, 13 m. W. of Kintyre; pop. 5743. Map 12.
Isleham, par. and vil., Cambridgeshire, 6½ m. N. of Newmarket; pop. 1490. Map 61.
Isleworth, par. and suburban town, Middlesex, 12 m. W.S.W. of London; pop. 29,908. Map 71.
Ivinghoe, market vil. and par., Buckinghamshire, 2 m. S.E. of Cheddington Junction; pop. 810. Map 71.
Ivybridge, urb. dist. and par., Devonshire, 10½ m. E.N.E. of Plymouth; pop. 1609. Map 88.
Iwerne Minster, par. and vil., Dorsetshire, 5 m. N. of Blandford; pop. 501. Map 87.
Ixworth, par. and vil., W. Suffolk, 7 m. N.E. of Bury St Edmunds; pop. 779. Map 62.
JACOBSTOW, par. and vil., Cornwall, 11 m. N.W. of Launceston; pop. 312. Map 84.
Jamestown, vil., in S. co. Leitrim, 3 m. S.E. of Carrick-on-Shannon. Map 92.
Jamestown, town and *q.s.* par., Dumbartonshire, 1 m. S.E. of Balloch; pop. 2389. Map 12.
Jarrow, mun. bor. and par., Durham, 4¼ m. W.S.W. of South Shields; pop. 32,018. Map 23.
Jeantown, vil., on W. side of Loch Carron, Ross and Cromarty. Map 2.
Jedburgh, bur., par. and co. town of Roxburghshire, 56 m. S.E. of Edinburgh; pop. 3057. Map 16.
Jeffreston, par. and vil., Pembrokeshire, 5½ m. S.S.W. of Narberth; pop. 419. Map 64.
Jemimaville, vil., Ross and Cromarty, 2 m. S.S.E. of Invergordon. Map 3.
Jervaulx Abbey, N.R. Yorkshire, 5 m. S.E. of Leyburn. Map 27.
Johnby, vil. and seat, Cumberland, 6 m. N.W. of Penrith. Map 21.
John o' Groats, house, Caithness-shire, 1½ m. W. of Duncansby Head. Map 3.
Johnshaven, fishing vil., Kincardineshire, 8½ m. N.E. of Montrose. Map 3.
Johnston, par. and vil., Pembrokeshire, 4½ m. W.S.W. of Haverfordwest; pop. 322. Map 64.
Johnstone, manufacturing town and police bur., Renfrewshire, 9½ m. W. of Glasgow; pop. 12,837. Map 8.
Juniper Green, *q.s.* par., in city and 4¾ m. from Princes Street sta., Edinburgh; pop. 1865. Map 10.
Jura, Isle of, isl. and par., Argyllshire; pop. 446. Map 12.
Jurby, par. and vil., Isle of Man, 6 m. N.W. of Ramsey; pop. 448. Map 24.
KAMES, vil., on Kyles of Bute, Argyllshire, 1½ m. S.W. of Tighnabruaich. Map 12.
Kanturk, market town, N. co. Cork, 36¼ m. N.W. of Cork; pop. 1630. Map 94.
Katrine, Loch, Perthshire and Stirlingshire, 8½ m. W. of Callander. Map 12.
Keadby, par. and vil., Lindsey, Lincolnshire, 4 m. S.E. of Crowle; pop. 681. Map 34.
Keady, town and par., in co. and 8 m. S.W. of Armagh; pop. 5202. Map 93.
Kearsley, urb. dist., Lancashire, 4 m. S.E. of Bolton; pop. 9736. Map 31.
Keelby, par. and vil., Lincolnshire, 6½ m. N.E. of Caistor; pop. 635. Map 43.
Kegworth, par. and town, Leicestershire, 5½ m. N.W of Loughborough; pop. 2139. Map 49.
Keighley, mun. bor., mkt. tn. and par., W.R. Yorkshire, 9 m. N.W. of Bradford; pop. 40,440. Map 32.
Keiss, fishing vil., Caithness-shire, 8 m. N. of Wick; pop. of *q.s.* par. 857. Map 3.
Keith, police bur. and par., Banffshire, 53½ m. N.W. of Aberdeen; pop. 4424. Map 3.
Kelso, market town and par., Roxburghshire, 52½ m. S.E. of Edinburgh; pop. 3855. Map 16.
Kelton, small port and seat, in co. and 3½ m. S. of Dumfries. Map 20.
Kelty, *q.s.* par. and mining town, Fifeshire, 5 m. S.E. of Kinross; pop. 7315. Map 10.
Kelvedon, par. and vil., Essex, 9 m. S.W. of Colchester; pop. 1547. Map 72.
Kelvedon Hatch, par. and vil., Essex, 3 m. S.E. of Chipping Ongar; pop. 469. Map 72.
Kempston, urb. dist. and par., in co. and 2 m. S. of Bedford; pop. 5390. Map 60.
Kendal, market town and par., Westmorland, 8¼ m. S.E. of Windermere; pop. 15,575. Map 26.
Kenfig, par. and ancient town, Glamorganshire, 3½ m. N. of Porthcawl; pop. 519. Map 66.
Kenilworth, urb. dist. and par., Warwickshire, 4 m. N. of Warwick; pop. 7592. Map 58.
Kenmare, town and par., Kerry, 19¾ m. S.E. of Headford Junction; pop. 2739. Map 94.
Kenmore, par. and vil., Perthshire, on r. Tay at its efflux from Loch Tay; pop. 1009. Map 5.
Kennoway, par. and vil., Fifeshire, 3 m. N.W. of Leven; pop. 1783. Map 7.
Kentford, par. and vil., W. Suffolk, 4½ m. N.E. of Newmarket; pop. 245. Map 62.
Kentisbeare, par. and vil., Devonshire, 3½ m. N.E. of Cullompton; pop. 724. Map 85.
Kenton, par. and vil., Devonshire, 6½ m. S.E. of Exeter; pop. 1826. Map 89.
Kenton, par. and vil., Northumberland, 3 m. N.W. of Newcastle-on-Tyne. Map 23.
Kessingland, coast par. and vil., E. Suffolk, 4½ m. S.W. of Lowestoft; pop. 2056. Map 63.
Keswick, urb. dist. and par., Cumberland, 12½ m. S.E. of Cockermouth; pop. 4635. Map 20.
Kettering, urb. dist. and par., Northamptonshire, 8 m. N. of Wellingborough; pop. 31,220. Map 60.
Kettlebridge, vil., Fifeshire, 2 m. S. of Ladybank Junction. Map 7.
Kettleholmbridge, ham., Dumfriesshire, 3 m. S.S.W. of Lockerbie. Map 20.
Kettlewell, par., W.R. Yorkshire, 13 m. N. of Skipton; pop. 374. Map 27.
Kew, eccl. par. and vil., on r. Thames, Surrey, 6 m. W. of London; pop. 4362. Map 71.
Keyingham, par. and vil., E.R. Yorkshire, 10 m. S.E. of Hull; pop. 595. Map 35.
Keynsham, market town and par., Somersetshire, 5 m. S.E. of Bristol; pop. 3837. Map 75.
Kidderminster, mun. bor., Worcestershire, 19 m. S.W. of Birmingham; pop. 28,914. Map 57.
Kidlington, par. and vil., Oxon, 5 m. N. of Oxford; pop. 1073. Map 70.

Kidsgrove, urb. dist., Staffordshire, 2½ m. N.N.W. of Tunstall ; pop. 9937.　Map 39.

Kidwelly, par., mun. bor. and port, Carmarthenshire, 9¼ m. N.W. of Llanelly ; pop. 3161.　Map 65.

Kilbarchan, town and par., Renfrewshire, 5 m. W. of Paisley ; pop. 7492.　Map 8.

Kilbeggan, town and par., Westmeath, 4 m. S.E. of Horseleap ry. sta. ; pop. 1265.　Map 93.

Kilbirnie, town and par., Ayrshire, 20½ m. S.W. of Glasgow ; pop. 8032.　Map 8.

Kilcock, market town and par., Kildare, 3½ m. N.W. of Maynooth ; pop. 986.　Map 93.

Kilconquhar, par. and vil., Fifeshire, 4 m. E. of Largo ; pop. 1319.　Map 7.

Kilcreggan, watering place, Dumbartonshire, 6 m. N.W. of Greenock.　Map 12.

Kilcullen, town and par., in co. and 5 m. E.S.E. of Kildare ; pop. 1293.　Map 95.

Kildare, market town, par. and cap. of co. Kildare, 30 m. S.W. of Dublin ; pop. 1971.　Map 95.

Kilfenora, par. and vil., co. Clare, 5 m. N.E. of Ennistimon ; pop. 1278.　Map 94.

Kilfinan, par. and vil., Argyllshire, on E. shore of Loch Fyne ; pop. 2199.　Map 12.

Kilfinnane, par. and town, co. Limerick, 5 m. S.E. of Kilmallock ; pop. 890.　Map 94.

Kilgarvan, par. and vil., co. Kerry, 6¾ m. N.E. of Kenmare ; pop. 2350.　Map 94.

Kilgetty, ham. and ry. sta., Pembrokeshire, 5 m. N. of Tenby.　Map 64.

Kilham, par. and vil., E.R. Yorkshire, 5½ m. N.E. of Great Driffield ; pop. 853.　Map 35.

Kilkee, watering place with ry. sta. in co. Clare, 9 m. N.W. of Kilrush ; pop. 1682.　Map 94.

Kilkeel, seaport town and par. in co. Down, 10 m. S.E. of Warrenpoint ry. sta. ; pop. 1620.　Map 93.

Kilkenny, mun. bor. with ry. sta., cap. of Kilkenny, 80 m. S.W. of Dublin ; pop. 10,056.　Map 95.

Kilkieran, ham. and bay, in co. and 28 m. W. of Galway.　Map 92.

Killala, seaport town and par., co. Mayo, 8 m. N.N.W. of Ballina ; pop. 872.　Map 92.

Killaloe, town and par., Clare, 17 m. N.E. of Limerick ; town pop. 821.　Map 94.

Killarney, par. and urb. dist., Kerry, 185½ m. S.W. of Dublin ; pop. 5325.　Map 94.

Killearn, par. and vil., Stirlingshire, 9½ m. N.W. of Lennoxtown ; pop. 1054.　Map 8.

Killeshandra, par. and town, in co. and 5 m. W. of Cavan ; pop. of town 561.　Map 93.

Killester, par. and vil., in co. and 2 m. N.E. of Dublin ; pop. 5325.　Map 95.

Killin, par. and vil., Perthshire, 39¼ m. N.W. of Stirling ; pop. 1502.　Map 12.

Killiney and Ballybrack, urb. dist. and par., co. Dublin, 2 m. S.E. of Dun-Laoghaire ; pop. 2069.　Map 95.

Killinghall, par. and vil., W.R. Yorkshire, 1 m. S. of Ripley ; pop. 1237.　Map 33.

Killorglin, par. and town, co. Kerry, 13 m. N.W. of Killarney ; pop. of town 1087.　Map 94.

Killybegs, seaport town and ry. sta., in co. and 19 m. W. of Donegal ; pop. 634.　Map 92.

Killyleagh, seaport town and par., co. Down, 4 m. E. of Crossgar ry. sta. ; pop. 1610.　Map 93.

Kilmacolm, par. and town, Renfrewshire, 17½ m. W. of Glasgow ; pop. 2852.　Map 8.

Kilmacow, par. and vil., co. Kilkenny, 6 m. N.W. of Waterford ; pop. 988.　Map 95.

Kilmacrenan, par. and vil., co. Donegal, 7 m. N.W. of Letterkenny ; pop. 4375.　Map 92.

Kilmallock, market town with ry. sta., in co. and 20¾ m. S. of Limerick ; pop. 1101.　Map 94.

Kilmany, par. and vil., Fifeshire, 5 m. N. of Cupar ; pop. 514.　Map 7.

Kilmarnock, mun. bur. and par., Ayrshire, 24¼ m. S.W. of Glasgow ; pop. 38,099.　Map 12.

Kilmaurs, town and par., Ayrshire, 2¼ m. N.W. of Kilmarnock ; pop. 1843.　Map 12.

Kilmun, q.s. par. and vil., Argyllshire, 7½ m. W. of Greenock ; pop. 1351.　Map 12.

Kilrea, town and par., Londonderry, 5¾ m. S.E. o Garvagh ; pop. 783.　Map 93.

Kilrenny, mun. bur. and par., Fifeshire, on Firth of Forth ; pop. 3325.　Map 7.

Kilronan, vil., Inishmore Isl., co. Galway ; pop. 459. Map 94.

Kilrush, seaport town, urb. dist. and par., Clare, 9 m. S.E. of Kilkee ; pop. 3346.　Map 94.

Kilsby, par. and vil., Northamptonshire, 7 m. N. of Daventry ; pop. 518.　Map 59.

Kilspindie, par. and vil., S.E. Perthshire, 2 m. N.W. of Errol sta. ; pop. 437.　Map 6.

Kilsyth, town, police bur. and par., Stirlingshire, 12¾ m. N.E. of Glasgow ; pop. 7551.　Map 9.

Kilwinning, town and par., Ayrshire, 26½ m. S.W. of Glasgow ; pop. 5324.　Map 12.

Kilworth, par. and vil., co. Cork, 3 m. N. of Fermoy ; pop. 990.　Map 94.

Kimberley, par. and town, in co. and 5 m. N.W. of Nottingham ; pop. 5158.　Map 49.

Kimbolton, market town and par., in co. and 10½ m. W.S.W. of Huntingdon ; pop. 902.　Map 60.

Kimbolton, par. and vil., Herefordshire, 2½ m. N.E. of Leominster ; pop. 526.　Map 57.

Kimpton, par. and vil., Hampshire, 5 m. W.N.W. of Andover ; pop. 387.　Map 76.

Kincardine, small seaport town, Fifeshire, 5½ m. S.E. of Alloa ; pop. 2112.　Map 9.

Kinder Scout, mtn., Peak dist., Derbyshire ; height 2088 ft.　Map 40.

Kineton, market town and par. Warwickshire, 6 m. W. of Fenny Compton ; pop. 950.　Map 59.

Kingham, par. and vil., Oxon, 4½ m. S.W. of Chipping Norton ; pop. 713.　Map 59.

Kinghorn, parl., mun. bur. and par., Fifeshire, 22½ m. N. of Edinburgh ; pop. 2001.　Map 10.

Kinglassie, par. and vil., Fifeshire, 6 m. N.W. of Kirkcaldy ; pop. 836.　Map 10.

Kingsand, vil., Cornwall, 4 m. S.W. of Plymouth. Map 88.

Kingsbarns, par. and vil., Fifeshire, 8 m. S.E. of St Andrews ; pop. 640.　Map 7.

Kingsbridge, urb. dist. and par., Devonshire, 11 m. S.W. of Totnes ; pop. 2978.　Map 89.

Kingsbury, urb. dist., Middlesex, on r. Brent ; pop. 16,636.　Map 71.

Kingsbury Episcopi, par. and vil., Somersetshire, 4 m. S. of Langport ; pop. 1114.　Map 86.

Kingsclere, market town and par., Hampshire, 9 m. N.W. of Basingstoke ; pop. 2243.　Map 76.

King's Cliffe, par. and vil., Northamptonshire, 12 m. W. of Peterborough ; pop. 974.　Map 50.

Kingscourt, town with ry. sta., Cavan, 47 m. N.W. of Dublin ; pop. 788.　Map 93.

Kingsheath, eccl. par. in S. of Birmingham ; pop. 14,765.　Map 58.

Kingskettle, ry. sta., Fifeshire, 1 m. S. of Ladybank Junction.　Map 7.

Kings Langley, par. and vil., Hertfordshire, 5 m. N. of Watford ; pop. 2504.　Map 71.

Kingsley, par. and vil., N.E. Hampshire, 4 m. S.E. of Alton ; pop. 1051.　Map 79.

King's Lynn, mun. bor. and seaport, Norfolk, 48½ m. N.W. of Norwich ; pop. 20,580.　Map 51.

Kings Norton, ward and eccl. par. in S. of Birmingham ; pop. 7490.　Map 58.

Kings Nympton, par. and vil., Devonshire, 3½ m. N. of Chulmleigh ; pop. 444.　Map 85.

Kings Somborne, par. and vil., Hampshire, 7 m. W.N.W. of Winchester ; pop. 1203.　Map 76.

Kingston-on-Soar, par. and vil., in co. and 10 m. S.S.W. of Nottingham ; pop. 241.　Map 49.

Kingston-on-Thames, mun. bor., Surrey, 3½ m. S. of Richmond ; pop. 39,052.　Map 80.

Kingstown (Dun Laoghaire), seaport and watering place, 6 m. S.E. of Dublin ; pop. 18,992. Map 93.

Kingswear, par. and vil., Devonshire, 35 m. S. of Exeter ; pop. 862. Map 89.

Kingswinford, par. and vil., Staffordshire, 3½ m. N. of Stourbridge ; pop. 22,067. Map 57.

Kingswood, par. and vil., Gloucestershire, 1½ m. S.W. of Wotton-under-Edge ; pop. 850. Map 68.

Kingswood, urb. dist., Gloucestershire, 3½ m. N.E. of Bristol ; pop. 13,297. Map 68.

Kingswood, par. and vil., Surrey, 3½ m. N.W. of Reigate ; pop. 1140. Map 80.

Kington, urb. dist., Herefordshire, 13¾ m. W. of Leominster ; pop. 1742. Map 56.

Kingussie, eccl. par. and police bur., Inverness-shire, 46½ m. S. of Inverness ; pop. bur. 1067. Map 3.

Kinlochewe, ham., Ross and Cromarty, 10 m. N.W. of Achnasheen ry. sta. Map 2.

Kinlochmoidart, seat and deer forest, Ardnamurchan par., Inverness-shire. Map 2.

Kinloch Rannoch, vil. and q.s. par., Perthshire, 21 m. W. of Pitlochry ; pop. 665. Map 12.

Kinnaird, par. and vil., Perthshire, 2½ m. W. of Inchture ; pop. 193. Map 6.

Kinnerley, par. and vil., Salop, 6 m. S.E. of Oswestry ; pop. 1022. Map 46.

Kinnesswood, vil. in co. and 5 m. E. of Kinross. Map 6.

Kinross, police bur., market tn. and par., Kinrossshire, 13¾ m. N. of Dunfermline ; pop. 2525. Map 6.

Kinsale, seaport, par. and urb. dist., in co. and 24 m. S. of Cork ; pop. 2881. Map 94.

Kintbury, par. and vil., S.W. Berkshire, 3½ m. E. of Hungerford ; pop. 1648. Map 76.

Kintore, police bur. and par., Aberdeenshire, 16 m. E. of Alford ; bur. pop. 756. Map 3.

Kinvarra, vil., Galway, 8 m. N.W. of Gort ; pop. 347. Map 94.

Kinver, town and par., Staffordshire, 3½ m. W.S.W. of Stourbridge ; pop. 2886. Map 57.

Kippen, par. and vil., in co. and 9 m. W. of Stirling ; pop. 1518. Map 8.

Kirby Grindalythe, par. and vil., E.R. Yorkshire, 8 m. S.E. of Malton ; pop. 146. Map 29.

Kirby-le-Soken, par. and vil., Essex, 2 m. W. of Walton-on-the-Naze ; pop. 1160. Map 73.

Kirby Malzeard, par. and vil., W.R. Yorkshire, 6 m. N.W. of Ripon ; pop. 523. Map 27.

Kirkbampton, par. and vil., Cumberland, 6½ m. W. of Carlisle ; pop. 387. Map 21.

Kirkbean, par. and vil., Kirkcudbrightshire, 12 m. S. of Dumfries ; pop. 679. Map 20.

Kirkbride, par. and vil., Cumberland, 12¾ m. W. of Carlisle ; pop. 408. Map 20.

Kirkburton, urb. dist., W.R. Yorkshire, 5 m. S.E. of Huddersfield ; pop. 3184. Map 32.

Kirkby, par., S.W. Lancashire, 7 m. N.E. of Liverpool ; pop. 1429. Map 38.

Kirkby Fleetham, par. and vil., N.R. Yorkshire, 4 m. N.N.E. of Bedale ; pop. 515. Map 28.

Kirkby-in-Ashfield, urb. dist., Nottinghamshire, 12 m. N.W. of Nottingham ; pop. 17,798. Map 41.

Kirkby Lonsdale, urb. dist., mkt. tn. and par., Westmorland, 4¾ m. N.W. of Ingleton ; pop. 1370. Map 26.

Kirkby Moorside, par. and market town, N.R. Yorkshire, 6½ m. W. of Pickering ; pop. 1695. Map 28.

Kirkby Stephen, market town and par., Westmorland, 10 m. S.E. of Appleby ; pop. 1542. Map 26.

Kirkby Thore, par. and vil., N. Westmorland, 4½ m. N.W. of Appleby ; pop. 469. Map 21.

Kirkcaldy, mun. bur. and par., Fifeshire, 26 m. N. of Edinburgh ; pop. 43,874. Map 10.

Kirkcudbright, mun. bur. and co. town, Kirkcudbrightshire, 30 m. S.W. of Dumfries ; pop. 2311. Map 19.

Kirkfieldbank, vil., in co. and 1 m. W. of Lanark. Map 14.

Kirkham, urb. dist., market town and par., N. Lancashire, 8 m. W. of Preston ; pop. 4031. Map 30.

Kirkheaton, urb. dist., W.R. Yorkshire, 2½ m. E. of Huddersfield ; pop. 2610. Map 32.

Kirkintilloch, police bur. and par., Dumbartonshire, 8 m. N.E. of Glasgow ; bur. pop. 11,817. Map 8.

Kirklington, urb. dist., par. and vil., N.R. Yorkshire, 5½ m. S.E. of Bedale ; pop. 251. Map 27.

Kirkliston, vil, with ry. sta., West Lothian, 10 m. W. of Edinburgh ; pop. 961. Map 10.

Kirkmaiden, par., Wigtown, 15 m. S. of Stranraer. Map 18.

Kirkmichael, par. and vil., Isle of Man, 6 m. N.E. of Peel ; pop. 809. Map 24.

Kirknewton, par. and vil., Midlothian, 10 m. S.W. of Edinburgh ; pop. 3000. Map 9.

Kirkoswald, par. and vil., Cumberland, 8 m. N.E. of Penrith ; pop. 475. Map 21.

Kirkpatrick, ry. sta. and vil., Dumfries, 7 m. S.E. of Ecclefechan. Map 20.

Kirkton of Auchterhouse, par. and vil., Angus, 12½ m. N.W. of Dundee by rail ; pop. 643. Map 7.

Kirkwall, cap. of Orkney Islands ; pop. 3517.

Kirkwhelpington, par. and vil., Northumberland, 12½ m. W. of Morpeth ; pop. 230. Map 17.

Kirn, q.s. par., Argyllshire, part of Dunoon. Map 12.

Kirriemuir, police bur. and par., Angus, 5 m. N.W. of Forfar ; pop. 3326. Map 7.

Kirtlebridge, vil., S.E. Dumfriesshire, 3 m. S.E. of Ecclefechan. Map 20.

Kirton, par. and vil., Holland, Lincolnshire, 4 m. S.S.W. of Boston ; pop. 2700. Map 51.

Kirton Lindsey, market town and par., Lincolnshire, 6¼ m. S.W. of Brigg ; pop. 1651. Map 42.

Knapton, par. and vil., Norfolk, 3 m. N.E. of N. Walsham ; pop. 348. Map 53.

Knapton, par., E.R. Yorkshire, 6 m. N.E. of Malton ; pop. 244. Map 29.

Knaresborough, urb. dist., mkt. tn., par., W.R. Yorks, 3½ m. N.E. of Harrogate ; pop. 5942. Map 33.

Knarsdale, par. and vil., Northumberland, 6½ m. S.S.W. of Haltwhistle ; pop. 379. Map 21.

Knighton, urb. dist., Radnorshire, 5½ m. N.N.W. of Presteigne ; pop. 1836. Map 56.

Knightsford Bridge, on r. Teme, Worcestershire, 5½ m. E.N.E. of Bromyard. Map 57.

Knott End, place, W. Lancashire, on r. Wyre, opposite Fleetwood. Map 30.

Knottingley, urb. dist. and par., W. R. Yorkshire, 2½ m. N.E. of Pontefract ; pop. 6842. Map 33.

Knowesgate, ry. sta., Northumberland, 10¼ m. N.E. of Reedsmouth. Map 17.

Knowsley, par. and vil., S.W. Lancashire, 3 m. N.W. of Prescot ; pop. 1175. 1 m. S.E. of vil. is **K. Hall**, seat of Earl of Derby. Map 38.

Knutsford, urb. dist., market town and par., N. Cheshire, 6 m. E.N.E. of Northwich ; pop. 5878. Map 39.

Kyle of Lochalsh, vil., Ross and Cromarty, 10½ m. S.W. of Strome Ferry ; pop. 505. Map 2.

LACEBY, par. and vil., Lindsey, Lincolnshire, 4 m. S.W. of Grimsby ; pop. 1102. Map 35.

Ladbroke, par. and vil., Warwickshire, 2 m. S. of Southam ; pop. 169. Map 59.

Ladybank, police bur., Fifeshire, 5½ m. S.W. of Cupar ; pop. 1128. Map 7.

Ladykirk, par. and ham., Berwickshire, 6 m. N. of Coldstream ; pop. 338. Map 11.

Laindon, par. and vil. Essex, 3½ m. S.S.E. of Billericay ; pop. 1205. Map 72.

Lairg, par. and vil., Sutherlandshire, 11 m. N. of Bonar Bridge ; pop. 328. Map 3.

Lakenheath, par. and vil., Suffolk, 4½ m. S.W. of Brandon ; pop. 1713. Map 62.

Laleham, par. and vil., Middlesex, 2 m. S.E. of Staines ; pop. 755. Map 71.

Lamberhurst, par. and town, Kent, 6½ m. S.E. of Tunbridge Wells; pop. 1508. Map 82.
Lambourn, town and par., Berkshire, 8 m. N. of Hungerford; pop. 2193. Map 69.
Lamerton, par. and vil., Devonshire, 2½ m. N.W. of Tavistock; pop. 545. Map 88.
Lamington, vil., Lanarkshire, 10 m. S. of Carstairs by rail. Map 15.
Lamlash, vil., Arran, 4 m. S.E. of Brodick. Map 12.
Lammermuir Hills, E. Lothian and Berwickshire. **Lammer Law**, 1733 ft. Map 12.
Lamonby, vil., Cumberland, 7½ m. N.W. of Penrith. Map 21.
Lampeter, mun. bor. and par., Cardiganshire, 12 m. S.E. of Aberayron; pop. 1742. Map 54.
Lampeter Velfrey, par., Pembrokeshire, 3 m. E. of Narberth; pop. 909. Map 64.
Lamport, par. and vil., in co. and 10 m. N. of Northampton; pop. 166. Map 59.
Lanark, mun. bur., par. and co. town of Lanarkshire, 32¼ m. S.E. of Glasgow by rail; bur. pop. 6178. Map 14.
Lancaster, mun. bor., spt., par. and co. town of Lancashire, 21 m. N. of Preston; pop. 43,396. Map 30.
Lanchester, par. and vil., Durham, 7½ m. N.W. of Durham; pop. 5091. Map 23.
Landore, vil., Glamorganshire, 1½ m. N.E. of Swansea. Map 66.
Lands End, Cornwall, the extreme S.W. point of Britain. Map 90.
Lanesborough, vil., in co. and 10 m. N.E. of Roscommon; pop. 254. Map 92.
Langbank, *q.s.* par. and vil., Renfrewshire, 4½ m. E. of Port Glasgow; pop. 457. Map 12.
Langdon, East, par. and vil., Kent, 3 m. N.N.E. of Dover; pop. 336. Map 83.
Langford, par. and vil., Oxon, 3 m. N.E. of Lechlade; pop. 268. Map 69.
Langham, par. and vil., Rutlandshire, 1½ m. N.W. of Oakham; pop. 558. Map 50.
Langholm, town and par., Dumfriesshire, 91½ m. S. of Edinburgh; pop. 2448. Map 15.
Langport, market town and par., Somersetshire, 11 m. N.W. of Yeovil; pop. 781. Map 86.
Langsett, par. and vil., W.R. Yorkshire, 3½ m. S.W. of Penistone; pop. 366. Map 40.
Langtoft, par. and vil., E.R. Yorkshire, 6½ m. N.W. of Great Driffield; pop. 470. Map 35.
Langton Matravers, par. and vil., Dorsetshire, 8 m. S.E. of Wareham; pop. 948. Map 87.
Langwathby, par. and vil., Cumberland, 4 m. N.E. of Penrith; pop. 272. Map 21.
Langworth, vil. and ry. sta., in co. and 6¼ m. N.E. of Lincoln. Map 42.
Lapford, par. and vil., Devonshire, 6 m. N.W. of Yeoford Junction; pop. 451. Map 85.
Larbert, par. and town, Stirlingshire, 2½ m. N.W. of Falkirk; pop. 12,301. Map 9.
Largo, par., Fifeshire, 3 m. N.E. of Leven; pop. 3215. Map 7.
Largs, police bur. and par., Ayrshire, 11 m. N. of Ardrossan by rail; pop. 6115. Map 12.
Larkhall, town and *q.s.* par., Lanarkshire, 3½ m. S.E. of Hamilton; pop. 14,055. Map 9.
Larne, town, par. and urb. dist., co. Antrim, 24 m. N. of Belfast; pop. 8036. Map 93.
Lasswade, bur. and par., Midlothian, 6 m. S.E. of Edinburgh; pop. 467. Map 10.
Latchingdon, par. and vil., N.E. Essex, 5 m. S.S.E. of Maldon; pop. 420. Map 73.
Latheron, coast par. and vil., Caithness-shire, 18 m. S.W. of Wick; pop. 3866. Map 3.
Lathom and Burscough, dist., Lancashire, now in Ormskirk. Map 30.
Latimer, par. and vil., Buckinghamshire, 3½ m. S.E. of Chesham; pop. 684. Map 71.
Lauder, royal and mun. bur., W. Berwickshire, 10½ m. E. of Fountainhall; pop. 628. Map 10.
Laugharne, par. and market town, in co. and 9 m. S.W. of Carmarthen; pop. 992. Map 65.
Laughton, par. and vil., E. Sussex, 6 m. N.E. of Lewes; pop. 634. Map 81.
Launceston, mun. bor. and market town, Cornwall, 18½ m. N.W. of Tavistock; pop. 4071. Map 88.
Laurencekirk, small market town and par., S. Kincardineshire; pop. 1316. Map 3.
Lavant, par. and vil., W. Sussex, 2½ m. N. of Chichester; pop. 697. Map 79.
Lavendon, par. and vil., Buckinghamshire, 2 m. N.E. of Olney; pop. 667. Map 60.
Lavenham, par. and vil., Suffolk, 10 m. N.E. of Bury St Edmunds; pop. 1620. Map 62.
Laxey, vil., Isle of Man, 6 m. N.E. of Douglas; pop. 1639. Map 24.
Laxfield, par. and vil., E. Suffolk, 6 m. N. of Framlingham; pop. 787. Map 63.
Laxton, par. and vil., Nottinghamshire, 3½ m. S.W. of Tuxford; pop. 396. Map 41.
Lazonby, par. and vil., Cumberland, 7 m. N.E. of Penrith; pop. 707. Map 21.
Leadburn, ham. and ry. sta., Midlothian, 9½ m. N. of Peebles. Map 10.
Leadgate, urb. dist., Durham, 1½ m. E.N.E. of Consett; pop. 6395. Map 22.
Leadhills, vil. and ry. sta., Lanarkshire, 5 m. S.W. of Elvanfoot sta.; pop. 820. Map 14.
Leafield, par. and vil., Oxfordshire, 4 m. N.W. of Witney; pop. 606. Map 69.
Lealholm Bridge, vil. and ry. sta., N.R. Yorkshire, 9 m. W.S.W. of Whitby. Map 28.
Leamington, mun. bor. and watering place, in co. and 2 m. E. of Warwick; pop. 29,662. Map 58.
Leasingham, par. and vil., Kesteven, Lincolnshire, 2 m. N. of Sleaford; pop. 299. Map 42.
Leatherhead, urb. dist. and town, Surrey, 4 m. S.W. of Epsom; pop. 6916. Map 78.
Leathley, par. and vil., W.R. Yorkshire, 3 m. N.E. of Otley; pop. 127. Map 32.
Lechlade, par. and market town, Gloucestershire, 3½ m. E.S.E. of Fairford; pop. 1048. Map 69.
Leconfield, par. and vil., E.R. Yorkshire, 3 m. N.W. of Beverley; pop. 284. Map 35.
Ledbury, urb. dist., in co. and 13 m. S.E. of Hereford; pop. 3283. Map 57.
Leeds, city, parl. and co. bor. and par., W.R. Yorkshire, 25 m. S.W. of York; pop. 482,789. Map 33.
Leek, urb. dist., market town and par., Staffordshire, 12½ m. S.E. of Macclesfield; pop. 18,556. Map 40.
Leeming, eccl. dist. and vil., N.R. Yorkshire, 1½ m. N.E. of Bedale; pop. 487. Map 27.
Lee-on-the-Solent, watering place, Hampshire, 3 m. W. of Fort Brockhurst. Map 77.
Lees, urb. dist., Lancashire, 1½ m. S.E. of Oldham; pop. 4738. Map 31.
Legerwood, par. and ham., Berwickshire, 3½ m. N.E. of Earlston; pop. 379. Map 16.
Leicester, city, parl. and co. bor., par., market town and co. town of Leicestershire, 29 m. N.W. of Northampton; pop. 239,111. Map 49.
Leigh, mun. bor. and par., S.W. Lancashire, 21 m. N.E. of Liverpool; pop. 45,313. Map 39.
Leigh, par. and vil., in co. and 4½ m. S.W. of Worcester; pop. 1094. Map 57.
Leighlinbridge, town, in co. and 8 m. S. of Carlow; on r. Barrow. Map 95.
Leigh-on-Sea, ward of Southend-on-Sea, co. bor., Essex. Map 72.
Leighterton, vil., W. Gloucestershire, 4½ m. E.S.E. of Wotton-under-Edge. Map 68.
Leighton Buzzard, urb. dist., par. and mkt. tn., Beds, 7 m. N.W. of Dunstable; pop. 7031. Map 71.
Leintwardine, par. and vil., Herefordshire, 7 m. W. of Ludlow; pop. 846. Map 56.

Leiston, urb. dist. and par., E. Suffolk, 4 m. E. of Saxmundham; pop. 4184. Map 63.

Leith, parl. bur. and seaport, forming 4 wards of city of Edinburgh. Map 10.

Leith Hill, Surrey, 4 m. S.W. of Dorking; alt. 965 ft., highest point in co. Map 78.

Leitholm, vil., Berwickshire, 5 m. N.W. of Coldstream. Map 12.

Leixlip, town, N. co. Kildare, par. partly also in co. Dublin; pop. 1528. Map 93.

Lelant, par. and vil., Cornwall, 3¼ m. S.E. of St Ives; pop. 1167. Map 90.

Lenham, town and par., Kent, 9 m. E.S.E. of Maidstone; pop. 1947. Map 82.

Lennoxtown, town, Stirlingshire, 11½ m. N. of Glasgow; pop. 2182. Map 8.

Lenzie, q.s. par. and S. sub. of Kirkintilloch, Dumbartonshire, 6¼ m. N.E. of Glasgow; pop. 3432. Map 8.

Leominster, mun. bor., in co. and 12 m. N. of Hereford; pop. 5707. Map 56.

Lepton, urb. dist., W.R. Yorkshire, 4¾ m. S.E. of Huddersfield; pop. 3322. Map 32.

Lerwick, seaport and cap. of Shetland Islands; pop. 4221.

Lesbury, par. and vil., Northumberland, 3½ m. E.S.E. of Alnwick; pop. 988. Map 17.

Leslie, market town and par., Fifeshire, 4¼ m. W. of Markinch; pop. 2477. Map 6.

Lesmahagow, par. and vil., Lanarkshire, 6 m. S.W. of Lanark; pop. 12,931. Map 14.

Letchworth, urb. dist., par., N. Herts, 2 m. N.E. of Hitchin; pop. 14,454. Map 61.

Letham, vil., Angus, 5 m. E. of Forfar. Map 7.

Letterkenny, urb. dist., mid co. Donegal, 25 m. S.W. of Londonderry; pop. 2194. Map 92.

Leuchars, par. and vil., Fifeshire, 5 m. N.W. of St Andrews; pop. 2765. Map 7.

Leven, town, Fifeshire, 5¾ m. N.E. of Thornton Junct.; pop. 7411. Map 10.

Leven, Loch, in co. Kinross, about 8½ m. in circuit; max. depth 83 ft. Map 6.

Lever, Little, urb. dist., Lancashire, 3 m. S.E. of Bolton; pop. 4944. Map 31.

Levisham, par. and vil., N.R. Yorkshire, 5 m. N.E. of Pickering; pop. 118. Map 29.

Lewes, mun. bor., par., mkt. tn. and co. tn. of Sussex, 8 m. N.E. of Brighton; pop. 10,785. Map 81.

Lewis, isl., largest and most northerly of Outer Hebrides; pop. 28,378. Map 2.

Leybourne, par. and vil., Kent, 5 m. N.W. of Maidstone; pop. 335. Map 82.

Leyburn, par. and small market town, N.R. Yorkshire, 16 m. W. of Northallerton; pop. 868. Map 27.

Leyland, urb. dist. and par., N. Lancashire, 4½ m. S. of Preston; pop. 10,573. Map 30.

Leysdown, par. and vil., Sheppey, Kent, 6 m. N.N.E. of Faversham; pop. 221. Map 83.

Leyton, urb. dist. and par., Essex, 1 m. N. of Stratford; pop. 128,317. Map 71.

Lezayre, par. and vil., Isle of Man, 1¾ m. S.W. of Ramsey; pop. 2643. Map 24.

Libberton, par. and vil., Lanarkshire, 5 m. N.W. of Biggar; pop. 541. Map 15.

Lichfield, mun. bor., city and co. in itself, 17 m. S.E. of Stafford; pop. 8508. Map 48.

Liddesdale, the valley of Liddel Water, Roxburghshire. Map 16.

Liddington, par. and vil., Wiltshire, 3 m. S.E. of Swindon; pop. 396. Map 69.

Lidgate, par. and vil., W. Suffolk, 6½ m. S.E of Newmarket; pop. 268. Map 62.

Lifford, town, Donegal, 15 m. S.W. of Londonderry; pop. 419. Map 93.

Lifton, par. and vil., Devonshire, 3¼ m. E. of Launceston; pop. 830. Map 88.

Lilliesleaf, par. and vil., Roxburghshire, 5 m. S.E. of Selkirk; pop. 246. Map 16.

Limavady, market town and urb. dist., in co. and 12½ m. N.E. of Londonderry; pop. 2667. Map 93.

Limerick, co. bor., city and co. in itself, 62 m. N. of Cork; pop. 39,690, parl. bor. pop. 62,403. Map 94.

Limpsfield, par. and vil., Surrey, 7 m. W. of Sevenoaks; pop. 2522. Map 80.

Lincoln, parl. and co. bor., co. town and co. in itself, 33 m. N.E. of Nottingham; pop. 66,246. Map 42.

Lindfield, par. and vil., E. Sussex, 1½ m. N.E. of Hayward's Heath; pop. 3061. Map 81.

Lindisfarne (or **Holy Island**), insular par., Northumberland, 6 m. N. of Belford; pop. 586. Map 17.

Lingdale, vil., N.R. Yorkshire, 4 m. E. of Guisborough. Map 28.

Lingfield, par. and vil., Surrey, 3½ m. N. of East Grinstead; pop. 4905. Map 80.

Linlithgow, royal and mun. bur. and co. tn., W. Lothian, 17½ m. W. of Edinburgh; pop. 3666. Map 9.

Linnhe, Loch, sea loch, Argyllshire and Invernessshire, extends 21 m. N.E. from Firth of Lorne. Map 12.

Linslade, urb. dist., Buckinghamshire, 2 m. N.W. of Leighton Buzzard; pop. 2433. Map 70.

Linthwaite, urb. dist., W.R. Yorkshire, on S. side of Huddersfield; pop. 9689. Map 31.

Lintrathen, par. and vil., Angus, 10 m. W.N.W. of Forfar; pop. 500. Map 3.

Liphook, vil., Hants, 8½ m. N.E. of Petersfield. Map 79.

Lisburn, town and urb. dist., cos. Antrim and Down, 7½ m. S.W. of Belfast. Map 93.

Liskeard, mun. bor. and par., Cornwall, 15 m. S.W. of Launceston; pop. 4266. Map 88.

Lismore, market town, Waterford, 14½ m. W. of Dungarvan; pop. 1474. Map 95.

Liss, par. and vil., Hants, 4 m. N.E. of Petersfield; pop. 2322. Map 79.

Listowel, urb. dist. and par., co. Kerry, 20 m. N.E. of Tralee; pop. 4392. Map 94.

Litcham, par. and vil., Norfolk, 8 m. N.E. of Swaffham; pop. 575. Map 52.

Litherland, urb. dist. and par., S.W. Lancashire, 1½ m. N. of Bootle; pop. 15,967. Map 38.

Littleborough, urb. dist., par. and town, S.E. Lancashire, 3¼ m. N.E. of Rochdale; pop. 12,028. Map 32.

Little Crosby, urb. dist., Lancashire, adjacent to Great Crosby; pop. 1086. Map 38.

Littlehampton, urb. dist. and par., Sussex, 3¼ m. S. of Arundel; pop. 10,181. Map 79.

Littleport, par. and vil., Isle of Ely, Cambridgeshire, 4½ m. N.E. of Ely; pop. 604. Map 61.

Litton Cheney, par. and vil., Dorsetshire, 5 m. S.E. of Bridport; pop. 253. Map 86.

Liverpool, parl. and co. bor., city and seaport, Lancashire, 31 m. W. of Manchester; pop. 855,539. Map 38.

Liversedge, par., in Spenborough urb. dist., W.R. Yorkshire, 6½ m. S.E. of Bradford. Map 32.

Liverton, par. and vil., N.R. Yorkshire, 6½ m. E. of Guisborough; pop. 1057. Map 28.

Lizard, The, peninsula, S.W. Cornwall, most southerly promontory in England. Map 90.

Llanarmon, par. and vil., Denbighshire, 5 m. S.E. of Ruthin; pop. 1157. Map 38.

Llanarth, par. and vil., Cardiganshire, 4 m. S.W. of Aberayron; pop. 1592. Map 54.

Llanbadarnfawr, vil., Cardiganshire, 1 m. E. of Aberystwyth. Map 54.

Llanbeblig, par. coterminous with bor. of Carnarvon; pop. 8469. Map 36.

Llanberis, small town and par., in co. and 9 m. S.E. of Carnarvon; pop. 2373. Map 36.

Llanbister, par. and vil., Radnorshire, 9¼ m. W.S.W. of Knighton; pop. 638. Map 56.
Llanbradach, vil., 9½ m. N. of Cardiff. Map 67.
Llandaff, par. and city, S.E. Glamorganshire, 2 m. N.W. of Cardiff; pop. 13,277. Map 74.
Llanddarog, par. and vil., in co. and 6 m. S. of Carmarthen; pop. 953. Map 65.
Llandilo, urb. dist. and par., in co. and 15 m. N.E. of Carmarthen; pop. 1886. Map 65.
Llandilo Abercowin, par., Carmarthenshire, 3 m. S.E. of St Clears; pop. 46. Map 65.
Llandissilio, par., Pembrokeshire, 2 m. N. of Clynderwen; pop. 346. Map 64.
Llandovery, mun. bor., Carmarthenshire, 11¼ m. N.E. of Llandilo; pop. 1980. Map 55.
Llandowror, par. and vil., Carmarthenshire, 2 m. S.W. of St Clears; pop. 194. Map 65.
Llandre, ry. sta., Cardiganshire, 6 m. N.E. of Aberystwyth. Map 45.
Llandrillo, par. and vil., Merionethshire, 5 m. S.W. of Corwen; pop. 556. Map 45.
Llandrindod Wells, urb. dist., Radnorshire, 5¾ m. N.N.E. of Builth Road; pop. 2925. Map 56.
Llandudno, Carnarvonshire, 3½ m. N.E. of Conway, wtg. place and lifeboat sta.; pop. 13,677. Map 37.
Llandybie, par. and vil., Carmarthenshire, 4½ m. S. of Llandilo; pop. 8019. Map 65.
Llandyfriog, par. and ham., Cardiganshire, 1½ m. E.N.E. of Newcastle Emlyn; pop. 777. Map 54.
Llandyssul, par. and town, Cardiganshire, 7 m. E. of Newcastle Emlyn; pop. 2688. Map 54.
Llanelly, mun. bor., par. and spt., Carmarthenshire, 10½ m. N.W. of Swansea; pop. 38,393. Map 65.
Llanerch-Aeron, par., Cardiganshire, 2 m. S.E. of Aberayron; pop. 133. Map 54.
Llanerchymedd, small town and par., Anglesey, 6½ m. S. of Amlwch; pop. 782. Map 36.
Llanfaes, locality, Breconshire, in Brecknock borough. Map 55.
Llanfair Caereinion, mkt. tn. and par., Montgomeryshire, 8 m. W. of Welshpool; pop. 1715. Map 46.
Llanfairfechan, urb. dist. and par., Carnarvonshire, 7¾ m. S.W. of Conway; pop. 3162. Map 37.
Llanfair Orllwyn, par., Cardiganshire, 3½ m. E. of Newcastle Emlyn; pop. 438. Map 54.
Llanfihangel Aberbythych, par., Carmarthenshire, 3 m. S.W. of Llandilo; pop. 1336. Map 65.
Llanfihangel-geneu'r-glynn, vil., Cardiganshire, 4 m. N.E. of Aberystwyth. Map 44.
Llanfihangel Ystrad, par. and ham., Cardiganshire, 6 m. S.E. of Aberayron; pop. 813. Map 54.
Llanfrechfa, Upper, urb. dist., Monmouthshire, 2½ m. N.W. of Caerleon; pop. 4482. Map 67.
Llanfyllin, mun. bor., Montgomeryshire, on r. Cain; pop. 1449. Map 46.
Llanfyrnach, par. and vil., Pembrokeshire, 15 m. S.S.E. of Cardigan; pop. 960. Map 65.
Llangadock, par. and town, Carmarthenshire, 6 m. N.E. of Llandilo; pop. 1545. Map 55.
Llangammarch Wells, vil. and sta., Breconshire, 7 m. W.S.W. of Builth. Map 55.
Llangathen, par. and vil., Carmarthenshire, 3 m. W. of Llandilo; pop. 619. Map 65.
Llangattock, par. and vil., Breconshire, near Crickhowell; pop. 921. Map 67.
Llangefni, urb. dist., Anglesey, 13 m. S. of Amlwch; pop. 1782. Map 36.
Llangennech, par. and vil., Carmarthenshire, 4 m. E.N.E. of Llanelly; pop. 2817. Map 65.
Llangerniew, par. and vil., Denbighshire, on r. Elwy, 7 m. N.E. of Llanrwst; pop. 817. Map 37.
Llangollen, mkt. tn., urb. dist. and par., Denbighshire, 22 m. S.W. of Chester; pop. 2937. Map 46.
Llangorse, par. and vil., Breconshire, 6 m. E. of Brecon; pop. 360 (**L. Lake,** 5 m. in circuit). Map 56.
Llangranog, coast par. and vil., Cardiganshire, 4 m. N.E. of Aberporth; pop. 763. Map 54.
Llangunilo, par. and sta., Radnorshire, 5¾ m. W. of Knighton; pop. 452. Map 56.
Llangunnor, par. and vil., in co. and 1 m. E. of Carmarthen; pop. 830. Map 65.
Llangurig, par. and vil., Montgomeryshire, 4½ m. S.W. of Llanidloes; pop. 1015. Map 55.
Llangybi, par. and vil., Carnarvonshire, 2½ m. N.W. of Afon Wen sta.; pop. 455. Map 44.
Llangybi, par. and vil., Cardiganshire, 4 m. N.E. of Lampeter; pop. 252. Map 54.
Llanidloes, mun. bor. and par., Montgomeryshire, 10½ m. S.W. of Newtown; pop. 2356. Map 45.
Llanilar, par. and vil., Cardiganshire, 6 m. S.E. of Aberystwyth; pop. 585. Map 54.
Llanllwchaiarn, coast par., Cardiganshire, 1¾ m. S. of New Quay; pop. 407. Map 54.
Llanllyfni, par. and vil., in co. and 7 m. S. of Carnarvon; pop. 4417. Map 36.
Llanpumpsaint, par. and vil., in co. and 5½ m. N. of Carmarthen; pop. 686. Map 65.
Llanrhaiadr-ym-Mochnant, par., Montgomeryshire; pop. 741. Map 41.
Llanrhystyd, vil., Cardiganshire, 8 m. S. of Aberystwyth. Map 54.
Llanrhystyd Road, ry. sta., Cardiganshire, 2½ m. S.S.E. of Aberystwyth. Map 54.
Llanrug, par., in co. and 3 m. E. of Carnarvon; pop. 2504. Map 36.
Llanrwst, mkt. tn. and urb. dist., Denbighshire, 12 m. S. of Llandudno Jun.; pop. 2366. Map 37.
Llansaintfraed-in-Elvel, par., Radnorshire, 4½ m. N.E. of Builth; pop. 218. Map 56.
Llansantffraid, par. and ham., Cardiganshire, 4½ m. N.E. of Aberayron; pop. 946. Map 54.
Llansantffraid Glan Conway, par. and vil., Denbighshire, 2 m. S.E. of Conway; pop. 1268. Map 37.
Llanstadwell, par. and vil., Pembrokeshire, 2 m. E. of Milford; pop. 1059. Map 64.
Llanstephan, par. and vil., in co. and 7 m. S.S.W. of Carmarthen; pop. 1131. Map 65.
Llantarnam, urb. dist., Monmouthshire, 3½ m. N. of Newport; pop. 7284. Map 67.
Llantrisant, par. and mkt. tn., S.E. Glamorganshire, 10½ m. N.W. of Cardiff; pop. 21,946. Map 66.
Llanwnda, par., in co. and 4½ m. S. of Carnarvon pop. 1855. Map 36.
Llanwnda, par. and ham., Pembrokeshire, 2½ m. N.W. of Fishguard; pop. 2751. Map 64.
Llanwrda, par. and vil., E. Carmarthenshire, 4 m. S.W. of Llandovery; pop. 460. Map 55.
Llanwrtyd, urb. dist. and par., Breconshire, 10 m. S.W. of Builth; pop. 742. Map 55.
Llanymynech, par. and vil., Shropshire, 6 m. S.S.W. of Oswestry; pop. 557. Map 46.
Llwchwr (Loughor), urb. dist., Glamorganshire, 8 m. N.W. of Swansea; pop. 26,595. Map 65.
Llyswen, par., Breconshire, 7 m. S.W. of Hay; pop. 219. Map 56.
Loanhead, town, Midlothian, 5 m. S.W. of Edinburgh; pop. 3940. Map 10.
Lochawe, vil. and ry. sta., Argyllshire, 2½ m. W. of Dalmally. Map 12.
Lochboisdale, ham. in S.E. of South Uist Island, Outer Hebrides, on Loch Boisdale. Map 2.
Loch Buy, ham. and loch in S. of Mull Island, Argyllshire. Map 12.
Lochcarron, or **Jeantown,** par. and vil., Ross and Crom., 5 m. N.E. of Stromeferry; pop. 1066. Map 2.
Lochearnhead, vil., Perthshire, at head of Loch Earn, 13 m. N.W. of Callander. Map 12.

Lochee, par. and dist., Angus, in N.W. of Dundee; pop. 2613. Map 7.

Lochgelly, town, police bur. and par., Fifeshire, 7½ m. N.E. of Dunfermline; pop. 9297. Map 10.

Lochgilphead, police bur. and par., Argyllshire, 2 m. N. of Ardrishaig; pop. 939. Map 12.

Lochgoilhead, par., Argyllshire, 18 m. (by water) N.W. of Greenock; pop. 974. Map 12.

Loch Indail, sea loch, on S. of Islay, Argyllshire. Map 12.

Lochington, par. and vil., E.R. Yorkshire, 8 m. S. of Great Driffield; pop. 448. Map 35.

Lochinver, vil., with pier, Sutherlandshire, on Loch Inver; pop. 260. Map 2.

Lochluichart, ham. and ry. sta., Ross and Cromarty, 17 m. W. of Dingwall. Map 2.

Lochmaben, royal and mun. bur., in co. and 9 m. N. of Dumfries; pop. 1014. Map 15.

Lochmaddy, seaport vil., North Uist, Outer Hebrides, on W. shore of Loch Maddy; pop. 219. Map 2.

Lochranza, q.s. par. and vil., on N. of Arran Island, Buteshire; pop. 1038. Map 12.

Lochwinnoch, par. and town, Renfrewshire, 8½ m. S.W. of Paisley; pop. 4224. Map 8.

Lockerbie, market tn. and police bur., Dumfriesshire, 14½ m. N.E. of Dumfries; pop. 2574. Map 20.

Lockerley, par. and vil., Hants, 5 m. N.W. of Romsey; pop. 563. Map 76.

Loddington, par. and vil., Northamptonshire, 4 m. W. of Kettering; pop. 333. Map 60.

Loddiswell, par. and vil., Devonshire, on r. Avon, 3 m. N.W. of Kingsbridge; pop. 641. Map 89.

Lo don, market town and par., Norfolk, 10½ m. S.E. of Norwich; pop. 1019. Map 53.

Loftus, urb. dist., N.R. Yorkshire, 4 m. S.E. of Saltburn; pop. 7631. Map 28.

Logierait, par. and vil., Perthshire, ¾ m. W. of Ballinluig sta., 8 m. N.W. of Dunkeld; pop. 1680. Map 6.

Lomond, Loch, largest loch in Scotland, 24 m. long, 5 m. broad, greatest depth 623 feet. Map 12.

Londesborough, par., E.R. Yorkshire; pop. 297. Map 34.

London, capital of England, in co. of London; administrative co. pop. 4,396,821, Greater London 8,202,818. Map 71.

London Colney, eccl. dist. and vil., on S.E. border of Hertfordshire, 3 m. S.E. of St Albans. Map 71.

Londonderry, city, spt. and co. bor., N.W. co. Londonderry, on W. side of r. Foyle; pop. 45,165. Map 93.

Longbenton, urb. dist. and par., Northumberland, 3½ m. N.E. of Newcastle; pop. 14,072. Map 23.

Longborough, par. and vil., Gloucestershire, 3 m. S.W. of Moreton-in-the-Marsh; pop. 423. Map 58.

Longbridge Deverill, par., Wiltshire, 3 m. S. of Warminster; pop. 624. Map 75.

Long Buckby, par. and vil., in co. and 10 m. N.W. of Northampton; pop. 2430. Map 59.

Long Compton, par. and vil., S. Warwickshire, 5 m. S.E. of Shipston-on-Stour; pop. 525. Map 58.

Long Eaton, urb. dist. and par., Derbyshire, 7 m. S.E. of Derby; pop. 22,339. Map 49.

Longford, market town and urb. dist., co. Longford, 76 m. N.W. of Dublin; pop. 3760. Map 93.

Longforgan, par. and vil., E. Perthshire, 5½ m. S.W. of Dundee; pop. 2032. Map 7.

Longformacus, par. and vil., Berwickshire, 6½ m. N.W. of Duns; pop. 250. Map 11.

Longframlington, par. and vil., Northumberland, 5½ m. E. of Rothbury; pop. 531. Map 17.

Longhirst, par. and vil., Northumberland, 2½ m. N.E. of Morpeth; pop. 417. Map 17.

Longhope, par. and vil., in co. and 9 m. W. of Gloucester; pop. 964. Map 68.

Longhorsley, eccl. par. and vil., Northumberland, 6 m. N.W. of Morpeth; pop. 652. Map 17.

Longhoughton, par. and vil., Northumberland, 5½ m. N.E. of Alnwick; pop. 600. Map 17.

Long Itchington, par. and vil., Warwickshire, 6½ m. E. of Leamington; pop. 1227. Map 59.

Long, Loch, sea loch, Argyllshire and Dumbartonshire, strikes 17 m. N. and N.E. from Firth of Clyde at Holy Loch to Arrochar. Map 12.

Long Marton, par., Westmorland, 3½ m. N.W. of Appleby; pop. 619. Map 21.

Long Melford, par. and town, W. Suffolk, 3 m. N.W. of Sudbury; pop. 2635. Map 62.

Longniddry, vil., East Lothian, 4¾ m. N.W. of Haddington; pop. 382. Map 10.

Longnor, par. and vil., Staffordshire, on r. Manifold, 6 m. S.E. of Buxton; pop. 444. Map 40.

Long Preston, par. and vil., W.R. Yorkshire, 4 m. S.E. of Settle; pop. 690. Map 34.

Longridge, urb. dist., N. Lancashire, 7 m. N.E. of Preston; pop. 4158. Map 31.

Long Riston, par. and vil., E.R. Yorkshire, 6 m. N.E. of Beverley; pop. 278. Map 35.

Longstock, par. and vil., Hants, 1 m. N. of Stockbridge; pop. 413. Map 76.

Long Sutton, urb. dist., Holland, Lincolnshire, 4½ m. E.S.E. of Holbeach; pop. 2902. Map 51.

Long Sutton, par. and vil., Somersetshire, 2¾ m. S.W. of Somerton; pop. 698. Map 86.

Longton, par. and vil., N. Lancashire, 5 m. S.W. of Preston; pop. 2543. Map 30.

Longton, par., Staffordshire, within the parl. and co. bor. of Stoke-upon-Trent; pop. 37,812. Map 39.

Longtown, market town, Cumberland, on r. Esk, 9 m. N.W. of Carlisle. Map 21.

Long Whatton, par. and vil., Leicestershire, 4½ m. N.W. of Loughborough; pop. 604. Map 49.

Looe, East, urb. dist., fishing port, Cornwall, 8¾ m. S. of Liskeard; pop. 2878. Map 88.

Looe, West, coast tn., Cornwall, 7 m. S. of Liskeard, opposite East Looe. Map 88.

Loose, par. and vil., Kent, 2½ m. S. of Maidstone; pop. 1910. Map 82.

Lorton, par. and vil., Cumberland, 4 m. S.E. of Cockermouth; pop. 326. Map 20.

Lossiemouth, seaport town and police bur., Morayshire, 5½ m. N.E. of Elgin; pop. 3914. Map 3.

Lostwithiel, mun. bor., par. and market town, Cornwall, 3¼ m. S. of Bodmin Road sta.; pop. 1325. Map 91.

Loughborough, mun. bor. and par., Leicestershire, 10½ m. N.W. of Leicester; pop. 26,945. Map 49.

Loughor, Glamorganshire. *See* Llwchwr. Map 65.

Loughrea, market town and par., co. Galway, on Lough Rea, 9 m. S.S.E. of Attymon; pop. 2778. Map 94.

Loughton, urb. dist. and par., Essex, 5 m. S.W. o Epping; pop. 7390. Map 72.

Louth, mun. bor., mkt. town and par., Lincolnshire, 30¾ m. N.E. of Lincoln; pop. 9678. Map 43.

Louth, par. and vil., co. Louth, on r. Glyde, 6 m. S.W. of Dundalk; pop. 3039. Map 93.

Lowdham, par. and vil., in co. and 7½ m. N.E. of Nottingham; pop. 985. Map 41.

Lowestoft, mun. bor. and seaport, E. Suffolk, 10 m. S. of Yarmouth; pop. 41,768. Map 53.

Lowick, par. and vil., Northumberland, 7 m. N.W. of Belford; pop. 874. Map 17.

Lowick, par., Lancashire, 5 m. N. of Ulverston; pop. 313. Map 25.

Loxley, par. and vil., Warwickshire, 4 m. S.E. of Stratford-on-Avon; pop. 221. Map 58.

Loyal, Loch, on E. side of Ben Loyal, Sutherlandshire, 5 m. S.E. of Tongue. Map 3.

Lubenham, par. and vil., Leicestershire, 3½ m. W. of Market Harborough; pop. 597. Map 49.

Lubnaig, Loch, Perthshire, 4 m. N.W. of Callander; length 4 m. Map 5.

Lucan, small town, par. and seat, in co. and 7 m. W. of Dublin ; pop. 1121. Map 93.

Luccombe, par. and vil., Somersetshire, 4 m. S.W. of Minehead ; pop. 581. Map 85.

Luddenden Foot, urb. dist. and par., W.R. Yorkshire, 6 m. W. of Halifax ; pop. 2881. Map 31.

Luddington, par. and vil., Lincolnshire, on r. Old Don, $4\frac{1}{2}$ m. N.E. of Crowle ; pop. 431. Map 34.

Ludgershall, par. and vil., Buckinghamshire, 6 m. S.E. of Bicester ; pop. 240. Map 70.

Ludgershall, par. and vil., E. Wiltshire, $6\frac{1}{2}$ m. N.W. of Andover ; pop. 1090. Map 76.

Ludgvan, urb. dist., Cornwall, 3 m. N.E. of Penzance ; pop. 1897. Map 90.

Ludlow, mun. bor., Salop, $27\frac{1}{4}$ m. S. of Shrewsbury ; pop. 5642. Map 57.

Luffenham, North and **South,** 2 pars., Rutlandshire, 7 m. S.E. of Oakham ; pop. 441 and 317. Map 50.

Lugwardine, par. and vil., in co. and 3 m. E.N.E. of Hereford ; pop. 686. Map 57.

Lulworth, West, coast par. and vil., Dorsetshire, $8\frac{1}{2}$ m. S.W. of Wareham ; pop. 797. Map 87.

Lumphanan, par. and vil., in co. and 7 m. W. of Aberdeen ; pop. 852. Map 3.

Lunan, par., Angus, and ry. sta. (**L. Bay**), 5 m. S.S.W. of Montrose ; pop. 327. Map 7.

Lundin Links, place and summer resort, Fifeshire, $7\frac{1}{4}$ m. E. of Thornton Junction. Map 7.

Lurgan, town and urb. dist., co. Armagh, 20 m. S.W. of Belfast ; pop. 12,553. Map 93.

Lurgashall, par. and vil., W. Sussex, 4 m. N.W. of Petworth ; pop. 610. Map 79.

Lusk, par. and vil., in co. and 14 m. N. of Dublin ; pop. 3742. Map 93.

Luss, par. and vil., Dumbartonshire, W. side of Loch Lomond ; pop. 670. Map 12.

Luton, mun. bor., par. and market town, Bedfordshire, $4\frac{1}{2}$ m. E.S.E. of Dunstable ; pop. 68,526. Map 71.

Lutterworth, par. and market town, Leicestershire, $7\frac{1}{4}$ m. N.E. of Rugby ; pop. 2092. Map 59.

Lybster, par. and vil., Caithness-shire, 13 m. S.W. of Wick ; pop. 1726. Map 3.

Lydbury North, par. and vil., Salop, $2\frac{1}{2}$ m. S.E. of Bishop's Castle ; pop. 710. Map 46.

Lydd, mun. bor., market town and par., Kent, $3\frac{1}{2}$ m. S.W. of New Romney ; pop. 2778. Map 83.

Lydford, par. and vil., S.W. Devonshire, $6\frac{3}{4}$ m. N. of Tavistock ; pop. 2232. Map 88.

Lydham, par., seat and vil., Shropshire, 2 m. N.E. of Bishop's Castle ; pop. 146. Map 46.

Lydney, par. and town, Gloucestershire, 8 m. N.E. of Chepstow ; pop. 3775. Map 68.

Lye and Wollescote, urb. dist., Worcestershire, $1\frac{1}{2}$ m. E. of Stourbridge ; pop. 12,245. Map 57.

Lyme Regis, mun. bor., seaport and par., Dorsetshire, $6\frac{1}{2}$ m. S.E. of Axminster ; pop. 2620. Map 86.

Lyminge, par. and vil., Kent, 4 m. N. of Hythe ; pop. 1398. Map 83.

Lymington, mun. bor., spt. and par., Hampshire, 20 m. S.W. of Southampton ; pop. 5157. Map 77.

Lymm, urb. dist. and par., Cheshire, 5 m. E.S.E. of Warrington ; pop. 5642. Map 39.

Lympstone, par. and vil., Devonshire, $8\frac{1}{2}$ m. S.E. of Exeter ; pop. 1068. Map 89.

Lyndhurst, par. and vil., Hampshire, New Forest, 9 m. W.S.W. of Southampton ; pop. 2562. Map 77.

Lynmouth, vil., Devonshire, 18 m. N.E. of Barnstaple. Map 84.

Lynton, urb. dist. and watering place, Devonshire, 18 m. N.E. of Barnstaple ; pop. 2012. Map 85.

Lyon, River, Perthshire, rises near W. border of co. and flows 34 m. E. through Glen Lyon. Map 5.

Lyonshall, par. and vil., Herefordshire, 2 m. E. of Kington ; pop. 692. Map 56.

Lytham St Anne's, urb. dist., Lancashire, 7 m. S.E. of Blackpool ; pop. 25,760. Map 30.

Lythe, par. and vil., N.R. Yorkshire, $3\frac{1}{2}$ m. N.W. of Whitby ; pop. 931. Map 29.

MABLETHORPE, urb. dist., watering place and par., Lincs, 13 m. E.S.E. of Louth ; pop. 3928. Map 43.

Macclesfield, mun. bor. and par., Cheshire, on r. Bollin, $17\frac{1}{2}$ m. S. of Manchester ; pop. 34,902. Map 39.

Macduff, bur., spt. and *q.s.* par., Banffshire, on r. Deveron, opposite Banff ; pop. 3276. Map 3.

Machrihanish, watering place, Kintyre, Argyllshire, 6 m. W. of Campbeltown. Map 12.

Machynlleth, par. and urb. dist., Montgomeryshire, $20\frac{3}{4}$ m. N.E. of Aberystwyth ; pop. 1892. Map 45.

Macroom, market town and par., co. Cork, $24\frac{1}{2}$ m. W. of Cork ; pop. 3556. Map 94.

Madron, urb. dist. and par., Cornwall, $1\frac{1}{2}$ m. N.N.W. of Penzance ; pop. 3276. Map 90.

Maenclochog, par. and vil., Pembrokeshire, 10 m. E.S.E. of Fishguard ; pop. 419. Map 64.

Maesteg, urb. dist., Glamorganshire, 8 m. N.W. of Bridgend ; pop. 25,552. Map 66.

Maghera, market town and par., co. Londonderry, $49\frac{1}{2}$ m. N.W. of Belfast ; pop. 6584. Map 93.

Magherafelt, market town and par., co. Londonderry, $42\frac{1}{2}$ m. N.W. of Belfast ; pop. 3977. Map 93.

Magor, par. and vil., Monmouthshire, $7\frac{1}{2}$ m. E. of Newport ; pop. 522. Map 67.

Maidenhead, mun. bor. and market town, Berkshire, $11\frac{1}{2}$ m. N.E. of Reading ; pop. 17,520. Map 78.

Maiden Newton, par. and vil., Dorsetshire, $7\frac{1}{2}$ m. N.W. of Dorchester ; pop. 597. Map 87.

Maids Moreton, par. and vil., Buckinghamshire, 1 m. N.E. of Buckingham ; pop. 351. Map 59.

Maidstone, mun. bor. and co. town of Kent, $41\frac{1}{2}$ m. S.E. of London ; pop. 42,259. Map 82.

Malahide, coast par., abbey ruins and vil., in co. and 9 m. N. of Dublin ; pop. 1174. Map 93.

Malborough, par. and vil., Devonshire, $3\frac{1}{4}$ m. S.W. of Kingsbridge ; pop. 630. Map 89.

Maldens and Coombe, The, urb. dist., Surrey, $9\frac{3}{4}$ m. S.W. of Waterloo, London ; pop. 23,412. Map 71.

Maldon, mun. bor., market town and r. port, Essex, 17 m. S.W. of Colchester ; pop. 6559. Map 72.

Malham, par., vil. and tourist resort, W.R. Yorkshire, $5\frac{1}{2}$ m. E. of Settle ; pop. 142. Map 31.

Malin, coast vil., co. Donegal, 25 m. N. of Londonderry ; pop. 129. Map 93.

Mallaig, vil., W. Inverness-shire, at entrance to Loch Nevis, $41\frac{3}{4}$ m. W. of Fort William. Map 2.

Malling, West, market town and par., Kent, 5 m. W.N.W. of Maidstone ; pop. 2365. Map 82.

Mallow, market town and par., co. Cork, on r. Blackwater, 21 m. N.W. of Cork ; pop. 5369. Map 94.

Mallwyd, urb. dist., Merionethshire, on r. Dyfi ; pop. 679. Map 45.

Malmesbury, mun. bor. and market town, Wiltshire, 16 m. N.W. of Swindon ; pop. 2334. Map 68.

Malpas, market town and par., in S.W. Cheshire, $13\frac{1}{2}$ m. S.E. of Chester ; pop. 1098. Map 38.

Maltby, urb. dist., W.R. Yorkshire, 6 m. E. of Rotherham ; pop. 10,013. Map 41.

Malton, urb. dist. and par., N.R. Yorkshire, 21 m. N.E. of York ; pop. 4418. Map 28.

Malvern, Great, urb. dist., in co. and $8\frac{1}{2}$ m. S.W. of Worcester ; pop. 15,632. Map 57.

Malvern Wells, par. and vil., Worcestershire, $2\frac{1}{2}$ m. S. of Great Malvern ; pop. 1815. Map 57.

Mamore, Gap of, mtn. pass, co. Donegal, 8 m. N.N.W. of Buncrana. Map 92.

Manaccan, par. and vil., Cornwall, $6\frac{1}{2}$ m. S.W. of Falmouth ; pop. 350. Map 90.

Manaton, par. and vil., Devonshire, $3\frac{1}{2}$ m. S. of Moreton Hampstead ; pop. 387. Map 89.

Manby, par. and vil., Lindsey, Lincolnshire, 4½ m. E.S.E. of Louth; pop. 137. Map 43.

Manchester, parl. and co. bor., city, par. and see of Bishop, S.E. Lancashire, 31 m. E. of Liverpool; pop. 766,333. Map 39.

Manea, par. and vil., Isle of Ely, Cambridgeshire, 10 m. N.W. of Ely; pop. 1463. Map 51.

Man, Isle of, in Irish Sea; area 141,263 acres; pop. 60,284. Capital, Douglas. Map 24.

Mangotsfield, urb. dist., Gloucestershire, 5 m. N.E. of Bristol; pop. 11,251. Map 68.

Manningtree, market town and par., Essex, 8 m. N.E. of Colchester; pop. 870. Map 73.

Manorbier, coast par. and vil., in co. and 5½ m. E.S.E. of Pembroke; pop. 656. Map 64.

Manorcunningham, vil., co. Donegal, 5 m. E. of Letterkenny; pop. 115. Map 93.

Manorhamilton, town, co. Leitrim, 23½ m. E. of Sligo; pop. 1013. Map 93.

Manorowen, coast par., Pembrokeshire, 1½ m. S.W. of Fishguard; pop. 194. Map 64.

Mansergh, par., Westmorland, 2 m. N. of Kirkby Lonsdale; pop. 180. Map 26.

Mansfield, mun. bor., mkt. tn. and par., Notts, 16 m. N. of Nottingham; pop. 46,075. Map 41.

Mansfield Woodhouse, urb. dist. and par., Notts, 1½ m. N. of Mansfield; pop. 13,707. Map 41.

Mapledurham, par. and vil., Oxon, 3½ m. N.W. of Reading; pop. 541. Map 70.

Mapledurwell, par. and vil., Hampshire, 3 m. S.E. of Basingstoke; pop. 209. Map 78.

Marazion, watering place and seaport, Cornwall, 3 m. E. of Penzance; pop. 1114. Map 90.

March, urb. dist., Cambridgeshire, 14½ m. E. of Peterborough; pop. 11,276. Map 51.

Marchington, par. and vil., Staffordshire, 3½ m. S.E. of Uttoxeter; pop. 504. Map 48.

Marden, par. and vil., Kent, 10 m. E.S.E. of Tonbridge; pop. 2484. Map 82.

Maree, Loch, Ross and Cromarty, 19 m. N.W. of Achnasheen. Map 2.

Maresfield, par. and vil., E. Sussex, 2 m. N. of Uckfield; pop. 3610. Map 81.

Margate, mun. bor., par. and pop. seaside resort, Kent, 4 m. N.N.W. of Ramsgate; pop. 31,312. Map 83.

Marhamchurch, par. and vil., Cornwall, 2 m. S.S.E. of Bude Haven; pop. 464. Map 84.

Market Bosworth, par. and market town, Leicestershire, 8 m. N.E. of Nuneaton; pop. 886. Map 49.

Market Deeping, par. and town, Kesteven, Lincolnshire, 7 m. S.S.E. of Bourne; pop. 888. Map 50.

Market Drayton, par., urb. dist. and mkt. tn., Shropshire, 18 m. N.E. of Shrewsbury; pop. 4749. Map 47.

Market Harborough, urb. dist. and par., in co. and 16 m. S.E. of Leicester; pop. 9312. Map 49.

Market Lavington, par. and vil., Wiltshire, 5½ m. S. of Devizes; pop. 904. Map 75.

Market Rasen, urb. dist., mkt. tn. and par., in co. and 13½ m. N.E. of Lincoln; pop. 2048. Map 42.

Market Warsop, urb. dist. and par., Nottinghamshire, 5 m. N.E. of Mansfield; pop. 7238. Map 41.

Market Weighton, market town and par., E.R. Yorkshire, 10 m. N.W. of Beverley; pop. 1717. Map 34.

Market Weston, par. and vil., W. Suffolk, 9 m. S.E. of Thetford; pop. 213. Map 62.

Markinch, police bur., Fifeshire, 4½ m. E. of Leslie; pop. 1988. Map 10.

Marks Tey, par. and vil., Essex, 5 m. W.S.W. of Colchester; pop. 585. Map 73.

Marlborough, mun. bor., Wiltshire, on r. Kennet, 11 m. S. of Swindon; pop. 3492. Map 76.

Marlesford, par. and vil., E. Suffolk, 4 m. S.E. of Framlingham; pop. 379. Map 63.

Marloes, par. and vil., Pembrokeshire, 7 m. W. of Milford Haven; pop. 316. Map 64.

Marlow, urb. dist., mkt. tn., par. and seat, Bucks, 5 m. N.W. of Maidenhead; pop. 5087. Map 70.

Marple, urb. dist. and par., Cheshire, 9 m. S.E. of Manchester; pop. 7390. Map 39.

Marrick, par. and vil., N.R. Yorkshire, 6½ m. W.S.W. of Richmond; pop. 172. Map 27.

Marsden, urb. dist. and par., W.R. Yorkshire, 7 m. S.W. of Huddersfield; pop. 5729. Map 31.

Marsden, coast vil., Durham, 2½ m. S.E. of South Shields. Map 23.

Marshfield, market town and par., Gloucestershire, 11½ m. E. of Bristol; pop. 1030. Map 68.

Marsh Gibbon, par. and vil., Buckinghamshire, 3½ m. E. of Bicester; pop. 521. Map 70.

Marske, par., N.R. Yorkshire, 2½ m. S.E. of Redcar; pop. 3547. Map 28.

Martham, par. and vil., Norfolk, 9 m. N.W. of Yarmouth; pop. 1335. Map 53.

Martin, par. and vil., Hampshire, 6 m. N.W. of Fordingbridge; pop. 384. Map 77.

Martin, vil. and ry. sta., Kent, 4 m. N.E. of Dover. Map 83.

Martindale, par., Westmorland, 10 m. S.W. of Penrith; pop. 195. Map 25.

Martlesham, par. and vil., E. Suffolk, 1½ m. S.W. of Woodbridge; pop. 676. Map 63.

Martock, par. and vil., Somersetshire, 7 m. N.W. of Yeovil; pop. 2065. Map 86.

Marton, par. and vil., Warwickshire, 6¾ m. N.E. of Leamington; pop. 392. Map 59.

Marton, par. and vil., N.R. Yorkshire, 3 m. S.S.E. of Middlesbrough; pop. 1062. Map 28.

Maryborough (Port Laoighise), mkt. and co. tn., Leix co., 51 m. S.W. of Dublin; pop. 3272. Map 95.

Maryhill, municipal ward in N.W. of city of Glasgow. Map 8.

Maryport, urb. dist., mkt. tn. and spt., Cumberland, 5¼ m. N.E. of Workington; pop. 10,182. Map 20.

Masham, urb. dist., par. and mkt. tn., N.R. Yorkshire, 8 m. N.W. of Ripon; pop. 1995. Map 27.

Massingham, Great and Little, 2 pars., Norfolk, 11 m. N.E. of King's Lynn; pop. 726 and 235. Map 52.

Matlock, urb. dist. and par., 17 m. N.W. of Derby pop. (**The Matlocks**) 10,599. Map 40.

Matlock Bath, urb. dist. and par., Derbyshire, 1 m. S. of Matlock. Map 40.

Matterdale, par., Cumberland, 8 m. E. of Keswick; pop. 245. Map 21.

Mauchline, small town and par., Ayrshire, 9½ m. S.E. of Kilmarnock; pop. 2357. Map 12.

Maughold, par. and vil., Isle of Man, 3½ m. S.E. of Ramsey; pop. 3481. Map 24.

Mawdesley, par. and vil., Lancashire, 8 m. N.W. of Wigan; pop. 1280. Map 30.

Maxton, par. and vil., Roxburghshire, 7 m. S.W. of Kelso; pop. 357. Map 16.

Maxwelltown, Kirkcudbrightsh., part of Dumfries. Map 20.

Maybole, market town, police bur. and par., Ayrshire, 9 m. S.W. of Ayr; pop. of par. 4210. Map 12.

Mayfield, par. and vil., Staffordshire, 2 m. S.W. of Ashbourne; pop. 1232. Map 40.

Mayfield, town and par., E. Sussex, 8 m. S. of Tunbridge Wells; pop. 2880. Map 81.

Maynooth, town, co. Kildare, 15 m. W. of Dublin; pop. 886. Map 95.

Mealsgate, vil., Cumberland, 5¾ m. S.W. of Wigton. Map 20.

Measham, par. and vil., Leicestershire, 8 m. N.W. of Market Bosworth; pop. 2425. Map 49.

Medbourne, par. and vil., Leicestershire, 6 m. N.E. of Market Harborough; pop. 380. Map 50.

Medina, r., Isle of Wight, flowing 12 m. N. to the Solent. Map 77.

Medmenham, par. and vil., Buckinghamshire, 3 m. S.W. of Marlow; pop. 425. Map 70.
Medomsley, par. and vil., Durham, $2\frac{1}{4}$ m. N.N.E. of Consett; pop. 6522. Map 22.
Medstead, par. and vil., Hampshire, $4\frac{1}{4}$ m. S.W. of Alton; pop. 776. Map 79.
Medway, r., Sussex and Kent, flowing 70 m. to the Thames. Map 80.
Meeth, par. and vil., Devonshire, $2\frac{1}{2}$ m. N. of Hatherleigh; pop. 202. Map 84.
Meifod, par. and vil., Montgomeryshire, 5 m. N.W. of Welshpool; pop. 1226. Map 46.
Meigle, par. and vil., Perthshire, $1\frac{1}{4}$ m. S.E. of Alyth; pop. 808. Map 7.
Meikleour, vil., Perthshire, 4 m. S. of Blairgowrie. Map 6.
Melbourn, par. and vil., in co. and 10 m. S.W. of Cambridge; pop. 1294. Map 61.
Melbourne, par. and vil., E.R. Yorkshire, 4 m. S.W. of Pocklington; pop. 365. Map 34.
Melbourne, town and par., in co. and $7\frac{1}{2}$ m. S.E. of Derby; pop. 3467. Map 49.
Melchbourne, par. and vil., Bedfordshire, 5 m. S.E. of Higham Ferrers; pop. 164. Map 60.
Meldon, par. and vil., Northumberland, 5 m. W.S.W. of Morpeth; pop. 134. Map 17.
Melksham, urb. dist. and market town, Wiltshire, $6\frac{1}{4}$ m. S. of Chippenham; pop. 3881. Map 75.
Melling, vil., N. Lancashire, $1\frac{1}{4}$ m. N.W. of Wennington Junction. Map 26.
Mellis, par. and vil., E. Suffolk, $3\frac{1}{2}$ m. S.W. of Diss; pop. 390. Map 62.
Melmerby, par. and vil., Cumberland, $8\frac{1}{2}$ m. N.E. of Penrith; pop. 219. Map 21.
Melrose, market town and par., Roxburghshire, $3\frac{3}{4}$ m. S.E. of Galashiels; pop. 2052. Map 16.
Melsonby, par. and vil., N.R. Yorkshire, $5\frac{1}{2}$ m. N.E. of Richmond; pop. 458. Map 27.
Meltham, urb. dist. and par., W.R. Yorkshire, 5 m. S.W. of Huddersfield; pop. 5051. Map 31.
Melton Constable, par. and vil., Norfolk, $5\frac{1}{2}$ m. S.W. of Holt; pop. 1034. Map 52.
Melton Mowbray, urb. dist., par. and market town, in co. and 14 m. N.E. of Leicester; pop. 10,437. Map 49.
Melvich, vil., Sutherlandshire, 17 m. W. of Thurso. Map 3.
Menai Bridge, urb. dist., Anglesey, 4 m. S.W. of Beaumaris; pop. 1675. Map 36.
Menstrie, *q.s.* par. and vil., Clackmannanshire, 4 m. N.W. of Alloa; vil. pop. 774. Map 9.
Meole Brace, par. and vil., Shropshire, $1\frac{1}{2}$ m. S. of Shrewsbury; pop. 2259. Map 46.
Meonstoke, par. and vil., Hants, 4 m. N.E. of Bishops Waltham; pop. 445. Map 77.
Mere, town and par., Wiltshire, 4 m. N.E. of Gillingham; pop. 1847. Map 75.
Mereworth, par. and vil., Kent, 7 m. W.S.W. of Maidstone; pop. 706. Map 82.
Meriden, par. and vil., Warwickshire, $5\frac{1}{2}$ m. N.W. of Coventry; pop. 848. Map 58.
Merrion, vil., in co. and 4 m. S.W. of Pembroke. Map 64.
Mersea Island, Essex, 8 m. S.E. of Colchester; **M. East** pop. 205, **M. West** pop. 2067. Map 73.
Mersey, r. Cheshire and Lancashire, flows 70 m. to the Irish Sea. Map 38.
Merstham, par. and vil., Surrey, 2 m. N.N.E. of Redhill; pop. 3597. Map 80.
Merthyr Tydfil, co. bor., Glamorganshire, 22 m. N.W. of Cardiff; pop. 71,099. Map 66.
Merton and Morden, urb. dist., Surrey, $7\frac{1}{2}$ m. S.W. of Waterloo sta., London; pop. 41,228. Map 71.
Methil, seaport vil. and *q.s.* par., Fifeshire, 1 m. S.W. of Leven; pop. of par. 12,295. Map 10.
Methley, urb. dist., W.R. Yorkshire, 7 m. S.E. of Leeds; pop. 4606. Map 33.
Methven, par. and vil., Perthshire, $7\frac{3}{4}$ m. W. of Perth; pop. 1772. Map 6.
Methwold, par. and vil., Norfolk, $3\frac{1}{2}$ m. S.E. of Stoke Ferry; pop. 1195. Map 52.
Mevagissey, fishing town and par., Cornwall, 5 m. S. of St Austell; pop. 1745. Map 91.
Mexborough, urb. dist. and par., W.R. Yorkshire, $5\frac{1}{2}$ m. N.E. of Rotherham; pop. 15,856. Map 41.
Micheldever, par. and vil., Hampshire, $8\frac{1}{2}$ m. N.E. of Winchester; pop. 958. Map 76.
Michelmersh, par. and vil., Hants, $3\frac{1}{2}$ m. N. of Romsey; pop. 1109. Map 76.
Mickleton, par. and vil., N.R. Yorkshire, 2 m. S.E. of Middleton-in-Teesdale; pop. 520. Map 22.
Mickletown, eccl. par., W.R. Yorkshire, $7\frac{1}{2}$ m. S.E. of Leeds; pop. 3293. Map 33.
Mid Calder, par. and vil., Midlothian, 10 m. S.W. of Edinburgh; vil. pop. 634. Map 9.
Middlebie, par. and vil., Dumfriesshire, 6 m. N.E. of Annan; pop. 1547. Map 20.
Middleham, par. and vil., N.R. Yorkshire, $2\frac{1}{2}$ m. S.E. of Leyburn; pop. 652. Map 27.
Middlesbrough, parl. and co. bor. and par., N.R. Yorks, 3 m. E. of Stockton; pop. 138,489. Map 28.
Middleton, mun. bor., mkt. tn. and par., S.E. Lancashire, $3\frac{1}{2}$ m. W. of Oldham; pop. 29,189. Map 31.
Middleton, par. and vil., Westmorland, 5 m. N. of Kirkby Lonsdale; pop. 209. Map 26.
Middleton, par. and vil., N. Lancashire, $4\frac{1}{2}$ m. S.W. of Lancaster; pop. 188. Map 30.
Middleton Cheney, par. and vil., Northamptonshire, $2\frac{1}{2}$ m. N.E. of Banbury; pop. 1093. Map 59.
Middleton-in-Teesdale, market town and par., Durham, 9 m. N.W. of Barnard Castle; pop. 1977. Map 22.
Middleton-on-the-Wolds, par., vil. and seat, E.R. Yorks, 8 m. N.W. of Beverley; pop. 628. Map 35.
Middleton Tyas, par. and vil., N.R. Yorkshire, 5 m. N.E. of Richmond; pop. 423. Map 27.
Middlewich, urb. dist. and par., Cheshire, $5\frac{1}{2}$ m. S.E. of Northwich; pop. 5458. Map 39.
Midgley, urb. dist., W.R. Yorkshire, $4\frac{1}{2}$ m. N.W. of Halifax; pop. 1882. Map 32.
Midhurst, par. and market town, Sussex, 9 m. E.S.E. of Petersfield; pop. 1890. Map 79.
Midlem, vil., N. Roxburghshire, $3\frac{1}{2}$ m. E. of Selkirk; pop. 98. Map 16.
Midsomer Norton, urb. dist. and par., Somersetshire, 10 m. S.W. of Bath; pop. 7490. Map 75.
Milborne Stileham, par., Dorsetshire; pop. 157. Map 87.
Mildenhall, par. and vil., Wiltshire, $1\frac{1}{2}$ m. E. of Marlborough; pop. 457. Map 69.
Mildenhall, market town and par., W. Suffolk, 12 m. N.W. of Bury St Edmunds; pop. 3370. Map 62.
Milford, eccl. par. and vil., Surrey, $1\frac{1}{2}$ m. S.W. of Godalming; pop. 1927. Map 78.
Milford Haven, urb. dist. and seaport, in co. and 6 m. W.N.W. of Pembroke; pop. 10,116. Map 64.
Milford-on-Sea, coast par. and vil., Hants, $3\frac{1}{2}$ m. S.W. of Lymington; pop. 1876. Map 77.
Millbrook, eccl. dist., par. and vil., Cornwall, 2 m. S.W. of Devonport; pop. 1959. Map 88.
Millom, urb. dist. and par., Cumberland, 6 m. S.W. of Broughton-in-Furness; pop. 7406. Map 25.
Millport, watering place and police bur., Buteshire, 24 m. S.W. of Greenock; pop. 2083. Map 12.
Millstreet, market town, Cork, $19\frac{3}{4}$ m. W. of Mallow Junction; pop. 1069. Map 94.
Milnathort, market town, Kinross-shire, $1\frac{1}{4}$ m. N.E. of Kinross Junction; pop. 1207. Map 6.
Milngavie, *q.s.* par. and town, Dumbartonshire, 7 m. N.W. of Glasgow; town pop. 5056. Map 8.

Milnrow, urb. dist. and par., S.E. Lancashire, 2 m. E.S.E. of Rochdale ; pop. 8624. Map 31.

Milnthorpe, par. and market town, Westmorland, 7 m. N. of Carnforth ; pop. 1025. Map 26.

Milton, urb. dist., Hants, on Christchurch Bay ; pop. 5299. Map 77.

Milton Abbas, par. and vil., Dorsetshire, 6 m. S.W. of Blandford ; pop. 578. Map 87.

Milton Abbot, par. and vil., Devonshire, 6 m. N.W. of Tavistock ; pop. 619. Map 88.

Milton Ernest, par. and vil., in co. and 4½ m. N.W. of Bedford ; pop. 340. Map 60.

Milton Regis, urb. dist., Kent, on N.W. side of Sittingbourne ; pop. 7481. Map 82.

Miltown Malbay, market town and watering place, co. Clare, 27 m. W. of Ennis ; pop. 995. Map 94.

Milverton, par. and market town, Somersetshire, 6¼ m. W. of Taunton ; pop. 1393. Map 86.

Minchinhampton, par. and town, Gloucestershire, 3½ m. S.E. of Stroud ; pop. 3722. Map 68.

Minehead, urb. dist. and market town, Somersetshire, 8 m. W.N.W. of Watchet ; pop. 6315. Map 85.

Minshull Vernon, par., Cheshire, 4½ m. N.W. of Crewe ; pop. 295. Map 39.

Minto, par. and vil., Roxburghshire, 6 m. N.E. of Hawick ; pop. 382. Map 16.

Mirfield, urb. dist. and par., W.R. Yorkshire, 4¾ m. N.E. of Huddersfield ; pop. 12,099. Map 32.

Missenden, Great, par. and vil., Buckinghamshire, 9 m. S.S.E. of Aylesbury ; pop. 2882. Map 70.

Missenden, Little, par. and vil., Buckinghamshire, 2 m. S.E. of Great Missenden ; pop. 1518. Map 70.

Misterton, par. and vil., Notts, on Chesterfield Canal, 5 m. N.W. of Gainsborough ; pop. 1668. Map 42.

Mitcham, mun. bor., Surrey, on r. Wandle, 2¼ m. S.E. of Wimbledon ; pop. 56,856. Map 71.

Mitcheldean, par. and vil., Gloucestershire, 5½ m. S.E. of Ross ; pop. 624. Map 68.

Mitchelstown, market town, co. Cork, 12 m. N. of Fermoy ; pop. 2268. Map 94.

Mobberley, par. and vil., Cheshire, 2¾ m. N.E. of Knutsford ; pop. 1550. Map 39.

Mochdre, par., Montgomeryshire, 3 m. S.W. of Newtown ; pop. 371. Map 46.

Modbury, small town and par., Devonshire, 3½ m. S.E. of Ivybridge ; pop. 1103. Map 89.

Moffat, watering place, Dumfriesshire, 2 m. N.E. of Beattock ; town pop. 2006. Map 15.

Mold, par., urb. dist. and market town, Flintshire, on r. Alyn, 6 m. S. of Flint ; pop. 5133. Map 38.

Molesey, urb. dist., Surrey, 3 m. S.W. of Kingston-on-Thames ; pop. 8460. Map 78.

Molton, North, par. and vil., Devonshire, 2¾ m. N.E. of South Molton ; pop. 993. Map 85.

Molton, South, mun. bor. and market town, Devonshire, 10½ m. S.E. of Barnstaple ; pop. 2831. Map 85.

Monaghan, par., urb. dist. and co. town of Monaghan, 52 m. S.W. of Belfast ; pop. 6923. Map 93.

Monasterevin, small market town and par., in co. and 6¾ m. W. of Kildare ; pop. 2010. Map 95.

Moniaive, vil. and ry. sta., Dumfriesshire, 7 m. S.W. of Thornhill ; pop. 573. Map 14.

Monifieth, town, Angus, 2 m. N.E. of Broughty Ferry ; pop. of par. 2984. Map 7.

Monkleigh, par. and vil., Devonshire, 3 m. N.W. of Torrington ; pop. 324. Map 84.

Monmouth, mun. bor., par. and co. tn., Monmouthshire, 19 m. S. of Hereford ; pop. 4731. Map 67.

Montacute, par. and vil., Somersetshire, 4 m. W. of Yeovil ; pop. 739. Map 86.

Montgomery, mun. bor., par. and co. tn., Montgomeryshire, 6¼ m. S. of Welshpool ; pop. 918. Map 46.

Montrose, parl., royal and mun. bur. and par., Angus, 90 m. N.E. of Edinburgh ; pop. 10,196. Map 3.

Monyash, par. and vil., Derbyshire, 5 m. W. of Bakewell ; pop. 350. Map 40.

Monzie, eccl. par. and vil., Perthshire, 3 m. N. by E. of Crieff ; pop. 447. Map 6.

Moorfoot Hills, chiefly in S.E. of Midlothian ; greatest alt. 2136 ft. Map 12.

Moorsholm, par., N.R. Yorkshire, 5 m. E.S.E. of Guisborough ; pop. 582. Map 28.

Morar, dist. and ry. sta., Inverness-shire. **Loch M.** is deepest loch in Scotland. Map 2.

Morchard Bishop, par. and vil., Devonshire, 6½ m. N.W. of Crediton ; pop. 894. Map 85.

Morda, vil., Shropshire, 1½ m. S. of Oswestry. Map 46.

Morebattle, par. and vil., Roxburghshire, 7 m. S. by E. of Kelso ; pop. 238. Map 16.

Morecambe and Heysham, mun. bor. and watering place, N. Lancs, 3½ m. N.W. of Lancaster ; pop. 24,586. Map 26.

Moreton Hampstead, town and par., Devonshire, 12¼ m. N.W. of Newton Abbot ; pop. 1636. Map 89.

Moreton-in-the-Marsh, market town and par., Glos., 4½ m. N. of Stow-on-the-Wold ; pop. 1442. Map 58.

Moreton Pinkney, par. and vil., Northamptonshire, 8 m. W. of Towcester ; pop. 362. Map 59.

Moreton Say, par. and vil., Shropshire, 3 m. W. of Market Drayton ; pop. 847. Map 47.

Morham, par., East Lothian, 3 m. S.E. of Haddington ; pop. 204. Map 10.

Morley, mun. bor. and par., W.R. Yorkshire, 5 m. S.W. of Leeds ; pop. 23,397. Map 32.

Morpeth, mun. bor. and par., Northumberland, 16½ m. N. by W. of Newcastle ; pop. 7390. Map 17.

Morriston, vil. and ry. stas., Glamorganshire, in N.E. suburbs of Swansea. Map 66.

Mortehoe, par. and vil., Devonshire, 5 m. S.W. of Ilfracombe ; pop. 1515. Map 84.

Mortimer, vil. and ry. sta., Berkshire, 7½ m. S.W. of Reading. Map 78.

Mortimers Cross, ham., Herefordshire, 5½ m. N.W. of Leominster. Map 56.

Mortlake, par., Surrey, Barnes urb. dist., 1½ m. N.E. of Richmond ; pop. 19,502. Map 71.

Morton, par. and vil., Kesteven, Lincolnshire, 3 m. N. of Bourne ; pop. 790. Map 50.

Morville, par. and vil., Shropshire, 3 m. W.N.W. of Bridgnorth ; pop. 366. Map 47.

Moss, par. and ry. sta., W.R. Yorkshire, 7 m. N. of Doncaster ; pop. 278. Map 34.

Moss Bank, vil., Prescot par., S.W. Lancashire, 1½ m. N.W. of St Helens. Map 38.

Mossend, tn., Lanarksh., 2 m. N. of Motherwell. Map 9.

Mossley, mun. bor., Lancashire, 2½ m. N. of Stalybridge ; pop. 12,041. Map 40.

Mostyn, vil., Whitford par., Flintshire, 3¼ m. N.W. of Holywell. Map 38.

Motcombe, par. and vil., Dorsetshire, 1½ m. N.W. of Shaftesbury ; pop. 1143. Map 87.

Motherwell and Wishaw, town, Lanarkshire, 2½ m. N.E. of Hamilton ; pop. 64,708. Map 9.

Mottingham, par. and vil., Kent, 1 m. S. of Eltham ; pop. 1804. Map 80.

Mottisfont, par. and vil., Hampshire, 4 m. N.W. of Romsey ; pop. 516. Map 76.

Mottistone, par. and vil., Isle of Wight, 6½ m. S.W. of Newport ; pop. 105. Map 77.

Mottram, urb. dist. and par., Cheshire, 3 m. W.N.W. of Glossop ; pop. 2636. Map 40.

Moulton, par. and vil., in co. and 4 m. N.E. of Northampton ; pop. 1347. Map 60.

Moulton, par. and vil., Holland, Lincolnshire, 4 m. E. of Spalding ; pop. 2345. Map 51.

Mountain Ash, urb. dist. and mining town, Glamorgan, 37½ m. S.E. of Aberdare ; pop. 38,381. Map 66.

Mount Bellew, small market town, co. Galway, 9 m. N. of Woodlawn; pop. 254. Map 94.

Mountmellick, market town with ry. sta., N. Leix co., 6 m. N. of Maryborough; pop. 2341. Map 95.

Mountnessing, par. and vil., Essex, 3 m. N.E. of Brentwood; pop. 1118. Map 72.

Mountrath, small market town and ry. sta., W. Leix co., 8 m. S.W. of Maryborough; pop. 1259. Map 95.

Mouswald, par. and vil., Dumfriesshire, 7 m. S.E. of Dumfries; pop. 466. Map 20.

Moville, small market town, co. Donegal, 19 m. N. by E. of Londonderry; pop. 1016. Map 93.

Moy, vil. and ry. sta., Inverness-shire, 14¾ m. S.E. of Inverness. Map 3.

Moy, small market town and ry. sta., co. Tyrone, 6¼ m. N. of Armagh; pop. 471. Map 93.

Much Birch, par. and vil., in co. and 6½ m. S. of Hereford; pop. 410. Map 66.

Much Hadham, par. and vil., Hertfordshire, 4 m. S.W. of Bishop's Stortford; pop. 1570. Map 72.

Much Wenlock, par. and ry. sta., Shropshire; pop. 1991. Map 47.

Muckhart, par., Perthshire, on r. Devon, 16 m. S.E. of Crieff; pop. 599. Map 6.

Mucking, par. and vil., Essex, on Thames, 4 m. N. of Tilbury; pop. 561. Map 72.

Muggleswick, par. and vil., Durham, 4 m. W. of Consett; pop. 368. Map 22.

Muirkirk, town and par., Ayrshire, 8 m. N.E. of Cumnock; pop. of par. 4726. Map 14.

Muker, par. and small town, N.R. Yorkshire, 5 m. N.W. of Askrigg; pop. 547. Map 27.

Mulbarton, par. and vil., Norfolk, 4 m. S.S.W. of Norwich; pop. 469. Map 53.

Mull, Isle of, Argyllshire, 7 m. W. of Oban; Isl. pop. 3389. Map 12.

Mullingar, co. town and par., co. Westmeath, 50 m. N.W. of Dublin; pop. of par. 8673. Map 93.

Mullion, par. and vil., Cornwall, 5½ m. N. of Lizard Head; pop. 954. Map 90.

Mumbles, seaport vil., Glamorganshire, 5 m. S.W. of Swansea. Map 66.

Muncaster, par. and vil., Cumberland, 1½ m. E. of Ravenglass; pop. 530. Map 25.

Mundesley, coast par. and vil., Norfolk, 5 m. N.E. of N. Walsham; pop. 1161. Map 53.

Munlochy, vil., Black Isle, Ross and Cromarty, 5½ m. S.W. of Fortrose; pop. 158. Map 3.

Murston, par. and vil., Kent, 1¼ m. N.E. of Sittingbourne; pop. 1603. Map 82.

Murthly, *q.s.* par., E. Perthshire, 4¼ m. S.E. of Dunkeld; pop. 739. Map 6.

Musgrave, Great, par., Westmorland, 4 m. N.W. of Kirkby Stephen; pop. 196. Map 26.

Musselburgh, parl. and mun. bur. and town, Midlothian, 6 m. E. of Edinburgh; pop. 16,996. Map 10.

Muthill, par. and vil., Perthshire, 3 m. S. of Crieff; pop. of par. 1287. Map 6.

Myddle, par. and vil., Shropshire, 7 m. N.W. of Shrewsbury; pop. 685. Map 46.

Mydroilin, vil., Cardigansh., 6 m. S. of Aberayron. Map 54.

Mynyddislwyn, urb. dist., Monmouthshire, 7 m. S.W. of Pontypool; pop. 16,201. Map 67.

Mytholmroyd, urb. dist. and par., N. div., W.R. Yorks, 1½ m. S.E. of Hebden Bridge; pop. 4467. Map 31.

NAAS, par. and urb. dist., co. Kildare, 20¼ m. S.W. of Dublin; pop. 3343. Map 95.

Naburn, par. and vil., E.R. Yorkshire, on r. Ouse, 4 m. S. of York; pop. 556. Map 34.

Nafferton, par. and vil., E.R. Yorkshire, 2 m. N.E. of Great Driffield; pop. 1237. Map 35.

Nailsea, par. and vil., Somersetshire, 8 m. W.S.W. of Bristol; pop. 1984. Map 74.

Nailsworth, urb. dist. and par., Gloucestershire, 4 m. S. of Stroud; pop. 3129. Map 68.

Nairn, mun. bur., par. and co. town of Nairnshire, 15½ m. E.N.E. of Inverness by rail; pop. 4201. Map 3.

Nannerch, par. and vil., Flintshire, 6½ m. N.W. of Mold; pop. 347. Map 38.

Nantlle, vil. and lake, in co. and 9 m. S.S.E. of Carnarvon. Map 36.

Nantwich, urb. dist. and par., Cheshire, 4 m. S.W. of Crewe; pop. 7132. Map 39.

Nantyglo and Blaina, urb. dist., Monmouthshire, 7½ m. S.W. of Abergavenny; pop. 13,190 Map 67.

Napton-on-the-Hill, par. and vil., Warwickshire, 3 m. E. of Southam; pop. 805. Map 59.

Narberth, urb. dist. and par., Pembrokeshire, 10½ m. N. of Tenby; pop. 1046. Map 64.

Narborough, par. and vil., in co. and 7 m. S.W. of Leicester; pop. 320. Map 49.

Naseby, par. and vil., Northamptonshire, 7 m. S.W. of Market Harborough; pop. 416. Map 59.

Nash, par. and vil., in co. and 5½ m. E. of Buckingham; pop. 237. Map 59.

Nash, par. and vil., Monmouthshire, 3½ m. S.E. of Newport; pop. 331. Map 67.

Nassington, par. and vil., Northamptonshire, 8 m. W.S.W. of Peterborough; pop. 491. Map 50.

Nateby, par. and vil., N. Lancashire, 2 m. S.W. of Garstang; pop. 305. Map 30.

Natland, par. and vil., Westmorland, 2 m. S. of Kendal; pop. 572. Map 26.

Naunton, par. and vil., Gloucestershire, 5 m. S.W. of Stow-on-the-Wold; pop. 404. Map 69.

Navan, urb. dist. and par., co. Meath, 16½ m. S.W. of Drogheda; pop. 3649. Map 93.

Navenby, par. and vil., Kesteven, in co. and 8¾ m. S. of Lincoln; pop. 824. Map 42.

Naver, r., Sutherlandshire, flows 19 m. N. from Loch Naver to the Pentland Firth. Map 3.

Navestock, par. and vil., Essex, 6 m. N. of Romford; pop. 720. Map 72.

Nayland, par. and vil., W. Suffolk, 8½ m. S.E. of Sudbury; pop. 1273. Map 62.

Neagh, Lough, Ulster, largest fresh water lake in British Isles. Map 93.

Neasham, par. and vil., Durham, 4 m. S.E. of Darlington; pop. 323. Map 27.

Neath, mun. bor. and par., Glamorganshire, 8 m. S.E. of Swansea; pop. 33,322. Map 66.

Needham Market, market town and par., Suffolk, 7 m. N.W. of Ipswich; pop. 1349. Map 62.

Needingworth, vil., Huntingdonshire, 2 m. N.E. of St Ives. Map 61.

Needles, The, group of rocks at western extremity of Isle of Wight. Map 77.

Neilston, town and par., Renfrewshire, 10 m. S.W. of Glasgow by rail; town pop. 3499. Map 8.

Nelson, mun. bor. and par., N.E. Lancashire, 3½m. N.E. of Burnley; pop. 38,306. Map 31.

Nenagh, urb. dist. and par., Tipperary, 27½ m. N.E. of Limerick; pop. 4517. Map 94.

Nenthall, vil., Cumberland, 2 m. E. of Alston. Map 22.

Nenthead, eccl. dist. and vil., Cumberland, 4 m. S.E. of Alston; pop. 780. Map 22.

Nenthorn, par. and vil., S.W. Berwickshire, on Eden Water; pop. 363. Map 16.

Ness, loch and r., Inverness-shire, on line of Caledonian Canal. Map 3.

Neston, urb. dist. and par., Cheshire, on Dee estuary, 12½ m. N.W. of Chester; pop. 5674. Map 38.

Netherbury, par. and vil., Dorsetshire, 12½ m. S.W. of Beaminster; pop. 1110. Map 86.

Nether Stowey, par. and vil., Somersetshire, 7 m. W.N.W. of Bridgwater; pop. 578. Map 74.

Nethybridge, vil., Inverness-shire, 5 m. S.S.W. of Grantown; pop. 478. Map 3.

Netley Marsh, par. and vil., Hampshire, 6 m. W. of Southampton; pop. 1396. Map 77.
Nettleham, par. and vil., Lindsey, in co. and 3 m. N.E. of Lincoln; pop. 381. Map 42.
Nevin, par. and town, Carnarvonshire, 6 m. N.W. of Pwllheli; pop. 1900. Map 36.
New Abbey, par. and vil., Kirkcudbrightshire, 7 m. S. of Dumfries; pop. 779. Map 20.
New Alresford, par., Hants, 6½ m. N.E. of Winchester; pop. 1709. Map 76.
Newark, mun. bor. and par., in co. and 18½ m. N.E. of Nottingham; pop. 18,055. Map 42.
New Barnet, eccl. par. and vil., S. Hertfordshire, 9¼ m. N.N.W. of London; pop. 4574. Map 71.
Newbiggin-by-the-Sea, urb. dist. and par., Northumberland, 7 m. N.E. of Morpeth; pop. 6904. Map 17.
Newbigging, vil., Lanarkshire, 3 m. S.E. of Carnwath. Map 10.
Newbigging, vil., Angus, 7½ m. N.E. of Dundee. Map 7.
Newbold-on-Avon, par. and vil., Warwickshire, 2 m. N.W. of Rugby; pop. 1699. Map 59.
Newborough, par. and vil., Staffordshire, 7 m. W.N.W. of Burton-on-Trent; pop. 496. Map 48.
New Bridge, vil., Monmouthshire, 5½ m. S.W. of Pontypool. Map 67.
Newbridge, place, Pembrokeshire, 3½ m. S. of Fishguard. Map 64.
Newbridge, urb. dist., in co. and 4½ m. N.E. of Kildare; pop. 2250. Map 95.
Newbridge-on-Wye, vil., Radnorshire, 7½ m. S.E. of Rhayader. Map 55.
New Brighton, ward of Wallasey co. bor., Cheshire, 4 m. N. of Birkenhead; watering pl. Map 38.
New Broughton, ham., Denbighshire, 1½ m. N.W. of Wrexham. Map 38.
New Buckenham, par. and vil., Norfolk, 4 m. S.E. of Attleborough; pop. 464. Map 53.
Newburgh, mun. bur. and par., Fifeshire, 7 m. N.W. of Ladybank Junction by rail; pop. 2152. Map 6.
Newburgh, eccl. dist. and ham., S.W. Lancashire, 5 m. N.E. of Ormskirk; pop. 554. Map 30.
Newburn, urb. dist., Northumberland, 5 m. W.N.W. of Newcastle; pop. 19,539. Map 23.
Newbury, mun. bor., Berkshire, on r. Kennet, 17 m. S.W. of Reading; pop. 13,336. Map 76.
Newby Bridge, vil., N. Lancashire, 5 m. N.W. of Cartmel. Map 25.
Newcastle, market town and par., in co. and 27½ m. S.W. of Limerick; pop. 2687. Map 94.
Newcastle, town, co. Down, 11 m. S.W. of Downpatrick; pop. 1765. Map 93.
Newcastle, Little, par. and vil., Pembrokeshire, 5½ m. S.S.E. of Fishguard; pop. 170. Map 64.
Newcastle Emlyn, urb. dist., Carmarthenshire, 9 m. E.S.E. of Cardigan; pop. 762. Map 54.
Newcastle-on-Tyne, city, co. bor. and spt., Northumberland, 268½ m. N. of London; pop. 283,145. Map 23.
Newcastleton, vil., Roxburghshire, 21 m. S.W. of Hawick; pop. 847. Map 16.
Newcastle-under-Lyme, mun. bor. and par., in co. and 16 m. N.N.W. of Stafford; pop. 23,246. Map 39.
Newchurch, par. and vil., Isle of Wight, 2½ m. N.W. of Sandown; pop. 707. Map 77.
New Cumnock, par. and town, Ayrshire, 5½ m. S.E. of Cumnock; pop. 1889. Map 14.
New Deer, par. and vil., Aberdeenshire, 13 m. W. of Peterhead; pop. 761. Map 3.
Newent, par. and market town, in co. and 8½ m. N.W. of Gloucester; pop. 2325. Map 57.
New Ferry, eccl. dist. in Birkenhead co. bor., Cheshire, on r. Mersey; pop. 11,244. Map 38.
New Forest, region, S.W. Hampshire; cap. Lyndhurst. Map 77.
Newgale, place, on coast of Pembrokeshire, 7 m. E.S.E. of St Davids. Map 64.
New Galloway, mun. bur. and town, in co. and 19 m. N. of Kirkcudbright; pop. 307. Map 19.
Newhaven, urb. dist. and par., E. Sussex, 9 m. E. of Brighton by rail; pop. 6790. Map 81.
New Holland, seaport, Lincolnshire, on r. Humber, 3½ m. N.E. of Barton-upon-Humber, opp. Hull. Map 35.
New Hutton, par., Westmorland, 3 m. E.S.E. of Kendal; pop. 246. Map 26.
Newick, par. and vil., E. Sussex, 7 m. N. of Lewes; pop. 965. Map 81.
New Inn, vil., in co. and 11 m. N.N.E. of Carmarthen. Map 65.
Newlyn, eccl. dist. and seaport, Cornwall, 1 m. S.W. of Penzance; pop. 3902. Map 90.
Newlyn, East, par. and vil., Cornwall, 7½ m. S.W. of St Columb; pop. 1097. Map 91.
Newmarket, town, with ry. sta., co. Cork, 5 m. N.W. of Kanturk; pop. 934. Map 94.
Newmarket, urb. dist. and racecourse, W. Suffolk, 14 m. E. of Cambridge; pop. 9753. Map 61.
New Mill, urb. dist., W.R. Yorkshire, 6 m. S.E. of Huddersfield; pop. 4538. Map 32.
New Mills, urb. dist. and par., Derbyshire, on r. Goyt, 6¼ m. N.W. of Chapel-en-le-Frith; pop. 8551. Map 40.
Newmilns, town and police bur., Ayrshire, 7 m. E. of Kilmarnock; pop. 3979. Map 14.
Newnham, urb. dist. and par., in co. and 11 m. S.W. of Gloucester by rail; pop. 1035. Map 68.
Newnham, ham. and ry. sta., Worcestershire, 3 m. N.E. of Tenbury. Map 57.
New Pitsligo, vil., Aberdeenshire, 4 m. W. of Strichen; pop. 1440. Map 3.
Newport, par., town and port, Pembrokeshire, 6½ m. E.N.E. of Fishguard; pop. 1292. Map 64.
Newport, urb. dist. and par., Salop, 11½ m. W.S.W. of Stafford; pop. 3439. Map 47.
Newport, par. and vil., Essex, 3 m. S.W. of Saffron Walden; pop. 914. Map 61.
Newport, seaport, mun. bur. and *q.s.* par., Fifeshire, 2 m. N.E. of Wormit; pop. 3275. Map 7.
Newport, co. bor., spt. and par., Monmouthshire, 12 m. N.E. of Cardiff by rail; pop. 89,198. Map 74.
Newport, mun. bor. and par., cap. of Isle of Wight, 91 m. from London; pop. 11,313. Map 77.
Newport Pagnell, urb. dist. and par., in co. and 14 m. N.E. of Buckingham; pop. 3957. Map 60.
Newquay, urb. dist. and par., Cornwall, 11 m. N. of Truro; pop. 5958. Map 90.
New Quay, urb. dist. and seaport, Cardiganshire, 5 m. S.W. of Aberayron; pop. 1112. Map 54.
New Radnor, par. and vil., Radnorshire, 6 m. N.W. of Kington; pop. 368. Map 56.
New Romney, mun. bor., par. and Cinque port, Kent, 8 m. S.W. of Hythe; pop. 1786. Map 83.
New Ross, r. port and urb. dist., Wexford, 13 m. N.E. of Waterford; pop. 5009. Map 95.
Newry, seaport, par. and urb. dist., co. Down, 44½ m. S. of Belfast by rail; pop. 11,963. Map 93.
Newton Abbot, urb. dist., Devonshire, 20½ m. S. of Exeter by rail; pop. 15,003. Map 89.
Newton Arlosh, eccl. dist., Cumberland, near Moricambe Bay; pop. 358. Map 20.
Newton-by-the-Sea, par. and vil., Northumberland, 7½ m. N.E. of Alnwick; pop. 243. Map 17.
Newton Heath, town, S. Lancashire, forming N.E. portion of Manchester parl. bor. Map 39.
Newton in Makerfield, urb. dist. and par., S.W. Lancashire, 15¾ m. W. of Manchester; pop. 20,150. Map 39.
Newtonmore, vil., with ry. sta., Inverness-shire, 3 m. S.W. of Kingussie; pop. 884. Map 3.
Newton Reigny, par. and vil., Cumberland, 2½ m. N.W. of Penrith; pop. 165. Map 21.

Newton Stewart, police bur., Wigtownshire, 23½ m. E. of Stranraer; pop. 1914. Map 18.

Newton Tracey, par. and vil., Devonshire, 5 m. S.W. of Barnstaple; pop. 121. Map 84.

Newtown and Llanllwchaiarn, urb. dist., in co. and 7½ m. S.W. of Montgomery; pop. 5152. Map 46.

Newtownards, township and par., co. Down, 9 m. E. of Belfast; pop. 9587. Map 93.

Newtonbarry, market town, Wexford, 12 m. S. of Tullow; pop. 884. Map 95.

Newtown St Boswells, vil., Roxburghshire, 3½ m. S.E. of Melrose; pop. 518. Map 16.

Newtown Stewart, market town, Tyrone, 23¾ m. S.E. of Londonderry; pop. 1012. Map 93.

Newtyle, par. and vil., Angus, 11 m. N.W. of Dundee; pop. 883. Map 7.

Neyland, urb. dist. and seaport, Pembrokeshire, 3½ m. E. of Milford; pop. 2161. Map 64.

Nigg, par. and vil., Ross and Cromarty, 4 m. N.E. of Cromarty; pop. 867. Map 3.

Nocton, par. and vil., Kesteven, in co. and 7 m. S.E. of Lincoln; pop. 553. Map 42.

Norden, urb. dist. and par., Lancashire, 2 m. W.N.W. of Rochdale; pop. 4348. Map 31.

Normanby, par. and vil., N.R. Yorkshire, 4½ m. S.W. of Pickering; pop. 143. Map 28.

Normanby, par. and vil., Lindsey, Lincolnshire, 3½ m. N.E. of Market Rasen; pop. 281. Map 42.

Normanton, ham. and seat, N.E. vicinity of Southwell, Nottinghamshire. Map 41.

Normanton, urb. dist. and par., W.R. Yorkshire, 3 m. N.E. of Wakefield; pop. 15,684. Map 33.

Normanton-upon-Trent, par. and vil., Nottinghamshire, 3½ m. S.E. of Tuxford; pop. 275. Map 42.

Northallerton, urb. dist., par. and mkt. tn., N.R. Yorks, 14 m. S.E. of Darlington; pop. 4787. Map 27.

Northam, urb. dist., Devonshire, 1½ m. N.W. of Bideford; pop. 5561. Map 84.

Northampton, parl. and co. bor. and cap. of Northamptonshire, 65¾ m. N.W. of London by rail; pop. 92,314. Map 59.

North Berwick, mun. bur. and par., E. Lothian, 22½ m. E.N.E. of Edinburgh by rail; pop. 3473. Map 10.

North Burton, par. and vil., E.R. Yorkshire, 7 m. N.W. of Bridlington; pop. 420. Map 29.

North Cave, par. and vil., E.R. Yorkshire, 14½ m. W.N.W. of Hull; pop. 1019. Map 34.

North Chapel, par. and vil., W. Sussex, 5 m. N.N.W. of Petworth; pop. 732. Map 79.

North Coates, par. and vil., Lindsey, Lincolnshire, 9 m. N.N.E. of Louth; pop. 241. Map 43.

North Curry, par. and vil., W. Somersetshire, 6 m. E. of Taunton; pop. 1363. Map 86.

North Darley, urb. dist., Derbyshire, 6 m. S.E. of Bakewell; pop. 4093. Map 40.

Northfleet, urb. dist., Kent, on r. Thames, 21¾ m. S.E. of London; pop. 16,429. Map 80.

North Kelsey, par. and vil., Lindsey, Lincolnshire, 5 m. W. of Caistor; pop. 822. Map 42.

Northleach, par. and vil., Gloucestershire, 10 m. N.E. of Cirencester; pop. 611. Map 69.

North Leverton, par. and vil., Nottinghamshire, 5½ m. E. of East Retford; pop. 374. Map 42.

Northlew, par. and vil., Devonshire, 3½ m. S.W. of Hatherleigh; pop. 628. Map 84.

North Molton, par. and vil., Devonshire, 2¾ m. N.E. of South Molton; pop. 993. Map 85.

Northolt, par. and vil., Middlesex, 4½ m. E. of Uxbridge; pop. 904. Map 71.

Northowram, former urb. dist., W.R. Yorkshire, now included in Halifax; pop. 2425. Map 32.

Northrepps, par. and vil., Norfolk, 3 m. S.S.E. of Cromer; pop. 559. Map 53.

North Shields, town and seaport, Northumberland, now in Tynemouth mun. bor. Map 23.

North Somercotes, par. and vil., Lindsey, Lincolnshire, 8 m. N.E. of Louth; pop. 1031. Map 43.

Northwich, urb. dist., Cheshire, 9½ m. S.E. of Warrington; pop. 18,728. Map 39.

Northwick, ham., Gloucestershire, 5½ m. S.W. of Thornbury. Map 68.

Northwold, par. and vil., Norfolk, 6½ m. N.W. of Brandon; pop. 1105. Map 52.

Northwood, vil., Middlesex, 2¼ m. S.E. of Rickmansworth. Map 71.

Norton, par. and vil., Durham, 2 m. N. of Stockton; pop. 330. Map 23.

Norton, urb. dist., E.R. Yorkshire, opposite Malton; pop. 3934. Map 28.

Norton sub Hamdon, par. and vil., Somersetshire, 5½ m. W. of Yeovil; pop. 428. Map 86.

Norton St Philip, par. and vil., Somersetshire, 6 m. S. of Bath; pop. 448. Map 75.

Norwich, parl. and co. bor., par., city and co. town of Norfolk, 114 m. N.E. of London by rail; pop. 126,207. Map 53.

Nottingham, city, co. bor. and co. town of Nottinghamshire, 123½ m. N.W. of St Pancras, London, by rail; pop. 268,801. Map 49.

Nunburnholme, par. and vil., E.R. Yorkshire, 4 m. N.W. of Market Weighton; pop. 189. Map 34.

Nuneaton, mun. bor. and par., Warwickshire, 9 m. N.N.E. of Coventry; pop. 46,305. Map 49.

Nunnington, par. and vil., N.R. Yorkshire, 4½ m. S.E. Helmsley; pop. 278. Map 28.

Nursling, par. and vil., Hampshire, 5 m. W.N.W. of Southampton; pop. 655. Map 77.

Nutfield, par. and vil., Surrey, 2 m. E. of Redhill; pop. 1828. Map 80.

OADBY, urb. dist., in co. and 3½ m. S.E. of Leicester; pop. 4724. Map 49.

Oakengates, urb. dist., Salop, 13½ m. E. of Shrewsbury; pop. 11,189. Map 47.

Oakham, urb. dist. and co. town of Rutlandshire, 11½ m. W. of Stamford; pop. 3191. Map 50.

Oakhill, vil. and eccl. par., Somersetshire, 2½ m. N.E. of Shepton Mallet; pop. 92. Map 75.

Oakley, par. and vil., in co. and 4 m. N.W. of Bedford; pop. 337. Map 60.

Oakley, Great, par. and vil., Northamptonshire, 5 m. N. of Kettering; pop. 204. Map 60.

Oaksey, par. and vil., Wiltshire, 6 m. S.W. of Cirencester; pop. 308. Map 68.

Oakworth, urb. dist. and par., W.R. Yorkshire, 3 m. S.W. of Keighley; pop. 3984. Map 31.

Oban, mun. bur., seaport and *q.s.* par., Argyllshire, 101 m. N.W. of Glasgow; pop. 5759. Map 12.

Ockendon, South, par. and vil., Essex, 5½ m. S.E. of Romford; pop. 1432. Map 72.

Oddington, par., Gloucestershire, 2½ m. E. of Stow-on-the-Wold; pop. 388. Map 58.

Odiham, market town and par., N.E. Hampshire, 6½ m. E.S.E. of Basingstoke; pop. 2683. Map 78.

Offham, par. and vil., Kent, 3 m. S.E. of Wrotham; pop. 386. Map 80.

Ogmore and Garw, urb. dist., Glamorganshire, 7 m. N. of Bridgend; pop. 26,979. Map 66.

Okeford Fitzpaine, par. and vil., Dorsetshire, 7 m. N.W. of Blandford; pop. 652. Map 87.

Okehampton, mun. bor. and par., Devonshire, 25¾ m. W. of Exeter; pop. 3352. Map 84.

Oldbury, urb. dist. and par., Worcestershire, 5 m. N.W. of Birmingham; pop. 35,918. Map 48.

Oldcastle, market town and par., Meath, 12¾ m. N.W. of Kells; pop. 673. Map 93.

Oldham, parl. and co. bor. and par., Lancashire, 6 m. N.E. of Manchester; pop. 140,309. Map 31.

Old Meldrum, police bur., Aberdeenshire, 19 m. N.W. of Aberdeen; pop. 980. Map 3.

Old Woking, locality, Surrey, in Woking urb. dist. Map 78.

Ollerton, par. and town, Nottinghamshire, on r. Maun, 9 m. N.E. of Mansfield; pop. 676. Map 41.

Olney, par. and town, Buckinghamshire, 11 m. S.E. of Northampton; pop. 2651. Map 60.

Omagh, urb. dist., Tyrone, 34 m. S.E. of Londonderry; pop. 4836. Map 93.

Ombersley, par. and vil., Worcestershire, 3½ m. W. of Droitwich; pop. 2066. Map 57.

Onchan, or **Conchan,** par., Isle of Man, partly in town of Douglas. Map 24.

Onibury, par. and vil., Salop, 5 m. N.W. of Ludlow; pop. 405. Map 56.

Oranmore, par. and vil., in co. and 5½ m. E. of Galway; pop. 164. Map 94.

Orchy, Bridge of, place, with ry. sta., Argyllshire, 12 m. N.E. of Dalmally. Map 12.

Orford, par. and fishing vil., E. Suffolk, 5½ m. S.W. of Aldeburgh; pop. 818. Map 63.

Orleton, par. and vil., Herefordshire, 5 m. S.S.W. of Ludlow; pop. 505. Map 56.

Ormesby, 2 pars. and vil., Norfolk, 4 m. N. of Yarmouth; pop. 1449. Map 53.

Ormesby, par. and vil., N.R. Yorkshire, 3 m. S.E. of Middlesbrough; pop. 428. Map 28.

Ormes Head, Great, Carnarvonshire, has lighthouse, 325 ft. above high water, seen 24 m. Map 37.

Ormes Head, Little, headland, on coast of Carnarvonshire, 2½ m. E. of Llandudno. Map 37.

Ormiston, par. and vil., East Lothian, 12 m. E.S.E. of Edinburgh; pop. 1841. Map 10.

Ormskirk, urb. dist., mkt. tn. and par., S.W. Lancashire, 12 m. N.E. of Liverpool; pop. 17,121. Map 30.

Orpington, par. and vil., Kent, 2½ m. S.E. of Chislehurst; pop. 7047. Map 80.

Orrell, urb. dist., Lancashire, 3 m. W.S.W. of Wigan; pop. 6951. Map 39.

Orsett, par. and vil., Essex, 3½ m. N. of Tilbury; pop. 1530. Map 72.

Orton, market vil. and par., Westmorland, 8 m. S.W. of Appleby; pop. 798. Map 26.

Osborne, former royal residence, Isle of Wight, 1 m. S.E. of East Cowes. Map 77.

Ossett, mun. bor. and par., W.R. Yorkshire, 2½ m. W. of Wakefield; pop. 14,838. Map 32.

Oswaldkirk, par. and vil., N.R. Yorkshire, 3 m. S. of Helmsley; pop. 191. Map 28.

Oswaldtwistle, urb. dist., Lancashire, 3 m. E.S.E. of Blackburn; pop. 14,221. Map 31.

Oswestry, mun. bor. and par., Salop, 17 m. N.W. of Shrewsbury; pop. 9754. Map 46.

Otford, par. and vil., Kent, 3 m. N. of Sevenoaks; pop. 857. Map 80.

Othery, par. and vil., Somersetshire, 6½ m. S.E. of Bridgwater; pop. 416. Map 74.

Otley, urb. dist., market town and par., W.R. Yorkshire, 6 m. E. of Ilkley; pop. 11,020. Map 32.

Otterburn, par. and vil., Northumberland, 8 m. N.E. of Bellingham; pop. 350. Map 17.

Ottershaw, eccl. par. and vil., Surrey, 2½ m. S.S.W. of Chertsey; pop. 783. Map 78.

Otterton, par. and vil., Devonshire, 3½ m. S.W. of Sidmouth; pop. 581. Map 89.

Ottery St Mary, urb. dist. and par., Devonshire, 12 m. N.E. of Exeter; pop. 3713. Map 85.

Ottringham, par. and vil., E.R. Yorks, 13 m. E. of Hull; pop. 516. Map 35.

Oughterard, market town, in co. and 17 m. N.W. of Galway; pop. 601. Map 94.

Oughtibridge, eccl. dist., N.W. suburb of Sheffield, W.R. Yorkshire; pop. 2328. Map 40.

Oulton, par. and vil., Cumberland, 2 m. N.W. of Wigton; pop. 307. Map 20.

Oulton, par. and vil., E. Suffolk, 1½ m. N.W. of Lowestoft; pop. 643. Map 53.

Oulton, vil. and par., W.R. Yorkshire, 5½ m. S.E. of Leeds; pop. 3752. Map 33.

Oundle, urb. dist. and par., Northamptonshire, 13¼ m. S.W. of Peterborough; pop. 2001. Map 50.

Outwell, par. and vil., Isle of Ely, Cambridgeshire, 5 m. S.E. of Wisbech; pop. 483. Map 51.

Over, par. and vil., in co. and 8¼ m. N.W. of Cambridge; pop. 896. Map 61.

Overstrand, coast par. and vil., Norfolk, 2 m. S.E. of Cromer; pop. 633. Map 53.

Overton, par. and ry. sta., Flintshire, 4½ m. N.W. of Ellesmere; pop. 1131. Map 46.

Overton, par. and vil., N. Lancashire, 3½ m. S.W. of Lancaster; pop. 367. Map 30.

Overton, par. and vil., Hants, 7¾ m. S.W. of Basingstoke; pop. 1779. Map 76.

Oxenhope, urb. dist., W.R. Yorkshire, 5 m. S.W. of Keighley; pop. 2276. Map 31.

Oxford, city and co. bor., Oxon, 63 m. W.N.W. of London; pop. 80,540. Map 70.

Oxnam, par. and ham., Roxburghshire, 4½ m. S.E. of Jedburgh; pop. 550. Map 16.

Oxshott, eccl. par., Surrey, 4½ m. S.W. of Surbiton; pop. 1245. Map 78.

Oxted, par. and vil., Surrey, 11 m. S.E. of Croydon; pop. 3284. Map 80.

Oxton, vil. and ry. sta., Berwickshire, 5 m. N.W. of Lauder; pop. 188. Map 10.

Oxwich, par. and vil., Glamorganshire, 10 m. W.S.W. of Swansea; pop. 194. Map 65.

PADGATE STATION, eccl. dist. and vil., Lancashire, 2 m. N.E. of Warrington; pop. 2101. Map 39.

Padiham, urb. dist., mfr. town and par., N.E. Lancashire, 3 m. W. of Burnley; pop. 11,632. Map 31.

Padstow, urb. dist., par. and seaport, Cornwall, 11 m. N.W. of Bodmin; pop. 1929. Map 91.

Paignton, urb. dist. and par., Devonshire, 2 m. S. of Torquay; pop. 18,405. Map 89.

Pailton, par. and vil., Warwickshire, 5 m. N.N.W. of Rugby; pop. 450. Map 59.

Painscastle, vil., Radnorshire, 5 m. N.W. of Hay. Map 56.

Painswick, par. and town, in co. and 6 m. S.E. of Gloucester; pop. 2639. Map 68.

Paisley, mun. bur., par. and r. port, Renfrewshire, 7¼ m. W. of Glasgow; pop. 86,441. Map 8.

Pakenham, par. and vil., W. Suffolk, 5 m. N.E. of Bury St Edmunds; pop. 829. Map 62.

Palgrave, par. and vil., E. Suffolk, 4 m. N.W. of Eye; pop. 693. Map 63.

Palling, coast par. and vil., Norfolk, 4 m. E. of Stalham; pop. 399. Map 53.

Pangbourne, par. and vil., Berkshire, 5½ m. N.W. of Reading; pop. 1936. Map 70.

Panteg, urb. dist., Monmouthshire, 1½ m. S.E. of Pontypool; pop. 11,500. Map 67.

Parkgate, vil., Cheshire, on Dee estuary, 13 m. N.W. of Chester. Sea bathing resort. Map 38.

Parkmill, ham., Gower peninsula, Glamorganshire, 9 m. W.S.W. of Swansea. Map 65.

Parknasilla, vil., co. Kerry, on west side of Sneen Harbour. Map 94.

Parkstone, dist. and ry. sta., in bor. of Poole, Dorsetshire. Map 87.

Parrog, seaside resort, Pembrokeshire, ½ m. N.W. of Newport. Map 64.

Parsley Hay Sta., on W. border of Derbyshire, 9 m. S.E. of Buxton. Map 40.

Parton, small seaport and par., Cumberland, 1½ m. N. of Whitehaven; pop. 1552. Map 24.

Paston, coast par. and vil., Norfolk, 4 m. N.E. of N. Walsham; pop. 281. Map 53.

Patcham, par. and vil., E. Sussex, 3 m. N. of Brighton; pop. 1768. Map 81.

Pateley Bridge, market town, W.R. Yorkshire, 14 m. N.W. of Harrogate; pop. 2558. Map 27.

Pathhead, vil., Midlothian, 5 m. S.E. of Dalkeith; pop. 465. Map 10.

Patrick Brompton, par., vil. and seat, N.R. Yorkshire, 3½ m. N.W. of Bedale; pop. 132. Map 27.

Patrington, small town and par., E.R. Yorkshire, 4 m. S.W. of Withernsea; pop. 1137. Map 35

Patterdale, par. and vil., Westmorland, $8\frac{1}{2}$ m. N. of Ambleside; pop. 961. Map 25.

Paul, urb. dist., Cornwall, $2\frac{1}{2}$ m. S. of Penzance; pop. 5813. Map 90.

Paulerspury, par. and vil., Northamptonshire, $2\frac{1}{2}$ m. S.E. of Towcester; pop. 804. Map 59.

Peacehaven, seaside garden city, E. Sussex, $6\frac{1}{2}$ m. E. of Brighton. Map 81.

Peak Forest, par. and vil., Derbyshire, 5 m. N.E. of Buxton; pop. 420. Map 40.

Peak, The, Kinder Scout, Derbyshire, 4 m. S.E. of Glossop; alt. 2088 ft. highest summit. Map 40.

Pebworth, par. and vil., Worcestershire, 5 m. N.N.W. of Chipping Campden; pop. 542. Map 58.

Peebles, mun. bur. and par., Peeblesshire, 23 m. S. of Edinburgh; pop. 5853. Map 15.

Peel, coast town, lifeboat and coastguard sta., I. of Man, $11\frac{1}{2}$ m. N.W. of Douglas; pop. 2690. Map 24.

Pegswood, par. and vil., Northumberland, 2 m. N.E. of Morpeth; pop. 2875. Map 17.

Pegwell, ham., Kent, 1 m. S.W. of Ramsgate. Map 83.

Pembrey, seaport and par., Carmarthenshire, 5 m. W. of Llanelly; pop. 5544. Map 65.

Pembridge, par. and vil., Herefordshire, 7 m. W. of Leominster; pop. 991. Map 56.

Pembroke, mun. bor. and spt., on Milford Haven, $9\frac{1}{2}$ m. W. of Tenby, Pembrokeshire; pop. 12,008. Map 64.

Penarth, urb. dist. and seaport town, Glamorganshire, 3 m. S. of Cardiff; pop. 17,710. Map 74.

Penbryn, coast par., in co. and 8 m. N.E. of Cardigan; pop. 1100. Map 54.

Pencader, vil., in co. and 10 m. N.N.E. of Carmarthen. Map 65.

Pendlebury, par., S.E. Lancashire, containing part of Swinton and Pendlebury; pop. 10,130. Map 39.

Penge, urb. dist., Kent, 7 m. S. of London Bridge Sta.; pop. 27,762. Map 80.

Penicuik, police bur. and par., S. Midlothian, 10 m. S. of Edinburgh; pop. 2750. Map 10.

Penistone, urb. dist. and par., W.R. Yorkshire, on r. Don, $12\frac{1}{2}$ m. N.W. of Sheffield; pop. 3264. Map 40.

Penkridge, small town and par., Staffordshire, 6 m. S. of Stafford; pop. 2570. Map 47.

Penmaenmawr, N. coast of Carnarvonshire, $4\frac{1}{2}$ m. S.W. of Conway, watering place; pop. 4021, Map 37.

Penn, par. and vil., Buckinghamshire, 4 m. S.W. of Amersham; pop. 1604. Map 70.

Penrhiwceiber, vil., with ry. stas., Glamorganshire, $1\frac{1}{4}$ m. S.E. of Mountain Ash. Map 66.

Penrhos, ham., Carmarthenshire, 7 m. N.W. of Llanelly. Map 64.

Penrhyn Bay, par., N.E. Carnarvonshire, 2 m. E. of Llandudno; pop. 1252. Map 37.

Penrhyndeudraeth, par. and vil., Merionethshire, $3\frac{1}{2}$ m. E. of Portmadoc; pop. 1949. Map 37.

Penrhyn Slate Quarries, Carnarvonshire, in S. vicinity of Bethesda. Map 36.

Penrice, par. and vil., Glamorganshire, 10 m. W.S.W. of Swansea; pop. 311. Map 65.

Penrith, urb. dist., market town and par., Cumberland, $17\frac{3}{4}$ m. S.E. of Carlisle; pop. 9065. Map 21.

Penruddock, vil. (alt. 857 ft.), Cumberland, $7\frac{1}{2}$ m. S.W. of Penrith. Map 21.

Penryn, mun. bor. and par., Cornwall, $3\frac{1}{2}$ m. N.W. of Falmouth; pop. 3414. Map 90.

Pensarn, locality, Anglesey, in Twrcelyn rural dist. Map 36.

Penshaw, par. and ry. sta., in co. and 8 m. N.E. of Durham; pop. 7265. Map 23.

Penshurst, par. and vil., Kent, 4 m. S.W. of Tonbridge; pop. 1531. Map 82.

Pentland Hills, extend through cos. of Midlothian, Peebles and Lanark. Map 12.

Pentraeth, par. and vil., Anglesey, 5 m. W. of Beaumaris; pop. 712. Map 36.

Pentre, ham., Flintshire, 2 m. E. of Hawarden. Map 38.

Pentyrch, par. and vil., Glamorganshire, 7 m. N.W. of Cardiff; pop. 2440. Map 67.

Penwortham, par. and vil., Lancashire, 2 m. S.W. of Preston; pop. 3999. Map 30.

Penybont, vil. and sta., Radnorshire, 4 m. N.E. of Llandrindod Wells. Map 56.

Pen-y-cae, par. and vil., Denbighshire, 2 m. W. of Ruabon; pop. 2037. Map 46.

Penzance, mun. bor., par. and seaport, Cornwall, 26 m. S.W. of Truro; pop. 11,342. Map 90.

Perranporth, vil., Cornwall, $7\frac{1}{2}$ m. N.W. of Truro. Map 90.

Perranzabuloe, par. and vil., Cornwall, $5\frac{1}{2}$ m. N.W. of Truro; pop. 2380. Map 90.

Perrott, South, par. and vil., Dorsetshire, 3 m. S.E. of Crewkerne; pop. 213. Map 86.

Perry Barr, dist. in N. of Birmingham. Map 48.

Pershore, market town, in co. and $8\frac{1}{2}$ m. S.E. of Worcester; pop. 4035. Map 57.

Perth, city, bur., par., r. port and co. town, Perthshire, 21 m. W.S.W. of Dundee; pop. 34,807. Map 6.

Peterborough, city and mun. bor., in Soke of Peterborough, Northamptonshire, on r. Nen, $14\frac{1}{2}$ m. W. of March; pop. 43,558. Map 51.

Peterchurch, par. and vil., Herefordshire, 11 m. W. of Hereford; pop. 528. Map 56.

Peterhead, mun. bur., spt.- tn. and par., Aberdeenshire, $44\frac{1}{4}$ m. N.E. of Aberdeen; pop. 12,545. Map 3.

Petersfield, urban dist. and par., Hants, 19 m. N.E. of Portsmouth; pop. 4386. Map 79.

Petersham, par. and vil., Surrey, 10 m. S.W. of London; pop. 592. Map 71.

Petham, par. and vil., Kent, 4 m. S.S.W. of Canterbury; pop. 562. Map 83.

Petherton, North, par. and vil., Somersetshire, 2 m. S. of Bridgwater; pop. 3179. Map 74.

Petherton, South, small town and par., Somersetshire, $4\frac{1}{2}$ m. N. of Crewkerne; pop. 1971. Map 86.

Pettaugh, par. and vil., E. Suffolk, 10 m. N. of Ipswich; pop. 171. Map 63.

Pettinain, par. and vil., Lanarkshire, 3 m. S. of Carstairs Junction; pop. 301. Map 9.

Petworth, par. and town, Sussex, $55\frac{1}{2}$ m. S.W. of London; pop. 2435. Map 79.

Pevensey, par. and vil., E. Sussex, 4 m. N.E. of Eastbourne; pop. 764. Map 81.

Pewsey, town and par., E. Wiltshire, 7 m. S. of Marlborough; pop. 1692. Map 76.

Philipstown, market town, E. Offaly, 8 m. E. of Tullamore; pop. 659. Map 93.

Philipstoun, vil., with ry. sta., West Lothian, $3\frac{1}{2}$ m. E. of Linlithgow. Map 9.

Phillack, urb. dist., Cornwall, $1\frac{1}{2}$ m. N.E. of Hayle; pop. 3232. Map 90.

Pickering, par. and urb. dist., N.R. Yorkshire, 11 m. N. of Malton; pop. 3668. Map 29.

Pickwell with Leesthorpe, par. and vil., Leicestershire, 6 m. S.E. of Melton Mowbray; pop. 170. Map 50.

Pickworth, par. and vil., Kesteven, Lincolnshire, 8 m. E.S.E. of Grantham; pop. 153. Map 50.

Piddletrenthide, par. and vil., Dorsetshire, 7 m. N. of Dorchester; pop. 504. Map 87.

Piercebridge, par. and vil., Durham, 5 m. W. of Darlington; pop. 204. Map 27.

Pilling, par. and vil., Lancashire, 5 m. W.N.W. of Garstang; pop. 1465. Map 30.

Pilsley, par. and vil., Derbyshire, 6 m. S.E. of Chesterfield; pop. 2885. Map 41.

Pilton, East, par. in mun. bor. of Barnstaple pop. 2276. Map 84.

Pimperne, par. and vil., Dorsetshire, 2 m. N.E. of Blandford; pop. 853. Map 87.

Pinchbeck, par. and vil., Holland, Lincolnshire, 3 m. N. of Spalding; pop. 1597. Map 51.

Pinhoe, par. and vil., Devonshire, 2½ m. N.E. of Exeter; pop. 1206. Map 85.

Pinner, par. and vil., Middlesex, 2½ m. N.W. of Harrow; pop. 9462. Map 71.

Pinxton, par. and vil., Derbyshire, 3 m. E. of Alfreton; pop. 5348. Map 41.

Pipegate, place and ry. sta., Salop, 5 m. N.E. of Market Drayton. Map 47.

Pirbright, par. and vil., Surrey, 5 m. N.W. of Guildford; pop. 3273. Map 78.

Pitcairngreen, vil., Perthshire, on r. Almond, 4½ m. N.W. of Perth. Map 6.

Pitlessie, vil., Fifeshire, 4 m. S.W. of Cupar. Map 7.

Pitlochry, vil., Perthshire, 28½ m. N.W. of Perth; pop. 2241. Map 6.

Pitminster, par. and vil., Somersetshire, 5½ m. S. of Taunton; pop. 1107. Map 86.

Pittenweem, mun. bur., seaport town and par., Fifeshire, 3½ m. N.E. of Elie; pop. 1619. Map 7.

Pittington, par. and vil., in co. and 3½ m. N.E. of Durham; pop. 2084. Map 23.

Pitton and Farley, par. and vil., Wiltshire, 4 m. E. of Salisbury; pop. 414. Map 76.

Plattlane, ham., Salop, 3½ m. S.W. of Whitchurch. Map 46.

Plaxtol, eccl. par., Kent, 5 m. E.S.E. of Sevenoaks; pop. 1054. Map 82.

Pleasley, par. and vil., Derbyshire, 3 m. N.W. of Mansfield; pop. 2510. Map 41.

Plowden, ry. sta., Salop, 4 m. E.S.E. of Bishop's Castle. Map 46.

Pluckley, par. and vil., Kent, 5½ m. N.W. of Ashford; pop. 900. Map 82.

Plumbland, par. and vil., Cumberland, 6 m. N.E. of Cockermouth; pop. 576. Map 20.

Plumpton, par. and vil., Sussex, 4½ m. N.W. of Lewes; pop. 713. Map 81.

Plumpton Hall, par. and vil., Cumberland, 4½ m. N.W. of Penrith; pop. 305. Map 21.

Plumstead, par., in met. bor. of Woolwich. Map 80.

Plymouth, co. bor. and naval sta., Devonshire, 246¾ m. S.W. of London; pop. 208,166. Map 88.

Plympton, market town, Devonshire, 4½ m. E. of Plymouth; pop. 1102. Map 88.

Plymstock, par. and vil., Devonshire, 3 m. S.E. of Plymouth; pop. 4121. Map 88.

Pocklington, urb. dist., par. and mkt. tn., E.R. Yorks, 7 m. N.W. of Market Weighton; pop. 2640. Map 34.

Podington, par. and vil., Bedfordshire, 4½ m. S.E. of Wellingborough; pop. 478. Map 60.

Polegate, vil., with ry. sta., Sussex, 4½ m. N.N.W. of Eastbourne. Map 81.

Polesworth, par. and vil., Warwickshire, 4 m. E.S.E. of Tamworth; pop. 6277. Map 48.

Pollington, par. and vil., W.R. Yorkshire, 2½ m. S.W. of Snaith; pop. 412. Map 33.

Polmont, vil. and ry. sta., Stirlingshire, 3 m. E. of Falkirk; pop. 5011. Map 9.

Polperro, town, Cornwall, 5½ m. E. of Fowey. Map 91.

Polstead, par. and vil., W. Suffolk, 4 m. S.W. of Hadleigh; pop. 643. Map 62.

Pomeroy, par. and vil., Tyrone, 8 m. N.W. of Dungannon; pop. 3413. Map 93.

Pontardawe, vil., with ry. sta., Glamorganshire, 8 m. N.E. of Swansea. Map 66.

Pontardulais, vil., Carmarthenshire and Glamorganshire, 6 m. N.E. of Llanelly. Map 65.

Pont-ar-Sais, place, in co. and 5 m. N.E. of Carmarthen. Map 65.

Pontefract, mun. bor., market town and par., W.R. Yorks, 10 m. E. of Wakefield; pop. 19,053. Map 33.

Ponteland, par. and vil., Northumberland, 8 m. N.W. of Newcastle-on-Tyne; pop. 1146. Map 23.

Pontesbury, par. and vil., Salop, 8 m. S.W. of Shrewsbury; pop. 2815. Map 46.

Pontlliw, ham. and ry. sta., Glamorganshire, 6½ m. N.N.W. of Swansea. Map 66.

Pont-newydd, ham., Breconshire, 3 m. E.N.E. of Crickhowell. Map 67.

Pontshaen, ham., Cardiganshire, 4 m. N. of Llandyssul. Map 54.

Pont Yates, vil., Carmarthenshire, 4 m. N.E. of Kidwelly. Map 65.

Pontyberem, par. and vil., Carmarthenshire, 6½ m. N.E. of Kidwelly; pop. 3025. Map 65.

Pontyclun, ham., Glamorganshire, 2 m. S.W. of Llantrisant. Map 66.

Pontypool, urb. dist. and par., Monmouthshire, 9¼ m. N. of Newport by rail; pop. 6788. Map 67.

Pontypridd, urb. dist. and par., Glamorganshire, 12 m. N.W. of Cardiff; pop. 42,737. Map 66.

Poole, mun. bor., par. and spt., Dorsetshire, 5 m. W. of Bournemouth; pop. 57,258. Map 87.

Poolewe, q.s. par. and vil. Ross and Cromarty, 27½ m. N.W. of Achnasheen; pop. 1294. Map 2.

Pooley Bridge, eccl. dist. and vil., Westmorland, 5½ m. S.S.W. of Penrith; pop. 236. Map 21.

Porchester, par. and vil., Hants, 4 m. N.W. of Portsmouth; pop. 993. Map 77.

Poringland, par. and vil., Norfolk, 5½ m. S.E. of Norwich; pop. 463. Map 53.

Porlock, par. and vil., Somersetshire, 5½ m. W. of Minehead; pop. 965. Map 85.

Portadown, market town and ry. sta., Armagh, 25 m. S.W. of Belfast; pop. 11,727. Map 93.

Portaferry, market and seaport town, E. co. Down, 8 m. N.E. of Downpatrick; pop. 1518. Map 93.

Portarlington, mkt. tn., with, ry. sta., cos. Leix and Offaly, 42 m. S.W. of Dublin; pop. 1951. Map 95.

Port Cardigan, at mouth of r. Teifi, 3 m. N.W. of Cardigan. Map 54.

Port Carlisle, ry. sta., N. Cumberland, 12 m. N.W. of Carlisle by rail. Map 20.

Port Dinorwic, seaport vil., Carnarvonshire, on Menai Strait. Map 36.

Port Ellen, seaport vil., Islay Isl., Argyllshire, 12 m. S.E. of Bowmore; pop. 750. Map 12.

Portencross, place, Ayrshire, 3 m. W.N.W. of West Kilbride. Map 8.

Port Erin, coast vil., lifeboat sta. and watering place, Isle of Man, 4½ m. W. of Castletown. Map 24.

Porteynon, par. and vil., Glamorganshire, 15 m. W.S.W. of Swansea; pop. 278. Map 65.

Port Glasgow, mun. bur., spt. and par., Renfrewshire, 20¼ m. N.W. of Glasgow; pop. 19,580. Map 12.

Porthcawl, urb. dist., Glamorganshire, 6 m. S.W. of Bridgend; pop. 6447. Map 66.

Porthleven, seaport town, Cornwall, 2½ m. S.W. of Helston; pop. 1592. Map 90.

Porth Nigel, bay, on S. coast Lleyn Prom., Carnarvonshire. Map 44.

Porthyrhyd, vil., in co. and 7½ m. E.S.E. of Carmarthen. Map 65.

Portincaple, place, E. side of Loch Long, Dumbartonshire, ½ m. W. of Whistlefield. Map 8.

Portinscale, vil., Cumberland, 1¼ m. W. of Keswick. Map 20.

Portishead, town and par., Somersetshire, 11½ m. W.N.W. of Bristol; pop. 3908. Map 74.

Portknockie, police bur., Banffshire, 5 m. N.E. of Buckie; pop. 1619. Map 3.

Portland, Isle of, urb. dist., par. and peninsula, in S. Dorsetshire; pop. 12,018. Map 87.

Portmadoc, urb. dist., Carnarvonshire, 11 m. E. of Pwllheli; pop. 3986. Map 36.

Portnacroish, vil., Argyllsh., 14 m. N.E. of Oban. Map 12.

Portobello, seaside resort, in city and 3 m. E. of G.P.O., Edinburgh. Map 10.

Port of Menteith, par. and ry. sta., Perthshire, 3 m. N.E. of Buchlyvie; pop. 1019. Map 8.

Portpatrick, par. and seaport, Wigtownshire, 7½ m. S.W. of Stranraer; pop. 1495. Map 18.

Portreath, seaport vil., Cornwall, 4 m. N.W. of Redruth. Map 90.

Portree, par. and spt. vil., I. of Skye, Inverness-shire, 60 m. S.E. of Stornoway; pop. 793. Map 2.

Portrush, urb. dist. and seaport town, Antrim, 67½ m. N.W. of Belfast; pop. 2107. Map 93.

Port St Mary, coast vil. and lifeboat sta., Isle of Man, 4¾ m. W. of Castletown. Map 24.

Portsea, dist. and ward, Hants, within co. bor. of Portsmouth; ward pop. 20,712. Map 77.

Portslade-by-Sea, urb. dist., E. Sussex, 4 m. W. of Brighton; pop. 9527. Map 81.

Portsmouth, co. bor., naval sta. and par., Hants, 27 m. S.E. of Southampton; pop. 249,288. Map 79.

Port Soderick, coast ham., Isle of Man, 3 m. S.W. of Douglas. Map 24.

Port Sonachan, ham., Argyllshire, 8½ m. S.W. of Dalmally. Map 12.

Portsoy, seaport town, police bur. and q.s. par., Banffshire, 8½ m. W. of Banff; pop. 1651. Map 3.

Portstewart, vil., co. Londonderry, 4 m. N.W. of Coleraine; pop. 1459. Map 93.

Port Sunlight, vil. and soapworks of Lever Bros. Ltd., 3 m. S.S.E. of Birkenhead, Cheshire. Map 38.

Port Talbot, mun. bor. and port, Glamorganshire, 10¾ m. S.E. of Swansea; pop. 40,672. Map 66.

Portumna, market town, Galway, 14½ m. W. of Parsonstown; pop. 873. Map 94.

Port Victoria, ry. sta., Kent, at mouth of r. Medway, 2 m. S.W. of Sheerness. Map 73.

Potter Street, vil., Essex, 2 m. S. of Harlow. Map 72.

Potters Bar, eccl. par. and vil., Middlesex, 12¼ m. N. of London; pop. 1752. Map 71.

Potton, market town and par., Bedfordshire, 4 m. N.E. of Biggleswade; pop. 2087. Map 60.

Potton, island, Essex, in estuary of river Roach. Map 73.

Poulton, eccl. dist., in Morecambe mun. bor., N. Lancashire; pop. 6956. Map 26.

Poulton-le-Fylde, urb. dist., small mkt. tn. and par., N. Lancs, 6 m. S. of Fleetwood; pop. 3366. Map 30.

Powfoot, ham., Dumfriesshire, 4 m. S.W. of Annan. Map 20.

Powick, par. and vil., in co. and 3 m. W. of Worcester; pop. 2640. Map 52.

Poyntzpass, vil., cos. Armagh and Down, 10 m. S. of Portadown Junction; pop. 348. Map 93.

Prawle, fishing vil., S. Devonshire, 7 m. S.E. of Kingsbridge. Map 89.

Prees, par. and vil., Shropshire, 4¼ m. S.E. of Whitchurch; pop. 1987. Map 47.

Preesall, urb. dist. and par., N. Lancashire, on r. Wyre, opposite Fleetwood; pop. 2043. Map 30.

Prendergast, par., Pembrokeshire, in bor. of Haverfordwest; pop. 1179. Map 64.

Prengwyn, ham., Cardiganshire, 2½ m. N.N.E. of Llandyssul. Map 54.

Prescot, urb. dist., mfg. and mkt. tn. and par., S.W. Lancs, 7¼ m. E. of Liverpool; pop. 9396. Map 38.

Prestatyn, par., small mkt. tn. and urb. dist., Flintshire, 4 m. E. of Rhyl; pop. 4511. Map 37.

Presteigne, urb. dist., Radnorshire, 6½ m. N.E. of New Radnor; pop. 1102. Map 56.

Preston, bor., par. and port, N. Lancashire, 28 m. N.E. of Liverpool; pop. 118,839. Map 30.

Preston, par. and vil., Dorsetshire, 3 m. N.E. of Weymouth; pop. 886. Map 87.

Preston Candover, par. and vil., Hants, 6 m. N. of Alresford; pop. 379. Map 76.

Preston-on-Wye, par. and vil., Herefordshire, 6½ m. S. of **Weobley;** pop. 301. Map 56.

Prestonpans, coast tn., police bur. and par., E. Lothian, 9½ m. E. of Edinburgh; pop. 2426. Map 10.

Prestwich, urb. dist. and par., Lancashire, 4½ m. N.W. of Manchester; pop. 23,876. Map 39.

Prestwick, town, Ayrshire, 38¼ m. S.W. of Glasgow; pop. 8538. Map 12.

Princes Risborough, market town and par., Bucks, 7½ m. S.S.W. of Aylesbury; pop. 2438. Map 70.

Princetown, eccl. dist. and vil., Devonshire, 21¼ m. N.N.E. of Plymouth; pop. 2061. Map 88.

Priors Marston, par. and vil., Warwickshire, 5 m. S.E. of Southam; pop. 451. Map 59.

Prudhoe, urb. dist. and par., Northumberland, 11 m. W. of Newcastle; pop. 9260. Map 22.

Puckeridge, vil., Hertfordshire, 6 m. N.E. of Ware. Map 71.

Pucklechurch, par. and vil., Gloucestershire, 4 m. S.W. of Chipping Sodbury; pop. 1283. Map 68.

Puddletown, par. and vil., Dorsetshire, 5 m. N.E. of Dorchester; pop. 761. Map 87.

Pudsey, mun. bor. and par., W.R. Yorkshire, 3 m. E. of Bradford; pop. 14,762. Map 32.

Puffin Island, or **Priestholm,** off E. point of Anglesey; area 58 acres. Map 37.

Pulborough, par. and market town, W. Sussex, 3¼ m. S.E. of Petworth; pop. 2065. Map 79.

Pulham Market, vil. and ry. sta., Norfolk, 3½ m. N.W. of Harleston. Map 63.

Puncheston, par. and vil., Pembrokeshire, 11 m. S.E. of Fishguard; pop. 204. Map 64.

Purfleet, urb. dist., Essex, 7 m. N.W. of Tilbury sta.; pop. 8511. Map 72.

Purley, vil., Surrey, 2½ m. S.S.W. of Croydon. Map 80.

Pwllheli, mun. bor. and seaport town, in co. and 21 m. S.W. of Carnarvon; pop. 3599. Map 44.

QUAINTON, par. and vil., Buckinghamshire, 6½ m. N.W. of Aylesbury; pop. 928. Map 70.

Quarry Bank, urb. dist., Staffordshire, 1½ m. S.E. of Brierley Hill; pop. 8100. Map 57.

Queenborough, mun. bor., Isle of Sheppey, Kent, 2 m. S.S.W. of Sheerness; pop. 2941. Map 73.

Queensbury, urb. dist. and par., W.R. Yorkshire, 4 m. N. of Halifax; pop. 5763. Map 32.

Queensferry, vil. and ry. sta., on r. Dee, in co. and 5½ m. S.E. of Flint. Map 38.

Queensferry, North, vil., with ry. sta., Fifeshire, 2 m. S. of Inverkeithing; pop. 1647. Map 10.

Queensferry, South, q.s. par., mun. bur. and spt. tn., West Lothian, 9½ m. W. of Edinburgh; pop. 1798. Map 10.

Queenstown, now **Cobh,** seaport, in co. and 13 m. S.E. of Cork; pop. 8209. Map 94.

Quendon, par. and vil., Essex, 6 m. S.W. of Saffron Walden; pop. 124. Map 61.

Quorndon, urb. dist. and par., Leicestershire, 2½ m. S.E. of Loughborough; pop. 2603. Map 49.

RADCLIFFE, urb. dist. and par., S.E. Lancashire, 3 m. S.W. of Bury; pop. 24,674. Map 31.

Radcliffe-on-Trent, par. and vil., in co. and 4¾ m. E. of Nottingham; pop. 2849. Map 49.

Radlett, eccl. dist. and vil., Hertfordshire, 5 m. S. of St Albans; pop. 2431. Map 71.

Radstock, urb. dist. and par., Somersetshire, 16 m. S.E. of Bristol; pop. 3622. Map 75.

Raglan, par. and vil., in co. and 7 m. S.W. of Monmouth; pop. 676. Map 67.

Rainford, urb. dist. and par., Lancashire, 4 m. N.W. of St Helens; pop. 3494. Map 38.

Rainham, par. and vil., Essex, 5 m. S.E. of Barking; pop. 2196. Map 72.

Rainhill, par. and vil., Lancashire, 9 m. E. of Liverpool; pop. 2463. Map 38.

Ramelton, market town, co. Donegal, 7 m. N.N.E. of Letterkenny; pop. 932. Map 93.

Rampside, eccl. dist. and vil., Lancashire, Dalton-in-Furness par.; pop. 481. Map 25.
Ramsbottom, urb. dist. and par., S.E. Lancashire, 4 m. N. of Bury; pop. 14,926. Map 31.
Ramsbury, par. and vil., Wiltshire, 5 m. N.W. of Hungerford; pop. 1504. Map 69.
Ramsey, seaport town, Isle of Man, 13 m. N. of Douglas; pop. 4642. Map 24.
Ramsey, urb. dist. and par., in co. and 10 m. N.E. of Huntingdon; pop. 5180. Map 61.
Ramsgate, mun. bor. and wtg. place, I. of Thanet, Kent, 74 m. S.E. of London; pop. 33,597. Map 83.
Randalstown, market town, in co. and 5 m. N.W. of Antrim; pop. 986. Map 93.
Rannoch, dist., loch and ry. sta., Perthshire and Argyllshire. Map 3.
Raphoe, mkt. tn. and par., co. Donegal, 6½ m. N.W. of Strabane; town pop. 705. Map 93.
Rastrick, now part of Brighouse mun. bor., W.R. Yorks, 3½ m. N. of Huddersfield. Map 32.
Rathdrum, market town and par., in co. and 9 m. S.W. of Wicklow; town pop. 680. Map 95.
Rathfriland, or **Rathfryland,** market town, co. Down, 9 m. N.E. of Newry; pop. 1365. Map 93.
Rathkeale, market town and par., in co. and 18 m. S.W. of Limerick; pop. 1550. Map 94.
Rathlin Island, par., off N. coast of co. Antrim; pop. 351. Map 93.
Rathmullan, vil., co. Donegal, on Lough Swilly, 7 m. N.E. of Ramelton; pop. 485. Map 93.
Rattray, Perthshire. *See* Blairgowrie and Rattray.
Raunds, urb. dist. and par., Northamptonshire, 4 m. S. of Thrapston; pop. 3683. Map 60.
Ravenglass, seaport and market town, Cumberland, 5 m. N.W. of Bootle. Map 25.
Raveningham, par. and vil., Norfolk, 3½ m. S.E. of Loddon; pop. 289. Map 53.
Ravenscar, seaside resort, N.R. Yorkshire, 8 m. S.E. of Whitby; pop. 496. Map 29.
Ravenstonedale, par. and vil., Westmorland, 4½ m. S.W. of Kirkby Stephen; pop. 831. Map 26.
Ravensworth, par. and vil., N.R. Yorkshire, 5 m. N.W. of Richmond; pop. 259. Map 27.
Raventhorpe, par., W.R. Yorkshire, a western ward of Dewsbury; pop. 6719. Map 32.
Rawdon, urb. dist. and par., W.R. Yorkshire, 5 m. N.E. of Bradford; pop. 4574. Map 32.
Rawmarsh, urb. dist. and par., W.R. Yorkshire, 2 m. N.N.E. of Rotherham; pop. 18,570. Map 41.
Rawtenstall, mun. bor. and par., N.E. Lancashire, 8 m. N. of Bury; pop. 28,575. Map 31.
Rayleigh, par. and urban dist., Essex, 7 m. W.N.W. of Southend; pop. 6256. Map 72.
Read, par. and vil., N.E. Lancashire, 2 m. E.S.E. of Whalley; pop. 904. Map 31.
Reading, co. bor., Berkshire, on r. Kennet, 36 m. W. of Paddington sta., London; pop. 97,153. Map 78.
Reay, par. and vil., Caithness, 10½ m. W. of Thurso; pop. 1355. Map 3.
Redcar, mun. bor. and par., Yorkshire, 7¾ m. N.E. of Middlesbrough; pop. 20,159. Map 23.
Redditch, urb. dist. and par., Worcestershire, 15½ m. S. of Birmingham; pop. 19,280. Map 58.
Redgrave, par. and vil., E. Suffolk, 7 m. N.W. of Eye; pop. 447. Map 62.
Redhill, residential dist., forming Eastern part of bor. of Reigate, Surrey. Map 80.
Redmarley D'Abitot, par. and vil., Gloucestershire, 5 m. S.E. of Ledbury; pop. 722. Map 57.
Redmire, par. and vil., N.R. Yorkshire, 4½ m. W. of Leyburn; pop. 238. Map 27.
Redruth, urb. dist. and par., Cornwall, 9 m. S.W. of Truro; pop. 9904. Map 90.
Red Wharf, on N.E. coast of Anglesey, 5½ m. N.W. of Beaumaris. Map 36.
Reedham, par. and vil., Norfolk, 8 m. S.W. of Yarmouth; pop. 840. Map 53.
Reepham with Kerdiston, par. and vil., Norfolk, 6½ m. W.S.W. of Aylsham; pop. 372. Map 53.
Reeth, par. and moorland vil., N.R. Yorkshire, 9 m. W. of Richmond; pop. 709. Map 27.
Reigate, mun. bor., Surrey, 24¼ m. S. of London; pop. 30,830. Map 80.
Reighton, par. and vil., E.R. Yorkshire, 6 m. N.W. of Bridlington; pop. 202. Map 29.
Renfrew, mun. bor. and co. town of Renfrewshire, 5 m. W. of Glasgow; pop. 14,986. Map 8.
Renton, town and *q.s.* par., in co. and 2¼ m. N. of Dumbarton; pop. 4923. Map 8.
Renwick, par. and vil., Cumberland, 3 m. N.E. of Kirkoswald; pop. 174. Map 21.
Repton, par. and vil., Derbyshire, 4¾ m. N.E. of Burton-on-Trent; pop. 1929. Map 48.
Reston, vil. and ry. sta., Berwickshire, 6¾ m. N.E. of Duns. Map 11.
Rettendon, par. and vil., Essex, 6½ m. S.E. of Chelmsford; pop. 851. Map 72.
Reynalton, par., Pembrokeshire, 4 m. S.S.W. of Narberth; pop. 62. Map 64.
Reynoldston, par. and vil., Glamorganshire, 12 m. W.S.W. of Swansea; pop. 278. Map 65.
Rhayader, market town and par., Radnorshire, 14 m. S. of Llanidloes; pop. 910. Map 55.
Rheidol Falls, ry. sta., Cardiganshire, 2½ m. W.N.W. of Devil's Bridge. Map 55.
Rhondda, urb. dist., Glamorganshire, 7½ m. N.W. of Pontypridd; pop. 141,344. Map 66.
Rhos-Goch, Anglesey, 3 m. S.W. of Amlwch. Map 36.
Rhosllanerchrugog, par. and vil., Denbighshire, 4 m. S.W. of Wrexham; pop. 11,139. Map 38.
Rhosneigr, vil., lifeboat and coastguard sta., 1½ m. W. of Llanfaelog, W. Anglesey. Map 36.
Rhos-on-Sea, vil. and seaside resort, Denbighshire and Carnarvonshire. Map 37.
Rhossili, par. and vil., Glamorganshire, 12 m. S.W. of Loughor; pop. 304. Map 65.
Rhostyllen, ham. and ry. sta., S.E. Denbighshire, 1¾ m. S.W. of Wrexham. Map 38.
Rhuddlan, par., Flintshire, on r. Clwyd, 3 m. N.W. of St Asaph; pop. 1701. Map 37.
Rhydowen, ham., Cardiganshire, 3½ m. N.N.E. of Llandyssul. Map 55.
Rhyl, watering place, par. and urb. dist., Flintshire, 6 m. S.W. of St Asaph; pop. 13,489. Map 37.
Rhymney, urb. dist. and par., Monmouthshire, 2½ m. W. of Tredegar; pop. 10,505. Map 66.
Ribbleton, par. and seat, Lancashire, 2 m. N.E. of Preston; pop. 78. Map 30.
Ribchester, town and par., N.E. Lancashire, 5½ m. N.N.W. of Blackburn; pop. 1450. Map 30.
Riccall, par. and vil., E.R. Yorkshire, 4 m. N. of Selby; pop. 739. Map 34.
Richard's Castle, par. and vil., Salop, 3½ m. S.W. of Ludlow; pop. 393. Map 56.
Richborough, ham. and ancient seaport, Kent, 1½ m. N.W. of Sandwich. Map 83.
Richmond, mun. bor., Surrey, on r. Thames, 9¾ m. S.W. of London; pop. 37,791. Map 71.
Richmond, mun. bor., par. and mkt. tn., N.R. Yorkshire, 15 m. S.W. of Darlington; pop. 4769. Map 27.
Rickmansworth, urb. dist. and par., Hertfordshire, 3½ m. S.W. of Watford; pop. 10,810. Map 71.
Riding, par. and ry. sta. **(R. Mill),** Northumberland, 5½ m. S.E. of Hexham; pop. 318. Map 22.
Ridsdale, vil., Northumberland, 1 m. S.S.E. of Woodburn ry. sta. Map 17.
Rigg, vil. and ry. sta., Dumfriesshire, 6 m. E. of Annan. Map 21.
Rillington, par. and vil., E.R. Yorkshire, 4¼ m. N.E of Malton; pop. 684. Map 29.

Ringwood, market town and par., Hants, 8 m. N. of Christchurch; pop. 5131. Map 77.

Ripley, urb. dist. and par., Derbyshire, 10 m. N.E. of Derby; pop. 13,415. Map 41.

Ripley, eccl. par. and vil., Surrey, $5\frac{1}{2}$ m. N.E. of Guildford; pop. 1557. Map 78.

Ripley, market vil. and par., W.R. Yorkshire, $3\frac{1}{2}$ m. N.W. of Harrogate; pop. 231. Map 32.

Ripon, city, mun. bor. and par., W.R. Yorkshire, $13\frac{3}{4}$ m. S. of Northallerton; pop. 8576. Map 27.

Rippingale, par. and vil., Kesteven, Lincolnshire, $5\frac{1}{2}$ m. N. of Bourne; pop. 435. Map 50.

Risca, urb. dist. and par., Monmouthshire, $6\frac{1}{2}$ m. N.W. of Newport; pop. 16,605. Map 67.

Riseley, par. and vil., in co. and 9 m. N. of Bedford; pop. 600. Map 60.

Rishton, urb. dist. and par., N.E. Lancashire, 3 m. N.E. of Blackburn; pop. 6631. Map 31.

Rishworth, urb. dist., W.R. Yorkshire, $4\frac{1}{2}$ m. S.S.W. of Sowerby Bridge; pop. 838. Map 31.

Riverhead, par. and vil., Kent, $1\frac{1}{2}$ m. N.W. of Sevenoaks; pop. 943. Map 82.

Rivington, par. and vil., mid. Lancashire, 4 m. S.E. of Chorley; pop. 238. Map 30.

Roberton, par., Roxburghshire; Church 5 m. W. of Hawick; pop. 383. Map 16.

Robertsbridge, or **Rotherbridge,** town, E. Sussex, on r. Rother, $4\frac{3}{4}$ m. N. of Battle. Map 82.

Robin Hood's Bay, fishing town, N.R. Yorkshire, 5 m. S.E. of Whitby. Map 29.

Roby, par. and seat, S.W. Lancashire, $5\frac{1}{2}$ m. E. of Liverpool; pop. of eccl. dist. 985. Map 38.

Rochdale, parl. and co. bor. and par., S.E. Lancashire, $10\frac{1}{2}$ m. N.E. of Manchester; pop. 90,278. Map 31.

Rochester, mun. bor. and r. port, Kent, 30 m. S.E. of London; pop. 31,196. Map 80.

Rochford, town and par., Essex, 3 m. N. of Southend; pop. 2077. Map 73.

Rock, par. and vil., Worcestershire, $4\frac{1}{2}$ m. S.W. of Bewdley; pop. 1534. Map 57.

Rockbourne, par. and vil., Hants, $3\frac{1}{2}$ m. N.W. of Fordingbridge; pop. 423. Map 77.

Rockcliffe, par. and vil., Cumberland, 4 m. N.W. of Carlisle; pop. 559. Map 21.

Rock Ferry, summer resort, Cheshire, on r. Mersey, in S. suburbs of Birkenhead. Map 38.

Rockingham, par. and vil., Northamptonshire, 10 m. N.E. of Market Harborough; pop. 163. Map 50.

Rodborough, par. and vil., Gloucestershire, $\frac{1}{2}$ m. S.W. of Stroud; pop. 3824. Map 68.

Rodbourne Cheney, par. and vil., Wiltshire, 2 m. N.W. of Swindon; pop. 2115. Map 69.

Rodlington, par. and vil., Salop, $4\frac{1}{2}$ m. N.W. of Wellington; pop. 483. Map 47.

Rodney Stoke, par. and vil., Somersetshire, 5 m. N.W. of Wells; pop. 608. Map 74.

Rogate, par. and vil., W. Sussex, 5 m. W. of Midhurst; pop. 1001. Map 79.

Rolleston, par. and vil., Staffordshire, 3 m. N.W. of Burton-on-Trent; pop. 764. Map 48.

Rolvenden, par. and vil., Kent, 3 m. W.S.W. of Tenterden; pop. 1194. Map 82.

Romaldkirk, par. and vil., N.R. Yorkshire, 5 m. N.W. of Barnard Castle; pop. 233. Map 27.

Romford, urb. dist. and market town, Essex, 6 m. S.W. of Brentwood; pop. 35,918. Map 72.

Romsey, mun. bor. and par., Hants, 10 m. S.W. of Southampton by rail; pop. 4863. Map 77.

Roos, par. and vil., E.R. Yorkshire, 7 m. E. of Hedon; pop. 455. Map 35.

Ropley, par. and vil., Hants, 4 m. E.S.E. of Alresford; pop. 1473. Map 79.

Ropsley, par. and vil., Kesteven, Lincolnshire, 5 m. E.S.E. of Grantham; pop. 519. Map 50.

Roscommon, par., market and co. town of Roscommon, 96 m. W.N.W. of Dublin; pop. 1830. Map 92.

Roscrea, market town, with ry. sta., Tipperary, $46\frac{3}{4}$ m. N.E. of Limerick by rail; pop. 2694. Map 95.

Rosehearty, vil. (police bur.), Aberdeenshire, $4\frac{1}{2}$ m. W. of Fraserburgh; pop. 1079. Map 3.

Rosemarket, par. and vil., Pembrokeshire, $3\frac{1}{2}$ m. N.E. of Milford; pop. 384. Map 64.

Roseneath, par. and vil., Dumbartonshire, $2\frac{1}{2}$ m. W. of Helensburgh; pop. 2770. Map 8.

Roslin, *q.s.* par. and vil., Midlothian, $6\frac{1}{2}$ m. S. of Edinburgh; pop. 1891. Map 10.

Rosliston, par. and vil., Derbyshire, $4\frac{1}{2}$ m. S. of Burton-on-Trent; pop. 467. Map 48.

Ross, urb. dist. and par., Herefordshire, 18 m. N.W. of Gloucester by rail; pop. 4738. Map 68.

Rossington, par. and vil., W.R. Yorkshire, $4\frac{3}{4}$ m. S.E. of Doncaster; pop. 3029. Map 41.

Rosslare, par. and vil., in co. and 6 m. S.E. of Wexford; pop. 667. Map 95.

Rosyth, vil., Fifesh., $1\frac{3}{4}$ m. N.W. of Queensferry. Map 10.

Rothbury, urb. dist. and par., Northumberland, 11 m. S.W. of Alnwick; pop. 1255. Map 17.

Rotherfield, par. and vil., Sussex, $8\frac{1}{2}$ m. S.W. of Tunbridge Wells; pop. 2178. Map 81.

Rotherham, co. bor., mkt. tn. and par., W.R. Yorkshire, 6 m. N.E. of Sheffield; pop. 69,689. Map 41.

Rothes, par. and police bur., Morayshire, $9\frac{3}{4}$ m. S.E. of Elgin; pop. 1292. Map 3.

Rothesay, mun. bur., co. tn. of Bute, Firth of Clyde, 19 m. S.W. of Greenock; pop. 9346. Map 12.

Rothley, par. and vil., Leicestershire, $1\frac{1}{2}$ m. S. of Mountsorrel; pop. 2264. Map 49.

Rothwell, urb. dist. and par., Northamptonshire, 4 m. N.W. of Kettering; pop. 4516. Map 60.

Rothwell, par. and vil., Lindsey, Lincolnshire, $2\frac{1}{2}$ m. S.E. of Caistor; pop. 198. Map 42.

Rothwell, urb. dist., W.R. Yorkshire, 4 m. S.E. of Leeds; pop. 15,639. Map 32.

Rottingdean, coast par. and vil., E. Sussex, 4 m. S.E. of Brighton; pop. 2769. Map 81.

Roughton, par. and vil., Norfolk, $3\frac{1}{2}$ m. S. of Cromer; pop. 479. Map 53.

Row (Rhu), par. and vil., Dumbartonshire, 2 m. N.W. of Helensburgh; vil., pop. 1136. Map 8.

Rowhedge, vil., Essex, 3 m. S.E. of Colchester. Map 73.

Rowley Regis, urb. dist. and par., Staffordshire, $2\frac{1}{2}$ m. S.E. of Dudley; pop. 41,238. Map 47.

Rowsley, Great, par. and vil., Derbyshire, $3\frac{1}{2}$ m. S.E. of Bakewell; pop. 338. Map 40.

Roxburgh, par. and vil., Roxburghshire, vil., 3 m. S.W. of Kelso; pop. 742. Map 16.

Roxby-cum-Risby, urb. dist., Lincoln, 8 m. N.W. of Brigg; pop. 548. Map 34.

Roydon, par. and vil., W. Essex, $4\frac{1}{2}$ m. W.S.W. of Harlow; pop. 1182. Map 71.

Royston, urb. dist., par. and vil., W.R. Yorkshire, 4 m. N.E. of Barnsley; pop. 7156. Map 33.

Royston, urb. dist. and par., Hertfordshire, $12\frac{1}{2}$ m. N.E. of Hitchin; pop. 3831. Map 61.

Royton, urb. dist. and par., S.E. Lancashire, 3 m. N. of Oldham; pop. 16,687. Map 31.

Ruabon, town and par., Denbighshire, $4\frac{1}{4}$ m. S.W. of Wrexham; pop. 3333. Map 38.

Ruddington, par. and vil., with ry. sta., in co. and $4\frac{1}{2}$ m. S. of Nottingham; pop. 2877. Map 49.

Rudgwick, par. and vil., W. Sussex, 6 m. N.W. of Horsham; pop. 1175. Map 79.

Rudham, East and **West,** 2 pars., Norfolk, $6\frac{1}{2}$ m. W. of Fakenham; pop. 639 and 346. Map 52.

Rudston, par. and vil., E.R. Yorkshire, 5 m. W. of Bridlington; pop. 492. Map 29.

Rugby, urb. dist. and par., in co. and $15\frac{3}{4}$ m. N.E. of Warwick; pop. 23,824. Map 59.

Rugeley, urb. dist. and par., in co. and $8\frac{1}{2}$ m. S.E. of Stafford; pop. 5263. Map 48.

Ruislip, urb. dist., Middlesex, 3½ m. N.E. of Uxbridge; pop. 16,038. Map 71.

Rum Island, Inner Hebrides, Inverness-shire, 15 m. N.W. of Ardnamurchan Point; pop. 149. Map 2.

Rumbling Bridge, place, border of Kinross-shire and Perthshire, 4¼ m. N.E. of Dollar. Map 7.

Runcorn, urb. dist., seaport and par., Cheshire, 12½ m. S.E. of Liverpool by rail; pop. 18,158. Map 38.

Rushall, par. and vil., Staffordshire, 1½ m. N.E. of Walsall; pop. 3256. Map 48.

Rushden, urb. dist. and par., Northamptonshire, 1¼ m. S. of Higham Ferrers; pop. 14,247. Map 60.

Rushyford, ham., Durham, 5 m. E.S.E. of Bishop Auckland. Map 23.

Ruskington, urb. dist. and par., Kesteven, Lincolnshire, 3½ m. N.N.E. of Sleaford; pop. 1101. Map 42.

Ruswarp, par. and vil., N.R. Yorkshire, in urb. dist. of Whitby; pop. 6195. Map 29.

Rutherglen, mun. bur. and par., Lanarkshire, 2 m. S.E. of Central sta., Glasgow; pop. 25,157. Map 8.

Ruthin, mun. bor., mkt. tn. and par., Denbighshire, on r. Clwyd, 7¾ m. S.E. of Denbigh; pop. 2912. Map 38.

Ruthwell, coast par. and vil., in co. and 9 m. S.E. of Dumfries; pop. 727. Map 20.

Ryburgh, par. and vil., Norfolk, 3 m. S.E. of Fakenham; pop. 550. Map 52.

Ryde, wtg. pl., mun. bor. and par., Isle of Wight, 20 m. from Southampton; pop. 10,519. Map 77.

Rye, mun. bor., par. and Cinque port, Sussex, 11 m. N.E. of Hastings by rail; pop. 3947. Map 82.

Ryhope, par. and vil., Durham, 3 m. S. of Sunderland; pop. 11,650. Map 23.

Ryton, urb. dist. and par., Durham, 6 m. W. of Newcastle; pop. 14,204. Map 22.

SABDEN, par. and vil., N.E. Lancashire, 5 m. N.W. of Burnley; pop. 1645. Map 31.

Saddleworth, urb. dist., W.R. Yorkshire, 12 m. S.W. of Huddersfield; pop. 12,577. Map 31.

Saffron Walden, mun. bor. and par., Essex, 43¾ m. N.E. of London; pop. 5930. Map 61.

Saham Toney, par. and vil., Norfolk, 1½ m. N.W. of Watton; pop. 882. Map 52.

St Abb's, vil., Berwickshire, 1½ m. N.E. of Coldingham; pop. 403. Map 11.

St Agnes, seaport and par., Cornwall, 8½ m. N.W. of Truro; pop. 3347. Map 90.

St Albans, mun. bor., city and par., Hertfordshire, 21½ m. N.W. of London by rail; pop. 28,625. Map 71.

St Andrews, mun. bur., spt. and par., Fifeshire, 13½ m. S.E. of Dundee by rail; bur. pop. 8269. Map 7.

St Anne's Chapel, ham., S. Devonshire, ½ m. N. of Bigbury. Map 89.

St Anne's-on-the-Sea. *See* Lytham.

St Asaph, city and par., Flintshire, 5¼ m. N. of Denbigh; pop. 1830. Map 37.

St Athan, par. and vil., Glamorganshire, 4½ m. S.S.E. of Cowbridge; pop. 444. Map 66.

St Austell, urb. dist. and par., Cornwall, 1½ m. W. of St Austell Bay; pop. 8295. Map 91.

St Bees, coast town and par., Cumberland, 5 m. S. of Whitehaven; pop. 1609. Map 24.

St Blazey, town and par., Cornwall, 4 m. E.N.E. of St Austell; pop. 3146. Map 91.

St Breock, par. and vil., Cornwall, 7 m. N.W. of Bodmin; pop. 713. Map 91.

St Briavals, par. and vil., Gloucestershire, 7¼ m. N.N.E. of Chepstow; pop. 1210. Map 68.

St Brides Minor, par., Glamorganshire, 2½ m. N. of Bridgend; pop. 1837. Map 66.

St Budeaux, par. and vil., Devonshire, 4 m. N.W. of Plymouth; pop. 1803. Map 88.

St Buryan, par. and vil., Cornwall, 5½ m. S.W. of Penzance; pop. 1132. Map 90.

St Clears, par., town and r. port, in co. and 8 m. S.W. of Carmarthen; pop. 931. Map 65.

St Columb Major, market town and par., Cornwall, 9 m. N.W. of St. Austell; pop. 2880. Map 91.

St Cyrus, par. and vil., Kincardineshire, 5¼ m. N.N.E. of Montrose; pop. 1306. Map 3.

St David's, city and par., Pembrokeshire, 14 m. N.W. of Haverfordwest; pop. 1543. Map 64.

St Dennis, par. and vil., Cornwall, 4 m. N.W. of St Austell; pop. 2158. Map 91.

St Dogmells, par., partly within the bor. of Cardigan; pop. 844. Map 54.

St Dogwells, par., Pembrokeshire, 6 m. S. of Fishguard; pop. 309. Map 64.

St Endellion, par. and vil., Cornwall, 9 m. N.W. of Bodmin; pop. 1047. Map 91.

St Ewe, par. and vil., Cornwall, 5 m. S.S.W. of St Austell; pop. 889. Map 91.

Saintfield, market town and par., co. Down, 15¼ m. S.E. of Belfast; pop. (town) 533. Map 93.

St Fillans, vil., with ry. sta., Perthshire, 11½ m. W. of Crieff; pop. 300. Map 5.

St Germans, market town and par., Cornwall, 9½ m. W.N.W. of Plymouth; pop. 1986. Map 88.

St Helens, par. and co. bor., Lancashire, 10 m. E.N.E. of Liverpool; pop. 106,793. Map 38.

St Helens, urb. dist. and par., Isle of Wight, 4 m. S.E. of Ryde; pop. 5478. Map 77.

St Ives, mun. bor., par. and seaport, Cornwall, 8 m. N.E. of Penzance; pop. 6687. Map 90.

St Ives, mun. bor. and par., in co. and 5¼ m. E. of Huntingdon; pop. 2664. Map 61.

St Johns, ham., Isle of Man, on r. Neb, 3 m. S.E. of Peel. Map 24.

St John's Chapel, ry. sta., Durham, 7 m. W. of Stanhope. Map 22.

St Just, urb. dist. and par., Cornwall, 7 m. W. of Penzance; pop. 4356. Map 90.

St Keverne, coast par. and vil., Cornwall, 8 m. S. of Falmouth; pop. 1745. Map 90.

St Leonards, western suburb of Hastings, Sussex. Map 81.

St Margaret at Cliffe, par. and vil., Kent, 3½ m. N.E. of Dover; pop. 1280. Map 83.

St Martin's, par. and vil., Salop, 5 m. N.E. of Oswestry; pop. 1459. Map 46.

St Mary Bourne, par. and vil., Hants, 3 m. N.W. of Whitchurch; pop. 1151. Map 76.

St Mary Cray, par. and vil., Kent, 4½ m. E.S.E. of Bromley; pop. 2178. Map 80.

St Mawes, market town, Cornwall, 3 m. E. of Falmouth. Map 91.

St Mellons, par. and vil., Monmouthshire, 4 m. N.E. of Cardiff; pop. 709. Map 67.

St Michaels-on-Wyre, eccl. dist. and vil., N. Lancashire, 3½ m. S.W. of Garstang; pop. 548. Map 30.

St Monans, par. and vil., Fifeshire, 3 m. S.W. of Anstruther; pop. 1796. Map 7.

St Neots, par. and vil., Cornwall, 4½ m. N.W. of Liskeard; pop. 1086. Map 88.

St Neots, urb. dist. and par., in co. and 8 m. S.W. of Huntingdon; pop. 4314. Map 61.

St Nicholas at Wade, par. and vil., Kent, 6½ m. S.W. of Margate; pop. 538. Map 83.

St Osyth, par. and vil., Essex, 10 m. S.E. of Colchester; pop. 1286. Map 73.

St Stephen, par. and vil., Hertfordshire, 2 m. S. of St Albans; pop. 1960. Map 71.

Salcombe, urb. dist., Devonshire, 3¼ m. S. of Kingsbridge; pop. 2383. Map 89.

Sale, urb. dist. and par., Chester, on r. Mersey, 5 m. S.W. of Manchester; pop. 28,063. Map 39.

Salehurst, par. and vil., E. Sussex, 5 m. N. of Battle; pop. 1978. Map 81.

Salford, city, parl. and co. bor. and par., S.E. Lancashire; pop. 223,442. Map 39.
Saline, par. and vil., Fifeshire, 5½ m. N.W. of Dunfermline; pop. 1379. Map 9.
Salisbury, mun. bor. and co. town of Wiltshire, 23 m. W. of Winchester; pop. 26,456. Map 76.
Salkeld, Great, par. and vil., Cumberland, 4½ m. N.E. of Penrith; pop. 394. Map 21.
Saltash, mun. bor. and par., Cornwall, 4 m. N.W. of Devonport; pop. 3603. Map 88.
Saltburn-by-the-Sea, urb. dist. and par., N.R. Yorkshire, 4½ m. S.E. of Redcar; pop. 3911. Map 28.
Saltcoats, police bur. and seaport, Ayrshire, 29½ m. S.W. of Glasgow by rail; pop. 10,173. Map 12.
Salterforth, par. and vil., W.R. Yorkshire, 8 m. S.W. of Skipton; pop. 643. Map 31.
Saltwood, par. and vil., Kent, ¾ m. N. of Hythe; pop. 861. Map 83.
Samlesbury, par. and vil., N.E. Lancashire, 3½ m. E. of Preston; pop. 835. Map 30.
Sampford Courtenay, par. and vil., Devonshire, 3¾ m. N.E. of Okehampton: pop. 731. Map 84.
Sandbach, urb. dist., market town and par., Cheshire, 4½ m. N.E. of Crewe; pop. 6411. Map 39.
Sandbank, *q.s.* par. and vil., Argyllshire, 2¾ m. N.W. of Dunoon; pop. 1257. Map 12.
Sanderstead, par. and vil., Surrey, 3 m. S.E. of Croydon; pop. 3351. Map 80.
Sandford, par. and vil., Devonshire, 2 m. N.W. of Crediton; pop. 961. Map 85.
Sandgate, urb. dist. and par., Kent, 1½ m. W.S.W. of Folkestone; pop. 2596. Map 83.
Sandhurst, par. and vil., S.E. Berkshire, 4½ m. S.E. of Wokingham; pop. 3802. Map 78.
Sandhurst, par. and vil., Kent, 6 m. S. of Cranbrook; pop. 898. Map 82.
Sandon, par. and vil., in co. and 5 m. N.E. of Stafford; pop. 477. Map 47.
Sandown, urb. dist. and par., Isle of Wight, 6½ m. S. of Ryde; pop. 6167. Map 77.
Sandringham, par. and royal seat, Norfolk, 6 m. N.E. of King's Lynn; pop. 96. Map 52.
Sandwich, mun. bor. and Cinque port, Kent, 5 m. S.W. of Ramsgate by rail; pop. 3287. Map 83.
Sandy, urb. dist., Bedfordshire, 3 m. N.W. of Biggleswade; pop. 3140. Map 60.
Sandygate, vil., Isle of Man, 2½ m. N.N.W. of Sulby. Map 24.
Sandylands, rising watering place, N.W. Lancashire, on S. side of Morecambe; pop. 3553. Map 30.
Sanquhar, mun. bur. and par., in co. and 26½ m. N.W. of Dumfries by rail; pop. 1753. Map 14.
Sarnau, ham., in co. and 9 m. N.E. of Cardigan. Map 54.
Sarre, par. and vil., Kent, 7 m. S.W. of Margate; pop. 147. Map 83.
Saundersfoot, seaport vil., Pembrokeshire, 2½ m. N. of Tenby. Map 64.
Sawbridgeworth, urb. dist. and par., Hertfordshire, 4 m. S. of Bishop's Stortford; pop. 2604. Map 72.
Sawley, par. and vil., W.R. Yorkshire, 5 m. S.W. of Ripon; pop. 312. Map 27.
Sawtry, vil., in co. and 8½ m. N.W. of Huntingdon. Map 60.
Saxmundham, urb. dist. and par., E. Suffolk, 23 m. N.E. of Ipswich; pop. 1259. Map 63.
Saxthorpe, par. and vil., Norfolk, 5 m. N.W. of Aylsham; pop. 276. Map 53.
Sca Fell and Pike, mts., Cumberland, 10½ and 10 m. S.W. of Keswick; alt. 3162 and 3210 ft. Map 25.
Scalby, urb. dist. and par., N.R. Yorkshire, 2½ m. N.W. of Scarborough; pop. 2771. Map 29.
Scaleby, par. and vil., Cumberland, 5 m. N.E. of Carlisle; pop. 358. Map 21.
Scales, vil., Lancashire, 4 m. N.W. of Ulverston. Map 25.
Scalford, par. and vil., Leicestershire, 3½ m. N. of Melton Mowbray; pop. 581. Map 49.
Scammonden, urb. dist., W.R. Yorkshire, 6 m. W. of Huddersfield; pop. 394. Map 31.
Scampston, par., E.R. Yorkshire, 5 m. N.E. of Malton; pop. 198. Map 29.
Scarborough, mun. bor., par., spt. and wtg. pl., N.R. Yorks, 42 m. N.E. of York; pop. 41,791. Map 29.
Scarcliffe, par. and vil., Derbyshire, 8 m. E.S.E. of Chesterfield; pop. 3442. Map 41.
Scartho, par. and vil., Lindsey, Lincolnshire, 2½ m. S.S.W. of Grimsby; pop. 744. Map 35.
Scole, par. and vil., Norfolk, 1½ m. E. of Diss; pop. 566. Map 63.
Scone, Old and **New,** par. and vil., Perthshire, 2 m. N.E. of Perth; pop. 2935. **S. Palace.** Map 6.
Scopwick, par. and vil., Kesteven, Lincolnshire, 8 m. N. of Sleaford; pop. 423. Map 42.
Scotby, eccl. dist. and vil., Cumberland, 2½ m. E. of Carlisle; pop. 769. Map 21.
Scotch Corner, N.R. Yorkshire, 4 m. N. of Catterick Bridge. Map 27.
Scotforth, par., Lancashire, forming a S. suburb of Lancaster; pop. 301. Map 30.
Scotlandwell, vil., Kinross-shire, 5 m. W. of Leslie. Map 6.
Scots Gap, ry. sta., Northumberland, 11 m. W. of Morpeth. Map 17.
Scotter, par. and vil., Lindsey, Lincolnshire, 3½ m. N.W. of Kirton-in-Lindsey; pop. 1043. Map 42.
Scourie, vil., Sutherlandshire, 43½ m. N.W. of Lairg; pop. 77. Map 2.
Scunthorpe, urb. dist. and par., Lincolnshire, 8 m. E. of Crowle; pop. 33,761. Map 34.
Seaford, urb. dist. and Cinque port, E. Sussex, 2¾ m. S.E. of Newhaven; pop. 6570. Map 81.
Seaham, coast par. and ry. sta., Durham, 5 m. S. of Sunderland; pop. 6488. Map 23.
Seaham Harbour, urb. dist. and spt., Durham, 5½ m. S. of Sunderland; pop. 19,394. Map 23.
Sea Houses, vil. and harbour, Northumberland, 4 m. N.E. of Chathill by rail. Map 17.
Seal, par. and vil., Kent, 1½ m. N.E. of Sevenoaks; pop. 1627. Map 82.
Seamer, par. and vil., N.R. Yorkshire, 3 m. S.W. of Scarborough; pop. 640. Map 29.
Seaton, urb. dist. and par., Devonshire, 7½ m. S.W. of Axminster; pop. 2351. Map 86.
Seaton Carew, eccl. dist. and ry. sta., Durham, in W. Hartlepool co. bor.; pop. 2170. Map 23.
Seaton Delaval, urb. dist. and par., Northumberland, 3 m. S.W. of Blyth; pop. 7377. Map 23.
Seaton Sluice, seaport, Northumberland, 3 m. S.E. of Blyth. Map 23.
Sedbergh, market town and par., W.R. Yorkshire, 14½ m. N.W. of Ingleton; pop. 2586. Map 26.
Sedgeberrow, par. and vil., Worcestershire, 3½ m. S.S.W. of Evesham; pop. 332. Map 58.
Sedgefield, market town and par., Durham, 8½ m. N.W. of Stockton; pop. 3111. Map 23.
Sedgemoor, marshy tract, Somersetshire, 8 m. S.E. of Bridgwater. Map 86.
Sedgley, urb. dist. and par., Staffordshire, 3 m. S. of Wolverhampton; pop. 19,261. Map 47.
Sedgwick, par. and seat, Westmorland, 3½ m. S. of Kendal; pop. 200. Map 26.
Sedlescombe, par. and vil., E. Sussex, 2½ m. N.E. of Battle; pop. 546. Map 81.
Seend, par. and vil., Wiltshire, 4 m. W. of Devizes; pop. 934. Map 75.
Sefton, par. and vil., Lancashire, 6 m. N. of Liverpool; pop. 296. Map 38.
Seghill, urb. dist. and par., Northumberland, 7 m. N.E. of Newcastle; pop. 2582. Map 23.
Selborne, par. and vil., Hampshire, 4 m. S.E. of Alton; pop. 2004. Map 79.

Selby, urb. dist., market town and par., W.R. Yorkshire, 14 m. S. of York; pop. 10,064. Map 33.
Selkirk, mun. bur. and co. town of Selkirkshire, 40 m. S.E. of Edinburgh; pop. 5667. Map 16.
Selling, par. and vil., Kent, 3½ m. S.E. of Faversham; pop. 722. Map 83.
Sellinge, par. and vil., Kent, 5 m. N.W. of Hythe; pop. 793. Map 83.
Selly Oak, a ward in the S.W. of Birmingham. Map 58.
Selsey, par. and vil., W. Sussex, 7 m. S. of Chichester; pop. 2307. Map 79.
Selston, par. and vil., Nottinghamshire, 7 m. S.W. of Mansfield; pop. 9285. Map 41.
Senghennydd, vil. and ry. sta., Glamorganshire, 11 m. N.N.W. of Cardiff. Map 67.
Senny, par., in co. and 8 m. S.W. of Brecknock; pop. 187. Map 66.
Settle, market town and par., W.R. Yorkshire, 15½ m. N.W. of Skipton; pop. 2389. Map 26.
Settrington, par. and vil., E.R. Yorkshire, 3 m. E. of Malton; pop. 448. Map 29.
Sevenoaks, urb. dist. and market town, Kent, 22 m. S.E. of London; pop. 10,482. Map 82.
Severn Stoke, par. and vil., Worcestershire, 2½ m. N.N.E. of Upton; pop. 555. Map 57.
Shadforth, par. and vil., in co. and 5 m. E.S.E. of Durham; pop. 2217. Map 23.
Shaftesbury, mun. bor., N. Dorsetshire, 3½ m. S.W. of Semley; pop. 2366. Map 87.
Shafton, par. and vil., W.R. Yorkshire, 4 m. N.E. of Barnsley; pop. 1290. Map 32.
Shakespeare's Cliff, on coast, Kent, 1 m. S. of Dover; alt. 350 ft. Map 83.
Shaldon, vil., Devonshire, at mouth of r. Teign. Map 89.
Shalfleet, par. and vil., Isle of Wight, 3½ m. E. of Yarmouth; pop. 835. Map 77.
Shalford, par. and vil., Essex, 4½ m. N.W. of Braintree; pop. 515. Map 72.
Shalford, par. and vil., Surrey, 1 m. S. of Guildford; pop. 3077. Map 78.
Shanagolden, par. and vil., in co. and 21 m. W.S.W. of Limerick; pop. 771. Map 94.
Shandon, vil., Dumbartonshire, on E. shore of Gare Loch, 5 m. N.W. of Helensburgh. Map 8.
Shankill, vil. and ry. sta., in co. and 9½ m. S.E. of Dublin. Map 95.
Shanklin, urb. dist. and par., Isle of Wight, 3 m. N.E. of Ventnor; pop. 5071. Map 77.
Shap, urb. dist. and par., Westmorland, 12 m. S.E. of Penrith; pop. 1227. Map 26.
Sharlston, par. and vil., W.R. Yorkshire, 4 m. S.E. of Wakefield; pop. 2776. Map 33.
Sharnbrook, par. and vil., in co. and 7 m. N.N.W. of Bedford; pop. 772. Map 60.
Shaw, eccl. dist. and vil., S.E. Lancashire, 3½ m. N. of Oldham; pop. 5121. Map 31.
Sheerness, urb. dist., spt. and dockyard, Kent, 51¾ m. E. of London; pop. 16,721. Map 73.
Sheffield, co. bor., mfg. tn. and par., W.R. Yorkshire, 53 m. S.W. of York; pop. 511,742. Map 41.
Shefford, market town and par., in co. and 10 m. S.E. of Bedford; pop. 849. Map 60.
Shelf, urb. dist., W.R. Yorkshire, 3 m. N.E. of Halifax; pop. 2600. Map 32.
Shelfield, vil., Staffs., 2½ m. N.E. of Walsall. Map 48.
Shelford, Great, par. and vil., in co. and 3 m. S. of Cambridge; pop. 1534. Map 61.
Shelley, urb. dist. and par., W.R. Yorkshire, 6 m. S.E. of Huddersfield; pop. 1566. Map 32.
Shelsley Beauchamp, par., Worcestershire, 7½ m. S.W. of Stourport; pop. 197. Map 57.
Shenfield, par. and vil., Essex, 1 m. N.E. of Brentwood; pop. 2604. Map 72.
Shenley, par. and vil., Hertfordshire, 5 m. N.W. of Barnet; pop. 1729. Map 71.
Shenstone, par. and vil., Staffordshire, 3 m. S. of Lichfield; pop. 2411. Map 48.
Shepley, urb. dist., W.R. Yorkshire, 7 m. S.E. of Huddersfield; pop. 1668. Map 32.
Shepperton, par. and vil., Middlesex, 2 m. E. of Chertsey; pop. 2858. Map 78.
Sheppey, Isle of, off N. coast of Kent, at mouth of the Thames. Map 83.
Shepshed, urb. dist., Leicestershire, 4 m. W. of Loughborough; pop. 5759. Map 49.
Shepton Mallet, market town and par., Somersetshire, 5 m. E.S.E. of Wells; pop. 4105. Map 75.
Sherborne, urb. dist. and par., Dorsetshire, 18 m. N. of Dorchester; pop. 6542. Map 87.
Sherborne St John, par. and vil., Hants, 2½ m. N.W. of Basingstoke; pop. 736. Map 76.
Sherburn, par. and vil., E.R. Yorkshire, 3½ m. S. of Brompton; pop. 581. Map 29.
Sherburn-in-Elmet, small market town and par., W.R. Yorks, 6¾ m. N. of Knottingley; pop. 1731. Map 33.
Shere, par. and vil., Surrey, 5 m. S.E. of Guildford; pop. 2596. Map 78.
Sheriff Hutton, vil., N.R. Yorkshire, 2½ m. N.W. of Flaxton sta. Map 28.
Sheringham, urb. dist. and par., Norfolk, 4 m. W.N.W. of Cromer; pop. 4141. Map 53.
Sherston, par. and vil., Wiltshire, 5½ m. S.W. of Malmesbury; pop. 1070. Map 68.
Shifnal, market town and par., Salop, 17 m. E.S.E. of Shrewsbury; pop. 3303. Map 47.
Shilbottle, par. and vil., Northumberland, 3 m. S. of Alnwick; pop. 799. Map 17.
Shildon and East Thickley, urb. dist., Durham, 3 m. S.E. of Bishop Auckland; pop. 12,690. Map 23.
Shillelagh, vil. and ry. sta., co. Wicklow, 5 m. S.W. of Tinahely. Map 95.
Shimpling, par. and vil., W. Suffolk, 4 m. N.W. of Lavenham; pop. 381. Map 62.
Shipdham, par. and vil., Norfolk, 4½ m. S.W. of E. Dereham; pop. 1272. Map 52.
Shipley, urb. dist. and par., W.R. Yorkshire, 3 m. N.W. of Bradford; pop. 30,243. Map 32.
Shipston-on-Stour, mkt. tn. and par., Warwickshire, 6½ m. E.N.E. of Chipping Campden; pop. 1365. Map 58.
Shipton-under-Wychwood, par. and vil., Oxon, 6 m. S.S.W. of Chipping Norton; pop. 667. Map 69.
Shirebrook, par. and vil., Derbyshire, 2¼ m. N.E. of Pleasley; pop. 11,309. Map 41.
Shirehampton, eccl. par., on r. Avon, in N.W. of Bristol; pop. 4009. Map 74.
Shirley, eccl. par. and vil., Warwickshire, 6¾ m. S.E. of Birmingham; pop. 3073. Map 58.
Shobdon, par. and vil., Herefordshire, 6½ m. W.N.W. of Leominster; pop. 298. Map 56.
Shoeburyness, urb. dist. and garrison town, Essex, 3 m. S.E. of Southend; pop. 6717. Map 73.
Sholing, eccl. dist. and ry. sta., Hants, in bor. of Southampton; pop. 7527. Map 77.
Shoreham, par. and vil., Kent, 4½ m. N. of Sevenoaks; pop. 1509. Map 80.
Shoreham-by-Sea, urb. dist., par. and spt., W. Sussex, 6 m. W. of Brighton; pop. 8757. Map 79.
Shorncliffe Camp, with ry. sta., Kent, 2 m. W. of Folkestone. Map 83.
Short Heath, Staffordshire, within parl. limits of Wolverhampton; pop. 5048. Map 47.
Shotley Bridge, vil., with ry. sta., Durham, in Benfieldside urb. dist. Map 22.
Shottery, vil., Warwickshire, on W. side of Stratford-on-Avon. Map 58.
Shouldham, par. and vil., Norfolk, 6 m. N.E. of Downham Market; pop. 447. Map 52.
Shrewsbury, mun. bor. and co. town, Salop, 42 m. N.W. of Birmingham; pop. 32,370. Map 47.

Shrewton, par. and vil., Wiltshire, 6 m. N.W. of Amesbury; pop. 634. Map 76.
Shrivenham, par. and vil., Berkshire, 6 m. N.E. of Swindon; pop. 592. Map 69.
Sible Hedingham, par. and vil., Essex, 3½ m. N.W. of Halstead; pop. 1762. Map 62.
Sibsey, par. and vil., Lindsey, Lincolnshire, 4½ m. N.E. of Boston; pop. 1063. Map 43.
Sidcup, urb. dist., Kent, 12 m. S.E. of Charing Cross sta., London; pop. 12,360. Map 80.
Sidestrand, coast par. and vil., Norfolk, 3 m. E.S.E. of Cromer; pop. 103. Map 53.
Sidlesham, par. and vil., W. Sussex, 4 m. S. of Chichester; pop. 801. Map 79.
Sidmouth, urb. dist. and par., Devonshire, 16 m. S.E. of Exeter; pop. 6126. Map 86.
Silchester, par. and vil., Hants, 7 m. N. of Basingstoke; pop. 390. Map 78.
Silecroft, vil., Cumberland, 10 m. S.E. of Ravenglass. Map 25.
Silloth, seaport town, Cumberland, 22¼ m. W.S.W. of Carlisle. Map 20.
Silsden, urb. dist. and par., W.R. Yorkshire, 4 m. N.W. of Keighley; pop. 4881. Map 31.
Silverdale, par. and vil., Lancashire, 3½ m. N.W. of Carnforth; pop. 895. Map 25.
Silverstone, par. and vil., Northamptonshire, 4 m. S.S.W. of Towcester; pop. 862. Map 59.
Singleton, Great, par., N. Lancashire, 5 m. E.N.E. of Blackpool; pop. 453. Map 30.
Sittingbourne, urb. dist., par. and seaport, Kent, 16 m. N.W. of Canterbury; pop. 20,175. Map 82.
Sizewell, coast ham., E. Suffolk, 6 m. E. of Saxmundham. Map 63.
Skateraw, vil., Kincardineshire, 6 m. N.E. of Stonehaven. Map 3.
Skegly, par. and vil., Nottinghamshire, 3 m. W. of Mansfield; pop. 6230. Map 41.
Skegness, urb. dist. and par., Lindsey, Lincolnshire, 5 m. N.E. of Wainfleet; pop. 9121. Map 43.
Skelmanthorpe, urb. dist. and par., W.R. Yorkshire, 6 m. S.E. of Huddersfield; pop. 3711. Map 32.
Skelmersdale, urb. dist. and par., S.W. Lancashire, 3½ m. E.S.E. of Ormskirk; pop. 6177. Map 30.
Skelmorlie, coast vil., Ayrshire, 4½ m. N.W. of Largs; par. pop. 1878. Map 12.
Skelton, par. and vil., N.R. Yorkshire, 4 m. N.W. of York; pop. 405. Map 33.
Skelton, par. and vil., Cumberland, 6½ m. N.W. of Penrith; pop. 591. Map 21.
Skelton, urb. dist. and par., N.R. Yorkshire, 3 m. N.E. of Guisborough; pop. 13,654. Map 28.
Skene, par. and ham., in co. and 8¾ m. W. of Aberdeen; pop. 1405. Map 3.
Skerries, seaport and watering place, in co. and 18 m. N. of Dublin; pop. 1770. Map 93.
Skerries, The, group of rocky isles off N.W. coast of Anglesey; lighthouse 75 ft. high. Map 36.
Skewen, dist. and ry. sta., Glamorganshire, on N. side of Neath. Map 66.
Skibbereen, urb. dist. and seaport, in co. and 54 m. S.W. of Cork; pop. 2620. Map 94.
Skidby, par. and vil., E.R. Yorkshire, 4 m. S.W. of Beverley; pop. 291. Map 35.
Skinburness, vil., Cumberland, 2 m. N.E. of Silloth. Map 20.
Skipsea, coast par. and vil., E.R. Yorkshire; pop. 286. Ruins of Saxon castle in vicinity. Map 35.
Skipton, urb. dist., market town and par., W.R. Yorks, 9 m. N.W. of Keighley; pop. 12,434. Map 32.
Skipwith, par. and vil., E.R. Yorkshire, 12¾ m. S.E. of York; pop. 226. Map 34.
Skirling, par. and vil., Peeblesshire, 2½ m. N.E. of Biggar; pop. 222. Map 15.
Skirwith, par. and vil., Cumberland, 6½ m. E.N.E. of Penrith; pop. 238. Map 21.
Skye, Isle of, Inverness-shire; pop. 11,031. Map 2.
Slaithwaite, urb. dist., par. and mkt. tn., W.R. Yorks. 4 m. S.W. of Huddersfield; pop. 5181. Map 31.
Slaley, par. and vil., Northumberland, 4½ m. S.E. of Hexham; pop. 585. Map 22.
Slamannan, par. and vil., Stirlingshire, 5½ m. S.W. o Falkirk; pop. 1610. Map 9.
Slane, par. and vil., Meath, 8 m. W. of Drogheda pop. 992. Map 93.
Sleaford, urb. dist., Kesteven, in co. and 21½ m. S.E. of Lincoln; pop. 7024. Map 42.
Sledmere, par. and vil., E.R. Yorkshire, 8 m. N.W. of Driffield; pop. 491. Map 29.
Sleights, vil., N.R. Yorkshire, 3½ m. S.W. of Whitby. Map 29.
Sligachan, place, Isle of Skye, 9 m. S. of Portree. Map 2.
Sligo, mun. bor., spt. and co. tn. of Sligo, 134 m. N.W. of Dublin by rail; pop. 11,439. Map 92.
Slinfold, par. and vil., W. Sussex, 4 m. W. of Horsham; pop. 979. Map 79.
Slingsby, par. and vil., N.R. Yorkshire, 6 m. W.N.W. of Malton; pop. 440. Map 28.
Slough, urb. dist. and market town, Buckinghamshire, 2 m. N.E. of Windsor; pop. 33,530. Map 71.
Slyne, par. and vil., N. Lancashire, 3 m. N. of Lancaster; pop. 695. Map 25.
Sma' Glen, Perthshire, 8¾ m. N. of Crieff. Map 6.
Smailholm, par. and vil., Roxburghshire, 6 m. N.W. of Kelso; pop. 261. Map 16.
Smallburgh, par. and vil., Norfolk, 12 m. N.E. of Norwich; pop. 346. Map 53.
Smallthorne, urb. dist., now in Stoke-on-Trent, 1½ m. E.N.E. of Burslem; pop. 14,013. Map 39.
Smarden, par. and vil., Kent, 8 m. W. of Ashford; pop. 992. Map 82.
Smeeth Road, ry. sta., Norfolk, 3¾ m. E. of Wisbech. Map 51.
Smethwick, co. and parl. bor., Staffordshire, 3½ m. N.W. of Birmingham; pop. 84,354. Map 48.
Smithfield, vil., N.W. Cumberland, 4¼ m. S.E. of Longtown. Map 21.
Snainton, par. and vil., N.R. Yorkshire, 9 m. S.W. of Scarborough; pop. 685. Map 29.
Snaith, market town and par., W.R. Yorkshire, 7 m. W. of Goole; pop. 1560. Map 34.
Snettisham, par. and vil., Norfolk, 4 m. S. of Hunstanton; pop. 1443. Map 52.
Snitterfield, par. and vil., Warwickshire, 3½ m. N.N.E. of Stratford-on-Avon; pop. 691. Map 58.
Snodland, par. and vil., Kent, 6 m. S.S.W. of Rochester by rail; pop. 4481. Map 80.
Snowdon, Mt., in co. and 9 m. S.E. of Carnarvon; alt. 3560 ft. Map 36.
Soham, market town and par., Cambridgeshire, 5 m. S.E. of Ely; pop. 4737. Map 61.
Solihull, market town and par., Warwickshire, 6½ m. S.E. of Birmingham; pop. 11,552. Map 58.
Solva, seaport vil., Pembrokeshire, 3 m. E. of St David's. Map 64.
Somerby, par. and vil., Leicestershire, 5 m. W. of Oakham; pop. 480. Map 50.
Somerby, Old, par. and vil., Kesteven, Lincolnshire, 3 m. S.E. of Grantham; pop. 185. Map 50.
Somerford, Great, par. and vil., Wiltshire, 4 m. S.E. of Malmesbury; pop. 421. Map 68.
Somerton, market town and par., Somersetshire, 4½ m. E.N.E. of Langport; pop. 1776. Map 86.
Sopley, par. and vil., Hants, 2½ m. N. of Christchurch; pop. 793. Map 77.
Soulby, par. and vil., Westmorland, 2 m. N.W. of Kirkby Stephen; pop. 200. Map 26.
Southall, urb. dist. and market town, Middlesex, 3½ m. N.W. of Brentford; pop. 38,932. Map 71.
Southam, market town and par., in co. and 9 m. S.E. of Warwick; pop. 1744. Map 59.

Southampton, co. bor., par., spt. and co. town of Hampshire, 79 m. S.W. of London by rail; co. bor. pop. 176,025. Map 77.

Southborough, urb. dist. and par., Kent, 1½ m. N. of Tunbridge Wells; pop. 7352. Map 82.

South Brent, par. and vil., S. Devonshire, 7 m. W. of Totnes; pop. 1601. Map 89.

South Crosland, urb. dist., W.R. Yorkshire, 3 m. S.W. of Huddersfield; pop. 2993. Map 32.

South Darley, urb. dist., Derbyshire, adjoining North Darley; pop. 731. Map 40.

Southend-on-Sea, co. bor. and spt., Essex, 3 m. W. of Shoeburyness; pop. 120,093. Map 72.

Southerness, vil., Kirkcudbrightshire, 10 m. S.E. of Dalbeattie. Map 20.

Southfleet, par. and vil., Kent, 3 m. S.W. of Gravesend; pop. 1311. Map 80.

Southgate, urb. dist., Middlesex, 2½ m. S.W. of Enfield station; pop. 55,570. Map 71.

South Harting, locality, W. Sussex, in Midhurst rural district. Map 79.

South Milford, par. and vil., W.R. Yorkshire, 12 m. E. of Leeds; pop. 1122. Map 33.

Southminster, par. and vil., Essex, 8 m. S.E. of Maldon; pop. 1592. Map 73.

South Molton, mun. bor. and par., Devonshire, 10½ m. S.E. of Barnstaple; pop. 2818. Map 85.

South Newton, par. and vil., Wiltshire, 2 m. N. of Wilton; pop. 407. Map 76.

South Ockendon, par. and vil., Essex, 5½ m. S.E. of Romford; pop. 1432. Map 72.

South Otterington, par. and vil., N.R. Yorkshire, 4 m. S. of Northallerton; pop. 292. Map 28.

Southowram, urb. dist., W.R. Yorkshire, adjoining Halifax; pop. 2570. Map 32.

Southport, wtg. pl., parl. and co. bor. and par., S.W. Lancs, 18½ m. N. of Liverpool; pop. 78,927. Map 30.

Southrepps, par. and vil., Norfolk, 4½ m. S.E. of Cromer; pop. 755. Map 53.

Southsea, residential dist. and watering place, Hants, on S. side of Portsmouth. Map 79.

South Shields, parl. and co. bor., Durham, 8 m. E. of Newcastle-on-Tyne; pop. 113,452. Map 23.

Southwell, market town, see of a bishop and par., Notts, 6 m. W. of Newark; pop. 3085. Map 41.

Southwick, par., Wiltshire, 2 m. S.W. of Trowbridge; pop. 754. Map 75.

Southwick, urb. dist., Sussex, 4 m. W. of Brighton; pop. 6138. Map 81.

South Wingfield, par. and vil., Derbyshire, 2 m. W. of Alfreton; pop. 1605. Map 41.

Southwold, mun. bor. and seaport, E. Suffolk, 11 m. S. of Lowestoft; pop. 2753. Map 63.

Sowerby, urb. dist. and par., W.R. Yorkshire, 4 m. S.W. of Halifax; pop. 14,679. Map 32.

Sowerby Bridge, dist., 2½ m. S.W. of Halifax. Map 32.

Soyland, urb. dist., W.R. Yorkshire, 4½ m. S.W. of Halifax; pop. 3057. Map 32.

Spalding, urb. dist., Holland, Lincolnshire, 14 m. S.W. of Boston; pop. 12,592. Map 51.

Spaldington, par. and vil., E.R. Yorkshire, 4 m. N. of Howden; pop. 547. Map 34.

Sparsholt, par. and vil., Hants, 2½ m. N.W. of Winchester; pop. 376. Map 76.

Sparsholt, par. and vil., Berkshire, 3½ m. W. of Wantage; pop. 286. Map 69.

Spean Bridge, ham. and ry. sta., Inverness-shire, 9½ m. N.E. of Fort William. Map 2.

Speen, par. and vil., Berkshire, 1½ m. N.W. of Newbury; pop. 1090. Map 70.

Spenborough, urb. dist., W.R. Yorkshire, 6 m. S.E. of Bradford; pop. 30,962. Map 32.

Spennymoor, urb. dist. and par., Durham, 4 m. N.E. of Bishop Auckland; pop. 16,361. Map 23.

Spettisbury, par. and vil., Dorsetshire, 3 m. S.E. of Blandford; pop. 426. Map 87.

Spilsby, town and par., Lindsey, Lincolnshire, 7 m. S.W. of Alford; pop. 1400. Map 43.

Spittal, coast town and watering place, Northumberland, near Berwick-on-Tweed; pop. 2268. Map 11.

Spittal, place, Roxburghshire, on Rule Water, 1½ m. E. of Denholm. Map 16.

Spofforth, par. and vil., W.R. Yorkshire, 3½ m. N.W. of Wetherby; pop. 799. Map 33.

Spondon, par. and vil., Derbyshire, 3 m. E. of Derby; pop. 3132. Map 49.

Spreyton, par. and vil., Devonshire, 7 m. E. of Okehampton; pop. 338. Map 85.

Springfield, vil. and ry. sta., Fifeshire, 3 m. S.W. of Cupar. Map 7.

Springhead, urb. dist., W.R. Yorkshire, on E. side of Oldham; pop. 4833. Map 40.

Sproatley, par. and vil., E.R. Yorkshire, 4 m. N. of Hedon; pop. 274. Map 35.

Sprouston, par. and vil., Roxburghshire, 2 m. N.E. of Kelso; pop. 776. Map 16.

Stackpole, coast par. and ham., in co. and 3 m. S. of Pembroke; pop. 225. Map 64.

Stacksteads, vil., S.E. Lancashire, 1½ m. S.W. of Bacup. Map 31.

Staffa, isl., Inner Hebrides, Argyllshire. Map 12.

Stafford, mun. bor., par. and co. tn., Staffordshire, 27 m. N.N.W. of Birmingham; pop. 29,485. Map 47.

Staindrop, par. and vil., Durham, 8 m. S.W. of Bishop Auckland; pop. 1347. Map 27.

Staines, urb. dist. and market town, S.W. Middlesex, 6 m. S.E. of Windsor; pop. 21,209. Map 71.

Stainforth, par. and vil., W.R. Yorkshire, 3 m. N. of Settle; pop. 198. Map 26.

Stainforth and Hatfield, par. and vil., W.R. Yorks, on r. Don, 9 m. N.E. of Doncaster; pop. 2217. Map 33.

Stainland, urb. dist. and par., W.R. Yorkshire, 3½ m. S.W. of Halifax; pop. 4246. Map 31.

Stainton, par., Durham, 2½ m. N.E. of Barnard Castle; pop. 302. Map 27.

Staintondale, coast par. and ry. sta., N.R. Yorkshire, 7 m. N.W. of Scarborough; pop. 355. Map 29.

Staithes, vil. and ry. sta., N.R. Yorkshire, 9 m. N.W. of Whitby. Map 29.

Stalbridge, town and par., Dorsetshire, 7 m. E. of Sherborne; pop. 1222. Map 87.

Stalham, par. and vil., Norfolk, 6 m. S.E. of N. Walsham; pop. 937. Map 53.

Stallingborough, par. and vil., Lincolnshire, 5 m. N.W. of Grimsby; pop. 508. Map 35.

Stalybridge, mun. bor. and par., Cheshire, on r. Tame, 7½ m. E. of Manchester; pop. 2483. Map 40.

Stambourne, par. and vil., Essex, 8 m. N.W. of Halstead; pop. 299. Map 62.

Stamford, mun. bor., Kesteven, Lincolnshire, 16½ m. N.W. of Peterborough; pop. 9946. Map 50.

Standish with Langtree, urb. dist., Lancashire, 3½ m. N.W. of Wigan; pop. 7262. Map 30.

Standlake, par. and vil., Oxon, 5 m. S.E. of Witney; pop. 510. Map 69.

Standon, par. and vil., Hertfordshire, 8 m. N.E. of Hertford; pop. 2485. Map 71.

Stanford Bridge, ham., Worcestershire, 7 m. S.W. of Stourport. Map 57.

Stanford-in-the-Vale, par. and vil., Berkshire, 4 m. S.E. of Faringdon; pop. 764. Map 69.

Stanford-le-Hope, par. and vil., Essex, 5 m. S.W. of Pitsea; pop. 3379. Map 72.

Stanhope, urb. dist. and par., Durham, 6 m. N.W. of Wolsingham; pop. 1746. Map 22.

Stanley, urb. dist., par. and vil., Durham, 4 m. N.E. of Lanchester; pop. 24,458. Map 23.

Stanley, urb. dist., W.R. Yorkshire, 2 m. N.E. of Wakefield; pop. 14,570. Map 33.

Stanley, vil. and *q.s.* par., Perthshire, 7 m. N. of Perth ; pop. 1240.　Map 6.

Stanmore, Great, par. and vil., N. Middlesex, 2 m. N.E. of Harrow ; pop. 1849.　Map 71.

Stanningfield, par. and vil., W. Suffolk, 5½ m. S. of Bury St Edmunds ; pop. 211.　Map 62.

Stannington, par. and vil., Northumberland, 4 m. S. of Morpeth ; pop. 1664.　Map 23.

Stanstead Abbots, par. and vil., Hertfordshire, 4 m. E. of Hertford ; pop. 1362.　Map 71.

Stanton Harcourt, par. and vil., Oxon, 4½ m. S.E. of Witney ; pop. 451.　Map 61.

Stansted, par. and vil., Kent, 7 m. N.E. of Sevenoaks ; pop. 426.　Map 82.

Stanwell, par. and vil., Middlesex, 2 m. N.E. of Staines ; pop. 2306.　Map 71.

Stanwix, par., Cumberland, on N. side of Carlisle ; pop. 681.　Map 21.

Stapleford, par. and vil., in co. and 4 m. S.E. of Cambridge ; pop. 514.　Map 61.

Stapleford, par., Leicestershire, 4 m. E. of Melton Mowbray ; pop. 133.　Map 50.

Stapleford-Abbots, par., Essex, 5 m. N. of Romford ; pop. 391.　Map 72.

Staplehurst, par. and vil., Kent, 8 m. S.S.E. of Maidstone ; pop. 1897.　Map 82.

Star, vil., Fifeshire, 1¾ m. N.E. of Markinch.　Map 7.

Staughton, Great, par. and vil., Huntingdonshire, 2½ m. S.E. of Kimbolton ; pop. 685.　Map 60.

Staunton, par. and vil., in co. and 7½ m. N.N.W. of Gloucester.　Map 57.

Staunton-on-Arrow, par., Herefordshire, 5 m. N.E. of Kington ; pop. 237.　Map 56.

Staunton-on-Wye, par. and vil., in co. and 9 m. W.N.W. of Hereford ; pop. 446.　Map 56.

Staveley, par., Derbyshire, 4 m. N.E. of Chesterfield ; pop. 12,646.　Map 41.

Staveley, par. and ham., N. Lancashire, 5 m. N. of Cartmel ; pop. 384.　Map 25.

Steeple Ashton, par. and vil., Wiltshire, 3 m. E. of Trowbridge ; pop. 667.　Map 75.

Stenhousemuir, town, Stirlingshire, 3 m. N.W. of Falkirk ; pop. 4601.　Map 9.

Stenton, par. and vil., East Lothian, 4 m. S.E. of East Linton ; pop. of vil. 113.　Map 11.

Steps, residential dist., Lanarkshire, 4½ m. N.E. of Glasgow ; pop. 2823.　Map 8.

Sterridge, vil., N. Devon, 3 m. S.E. of Ilfracombe. Map 84.

Stetchworth, par. and vil., Cambridgeshire, 3 m. S. of Newmarket ; pop. 659.　Map 61.

Stevenage, urb. dist. and par., Hertfordshire, 4 m. S.E. of Hitchin ; pop. 5476.　Map 71.

Stevenston, town and par., Ayrshire, 28 m. S.W. of Glasgow ; pop. 8224.　Map 12.

Stewarton, town, police bur. and par., Ayrshire, 18 m. S.W. of Glasgow ; pop. 2749.　Map 8.

Stewartstown, market town, with ry. sta., Tyrone, 8½ m. N.E. of Dungannon ; pop. 623.　Map 93.

Stewkley, par. and vil., Buckinghamshire, 4 m. N.W. of Leighton Buzzard ; pop. 1018.　Map 60.

Steyning, par. and market town, W. Sussex, 5 m. N.W. of Shoreham ; pop. 1875.　Map 79.

Steynton, par. and ham., Pembrokeshire, 1½ m. N.N.E. of Milford ; pop. 1408.　Map 64.

Stichill, par., Roxburghshire and Berwickshire, 3½ m. N. of Kelso ; pop. 523.　Map 16.

Stickford, par. and vil., Lindsey, Lincolnshire, 5 m. S.W. of Spilsby ; pop. 404.　Map 43.

Sticklepath, vil., Devonshire, 3½ m. E.S.E. of Okehampton.　Map 84.

Stiffkey, par. and vil., Norfolk, 3½ m. E. of Wells ; pop. 521.　Map 52.

Stillingfleet, par. and vil., E.R. Yorkshire, 7 m. S. of York ; pop. 317.　Map 34.

Stillington, par. and vil., N.R. Yorkshire, 4 m. S.E. of Easingwold ; pop. 510.　Map 28.

Stilton, par. and vil., Huntingdonshire, 2 m. N.W. of Holme ; pop. 455.　Map 50.

Stirling, par., bur. and co. town of Stirlingshire, 20½ m. N.E. of Glasgow ; pop. 22,593.　Map 9.

Stithians, par. and vil., Cornwall, 4 m. S.E. of Redruth ; pop. 1522.　Map 90.

Stockbridge, par. and vil., Hants, 6½ m. S. of Andover ; pop. 862.　Map 76.

Stockbury, par. and vil., Kent, 4 m. S.W. of Sittingbourne ; pop. 481.　Map 82.

Stockcross, eccl. dist. and vil., Berkshire, 2 m. N.W. of Newbury ; pop. 514.　Map 76.

Stockingford, eccl. dist. and vil., Warwickshire, 1½ m. W. of Nuneaton ; pop. 10,598.　Map 48.

Stockland, par. and vil., Devonshire, 5 m. N.W. of Axminster ; pop. 731.　Map 86.

Stockport, co. bor. and par., Cheshire and Lancashire, 5½ m. S.E. of Manchester ; pop. 125,505.　Map 39.

Stocksbridge, urb. dist., W.R. Yorkshire, 7½ m. N.W. of Sheffield ; pop. 9253.　Map 40.

Stockton Heath, par. and vil., Cheshire, 1½ m. S. of Warrington sta.　Map 39.

Stockton-on-Tees, parl. and mun. bor., Durham, 4 m. S.W. of Middlesbrough ; pop. 67,724.　Map 28.

Stockton-on-Teme, par. and vil., Worcestershire, 6½ m. S.W. of Bewdley ; pop. 115.　Map 57.

Stockton-on-the-Forest, par. and vil., N.R. Yorkshire, 4½ m. N.E. of York ; pop. 393.　Map 34.

Stockwith, East, par. and vil., Lindsey, Lincolnshire, 3½ m. N.E. of Gainsborough ; pop. 314.　Map 42.

Stogumber, par. and vil., Somersetshire, 5 m. S.E. of Watchet ; pop. 722.　Map 85.

Stogursey, par. and vil., Somersetshire, 7½ m. N.W. of Bridgwater ; pop. 886.　Map 74.

Stoke, par. and vil., Kent, 7 m. N.E. of Rochester ; pop. 686.　Map 72.

Stoke-by-Clare, par. and vil., W. Suffolk, 2 m. S.W. of Clare ; pop. 427.　Map 62.

Stoke Canon, par. and vil., Devonshire, 3½ m. N.E. of Exeter ; pop. 360.　Map 85.

Stoke Climsland, par., Cornwall, 7½ m. W. of Tavistock ; pop. 1578.　Map 88.

Stoke Ferry, par. and vil., Norfolk, 6 m. S.E. of Downham Market ; pop. 589.　Map 52.

Stoke Fleming, coast par. and vil., Devonshire, 2½ m. S.W. of Dartmouth ; pop. 602.　Map 89.

Stoke-in-Teignhead, coast par. and vil., Devonshire, 2 m. S.W. of Teignmouth ; pop. 469.　Map 89.

Stoke-on-Trent, city, co. bor. and par., Staffordshire, 16 m. N. of Stafford ; pop. 276,619.　Map 39.

Stoke Poges, vil., Buckinghamshire, 2 m. N. of Slough. Map 71.

Stokesley, market town and par., N.R. Yorkshire, 8½ m. S.E. of Stockton ; pop. 1641.　Map 28.

Stone, urb. dist. and par., in co. and 7 m. N. of Stafford ; pop. 5952.　Map 47.

Stonegrave, par. and vil., N.R. Yorkshire, 5 m. S.E. of Helmsley ; pop. 98.　Map 28.

Stonehaven, bur. spt. and co. town of Kincardineshire, 16 m. S.W. of Aberdeen ; pop. 4185. Map 3.

Stonehenge, group of large standing stones, Salisbury Plain, Wiltshire, 2 m. W. of Amesbury.　Map 76.

Stonehouse, town and par., Lanarkshire, 7 m. S.E. of Hamilton ; pop. 3555.　Map 9.

Stonehouse, par. and vil., Gloucestershire, 3 m. W. of Stroud ; pop. 2393.　Map 68.

Stonehouse, par., Devonshire, in co. bor. of Plymouth ; pop. 13,857.　Map 88.

Stoney Middleton, par. and vil., Oxon, 3 m. W.N.W. of Bicester ; pop. 256.　Map 70.

Stony Stratford, market town, in co. and 8 m. N.E. of Buckingham ; pop. 1992.　Map 60.

Storeton, par. and vil., Cheshire, 3 m. S.W. of Birkenhead ; pop. 279.　Map 38.

Stornoway, bur., seaport and par., Lewis, Isl., Outer Hebrides ; town pop. 3771. Map 2.

Storrington, par. and vil., W. Sussex, 6½ m. N.E. of Arundel ; pop. 1388. Map 79.

Stoughton, par., W. Sussex, 6 m. N.W. of Chichester ; pop. 615. Map 79.

Stoughton, eccl. dist. and ham., Surrey, 1½ m. N.N.W. of Guildford. Map 78.

Stourbridge, mun. bor., Worcestershire, 11½ m. W. of Birmingham ; pop. 19,903. Map 57.

Stourport, urb. dist., Worcestershire, 4 m. W. of Kidderminster ; pop. 5949. Map 57.

Stourton, par. and vil., Wiltshire, 3 m. N.W. of Mere ; pop. 418. Map 75.

Stourton Caundle, par. and vil., Dorsetshire, 4½ m. N.W. of Sturminster Newton ; pop. 254. Map 87.

Stow, par. and vil., Midlothian, 6¼ m. N. of Galashiels ; pop. 493. Map 10.

Stow Bardolf, par. and vil. (**Stowbridge**), Norfolk, 2½ m. N.N.E. of Downham Market ; pop. 1275. Map 52.

Stowmarket, urb. dist. and par., E. Suffolk, 12½ m. N.W. of Ipswich ; pop. 4296. Map 62.

Stow-on-the-Wold, urb. dist. and par., Glos., 4 m. S.S.W. of Moreton-in-the-Marsh ; pop. 1266. Map 58.

Strabane, urb. dist., co. Tyrone, 14 m. S.W. of Londonderry ; pop. 5107. Map 93.

Strachur, par. and vil., Argyllshire, on E. side of Loch Fyne ; pop. 548. Map 12.

Stradbally, market town and par., Leix co., 6 m. E.S.E. of Maryborough ; pop. 1092. Map 95.

Stradbally, coast par. and vil., Waterford, 8 m. N.E. of Dungarvan ; pop. 1251. Map 95.

Stradbroke, par. and town, E. Suffolk, 5½ m. E. of Eye ; pop. 927. Map 63.

Stradishall, par. and vil., W. Suffolk, 5 m. N. of Clare ; pop. 263. Map 62.

Straiton, par. and vil., Ayeshire, 7 m. S.E. of Maybole ; pop. 1166. Map 12.

Straits, vil., Lancashire, 4½ m. S. of Preston. Map 30.

Stranraer, mun. bur., spt. and par., Wigtownshire, at head of Loch Ryan ; pop. 6490. Map 18.

Strata Florida, par. and ham., Cardiganshire, 5 m. N.N.E. of Tregaron ; pop. 440. Map 55.

Stratford, populous dist. in mun. bor. of West Ham, Essex, 3½ m. N.E. of London. Map 71.

Stratford-on-Avon, mun. bor., in co. and 8 m. S.W. of Warwick ; pop. 11,616. Map 58.

Stratford Tony, par., Wiltshire, 4 m. S.W. of Salisbury ; pop. 86. Map 76.

Strathallan, valley of r. Allan, Perthshire and Stirlingshire. Map 6.

Strathaven, town, Lanarkshire, 7 m. S. of Hamilton ; pop. 4207. Map 14.

Strathblane, par. and vil., Stirlingshire, 11 m. N. of Glasgow ; pop. 1275. Map 8.

Strathearn, valley of r. Earn, Perthshire, 32 m. in length. Map 6.

Strathkinnes, q.s. par. and vil., Fifeshire, 3 m. W. of St Andrews ; pop. 851. Map 7.

Strathmiglo, par. and vil., Fifeshire, 6½ m. W. of Ladybank Junction ; pop. 1609. Map 6.

Strathpeffer, vil., Ross and Cromarty, 5 m. W. of Dingwall ; pop. 875. Map 3.

Strathyre, vil. and ry. sta., Perthshire, 8 m. N.W. of Callander. Map 5.

Stratton and Bude, urb. dist., Cornwall, 16 m. N.W. of Launceston ; pop. 3836. Map 84.

Stratton-on-the-Fosse, par. and vil., Somersetshire, 7½ m. W.N.W. of Frome ; pop. 412. Map 75.

Streatley, par. and vil., Berkshire, 6 m. S. of Wallingford ; pop. 793. Map 70.

Street, urb. dist. and par., Somersetshire, 2 m. S.W. of Glastonbury ; pop. 4453. Map 74.

Street Cobham, ham., N. Surrey, ½ m. N.W. of Cobham. Map 78.

Strensall, par. and vil., N.R. Yorkshire, 6 m. N.N.E. of York ; pop. 738. Map 34.

Stretford, urb. dist., Lancashire, 4 m. S.W. of Manchester ; pop. 56,795. Map 39.

Stretton, par. and vil., Cheshire, 3½ m. S. of Warrington ; pop. 352. Map 39.

Stretton-on-Dunsmore, par. and vil., Warwickshire, 7 m. S.E. of Coventry ; pop. 612. Map 59.

Strichen, par. and vil., Aberdeenshire, 10 m. S.W. of Fraserburgh ; pop. 2243. Map 3.

Strokestown, market town, in co. and 12 m. N.E. of Roscommon ; pop. 801. Map 92.

Strome Ferry, vil., Ross and Cromarty, on Loch Carron, 53 m. S.W. of Dingwall. Map 2.

Strone, watering place, Argyllshire, 6 m. N.W. of Greenock by water. Map 12.

Strood Intra, par. and town, Kent, on left bank of r. Medway ; pop. 10,283. Map 82.

Stroud, urb. dist. and par., in co. and 12 m. S. of Gloucester : pop. 8360. Map 68.

Studland, par. and vil., Isle of Purbeck, Dorsetshire, 5 m. E. of Corfe Castle ; pop. 691. Map 87.

Sturminster Newton, market town and par., Dorsetshire, 9 m. N.W. of Blandford ; pop. 1619. Map 87.

Sturry, par. and vil., Kent, 2½ m. N.E. of Canterbury ; pop. 1386. Map 83.

Sturton, par. and vil., Lindsey, Lincolnshire, 6 m. S.E. of Gainsborough ; pop. 539. Map 42.

Sudbourne, par. and vil., E. Suffolk, 4 m. S.W. of Aldeburgh ; pop. 462. Map 63.

Sudbury, vil., Middlesex, 3 m. S.E. of Harrow. Map 71.

Sudbury, mun. bor. and par., W. Suffolk, 21 m. W. of Ipswich ; pop. 7007. Map 62.

Sulby, vil., Isle of Man, 4 m. W. of Ramsey, on r. Sulby. Map 24.

Sully, coast par. and ry. sta., Glamorganshire, 6 m. S.W. of Cardiff ; pop. 576. Map 67.

Sunbury-on-Thames, urb. dist. and par., Middlesex, 4½ m. W. of Kingston ; pop. 13,329. Map 78.

Sunderland, co. bor., spt. and par., Durham, 12 m. S.E. of Newcastle ; pop. 185,870. Map 23.

Sunderland, North, par. and vil., Northumberland, 7 m. S.E. of Belford ; pop. 1449. Map 17.

Sundridge, par. and vil., Kent, 3 m. W. of Sevenoaks ; pop. 1814. Map 80.

Sunningdale, par. and vil., Berkshire, 8 m. S.W. of Staines ; pop. 1657. Map 78.

Sunninghill, par. and vil., Berkshire, 5 m. S.W. of Windsor ; pop. 5839. Map 78.

Surbiton, urb. dist., Surrey, 12 m. S.W. of Waterloo sta., London ; pop. 29,396. Map 78.

Sutton, par. and vil., Kent, 3½ m. S.W. of Deal ; pop. 144. Map 83.

Sutton, par., in co. and 4 m. N.E. of Hereford ; pop. 351. Map 57.

Sutton and Cheam, urb. dist., Surrey, 4½ m. S.W. of Croydon ; pop. 46,488. Map 80.

Sutton at Hone, par. and vil., Kent, 7 m. S.W. of Gravesend ; pop. 5804. Map 80.

Sutton Benger, par. and vil., Wiltshire, 4 m. N.E. of Chippenham ; pop. 327. Map 75.

Sutton Bridge, urb. dist., Holland, Lincolnshire, 7 m. N. of Wisbech ; pop. 2837. Map 51.

Sutton Coldfield, mun. bor. and par., Warwickshire, 7 m. N.E. of Birmingham ; pop. 29,924. Map 48.

Sutton-in-Ashfield, urb. dist., mfg. mkt. tn. and par., Notts, 3 m. S.W. of Mansfield ; pop. 25,151. Map 41.

Sutton St Edmund, par. and vil., Holland, Lincolnshire, 6½ m. N.W. of Wisbech ; pop. 677. Map 51.

Sutton St James, par. and vil., Holland, Lincolnshire, 3½ m. S.W. of Long Sutton sta. ; pop. 676. Map 51.

Sutton Valence, par. and vil., Kent, 4 m. N.E. of Staplehurst; pop. 1174. Map 82.
Swadlincote, urb. dist. and par., Derbyshire, 5 m. S.E. of Burton-on-Trent; pop. 20,305. Map 48.
Swaffham, urb. dist. and par., Norfolk, 15 m. S.E. of King's Lynn; pop. 2783. Map 52.
Swaffham Bulbeck, par. and vil., in co. and 7 m. E.N.E. of Cambridge; pop. 639. Map 61.
Swaffham Prior, par. and vil., in co. and 8 m. N.E. of Cambridge; pop. 892. Map 61.
Swafield, par. and vil., Norfolk, 2 m. N. of North Walsham; pop. 148. Map 53.
Swainswick, par. and vil., Somersetshire, 2½ m. N.E. of Bath; pop. 502. Map 75.
Swallowcliffe, par. and vil., Wiltshire, 1½ m. S.E. of Tisbury; pop. 236. Map 87.
Swallowfield, par. and vil., S. Berkshire, 6 m. S. of Reading; pop. 1587. Map 78.
Swanage, urb. dist. and par., Dorsetshire, 9 m. S.E. of Wareham; pop. 6276. Map 87.
Swanbach, vil., Cheshire, 6 m. S. of Nantwich. Map 47.
Swanley Junction, vil. and ry. stn., Kent, 4 m. S.E. of Sidcup. Map 80.
Swanscombe, urban dist. and par., Kent, on r. Thames, W. of Northfleet; pop. 8541. Map 72.
Swansea, parl. and co. bor., spt. and par., Glamorganshire, 32½ m. S.W. of Merthyr Tydfil, and 192¾ m. W. of London by rail; pop. 164,825. Map 66.
Swanton Abbot, par. and vil., Norfolk, 3 m. S.W. of North Walsham; pop. 443. Map 53.
Swanton Morley, par. and vil., Norfolk, 3½ m. N.E. of East Dereham; pop. 546. Map 52.
Swanton Novers, par., Norfolk, 6 m. E.N.E. of Fakenham; pop. 270. Map 52.
Swanwick, eccl. dist. and vil., Derbyshire, in par. of and 2½ m. S.W. of Alfreton; pop. 2034. Map 41.
Swarkeston, par. and vil., Derbyshire, 5 m. S. of Derby; pop. 155. Map 49.
Swavesey, par. and vil., Cambridgeshire, 3½ m. S.E. of St Ives; pop. 830. Map 61.
Swefling, par. and vil., E. Suffolk, 2½ m. W. of Saxmundham; pop. 236. Map 63.
Swepstone, par. and vil., Leicestershire, 5 m. N.W. of Bosworth; pop. 630. Map 49.
Swinbrook, par. and vil., Oxon, 2 m. E. of Burford; pop. 167. Map 69.
Swindon, mun. bor. and par., Wiltshire, 10½ m. N. of Marlborough; pop. 62,407. Map 69.
Swinefleet, par. and vil., W.R. Yorkshire, 2½ m. S.E. of Goole; pop. 1126. Map 34.
Swineford, market town, co. Mayo, 22 m. S.W. of Ballymote; pop. 1302. Map 92.
Swineshead, par. and vil., Bedfordshire, 3 m. S.W. of Kimbolton; pop. 129. Map 60.
Swineshead, town and par., Lincolnshire, 6 m. S.W. of Boston; pop. 1895. Map 51.
Swinton, urb. dist. and par., W.R. Yorkshire, 10½ m. N.E. of Sheffield; pop. 13,820. Map 41.
Swinton, par. and vil., Berwickshire, 5½ m. S.E. of Duns; pop. 689. Map 11.
Swinton and Pendlebury, urb. dist., Lancashire, 4 m. N.W. of Manchester; pop. 32,761. Map 39.
Swords, town and par., in co. and 8 m. N. of Dublin; pop. of town 907. Map 93.
Swyre, par. and vil., Dorsetshire, 5 m. S.E. of Bridport; pop. 111. Map 86.
Syderstone, par. and vil., Norfolk, 4½ m. W.N.W. of Fakenham; pop. 429. Map 52.
Sydling St. Nicholas, par. and vil., Dorsetshire, 8 m. N.N.W. of Dorchester; pop. 346. Map 87.
Sykehouse, par. and vil., W.R. Yorkshire, 4 m. S.S.W. of Snaith; pop. 453. Map 33.
Synod, ham., Cardiganshire, 3½ m. S.S.E. of New Quay. Map 54.
Syston, par. and vil., Kesteven, Lincolnshire, 3 m. N. of Grantham; pop. 172. Map 50.
Syston, par. and vil., in co. and 5 m. N.N.E. of Leicester; pop. 3214. Map 49.
TADCASTER, market town, W.R. Yorkshire, 14 m. S.E. of Harrogate; pop. 4005. Map 34.
Taddington, par. and mining vil., Derbyshire, 5½ m. N.W. of Bakewell; pop. 384. Alt. 1050 ft.; claims to be highest vil. in England. Map 40.
Tadley, par. and vil., Hants, 6½ m. N.N.W. of Basingstoke; pop. 1269. Map 78.
Tain, bur., seaport and par., Ross and Cromarty, 25½ m. N.E. of Dingwall; pop. 1383. Map 3.
Talaton, par. and vil., Devonshire, 3 m. N.W. of Ottery St Mary; pop. 397. Map 85.
Talgarth, market town, Breconshire, 12 m. S.W. of Hay; pop. 1881. Map 56.
Taliesin (Tre Taliesin), ham., Cardiganshire, 1½ m. N. of Talybont. Map 45.
Talkin, vil., N. Cumberland, 1½ m. S. of Brampton (**T. Tarn**, alt. 419 ft.). Map 21.
Tallentire, par. and vil., Cumberland, 3 m. N.W. of Cockermouth; pop. 202. Map 20.
Talsarn, ham., Cardiganshire, 5½ m. N.N.W. of Lampeter. Map 54.
Talybont, ham., Cardiganshire, 6½ m. N.E. of Aberystwyth. Map 45.
Tamworth, mun. bor. and par., in co. and 22 m. S.E. of Stafford; pop. 7510. Map 48.
Tanfield, urb. dist. and par., Durham, 7 m. S.W. of Gateshead; pop. 9236. Map 23.
Tanworth, par. and vil., Warwickshire, 4 m. N.W. of Henley-in-Arden; pop. 2839. Map 58.
Taplow, par. and vil., Buckinghamshire, on r. Thames, 1½ m. E. of Maidenhead; pop. 1502. Map 70.
Tarbert, *q.s.* par. and seaport, Argyllshire, 13½ m. S. of Lochgilphead; pop. 1983. Map 12.
Tarbert, seaport town, co. Kerry, 10 m. N.E. of Listowel; pop. 354. Map 94.
Tarbet, ham. and ry. sta., on W. shore of Loch Lomond, Dumbartonshire. Map 12.
Tarleton, par. and vil., S.W. Lancashire, 8 m. S.W. of Preston; pop. 2115. Map 30.
Tarporley, urb. dist., Cheshire, 10 m. E.S.E. of Chester; pop. 2152. Map 39.
Tarrington, par. and vil., in co. and 7 m. E. of Hereford; pop. 410. Map 57.
Tattenhall, market town and par., in co. and 7½ m. S.E. of Chester; pop. 1055. Map 38.
Tattershall, par. and vil., Lindsey, Lincolnshire, 11 m. N.W. of Boston; pop. 424. Map 43.
Taunton, mun. bor. and co. town of Somersetshire, 44¾ m. S.W. of Bristol; pop. 25,177. Map 86.
Tavistock, urb. dist. and par., Devonshire, 14½ m. N. of Plymouth; pop. 4453. Map 88.
Tawton, North, par. and town, Devonshire, 6½ m. N.E. of Okehampton; pop. 1408. Map 85.
Tay, largest r. of Scotland, flows from Loch Tay and expands into the Firth of Tay. Map 5.
Taynton, par. and vil., Oxon, 1½ m. N.W. of Burford; pop. 215. Map 69.
Taynuilt, vil. and ry. sta., Argyllshire, 13 m. E. of Oban. Map 12.
Tayport, bur. and par., Fifeshire, on Firth of Tay, opposite Dundee; pop. 3164. Map 7.
Tebay, par. and vil., Westmorland, 7½ m. S.E. of Shap; pop. 1030. Map 26.
Tedburn St Mary, par. and vil., Devonshire, 4 m. S.W. of Crediton; pop. 449. Map 85.
Teddington, urb. dist., Middlesex, on r. Thames, 1½ m. N.W. of Kingston; pop. 23,362. Map 71.
Tees, River, flows 70 m. to North Sea between Hartlepool and Redcar. Map 23.
Teignmouth, urb. dist., par. and seaport, Devonshire, 15 m. S. of Exeter; pop. 10,019. Map 89.
Temple Ewell, par. and vil., Kent, 2½ m. N.W. of Dover; pop. 1034. Map 83.
Temple Grafton, par., Warwickshire, 5 m. W. of Stratford-on-Avon; pop. 314. Map 58.

Templemore, urb. dist. and par., Tipperary, 79 m. S.W. of Dublin; pop. 2230. Map 95.

Templenewsam, par. and seat, W.R. Yorkshire, 4 m. E. of Leeds; pop. 3370. Map 33.

Templepatrick, par. and vil., co. Antrim, 9 m. N.W. of Belfast; pop. 2673. Map 96.

Templeton, vil., Pembrokeshire, in par. and 2 m. S. of Narberth. Map 64.

Tempsford, par., vil. and seat, Bedfordshire, 5½ m. N.N.W. of Biggleswade; pop. 468. Map 60.

Tenbury, market town, Worcestershire, 5 m. E. of Woofferton Junction; pop. 1922. Map 57.

Tenby, mun. bor. and seaport, in co. and 9½ m. E. of Pembroke; pop. 4108. Map 64.

Tendring, par. and vil., Essex, 9 m. E. of Colchester; pop. 791. Map 73.

Tenterden, mun. bor. and par., Kent, 7 m. E.S.E. of Cranbrook; pop. 3473. Map 82.

Terenure, vil., in co. and 3 m. S. of Dublin; pop. 4697. Map 95.

Ternhill, ham. with ry. sta., Salop, 3 m. S.W. of Market Drayton. Map 47.

Terregles, par., E. Kirkcudbrightshire, 2 m. W. of Dumfries; pop. 428. Map 20.

Terrington St Clement and **St John**, 2 pars., Norfolk, 4 m. W. of King's Lynn; pop. 2689 and 818. Map 51.

Tetbury, urb. dist. and par., Gloucestershire, 8 m. S.E. of Stroud; pop. 2237. Map 68.

Tetford, par. and vil., Lincolnshire, 6 m. N.E. of Horncastle; pop. 367. Map 43.

Tettenhall, urb. dist., Staffordshire, 2 m. N.W. of Wolverhampton; pop. 5767. Map 47.

Teviotdale, the vale of the Teviot, Roxburghshire. Map 16.

Teviot, River, Roxburghshire, flows 37 m. N.E. to the Tweed at Kelso. Map 16.

Tewkesbury, mun. bor. and par., Gloucestershire, 8 m. N.W. of Cheltenham; pop. 4352. Map 57.

Teynham, par. and vil., Kent, 3¼ m. N.W. of Faversham; pop. 1734. Map 83.

Thame, urb. dist. and par., Oxon, 48 m. N.W. of London; pop. 3019. Map 70.

Thames Ditton, par. and vil., Surrey, on r. Thames, opposite Hampton Court Palace; pop. 8450. Map 78.

Thanet, Isle of, in N.E. extremity of Kent, contains wtg. pls., Margate, Ramsgate and Broadstairs. Map 83.

Thankerton, vil., Lanarkshire, on r. Clyde, 5 m. S. of Carstairs; pop. 290. Map 14.

Thatcham, par. and vil., Berkshire, 3 m. E. of Newbury; pop. 2459. Map 76.

Thaxted, small town and par., Essex, 7 m. N. of Dunmow; pop. 1596. Map 72.

Theale, par. and vil., Berkshire, 5 m. S.W. of Reading; pop. 1021. Map 78.

Theberton, par. and vil., E. Suffolk, 4 m. N.E. of Saxmundham; pop. 477. Map 63.

Theddingworth, par. and ry. sta., Leicestershire, 5½ m. S.W. of Market Harborough; pop. 193. Map 59.

Thetford, mun. bor., Norfolk, 14 m. N. of Bury St Edmunds; pop. 4097. Map 62.

Thirsk, par. and market town, N.R. Yorkshire, 22½ m. N.W. of York; pop. 2755. Map 28.

Thomastown, market town and par., in co. and 11 m. S.S.E. of Kilkenny; town pop. 959. Map 95.

Thormanby, par., N.R. Yorkshire, 4 m. N.W. of Easingwold; pop. 102. Map 28.

Thornaby-on-Tees, mun. bor. and par., N.R. Yorkshire, opposite Stockton; pop. 21,233. Map 28.

Thornbury, par. and market town, Gloucestershire, 12 m. N. of Bristol; pop. 2493. Map 68.

Thornby, par. and vil., in co. and 11 m. N.N.W. of Northampton; pop. 214. Map 59.

Thorndon, par. and vil., E. Suffolk, 3 m. S. of Eye; pop. 553. Map 63.

Thorne, market town and par., W.R. Yorkshire, on r. Don, 9 m. N.E. of Doncaster; pop. 6076. Map 34.

Thorner, par. and vil., W.R. Yorkshire, 6 m. N.E. of Leeds; pop. 1017. Map 33.

Thorney, par., Isle of Ely, Cambridgeshire, 7 m. N.E. of Peterborough; pop. 2165. Map 51.

Thornham, par. and vil., Kent, 3½ m. E. of Maidstone; pop. 716. Map 82.

Thornhill, vil. with ry. sta., in co. and 14 m. N.W. of Dumfries; pop. 1577. Map 14.

Thornhill, vil., Perthshire, 9¼ m. N.W. of Stirling. Map 8.

Thornton, vil. with ry. sta., Fifeshire, 3 m. S. of Markinch; pop. 1960. Map 10.

Thornton Cleveleys, urb. dist., Lancashire, 4 m. S.S.W. of Fleetwood; pop. 10,144. Map 30.

Thornton Dale, par. and vil., N.R. Yorkshire, 3 m. E. of Pickering; pop. 1186. Map 29.

Thornton Steward, par., N.R. Yorkshire, 5 m. S.E. of Leyburn; pop. 222. Map 27.

Thorpe, par. and vil., Derbyshire, on r. Dove, 3 m. N.W. of Ashbourne; pop. 196. Map 40.

Thorpe-le-Soken, small town and par., Essex, 4½ m. W. of Walton-on-the-Naze; pop. 1130. Map 73.

Thorpe Market, par. and vil., Norfolk, 4 m. N.W. of N. Walsham; pop. 231. Map 53.

Thorpeness, fishing and garden vil., E. Suffolk, 2 m. N.N.E. of Aldeburgh. Map 63.

Thorpe Thewles, vil. with ry. sta., Durham, 4 m. N.W. of Stockton. Map 23.

Thorrington, par., Essex, 7 m. S.E. of Colchester; pop. 397. Map 73.

Thorverton, par. and vil., Devonshire, 7 m. N. of Exeter; pop. 737. Map 85.

Thrapston, market town and par., Northamptonshire, 8½ m. S.W. of Oundle; pop. 1662. Map 60.

Threapwood, par. and vil., Cheshire, 3 m. S.W. of Malpas; pop. 294. Map 38.

Three Bridges, vil. and ry. sta., Sussex, 8½ m. S. of Redhill Junction. Map 81.

Three Cocks Junction, ry. sta., Breconshire, 5 m. S.W. of Hay. Map 56.

Threlkeld, par. and vil., Cumberland, 3¼ m. N.E. of Keswick; pop. 559. Map 21.

Threshfield, par. and vil., W.R. Yorkshire, 8 m. N. of Skipton; pop. 403. Map 31.

Thriplow, par. and vil., in co. and 7 m. S. of Cambridge; pop. 381. Map 61.

Thringstone, par., Leicestershire, 4 m. E. of Ashby-de-la-Zouch; pop. 1447. Map 49.

Thropton, par. and vil., Northumberland, 2 m. W. of Rothbury; pop. 233. Map 17.

Throston, par., Durham, within mun. bor. of Hartlepool; pop. 8569. Map 23.

Thurlby, par. and vil., Kesteven, Lincolnshire, 2 m. S. of Bourne; pop. 762. Map 50.

Thurles, urb. dist. and par., Tipperary, 29 m. N. of Clonmel; pop. 4796. Map 95.

Thurlston, urb. dist., W.R. Yorkshire, 1½ m. N.W. of Penistone; pop. 2640. Map 32.

Thurlton, par. and vil., Norfolk, 3½ m. E. of Loddon; pop. 320. Map 53.

Thurmaston, urb. dist. and par., in co. and 3½ m. N.E. of Leicester; pop. 3723. Map 49.

Thurnscoe, urb. dist., W.R. Yorkshire, 2 m. N.E. of Darfield; pop. 10,540. Map 41.

Thurso, spt., police bur. and par., Caithness-shire, 20¾ m. N.W. of Wick by rail; pop. 2946. Map 3.

Thurstonland and Farnley Tyas, urb. dist., W.R. Yorkshire, 4½ m. S.E. of Huddersfield; pop. 3980. Map 32.

Thurton, par. and vil., Norfolk, 2½ m. N.W. of Loddon; pop. 221. Map 53.

Thwing, par. and vil., E.R. Yorkshire, 6 m. N.W. of Hunmanby; pop. 307. Map 29.

Tibenham, par. and vil., Norfolk, 2 m. N.W. of Tivetshall; pop. 476. Map 63.
Tibshelf, par. and vil., Derbyshire, 4 m. N.E. of Alfreton; pop. 4053. Map 41.
Tichborne, par. and vil., Hants, 2 m. S.W. of Alresford; pop. 263. Map 76.
Tickhill and Wadworth, urb. dist. and par., W.R. Yorkshire, 4 m. W. of Bawtry; pop. 2297. Map 41.
Ticklerton, ham., S. Salop, 2¾ m. S.E. of Church Stretton. Map 46.
Tideswell, par. and small town, Derbyshire, 6½ m. E.N.E. of Buxton; pop. 1972. Map 40.
Tidworth, North, par. and vil., Wiltshire, 2 m. S.W. of Ludgershall; pop. 1253. Map 76.
Tilbury, urb. dist., Essex, on r. Thames, 22 m. E. of London; pop. 16,826. Map 80.
Tillicoultry, town, police bur. and par., Clackmannanshire, 3 m. S.W. of Dollar; pop. 2953. Map 9.
Tilshead, par. and vil., Wiltshire, on Salisbury Plain, 9 m. S. of Devizes; pop. 395. Map 75.
Timperley, par. and vil., Cheshire, 1½ m. N.E. of Altrincham; pop. 4263. Map 39.
Tinahely, vil, with ry. sta., Wicklow, 14 m. W. of Arklow; pop. 392. Map 95.
Tinsley, par., W.R. Yorkshire, in bor. and 3½ m. N.E. of Sheffield; pop. 7365. Map 41.
Tintagel Head, par., Cornwall, 5 m. N.W. of Camelford; pop. 1307. Map 91.
Tintern Abbey, ruin, on r. Wye, Monmouthshire, 4 m. N. of Chepstow. Map 68.
Tintinhull, par. and vil., Somersetshire, 4½ m. N.W. of Yeovil; pop. 488. Map 86.
Tintwistle, par. and vil., Cheshire, on r. Etherew, 3½ m. E. of Stalybridge; pop. 1530. Map 40.
Tipperary, urb. dist. and par., Tipperary, 25 m. S.E. of Limerick; pop. 5554. Map 95.
Tipton, urb. dist. and par., Staffordshire, 8½ m. N.W. of Birmingham; pop. 35,792. Map 47.
Tiptree, railway station, Essex, 3½ m. S.E. of Kelvedon. Map 73.
Tisbury, town and 2 pars. (**E.** and **W.**), Wiltshire, 12¾ m. W. of Salisbury; pop. **E. T.** 729, **W. T.** 691. Map 87.
Titchfield, par. and vil., Hants, 2 m. W. of Fareham; pop. 1915. Map 77.
Titchmarsh, par. and vil., Northamptonshire, 2 m. N.E. of Thrapston; pop. 620. Map 60.
Titterstone Clee Hill, Salop, 6 m. N.E. of Ludlow; altitude 1749 ft. Map 57.
Tiverton, par. and vil., Cheshire, 1½ m. S.E. of Tarporley; pop. 565. Map 39.
Tiverton, mun. bor. and par., Devonshire, 12 m. N. of Exeter; pop. 9611. Map 85.
Tobercurry, market town, in co. and 21¾ m. S.W. of Sligo; pop. 829. Map 92.
Tobermore, vil., S.E. co. Londonderry, 5 m. N.W. of Magherafelt; pop. 342. Map 93.
Tobermory, spt. and police bur., Mull Island, Argyllshire, 28 m. N.W. of Oban; pop. 771. Map 12.
Toddington, town and par., Bedfordshire ,4½ m. N. of Dunstable; pop. 2001. Map 71.
Todmorden, par., mun. bor., mfg. mkt. town, W.R. Yorks, 8¾ m. S.E. of Burnley; pop. 22,223. Map 31.
Toft Monks, par. and vil., Norfolk, 3 m. N.E. of Beccles; pop. 344. Map 53.
Tollesbury, par. and vil., Essex, 7 m. E.N.E. of Maldon; pop. 1721. Map 73.
Tolleshunt d'Arcy, par. and vil., Essex, 2 m. N.W. of Tollesbury; pop. 861. Map 73.
Tolworth, par. and vil., Surrey, 2 m. S. of Kingston-on-Thames; pop. 5387. Map 78.
Tomintoul, *q.s.* par. and vil., Banffshire, 14½ m. S. of Ballindalloch; pop. 596. Map 3.
Tonbridge, urb. dist. and market town, Kent, 29½ m. S.E. of London; pop. 16,332. Map 82.
Tongue, par. and vil., on N. coast of Sutherlandshire; pop. 1350. Map 3.
Ton-gwynlais, place, Glamorganshire, 3 m. N.W. of Llandaff. Map 67.
Ton-yr-efail, place, with ry. sta., Glamorganshire, 5 m. N.W. of Llantrisant sta. Map 66.
Topcliffe, par. and vil., N.R. Yorkshire, 4½ m. S.W. of Thirsk; pop. 490. Map 28.
Toppesfield, par. and vil., Essex, 6½ m. N.W. of Halstead; pop. 535. Map 62.
Topsham, town and par., Devonshire, 5¼ m. N.W. of Exmouth; pop. 3255. Map 89.
Torbryan, par. and vil., Devonshire, 4½ m. S.W. of Newton Abbot; pop. 443. Map 89.
Torksey, par. and vil., in co. and 9¾ m. N.W. of Lincoln; pop. 191. Map 42.
Tormaston, par. and vil., Gloucestershire, 4 m. S.E. of Chipping Sodbury; pop. 311. Map 75.
Torpenhow, par., Cumberland, 7 m. N.E. of Cockermouth; pop. 281. Map 20.
Torphichen, par. and vil., West Lothian, 2½ m. N. of Bathgate; pop. 4486. Map 9.
Torpoint, urb. dist. and par., Cornwall, opposite Devonport; pop. 3975. Map 88.
Torquay, mun. bor., watering place and seaport, Devonshire, 23 m. S. of Exeter; pop. 46,165. Map 89.
Torrington, par. and vil., Devonshire, 4½ m. W.N.W. of Hatherleigh; pop. 581. Map 84.
Torryburn, par. and vil., Fifeshire, 2½ m. E. of Culross; pop. 2224. Map 9.
Torthorwald, par. and vil., Dumfriesshire, 4 m. N.E. of Dumfries; pop. 801. Map 20.
Totland, par., Isle of Wight, 3 m. S.W. of Yarmouth; pop. 1689. Map 77.
Totley, par. and vil., Derbyshire, 6 m. S.W. of Sheffield; pop. 1341. Map 40.
Totnes, mun. bor. and par., Devonshire, 22 m. S.W. of Exeter; pop. 4525. Map 89.
Tottenham, urb. dist. and par., Middlesex, in N. suburbs of London; pop. 157,748. Map 71.
Totternhoe, par. and vil., Bedfordshire, 2 m. W. of Dunstable; pop. 449. Map 71.
Tottington, urb. dist. and par., S.E. Lancashire, 2½ m. N.W. of Bury; pop. 6532. Map 31.
Totton, vil., with ry. sta., Hants, 4 m. W. of Southampton. Map 77.
Towcester, market town and par., in co. and 8½ m. S.W. of Northampton; pop. 2383. Map 59.
Tow Law, urb. dist. and par., Durham, 8 m. N.W. of Bishop Auckland; pop. 3556. Map 22.
Towyn, wtg. pl. and urb. dist., Merionethshire, 3 m. N.W. of Aberdovey; pop. 3,803. Map 44.
Towyn, dist., Abergele par., Denbighshire. Map 37.
Tralee, spt., urb. dist. and par., Kerry, 31½ m. N.E. of Dingle by rail; pop. 10,536. Map 94.
Tramore, market town and watering pl., in co. and 7½ m. S. of Waterford; pop. 1812. Map 95.
Tranent, police bur., E. Lothian, 9½ m. E. of Edinburgh; pop. 4526. Map 10.
Traquair, par. and vil., Peeblesshire, 1½ m. S. of Innerleithen; pop. 556. Map 15.
Trawden, urb. dist., Lancashire, 2 m. S.E. of Colne; pop. 2548. Map 31.
Trearddwr, seaside resort, Anglesey, 12 m. S. of Holyhead. Map 36.
Tredegar, urb. dist. and par., Monmouthshire, 7 m. E.N.E. of Merthyr Tydfil; pop. 23,195. Map 67.
Treeton, par., W.R. Yorkshire, 3½ m. S. of Rotherham; pop. 1903. Map 41.
Treffgarne, par. and ham., Pembrokeshire, 5 m. N. of Haverfordwest; pop. 79. Map 64.
Treforest, ham., with ry. stas., Glamorganshire, 11¾ m. N.W. of Cardiff. Map 66.
Tregaron (Caron-is-Clawdd), par., Cardiganshire, 9½ m. N.E. of Lampeter; pop. 1364. Map 55.

Treharris, vil. and ry. sta., Glamorganshire, 5 m. N.E. of Pontypridd. Map 67.
Treig, Loch, Inverness-shire, extends 5 m. N. and S. r. Treig flows into Spean 6 m. E. Br. of Roy. Map 2.
Tremadoc, small town, Carnarvonshire, 4½ m. N.E. of Criccieth. Map 36.
Trentham, par. and vil., Staffordshire, 3 m. S. of Stoke-upon-Trent; pop. 3141. Map 47.
Treorky, vil., with ry. sta., Glamorganshire, 8¾ m. N.W. of Pontypridd. Map 66.
Trevalga, coast par. and vil., Cornwall, 4 m. N.W. of Camelford; pop. 105. Map 91.
Trim, urb. dist. and par., Meath, 29 m. N.W. of Dublin; pop. 1488. Map 93.
Trimdon, par. and vil., Durham, 8 m. S.E. of Durham; pop. 5410. Map 23.
Trimingham, coast par. and vil., Norfolk, 5 m. S.E. of Cromer; pop. 259. Map 53.
Trimsuran, ham., Carmarthenshire, 3 m. S.E. of Kidwelly. Map 65.
Tring, urb. dist. and par., Hertfordshire, 5 m. N.W. of Berkhampstead by rail; pop. 4364. Map 71.
Troon, police bur. and *q.s.* par., Ayrshire, 6½ m. N. of Ayr; pop. 8544. Map 12.
Trossachs, mountain defile, Perthshire, 8 m. W. of Callander. Map 5.
Troutbeck, par. and vil., Westmorland, 3 m. S.E. of Ambleside; pop. 486. Map 25.
Trowbridge, urb. dist. and market town, Wiltshire, 11¾ m. S.S.W. of Chippenham; pop. 12,011. Map 75.
Trull, par. and vil., Somersetshire, 2 m. S.S.W. of Taunton; pop. 9855. Map 86.
Trumpington, par. and vil., in co. and 2 m. S. of Cambridge; pop. 820. Map 61.
Trunch, par. and vil., Norfolk, 3 m. N. of N. Walsham; pop. 377. Map 53.
Truro, mun. bor., seaport and par., Cornwall, 11¾ m. N. of Falmouth by rail; pop. 11,074. Map 90.
Tuam, town and par., Galway, 15½ m. N.N.W. of Athenry; pop. 3288. Map 94.
Tuddenham, par. and vil., E. Suffolk, 3 m. N.E. of Ipswich; pop. 337. Map 63.
Tulla, market town and par., Clare, 10 m. E.N.E. of Ennis; pop. 2660. Map 94.
Tullamore, assize town and urb. dist., Offaly, 58 m. W. of Dublin; pop. 4924. Map 93.
Tulliallan, par., containing Kincardine, Fifeshire, on r. Forth; pop. 2298. Map 9.
Tullibody, vil., Clackmannanshire, 2¼ m. N.W. of Alloa; pop. 879. Map 9.
Tullow, market town, in co. and 9 m. S.E. of Carlow; pop. 1894. Map 95.
Tumble, vil., in co. and 10 m. S.E. of Carmarthen. Map 65.
Tumley, par. and vil., Lindsey, Lincolnshire, 6 m. S. of Horncastle; pop. 264. Map 43.
Tunbridge Wells, mun. bor. and par., Kent, 34½ m. S.E. of London; pop. 35,367. Map 82.
Tunstall, par. and vil., N. Lancashire, 3 m. S. of Kirkby Lonsdale; pop. 96. Map 26.
Tunstall, par., Staffordshire, 2¼ m. N.E. of Newcastle-under-Lyme; pop. 22,740. Map 39.
Tunstall, par. and vil., Kent, 1½ m. S.W. of Sittingbourne; pop. 265. Map 82.
Tupton, par. and seat, Derbyshire, 3 m. S. of Chesterfield; pop. 2034. Map 41.
Turkdean, par. and vil., Gloucestershire, 2 m. N. of Northleach; pop. 133. Map 69.
Turnershill, eccl. dist. and ham., E. Sussex, 3½ m. S.W. of East Grinstead; pop. 820. Map 81.
Turriff, police bur. and par., Aberdeenshire, 12 m. S. of Macduff; pop. 2298. Map 3.
Turton, urb. dist., Lancashire, 5 m. N. of Bolton; pop. 11,847. Map 31.
Turvey, par. and vil., in co. and 7 m. N.W. of Bedford; pop. 849. Map 60.
Tutbury, town and par., Staffordshire, 4½ m. N.E. of Burton-on-Trent; pop. 2062. Map 48.
Tuxford, small market town and par., Nottinghamshire, 6¾ m. S. of Retford; pop. 1191. Map 41.
Tweedmouth, par. and seaport, Northumberland, at mouth of r. Tweed; pop. 5151. Map 11.
Twickenham, urb. disr., Middlesex, on r. Thames, 11¼ m. S.W. of London; pop. 39,909. Map 78.
Twizell, par. and vil., Northumberland, 3 m. N.E. of Cornhill; pop. 223. Map 17.
Two Bridges, place, with inn, Devonshire, 8 m. E. of Tavistock. Map 88.
Twyford, par. and vil., Hants, 3 m. S. of Winchester; pop. 2214. Map 76.
Twyford, par. and vil., Berkshire, 4½ m. N.E. of Reading; pop. 1269. Map 70.
Twyford, par. and vil., Leicestershire, 6 m. S.S.W. of Melton Mowbray; pop. 333. Map 49.
Tydd, ry. sta., Holland, Lincolnshire, 5 m. S. of Wisbech. Map 51.
Tyldesley (with Shakerley), urb. dist. and par., S.W. Lancashire, 5 m. S. of Bolton; pop. 14,848. Map 39.
Tylorstown, ry. sta., Glamorganshire, between Porth sta. and Ferndale sta. Map 66.
Tyndrum, vil., with ry. stas., Perthshire, 34¼ m. N.W. of Callander. Map 4.
Tyne, River, flows through Northumberland and Durham, and is 30 m. in length. Map 22.
Tynemouth, parl. and co. bor. and par., Northumberland, 8 m. N.E. of Newcastle; pop. 64,913. Map 23.
Tywardreath, par. and vil., Cornwall, 5 m. N.E. of St Austell; pop. 2512. Map 91.
UCKFIELD, urb. dist. and par., Sussex, 50 m. S. of London; pop. 3557. Map 81.
Uddingston, town and *q.s.* par., Lanarkshire, 7 m. S.E. of Glasgow; pop. 8414. Map 9.
Uffculme, par. and vil., Devonshire, 7½ m. E. of Tiverton; pop. 1551. Map 85.
Uffington, par. and vil., Berkshire, 4 m. S.E. of Faringdon; pop. 480. Map 69.
Ufford, par. and vil., E. Suffolk, 3 m. N.E. of Woodbridge; pop. 432. Map 63.
Uist, North, isl. and par., Outer Hebrides, Inverness-shire; pop. 2579. Map 2.
Uist, South, isl. and par., Outer Hebrides, Inverness-shire; pop. 3235. Map 2.
Ulceby, par. and vil., Lindsey, Lincolnshire, 6 m. S. of New Holland; pop. 924. Map 35.
Uldale, par. and vil., Cumberland, 7½ m. S. of Wigton; pop. 228. Map 20.
Uley, par. and vil., Gloucestershire, 6 m. S.W. of Stroud; pop. 967. Map 68.
Ulgham, par. and vil., Northumberland, 4½ m. N.E. of Morpeth; pop. 1125. Map 17.
Ullapool, *q.s.* par. and vil., Ross and Cromarty, 32 m. N.W. of Garve ry. sta.; pop. 598. Map 2.
Ullswater, lake, 7½ m. long, Cumberland and Westmorland, 5 m. S.W. of Penrith. Map 25.
Ulverston, urb. dist., spt. and par., N. Lancashire, 8 m. N.E. of Barrow-in-Furness; pop. 9235. Map 25.
Upavon, par. and vil., Wiltshire, 4 m. S.W. of Pewsey; pop. 767. Map 76.
Upchurch, par. and vil., Kent, 5 m. E. of Chatham; pop. 1312. Map 82.
Uphall, par. and vil., West Lothian, 13½ m. W.S.W. of Edinburgh; pop. 3441. Map 9.
Upholland, urb. dist., Lancashire, 4 m. W. of Wigan; pop. 5480. Map 39.
Upminster, par. and vil., Essex, 3 m. S.E. of Romford; pop. 3559. Map 72.
Upper Clatford, par., Hampshire, 1 m. S. of Andover; pop. 688. Map 76.
Upper Tean, eccl. dist. and vil., Staffordshire, 2½ m. S. of Cheadle; pop. 1314. Map 48.

Uppingham, market town, Rutlandshire, 6 m. S. of Oakham; pop. 2453. Map 50.

Upton-on-Severn, market town, Worcestershire, 6 m. S.E. of Malvern; pop. 2004. Map 57.

Upwell, par. and vil., Cambridgeshire, 5 m. S.E. of Wisbech; pop. 1583. Map 51.

Urmston, urb. dist. and par., S.E. Lancashire, 5 m. S.W. of Central sta., Manchester; pop. 9284. Map 39.

Usk, par. and urb. dist., in co. and 12 m. S.W. of Monmouth; pop. 1315. Map 67.

Uttoxeter, urb. dist. and par., in co. and 13 m. N.E. of Stafford; pop. 5907. Map 48.

Uxbridge, urb. dist. and par., Middlesex, 16 m. N.W. of London; pop. 31,866. Map 71.

VALENTIA ISLAND, isl. and par., S.W. co. Kerry, 4 m. S.W. of Cahirciveen; pop. 1625. Map 94.

Velindre, ham., E. Breconshire, 4½ m. S.W. of Hay. Map 56.

Velindre-farchog, ham., Pembrokeshire, 2½ m. E. of Newport. Map 64.

Vennacher, Loch, Perthshire, 2¼ m. S.W. of Callander; is 3¾ m. in length. Map 5.

Ventnor, urb. dist. and par., Isle of Wight, 11 m. S. of Ryde; pop. 5112. Map 77.

Vernhams Dean, par. and vil., Hampshire, 7 m. N. of Andover; pop. 449. Map 76.

Verwood, par., vil. and ry. sta., Dorsetshire, 3½ m. S.E. of Cramborne; pop. 1217. Map 77.

Voil, Loch, Perthshire, 3 m. W. of Balquhidder; is 3½ m. in length. Map 5.

Vowchurch, par. and vil., in co. and 10 m. W.S.W. of Hereford; pop. 281. Map 56.

Vyrnwy, lake and river, Montgomeryshire, forming Liverpool's chief water supply. Map 45.

WADDESDON, par. and vil., Buckinghamshire, 5½ m. N.W. of Aylesbury; pop. 1439. Map 70.

Wadebridge, urb. dist. and par., Cornwall, 7 m. N.W. of Bodmin; pop. 2460. Map 91.

Wadhurst, par. and vil., Sussex, 6 m. S.E. of Tunbridge Wells; pop. 3674. Map 82.

Wadworth, par., vil. and seat, W.R. Yorkshire, 4 m. S. of Doncaster; pop. 710. Map 41.

Wainfleet, market town and par., Lindsey, Lincolnshire, 8½ m. S.E. of Spilsby; pop. 1375. Map 43.

Wakefield, city, parl. and co. bor. and par., W.R. Yorkshire, 9 m. S. of Leeds; pop. 59,115. Map 33.

Wakering, Great, par. and vil., Essex, 4½ m. E.N.E. of Southend; pop. 1826. Map 73.

Walkerburn, vil. and *q.s.* par., Peeblesshire, 1¾ m. E. of Innerleithen; pop. 1110. Map 15.

Walkeringham, par. and vil., Nottinghamshire, 4 m. N.W. of Gainsborough; pop. 973. Map 42.

Walkern, par. and vil., Hertfordshire, 3 m. E. of Stevenage; pop. 700. Map 71.

Walkington, par. and vil., E.R. Yorkshire, 3 m. S.W. of Beverley; pop. 1199. Map 35.

Wall, par. and vil., Northumberland, 3¼ m. N.W. of Hexham; pop. 381. Map 22.

Wallasey, co. bor. and par., Cheshire, in Wirral Peninsula, 3 m. N.W. of Birkenhead; pop. 97,465. Map 38.

Wallbottle, par. and vil., Northumberland, 5 m. W. of Newcastle-on-Tyne; pop. 3080. Map 23.

Wall Grange, sta., Staffordshire, between Leek and Endon. Map 40.

Wallingford, mun. bor., Berkshire, 14½ m. N.W. of Reading; pop. 2840. Map 70.

Wallington, par. and vil., Surrey, 2½ m. S.W. of West Croydon; pop. 9223. Map 80.

Wallsend, mun. bor. and par., Northumberland, 4 m. E.N.E. of Newcastle; pop. 44,582. Map 23.

Walmer, urb. dist., Kent, 1¼ m. S.S.W. of Deal; pop. 5324. Map 83.

Walney Island, eccl. dist., N. Lancashire, in Dalton-in-Furness par.; pop. 8013. Map 25.

Walpole, ry. sta., Norfolk, 8½ m. W. of King's Lynn. Map 51.

Walpole, par. and vil., E. Suffolk, 2½ m. S.W. of Halesworth; pop. 325. Map 63.

Walsall, parl. and co. bor. and par., Staffordshire, 8 m. N.W. of Birmingham; pop. 103,102. Map 48.

Walsden, eccl. dist., W.R. Yorkshire, 7 m. N.E. of Rochdale; pop. 4292. Map 31.

Walsgrave-on-Sowe, par. and vil., Warwickshire, 3½ m. N.E. of Coventry; pop. 2060. Map 59.

Walsham, North, urb. dist. and par., Norfolk, 16 m. N. of Norwich; pop. 4137. Map 53.

Walsham, South, par. and vil., Norfolk, 9 m. E.N.E. of Norwich; pop. 509. Map 53.

Walsingham, Great, par., Norfolk, 3½ m. S.S.E. of Wells; pop. 295. Map 52.

Walsingham, Little, par. and town, Norfolk, 4½ m. S. of Wells; pop. 788. Map 52.

Walsoken, urb. dist., Norfolk, 1 m. N.E. of Wisbech; pop. 4058. Map 51.

Waltham, market town and par., Lindsey, Lincolnshire, 4½ m. S. of Grimsby; pop. 978. Map 43.

Waltham Cross, eccl. par. and vil., Hertfordshire, on S. side of Cheshunt. Map 71.

Waltham, Great, par. and vil., Essex, 4 m. N. of Chelmsford; pop. 2029. Map 72.

Waltham (W. Holy Cross) (Abbey), urb. dist. and par., Essex, 15 m. N. of London; pop. 7116. Map 71.

Waltham-on-the-Wold, par. and vil., Leicestershire, 5 m. N.E. of Melton Mowbray; pop. 484. Map 50.

Waltham St Lawrence, par. and vil., Berkshire, 2½ m. N.E. of Twyford; pop. 960. Map 70.

Walthamstow, municipal bor., S.W. Essex, 6 m. N.E. of Liverpool St. sta., London; pop. 132,965. Map 71.

Walton, vil., Staffordshire, ½ m. S. of Stone. Map 47.

Walton, par. and vil., Cumberland, 2½ m. N. of Brampton; pop. 286. Map 21.

Walton-in-Gordano, coast par. and vil., Somersetshire, 1½ m. N.E. of Clevedon; pop. 732. Map 74.

Walton-le-dale, urb. dist. and par., Lancashire, 2 m. S.E. of Preston; pop. 12,718. Map 30.

Walton-on-Thames, urb. dist., Surrey, 17 m. S.W. of London; pop. 17,953. Map 78.

Walton-on-the-Naze, urb. dist. and par., Essex, 7 m. S. of Harwich; pop. 3066. Map 73.

Wanborough, par., ham. and ry. sta., Surrey, 3½ m. W. of Guildford; pop. 303. Map 78.

Wanstead, urb. dist., Essex, 7 m. N.E. of London; pop. 19,183. Map 71.

Wanstrow, par. and vil., Somersetshire, 6½ m. E.N.E. of Shepton Mallet; pop. 305. Map 75.

Wantage, urb. dist. and par., Berkshire, 9 m. S.W. of Abingdon; pop. 3424. Map 69.

Warblington, urb. dist. and par., Hants, 1 m. S.E. of Havant; pop. 4320. Map 79.

Warboys, par. and vil., Huntingdonshire, 3½ m. S.S.E of Ramsey; pop. 1720. Map 61.

Warcop, par. and vil., Westmorland, 5 m. S.E. of Appleby; pop. 577. Map 26.

Warden, par. and vil., Northumberland, 3 m. N.W. of Hexham; pop. 828. Map 22.

Wardington, par. and vil., Oxon, 4 m. N.E. of Banbury; pop. 594. Map 59.

Wardle, urb. dist. and par., S.E. Lancashire, on N.E. side of Rochdale; pop. 4793. Map 31.

Wardlow, par. and vil., Derbyshire, 2 m. S.E. of Tideswell; pop. 124. Map 40.

Ware, urb. dist. and par., Hertfordshire, 22½ m. N. of London by rail; pop. 6171. Map 71.

Wareham, mun. bor., Dorsetshire, 15 m. E. of Dorchester; pop. 2057. Map 87.

Warfield, par. and vil., Berkshire, 5 m. N.E. of Wokingham; pop. 2499. Map 70.

Wargrave, par. and vil., E. Berkshire, 3 m. S.E. of Henley-on-Thames; pop. 2383. Map 70.

Wark, par. and vil., Northumberland, 9 m. N.W. of Hexham; pop. 738. Map 22.

Warkworth, par. and seaport, Northumberland, 7 m. S.E. of Alnwick; pop. 1042. Map 17.

Warley, Great, par. and vil., Essex, $3\frac{1}{2}$ m. S. of Brentwood; pop. 2088. Map 72.

Warley Street, ham., $1\frac{1}{2}$ m. N.N.W. of Great Warley, Essex. Map 72.

Warlingham, par. and vil., Surrey, 5 m. S.E. of Croydon; pop. 3897. Map 80.

Warmfield, par. and vil., W.R. Yorkshire, 3 m. E. of Wakefield; pop. 1094. Map 33.

Warmington, par. and vil., Warwickshire, $5\frac{1}{2}$ m. N.W. of Banbury; pop. 245. Map 59.

Warminster, urb. dist. and market town, Wiltshire, 9 m. S. of Trowbridge; pop. 5176. Map 75.

Warmley, eccl. dist. and vil., Gloucestershire, 5 m. E. of Bristol; pop. 2830. Map 75.

Warnborough, South, par. and vil., Hants, $2\frac{1}{2}$ m. S.W. of Odiham; pop. 279. Map 78.

Warnham, par. and vil., Sussex, 2 m. N.W. of Horsham; pop. 1227. Map 79.

Warren Point, spt., urb. dist. and par., co. Down, 6 m. S.E. of Newry; pop. 1938. Map 93.

Warrington, co. bor. and par., S.W. Lancashire, midway between Liverpool and Manchester; pop. 79,322. Map 39.

Warsop, urb. dist., Nottinghamshire, $5\frac{1}{2}$ m. N.E. of Mansfield; pop. 10,748. Map 41.

Warter, par. and vil., E.R. Yorkshire, 4 m. E. of Pocklington; pop. 436. Map 34.

Warton, par., vil. and seat, W. Lancashire, 3 m. S.S.W. of Kirkham; pop. 684. Map 30.

Warton, par. and vil., N. Lancashire, $6\frac{1}{2}$ m. N. of Lancaster; pop. 1678. Map 26.

Warwick, mun. bor. and co. town of Warwickshire, 108 m. N.W. of London; pop. 13,459. Map 58.

Warwick, par. and vil., Cumberland, on r. Eden, 4 m. E. of Carlisle; pop. 262. Map 21.

Washington, urb. dist. and par., Durham, 6 m. W. of Sunderland; pop. 16,989. Map 23.

Wash, River, rises Leicestershire and flows 20 m. E to the Welland, near Stamford. Map 50.

Wash, The, estuary of rivers Ouse, Welland, Nene and Witham, Lincolnshire and Norfolk. Map 51.

Wast Water, lake, Cumberland, 14 m. S.W. of Keswick. Map 25.

Watchet, urb. dist., Somersetshire, $16\frac{3}{4}$ m. N.W. of Taunton; pop. 1936. Map 85.

Waterbeach, par. and vil., Cambridgeshire, 5 m. N.E. of Cambridge; pop. 1363. Map 61.

Waterbeck, vil., Dumfriesshire, 7 m. S.E. of Lockerbie. Map 20.

Waterfoot, eccl. dist. and vil., Lancashire; pop. 2873. Map 31.

Waterford, co. bor. and seaport, Waterford, 77 m. S.E. of Limerick; pop. 26,646. Map 95.

Waterhouses, vil., Staffordsh., $7\frac{1}{2}$ m. S.E. of Leek. Map 40.

Waterhouses, eccl. dist. and vil., in co. and $5\frac{1}{2}$ m. W. of Durham. Map 23.

Waterlooville, par. and vil., Hants, $3\frac{1}{2}$ m. N.N.W. of Havant; pop. 1033. Map 79.

Waterloo with Seaforth, urb. dist. and town, Lancs, 4 m. N. of Liverpool; pop. of urb. dist. 31,180. Map 38.

Watford, mun. bor. and market town, S.W. Hertfordshire, 8 m. S.W. of St Albans; pop. 56,799. Map 71.

Watford, par. and vil., Northamptonshire, $4\frac{1}{2}$ m. N.E. of Daventry; pop. 336. Map 59.

Wath, place, Cumberland, 1 m. from Cleator Moor. Map 24.

Wath, par. and vil., N.R. Yorkshire, 4 m. N. of Ripon; pop. 192. Map 27.

Wath-upon-Dearne, urb. dist. and par., W.R. Yorks 8 m. S.E. of Barnsley; pop. 13,653. Map 41.

Watling Street, Roman military road, which extended from E. coast of Kent into North Wales. Map 83.

Watlington par. and town, Oxon, 8 m. N.E. of Wallingford; pop. 1386. Map 70.

Watlington, par. and vil., Norfolk, 6 m. S. of King's Lynn; pop. 590. Map 52.

Watten, par. and vil., Caithness-shire, $7\frac{1}{2}$ m. N.W. of Wick; pop. 934. Map 3.

Watton, market town and par., Norfolk, $13\frac{1}{4}$ m. N.N.E. of Thetford; pop. 1331. Map 52.

Wavendon, par. and vil., Buckinghamshire, 5 m. S.E. of Newport Pagnell; pop. 465. Map 60.

Weald, par. and vil., W. Kent. $2\frac{1}{2}$ m. S. of Sevenoaks; pop. 912. Map 82.

Weald, South, par. and vil., Essex, $1\frac{1}{2}$ m. W. of Brent wood; pop. 5682. Map 72.

Weald Basset, North, par. and vil., Essex, $2\frac{3}{4}$ m. N.E. of Epping; pop. 1239. Map 72.

Wealdstone, urb. dist. and par., Middlesex, 1 m. N.E. of Harrow; pop. 27,001. Map 71.

Wear Head, vil. and ry. sta., W. Durham, $8\frac{1}{2}$ m. W. of Stanhope. Map 22.

Weaverham, par. and vil., Cheshire, 3 m. W.N.W. of Northwich; pop. 2111. Map 39.

Weaverthorpe, ry. sta., E.R. Yorkshire, 1 m. N. of Sherburn. Map 29.

Wedmore, par. and vil., Somersetshire, $4\frac{1}{2}$ m. S. of Axbridge; pop. 2385. Map 74.

Wednesbury, mun. bor. and par., Staffordshire, 8 m. N. of Birmingham by rail; pop. 31,534. Map 48.

Wednesfield, urb. dist., Staffordshire, in parl. bor. of Wolverhampton; pop. 9333. Map 47.

Weedon, par. and vil., Buckinghamshire, 3 m. N. of Aylesbury; pop. 325. Map 70.

Weedon Beck, par. and vil., Northamptonshire, 4 m. S.E. of Daventry; pop. 2020. Map 59.

Weeford, par. and vil., Staffordshire, $3\frac{1}{2}$ m. S.E. of Lichfield; pop. 245. Map 48.

Weekley, par. and vil., Northamptonshire, $1\frac{3}{4}$ m. N.E. of Kettering; pop. 223. Map 60.

Week St Mary, par. and vil., Cornwall, 11 m. N.W. of Launceston; pop. 452. Map 88.

Weeley, par., vil. and ry. sta., Essex, $6\frac{1}{2}$ m. W. of Walton-on-the-Naze; pop. 648. Map 73.

Weem, par. and vil., Perthshire, 1 m. N.W. of Aberfeldy; pop. 429. Map 6.

Weeting with Bromehill, par. and vil., Norfolk, $1\frac{1}{2}$ m. N. of Brandon; pop. 312. Map 62.

Weeton, par. and vil., N. Lancashire, 3 m. N.W. of Kirkham; pop. 361. Map 30.

Weetslade, urb. dist., Northumberland, 3 m. N.W. of Longbenton; pop. 7736. Map 23.

Welbeck, par. and ry. sta., Nottinghamshire, $3\frac{1}{2}$ m. S.W. of Worksop; pop. 77. Map 41.

Welbourn, par. and vil., Kesteven, in co. and 12 m. S. of Lincoln; pop. 524. Map 42.

Welby, par. and vil., Kesteven, Lincolnshire, 4 m. N.E. of Grantham; pop. 312. Map 50.

Wellingborough, urb. dist. and par., in co. and $10\frac{1}{4}$ m. N.E. of Northampton; pop. 21,221. Map 60.

Wellington, par. and vil., in co. and 5 m. N. of Hereford; pop. 625. Map 56.

Wellington, urb. dist. and par., Salop, 10 m. E. of Shrewsbury by rail; pop. 8185. Map 47.

Wellington, urb. dist. and par., Somersetshire, 7 m. S.W. of Taunton by rail; pop. 7128. Map 86.

Wellington Heath, par. and vil., Herefordshire, 2 m. N. of Ledbury; pop. 421. Map 57.

Wells, urb. dist., par. and seaport, Norfolk, 31 m. N.E. of King's Lynn; pop. 2505. Map 52.

Wells, mun. bor. and ancient city, Somersetshire, 19 m. S.W. of Bath; pop. 4833. Map 74.

Welnetham, Little, par., Suffolk, $3\frac{1}{2}$ m. S.E. of Bury St Edmunds; pop. 123. Map 62.

Welney, par. and vil., Norfolk, 8 m. S.W. of Downham Market; pop. 366. Map 51.

Welshampton, par. and vil., Salop, $2\frac{3}{4}$ m. E. of Ellesmere; pop. 432. Map 46.

Welsh Newton, par., S. Herefordshire, $3\frac{1}{2}$ m. N. of Monmouth; pop. 202. Map 67.

Welshpool, mun. bor., Montgomeryshire, $19\frac{3}{4}$ m. S.W. of Shrewsbury; pop. 5637. Map 46.

Welton, par. and vil., Northamptonshire, 2 m. N.E. of Daventry; pop. 339. Map 59.

Welton, par. and vil., E.R. Yorkshire, $9\frac{1}{2}$ m. W. of Hull; pop. 696. Map 35.

Welton, par. and vil., in co. and 6 m. N.N.E. of Lincoln; pop. 637. Map 42.

Welton-le-Marsh, par. and vil., Lindsey, Lincolnshire, 5 m. N.E. of Spilsby; pop. 289. Map 43.

Welwyn, par. and urb. dist., Hertfordshire, 4 m. N. of Hatfield; pop. 8585. Map 71.

Wem, urb. dist. and par., Salop, $10\frac{1}{2}$ m. N. of Shrewsbury; pop. 2157. Map 46.

Wembley, urb. dist., Middlesex, $2\frac{1}{2}$ m. S.E. of Harrow; pop. 48,546. Map 71.

Wembury, par. and vil., Devonshire, 6 m. S.E. of Plymouth; pop. 501. Map 88.

Wemyss Bay, watering place, Renfrewshire, 8 m. S.W. of Greenock. Map 12.

Wendling, par. and vil., Norfolk, 4 m. W. of East Dereham; pop. 302. Map 52.

Wendover, market town and par., Buckinghamshire, 5 m. S.E. of Aylesbury; pop. 2366. Map 70.

Wendron, par. and vil., Cornwall, $2\frac{1}{2}$ m. N.E. of Helston; pop. 3281. Map 90.

Wenlock, mun. bor., Staffordshire, 14 m. S.E. of Shrewsbury; pop. 14,152. Map 47.

Wennington, par., N. Lancashire, 11 m. N.E. of Lancaster; pop. 120. Map 26.

Wennington, par. and vil., Essex, 5 m. S.E. of Romford; pop. 432. Map 72.

Wensley, par. and vil., N.R. Yorkshire, $1\frac{1}{2}$ m. S.W. of Leyburn; pop. 202. Map 27.

Wentnor, par. and vil., Salop, 5 m. N.E. of Bishop's Castle; pop. 432. Map 46.

Wenvoe, par. and vil., Glamorganshire, 5 m. S.W. of Cardiff; pop. 495. Map 67.

Weobley, town, Herefordshire, $7\frac{1}{2}$ m. S.W. of Leominster; pop. 601. Map 56.

Wereham, par. and vil., Norfolk, 6 m. S.E. of Downham; pop. 467. Map 52.

West Acre, par. and vil., Norfolk, 5 m. W. of Swaffham; pop. 339. Map 52.

West Allen Dale, valley of the West Allen r., Northumberland, $3\frac{1}{2}$ m. S.W. of Staward ry. sta. Map 22.

Westbourne, par. and vil., W. Sussex, 3 m. N.E. of Havant; pop. 3562. Map 79.

West Bridgford, par. and urb. dist., in co. and 2 m. S.E. of Nottingham; pop. 17,821. Map 49.

West Bromwich, parl. and co. bor., Staffordshire, $4\frac{1}{2}$ m. N.W. of Birmingham; pop. 81,281. Map 48.

Westbury, par. and vil., Salop, 9 m. W.S.W. of Shrewsbury; pop. 1064. Map 46.

Westbury, par. and vil., Somersetshire, 4 m. N.W. of Wells; pop. 532. Map 74.

Westbury, urb. dist. and market town, Wiltshire, $4\frac{1}{2}$ m. S. of Trowbridge; pop. 4044. Map 75.

Westbury Leigh, place, on S. side of Westbury, Wiltshire. Map 75.

Westbury-on-Severn, urb. dist., par. and vil., Glos., 8 m. S.W. of Gloucester; pop. 1746. Map 68.

Westbury-on-Trym, 2 eccl. pars. in N.W. of Bristol; pop. 8971 and 3626. Map 68.

West Butterwick, par. and vil., Lindsey, Lincolnshire, $5\frac{1}{2}$ m. N.E. of Epworth; pop. 624. Map 34.

West Calder, par. and market town, Midlothian, $15\frac{3}{4}$ m. S.W. of Edinburgh; pop. (town) 3350. Map 9.

West Cornforth, mining vil., with ry. sta., Durham, $4\frac{1}{2}$ m. N.W. of Sedgefield. Map 23.

Westcot Barton, par. and seat, Oxon, 6 m. N. of Woodstock; pop. 132. Map 69.

Westcott, par. and vil., Buckinghamshire, 7 m. N.W. of Aylesbury; pop. 270. Map 70.

Westdean, par. and vil., W. Sussex, $4\frac{1}{2}$ m. N. of Chichester; pop. 681. Map 79.

Westerham, par. and market town, Kent, 6 m. W. of Sevenoaks; pop. 3162. Map 80.

Westgate, eccl. dist. and vil., Durham, $5\frac{1}{2}$ m. W. of Stanhope; pop. 693. Map 22.

Westgate-on-Sea, watering place and par., Kent, 2 m. W.S.W. of Margate; pop. 5096. Map 83.

West Gordon, vil., Berwickshire, 4 m. S.W. of Greenlaw; pop. 322. Map 11.

West Grinstead, par. and vil., Sussex, $6\frac{3}{4}$ m. S. of Horsham; pop. 1515. Map 79.

West Ham, co. bor., Essex, in E. of London, opposite Greenwich; pop. 294,086. Map 71.

Westham, par. and vil., E. Sussex, $\frac{1}{2}$ m. W.S.W. of Pevensey sta.; pop. 1439. Map 81.

West Heslerton, par., E.R. Yorkshire, $8\frac{1}{2}$ m. N.E. of Malton; pop. 288. Map 29.

Westhoughton, urb. dist. and par., S.E. Lancs, 5 m. E. of Wigan by rail; pop. 16,018. Map 30.

West Kilbride, small town and par., Ayrshire, $4\frac{1}{4}$ m. N.W. of Ardrossan; pop. 3588. Map 12.

West Kirby, part of Hoylake and West Kirby urb. dist., Cheshire. Map 38.

West Linton, par. and vil., Peeblesshire, 15 m. S.W. of Edinburgh; pop. 1292. Map 10.

West Melton, par. and vil., W.R. Yorkshire, $5\frac{1}{2}$ m. N. of Rotherham; pop. 4745. Map 41.

West Meon, par. and vil., Hants, $12\frac{1}{2}$ m. S.W. of Alton; pop. 751. Map 79.

Westminster, city. and met. bor., London; pop. 129,535. Map 71.

Westnewton, par. and vil., Cumberland, 2 m. N.W. of Aspatria; pop. 323. Map 20.

Weston, par. and vil., Cheshire, $1\frac{1}{2}$ m. S.W. of Runcorn; pop. 2246. Map 38.

Weston, par. and vil., Somersetshire, 2 m. N.W. of Bath; pop. 1549. Map 75.

Weston-super-Mare, urb. dist. and wtg. pl., Somersetshire, 19 m. S.W. of Bristol; pop. 28,555. Map 74.

Weston Zoyland, par. and vil., Somersetshire, $3\frac{1}{2}$ m. S.E. of Bridgwater; pop. 611. Map 74.

Westow, par. and vil., E.R. Yorkshire, 5 m. S.W. of Malton; pop. 248. Map 28.

Westport, urb. dist. and seaport town, Mayo, 160 m. N.W. of Dublin; pop. 3490. Map 92.

Westruther, par. and vil., Berwickshire, $7\frac{1}{2}$ m. N.E. of Lauder; pop. 448. Map 11.

Westward Ho, coast vil. and watering place, Devonshire, 3 m. N.W. of Bideford. Map 84.

Westwell, par. and vil., Kent, 3 m. N.N.W. of Ashford; pop. 849. Map 83.

West Wemyss, vil. and *q.s.* par., Fifeshire, 2 m. N.E. of Dysart; pop. (par.) 2497. Map 10.

Wetheral, par. and vil., Cumberland, 4 m. S.E. of Carlisle; pop. 3418. Map 21.

Wetherby, par. and market town, W.R. Yorkshire, 8 m. S.E. of Harrogate; pop. 2126. Map 33.

Wetherden, par. and vil., E. Suffolk, 4 m. N.W. of Stowmarket; pop. 471. Map 62.

Wethersfield, par. and vil., Essex, 6 m. N.W. of Braintree; pop. 986. Map 72.

Wetwang, par. and vil., E.R. Yorkshire, $6\frac{1}{2}$ m. W. of Driffield; pop. 484. Map 34.

Wexford, mun. bor., spt. and cap., Wexford, $92\frac{3}{4}$ m. S. of Dublin; pop. 11,870. Map 95.

Weybourne, par. and vil., Norfolk, 3 m. N.E. of Holt; pop. 362. Map 53.

Weybridge, urb. dist. and par., Surrey, $2\frac{1}{2}$ m. S.E. of Chertsey; pop. 7359. Map 78.

Weyhill, vil., Hants, 4 m. W. of Andover. Map 76.

Weymouth and Melcombe Regis, mun. bor., par. and seaport, Dorsetshire, 7½ m. S. of Dorchester; pop. 21,982.   Map 87.

Whaddon, par. and vil., Cambridgeshire, 4 m. N. of Royston; pop. 226.   Map 61.

Whaddon, par. and vil., Buckinghamshire, 4½ m. S.E. of Stony Stratford; pop. 273.   Map 60.

Whaley Bridge, vil., Cheshire, on r. Goyt, 10¼ m. S.E. of Stockport.   Map 40.

Whalley, par. and vil., N.E. Lancashire, 3½ m. S. of Clitheroe; pop. 1379.   Map 31.

Whalton, par. and vil., Northumberland, 5 m. S.W. of Morpeth; pop. 312.   Map 17.

Whaplode, par. and vil., Holland, Lincolnshire, 2¼ m. W. of Holbeach; pop. 2357.   Map 51.

Wharram-le-Street, par., E.R. Yorkshire, 7 m. S.E. of Malton; pop. 121.   Map 29.

Whatfield, par. and vil., W. Suffolk, 3 m. N. of Hadleigh; pop. 274.   Map 62.

Whatlington, par. and vil., E. Sussex, 2 m. N. of Battle; pop. 281.   Map 82.

Wheathampstead, par. and vil., Hertfordshire, 5 m. N.E. of St Albans; pop. 2870.   Map 71.

Wheatley, urb. dist. and par., Oxon, 5 m. E. of Oxford; pop. 1269.   Map 70.

Wheatley, North, par. and vil., Nottinghamshire, 5 m. N.E. of Retford; pop. 357.   Map 41.

Whetstone, eccl. par. and vil., N.E. Middlesex, 2 m. S.E. of Barnet; pop. 3627.   Map 71.

Whetstone, par. and vil., Leicestershire, 5½ m. S.W. of Leicester; pop. 1388.   Map 49.

Whickham, urb. dist. and par., Durham, 3½ m. W.S.W. of Gateshead; pop. 20,782.   Map 23.

Whimple, par. and vil., Devonshire, 8½ m. N.E. of Exeter; pop. 744.   Map 85.

Whippingham, par. and vil., Isle of Wight, 2½ m. N.E. of Newport; pop. 2033.   Map 77.

Whipsnade, par., Bedfordshire, 3 m. S. of Dunstable. Map 71.

Whissendine, par. and vil., Rutlandshire, 5 m. N.W. of Oakham; pop. 566.   Map 50.

Whitburn, par. and vil., Durham, 3½ m. N. of Sunderland; pop. 5291.   Map 23.

Whitburn, par. and town, West Lothian, 2¼ m. S.W. of Bathgate; pop. (town) 2440.   Map 9.

Whitby, urb. dist., par., spt. and mkt. tn., N.R. Yorks, 20 m. N.W. of Scarborough; pop. 11,441. Map 29.

Whitchurch, par. and vil., Buckinghamshire, 4 m. N. of Aylesbury; pop. 635.   Map 70.

Whitchurch, urb. dist. and par., Salop, 18¾ m. N. of Shrewsbury; pop. 6016.   Map 46.

Whitchurch, par. and vil., Herefordshire, 4½ m. N.E. of Monmouth; pop. 764.   Map 67.

Whitchurch, par. and vil., Devonshire, 1½ m. S.E. of Tavistock; pop. 1477.   Map 88.

Whitchurch, town and par., Hants, 7 m. N.E. of Andover; pop. 2461.   Map 76.

Whitchurch, par. and vil., Glamorganshire, 1 m. N.W. of Llandaff; pop. 11,287.   Map 74.

Whitechurch, par., Pembrokeshire, 6½ m. S. of Cardigan; pop. 241.   Map 64.

White Colne, par. and vil., Essex, 4 m. E.S.E. of Halstead; pop. 348.   Map 73.

Whitefield, urb. dist. and par., S.E. Lancashire, 6 m. N.N.W. of Manchester; pop. 9107.   Map 31.

Whitehaven, mun. bor., spt. and par., Cumberland, 38 m. S.W. of Carlisle; pop. 21,142.   Map 24.

Whiteparish, par. and vil., Wiltshire, 8 m. S.E. of Salisbury; pop. 839.   Map 76.

Whiteshill, par. and vil., Gloucestershire, 1½ m. N.W. of Stroud; pop. 1364.   Map 68.

Whitford, par. and vil., Flintshire, 3 m. N.W. of Holywell; pop. 3295.   Map 38.

Whithorn, mun. bur. and par., Wigtownshire, 12¼ m. S. of Wigtown; pop. (bur.) 951.   Map 19.

Whiting Bay, *q.s.* par., vil. and bay, Arran Island, 4 m. S.E. of Lamlash; pop. 2034.   Map 12.

Whitkirk, eccl. dist. and vil., W.R. Yorkshire, 4 m. E. of Leeds; pop. 3525.   Map 33.

Whitland, vil. and ry. sta., Carmarthenshire, 6 m. E.N.E. of Narberth.   Map 65.

Whitley and Monkseaton, urb. dist., Northumberland; pop. 24,210 (contains **Whitley Bay**).   Map 23.

Whitley Bay, watering place, Northumberland, 2½ m. N. of North Shields.   Map 23.

Whitley, Upper, urb. dist. and par., W.R. Yorkshire, 6 m. E. of Huddersfield; pop. 932.   Map 32.

Whitney, par. and vil., Herefordshire, 4 m. N.E. of Hay; pop. 197.   Map 56.

Whitrigg, ham., Cumberland, 1 m. S. of Torpenhow. Map 20.

Whitstable, urb. dist. and par., Kent, 6 m. N.W. of Canterbury; pop. 11,201.   Map 83.

Whittingham, par. and vil., Northumberland, 8½ m. W. of Alnwick; pop. 437.   Map 17.

Whittingham, par. and vil., Lancashire, 5 m. N.E. of Preston; pop. 4032.   Map 30.

Whittington, par. and vil., N. Lancashire, 2 m. S.W. of Kirkby Lonsdale; pop. 306.   Map 26.

Whittington, par. and vil., Salop, 2½ m. E.N.E. of Oswestry; pop. 2729.   Map 46.

Whittington, par. and vil., Staffordshire, 2½ m. S.E. of Lichfield; pop. 2525.   Map 48.

Whittlesey, urb. dist., Isle of Ely, Cambridgeshire, 5¼ m. E. of Peterborough; pop. 8299.   Map 51.

Whitton, par. and vil., Lincs, on r. Humber, 8 m. W.N.W. of Barton-upon-Humber; pop. 183. Map 34.

Whittonstall, par. and vil., Northumberland, 3 m. N.W. of Shotley Bridge; pop. 162.   Map 22.

Whitwood, urb. dist., W.R. Yorkshire, 4½ m. N.W. of Pontefract; pop. 6196.   Map 33.

Whitworth, urb. dist. and par., S.E. Lancashire, 3 m. N. of Rochdale; pop. 8360.   Map 31.

Wibsey, eccl. dist., W.R. Yorkshire, in S.W. of co. bor. of Bradford; pop. 4647.   Map 32.

Wick, mun. bur., spt., par. and co. town, Caithness-shire, 161½ m. N.E. of Inverness; bur. pop. 7548. Map 3.

Wickford, par. and vil., S. Essex, 8 m. S.S.E. of Chelmsford; pop. 1475.   Map 72.

Wickham, par. and vil., Hants, 4 m. N. of Fareham; pop. 1146.   Map 77.

Wickham Bishops, par. and vil., Essex, 2¼ m. S. of Witham; pop. 498.   Map 72.

Wickham Market, par. and town, E. Suffolk, 5 m. N.N.E. of Woodbridge; pop. 1259.   Map 63.

Wicklow, assize and spt. tn. and cap. of Wicklow, 28¼ m. S. of Dublin; pop. 3027.   Map 95.

Wickwar, par. and small town, Gloucestershire, 4 m. N. of Chipping Sodbury; pop. 769.   Map 75.

Widdrington, par. and vil., Northumberland, 7 m. N.E. of Morpeth; pop. 802.   Map 17.

Widnes, mun. bor. and par., S.W. Lancashire, 12¼ m. S.E. of Liverpool; pop. 40,608.   Map 39.

Wield, par., Hants, 7 m. W. of Alton; pop. 241. Map 79.

Wigan, parl. and co. bor., mfg. tn. and par., S.W. Lancs, 15 m. S. of Preston; pop. 85,357.   Map 30.

Wiggenhall St Mary Magdalen, par. and vil., Norfolk, 6 m. S.W. of King's Lynn; pop. 728.   Map 51.

Wigginton, par. and vil., Hertfordshire, 1½ m. S.E. of Tring; pop. 696.   Map 71.

Wigginton, par. and vil., Staffordshire, 1½ m. N. of Tamworth; pop. 1523.   Map 48.

Wiggonby, vil., Cumberland, 4 m. N.E. of Wigton. Map 20.

Wighton, par. and vil., Norfolk, 2 m. N. of Walsingham; pop. 412.   Map 52.

Wigley, ham., Hants, 5 m. N.W. of Southampton. Map 77.

Wigmore, par. and vil., Herefordshire, 8½ m. N.W. of Leominster; pop. 345.   Map 56.

Wigston Magna, urb. dist. and par., in co. and 6 m. S.E. of Leicester; pop. 11,393. Map 49.
Wigtoft, par. and vil., Holland, Lincolnshire, 6½ m. S.W. of Boston; pop. 712. Map 51.
Wigton, urb. dist. and par., Cumberland, 11¾ m. S.W. of Carlisle; pop. 3521. Map 20.
Wigtown, mun. bor., spt., par. and co. tn., Wigtownshire, 7¼ m. S. of Newton Stewart; pop. 1261. Map 19.
Wilbarston, par. and vil., Northamptonshire, 6 m. E. of Market Harborough; pop. 468. Map 50.
Wilbraham, Great and **Little**, 2 pars., in co. and 6 m. E. of Cambridge; pop. 444 and 348. Map 61.
Wilburton, par. and vil., Isle of Ely, Cambridgeshire, 5¼ m. S.W. of Ely; pop. 497. Map 61.
Wilby, par. and vil., Northamptonshire, 2 m. S.W. of Wellingborough; pop. 418. Map 60.
Wilcot, par. and vil., Wiltshire, 1½ m. W.N.W. of Pewsey; pop. 531. Map 76.
Wilkieston, vil., Midlothian, 3 m. E. of Mid-Calder; pop. 425. Map 9.
Willaston, par. and vil., Cheshire, 2½ m. S.W. of Crewe; pop. 2764. Map 39.
Willenhall, urb. dist. and par., Staffordshire, 3 m. E. of Wolverhampton; pop. 21,147. Map 48.
Willerby, par., E.R. Yorkshire, 5 m. N.W. of Hull; pop. 1319. Map 35.
Willesborough, par. and vil., Kent, 2½ m. S.E. of Ashford; pop. 4748. Map 83.
Willesden, urb. dist., Middlesex, 7 m. N.W. of St Paul's, London; pop. 184,410. Map 71.
Willingdon, par. and vil., E. Sussex, 2½ m. N.N.W. of Eastbourne; pop. 884. Map 81.
Willingham, par. and vil., Cambridgeshire, 5½ m. E. of St Ives; pop. 1657. Map 61.
Willington, par. and vil., Derbyshire, 4½ m. N.E. of Burton-on-Trent; pop. 631. Map 48.
Willington, urb. dist. and par., Durham, 5 m. N. of Bishop Auckland; pop. 8960. Map 23.
Williton, par. and market town, N. Somersetshire, 14 m. N.W. of Taunton; pop. 1131. Map 85.
Willoughby, par. and vil., Warwickshire, 5 m. S. of Rugby; pop. 306. Map 59.
Willoughby Waterless, par. and vil., Leicestershire, 6 m. N.E. of Lutterworth; pop. 210. Map 49.
Wilmslow, urb. dist. and par., Cheshire, 6 m. S.W. of Stockport; pop. 9760. Map 39.
Wilsontown, mining vil., Lanarkshire, 9¼ m. N.W. of Carstairs. Map 9.
Wilton, mun. bor., Wiltshire, 2½ m. N.W. of Salisbury; pop. 2193. Map 76.
Wilton, *q.s.* par., Roxburghshire, within bur. of Hawick; pop. 3436. Map 16.
Wimbledon, mun. bor., Surrey, 7½ m. S.W. of Waterloo sta., London; pop. 59,520. Map 71.
Wimborne Minster, urb. dist. and par., Dorsetshire, 7 m. N. of Poole; pop. 3895. Map 77.
Wincanton, market town and par., Somersetshire, 19½ m. S.E. of Glastonbury; pop. 1711. Map 87.
Winchburgh, *q.s.* par. and vil., West Lothian, 12 m. W. of Edinburgh; pop. 1742. Map 9.
Winchcomb, par. and market town, Gloucestershire, 6 m. N.E. of Cheltenham; pop. 2741. Map 58.
Winchelsea, par. and ancient town, E. Sussex, 8 m. N.E. of Hastings; pop. 152. Map 82.
Winchester, mun. bor. and co. tn. of Hants, on r. Itchen, 12 m. S.E. of Southampton; pop. 22,969. Map 76.
Winchfield, par. and vil., Hants, 4 m. W. of Farnborough; pop. 445. Map 78.
Windermere and **Lake**, Westmorland and Lancashire, pop. 5701. Lake 10½ m. long. Map 25.
Windlesham, par. and urb. dist., Surrey, 1½ m. N.E. of Bagshot; pop. 5254. Map 78.
Windsor, New, mun. bor., Berkshire, on r. Thames, 21¼ m. W. of London; pop. 20,284. Map 78.
Windygates, vil., Fifeshire, 3½ m. N.E. of Thornton Junction; pop. 1639. Map 7.
Winford, par. and vil., Somersetshire, 6 m. S.W. of Bristol; pop. 791. Map 74.
Winforton, par. and vil., Herefordshire, 5½ m. N.E. of Hay; pop. 120. Map 56.
Wing, par. and vil., Buckinghamshire, 2½ m. S.W. of Leighton Buzzard; pop. 1498. Map 70.
Wingate, par. and vil., Durham, 8 m. W.N.W. of Hartlepool; pop. 11,424. Map 23.
Wingfield, North, par. and vil., Derbyshire, 4½ m. S. of Chesterfield; pop. 5169. Map 41.
Wingfield, South, par. and vil., Derbyshire, 2 m. W. of Alfreton; pop. 1605. Map 41.
Wingham, par. and vil., Kent, 6 m. E. of Canterbury; pop. 1240. Map 83.
Winsford, urb. dist., Cheshire, 5 m. S. of Northwich; pop. 10,997. Map 39.
Winsham, par. and vil., Somersetshire, 4 m. S.E. of Chard; pop. 690. Map 86.
Winslow, market town and par., in co. and 6½ m. S.E. of Buckingham; pop. 1532. Map 59.
Winster, par. and small town, Derbyshire, 4 m. W. of Matlock; pop. 684. Map 40.
Winterbourne, par. and vil., Gloucestershire, 6½ m. N.E. of Bristol; pop. 3368. Map 68.
Winterbourne Earls, par., Wiltshire, 3½ m. N.E. of Salisbury; pop. 250. Map 76.
Winterbourne St Martin, par. and seat, Dorsetshire, 3 m. S.W. of Dorchester; pop. 422. Map 87.
Winteringham, par. and vil., Lincolnshire, 6½ m. W. of Barton-upon-Humber; pop. 747. Map 34.
Winterslow, par. and vil., Wiltshire, 6 m. N.E. of Salisbury; pop. 788. Map 76.
Winterton, urb. dist., mkt. tn. and par., Lincolnshire, 5 m. N. of Scunthorpe; pop. 1958. Map 34.
Winterton, coast par. and vil., Norfolk, 8 m. N. of Yarmouth; pop. 967. Map 53.
Wintringham, par. and vil., E.R. Yorkshire, 6 m. E.N.E. of Malton; pop. 280. Map 29.
Winwick, par. and vil., S.W. Lancashire, 2½ m. N. of Warrington; pop. 1869. Map 39.
Wirksworth, urb. dist., par. and market town, Derbyshire, 13¾ m. N.W. of Derby; pop. 3911. Map 40.
Wisbech, mun. bor., Isle of Ely, Cambridgeshire, 22 m. N.E. of Peterborough; pop. 12,005. Map 51.
Wisborough Green, par. and vil., W. Sussex, 5 m. N.E. of Petworth; pop. 1572. Map 79.
Wishaw. *See* Motherwell and Wishaw.
Wisley, par. and ham., Surrey, 3½ m. S.S.W. of Weybridge; pop. 273. Map 78.
Wistanstow, par. and vil., Salop, 5½ m. S. of Church Stretton; pop. 885. Map 46.
Witchampton, par. and vil., Dorsetshire, 4 m. N.W. of Wimborne; pop. 435. Map 87.
Witham, urb. dist. and par., Essex, 9 m. N.E. of Chelmsford; pop. 4367. Map 72.
Witheridge, par. and vil., Devonshire, 8 m. E. of Chulmleigh; pop. 759. Map 85.
Withernsea, urb. dist. and par., E.R. Yorkshire, 4 m. N.E. of Patrington; pop. 4251. Map 35.
Withersfield, par. and vil., W. Suffolk, 2 m. N.W. of Haverhill; pop. 485. Map 61.
Witherslack, par. and vil., Westmorland, 7 m. S.W. of Kendal; pop. 401. Map 25.
Withiel, par. and vil., Cornwall, 5 m. W.N.W. of Bodmin; pop. 329. Map 91.
Withington, par. and vil., in co. and 4½ m. N.E. of Hereford; pop. 756. Map 57.
Withington, par. and vil., Gloucestershire, 7½ m. S.E. of Cheltenham; pop. 555. Map 69.
Withnell, urb. dist. and par., N. Lancashire, 5 m. S.W. of Blackburn; pop. 3040. Map 30.
Witley, par. and vil., Surrey, 3 m. S.S.W. of Godalming; pop. 4289. Map 79.
Witnesham, par. and vil., E. Suffolk, 4½ m. N.N.E. of Ipswich; pop. 511. Map 63.

Witney, urb. dist. and par., Oxon, 5 m. N.E. of Bampton ; pop. 3409. Map 69.

Wittering, par., Soke of Peterborough, Northamptonshire, 3½ m. S.E. of Stamford ; pop. 192. Map 50.

Wittersham, par. and vil., Kent, 4½ m. N.N.W. of Rye ; pop. 643. Map 82.

Witton-le-Wear, par. and vil., Durham, 4½ m. W.N.W. of Bishop Auckland ; pop. 2432. Map 23.

Wiveliscombe, urb. dist. and mkt. tn., Somersetshire, 9½ m. W.N.W. of Taunton ; pop. 1262. Map 85.

Wivelsfield, par. and vil., E. Sussex, 2 m. S.S.E. of Hayward's Heath ; pop. 2233. Map 81.

Wivenhoe, urb. dist., r. port and par., Essex, 4 m. S.E. of Colchester ; pop. 2193. Map 73.

Woburn, town and par., Buckinghamshire, 4 m. S.E. of Wycombe ; pop. 4648. Map 70.

Woburn, market town and par., Bedfordshire, 6 m. N.E. of Leighton Buzzard ; pop. 1062. Map 60.

Woburn Sands, par. and vil., Buckinghamshire, 3 m. N.E. of Fenny Stratford ; pop. 1131. Map 60.

Woking, town and par., Surrey, on r. Wey, 6 m. N. of Guildford ; pop. 29,927. Map 78.

Wokingham, mun. bor., S.E. Berkshire, 7 m. S.E. of Reading ; pop. 7294. Map 78.

Woldingham, par. and ham., Surrey, 2 m. E. of Caterham ; pop. 646. Map 80.

Wollaston, par. and vil., Northamptonshire, 3½ m. S.S.E. of Wellingborough ; pop. 2339. Map 60.

Wollaton, par. and vil., Nottinghamshire, 3 m. W. of Nottingham ; pop. 551. Map 49.

Wolsingham, town and par., Durham, 10 m. N.W. of Bishop Auckland ; pop. 3535. Map 22.

Wolstanton, United, urb. dist. and par., Staffordshire, 2 m. N.E. of Newcastle-under-Lyme ; pop. 30,528. Map 39.

Wolston, par. and vil., Warwickshire, 6 m. W. of Rugby ; pop. 962. Map 59.

Wolverhampton, parl. and co. bor., Staffs, 12¾ m. N.W. of Birmingham ; co. bor. pop. 133,190. Map 47.

Wolverley, par. and vil., Worcestershire, 2 m. N. of Kidderminster ; pop. 2217. Map 57.

Wolverton, urb. dist. and par., Buckinghamshire, 2 m. N.E. of Stony Stratford ; pop. 12,870. Map 60.

Wolvey, par. and vil., Warwickshire, 5 m. S.E. of Nuneaton ; pop. 686. Map 49.

Wolviston, par. and vil., Durham, 4½ m. N. of Stockton ; pop. 642. Map 23.

Wombourn, par. and vil., Staffordshire, 4½ m. S.W. of Wolverhampton ; pop. 1670. Map 47.

Wombwell, urb. dist., W.R. Yorkshire, 4½ m. S.E. of Barnsley ; pop. 18,365. Map 41.

Wonersh, par. and vil., Surrey, 3 m. S.E. of Guildford ; pop. 2023. Map 78.

Wonston, par. and vil., Hants, 6 m. N. of Winchester ; pop. 910. Map 76.

Woodborough, par. and vil., in co. and 7½ m. N.E. of Nottingham ; pop. 682. Map 41.

Woodbridge, urb. dist. and par., E. Suffolk, 8 m. N.E. of Ipswich ; pop. 4734. Map 63.

Woodburn, West, vil., Northumberland, 4 m. N.E. of Bellingham. Map 17.

Woodbury, par. and vil., Devonshire, 7 m. S.E. of Exeter ; pop. 1533. Map 89.

Woodchester, par. and vil., Gloucestershire, 2½ m. S.W. of Stroud ; pop. 856. Map 68.

Woodchurch, par. and vil., Kent, 4 m. E.N.E. of Tenterden ; pop. 1044. Map 83.

Woodford, urb. dist. and par., Essex, 4½ m. N.E. of Stratford ; pop. 23,946. Map 72.

Wood Green, urb. dist. and par., Middlesex, 5 m. N. of London ; pop. 54,190. Map 71.

Woodhall Spa, urb. dist. and par., Lindsey, Lincolnshire, 6½ m. S.W. of Horncastle ; pop. 1372. Map 43.

Woodham Ferrers, par. and vil., Essex, 6 m. S.W. of Maldon ; pop. 1168. Map 72.

Woodhay, East, par. and vil., Hants, 4½ m. S.W. of Newbury ; pop. 1672. Map 76.

Woodstock, mun. bor. and par., in co. and 8 m. N.W. of Oxford ; pop. 1484. Map 69.

Woodville, par. and vil., Derbyshire, 3½ m. N.W. of Ashby-de-la-Zouch ; pop. 3146. Map 48.

Wofferton, vil. and ry. junction, Salop, 4 m. S. of Ludlow. Map 57.

Woolavington, par. and vil., Somersetshire, 4½ m. N.E. of Bridgwater ; pop. 328. Map 74.

Wooler, par. and town, Northumberland, 15 m. S. of Berwick ; pop. 1577. Map 17.

Woolhampton, par. and vil., Berkshire, 7 m. E. of Newbury ; pop. 609. Map 76.

Woolhope, par. and vil., in co. and 7 m. S.E. of Hereford ; pop. 536. Map 57.

Woolley, par. and vil., W.R. Yorkshire, 5½ m. S. of Wakefield ; pop. 974. Map 33.

Woolpit, par. and vil., W. Suffolk, 5 m. N.W. of Stowmarket ; pop. 734. Map 62.

Woolwich, met. bor. in E. of co. of London, on r. Thames ; pop. 146,944. Map 72.

Wootton, North, par. and vil., Norfolk, 3 m. N. of King's Lynn ; pop. 331. Map 52.

Wootton Basset, market town and par., Wiltshire, 6 m. W.S.W. of Swindon ; pop. 2112. Map 69.

Wootton Wawen, par. and vil., Warwickshire, 7 m. N.W. of Stratford-on-Avon ; pop. 1985. Map 58.

Woore, par. and vil., Salop, 7 m. N.E. of Market Drayton ; pop. 877. Map 47.

Worcester, parl. and co. bor., city and co. town of Worcestershire, 22 m. S.W. of Birmingham ; pop. 50,497. Map 57.

Worcestershire Beacon, on border of cos. Worcester and Hereford ; alt. 1395 ft. Map 57.

Worfield, par. and vil., Salop, 3 m. N.E. of Bridgnorth ; pop. 1475. Map 47.

Workington, mun. bor., spt. and par., Cumberland, 6½ m. N. of Whitehaven ; pop. 24,691. Map 20.

Worksop, municipal bor. and par., Notts, on r. Ryton, nr. N. extremity of Sherwood Forest, 26 m. N. of Nottingham ; pop. 26,286. Map 41.

Worle, par. and vil., Somersetshire, 2½ m. N.E. of Weston-super-Mare ; pop. 1490. Map 74.

Worleston, par. and vil., Cheshire, 1¾ m. N. of Nantwich ; pop. 463. Map 39.

Worlingworth, par. and vil., E. Suffolk, 5 m. N.W. of Framlingham ; pop. 504. Map 63.

Wormit, q.s. par. and bay, Fifeshire, on Firth of Tay and 2 m. W. of Newport ; pop. 1056. Map 7.

Worplesdon, par. and vil., Surrey, 3 m. N.W. of Guildford ; pop. 2593. Map 78.

Worsborough, urb. dist., W.R. Yorkshire, 2½ m. S. of Barnsley ; pop. 12,397. Map 33.

Worsley, urb. dist., Lancashire, 6 m. S. of Manchester ; pop. 14,503. Map 39.

Worthing, mun. bor. and par., W. Sussex, 10½ m. W. of Brighton ; pop. 46,230 (estimated,193 5) 53,840. Map 79.

Wortley, par. and vil., W.R. Yorkshire, 6 m. S.W. of Barnsley ; pop. 885. Map 40.

Wotton-under-Edge, par. and town, Gloucestershire, 9½ m. S.W. of Stroud ; pop. 3010. Map 68.

Wouldham, par. and vil., Kent, 3 m. S.W. of Rochester ; pop. 1077. Map 80.

Wragby, small town and par., Lindsey, Lincolnshire, 7 m. S.S.E. of Market Rasen ; pop. 463. Map 42.

Wrangle, coast par. and vil., Holland, Lincolnshire, 8 m. N.E. of Boston ; pop. 1142. Map 43.

Wrawby, par. and vil., Lindsey, Lincolnshire, 1½ m. N.E. of Brigg ; pop. 847. Map 35.

Wraxall, par. and vil., Somersetshire, 6 m. W. of Bristol ; pop. 813. Map 74.

Wreay, par. and vil., Cumberland, 5 m. S.E. of Carlisle ; pop. 140.　Map 21.

Wrecclesham, eccl. par. and vil., Surrey, 1¼ m. S.W of Farnham ; pop. 1857.　Map 78.

Wrentham, par. and vil., E. Suffolk, 4 m. N. of Southwold ; pop. 944.　Map 63.

Wrexham, mun. bor. and par., Denbighshire, 10 m. S.W. of Chester ; pop. 18,567.　Map 38.

Wribbenhall, par., Worcestershire, an E. suburb of Bewdley ; pop. 1420.　Map 57.

Wrington, par. and vil., Somersetshire, 6½ m. N.E. of Axbridge ; pop. 1369.　Map 74.

Wrockwardine, par. and vil., Salop, 2 m. W. of Wellington ; pop. 1051.　Map 47.

Wrotham, urb. dist. and town, Kent, 6 m. N.E. of Sevenoaks ; pop. 4510.　Map 80.

Wroughton, par. and vil., Wiltshire, 3 m. S. of Swindon ; pop. 2462.　Map 69.

Wroxeter, par. and vil., Salop, 6 m. S.E. of Shrewsbury ; pop. 551.　Map 47.

Wroxham, par. and vil., Norfolk, 7 m. N.E. of Norwich ; pop. 900.　Map 53.

Wybunbury, par. and vil., Cheshire, 3 m. S. of Crewe ; pop. 671.　Map 39.

Wycombe, Chepping, mun. bor., Buckinghamshire, 10 m. N. of Maidenhead ; pop. 27,987.　Map 70.

Wye, market town and par., Kent, 10 m. S.W. of Canterbury ; pop. 1390.　Map 83.

Wyke, ry. sta., W.R. Yorkshire, 4 m. S.W. of Bradford.　Map 32.

Wyke Regis, par. and vil., Dorsetshire, 2 m. S.W. of Weymouth ; pop. 2397.　Map 87.

Wylam, par. and vil., Northumberland, 8¼ m. W. of Newcastle ; pop. 1487.　Map 22.

Wylye, par. and vil., Wiltshire, 10 m. N.W. of Salisbury ; pop. 356.　Map 75.

Wymeswold, par. and vil., Leicestershire, 4½ m. N.E. of Loughborough ; pop. 777.　Map 49.

Wymington, par. and vil., Bedfordshire, 3 m. S. of Higham Ferrers ; pop. 516.　Map 60.

Wymondham, par. and town, Norfolk, 10 m. S.W. of Norwich ; pop. 4814.　Map 53.

Wymondham, par. and vil., Leicestershire, 6 m. E. of Melton Mowbray ; pop. 610.　Map 50.

YALDING, par. and vil., Kent, 6½ m. S.W. of Maidstone ; pop. 2555.　Map 82.

Yapton, par. and vil., W. Sussex, 3½ m. S.W. of Arundel ; pop. 712.　Map 79.

Yarcombe, par. and vil., Devonshire, 7 m. N.E. of Honiton ; pop. 536.　Map 86.

Yardley Gobion, par. and vil., Northamptonshire, 3¼ m. N.W. of Stony Stratford ; pop. 416.　Map 59.

Yarm, market town and par., N.R. Yorkshire, 4 m. S.S.W. of Stockton ; pop. 171.　Map 28.

Yarmouth, seaport and par., Isle of Wight, 10 m. W. of Newport ; pop. 893.　Map 77.

Yarmouth, Great, parl. and co. bor., Norfolk, 19 m. E. of Norwich ; pop. 56,769.　Map 53.

Yarnton, par. and vil., in co. and 4 m. N.W. of Oxford ; pop. 309.　Map 70.

Yarpole, par. and vil., Herefordshire, 5 m. N.W. of Leominster ; pop. 463.　Map 56.

Yatton, par. and vil., Somersetshire, 12 m. S.W. of Bristol ; pop. 2176.　Map 74.

Yeadon, urb. dist. and par., W.R. Yorkshire, 3 m. S. of Otley ; pop. 7671.　Map 32.

Yealmbridge, ham., Devonshire, 1 m. N.E. of Yealmpton.　Map 88.

Yealmpton, par. and vil., Devonshire, 7 m. E.S.E. of Plymouth ; pop. 878.　Map 88.

Yeardsley cum Whaley, urb. dist., Cheshire, 7½ m. N.E. of Macclesfield ; pop. 1745.　Map 40.

Yeldham, Great, par. and vil., Essex, 6½ m. N.W. of Halstead ; pop. 581.　Map 62.

Yelverton, residential dist., Devonshire, 5 m. S.E. of Tavistock.　Map 88.

Yelverton, par., Norfolk, 6 m. S.E. of Norwich ; pop. 567.　Map 53.

Yeovil, mun. bor. and par., Somersetshire, 50¼ m. S. of Bristol ; pop. 19,078.　Map 86.

Yerbleston, par., Pembrokeshire, 4½ m. S.W. of Narberth ; pop. 79.　Map 64.

Yester, par., East Lothian, 4 m. S.S.E. of Haddington ; pop. 778.　Map 10.

Yetholm, par. and vil., Roxburghshire, 7½ m. S.E. of Kelso ; pop. 772.　Map 16.

Yetminster, par. and vil., Dorsetshire, 4½ m. S.E. of Yeovil ; pop. 522.　Map 87.

Yiewsley, par. and urb. dist., Middlesex, 2½ m. S. of Uxbridge ; pop. 13,057.　Map 71.

York, parl. and co. bor., co. tn. of Yorks, and co. in itself, 188 m. N.W. of London ; pop. 84,810.　Map 33.

York Town, eccl. par. and vil., Surrey, 3 m. S.W. of Bagshot ; pop. 5415.　Map 78.

Youghal, seaport town, urb. dist. and par., Cork, 26¾ m. E. of Cork ; pop. 5340.　Map 95.

Youlgreave, par. and mining vil., Derbyshire, 3¼ m. S.W. of Bakewell ; pop. 1214.　Map 40.

Yoxall, par. and vil., Staffordshire, 8 m. S.W. of Burton-on-Trent ; pop. 1025.　Map 48.

Yoxford, par. and vil., E. Suffolk, 4 m. N. of Saxmundham ; pop. 978.　Map 63.

Yspitty Ystwyth, par. and ham., Cardiganshire, 8 m. N.N.E. of Tregaron ; pop. 476.　Map 55.

Ystalyfera, locality, Glamorganshire, 11 m. N.E. of Swansea.　Map 66.

Ystradvellte, par. and ham., Breconshire, 10 m. N.W. of Merthyr Tydfil ; pop. 613.　Map 66.

Ystradyfodwg, locality, Glamorganshire, in Rhondda urb. dist., 7½ m. N.W. of Pontypridd.　Map 66.

ZEALS, par. and vil., Wiltshire, 1½ m. W. of Mere ; pop. 379.　Map 75.

Zennor, par., Cornwall, 4¾ m. S.W. of St Ives ; pop. 298.　Map 90.

THE POCKET SERIES

OF

TOURING MAPS

By J. G. BARTHOLOMEW, F.R.G.S.

LIST OF SPECIAL DISTRICT MAPS & TOWN PLANS.

Those marked with an asterisk are price 1/- Net each, mounted on Cloth and in Case.   The other larger Maps are 1/- Net, Paper; and 2/- Net, Cloth.

DISTRICT MAPS.

Aldershot Dist. Scale, 2 m. to in.
British Isles, Railway Map.
*Cambridgeshire. Scale, 4 m. to in.
*Edinburgh, Env. of. Sc. 2 m. to in.
*Glasgow, Envs. of.   Do.
*Hampshire. Sc., 4 m. to in.
Isle of Wight, with Guide. 1 in. to m.
*Kent, County of. 4 m. to inch.
Keswick, Ullswater, &c. 1 inch to m.
*Lake District and Windermere.
 3 miles to inch.
*Liverpool & Environs.   4 m. to inch.

London & Envs. 50 Mile Radius Map.
 4 miles to inch.
London & Envs. Sc. 1 in. to m.
*Manchester & Envs. Sc. 4 m. to in.
Melrose Pocket Guide. 1/-.
*Northumberland Co. Sc. 4 m. to in.
Salisbury Plain Dist. Sc. 2 m. to in.
*Somersetshire.   Do.
*Surrey & Sussex.   Do.
Thames, The River. Sc. 2 m. to in.
Windermere & Morecambe Bay.
 Sc. 1 m. to in.
Yorkshire. Sc. 4 m. to in.

SPECIAL CYCLISTS' MAPS.

Scale, Half-an-inch to Mile. Coloured to show Cycling Roads.
Price 1/6 Net each, mounted on cloth.

London : Northern District. | London : Southern District.
Leeds and Sheffield Districts.

TOWN PLANS.

*Birmingham, with Index.
*Dublin, with Index, Guide and
 Environs.
*Durham, with Environs.
*Eastbourne, with Index and Guide.
*Edinburgh, with Index.
Glasgow, with Index.
*Hastings & St. Leonards, with
 Index and Guide.
*Harrogate, with Environs.
*Hull, with Index and Guide.

Liverpool, with Index.
London, with Index & Guide.
London, City. Scale, 12 in. to m.
London, East.
London, South.
London, North.
London, West.
Manchester, with Index.
*Oxford, with Environs.
Plymouth and Devonport.
*York, with Environs.

SPECIAL MAPS on Scale of 10 Miles to Inch.

ENGLAND & WALES, GEOLOGICAL, by Sir ARCHIBALD GEEKIE.   Cloth, 12/6
SCOTLAND,   Do.   Do.   Cloth, 7/6
 Do.   Coloured to show Height of Land.   Paper, 1/-: Cloth, 2/-
 Do.   Naturalist's Map, showing Faunal Areas, &c.   Do.

*THIS SERIES is now to be had at all the leading
Booksellers and Railway Bookstalls.*

The Geographical Institute

JOHN BARTHOLOMEW & Cº
Geographers, Map Draughtsmen, Engravers, and Printers
Under Direction of J. G. Bartholomew, F.R.G.S., F.R.S.E.

GENERAL MAPS FOR TOURISTS
AND CYCLISTS.

Scale, 10 Miles to Inch ; showing Main Driving and Cycling Roads.

ENGLAND and WALES in Two Sections.

Northern Section. Paper, 1s. ; Cl., 2s.
Southern Section. Paper, 1s. ; Cl., 2s.
Complete in one Sheet. Cloth, 3s.

SCOTLAND. Paper, 1s. ; Cloth, 2s.
IRELAND. Paper, 1s. ; Cloth, 2s.

Contoured Touring Map of England & Wales, for Cyclists.
Scale, 13 Miles to inch. Paper, 1s. ; Cloth, 2s.

THE SURVEY GAZETTEER OF THE BRITISH ISLES.
Topographical, Statistical, and Commercial. With appendices and Special Maps.
Reduced Price—Half-Morocco, 12s. 6d, net.

Pall Mall Gazette.—"One of the most comprehensive and accurate works of its kind."

Complete Prospectus on application.

WORLD SERIES OF TOURING MAPS.

General Railway Map of British Isles. Scale, 19 m. to in. Paper, 1s. ; Cl., 2s.
Railway Map of Europe. Scale, 86 m. to in. Paper, 1s. ; Cloth, 2s.
Route Chart of World. Mercator's Projection. Paper, 1s. ; Cloth, 1s. 6d.
Map of South America. Scale, 1 : 10,000,000. Paper, 2s. ; Cloth, 3s.
Route Chart to India and the East. Paper, 1s. ; Cloth, 1s. 6d.
China, Japan, and Korea. Scale, 1 : 6,060,000. Paper, 1s. ; Cloth, 2s.
General Map of Africa. Scale, 1 : 12,000,000. Paper, 1s. ; Cloth, 2s.
Tourist's Map of Egypt. Scale, 1 : 1,000,000. Paper, 2s. ; Cloth, 3s.
Central and South Africa. Scale, 1 : 5,600,000. Paper, 2s. ; Cloth, 3s.
Tourist's Map of South Africa. Scale, 1 : 2,500.000. Paper, 2s. ; Cloth, 3s.
Chart of Oceania and the Pacific. Mercator's Projection. Paper, 2s. ; Cl., 3s.
Commercial Map of Australia. Scale, 1 : 6,000,000. Paper, 2s. ; Cloth, 3s.
United States & Part of Canada. Scale, 1 : 5,000,000. Paper, 2s. ; Cloth, 3s.

THE ABOVE PRICES ARE NET.